PRINCIPLES OF LEARNING

FROM LABORATORY TO FIELD

DOUGLAS J. NAVARICK

California State University, Fullerton

ADDISON-WESLEY PUBLISHING COMPANY *Reading, Massachusetts*
Menlo Park, California
London • Amsterdam
Don Mills, Ontario
Sydney

Library of Congress Cataloging in Publication Data

Navarick, Douglas J.   1946-
    Principles of learning.

    Bibliography: ˊp.
    Includes index.
    1. Learning, Psychology of. 2. Behaviorism
(Psychology) I. Title.
LB1051.N336   153.1'5   78-62546
ISBN 0-201-05204-0

ISBN 0-201-05204-0
CDEFGHILKL-MA-89876543210

To the memory of Irving Navarick

ACKNOWLEDGMENTS

The author wishes to thank the copyright owners for permission to reprint in this text the following figures, tables, and quotations:

Fig. 1.1 After Ernest R. Hilgard, "A Perspective on the Relationship Between Learning Credit Line Theory and Educational Practices," in *Theories of Learning and Instruction,* Sixty-third Yearbook of the National Society for the Study of Education, Part 1, ed. Ernest R. Hilgard. Chicago: University of Chicago Press, 1964, p. 406. Reprinted by permission.

Fig. 1.6 From J. P. Hailman, How an instinct is learned, *Scientific American,* December 1969, 99. Copyright © *Scientific American,* Inc., 1969. All rights reserved.

Table 2.1 and Fig. 2.2 From M. A. H. Russell, E. Armstrong, and U. A. Patel, Temporal contiguity in electric aversion therapy for cigarette smoking, *Behavior Research and Therapy,* **14,** 1976, 107, 111. Reprinted with permission of Pergamon Press, Ltd.

Table 2.2 From A. R. Luria, *The Role of Speech in the Regulation of Normal and Abnormal Behavior.* New York: Liveright, 1961. Reprinted by permission.

Figs. 3.1, 3.2, and 3.3 From B. F. Skinner, *The Behavior of Organisms: An Experimental Analysis,* © 1938, renewed 1966, pp. 49, 67, 75. Reprinted by permission of Prentice-Hall, Inc., Englewood Cliffs, N.J.

Figs. 3.4 and 3.5 From R. V. Hall, D. Lund, and D. Jackson, Effects of teacher attention on study behavior, *Journal of Applied Behavior Analysis,* **2,** 1969, 143-157. Copyright 1969 by the society for the Experimental Analysis of Behavior, Inc. Reprinted by permission.

Fig. 3.6 From A. V. Wolf and N. A. Crowder, *An Introduction to Body Fluid Metabolism,* Baltimore, The Williams & Wilkins Co., 1964. Reprinted by permission.

(continued on page 423)

Learning: An Applied Approach

No psychological process is more fundamental than the learning process. Thought, emotion, and action are subject to its laws. Its influence is felt every day in the innumerable adjustments we make to a changing environment. Learning is a part of life. Yet, quite unnecessarily we seem to have separated learning from life in the pursuit of traditional instructional goals. We have rightfully endeavored to convey to students enrolled in the general introductory course in learning the importance of seeking knowledge in a rigorous scientific manner. We have explained that in designing or interpreting research one must take into account not only the factors of immediate interest but any additional factors that could influence the outcome of the research. The psychology of learning has long emphasized laboratory experimentation as a means of investigation and we have encouraged students to accept the artificiality that this sort of inquiry entails for the sake of the greater understanding it provides. Although students have generally gone along with us, I do not think they have accepted the invitation unconditionally. I believe that most students have tolerated the artificiality of laboratory experimentation with the expectation that what they learn will be applicable to what they experience outside the laboratory. The traditional content of a general learning course contains relatively little discussion of applications and is likely to frustrate those who seek to relate laboratory research to themselves and to society.

From several years of experience as an instructor in a general learning course I have gained the impression that students have two major reasons for desiring a discussion of applications of laboratory research. One is practical; the applications show students how they can turn principles of learning to their own economic, professional, or social advantage. The other basis for interest in applications is intellectual. Quite rightly, I think, students seek some assurance that we have not drifted from reality to artifact in our pursuit of scientific rigor. They seek some indication that the principles we have selected for examination in an introductory course are powerful ones—principles sufficiently robust to withstand the innumerable extraneous influences on behavior in natural settings. This dual interest in applications does not mean that students expect instructors to match every laboratory finding presented in class with a corresponding application. Students, like everyone else, are naturally curious and can become as enthusiastic over "basic" research as any basic researcher. It is a question of emphasis, and the traditional emphasis in introductory courses on learning has, in my judgment, been misplaced. You can see its deleterious effects in the downturned eyes, the glances at the clock, the unfilled seats. And you can see it mirrored in our textbooks, which for the most part have been formal, dull, and remote from a student's concerns.

I started to write this book during my first year of teaching. Perhaps because I had so recently been a student myself I felt rather keenly my students' frustrations with the traditional content of a learning course. After all, as a student, I, too, had been a victim of dull textbooks. (Who hasn't?) I remembered the many times that I would stop part way through a reading assignment and thumb ahead to see how many pages were left. To me, this was a clear sign that a book had failed to do justice to its subject. I knew that more could be expected for there were also occasions on which I would stop and thumb *back* through all the pages I had read, surprised that I had accomplished so much in so little time. It has long seemed to me that a disproportionate number of learning texts have been members of the former category, the kind of book that causes students to thumb ahead. I wanted to write the other kind of book.

Throughout the project I have had two basic aims: to give the reader a strong sense of the practical value of the major principles of learning, and to instill an appreciation for the ingenuity of the methods used to establish those principles. My approach to the first objective has been to juxtapose discussions of laboratory work and applied work within each chapter. Much of the applied work selected for discussion is essentially basic research conducted in an educational or clinical setting and comes from journals that experimental learning psychologists may not routinely consult, for example, the *Journal of Educational Psychology,* the *Journal of Special Education, Behavior Research and Therapy,* and the *Journal of Applied Behavior Analysis.* Other sections dealing with applications focus on work with a purely educational or clinical goal, for example, Maria Montessori's work on the teaching of simple concepts to young children and Anne Sullivan's work with Helen Keller in the field of language acquisition. Applications were selected for discussion which seemed particularly thought-provoking and which clearly illustrated important principles established by laboratory research. No attempt has been made to provide a comprehensive account of the technical issues and problems that exist within a given area. It has been my intent only to suggest the kinds of applications that are possible and to stimulate further inquiry.

With respect to my second major aim—enhancing appreciation for research methodology—I have frequently devoted more space than tends to be customary in learning texts to developing the rationale, procedure, results, and implications of studies. It seems to me that students enrolled in a first course in learning need this kind of extended development to visualize what an investigator has done. A brief account cannot adequately convey the logic and subtlety of the investigator's approach. Because of space limitations, the strategy of providing fuller treatments of selected studies necessitated a reduction in the number of studies included in the text. The reader will soon discover that the book is not encyclopedic. However, a glance at the Table of Contents will show that the book is nevertheless comprehen-

LEARNING: AN APPLIED APPROACH

sive in scope, with entire chapters devoted to such diverse topics as conditioning, language acquisition, concept formation, mnemonics, and the history of theories of learning. The book is also comprehensive in the sense that it provides balanced coverage of associative and cognitive approaches to learning, its central theme being that while the two approaches have often offered competing theoretical interpretations, they have generated complementary facts and are both essential to a full understanding of the learning process.

The book has benefited immeasurably from the detailed comments of many reviewers. To all of them I extend my sincerest thanks and express the hope that they will take some measure of satisfaction in having contributed to the finished product. I am particularly indebted to the editors and staff of Addison-Wesley, whose efficiency, dedication, and cooperative spirit were instrumental in bringing the book to fruition. Roger Drumm was the editor who initially gave me the opportunity to perform this experiment, and Stuart Johnson has since been a continuing source of encouragement and helpful advice. I am greatly appreciative of the confidence they have shown both in me and in the project.

Fullerton, California
August 1978

D. J. N.

Contents

CONTENTS

CHAPTER 1

Introduction: The Psychology of Learning in a Social Context

How psychologists study the processes of learning is the principal focus of this book. But before a discussion of "how" can be truly meaningful, we must have a satisfactory answer to the question, "Why?" Why do psychologists study learning, and why should you read this book?

"Why" is a question people are increasingly asking about scientific research in general (Shaffer, 1977). It is a question with serious consequences for the future of science, for much scientific research can proceed only with the public's consent. Research is expensive. An investigator may require thousands of dollars worth of equipment and a team of assistants to carry out a research program. Who pays the salaries of the assistants and the bills for the equipment? To a large extent, tax-payers do; the federal government is the major source of funds for scientific research. Because Congress must approve federal expenditures, congressmen give expression to many of the public's concerns over the value of scientific knowledge. Perhaps the loudest voice on the issue of research has been that of Senator William Proxmire of Wisconsin. His denunciations of research projects he considers frivolous have produced applause in some circles and resentment in others. Whatever the validity of his views, the Senator reflects widespread suspicion that scientific knowledge may not be worth its cost.

At budget hearings involving representatives of the scientific community, Proxmire's questioning is typically barbed and searching. One notable exchange (Schaar, 1977) took place in February 1977 with the Director of the National Science Foundation, Richard C. Atkinson, a psychologist whose work on memory we will examine in Chapter 10. Proxmire wished to know why the NSF had recently allocated $49,600 for a project to study the taste preferences of rats. The investigator planned to offer rats foods that initially were unpalatable—coffee and chili peppers—and to seek ways of making the foods palatable. The Senator asked, "How would you justify this kind of spending to the average American taxpayer who is making $10-11,000 a year?"

Atkinson replied that rodents pose a serious economic problem because they consume a large portion of U.S. agricultural production. "So the whole idea of understanding the behavior of rodents, their preferences in terms of tastes and foods, is a very useful enterprise." Proxmire saw a different purpose in the research. "I think the purpose of this study is not to find out what rats like, but how it affects human beings. I doubt if there is going to be much of a market for chili and coffee among rats. Especially these days with the cost of coffee."

Another official of the NSF interjected that the eating habits of rats were similar to those of humans. Therefore, by studying how rats acquire food preferences, we might achieve insights into the development of food preferences in people. The Senator was unimpressed. "Let's assume on the one hand that these rats really go mad for coffee and chili and prefer it to anything else after they have developed a taste for it. What have you got besides hungry rats? . . . I don't see that you have really determined, no matter what the finding is, anything that is of any value to human beings. . . ." Atkinson suggested potential applications of the research. "These types of studies with lab rats open new areas . . . the study of hunger and obesity . . . that can't really be studied with human beings. We're now breaking through in dramatic ways. . . ."

The debate continued.

Proxmire: "If you wanted to study obesity, coffee would be the *last* thing you would use because there are no calories in coffee."

Atkinson: "You are too fast afoot, Senator."

Proxmire: "I haven't seen many people who have gotten obese on chili either!"

Although the exchange was lighthearted, its underlying theme was deadly serious. "How," the Senator asks, "can you justify having the taxpayers paying for basic research when it doesn't always have an objective that relates to some kind of human end?" What is the social value of scientific knowledge? It is a simple question, but the answer is complex.

SCIENCE AND SOCIETY

There are two broad categories of scientific activity: "basic research" and "applied research." Although the definitions of basic and applied research are clear in abstract terms, categorizing a research project as either basic or applied is often difficult. Many projects have features characteristic of both categories, and this ambiguity is one reason why the social value of scientific knowledge is difficult to assess.

Basic research is research motivated by curiosity; the investigator seeks knowledge for the sake of knowledge. Because the needs of society are secondary considerations in the design of the research—or perhaps not considerations at all—the knowledge gained from basic research often seems useless. No specific use for the knowledge can be identified in the immediate or the foreseeable future. In contrast, applied research is motivated by a specific social need. The investigator has the objective of producing knowledge that will be usable in a particular setting and takes details of that setting into account when designing the research. Consequently, society can clearly perceive a use for the knowledge gained from applied research. Two considerations are thus involved when categorizing a research project as basic or applied: the motivation behind the investigator's choice of experimental variables, and the clarity with which we can perceive a social use for the knowledge.

Dividing research into two categories, basic and applied, is useful, but the practice can be misleading. Sharp distinctions between projects often cannot be made. For example, many experiments motivated by curiosity (basic research) are performed under conditions that approximate "real-world" settings (applied research). On the other hand, some experiments motivated by a social need (applied research) are performed under conditions that resemble a laboratory setting (basic research). To take into account these complex relationships, Hilgard (1964) suggested that we conceptualize the psychology of learning as a series of graded steps leading from pure basic research at one extreme to political and industrial activity at the other. Figure 1.1 illustrates Hilgard's view of the steps leading from basic research on learning to innovations in the field of education. Although education is the major beneficiary of research on learning, we could imagine a similar series of steps leading to innovations in psychotherapy.

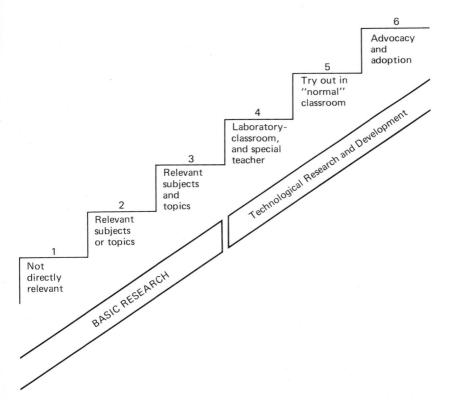

Fig. 1.1 A way of conceptualizing the relationship between basic research on learning and technological research and development in education. (After Hilgard, 1964)

Hilgard defines three categories of basic research and three categories of "technological research and development." The motivation of investigators in each of the basic research categories is curiosity, but as we go from Step 1 to Step 3, the experimental conditions increasingly approximate classroom settings. Thus, going from Step 1 to Step 3, we can see with increasing clarity the social value of the knowledge gained from the research.

The conditions of Step 1 experiments are totally unlike conditions prevailing in a classroom. Subjects in the experiments are often lower animals (rats, pigeons, and monkeys are most common), or if the subjects are human beings, the experimental tasks are highly artificial; no counterparts exist in the classroom. The maze in Fig. 1.2 permits the experimenter to study how practice affects learning in rats. Food is placed in the goal box, and then the rat is released from the start box. The experimenter measures learning as a decrease in the number of blind alleys the rat selects from one trial to the next, or a decrease in the time it takes the rat to reach the goal box. The mirror-tracing device in Fig. 1.3 has provided information about how people learn visual-motor coordination. The subject traces a star with his or her hand visible only through a mirror which reverses the visual field. Whenever the subject touches a line, the experimenter records an error, and initially there are many errors, as the sample drawing at the top demonstrates. But the number of errors gradually decreases from one trial to the next as the subject's visual-motor coordination improves.

An experiment is at Step 2 if it meets at least one of the following criteria: (1) the subjects are school-age children; (2) the experimental task resembles an educational task. Many experiments on learning are at Step 2. They employ adult human beings as subjects, and so do not meet the first criterion, but the subjects work at tasks which resemble educational tasks to some extent. For example, the experimenter may ask subjects to learn a long list of words (much as a teacher might ask students to learn the "ABCs") and strictly control the duration of exposure to each word. Later, the subjects try to recall the list, thereby giving the experimenter a

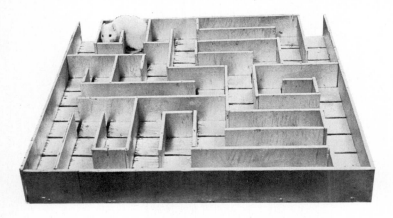

Fig. 1.2 Basic research on learning, Step 1: A rat in a maze. (Robert Smith, Black Star)

THE PSYCHOLOGY OF LEARNING IN A SOCIAL CONTEXT

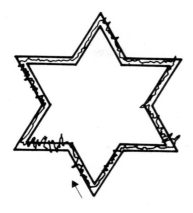

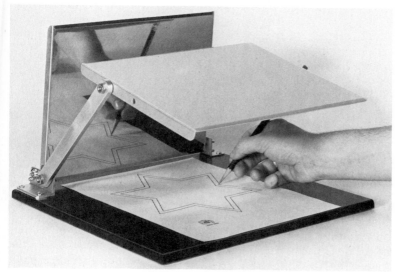

Fig. 1.3 Basic research on learning, Step 1: Mirror-tracing device with sample response sheet. (By courtesy of Lafayette Instrument Co., Lafayette, Ind.)

measure of retention. The memory drum in Fig. 1.4 is a standard laboratory device for presenting items on a time schedule. Whenever the drum rotates, a new item or set of items appears in the window.

Experiments at Step 3 meet both of the criteria described in the preceding paragraph. Because the subjects are school-age children, the experimental materials are likely to be school materials—for example, mathematical problems, foreign vocabulary, or reading primers. Textbooks on the psychology of learning have traditionally focused on research at Steps 1 and 2; in this book, we shall also give close attention to research at Step 3.

Fig. 1.4 Basic research on learning, Step 2: A memory drum for timed presentation of verbal items. (By courtesy of Ralph Gerbrands Co., Arlington, Mass.)

Technological research and development

The goal of technological research and development is to make classroom instruction more effective and efficient. Technological research has the responsibility for creating and evaluating new instructional techniques, materials, and apparatus. Technological development brings the fruits of technological research to society; if studies have shown that a new approach works, it is publicized and packaged for mass distribution.

In the sequence of steps leading from basic research to educational innovation, Steps 4 and 5 constitute the phase of technological research. Research at Step 4 is performed in a setting that resembles a classroom in some ways and a laboratory in other ways. Special facilities may be set up in a school or university for use by a few students. The setting resembles a laboratory in that it is somewhat artificial—the facilities are on a small scale and are not part of a regular instructional program. Yet there are also elements of realism, for the students use the facilities much as they would under normal classroom conditions. For example, to assess the effectiveness of computer-assisted instruction, several computer consoles like that in Fig. 1.5 might be set up for use by a few representative students. Instruction from the computer would supplement or replace instruction from the regular teacher on

Fig. 1.5 Technological research, Steps 4 and 5: A console for use in computer-assisted instruction. (Bob Peterson, Life Magazine, © 1966 Time, Inc.)

some subject. If tests of the system gave promising results, research would advance to Step 5, where regular teachers would integrate expanded versions of the system into their normal classroom routine. Some changes in the system might become necessary as reports from the field accumulated, but if the system facilitated learning and was economically feasible, efforts would probably be made to distribute the system more widely. Advocacy of the system before community groups and school boards, and production of the necessary materials and equipment, would constitute the final step in educational innovation, the phase of technological development.

The process of innovation

The foregoing discussion may have given the impression that educational innovation is typically an orderly process in which principles of learning discovered in the laboratory are taken step-by-step to the classroom. Although experiments on learning do fall on a continuum of increasing relevance to educational problems, the actual process of innovation often has not followed predictable steps. For example, there has been a long-standing tendency to jump from basic research at Steps 1 and

8

2 directly to technological development at Step 6. Hilgard (1964) describes such a case involving the construction of elementary-school books. An influential educational psychologist, E. L. Thorndike (whose work we shall examine in detail later), suggested that the words used in elementary-school readers be ones that appear frequently in print media such as newspapers and books. Research at Step 2 indicated that lists of common words were easier to memorize than lists of uncommon words. Educators embraced Thorndike's recommendation without taking the intermediate technological steps to verify with books what had been found with simple lists. Eventually, it became evident that children could learn uncommon words in the context of meaningful passages, and a revolt developed against the constraints upon word selection that Thorndike had engendered.

Unjustified leaps from the laboratory to the classroom are not the only departures from an orderly process of innovation. Often, innovations have evolved in educational settings without assistance from laboratory research. During the early part of this century, Maria Montessori, an Italian educator, developed instructional materials for preschool children that are today used throughout the world (we shall explore her approach to early childhood education in Chapter 8). Montessori accomplished these innovations by observing children in an informal way rather than by conducting formal experiments. Many recent reform movements have similarly originated in educational settings (Woodring, 1964). For example, a commission established by the National Association of Secondary School Principals developed far-reaching proposals for reorganizing the nation's secondary schools. These proposals, informally designated the Trump plan after the director of the commission, called for such fundamental changes as replacement of class periods of constant duration by class periods of variable duration, and replacement of classes of constant size by classes of variable size. Woodring (1964) notes that while nothing in the Trump plan was inconsistent with principles of learning derived from basic research, basic research did not play an explicit role in the formulation of the plan.

To be sure, laboratory principles have engendered some lasting educational innovations. Techniques of programmed instruction, which are widely used in textbooks and teaching machines, originated in laboratory work with lower animals (we shall explore the relationship between programmed instruction and laboratory principles in Chapter 3). But the history of educational innovation has not generally been one of close cooperation between educational technologists and psychologists engaged in basic research. This division between fields has been institutionalized on many university campuses by the establishment of separate departments of psychology and educational psychology. Perhaps educational technologists have felt that there is little in basic research on learning that would be helpful to them in solving practical problems. Perhaps basic researchers have felt that there is little in educational technology that would challenge them intellectually or provide an opportunity for significant scientific discovery. Both attitudes are misperceptions of the benefits to be gained from communication and cooperative efforts between the two fields.

THE PSYCHOLOGY OF LEARNING IN A SOCIAL CONTEXT

How basic research can help

A time-worn expression warns us that "appearances can be deceiving." This admonition is particularly apt when we consider the question of whether basic research yields significant benefits for society. At the time that basic research is performed, it often *appears* to be unrelated to social problems. Yet, history shows that discoveries made by basic researchers have been pivotal events in the development of many technological innovations. These discoveries might not have been made had the investigators tried to make their studies fit preconceived notions of what was "relevant."

That was a central conclusion reached by a task force set up by the National Institute of Mental Health to study the Institute's scientific activities and make recommendations for the future. The report of this Research Task Force was published in 1975 by NIMH in a volume entitled, *Research in the Service of Mental Health*. One of the task force's objectives was to study the processes responsible for scientific discovery and technological innovation. The focus of the study was an historical analysis performed by the National Research Council, under the sponsorship of NIMH, of the events leading to a major innovation in psychiatry, the development of a tranquilizer called chlorpromazine. Unlike sedatives of the barbiturate variety, chlorpromazine produces a state of "euphoric quietude," which is desirable in some forms of psychotherapy. The chemical from which chlorpromazine was ultimately derived—phenothiazine—was synthesized by a German researcher in 1883. No one anticipated at the time that phenothiazine would eventually lead to a breakthrough in the treatment of mental illness. In fact, the chemical was initially put to an entirely different use in the manufacture of artificial dyes. It was in 1950, more than a half-century after the discovery of phenothiazine, that a research chemist working in a French pharmaceutical laboratory synthesized chlorpromazine. In the intervening years, one would hardly have suspected that science was moving steadily closer to this major accomplishment. Summarizing the events, Seymour S. Kety of the National Research Council wrote the following:

> There were many crucial discoveries, along numerous devious pathways, in ways that could not have been anticipated, to the synthesis of chlorpromazine . . . and its application in psychiatry. Those crucial contributions came from basic research and applied research, organic chemistry, biochemistry, physiology, pharmacology, surgery, experimental psychology, and eventually psychiatry. . . . The logic of a master plan was completely lacking; in its stead were a multitude of smaller plans, creative and logical but none having as its goal a treatment of mental illness. . . . One conclusion, immediately apparent and rather surprising, is that none of the crucial findings or pathways that led, over a century, to the ultimate discovery of chlorpromazine and was essential to it would have been called relevant to the treatment of mental illness even by the most sophisticated judge. (Quoted in NIMH, *Research in the Service of Mental Health*, 1975, pp. 147-148)

The NIMH task force emphasized that the discovery of chlorpromazine was not an isolated example of the social value of scientific knowledge: ". . . there are few 20th century advances that are not indebted in this way to basic scientific research" (1975, p. 148). Essential for progress in the field of mental health, the task force concluded, was a balanced program of basic and applied research.

The climate for innovation   Perhaps you have sensed an inconsistency in the suggestion that basic research on learning contributes significantly to technological progress. If basic research on learning is really important, why has it been possible to create educational innovations without assistance from the laboratory? Is it not possible that technology simply does not require this particular line of research? That possibility exists, but to fully appreciate the importance of basic research on learning we must look more closely at how it influences technological efforts.

In the past 10 years there have been two major innovations with clear links to the laboratory: programmed instruction, which was mentioned earlier, and an approach to psychotherapy called a "token economy." Token economies are essentially systems for rewarding, and thereby strengthening, socially desirable behavior. These systems are prevalent in institutions like mental hospitals and reformatories where the need for behavior change is strong and therapists have great control over the individual's environment. When we examine these technologies in Chapter 3, and the laboratory research on which they are based, consider carefully the nature of the contribution basic research has made. Were the laboratory experiments really necessary? Was there any discovery that had to be made before educators and therapists could institute changes in their respective fields? It would be difficult to argue that progress in these fields would have been impossible without the help of basic research. Yet, basic research did help. It helped in a subtle way—by creating an intellectual climate that was conducive to innovation. Certain techniques had been found to be highly effective in laboratory settings. Individuals who faced challenges in the fields of education and therapy were aware of these techniques and essentially said, "Well, let's try this procedure. Maybe it will work here, too." In other words, basic research was a source of ideas. It changed the way people looked at problems. While laboratory research was not essential to the development of programmed instruction and token economies, it apparently accelerated the process of innovation. Perhaps education and psychotherapy would be further ahead today had there been more such communication in the past.

The relevance of rats   For decades, psychologists have studied the behavior of lower animals in an effort to understand the behavior of human beings. Perhaps that notion seems paradoxical to you. After all, if the objective is to understand people, why not study people? Skepticism about animal research is widespread (recall Senator Proxmire's assault on the chili-eating rats!), and some additional words on the problem would perhaps be useful here.

Some research must be done with animals rather than people. The investigators are interested in studying the effects of extremely aversive events, such as traumatic punishment, and ethical considerations preclude the use of human subjects. (Of course, one could argue that it is also unethical to inflict pain on lower animals.) Where ethics are not an issue, the rationale for studying animal behavior is usually that animals are simpler than people and that it is easier to identify and control the factors that influence animal behavior. By careful study of animals, we may discover leads that will give us a head start in our search for the factors that influence human behavior. Whether this is the most efficient way to learn about human behavior is debatable. But it is clear that the study of animals has advanced our understanding of human behavior and contributed significantly to society. Programmed instruction and token economies are just two examples of technological innovations that originated in laboratory work with lower animals.

Generalizing from animal behavior to human behavior must always be done cautiously, for human beings are in many ways unique. Specialists in animal learning are routinely cautious about generalizing; they recognize that studies with human subjects will not necessarily corroborate findings from animal research. But the skepticism that many people show toward animal research goes well beyond caution. It is more a refusal to accept any animal research as relevant to the understanding of human behavior. The attitude is a puzzling one, for the same people may generalize from human behavior to animal behavior without qualification. To say that a dog "wants to go out" is to generalize across species. Do not people also want things? To say that a dog "expects" food when it drools is to generalize across species. Do not people have expectations? To say that a cat feels "affection" when it purrs, or "anger" when it hisses, or "fear" when it runs away, is to generalize across species. Are not affection, anger, and fear human emotions? Animals and people often behave in similar ways in similar circumstances, and the inclination to project human traits onto animals is very strong. So common is this practice that it has a name—**anthropomorphism.** Why, then, is there a reluctance to accept generalizations in the reverse direction—from animals to people? Perhaps the practice is unacceptable because it seems to lower the status of human beings. Anthropomorphism, on the other hand, may be acceptable because it seems to elevate animals while leaving the status of human beings intact. Whatever the reason for these contradictory attitudes, we should recognize that cautious generalization from animal behavior to human behavior can tell us much about ourselves.

Your stake in basic research   "Why do psychologists study learning, and why should you read this book?" Those were questions posed at the beginning of the chapter and we are now in a good position to answer them. Psychologists study learning because it is a pervasive phenomenon and they wish to know more about it. Learning is the means by which we adjust to the demands of everyday life. It is the capacity which enables us to benefit not only from our own experience but— through the written and spoken word—from the experience of other people.

Improved understanding of the factors that influence learning can help in efforts to improve the human condition. But a desire to improve the human condition is not the principal reason why psychologists study learning; their primary motivation is curiosity, a desire to know.

Most of the principles that we shall explore in this book come from basic research supported by federal funds. Through your tax dollars you have made a real, personal investment in that research. Whether you realize a return on your investment will depend largely on your own efforts. Principles of learning discovered through basic research have made significant contributions to society, but technologists—educational, clinical, industrial—have only begun to tap this rich store of knowledge. It may be years before their efforts make contact with your life. You can realize the fullest benefits from principles of learning by using your own ingenuity to find applications of the principles in your daily life.

Of course, practical applications are not the only benefits that science offers. Scientific investigation is, in a sense, an art. Like a drama, a symphony, or a painting, an experiment is an act of creation. It, too, can stimulate the imagination and alter one's views. Such is the appeal of science to a scientist. Vincent Dethier, a biologist of international stature, has eloquently described the psychology of a scientist in his little book, *To Know a Fly* (1962). The book is about Dethier himself, and he epitomizes the scientific attitude with the assertion that, "A properly conducted experiment is a beautiful thing. It is an adventure, an expedition, a conquest (p. 18)." Those who can appreciate science in this emotional sense have available to them a unique opportunity for personal enrichment. An appreciation of science for its own sake is an attitude well worth cultivating.

The challenge of technology

Progress rather than curiosity is the primary motivation behind technological research on learning. Nevertheless, technological research can be as intellectually demanding and gratifying as basic research. A common misperception of technological research in general is that it involves only straightforward, cookbook applications of scientific principles. In reality, technological advances are as much products of creative thinking as scientific advances. Technology relies only partly on knowledge gained from basic research, for rarely can a technologist find a body of scientific knowledge that has anticipated all of the problems he or she faces. Much remains to be learned in the field. In the pursuit of knowledge the technologist may rely on rigorous scientific methodology in some circumstances, but more often the technologist must also play hunches and test them in a trial-and-error fashion. In a provocative historical survey of technological developments, Ferguson (1977) concludes that nonscientific modes of thought have heavily influenced technological decisions: "Pyramids, cathedrals, and rockets exist not because of geometry, theory of structures, or thermodynamics, but because they were first a picture—literally a vision—in the minds of those who built them

(p. 827)." To the student of learning, as well as to society, technological endeavors offer many rewards.

THE NATURE OF LEARNING

Have we gotten ahead of ourselves? Here we are well into the first chapter and we have yet to consider a formal definition of learning. How can we have gotten this far without one? Indeed, one might ask: How could the psychology of learning have gotten this far without one? For while research on learning has advanced significantly over the years, there is no single, universally accepted definition of learning. An angry judge once remarked that he could not formally define "pornography," but he sure knew it when he saw it. The term "learning" gives rise to a similar paradox. Notwithstanding the difficulty of developing a formal definition, examples of learning are usually easy to identify. Consider the rat in the maze in Fig. 1.2. On the first occasion that the rat enters the maze, it makes many wrong turns and its time to reach the goal is quite long. On the next trial, there are fewer wrong turns and the running time is shorter. Several trials later, the rat goes directly and speedily to the goal. Learning has clearly taken place. Or, consider the mirror-tracing device in Fig. 1.3. The first time the individual attempts the task, his or her pen touches the borders of the star many times. On later trials, the subject traces the star without an error. This, too, is a clear example of learning.

During the last World Series you probably noticed that the fans in the home ballparks of the contending teams held considerably different opinions about which of the teams should win the Series. Obviously, the preferences of the fans were learned. So, too, are political attitudes, and prejudices, and social skills, and fears of dogs and cats, and . . . the list if virtually endless.

Examples of unlearned behavior are also easy to identify, although on closer examination the behavior often reveals a learned component. The main clue that behavior is not entirely learned is its prevalence in all members of a species or subgroup of a species such as males or females. When the doctor taps your knee, your leg jumps. When you eat candy, your mouth waters. And when you enter a dark room, the pupils in your eyes dilate. Whatever your personal background, these stimuli will reliably elicit their responses. You have many such inborn **reflexes.** Another form of unlearned behavior, called a **tropism,** involves a general orientation toward or away from a particular kind of stimulus. If there was an annoying fly in your room, by darkening the room and lighting a candle you could induce it to "commit suicide." Because the fly has a tropism that favors bright areas, it might fly directly into the flame. More complex than reflexes and tropisms are **instincts,** which often consist of a chain of reactions. A striking example is the feeding behavior of young laughing gulls, a species of seagull that breeds in the coastal marshlands of eastern North America (Hailman, 1969). The laughing gull chick obtains food from the parent by performing a sequence of two pecks (Fig. 1.6). When the parent lowers its head (panel a), the chick pecks at the parent's beak and strokes it

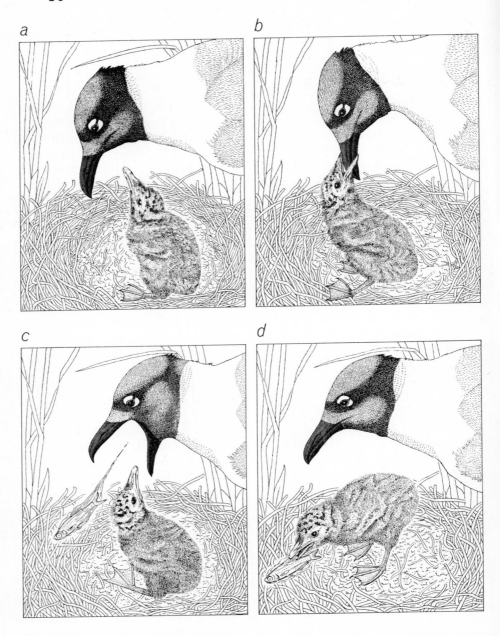

Fig. 1.6 Instinctive feeding behavior of the laughing gull chick. (a) Parent gull triggers feeding behavior by lowering head; (b) Chick grabs beak and strokes it downward ("begging peck"); (c) Parent regurgitates partly digested fish; (d) Chick tears at fish and swallows pieces ("feeding pecks"). (From Hailman, 1969)

THE PSYCHOLOGY OF LEARNING IN A SOCIAL CONTEXT

downward (panel b). This is a "begging peck." In response to the begging peck, the parent regurgitates a bit of partly digested food (panel c), which the chick tears at with a type of action called a "feeding peck" (panel d). The begging and feeding pecks are **fixed action patterns;** each has a characteristic form that varies little from one chick to another. Those actions of the parent that elicit begging and feeding pecks are called **releasers.**

Hailman (1969) presents evidence that much of the chick's feeding behavior is learned. In one experiment, chicks were reared in a dark incubator for 24 hours after hatching. Upon emerging from the incubator, the chicks encountered a series of models resembling an adult gull's head in varying degrees. The models were pictures drawn on cards that swung back and forth to simulate the natural movement of the adult. Hailman found that chicks without prior visual experience pecked vigorously at any model showing a beak which was at least partly red (the natural color of a laughing gull's beak.) In the most extreme comparison, the chicks were found to peck heartily at a model showing a beak without a head (a kind of "Cheshire" seagull), but to peck very little at a model showing a head without a beak. In contrast, older chicks which had received visual experience in the nest for a week pecked vigorously only at models that closely resembled an adult laughing gull. It appears that while the chick inherits a fixed action pattern to the releaser of a beak, experience teaches the chick to recognize its parent, and the influence of the releaser is eventually modified.

Experience is the common denominator of all the examples of learning we have examined. Experience took the form of repetitive practice in the maze and mirror-drawing situations. In the cases of preferences and prejudices, the precipitating experiences are undoubtedly more complex. If a particular form of behavior occurred without prior opportunity for relevant experience, we could say that the behavior was inborn. Such was the nature of the evidence Hailman (1969) presented to show that the laughing gull chick inherits a fixed action pattern of pecking at a beak.

Not all behavior changes brought about by experience can be taken as signs of learning. Suppose that our rat became an expert at running the maze, and our human subject became an expert at mirror-tracing. If we continued to administer practice trials without a break, we would eventually observe a deterioration in the subjects' performances. The rat would slow down and perhaps make more wrong turns. The mirror-tracer would hit the borders of the star more frequently. These are behavior changes, but they are not signs of learning. The rat became satiated with food. The human subject became tired or bored. In general, to say that a change in behavior has resulted from learning, we must be able to rule out alternative interpretations in terms of fatigue and shifts in motivation. We can do this by showing that the behavior change is relatively permanent. Despite fluctuations in performance, if learning has taken place, the subject should continue to be *capable* of the behavior indefinitely. Put the rat in the maze again after three days of food deprivation and it will show you what it is capable of. Offer the mirror-tracer $50 for an errorless trial, and chances are you will see an errorless trial.

THE NATURE OF LEARNING

With the foregoing considerations in mind, how would you interpret the following situation? You go to bed early one night and encounter unexpected difficulties in going to sleep—your neighbor is playing his or her stereo set very loudly. Thirty minutes pass before you can even close your eyes. Eventually, the noise ceases to arouse you and you fall asleep. A behavior change occurred: You **habituated** to the noise. As the night wore on, you became progressively less responsive to the stimulus of noise. Would you say that you habituated because you "learned" to cope with the noise? From this incident alone, one could not rule out an alternative interpretation in terms of sensory adaptation. It is possible that after extended exposure to the noise, the stimulus simply did not fully register in your brain. If the same predicament arose in the future, and you fell asleep sooner than you did the first time, we could attribute at least part of the habituation to learning, the part which was relatively permanent. Research in laboratory settings has shown that habituation often does have such a permanent effect.

Learning vs. performance

The distinction between capability, or level of learning, and performance is an important one, both theoretically and practically. Theoretically, the distinction implies that learning is not directly observable but rather reflected, sometimes inaccurately, in behavior. Practically, the distinction implies that we should not jump to conclusions about a person's capabilities on the basis of poor performance, for there may be much "beneath the surface." Experiments have shown that organisms can learn much without giving full evidence of what they have learned in their behavior. This phenomenon, called **latent learning,** was dramatically illustrated in a classic experiment by Tolman and Honzik (1930). Three groups of rats ran a maze once a day for 17 days. One group always found food in the goal box and, not surprisingly, these rats made progressively fewer wrong turns from day to day. Another group never found reward in the goal box. Although the unrewarded rats made many errors throughout the experiment, they did exhibit a slight improvement from day to day. Perhaps removal from the maze upon reaching the goal box was a reward in itself. A third group found no food for the first 10 days of the experiment, and was also making many errors. But on Day 11, and every day thereafter, things looked up. Rats in the third group now found food. The effect of introducing reward in the middle of the experiment was startling. On Day 12, the rats showed a sharp drop in errors and their performance matched that of the rats that had found food reward since Day 1. On subsequent days, rats in the third group even outperformed the others. Apparently, the rats in all of the groups had learned equal amounts about the maze, but the extent to which they exhibited learning depended on their motivation to perform.

As the foregoing discussion suggests, it is difficult to examine learning in isolation from other kinds of processes. Motivation must also be taken into account. So, too, must memory, our ability to retain traces of past experiences. For without memory, past experiences could not possibly influence our capabilities. Thus, this is a book about motivation and memory, as well as learning. Our goal is to explore the processes of learning, memory, and motivation as they relate to science, society, and, of course, *you*.

SUMMARY

There are two broad classes of scientific activity: basic research and applied research. In categorizing a research project as basic or applied, we must consider two factors: (1) the motivation behind the investigator's choice of variables: (2) the clarity with which we can perceive a social use for the knowledge obtained. Basic research is motivated by curiosity, an interest in knowledge for the sake of knowledge. Because basic research is typically conducted in artificial settings, it may be hard to perceive a social use for the knowledge. Applied research is motivated by specific social needs. Because it is conducted in "real-world" settings, the social value of the knowledge is evident.

In reality, there is no sharp boundary between basic and applied research. Hilgard suggested a system of categorization consisting of six steps leading from basic research on learning to technological research and development in the field of education. Basic research (Steps 1-3) is said to be motivated by curiosity, technological research and development (Steps 4-6) by social needs. As one goes from Step 1 to Step 3 in the basic research category, the experimental settings increasingly approximate classroom conditions. At Step 1, the tasks are very different from those found in classrooms, and the subjects are often lower animals. At Step 2, the experimental tasks resemble educational tasks, or the subjects are school-age children. At Step 3, both of the Step 2 criteria are met.

Technological research (Steps 4 and 5) has the goal of creating and testing new techniques, materials, and apparatus. Step 4 research is on a small scale and is administered by a special teacher who has been trained for this purpose. Step 5 research is on a large scale; regular teachers integrate the new educational strategies into their normal classroom routines. Technological development (Step 6) has the objective of distributing the products of technological research. This involves advocacy, marketing, and manufacturing.

Historically, the process of educational innovation has not followed predictable steps. Two common departures from an orderly process of innovation have been premature leaps from the laboratory to the classroom (Thorndike example), and the introduction of classroom techniques without prior laboratory research (Montessori example). Communication between educational technologists and basic researchers has perhaps been impeded by misperceptions of what each field offers the other.

In general, basic research has made many technological contributions. Progress toward a technological breakthrough has usually been hard to detect because the research projects contributing to a discovery have had purposes unrelated to that discovery. Basic research on learning in particular has contributed significantly to education and psychotherapy. The text suggests that basic research has contributed mainly by serving as a source of ideas to technologists confronted with difficult problems. In this sense, basic research on learning has created a climate conducive to technological innovation. From a more personal standpoint, basic research offers another sort of benefit: It can be appreciated for its own sake, much as one would appreciate a well-written novel or an elegantly composed symphony.

A common misperception of technological research is that it consists of "cookbook" applications of scientific principles. Actually, technological research can be highly creative, involving both intuitive thought and rigorous scientific methodology.

Although scientific research on learning has been going on for decades, there is no single, universally accepted definition of learning. One crucial aspect of learning is that it arises from experience. If an organism exhibited behavior without having had relevant prior experience, we would say that the behavior was genetic in origin. A clue that behavior is not entirely learned is the prevalence of the behavior among all members of a species or species subgroup. There are three kinds of behavior with a genetic component. "Reflexes" are relatively simple responses that are reliably elicited by stimuli. When the stimulus is present, the response occurs. "Tropisms" are general orientations toward or away from a stimulus. "Instincts" consist of sequences of reactions, each a fixed action pattern having a characteristic form that varies little from one member of the species to the other. Stimuli which elicit fixed action patterns are called "releasers."

Not all changes in behavior that arise from experience are signs of learning. Temporary changes in behavior due to fatigue or shifts in motivation must be distinguished from changes due to learning. One way to do this is to show that an organism continues to be capable of exhibiting the behavior despite temporary fluctuations in performance. This criterion is particularly important in the interpretation of "habituation," a progressive decline in responsiveness to a repeated stimulus. If an organism habituates to the stimulus faster as experience with the stimulus increases, at least part of the habituation can be attributed to learning. Otherwise, sensory adaptation is probably responsible.

"Latent learning" refers to a change in an organism's capabilities that is not fully apparent in behavior. Tolman and Honzik demonstrated latent learning in rats by administering trials in a maze without reward. Little learning was evident in performance, as errors dropped only slightly from trial to trial. After food was introduced, errors dropped sharply, indicating that the rats had learned the route to the goal box on earlier trials but had not exhibited learning because there was no incentive to do so. Latent learning emphasizes the distinction between learning and performance. It also shows the importance of studying learning in relation to motivation, as both motivation and learning influence performance. To fully understand learning, one must also consider the processes of memory, for learning would not be possible without the ability to remember past experiences. Thus the psychology of learning is necessarily concerned with the complex interrelationships among learning, memory, and motivation.

THE PSYCHOLOGY OF LEARNING IN A SOCIAL CONTEXT

STUDY QUESTIONS

1. What are the two major characteristics of basic research? Of applied research?

2. With specific reference to the points listed below, describe Hilgard's conceptualization of the steps leading from basic research on learning to technological research and development in education:

    a) The feature that distinguishes basic research (Steps 1–3) from applied research (Steps 4–6).

    b) The general features of Step 1 research; indicate why mirror-tracing experiments are classified as Step 1 research.

    c) The two criteria to be considered when deciding whether research is at Step 2.

    d) How Step 3 research differs from Step 2 research. Why would experiments using memory drums and adults as subjects be categorized at Step 2 rather than Step 3 or Step 1?

    e) The goals of technological research and technological development.

    f) How Step 4 research differs from Step 5.

    g) The nature of activities at Step 6.

3. Give two examples of cases in which the process of innovation in education has not followed the orderly progression of steps conceptualized by Hilgard.

4. Using the example of the discovery of chlorpromazine, explain how basic research can lead to a technological breakthrough without giving evidence that progress toward that achievement is being made.

5. According to the author, how has basic research on learning created a climate conducive to technological innovation?

6. What are the two major reasons why psychologists use lower animals in research on learning?

7. What is "anthropomorphism"? Give two examples.

8. Explain how technological research involves more than mere cookbook application of scientific principles.

9. What is the main clue that a particular bit of behavior is at least partly genetic in origin?

10. Define and give examples of an inborn *reflex* and a *tropism*.

11. Using the example of the feeding behavior of the laughing gull chick, describe the concept of instinctive behavior. Your answer should: (a) mention the two kinds of peck exhibited by the chick and the stimuli that produce them: (b) include definitions of the terms *fixed action pattern* and *releaser*.

12. What part of the laughing gull chick's feeding behavior is genetic in origin? What part is learned? How did Hailman demonstrate the learned and genetic components?

13. What is the common denominator of all instances of learning?

14. How can one demonstrate that a change in behavior resulted from learning rather than from fatigue or a shift in motivation? State a general rule and give an example.

15. What is *habituation*? How can one demonstrate that habituation is a form of learning?

16. Describe Tolman and Honzik's experiment on latent learning, indicating the procedure and results for each of the three groups. How do the results support a distinction between learning and performance?

CHAPTER 2

Classical Conditioning: Principles of Association

In 1904, Ivan Petrovich Pavlov became the first physiologist to win the Nobel Prize. News of the award is said to have stunned him, but the scientific community could not have been too surprised by Pavlov's selection. His accomplishments in the study of digestion had already brought him international recognition. For years, Pavlov had ranked among the leading scientists of Russia, and his book, *Lectures on the Work of the Digestive Glands,* had been translated into German, French, and English. Few scientific books have achieved such wide distribution.

Perhaps the greatest surprise occasioned by the award came during Pavlov's acceptance speech in Sweden. Instead of reviewing and enlarging upon his discoveries in digestion, as would be customary, Pavlov spoke enthusiastically about an entirely different subject, avoiding any discussion of the research for which he received the prize. The speech, entitled, "The First Sure Steps Along the Path of a New Investigation," signalled to all that his interests had radically changed. The new investigation to which he referred was the study of "conditioned reflexes," a phenomenon he had only recently discovered. Conditioned reflexes are now familiar to every student of psychology. Ring a bell just before giving a hungry dog a bit of food. The dog will salivate when he receives the food but not when he hears the bell. After ringing the bell and presenting the food several more times, you will find that the dog now salivates in response to the bell. The salivation produced by the food is an inborn or "unconditioned" reflex and the salivation produced by the bell is an acquired or "conditioned" reflex.

At the age of 55, Pavlov would have surprised no one had he announced in Sweden that he planned to continue his successful work on digestion. Indeed, just five years before the award that was his intention. He stated in a speech then that, "We shall in the end arrive at a knowledge as accurate and complete of the process of diseases of the alimentary canal [the gastrointestinal tract] as we now have of its admirably beautiful work under normal conditions (Babkin, 1949, p. 280)." But in succeeding years Pavlov devoted progressively less time to research on digestion, and eventually his laboratory abandoned the field entirely. Why did Pavlov consider the discovery of conditioned reflexes to be so important? From the perspective of the modern world—a world of space shuttles, jets, and microcomputers—

Biographical information on Pavlov is from B. P. Babkin, *Pavlov.* Chicago: University of Chicago Press, 1949.

Pavlov's enthusiasm may be hard to understand. It is only when we view conditioned reflexes as Pavlov did, in historical context, that we can fully appreciate their significance.

THE CONCEPT OF THE REFLEX IN THE HISTORY OF PSYCHOLOGY

The concept of the reflex has major implications for how we view ourselves and others. Philosophically, it represents a challenge to a belief that for many people has the status of a truism, and that is a basic assumption of religions and legal systems throughout the world. The belief in question is that of "free will," the idea that people can do as they wish whatever the pressures acting on them to do otherwise. If you say that something a person has done was a reflex, you are implying that the action was automatic, compelled, beyond the individual's control. You are denying free will.

The French philosopher, Descartes (1569-1650) introduced the concept of the reflex at a time when holding such views could be dangerous. Free will lay at the core of Church doctrine, and the Church exercised a powerful influence over people's lives. Denial of free will could have earned Descartes harsh censure or worse had he not softened his views. Descartes compromised. Only a small part of our behavior is reflexive, he said. The major part is the expression of a free will.

Descartes apparently took his concept of the reflex from observations of machines. At the Royal Fountains in France, engineers had constructed life-like animated dolls for the amusement of strollers. Mythical figures, monsters, and warriors performed elaborate routines as the strollers approached them. Unknowingly, a person would step on a hidden pedal along the path and a bathing Diana would run off behind the bushes. If the person pursued her, and happened to step on another pedal, Neptune emerged and threateningly displayed his trident. What gave the dolls realism was not movement alone, but movement in response to the environment. Had Diana run to the bushes on a time schedule, independently of approaching strollers, her movements would have seemed much less natural.

To make the machines responsive to the world, the engineers applied hydraulic principles. Inside the dolls was an elaborate system of pipes. When a stroller stepped on a pedal, water flowed from a central reservoir through the pipes and provided the energy for movement. Now, if the movements of Diana and Neptune were governed by mechanical principles, and their movements resembled human behavior, might not human behavior itself be governed by mechanical principles? Descartes maintained that some of it operated on principles similar to those employed by the engineers. Imagine that a barefoot boy has stepped on a hot cinder. The heat creates activity in a sense organ of the foot, and a hollow, tubular nerve attached to the organ carries the information to the brain. Upon receiving the message, the brain opens a reservoir and releases a substance, "animal spirits," into the nerve. The animal spirits flow through the nerve into the muscles of the foot. As the animal spirits enter the muscles, the muscles swell, thereby causing the foot to move away from the cinder. Note that the boy does not exercise any conscious control over the action; it runs off automatically.

CLASSICAL CONDITIONING: PRINCIPLES OF ASSOCIATION

There is much in Descartes' theory that a modern reader might find amusing. For example, no one today speaks of "animal spirits" or hollow, tube-like nerves. But the essential features of Descartes' system come surprisingly close to our modern concept of the reflex. Reflexes start when a physical event excites a sense organ. Sensory nerves carry the information by means of a chemical process to a point in the spinal cord or brain. The message thereupon goes to intermediary cells acting as a kind of switchboard, and then to appropriate motor nerves (a distinction between sensory and motor nerves came hundreds of years after Descartes). When the nerve impulses reach the muscles, the muscles contract (they do not swell, or increase in volume, as Descartes imagined). The nerves might run to glands instead of muscles, in which case glandular secretion rather than movement would be the consequence of stimulation. Most reflexes are difficult to control through an act of will. For example, try to hold your leg still after the doctor has tapped your knee, or to keep your mouth dry after sucking on a lemon. Once the stimulus occurs, the response follows, and the predictability of reflexive responses gives them a mechanical quality very much like that of Diana's and Neptune's movements. But how much further can we extend the analogy between ourselves and animated dolls? *All* of their behavior is mechanical in nature. To what extent is ours?

Body and soul

As mentioned earlier, Descartes maintained that relatively little human behavior was mechanical. He considered to be mechanical those actions we would today regard as unconditioned reflexes. According to Descartes, most human behavior originated in the "soul" and was free of the environmental compulsion which characterized reflexes. The soul had no physical dimensions. It existed in an entirely different realm than the brain, nerves, and muscles. Because physical laws did not operate in this mental world, the soul could initiate any actions it wished at any time. To initiate behavior, the soul commanded the brain to release animal spirits from the reservoir. The animal spirits flowed through the same system of nerves, and entered the same muscles, as they did when released by an external stimulus. But the behavior was voluntary in nature, not mechanical; no stimulus made the behavior happen.

For Descartes, then, the concept of a stimulus was central to the distinction between voluntary and involuntary behavior. An observable, physical event always preceded an involuntary act; no stimulus consistently preceded a voluntary act. By implication, an involuntary act was predictable, for if you saw the stimulus, you knew the response would follow. A voluntary act was inherently unpredictable because of the absence of a reliable signal. For example, if you had seen the barefoot boy discussed earlier step on the hot cinder, you could have predicted that he would soon lift his leg; this was a mechanical, involuntary act. But the boy could lift the same foot at other times in the act of walking, running, or jumping, and you might not be able to predict these actions. A person could do any of these things in the absence of a clear signal. Over the centuries, physiologists, and later psychologists, have sought to classify actions as either voluntary or involuntary, and their

THE CONCEPT OF THE REFLEX IN THE HISTORY OF PSYCHOLOGY

decisions have usually turned on this point. If one could show that a stimulus reliably predicted a response, that bit of behavior passed from the category of voluntary action to the category of involuntary action.

Free will and morality Voluntary or involuntary—what does it matter? The controversy over free will has many implications, but perhaps the most important bears on one's sense of morality. You can hold people morally responsible for their actions only to the extent that they have freedom of choice. Moral judgments of "right" and "wrong" make no sense when applied to actions performed under compulsion. Suppose, for example, that a teenager who has been walking behind a little old lady for several blocks suddenly pushes her down, causing serious injury. Was the assault on the woman morally wrong? Many people would view it that way and would want to see the assailant punished. Imagine, now, that the same teenager who has been walking behind the same little old lady suddenly trips. Reflexively, he thrusts his arms forward and happens to push the woman down, causing serious injury. Was the action morally wrong? One could hardly attach moral significance to the behavior since the boy did not intend to do harm. Looking at the situation from Descartes' standpoint, the behavior did not originate in the "soul" but in the environment.

According to a philosophical doctrine called **determinism,** no human action is free of compulsion. For every action, there is an identifiable cause, just as there are identifiable causes for sunsets, tides, and changes in the weather. To a determinist, it is as meaningless to call the assault on the woman wrong as it is to call the act of tripping wrong. This does not mean that determinists are unconcerned about crime. They are as opposed to crime as anyone else, but they take a practical approach to the problem, not a moralistic approach. A common moralistic attitude is that criminal offenders should be punished because they "deserve" to be punished. Before determinists favored the use of punishment, they would wish to know how effective it actually was in reducing crime, and under what conditions it worked best.

People commonly strike a compromise between free will and determinism, viewing some kinds of behavior as compelled and some kinds as free. Of course, that was also Descartes position, but far more behavior is seen as involuntary today than in Descartes' time. As we shall see, Pavlov's work on conditioned reflexes has done much to change people's attitudes.

Conditioned reflexes and the mind

Descartes arrived at his concept of the reflex through speculation rather than experimentation. Actual observations of reflexes during the 17th, 18th, and 19th centuries confirmed the essential features of Descartes' concept and revealed many subtle features that Descartes had not contemplated. Some of the reflexes studied by physiologists were highly complex, and up to the middle of the 19th century, physiologists believed such reactions to originate in the mind. The "wash reflex" of the frog illustrates how much thinking has changed since the 19th century (Babkin, 1949). To eliminate any influence of the frog's brain, the brain was surgically separated from the spinal cord, making the animal a "spinal" preparation. When an irritant, acetic acid, was painted on the right side of the frog's back, the right hind leg came up and scratched the area of irritation. At this point, the relationship between stimulus and response was simple and direct; there was little reason to talk about mental activity. But then the right leg was amputated. When acid was again applied on the right side of the back, the *left* leg came up and scratched the irritated area. The frog seemed to have a purpose in mind—to wash off the acid by whatever means were available. The physiologist Pfluger regarded the wash reflex as evidence that the frog had a mind in its spinal cord! You would have to look long and hard to find a physiologist today with a similar interpretation. No longer is the sheer complexity of an action taken as a sign that the action originated in the mind.

For centuries, then, the mind reigned supreme as the initiator of behavior. The stimulus had a minor influence, initiating only simple, inborn reflexes. In opposition to these generally accepted views, the 19th century Russian physiologist, I. M. Sechenov, advanced the radical thesis that *all* behavior was reflexive, from the simplest spinal reactions to the most complex activities involving the brain. Every action was part of a three-phase sequence beginning with sensory excitation, continuing with an internal phase in which nerve impulses followed certain paths, and terminating in muscular movement. The variability of so-called "voluntary" behavior was an illusion arising from unnoticed changes in the environment and the body. If one could somehow hold all the internal and external factors constant, a given stimulus would always produce the same movement. But what of thinking? Do not thoughts exist? A thought, said Sechenov, was nothing more than "the first two-thirds" of a reflex. Sensory excitation initiated a train of nerve impulses which we experienced as thought. The final phase of the reflexive sequence—muscular movement—was suppressed through a process of inhibition, a process Sechenov had clearly demonstrated in animals and human beings.

Sechenov asserted that connections between physical stimuli and thoughts emerged through a process of association. At the same time that we experienced a thought, we also received impulses from sense organs throughout the body. The simultaneous occurrence of a thought and a pattern of stimulation created a link between them, so that on future occasions when we encoutered the stimulus pattern we also experienced the thought. The stimuli could be so inconspicuous that the thought would seem to arise spontaneously in the mind. Sechenov illustrated the process of association with the following example:

> I devote my daytime to physiology, but in the evening, while going to bed, it is my habit to think of politics. It happens, of course, that among other political matters I sometimes think of the Emperor of China. This acoustic trace [the sound of the words] becomes associated with the various sensations (muscular, tactile, thermic, etc.) which I experience when lying in bed. It may happen one day, that owing to the fatigue or the lack of work,

I lie down on my bed in the daytime and lo! all of a sudden I notice that I am thinking of the Emperor of China. (Sechenov, *Reflexes of the Brain*, 1863; quoted in Babkin, 1949, p. 289)

The concept of association did not originate with Sechenov. Thousands of years earlier, Aristotle spoke of association in relation to memory, and the concept was further developed by a succession of British philosophers including Thomas Hobbes (1588-1679), John Locke (1632-1704), and George Berkeley (1685-1753). Basically, these philosophers took the position that all knowledge of the world came through the senses, that simple sense impressions became linked together through a process of association, and that clusters of sense impressions constituted "ideas." Sechenov was particularly influenced by Locke, who in 1700 similarly regarded the joint occurrence of two events as a powerful determinant of association:

A man has suffered pain or sickness in a place; he saw his friend die in such a room; though these have in nature nothing to do with one another, yet when the idea of the place occurs to mind, it brings (the impression being once made) that of the pain and displeasure with it: he confounds them in his mind, and can as little bear the one as the other. (Locke, 1700; reprinted in Dennis, 1948, p. 67)

Although Locke and Sechenov both saw great significance in the concept of association, they approached it very differently. Locke studied association through **introspection,** by "looking inward" at the mental events. Sechenov, who considered mental events to be reflexes firmly grounded in the physical world, felt that association should be studied in the same way as reflexes, by physiological methods. Sechenov never performed a physiological investigation of association, however. It was Pavlov who brought Sechenov's ideas to fruition.

Dr. Wolfson vs. Dr. Snarsky   Pavlov's chief concern in his studies of digestion had been the role of reflex action in glandular secretion. The research had fundamental significance for biology because for thousands of years the prevailing view had been that bodily fluids, or "humors," regulated the various functions of the body. Pavlov vigorously opposed the humoral view and held steadfastly to the supremacy of nervous regulation (we know today that both hormonal and nervous regulation are important). A deep interest in reflex action was thus present before Pavlov started work on conditioned reflexes.

Pavlov's studies of conditioned reflexes evolved directly from his studies of digestion. To investigate the secretions of the digestive glands, Pavlov would introduce food into the mouth or stomach of a dog. A tube implanted in the glands or the wall of the intestine carried the secretions outside the animal where Pavlov could measure the volume. By cutting various nerves serving the glands and intestine, Pavlov could deduce the role of these nerves in the regulation of digestion. There was a complicating factor, however. The dogs often salivated at the mere sight of food, so that the total volume of saliva Pavlov measured really represented more than a direct response to food in the mouth. This phenomenon, previously described by many investigators, had acquired the label of "psychic secretion" because the salivation seemed to arise from mental activity in the animal—the anticipation of food. To make his study of digestion complete, Pavlov felt that he ought to investigate this "psychic secretion," and initially he accepted the mental interpretation of it. But his views gradually changed. Two research associates who assisted him in the investigation approached the problem in opposite ways. One colleague, Dr. Wolfson, took an objective approach, observing external events and their interrelations. The other colleague, Dr. Snarsky, undertook a subjective approach. He assumed that the inner world of the dog was similar to ours and that we could understand psychic secretion by considering how we would feel under similar conditions. After a period of indecision over the relative merits of the two approaches, Pavlov came to feel that Wolfson's method of investigation was more promising. The objective analysis seemed to be producing facts while the subjective analysis seemed to be yielding only speculations. To reassure himself that the objective analysis was more appropriate, Pavlov sought facts about "psychic secretion" that a subjective interpretation could not readily explain. Eventually, facts did emerge which strengthened Pavlov's resolve to follow the objective path.

An experiment in 1901–1902 with I. F. Tolochinov—the first ever on conditioned reflexes—was a turning point for Pavlov (Babkin, 1949). A dog that customarily salivated at the sight of food was shown the food several times without being allowed to eat it. Gradually, the salivation decreased and eventually it disappeared. Thus far, the subjective approach encountered no difficulties; one could easily attribute the absence of salivation to the animal's no longer anticipating the food. But how might one explain the following phenomenon subjectively? Pavlov gave the dog a whiff of mustard oil, a highly aversive substance to dogs, and then displayed the food again without allowing the dog to eat it. Surprisingly, the dog salivated. Why should the animal now anticipate the food? Pavlov felt the phenomenon had no clear subjective interpretation and must have arisen from a physiological process of some kind. Subsequent experiments demonstrated that any arbitrary stimulus, such as a tone or light, could evoke secretion if it was presented several times before the delivery of food. The reaction was highly predictable. It exhibited none of the variability that was supposed to characterize voluntary acts originating in the mind. Moreover, the secretion never occurred in the absence of the stimulus. Why did not the thought of food occur spontaneously at other times? Pavlov saw no reason to regard the secretion as anything but a reflex, a special sort of reflex acquired through a process of association.

For Pavlov, these early investigations of conditioned reflexes apparently had great personal significance. After his decision to give up the study of digestion, Pavlov became more fully aware of his reasons for doing so. He recalled that as a youth he had read Sechenov's book, *Reflexes of the Brain* (1963), which interpreted our subjective world in physiological terms. At the time, the boldness and innovativeness of the theory impressed Pavlov deeply. Later, as the phenomenon of conditioned reflexes unfolded, the earlier enthusiasm over the reflex theory of thought must have been reawakened. Conditioned reflexes seemed to confirm Sechenov's basic insights and to offer a way of investigating the most complex functions of the brain. Pavlov always viewed his studies of conditioned reflexes as studies of the cerebral cortex. From each new relationship between stimulus and response Pavlov deduced some new feature of cortical function. It is ironic that today we view the relationships between stimulus and response as basic facts, and the deductions about the brain as little more than historical curiosities.

Pavlov's role in the development of behaviorism

During the early part of this century, as Pavlov's work became better known in the United States, American psychology underwent major changes. Dissatisfaction had been growing with investigations of conscious experience through introspection. Each person's inner world was necessarily private, open to observation by no one else. When one observer's introspective report differed from another's report, was one observer right and the other wrong? Or were both right, each accurately describing an experience that happened to differ from the other observer's experience? To establish hard facts, psychology seemed to require a subject matter that was open to public observation, and conditioned reflexes had much to offer. Conditioned reflexes took place outside the individual, thus enabling psychologists to study the processes of learning without reference to mental activity. Association, long the subject of philosophical speculation, was now open to objective scientific investigation. John B. Watson rallied American psychologists around the conditioned reflex concept, and the "behavioristic" movement was born. (It is noteworthy that Pavlov rather resented falling into the hands of American psychologists. Their willingness to speak of "learning" without discussion of his neurological principles upset him. He presented his views in a forceful article published in the United States entitled "The Reply of a Physiologist to Psychologists" (Pavlov, 1932).)

The conditioned reflex concept nourished behaviorism in its infancy and provided the framework for its subsequent development. New procedures, new viewpoints have evolved, but we still clearly see Pavlov's influence in the writings of behaviorists—the assumption of determinism, the avoidance of mentalistic interpretations, the emphasis on association as a fundamental process in learning. Let us now see what research on conditioned reflexes has taught us about the processes of learning.

ELEMENTS OF THE ASSOCIATIVE PROCESS

Although Pavlov's method of producing conditioned reflexes may seem to be quite simple, in practice it is remarkably complex. The timing of the stimuli, the intensity of the stimuli, the subject's level of arousal, the presence in the room of distracting stimuli—all of these contribute to the final result. In addition, the effects of training may extend to stimuli not included in the experimental procedure. Almost until the day he died in 1936, some 35 years after his first experiment on conditioned reflexes, Pavlov worked tirelessly to unravel the effects of such variables. His work not only established basic facts about learning, but created a new field of research. Known today as **classical,** or **Pavlovian conditioning** (we shall consider another type of conditioning in Chapter 3), this field continues to generate important principles of learning.

Classical conditioning procedures vary in complexity, but they all involve four basic features—a **conditioned stimulus** (CS), a **conditioned response** (CR), an **unconditioned stimulus** (UCS), and an **unconditioned response** (UCR). To interpret learning in terms of classical conditioning, one must identify these four elements. For example, consider the case of the dog that learned to salivate when it heard a bell. Initially, the dog salivated only when food was placed in its mouth. Since this reflex was inborn and required no training, the food would be considered a UCS and the salivation in response to food a UCR. After the dog heard the bell then received food several times, it salivated in response to the sound as well as the food. The sound became a CS and the salivation which it elicited became a CR. Note that the CR and UCR were physically the same response—salivation. What made one conditioned and the other unconditioned was the nature of the stimuli that elicited them, sound or food.

In some situations, elements of the classical conditioning procedure may take unusual forms. For example, Mowrer (1938) developed a classical conditioning treatment for bedwetting that is still widely used. Bedwetting usually occurs while the child sleeps. The objective of Mowrer's technique is to awaken the child before bedwetting occurs so that he or she may go to the bathroom. A special pad is placed on the bed which causes a bell to ring loudly when the pad becomes wet with urine. This awakens the child. Since the child requires no training to wake up in response to a loud sound, the bell would be a UCS and the arousal which it elicits would be a UCR. Prior to urination and the ringing of the bell, a complex neuromuscular pattern develops, one component of which is bladder distension. Because this pattern consistently precedes the ringing of the bell, it comes to do what the sound of the bell does—it awakens the child. The child thereby avoids urinating in bed and the problem is solved. In terms of classical conditioning, the neuromuscular pattern is a CS and the arousal which it elicits is a CR.

For centuries, philosophers maintained that two experiences would become associated if they occurred at the same time. A similar principle applies to the formation of conditioned reflexes. Conditioning is generally more effective when the UCS follows the CS quickly than when the UCS follows the CS after a long delay. The importance of **temporal contiguity,** or closeness in time, of CS and UCS has been demonstrated in many kinds of situations. For example, Peterson, Wright, and Hanlow (1969) used Mowrer's bedwetting technique under two conditions, one in which the bell rang as soon as the bed pad became wet, and one in which the bell rang about 3 minutes later. The subjects were children ranging in age from 4 through 13 years, who wet their beds on most nights. The children's parents recorded the number of wet nights for one week prior to treatment and then for the three-week duration of treatment. Records were also kept on a control group who received no treatment while the study was in progress (they did receive treatment when the study was over). Although the three groups showed about the same number of wet nights prior to treatment, they differed considerably from one another after the third week of treatment. The control subjects averaged 4.7 wet nights during the final week, subjects in the nondelay or temporal contiguity group averaged 2.2 wet nights, and children in the delay group averaged 3.9 wet nights. The improvement in the delay group may have arisen from classical conditioning to some extent, but nonconditioning factors were probably more important (e.g., the additional attention the children received).

Biological limits on contiguity

It was long thought that contiguity between any CS and any UCS would produce a CR. Recently, however, investigators have discovered some biological limits on the contiguity principle. Contiguity between a CS and a UCS may not result in a CR if the association is an "unnatural" one. Alternatively, if the association has some special biological significance for the species, a CR may develop even when the UCS follows the CS by a long delay. Garcia and Koelling (1966) demonstrated that rats make selective associations among four kinds of stimulus conditions: tastes, sickness, pain, and audiovisual events in the environment. The experiment was divided into three parts, in each of which the rats were deprived of water for a period of time and then given access to water. They did not drink just ordinary water, however. During the first phase of the study, there were two kinds of fluids—"tasty" water and "bright-noisy" water. The "tasty" water was in some cases sweet and in other cases salty. The "bright-noisy" water was flavorless but had a unique feature; whenever the rats licked the drinking spout, they saw a light flash and heard clicks. The purpose of this initial phase was to see how much of the two fluids the rats would drink before they encountered the experimental conditions. These conditions, which were introduced during the second phase, were designed to make the fluids aversive and thereby cause the rats to drink less of them. The rats now drank a concoction that was both "tasty" and "bright-and-noisy." Some of the rats got sick as they were drinking; the experimenter gave them heavy doses of X rays or spiked the fluid with poison. Other rats experienced pain while they were drinking; whenever they licked the spout, the experimenter shocked them. During this second phase, the rats drank less and less fluid from one session to the next, indicating that the fluid was becoming aversive through association with sickness or pain. In terms of classical conditioning, the X rays and the shock were UCSs and the discomforts they produced were UCRs, since no training was required to produce these reactions. But what was the CS that had acquired aversive properties? Was the taste aversive? The audiovisual effects? Or was the whole thing unpleasant? The third phase of the study provided the answer. The stimuli were separated into two fluids as in the first phase—"tasty" water and "bright-noisy" water. Consumption of each type of fluid was compared with consumption of the same type before introduction of the aversive conditions. A decrease in consumption would indicate that the stimuli characterizing the fluid were aversive. Garcia and Koelling found that the taste stimuli became aversive when the UCS was sickness but not when the UCS was pain. In contrast, the audiovisual stimuli became aversive when the UCS was pain but not when the UCS was sickness. In other words, when a rat gets sick, it naturally assumes that "It must have been something I ate," rather than "something I saw or heard." When a rat experiences pain, it assumes that "It must have been something I saw or heard," rather than "something I ate." So strong is the natural tendency to associate tastes with sickness that the association will develop even if the sickness follows the meal by several hours (Revusky and Garcia, 1970). A similar tendency in humans may explain why cancer patients occasionally develop food aversions after radiation therapy (Wallace, 1976).

Temporal relationships between CS and UCS

As a general rule, with the exceptions noted above, temporal contiguity between CS and UCS leads to the formation of a CR. A more precise definition of temporal contiguity is possible when we consider the CS-UCS relationship in greater detail. Several methods that experimenters have used to present the CS and UCS are illustrated in Fig. 2.1. Pavlov invented the procedures, introduced the terminology, and studied the effects of the procedures before other investigators. However, the definitions have changed somewhat over the years and we shall stay with the modern meanings. In **simultaneous conditioning** the CS and UCS are presented at exactly the same time. For example, the experimenter might ring a bell and at precisely the same moment place food into the mouth of a dog. In **delayed conditioning,** the CS begins before the UCS and continues until the UCS is presented. The experimenter would be using the delayed procedure if he or she rang the bell for a few seconds, and then gave food while the bell stayed on. **Trace conditioning** is like delayed conditioning except that the CS is turned off before the UCS is presented. **Backward conditioning** is what the name implies, a reversal of the usual order of events. Instead of presenting the CS before the UCS, the experimenter presents the UCS before the CS. Finally, there is **temporal conditioning,** in which time serves as the CS. The experimenter presents the UCS at constant intervals so that the passage of time will come to signal the approach of the UCS. Under these conditions, time actually does become a CS. Pavlov (1927) described an experiment in which a dog received food at 30-minute intervals. After a period of training, test trials were introduced in which the UCS was omitted. Despite the omission of the UCS, the dog salivated at about every thirtieth minute, showing no signs of a reaction earlier in the interval.

Intuitively, you might expect simultaneous conditioning to be the most effective method of presentation since it maximizes the temporal contiguity between CS and UCS. Actually, simultaneous conditioning is an ineffective method, producing no reliable CRs. The reason for this counterintuitive result is not known. Would you

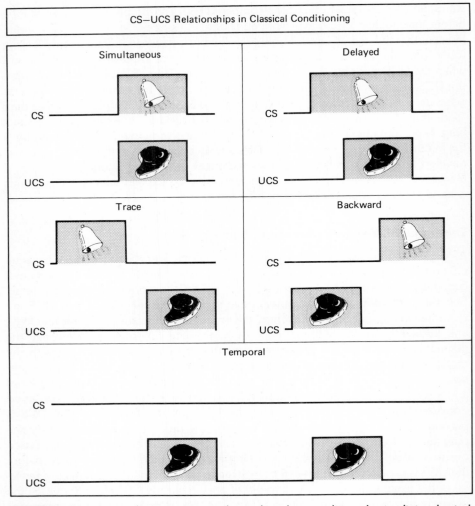

Fig. 2.1 Five ways of presenting conditioned and unconditioned stimuli in classical conditioning.

expect backward conditioning to be an effective method of presentation? From a mentalistic standpoint, a backward-conditioned CR would make no sense. One responds to the CS in anticipation of the UCS, and there can be no anticipation when the CS follows the UCS. However, backward conditioning does bring the CS close to the UCS in time, so that a form of temporal contiguity is present. If conditioning is a mechanical process of association, backward-conditioned CRs should not be too surprising. The effectiveness of backward conditioning is in doubt; some experiments yield positive results, others negative, and the reasons for the differences are not entirely clear (Razran, 1956). Pavlov (1927) maintained, and decades of research by other investigators have confirmed, that conditioning is most effective when the CS precedes the UCS. An interval of 0.5 second between the onset of the CS and the presentation of the UCS seems to be optimal in a variety of situations.

Spooner and Kellogg (1947) demonstrated many of the foregoing relationships with college students as subjects. A shock to the finger was the UCS and a buzzer was the CS. Finger withdrawal, a natural reaction to the shock, was the response selected for conditioning. Subjects could not avoid the shock by withdrawing their finger in advance. This was an important feature of the procedure, for if subjects could avoid the shock, subjects in some groups might receive more shocks than subjects in other groups. It would then be impossible to determine the effects of the experimental variable. Three trace conditioning groups received the CS before the UCS; the interval between onset of the CS (buzz) and UCS (shock) was 0.5, 1.0, or 1.5 seconds. Two backward conditioning groups took the UCS before the CS at intervals of 0.25 and 0.5 second. A simultaneous conditioning group was also included. All of the forward conditioning groups showed an increase in CRs with practice, but the group with the CS-UCS interval of 0.5 second showed the highest level of conditioning. The simultaneous and backward groups did occasionally respond to the CS, but their performance deteriorated with practice, a rather peculiar result. Forward and backward CRs differed in still another way: backward CRs occurred sooner after onset of the buzz than did the forward CRs. Backward CRs occurred within 0.2 second of the buzz, forward CRs after more than 0.5 second. Because of these differences in acquisition and speed of response, Spooner and Kellogg maintained that backward (and simultaneous) CRs reflected a different process than did forward CRs. They did not regard the backward CRs as evidence of true conditioning.

One explanation that has been offered for backward CRs is that they are the result of **pseudoconditioning.** Repeated presentations of the UCS may heighten a subject's sensitivity to stimuli. Sensitivity may become so high that the CS will trigger a response even though it has never occurred contiguously with the UCS. One way to assess the effects of pseudoconditioning is to present the CS and UCS in random orders. If CRs occur as often with random presentation as with contiguous presentation, responses with contiguous presentation are attributable to pseudoconditioning. Using the random control procedure, Champion and Jones (1961) were able to rule out pseudoconditioning as the cause of backward CRs in their experiment. From all of the discrepancies in the data on backward conditioning, it is clear that backward conditioning is at best a weak method of producing CRs.

Forward conditioning may be accomplished either with the "trace" procedure or the "delayed" procedure. Which is more effective? Trace and delayed conditioning give similar results when the interval between CS onset and UCS presentation is short (e.g., a few seconds). When the CS-UCS interval is relatively long (e.g., a minute), delayed conditioning is more effective (Manning, Schneiderman, and

ELEMENTS OF THE ASSOCIATIVE PROCESS

Lordahl, 1969). We see, then, that classical conditioning is not at all a "simple" form of learning. The success of conditioning depends heavily upon the details of CS and UCS presentation. If the learning process is this complicated at the level of conditioned reflexes, consider how much more complex it must be at the level of concept formation or language acquisition. Psychologists who seek to gain a full understanding of the learning processes certainly face a formidable challenge.

The process of inhibition

Recall Pavlov's first experiment on conditioned reflexes, the one conducted with Tolochinov. A dog which initially salivated at the sight of food (CS) stopped salivating after being shown the food several times (UCS) without being allowed to eat it. We may interpret this finding as evidence that a CS requires **reinforcement** by a UCS in order to remain effective. Presentation of the CS without the UCS results in the gradual loss, or **extinction,** of the CR. Pavlov introduced these well-known terms; so basic have they become that they are used by psychologists to describe phenomena produced by other types of conditioning. We shall encounter them again in an entirely different context in Chapter 3.

The experiment with Tolochinov illustrates extinction, but it certainly does not tell the whole story of extinction. Some unusual phenomena go along with extinction which seem to reveal features of the underlying process. Someone with a mentalistic viewpoint would probably say that extinction takes place because the organism stops anticipating the UCS. How well do you think the mentalistic viewpoint accounts for the following facts? Once, during a lecture, Pavlov (1927, pp. 48–59) performed a demonstration in which he conditioned the salivary response of a dog to the sound of metronome beats. The metronome (CS) started 30 seconds before the presentation of food (UCS) and continued during the entire 30-second interval (delayed conditioning procedure). On the first extinction trial, Pavlov counted 10 drops of saliva and observed that the first drop came three seconds after onset of the CS. Six trials later Pavlov counted three drops of saliva and observed a delay of 13 seconds. Extinction was almost complete; the CR was very weak. Pavlov then continued his lecture and 23 minutes later stopped to conduct another extinction trial. Now he counted six drops, with the first drop coming five seconds after the metronome started. Both the magnitude and speed of the response increased despite the absence of reinforcement. Pavlov regarded this **spontaneous recovery** as evidence that extinction does not destroy the CR. Rather, extinction inhibits the CR. With the passage of time, the **internal inhibition** produced by extinction subsides so that the response is again free to occur. Spontaneous recovery eventually stops, however, with the presentation of more extinction trials.

Another phenomenon which Pavlov regarded as evidence for inhibition occurs during extinction if the experimenter suddenly introduces a novel stimulus, such as the mustard oil in the experiment by Tolochinov. Presentation of the CS will again produce the CR, an effect Pavlov called **disinhibition.** If the experimenter introduced the novel stimulus during training, just the opposite effect of dis-inhibition would occur—the strength of the response would decrease. Pavlov labeled this effect **external inhibition.**

AVERSION THERAPY: DOES IT WORK?

When the drug, apomorphine, is injected under the skin, it produces nausea within 10 minutes. In sufficiently large doses, it causes vomiting. Pavlov (1927, p. 35) injected apomorphine into one of his dogs, and one or two minutes later sounded a tone. While the tone was on, the drug began to take effect. The dog became restless, wet its lips, salivated, and looked as if it were about to vomit. After repeating the procedure, Pavlov found that the sound alone came to evoke all the symptoms of nausea, although to a lesser degree. The reaction was clearly interpretable as a conditioned reflex despite the novelty of the situation. Apomorphine excited certain internal organs (UCS), the consequence of which was nausea (UCR). Through temporal contiguity with the UCS, the tone (CS) acquired the power to elicit nausea (CR).

With Pavlov's experiment in mind, how would you interpret the following case study? (Raymond, 1964). Mr. "X", age 63, is a company director whose experience and expertise have earned him the respect of his colleagues. However, Mr. X is also an alcoholic, and his actions have so embarrassed the company that his colleagues now actively seek his resignation. He attends meetings of Alcoholics Anonymous, but the requirement of total abstinence from alcohol is becoming very difficult to tolerate. **Aversion therapy** is suggested, and Mr. X agrees to enter a program "in a week or two," which is a polite way of saying "no." Ten days later Mr. X unexpectedly arrives at the hospital at which treatment is administered. He vaguely recalls having made a suicide attempt during a drinking bout and is very frightened. Because of his poor physical condition, aversion therapy is delayed for a few weeks. When therapy begins, he receives an injection of apomorphine. Seven minutes later, the therapist leads Mr. X to an adjoining room that is quiet and sparsely furnished. The therapist asks Mr. X to take one small drink and to indicate when he feels nauseous. The main purpose of the first session is to determine the precise moment of nausea so that the drink may be administered just prior to its peak. Subsequent sessions are administered twice daily for 17 days. Then the therapist conducts a test. Unknown to Mr. X, the therapist administers a neutral salt solution instead of apomorphine. When Mr. X enters the treatment room seven minutes later to take his drink, he finds not only the alcoholic beverage, but an array of soft drinks such as tonic water and tomato juice. The therapist tells Mr. X that he may choose any drink he wishes, and while Mr. X makes up his mind, the therapist discourages conversation. The atmosphere is tense. Finally, Mr. X chooses a soft drink, and the therapist, now encouraging conversation, assures Mr. X that there will be no nausea during this session. Mr. X receives apomorphine treatments for three more days and then encounters a second test. Again he chooses the soft drink. Treatments and tests continue until Mr. X is released from the hospital about a month after entering. Three years later, Mr. X reports, and his family confirms, that he has not taken a drink during the entire period. He has resumed an active and successful career with the company.

The procedure used by the therapist to help Mr. X was obviously similar to the procedure Pavlov used to condition the dog. But was classical conditioning really responsible for the therapist's results? Temporal contiguity between alcohol and the effects of apomorphine was only one element in a complex situation. The suicide attempt, the sympathy and interest of the therapist, the month-long hospital stay—these or other factors may have been responsible for the dramatic change in Mr. X. Case studies may strongly suggest that a particular variable is effective, but they are usually open to many interpretations. Experiments are necessary to clarify the factors contributing to a clinical outcome.

Although aversion therapy is a common treatment for alcoholism, there is little experimental evidence to support its effectiveness. To be sure, many therapists have reported positive results, but experimental designs have often had defects and the results of studies have been inconsistent. In a review of aversive conditioning studies with alcoholics, Davidson (1974) concluded that a therapist could not say with any confidence what outcomes were likely when giving aversion therapy to alcoholics. The need for rigorous experimental tests extends to many other areas in which aversion therapy is practiced, for example, smoking, obesity, and homosexuality. Russell, Armstrong, and Patel (1976) observed that, "Unfortunately, the scientific rigor of practitioners in the clinic has not matched that of laboratory work of experimental psychologists." (p. 103) They performed an experiment with cigarette smokers that illustrates the kind of detailed analysis possible in clinical work.

The investigators first screened participants in a smoker's clinic at a hospital to identify the heaviest and most dependent smokers. The participants had previously reported the number of cigarettes they usually smoked per day. To check the accuracy of the reports, the investigators gave the participants booklets to record cigarette consumption over a one-week period. The booklets also served a second purpose: It was possible that simply by paying more attention to the number of cigarettes they smoked, the participants would come to smoke less, even though the instructions stated that they should smoke in the usual way. Since subjects would be counting the number of cigarettes they smoked during treatment, it was important to know in advance the size of any such self-monitoring effect. At the end of the week, the smokers were given another booklet to record cigarette consumption for a second week. Unlike the previous instructions, the instructions now were to cut down on smoking as much as possible. The investigators wished to include those smokers with the least self-control as they would probably be the most difficult cases to treat. Also, it was important to know how much the subjects could do for themselves to evaluate the efficiency of treatment. Because aversion therapy requires considerable time and effort, its effects should greatly exceed those of mere self-control. Participants who were finally selected for the study recorded their cigarette consumption for an additional six days, smoking freely during the first three and again exercising self-control during the second three. This was a check on the reliability of the previous assessment. We see, then, that an adequate test of a clinical treatment requires a careful analysis even before treatment begins.

The investigators employed electric shock as the aversive stimulus, and arranged their experimental conditions to study several components of electric aversion therapy as it is commonly practiced. Subjects in Group A received true aversion therapy; subjects in other groups to be described underwent treatments that were missing one or more components of the regular procedure. The subjects in Group A attended 10 sessions over a four-week period, each session starting with a 10- to 15-minute interview with a sympathetic therapist. During the interview the subjects reported on their progress since the previous session and discussed problems related to cigarette withdrawal. The therapist encouraged the subjects by expressing confidence that the subjects could stop smoking completely. After the interview, the subjects entered another room for the aversive conditioning treatment. (For reasons soon to be discussed, the treatment was administered by a second therapist, not by the interviewer.) The subjects sat down with their backs to the therapist and found on a nearby table an ash tray, some matches, and their favorite brand of cigarettes. Treatment consisted of periods of shock in alternation with periods of rest. When a shock period started, the subject was instructed to light up and smoke continuously until a buzzer sounded. Three out of four times a one-second shock to the forearm came 0.5 second after the buzzer. On a random 25% of the trials the shock was omitted to make adaptation to the shock less likely. The shock periods varied in duration so that shocks were contiguous with all phases of the smoking sequence—handling the pack, lighting up, smoking, and finishing. Also, because the subjects never knew when the buzzer and shock would come, they waited tensely for it throughout the period. This tension was apparently more aversive than the shock itself. No shocks were presented during the rest periods, however, so the subjects could occasionally relax. Note that this situation is the reverse of that which smokers normally experience. They usually feel tense when *not* smoking and feel relief after lighting up. By reversing the conditions, the investigators hoped to break any associations that might have developed between smoking and relaxation.

Subjects in Group B underwent simulated therapy. The procedure was the same as for Group A except that smoking periods never terminated with shock. Instead, shock *preceded* the smoking periods and terminated the periods in which subjects did not smoke. Groups A and B received the same number of shocks, but for Group A shock was contiguous with smoking while for Group B shock was non-contiguous with smoking. Group C was a satiation group. Subjects in Group C lit up and smoked as often as the other subjects without getting shocked. The objective here was to see whether the heavy smoking itself had therapeutic value. Group D had only the 10-15 minute interviews with the therapist; there was no further treatment. Possibly just having a sympathetic ear could help the subjects. To make sure that the interviewer treated subjects in the different groups similarly, he did not administer the smoking sessions and did not know who was whom. Group E did

Table 2.1 Experimental conditions in study of aversion therapy for cigarette smoking. (From Russell, Armstrong, and Patel, 1976)

	Shocks contiguous with smoking	Shocks noncontiguous with smoking	Nonshock components of smoking sessions	Therapist contact and support
Group A	+	0	+	+
Group B	0	+	+	+
Group C	0	0	+	+
Group D	0	0	0	+
Group E	0	0	0	0

not go to the hospital at all after the first interview. Table 2.1 summarizes the experimental conditions. Factors that might contribute to the outcome are shown at the top: shocks contiguous with smoking, shocks noncontiguous with smoking, nonshock components of the smoking session, and therapist contact and support. For each group, if a particular factor was present, a "+" appears in the column headed by the factor; if the factor was absent, a "0" appears. As one goes from Group A to Group E, more and more elements of the standard procedure are withdrawn. Which factors *must* be present for aversion therapy to work?

Figure 2.2 gives the answer. It shows the average daily cigarette consumption during the pre-treatment period and during a two-week post-treatment period. The numerals I–VIII represent occasions on which subjects reported cigarette consumption. The post-treatment results are surprising indeed (dare one say "shocking"?). Although Groups A, B, C, and D smoked far fewer cigarettes than Group E (no treatment at all), they did not differ reliably from one another. Therapist contact and support—a sympathetic ear—was all the subjects needed. The pretreatment conditions produced substantial effects, too. The drop in cigarette consumption between I and II is a self-monitoring effect. Simply by keeping track of the number of cigarettes one smokes, it is possible to cut down. The drop between II and III is a self-control effect. Through a method of their own invention, the subjects managed to cut down slightly. Overall, aversion therapy fared poorly, ranking lower in influence than a sympathetic ear, self-monitoring, and self control.

Perhaps the problem lay in the investigators' choice of aversive stimulus. Recall the experiment by Garcia and Koelling (1966) which showed that rats associated tastes with sickness but not with pain produced by shock. The taste of the cigarettes might have also become aversive, and deterred consumption, had the investigators employed apomorphine instead of shock. Raymond (1964) reported a case study of a teenage smoker successfully treated with apomorphine. In a similar vein, Revusky and Taukulis (1975) suggested that sickness may be the aversive agent of choice with alcoholics. The study by Russell, Armstrong, and Patel (1976) is an example of the kind of research that would be necessary to test this notion with smokers.

CLASSICAL CONDITIONING: PRINCIPLES OF ASSOCIATION

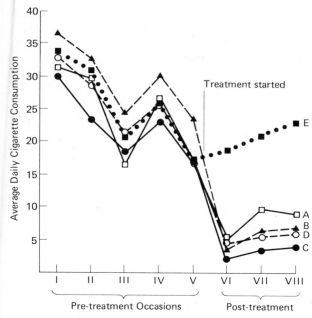

Fig. 2.2 Daily cigarette consumption under the five experimental conditions set up to test the effectiveness of aversion therapy. The pretreatment observation occasions were: I, Subjects estimate the number of cigarettes they smoked before beginning of study; II, Subjects smoke freely, simply monitor the number of cigarettes consumed; III, Subjects attempt to exercise "self-control"; IV, Subjects return to unrestricted, self-monitoring condition; V, Subjects again attempt to exercise self-control. The post-treatment measurements were taken over a two-week period immediately following the last treatment session. (From Russell, Armstrong, and Patel, 1976)

CONTIGUITY OR "CONTINGENCY"?

Biological constraints on the associability of stimuli, like the constraints mentioned above, limit the generality of the contiguity principle. But the contiguity principle may have another, much more serious limitation—it may be *wrong*. Although pairing a CS with a UCS usually does produce a CR, the pairing itself may not be responsible for the CR. Perhaps this sounds like a contradiction, but it is actually a very keen insight, one which raises fundamental questions about the nature of classical conditioning. The insight was that of Robert A. Rescorla, then a graduate student, who in the course of research on classical conditioning discovered that previous investigators had overlooked something significant. In a well-known article (Rescorla, 1967), Rescorla drew attention to this new dimension of classical conditioning, and in doing so proved that one need not have a Ph.D. to make important contributions to psychology.

Rescorla's concept can be illustrated by the following example. Suppose that we conducted a classical conditioning experiment in which subjects received 100

CS-UCS pairings. After the session we noted that a strong CR had developed. We then repeated the experiment with the next subject in the group, but after the session we discovered that no CR has developed. Eventually we found that the equipment had gone haywire and delivered 100 UCSs in addition to the 100 CS-UCS pairings. None of the extra UCSs was contiguous with a CS, that is, the UCSs occurred either a long time before or a long time after the CSs. On the basis of our current belief about the role of contiguity in classical conditioning, this would be a puzzling phenomenon. Both subjects had 100 CS-UCS pairings. If temporal contiguity between CS and UCS is the basic requirement for conditioning, both subjects should have acquired CRs, regardless of the extra UCSs in the second case.

Rescorla would probably give the following sort of explanation. Contiguity between CS and UCS is not sufficient to produce a CR. Organisms are sensitive to the amount of information the CS provides about the occurrence of the UCS. For conditioning to take place, the CS must be a useful predictor of the UCS, and only in the first case was the CS a useful predictor. When the CS was presented, the subject could predict that the UCS would soon follow; when a period of time elapsed without a CS, the subject could predict that there would be no UCS. In the second case, the CS was not a useful predictor of the UCS. True, when the CS was presented, the subject could predict that a UCS would soon follow. But when a period of time elapsed without a CS, many UCSs still occurred. Because the CS failed to predict these UCSs, it was an unreliable signal. For the first subject, we would say that the UCS was contingent, or conditional, on the CS. For the second subject, we would say that the UCS was not contingent on the CS. According to Rescorla, a CS predicts the UCS, and comes to elicit a CR, only when a contingency exists between the CS and UCS. Rescorla (1966) showed that the "accident" which occurred in our hypothetical experiment could actually be made to happen when experimental conditions were appropriately arranged.

What makes Rescorla's contingency concept particularly important is its implication that many research designs in classical conditioning are flawed. To demonstrate that conditioning has taken place in an experiment, investigators usually try to show that the CRs resulted specifically from CS-UCS pairings rather than from nonassociative factors such as pseudoconditioning. A control group is commonly included in classical conditioning experiments to indicate how much influence nonassociative factors have had. Rescorla argued that traditional control procedures based on the contiguity view did not serve their purpose, and that only an alternative procedure based on the contingency view was appropriate. Essentially, the procedure Rescorla advocated involved conditions similar to those prevailing in the hypothetical experiment, above, in which extra, unpaired UCSs were accidentally administered. The CSs and UCSs are presented at random intervals so that no contingency exists between the CS and UCS. Some CSs occur without being followed by UCSs, some UCSs occur without having been preceded by CSs, and some CSs and UCSs occur contiguously. The latter feature of the procedure is the major innovation. Investigators have long used a randomized control procedure in which no CSs and UCSs have been permitted to occur contiguously. This was the approach taken by Champion and Jones (1961) in the experiment on backward conditioning discussed earlier. Rescorla maintained that deliberate exclusion of CS-UCS pairings was inappropriate because it taught the subject a negative contingency: If the CS occurs, there will be no UCS. The negative contingency could result in suppression, or inhibition, of any tendency to respond to the CS and thereby lead to an overestimate of the effect of CS-UCS pairings in the experimental group.

The issues raised by Rescorla are still a source of controversy in the field of classical conditioning. That issues so fundamental to our understanding of the associative process are still unresolved underscores the uncertain state of knowledge in the psychology of learning generally. The field is young and is changing rapidly. None of its concepts or principles can be regarded as absolute truths. To the innovative and enterprising investigator, the psychology of learning offers many opportunities for making major contributions to scientific knowledge.

GENERALIZATION AND DISCRIMINATION

Somewhere in the world may walk a man with an intense fear of white rats, dogs, Santa Claus masks, and fur coats. His name is Albert, and his problem began in 1920 when John B. Watson and his colleague, Rosalie Rayner, deliberately created those peculiar fears to make a point. They wanted to demonstrate that human fears were acquired in much the same way that Pavlov's dogs acquired conditioned salivary responses. In this way, Watson sought to underscore the relevance of the conditioned reflex concept to our understanding of human behavior. Albert was then an infant in a foundling home and was selected for the study because he was initially fearless. Conditioning started with the presentation of a white rat. When Albert approached the animal, the experimenter struck a steel bar behind the child's head. The sharp sound (UCS) caused Albert to startle and cry (UCR). The experimenter repeated the procedure several times, presenting the rat then striking the bar. Eventually Albert started to cry (CR) when he saw the rat (CS) and tried to crawl away from it. This fear **generalized** to objects that resembled the rat but had not actually been associated with the sound—a dog, a Santa Claus mask, a coat. Watson and Rayner concluded that fears acquired naturally are also products of conditioning and generalization.

Pavlov (1927) had discovered the generalization process in his work with salivary CRs. If a CR was established to a tone of a certain pitch, other tones acquired the power to elicit the response. The more similar these tones were to the original one, the stronger was the response. Pavlov was able to confine the response to a narrow range of tones by initiating a process of **discrimination.** He paired one tone with food and presented a slightly different tone without food. After several alternations between the tones, the dog stopped salivating to the nonreinforced tone but continued to salivate to the reinforced tone. Pavlov discovered that such discrimination training could trigger "neurotic" symptoms in the animals. In one experiment he repeatedly fed a dog after projecting a luminous circle on a screen. Then he projected an elipse that was clearly distinguishable from the circle.

When the discrimination was established, the shape of the elipse was brought closer and closer to that of the circle, until the two stimuli were very difficult to distinguish. Although the dog did succeed in discriminating them, and maintained the discrimination for a few weeks, the discrimination deteriorated and eventually disappeared altogether. At the same time, the behavior of the dog changed dramatically. Previously a quiet and friendly animal, the dog now barked violently on being taken to the experimental room, squealed when placed in the apparatus, tore the apparatus off with its teeth, and chewed up tubes connecting its room with that of the observer next door. So great was the conflict created by the discrimination that the dog apparently suffered a "nervous breakdown."

Generalization and extinction

Reinforcement establishes a CR. Extinction eliminates a CR. Just as the effects of reinforcement generalize to new stimuli, so, too, do the effects of extinction generalize. Pavlov demonstrated this symmetry with dogs as subjects and Bass and Hull (1934) extended the principle to human subjects. In Bass and Hull's experiment, the subjects undressed and lay down on their stomachs in the manner illustrated in Fig. 2.3. Special vibrating devices stimulated four points along the left side

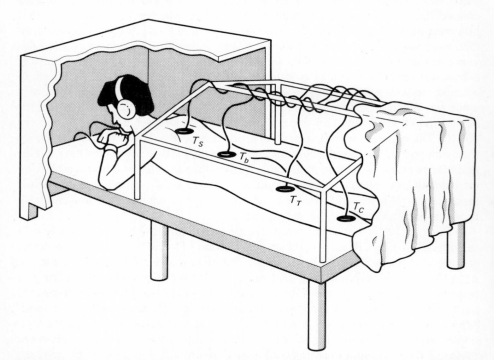

Fig. 2.3 Bass and Hull's apparatus for studying generalization of reinforcement and extinction across parts of the human body. (From Bass and Hull, 1934)

CLASSICAL CONDITIONING: PRINCIPLES OF ASSOCIATION

of the body—the shoulder, the small of the back, the thigh, and the calf. In some cases, stimulation of the shoulder served as a CS while in other cases stimulation of the calf served as a CS. The remaining points were used in a test for generalization. The UCS was a shock to the right wrist, and the response chosen for conditioning was a physiological indicator of anxiety, the galvanic skin response (GSR). The GSR measures the extent to which the skin conducts electricity. Sweating, a common response to anxiety, increases the conductivity of the skin, thereby registering a strong GSR. Bass and Hull observed the GSR on the left hand as they paired the CS with the UCS. They first examined the effects of reinforcement by reinforcing only one of the four points, the shoulder or the calf. After they established the CR, they stimulated each of the remaining points to see if the response generalized. The reinforcement gradient in Fig. 2.4 shows the reactions. The point "0" is the CS; the points "1, 2, 3" are locations increasingly distant from the CS. The strongest response occurred at the CS and progressively weaker responses occurred at points 1, 2, and 3. In other words, the more similar the test stimulus was to the CS, the stronger was the tendency to make the response. Bass and Hull studied the effects of extinction by reinforcing all four points on the body. Then they extinguished the response at either the shoulder or the calf, thereby creating a kind of negative CS. After they extinguished the CR, they stimulated each of the remaining points to see

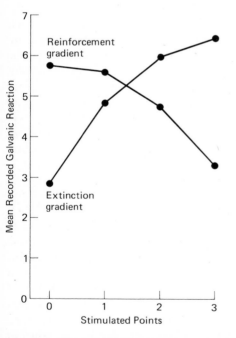

Fig. 2.4 Bass and Hull's generalization gradients for reinforcement and extinction. The "0" point is the part of the body that served as the CS. Points 1, 2, and 3 are locations at increasing distances from the CS. (After Bass and Hull, 1934)

GENERALIZATION AND DISCRIMINATION

if the effects of extinction generalized. The "extinction gradient" in Fig. 2.4 shows that the "negative" CS elicited the weakest response and points 1, 2, and 3 elicited progressively stronger responses. Thus the tendency to inhibit the response generalized much as the tendency to make the response had generalized earlier. The more similar the test stimulus was to the negative CS, the stronger was the tendency to inhibit the response. Generalization, then, is a by-product of both extinction and reinforcement.

Systematic desensitization: Pavlovian therapy for fear

The case of little Albert demonstrated that classical conditioning can create fears. Under different circumstances, classical conditioning can eliminate fears. The generalization principle is the basis of a highly effective treatment for phobias called "systematic desensitization" (Wolpe, 1958; Wolpe and Lazarus, 1966). Mary Cover Jones (1924) discovered the procedure while searching for ways to treat children's fears. She tested a variety of techniques with young children for whom she could identify specific fear objects, such as masks, snakes, frogs, and rabbits. Most of the techniques she tried were ineffective. For example, one four-year-old named Arthur had an intense fear of frogs. Jones tried a distraction technique with Arthur in which she placed some crayons he wanted on a table beside a frog. The reasoning was that perhaps Arthur would be so preoccupied playing with the crayons that he would ignore the frog. It did not quite work out that way. Arthur walked cautiously to the table, then suddenly grabbed the crayons and ran. Another ineffective technique was social pressure. Jones presented the fear object while other children were present. Rather than risk ridicule by the other children, the child might try to act in a courageous manner. Jones brought Arthur and four other boys into a room to see an aquarium containing frogs. Arthur boldly swaggered up to the aquarium, and for a moment it seemed that the technique had worked. But when a companion picked up a frog and offered it to Arthur, Arthur ran out of the room screaming. Jones successfully used an extinction procedure with another child who feared white rats (his name was Godfried, not Albert, unfortunately). Initially when she presented the rat, the child cried and moved as far away from it as possible. But after a few more presentations, the child stopped crying and made no effort to withdraw. The fear had extinguished. Jones believed that the extinction procedure was less than ideal because it left the child indifferent to the object rather than interested in it. Jones favored a technique which eliminated the fear response by substituting a positive reaction for it. She employed this **counterconditioning** approach with a two-year-old named Peter, who feared rabbits. While Peter sat in a highchair eating candy, Jones brought a rabbit to within four feet of the chair. Peter protested, "I want you to put bunny outside." Jones then moved the rabbit back 20 feet from the highchair. Now Peter tolerated the animal, although he did keep a watchful eye on it. Seeing that Peter tolerated the rabbit at 20 feet, Jones kept it there awhile, then moved it a bit closer. Because the change was so small, Peter continued to eat the candy without protesting. Over a six-week period, Jones moved the rabbit closer and closer until she was able to place the animal on the highchair. Peter was not simply indifferent to the rabbit. He petted and played with it, and even asked for it one day when it had not been brought in. The gratification produced by eating candy had been conditioned to the rabbit and replaced the fear.

Figure 2.5 illustrates the role of generalization in Jone's procedure. Let us say that the candy is a UCS and the gratification—or positive response—elicited by the candy is a UCR. The visual stimulus of the rabbit at 20 feet becomes a CS through pairing with the candy and produces a generalization gradient extending a few feet forward. Jones moves the rabbit forward into an area covered by the generalization gradient so that the rabbit continues to elicit a positive response. The magnitude of this response is smaller, however, than the magnitude of response produced by the CS at 20 feet. The response is sufficiently strong to enable Jones to keep the rabbit at the new position without causing Peter to protest. The rabbit now acquires the power to elicit the full-blown response at the shorter distance. As it did at the greater distance, the stimulus produces a generalization gradient extending a few feet forward, thereby enabling Jones to move the rabbit still closer. This continues until the rabbit can be placed on the highchair.

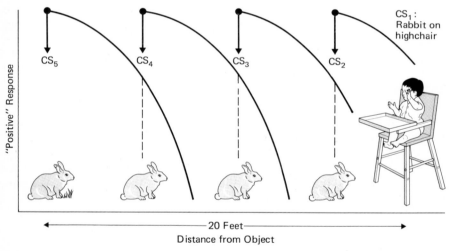

Fig. 2.5 Generalization gradients assumed to underlie Mary Cover Jones's counterconditioning treatment for a child's fear of rabbits. The rabbit is initially placed at the position labeled, CS_5, which is located 20 feet from the child. While the child eats candy, a "positive response" becomes associated with the visual stimulus of the rabbit and replaces the fear response. The strength of the positive response is represented by the point above the rabbit. As a result of generalization, presentation of the rabbit at closer distances produces weaker positive responses, the magnitudes of which are represented by the curved line extending forward from CS_5. The child tolerates the rabbit at the next position because of a substantial positive response at that distance, indicated by the vertical dashed line. Holding the rabbit at this position while the child eats makes the new visual stimulus a CS (CS_4). The generalization gradient extending forward from CS_4 permits Jones to move the rabbit still closer. Eventually, the child enjoys having the rabbit on the highchair.

GENERALIZATION AND DISCRIMINATION

Systematic desensitization differs from Jones' procedure in two main ways. First, relaxation rather than gratification from eating replaces the fear response. Second, systematic desensitization employs imagined scenes as stimuli rather than physical objects. As described by Wolpe and Lazarus (1966) systematic desensitization proceeds in three phases: (1) training in relaxation; (2) construction of an anxiety hierarchy, a set of imagined scenes that evoke different levels of anxiety; and (3) the pairing of the scenes with relaxation.

The relaxation training employs principles originally developed by Jacobson (1938). The patient learns to relax muscles throughout the body to a degree rarely experienced by most people. The therapist gives instruction separately for muscles in the arms, head, mouth, neck, shoulders, back, abdomen, thorax, and legs. The first step in training a muscle group is to increase the patient's awareness of the sensations produced by tension in those muscles. Then the therapist instructs the patient to relax the muscles "beyond what seems to be the furthest point," to "keep trying to go further and further in the negative direction" (Wolpe and Lazarus, 1966, pp. 62-63). The muscles of the head are particularly important from an emotional standpoint and they receive considerable attention. The therapist contracts the "eye-brow raising" and "frowning" muscles in the forehead so that the patient can see the anxious expression so produced. The therapist then relaxes the muscles step by step until no further changes are visible. The patient is told that despite the lack of visible change, the relaxation is continuing beneath the surface. It is the patient's objective to achieve this deeper state of relaxation.

Systematic desensitization is useful for treating a wide variety of phobias— fears of snakes, heights, confining places, examination-taking, being scrutinized, being devalued, seeing discord between people, and many others. One reason the technique is so widely applicable is that it does not require the therapist to stage the frightening scenes. The patient imagines them, and the effects of treatment usually generalize to the "real" world. The patient and therapist work together to create a set of scenes varying in fearfulness. The scenes are ranked so that the least anxiety-arousing is at the bottom of the list and the most anxiety-arousing is at the top. Listed below is the anxiety hierarchy of a woman who feared discord between people:

1. Her mother shouts at a servant.
2. Her young sister whines to her mother.
3. Her sister engages in a dispute with her father.
4. Her mother shouts at her sister.
5. She sees two strangers quarrel.

After the patient has learned to relax, and the anxiety hierarchy has been constructed, the desensitization procedure is performed. The patient sits back comfortably and initially imagines a neutral scene such as a familiar street corner. The patient signals the therapist by raising a finger if the scene creates any anxiety. If it does, the therapist stops the procedure and helps the patient relax. They go back to the neutral scene, and if a period of time elapses without anxiety, the therapist instructs the patient to imagine the lowest scene in the anxiety hierarchy. If a period elapses without anxiety, the patient proceeds to the next scene. Usually, the next scene does not arouse anxiety because the relaxation response has generalized from the previous scene. The patient imagines this scene for awhile, and then proceeds to the next one, continuing up the hierarchy until the most anxiety-arousing scene is encountered. If at any point the patient experiences anxiety, the scene is discontinued and the patient imagines a scene that elicits relaxation. As in Jones' procedure, the success of treatment depends upon the gradual approach to the final stimulus. Figure 2.6 illustrates the role of generalization in making possible this gradual approach. The patient begins by imagining a scene in which two strangers

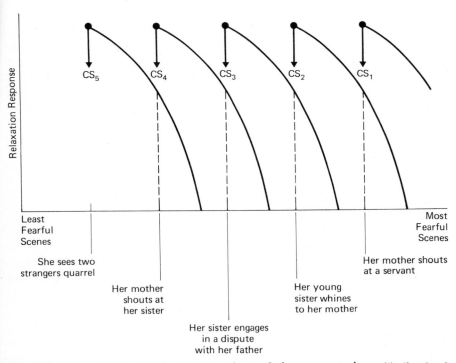

Fig. 2.6 Generalization gradients assumed to underlie systematic desensitization treatment for a patient's fear of discord. The patient has ranked the scenes described along the horizontal axis according to the amount of fear they evoke. She imagines first the least fearful scene (CS_5) while remaining in a relaxed state. Eventually, the relaxation response becomes associated with CS_5, replacing the fear response. The strength of the fear response is indicated by the point above the description of the scene. Extending forward from this point is the gradient representing generalization of relaxation to the next scene in the list. This scene evokes sufficient relaxation (indicated by the vertical dashed line) to enable the patient to imagine the scene with minimal fear. With continued training, relaxation increases and generalizes to the next scene. The process continues until the patient can imagine all the scenes while remaining relaxed. As a result of treatment, relaxation generalizes to the actual events and counteracts the fear they once produced.

GENERALIZATION AND DISCRIMINATION

quarrel. This scene comes to elicit a full-blown relaxation response and produces a generalization gradient which extends forward to the next scene: her mother shouts at her sister. Because of generalization from the previous scene, the patient has a head start on the current one and does not have far to go to achieve the full relaxation response. This scene now produces a generalization gradient so that the patient can move a step higher in the hierarchy with minimal anxiety. The process is essentially the same as that with Peter (Fig. 2.5) with one important difference: the basis of similarity between the stimuli. In Peter's case, the basis of similarity was physical; the dimension of distance is recognizable by anyone. Given a point 20 feet away and another 10 feet away, most people would say that the point 10 feet away was closer. Generalization along such physical dimensions is known as **primary stimulus generalization.** In the patient's case, the basis of similarity was something the patient had learned. Not everyone would regard the scene of a mother shouting at a child as more threatening than the scene of two strangers quarreling. Generalization along such learned dimensions is called **secondary stimulus generalization.** The practice of systematic desensitization requires attention to many details. For example, the number of exposures to a scene and the duration of each exposure are factors in the outcome (Ross, 1973). A thorough investigation of the many variables involved in systematic desensitization would facilitate its use and contribute importantly to our understanding of the associative process.

THE SECOND SIGNALLING SYSTEM

Pavlov (1927) believed that conditioned reflexes had great biological significance. The capacity to acquire conditioned reflexes gave animals an advantage in the struggle for survival. In the natural environment, some stimuli were beneficial and others were harmful. To a hungry animal, food was beneficial; to a small animal, a beast of prey might be harmful. Once the stimulus was encountered, the animal had to react appropriately or die. The hungry animal had to eat; the small animal had to fight or run. The chances for survival increased when animals learned to respond to events that signalled the approach of the stimuli. As a bird of prey circled an area, it might cast a shadow that signalled its presence. The intended victim that learned an aversive reaction to the shadow could avoid the fight by hiding. Similarly, some substances encountered by an animal were nutritious while others were poisonous. The animal that learned to distinguish them on the basis of appearance or smell would have a better chance of survival than an animal that simply ate what was there and took the consequences. Pavlov believed that a major evolutionary accomplishment of the human species was its development of language. Language served as a second signalling system, supplementing the signals provided by the environment. Lower animals depended on the physical cues (the first signalling system) in preparing for impending events. Humans could use words to describe the physical cues and could thus take action before the physical cues appeared. According to Pavlov, although language belongs to another system, it operates on the same principles as regular conditioned reflexes. Experimental tests of this notion, particularly by psychologists in Russia (Hartman, 1965), have revealed some fascinating parallels between the two systems.

Riess (1940) conditioned the GSR to words printed on cards. A word such as "surf" or "urn" was displayed for five seconds (CS), after which a loud buzzer was sounded (UCS). After the words elicited strong GSRs, generalization was tested to two types of words, homophones (words that had the same sound as the CSs but different meanings) and synonyms (words that had the same meaning as the CSs but different sounds). For example, with the CS "surf" the homonym was "serf" and the synonym was "wave." For the CS "urn" the homonym was "earn" and the synonym was "vase." Generalization to homonyms would represent primary stimulus generalization since the basis of similarity would be a physical one. Generalization to synonyms would represent secondary stimulus generalization because the meanings of the words must be learned. Riess found that synonyms elicited higher GSRs than homonyms; meaning took precedence over sound. In a later study, Riess (1946) tested four age groups, averaging 7 years 9 months, 10 years 8 months, 14 years 0 months, and 18 years 6 months. In addition to synonyms and homonyms, Riess included antonyms (words opposite in meaning to the CSs) during the generalization test. Generalization occurred to all of the words, but the youngest group generalized most to homophones, the next oldest groups generalized most to *antonyms*, and the two oldest groups generalized most to synonyms. Why the antonyms elicited such strong responses in the younger group is unexplained.

Sentences as well as words may serve as CSs. Razran (1949) demonstrated that conditioned salivary responses to a sentence generalized most to sentences with meanings consistent with that of the CS. Generalization was lower to sentences with meanings inconsistent with that of the CS, even though these sentences may have had many words in common with the CS. For example, one CS sentence was "Poverty is degrading." Generalization was greater to the sentence "Wealth is uplifting" (meaning consistent with CS) than to the sentence "Poverty is not degrading" (meaning inconsistent with CS). Such experiments on **semantic conditioning** provide striking evidence that parallels do exist between the two signalling systems.

The regulatory function of speech

For speech to provide an evolutionary advantage, it must influence action. One must not only speak, but act appropriately in response to speech. This regulatory function of speech is not inborn; it emerges gradually during the first five years of life. Luria (1961) followed the development of the regulatory function of speech using a simple, but revealing, experimental procedure. He had children of different ages squeeze a rubber bulb in response to instructions of varying degrees of complexity. From the children's responses, Luria identified four stages of development (Table 2.2).

Table 2.2 Stages in the development of the "second signalling system" (Luria, 1961)

Stage	Ages	Features	Examples
1	Birth–2½ yrs.	Speech possesses initiating function, but lacks inhibitory function; verbal instructions fail to regulate subsequent courses of action; child cannot coordinate speech and motor reactions to a sensory stimulus.	Child cannot respond appropriately to instruction "When you see the light, squeeze the balloon"; also fails to perform sequence: light–"go"–press.
2	2½–4½ yrs.	Speech-motor coordination possible, but regulatory influence of speech based on initiating function, not meaning; speech still lacks inhibitory function.	Child can perform sequence light–"go"–press–"go"–press; cannot obey instruction "When the light appears, press twice"; also child presses in response to own speech command "Don't press."
3	4½–5½ yrs.	Speech exercises regulatory influence based on specific meaning; has acquired inhibitory function; speech largely external.	Child obeys instruction to press in response to one signal but not another; stops pressing in response to "Don't press."
4	5½ and over.	Speech internalized.	

In the earliest stage (birth to 2½ years), speech has only an impellant or initiating function. It lacks an inhibitory function to terminate actions. If you instructed a child to squeeze a bulb, the child would do so but would have difficulty stopping. Even the instruction "That's enough" would be without effect. There are two additional deficiencies at this stage. First, speech lacks a preparatory function whereby it regulates a future course of action. For example, the child fails to respond to the instruction "When you see the light, squeeze the balloon." Another deficiency is that the child cannot coordinate speech and motor reactions to a stimulus. The child is unable to perform a simple sequence in which he or she is to say "go" when a light appears, then press the bulb.

During the second stage (2½ to 4½ years of age), speech-motor coordination emerges. However, the regulatory function of speech is still primitive. The impellant or initiating function of speech still dominates the child, and the meaning of the words is of secondary importance. For example, if you gave the instruction "When the light appears, press twice," the child would probably press many times. The inhibitory function of speech is also undeveloped. Luria gave children the task of saying "Don't press" when a signal was presented, and then not pressing. The children said "Don't press," but they pressed anyway. They spoke but did not "listen" to what they said.

During the third stage (4½ to 5½ years), all of the functions of speech are present—the impellant, the preparatory, the inhibitory—and there is good speech-motor coordination. But speech commands come mainly from other people rather than from the children themselves. In the final phase, which starts at about 5½ years, children internalize speech; they issue their own commands. The capacity for internalized speech opens the way to further intellectual development and, in Luria's terms, makes of the child a "self-regulating system."

SUMMARY

Introduced by Descartes in the 17th century, the concept of the reflex has had a major impact on both philosophy and psychology. A reflex is an involuntary response of a muscle or gland to the excitation of a sense organ. Once the stimulus is applied, the response must occur; no act of will can prevent the reflex from running its course. Descartes regarded reflexes as primitive, inborn modes of behavior that made up a very small part of a human being's total activity. Most human behavior was said to be voluntary in nature, originating in the mind rather than in the physical world. Pavlov's discovery of conditioned reflexes made possible an extension of Descartes' conceptualization of involuntary behavior to human behavior in general. It also provided an objective means of studying a process long thought to underly much human learning, the process of association. Philosophers had speculated that two sense impressions would become linked in the mind if they were experienced at about the same time. Pavlov showed that a similar principle of "temporal contiguity" governed the formation of conditioned reflexes. If the stimulus for an inborn reaction was repeatedly paired with some arbitrary event, that event would come to elicit the reaction. Like an unconditioned reflex, a conditioned reflex was highly predictable, a fact which suggested to Pavlov that the behavior was involuntary in nature.

Temporal contiguity between a CS and UCS is ordinarily essential for the development of a CR. However, many additional factors influence the course of learning and must be taken into account. For conditioning to be most effective, the onset of the CS should precede the onset of the UCS by about 0.5 seconds (the precise optimal value depends on experimental conditions). At short CS-UCS intervals it makes little difference whether the CS is kept on while the UCS is presented (delayed conditioning) or whether it is terminated before the UCS is presented (trace conditioning). At long CS-UCS intervals, however, delayed conditioning is more effective than trace conditioning. Simultaneous presentation of the CS and UCS is an ineffective procedure despite the fact that it maximizes the temporal contiguity between the CS and UCS. Also, presentation of the UCS before the CS is at best an unreliable method of producing CRs even with a short UCS-CS interval. In general, learning is most likely to occur when the CS acts as a signal for, or predicts the occurrence of, the UCS. Rescorla has developed a conceptualization of classical conditioning which relates associative learning to conditions in which the occurrence of the UCS is contingent on the occurrence of the CS. This contingency view is in contrast to the traditional view that the number of CS-UCS pairings is the primary determinant of associative learning.

In addition to the temporal relationship between the CS and UCS, the biological significance of the stimuli influences the course of learning. Studies on the conditioning of taste aversions have shown that if the CS and UCS do not go together in nature, an animal may not associate the stimuli even if they are contiguous. On the other hand, if the relationship is a natural one, associative learning may occur over very long CS-UCS intervals. These biological factors are potentially important considerations in the design of aversion therapy programs for the treatment of alcoholism and cigarette smoking.

To maintain its ability to elicit CRs, the CS requires continual reinforcement by the UCS. Presentation of the CS without the UCS results in the gradual weakening, or extinction, of the CR. After extinction has occurred, the CR will reappear at some strength if the CS is presented after a period of time (spontaneous recovery) of if a novel stimulus is introduced before presentation of the CS (disinhibition). Introduction of a novel stimulus during training results in the disappearance of the CR (external inhibition).

As a by-product of classical conditioning, stimuli other than the CS may acquire the power to elicit the CR (generalization). The extent to which they do so depends upon how similar they are to the CS. Extinction of a CR also leads to a kind of generalization, with stimuli similar to the CS acquiring the power to inhibit the CR. "Primary stimulus generalization" is the term used to refer to generalization across physical dimensions of similarity. Secondary stimulus generalization is involved when the basis of similarity is psychological, for example, the anxiety hierarchy in the systematic desensitization treatment for phobias. Generalization can be reduced by alternating CS-UCS pairings with presentations of other stimuli without the UCS. The result is stimulus discrimination, a CR to the CS but not to the other stimuli.

Pavlov distinguished between two systems of conditioned reflexes. One, the first signalling system, involved the learning of reactions to physical cues that signalled impending events of biological significance to the species. Both human beings and lower animals were said to have this capacity. The second signalling system, considered to be unique to human beings, involved the learning of reactions to words that described physical cues. Studies of semantic conditioning have supported Pavlov in demonstrating that words can function as CSs and produce effects similar to those found in conventional classical conditioning, such as stimulus generalization. Luria has identified three basic functions of speech in the regulation of behavior: the impellant, the preparatory, and the inhibitory. These regulatory functions apparently develop in stages during the first five years of life.

STUDY QUESTIONS

1. What is meant by the term "free will"?

2. Describe the operation of the animated dolls at the Royal Fountains of France from which Descartes took his concept of the reflex. What made the dolls seem realistic? Describe the hydraulic mechanism responsible for the dolls' movements.

3. Using the example of the barefoot boy, describe Descartes' concept of the reflex, relating it to the hydraulic mechanism discussed in Question 2.

4. State the three basic features of our modern concept of the reflex.

5. According to Descartes, what features characterize voluntary and involuntary actions?

6. Define "determinism." Using the example of the teenager and the little old lady, contrast the moral implications of the deterministic and nondeterministic views of human behavior.

7. Describe the "wash reflex" of the frog. How does it illustrate the orientation of 19th century physiologists toward the interpretation of complex behavior?

8. According to Sechenov, what is a "thought"? Using the "Emperor-of-China" example, explain Sechenov's theory of how thoughts become associated with physical stimuli. How did Sechenov's approach to the concept of association differ from Locke's?

9. What did physiologists of Pavlov's day mean by "psychic secretion"? How did the phenomenon get this label?

10. Describe the two approaches to the study of "psychic secretion" which Pavlov contemplated. Why did Tolochinov's experiment persuade Pavlov to adopt the objective approach? Why did Pavlov come to regard "psychic secretion" as a conditioned reflex?

11. State three contributions Pavlov made to the development of behaviorism.

12. State the principle of temporal contiguity as it applies to classical conditioning. Illustrate the principle using the experiment by Peterson, Wright, and Hanlow on the treatment of bedwetting.

13. In general terms, what are the biological limits on the contiguity principle? State the rationale, procedure, and results of the experiment by Garcia and Koelling on the conditioning of taste aversions.

14. Define the following conditioning procedures and compare their effectiveness in producing CRs: "simultaneous," "delayed," "trace," "backward," "temporal."

15. Define "pseudoconditioning."

16. Define and give examples of "extinction," "spontaneous recovery," "disinhibition," "external inhibition," "internal inhibition."

54

17. State the rationale, procedure, and results of the experiment by Russell, Armstrong, and Patel involving an aversion therapy treatment for cigarette smoking. What precautions does the experiment suggest one should take when interpreting clinical case studies?

18. Using the example of the hypothetical experiment that goes "haywire," describe Rescorla's concept of a CS-UCS contingency. Indicate how the contingency view of associative learning differs from the traditional, "pairings" view.

19. What is the purpose of a control group in classical conditioning? What kind of control group did Rescorla propose? Why did he maintain that the traditional randomization procedure was inappropriate?

20. Define and give examples of: "stimulus generalization," "stimulus discrimination."

21. Explain Bass and Hull's procedure for measuring the generalization gradients produced by extinction and reinforcement.

22. Describe Mary Cover Jones's procedure for eliminating a child's fear of rabbits. Identify the CS, UCS, CR, and UCR. Indicate how stimulus generalization enabled Jones to move the rabbit progressively closer to the child.

23. Describe the three phases of the systematic desensitization procedure. Indicate how stimulus generalization permits the patient to move progressively closer to the highest scene on the anxiety hierarchy.

24. Define and give examples of "primary stimulus generalization," "secondary stimulus generalization."

25. Describe Pavlov's concept of the second signalling system. How was this system said to differ from the first signalling system? How was it supposed to be similar?

26. Describe Riess's strategy for investigating stimulus generalization in semantic conditioning. Use the CS words "surf" and "earn" to illustrate the tests for primary and secondary stimulus generalization. Which type of generalization was stronger? What age-related changes take place in semantic generalization across homonyms, synonyms, and antonyms?

27. What does Luria mean by the "impellant," "preparatory," and "inhibitory" functions of speech? Illustrate using the example of the rubber bulb task.

28. According to Luria, what features characterize the four stages in the development of the regulatory functions of speech?

CHAPTER 3

Operant Conditioning: Principles of Behavior Change

Robbie is an elementary school pupil in the most economically deprived area of Kansas City, Kansas. His teacher reports that he is a highly disruptive student. Instead of working on assignments, he plays with toys that he has brought from home, jokes with classmates, snaps rubber bands, slowly drinks milk served earlier and then plays with the carton, or otherwise creates a disturbance. The situation is a serious one. Robbie must acquire basic intellectual skills now if he is to absorb work in later grades. Failure in school and the attendant frustration may encourage Robbie to drop out, and his future will indeed be bleak. To the extent that Robbie distracts his classmates, they will find learning that much more difficult, and they may also experience frustration. The teacher, for her part, may well complain that she spends more time policing the class than she does teaching it. In short, it is a situation that can be allowed to continue only at substantial cost to all.

Why will Robbie not study? It would be easy to say that he is just lazy or just a troublemaker. But such explanations fail to point us in the direction of positive remedial action. They fail to provide guidance because they are examples of the common **nominal fallacy,** an attempt to explain an action by labeling it. Why is this a fallacy? The practice of labeling is an exercise in circular reasoning; one infers a trait (for example, laziness) from something a person does (here, "fooling around"), and then uses this trait to explain the behavior. The circularity of the nominal fallacy may be readily exposed by asking its advocate two simple questions: (1) Why won't Robbie study? Answer: He is lazy. (2) How do you know he is lazy? Answer: He won't study. We are back where we began. We have added nothing to our original observation.

It is clear that we shall have to look elsewhere for a solution to the problem. Perhaps the answer lies in the consequences of Robbie's actions. What does he gain by acting as he does? Under what conditions does acting in this way pay off? Can the situation be altered in such a manner that study behavior now pays and disruptive behavior does not? Increasingly, individuals who must deal with behavioral problems are asking these kinds of questions and finding that they make progress. To fully appreciate the significance of this approach, let us briefly consider the work of one of its developers, B. F. Skinner, whose ideas have had a worldwide impact. After exploring some of these ideas in the simplified world of the laboratory, we shall return to our Kansas City classroom to see how they were used to improve Robbie's study behavior.

THE SKINNER BOX: WHAT RATS
HAVE TO SAY ABOUT HUMAN NATURE

In 1938, Skinner published a book setting forth a new approach to the study of behavior. The book was boldly entitled, *The Behavior of Organisms*, but, surprisingly, all of its conclusions were based upon the behavior of a single species— the albino rat! Skinner contended, as had Pavlov years earlier, that the behavior of human beings had much in common with the behavior of lower animals. Like Pavlov, Skinner adopted the strategy of studying a single species intensively on the assumption that the findings would have broad generality. Of course, there was no proof that rats could adequately stand in for people in psychological research, but neither had there been any proof that dogs could stand in for people. To Skinner, the value of the approach he was developing was an experimental question and should not be prejudged. That the approach is indeed a useful one will become evident later in the chapter when we examine its many applications. It would not be an exaggeration to say that Skinner's impact on modern behaviorism is comparable in magnitude to Pavlov's impact on early behaviorism.

Skinner's experiments were carried out with a small chamber like the one illustrated in Fig. 3.1. Popularly called a "Skinner box" now (a term Skinner himself has never used), the apparatus was assumed to represent in a highly simplified form many important aspects of the human environment. The advantages of simplification were precision in the measurement of behavior and rigor in the control of events likely to influence the behavior. The behavior selected for study was the response of pressing a bar. Normally, a rat would press the bar by lifting its fore-

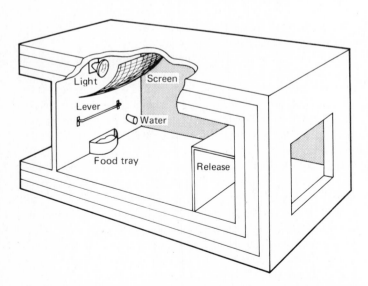

Fig. 3.1 Diagram of the experimental chamber employed by Skinner in his early studies of operant conditioning in rats. (From Skinner, 1938)

legs and pushing down on the bar with one or both of them. A response was recorded if the downward force exceeded some minimum value regardless of how the rat accomplished the act, with one paw or two. For Skinner, the important feature of a response was the change that it made in the environment, not the particular muscles that caused the action. Any such class of movements that changed the environment in a particular way was called an **operant**. The term was meant to convey the idea that the organism was operating upon, or manipulating, its environment. In contrast, the glandular secretions that Pavlov had studied were regarded as physiological responses without noticeable effect on the environment. Skinner believed that reflexes of all sorts were basically insensitive to the effects they had on the environment and should be distinguished from operants. Reflexive actions were referred to as **respondents** to emphasize their status as direct responses to stimuli, conditioned or unconditioned.

The principle of reinforcement

Upon entering the Skinner box for the first time, the rat, which has been deprived of food, is trained to eat from the food tray beneath the lever. When a mechanical device behind the chamber wall operates, a tiny pellet of food drops into the dish. The rat learns to turn promptly to the dish and seize a pellet in response to the sound of the food dispenser. Eventually, the rat will be trained to press the lever to produce the food pellets, but in the early phase of an experiment the lever is likely to be disconnected from the food dispenser. The purpose is to see how many times the rat presses the bar by chance. To say that the training procedure was effective, it will be necessary to show that the frequency of responses after training exceeds the frequency of responses before training. The response frequency before conditioning has been performed is known as the **operant level** of the response.

Suppose, now, that the bar has been connected to the food dispenser so that when the bar is pressed a food pellet will drop into the dish. You can see the result in Fig. 3.2, which illustrates the performance of one typical subject. The graph is

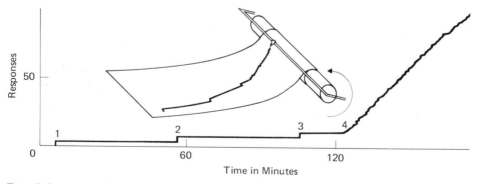

Fig. 3.2 A cumulative record illustrating a rat's acquisition of bar-pressing. The insert shows how the graph was made. (After Skinner, 1938)

THE SKINNER BOX: WHAT RATS HAVE TO SAY ABOUT HUMAN NATURE

called a **cumulative record** and in a sense was drawn by the rat while the experimental session was in progress. Cumulative records are made with the kind of device shown in the insert. A sheet of paper rolls over the drum at a constant speed. In the diagram, the drum is turning counterclockwise so that the paper is moving from right to left. Every time the rat responds, the pen moves up one notch, so that if the rat responds rapidly (short pauses between responses), the pen will draw a diagonal line with a steep slope. If the rat responds more slowly, the slope will be shallower. And if the rat does not respond at all, the pen will draw a horizontal line. The **cumulative recorder** is a standard device in modern operant conditioning laboratories.

The cumulative record reveals little responding during most of the session. Responses occurred at points 1, 2, and 3 in the figure but they were widely separated in time. The long pauses between responses reflect a low operant level. Suddenly, the fourth response opened a virtual floodgate, and responses poured out in rapid sequence. In the language of operant conditioning, the term **reinforcement** is used to refer to any such procedure in which a stimulus administered after a response increases the subsequent frequency of the response. The stimulus that produces an increase in response probability is called a **reinforcer.** Why do we not simply say that the food was a reward? While in the present situation that term makes sense, there are many other situations in which it would seem awkward even though reinforcement had occurred. For example, one could say that the reinforcer for turning on a vacuum cleaner is the sound of the motor. One would not flip the switch if the motor failed to operate. Yet the sound of the motor could hardly be said to provide a sense of gratification or pleasure, which is the effect a reward is usually assumed to have.

An important feature of reinforcement is that a response need not cause or produce the reinforcer to be strengthened by it. Any response followed by a reinforcer will tend to recur even if the reinforcer appeared by chance. Behavior that is maintained by reinforcers it does not actually produce is said to be **superstitious.** Skinner (1948) produced supersitions in pigeons by delivering grain every 15 seconds without reference to what the birds were doing. Soon, the pigeons acquired elaborate rituals such as turning in circles, hopping, and swinging their heads like pendulums. One chance reinforcement had made the response more likely to occur at the time of another reinforcement. This further strengthened the response, made it more likely to occur at the time of another reinforcement, and so on. Indian rain dances, the bowler's "body English" and countless other superstitions (many of which we are probably unaware because they seem to be effective) have probably been acquired under similar circumstances.

Skinner's rats vs. Pavlov's dogs   It may have occurred to you that Skinner's use of the term reinforcement differs considerably from Pavlov's. In Chapter 2 we saw that Pavlov's dogs would salivate in response to a bell (CS) if it regularly preceded the presentation of food (UCS). Pavlov did not require the dogs to salivate in order to receive food; the food followed the bell regardless of the dogs' behavior.

Nevertheless, the UCS had reinforced the power of the bell to elicit salivation. In Skinner's procedure, there was no CS in Pavlov's sense—a stimulus that consistently preceded the conditioned response and elicited it. Skinner, unlike Pavlov, waited until the conditioned response occurred and then gave food, without regard to any CS. Since the lever press was instrumental, or necessary for reinforcement, operant conditioning also carries the label of **instrumental conditioning.** Because of these basic differences in procedures, many theorists have argued that Skinner's rats and Pavlov's dogs acquired their respective conditioned responses for different reasons. Other theorists have disagreed, and the controversy continues to the present time. We shall examine the issue in greater detail in Chapter 6.

Extinction

One implication of the principle of reinforcement is that withdrawal of a reinforcer should lead to a decrease in responding. The term **extinction** refers to this witholding of the reinforcer and to the consequent decline in response strength. While it may seen obvious that the witholding of reinforcement will weaken a response, it is less obvious that extinction occurs in roughly the same way across a wide variety of species, including man. For purposes of later comparison with human subjects, let us examine the way in which extinction occurs in a rat. In one experiment, Skinner (1938) allowed rats to make 100 reinforced responses before withdrawing reinforcement. You can see the result in Fig. 3.3, which presents the cumulative records for four rats. Responding declined gradually rather than coming to an abrupt end. The dashed lines over the curves in Fig. 3.3 are theoretical lines

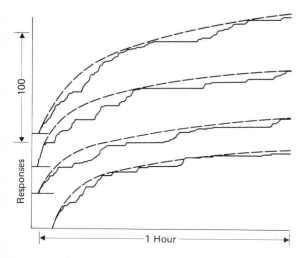

Fig. 3.3 Cumulative records of extinction in four rats. The dashed lines are theoretical estimates of the level of responding one might expect if there were no complicating factors. (From Skinner, 1938)

THE SKINNER BOX: WHAT RATS HAVE TO SAY ABOUT HUMAN NATURE

drawn by Skinner to suggest the form that the curves might have taken had there been no complicating factors. Each rat appears to drop below the line temporarily and then speed up to meet it. Perhaps the rat becomes emotional when it responds without its customary reinforcement and the emotionality temporarily suppresses the behavior. Whatever the reason for this "on-off" pattern of responding, the general form of the curves is the same for all rats. The resilience of this phenomenon could be demonstrated by removing the rats from the apparatus after extinction was complete and then returning them awhile later. The response would spontaneously recover some of its original strength, and one would observe a second extinction curve similar in form to the first. Now, if humans and rats behave according to the same basic principles, as Skinner contended, then we should expect to find a similar pattern when a human being undergoes extinction. The finding of such a pattern would not prove Skinner correct, of course, but it would make the argument a bit more provocative. As we shall see, there are many kinds of situations in which we may look for similarities between the species, and to the extent that we find them, the rat speaks that much more directly to man.

BACK TO KANSAS CITY

It is quite a leap from a Skinner box to a classroom but several rules implicit in our analysis of lever pressing did prove helpful in improving Robbie's study behavior. From the standpoint of operant conditioning, whenever we wish to strengthen behavior, we should:

1. *Define the behavior as specifically as possible.* Skinner defined the lever press in terms of a minimum force that the rat had to exert. As a result, recognizing that a response had occurred was easy. Similarly, we should make it easy to recognize that studying has occurred by defining it in concrete terms. Possible definitions of studying would be facing and listening to a classmate for five seconds as the classmate recites, or holding a pencil on the appropriate page of a workbook for a period of ten seconds.

2. *Develop a procedure for recording the behavior and counting its frequency.* The cumulative record of lever pressing clearly showed that conditioning had occurred (Fig. 3.2). To provide evidence that our conditioning procedures increased studying, we should show that the amount of studying after conditioning exceeded the amount of studying before conditioning; that is, the conditioned behavior should exceed the operant level.

3. *Identify a reinforcer.* When a rat is deprived of food, food naturally becomes a reinforcer. Deprivation is usually unnecessary with human subjects because reinforcers often already exist in the situation. For example, most people naturally respond for such social reinforcers as attention, approval, and affection. If a stimulus is a reinforcer, it will increase the frequency of response above the operant level.

4. *Make the behavior necessary for obtaining the reinforcer.* Skinner increased lever pressing by witholding food pellets until the rat pressed the lever. When the response occurred, the reinforcer immediately followed. Similarly, in using reinforcement to increase human behavior, we should require the subject to perform the desired behavior before we deliver the reinforcer, and we should provide the reinforcer after the response as quickly as possible.

With the cooperation of Robbie's teacher, three investigators (Hall, Lund, and Jackson, 1968) undertook to increase Robbie's studying using the foregoing rules. Let us consider the application of each rule in turn:

1. Study behavior was defined as having pencil on paper for a period of five seconds. The behavior was recorded during a 30-minute work period in which writing was considered appropriate behavior.

2. Study behavior was recorded by placing observers in the rear or on the side of the classroom. The observers used a kind of "score" sheet, a sample of which is shown in Fig. 3.4. The sheet was divided into a series of columns, each representing a 10-second observation interval. Every 10 seconds, the observers determined whether Robbie had kept his pencil on the paper for at least five seconds. If he had, the observers placed the letter "S" in the upper box of the column. If Robbie had not studied for at least five seconds, they placed the letter "N" (nonstudy) in the box. In addition to recording the behavior of Robbie, the observers recorded the behavior of the teacher. They placed a "T" in the middle box if the teacher talked to Robbie during the 10-second observation interval, and a slash mark in the bottom box if the teacher was within three feet of him. Thus, by scanning the score sheet, we could determine what sorts of things Robbie and his teacher were doing during the work period. Moreover, we could calculate the amount of study behavior with a relatively simple formula. For every 30-minute session, there were 180 columns (six boxes per minute). It was possible to calculate the percentage of time that Robbie studied by adding up the number of columns in which "S"s appeared and

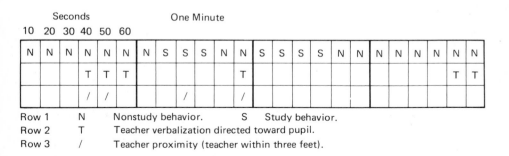

Fig. 3.4 Sample of the record sheet used by observers in study of disruptive classroom behavior. The entries on the sheet are hypothetical. (From Hall, Lund, and Jackson, 1968)

dividing by 180, the number of columns possible. If 36 columns contained "S"s, Robbie would have studied 20 percent of the time. Having developed a method of quantifying the behavior (that is, a method of determining how much behavior occurred), it became possible to test the effectiveness of the conditioning procedure in a precise way.

3. The investigators decided to use the attention of the teacher as a reinforcer for studying. Indeed, there was evidence that teacher attention may have been responsible for Robbie's disruptive behavior. Notice the pattern of "N"s and "T"s on the sample score sheet in Fig. 3.4. Beneath many "N"s appears a "T," but no "T" appears beneath the "S"s. The teacher paid relatively little attention to Robbie when he studied but paid considerable attention to him when he was disruptive, presumably to scold or threaten him. It was a good bet that teacher attention would be an effective reinforcer for studying.

4. To make studying necessary for reinforcement, the observers signalled the teacher to pay attention to Robbie at appropriate times by holding up a piece of colored paper. The teacher might then say, "Very good work, Robbie," or, "I see you are studying," or a similar statement. The observers never permitted the teacher to give attention to nonstudy behavior.

You can see the results of conditioning in Fig. 3.5. The percentage of time spent studying is shown for a series of 36 observation sessions. The baseline represents the way things were prior to conditioning and the amount of studying was quite low, about 30 percent; we may consider this value the operant level of studying. Immediately upon introduction of the reinforcement (labeled Reinforcement$_1$ in the figure) studying increased and reached a level of about 80 percent. The dramatic increase in studying was strong evidence that teacher attention was an effective reinforcer, but the objection could be raised that the increase was coincidental. Perhaps Robbie's parents increased pressure on him to study at the same time reinforcement was introduced. If reinforcement was the important factor, then removal of reinforcement for studying (extinction) and a return to the original conditions in which disruptive behavior received attention should have reduced the amount of studying. A reversal procedure was therefore conducted in which the classroom situation reverted to its original state. The result was a drop in studying. To make the demonstration even more convincing, reinforcement was introduced again (Reinforcement$_2$) and as you can see, studying increased. There can be little question that reinforcement was responsible for the changes in study behavior. The strategy employed to test the effectiveness of reinforcement is a popular one and has been used in a wide variety of settings. It is called an **ABA experimental design,** where the letter "A" represents the baseline condition (here, no reinforcement for studying) and the letter "B" represents the experimental condition in which a variable is introduced (here, reinforcement for studying). The assumption is that if the experimental variable is effective, introducing it in condition B should change the behavior in some way. If the effect of the variable is reliable, then removing the variable should "reverse" the effect, that is, return the behavior to the level asso-

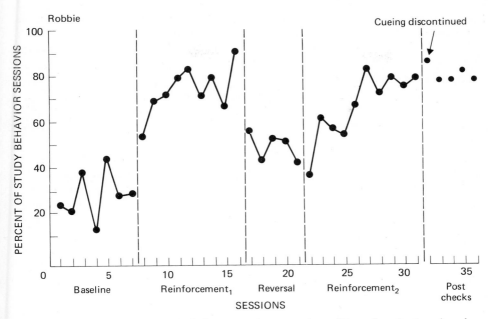

Fig. 3.5 Robbie's level of study behavior under normal conditions (baseline) and under reinforcement conditions, in which teacher paid attention to study behavior but ignored disruptive behavior. Post-checks were conducted 4, 6, 7, 12, and 14 weeks after the last reinforcement condition. Observers did not cue the teacher to attend to the child during these sessions. The implication of the results is that the teacher was able to perform this function without assistance. (From Hall, Lund, and Jackson, 1968)

ciated with condition A. The more subjects tested with the design, and the more subjects exhibiting **reversibility,** the more general would be the effect of the experimental variable. Hall, Lund, and Jackson (1968) were able to show that teacher attention had reliable effects on the study behavior of several children in addition to Robbie, thereby demonstrating that the procedure had generality.

SELF-DESTRUCTIVE CHILDREN: CAN YOU DIAGNOSE THE PROBLEM?

The successful use of operant conditioning to increase Robbie's study behavior helps to build a conceptual bridge between the Skinner box and the "real world." Of course, this demonstration does not prove that humans are just like rats, but it does show that the principles of operant conditioning, originally developed with lower animals, may be helpful in formulating solutions to human problems. When a problem arises, the situation is often so complex that it is difficult to know what aspects of the situation are important, and thus where to look for a solution. The concepts of operant conditioning help give direction to our efforts; they make us sensitive to aspects of the situation that may prove to be important.

Perhaps our analysis of Robbie's problem has influenced your outlook on behavior; perhaps not. Whatever one's outlook, urgent problems exist and solutions would be welcome from any source. Let us consider one such problem. Many severely retarded children who are maintained in hospitals exhibit self-destructive behavior. For no apparent reason, these children inflict injury on themselves by banging their arms against sharp corners, hitting their heads with their fists, or biting themselves. The self-destructive behavior may be so serious that restraint in a straight-jacket becomes necessary. If restraints are used over a sufficiently long period of time, the child's bones may undergo structural changes due to demineralization. Even if restraints are unnecessary to maintain the survival of the child, the occasional self-destructive acts create psychological problems of their own, such as anxiety and depression, and these problems further complicate treatment. Here is an urgent human problem; what is your solution? Why not take a moment to think about the situation? Close the book, and when you feel you have an answer, or when no answer seems to be forthcoming, pick up the book again to see what was actually done.

Diagnosis and treatment   What is your solution? Perhaps it is similar to one tried by two therapists (Lovaas and Simmons, 1969), who reasoned that the self-destructive behavior may have been operant behavior that the hospital environment was reinforcing. The hospital was understaffed and the attendants had little time to pay attention to a child who was quiet and in no danger. But the attendants wasted no time going to the aid of a child who was punching his head with his fist. Perhaps the attention of the staff had actually reinforced this self-destructive behavior, and if that were so, perhaps withdrawal of the reinforcement would produce extinction. Two children were placed in a room for 1.5 hours per day, and the attendants were instructed not to enter the room when the child committed a self-destructive act. The children had been judged medically able to withstand the injury that they may have inflicted on themselves. If attention from the staff were the source of reinforcement, the self-destructive behavior should have gradually decreased. That is precisely what happened. In the more severe case, the child made 2750 self-destructive acts during the first 1.5-hour extinction session. During the second session, the number of self-destructive acts dropped to less than 2000, and during the fourth session it dropped to less than 1000. By the tenth session, the number of self-destructive acts was zero. The extinction process here was thus similar to that shown by the rats whose food pellets were withdrawn: a gradual slowing-down of responding. Perhaps you are wondering why the self-destructive behavior declined gradually, while Robbie's study behavior dropped abruptly when teacher attention was withdrawn (the reversal period, Fig. 3.5). The reason for the difference may be that Robbie's teacher not only withdrew attention from studying during the reversal period, but gave attention for disruptive behavior. Since one cannot study and be disruptive simultaneously, the reinforcement of disruptive behavior may have accelerated the reduction in study behavior. Whatever the reason, both cases—Robbie's and the self-destructive children's—show that the consequences of one's actions are important determinants of behavior.

RESPONSE SHAPING: THE PSYCHOLOGIST AS SCULPTOR

To increase Robbie's study behavior, the investigators waited until studying occurred and then reinforced it. This was a practical approach because the operant level of studying was relatively high; prior to conditioning, Robbie was already studying about 30 percent of the time. But suppose the operant level was much lower, or zero. Waiting for the behavior to occur would be quite impractical. In general, when the operant level of a response is substantially greater than zero, we may strengthen the behavior by simply waiting until it occurs and providing reinforcement. But when the operant level is very low or zero, we must take steps to hasten the appearance of the behavior. **Shaping** is a technique that induces an organism to make a response that ordinarily rarely occurs. Shaping involves the reinforcement of successive approximations to the desired behavior, a gradual progression from what the organism is presently able to do to what the shaper would like the organism to do.

Skinner (1953) has likened the shaping of behavior to the artistry of the sculptor. Just as the sculptor's clay initially lacks form, so the psychologist's material, behavior, often initially lacks direction. Both carve out a distinctive new creation through the careful selection of intermediate forms, through the production of successive approximations to the final objective. The art of behavioral sculpturing has particular relevance to the fields of therapy and education, where the objective is frequently to develop new forms of behavior. In therapy, an individual may be so lacking in normal social behavior that the shaper must virtually create a "new" person. For example, schizophrenic children typically show little contact with reality and live in what amounts to a private world. They exhibit minimal responsiveness to other people and may utter few sounds that could be interpreted as meaningful speech. Two therapists (Hingtgen and Trost, 1964; reprinted in Ulrich, Stachnik, and Mabry, 1966) initiated a program to shape vocal responses and mutual physical contact in pairs of schizophrenic children. The children, who ranged in age from five to seven and one-half years, had previously been taught to operate a coin-dispensing device by pulling a lever, and to insert the coin in another device to obtain candy. The treatment consisted of two daily 30-minute training sessions, in the first of which the child was left alone in a room and reinforced with coins for vocal responses, and in the second of which pairs of children were reinforced for touching one another.

The program for shaping vocal responses required, first, that the child make any sound at all, such as humming, coughing, or giggling. Then, to receive reinforcement, the child had to make the sound more discrete, that is, to shorten the duration of the sound. Once the child was making discrete sounds, reinforcement was given for sounds that resembled syllables, for example, "ah," "uh," and "da."

Finally, reinforcement was given for responses on an intermittent rather than a continuous basis. The response that produced reinforcement was unpredictable, but on the average it was necessary to make three responses for one coin. The shaping procedure succeeded in increasing the vocalizations of three of four children tested from an operant level of virtually zero to a frequency of about five vocalizations per minute. Hopefully, these primitive sounds could later be used to establish words, and ultimately the words could be strung together to form sentences.

The shaping of cooperative behavior involved a program of four steps. With two children now in the room, one coin was delivered (and was taken by whichever child reached it first) if either child touched the other with his hand. This initial step was broken down into successive approximations to the target response beginning with physical closeness, then "accidental" bodily contact, and finally hand-to-body contact. The second step required either child to touch the other and make a vocal response at the same time. The third step was equivalent to the second except that it became necessary for one child to touch the other with two hands. Finally, both children had to touch each other with two hands and vocalize. The result of shaping was a substantial increase in cooperative behavior from an operant level of virtually zero to about two social acts per minute. Moreover, the treatment yielded dividends in that the new social behavior generalized to novel situations outside the treatment room. For example, after watching his father use a water hose for some time, one child touched him and said "ba," one kind of social response that had previously been conditioned in the training room. The father gave the child the hose and thereafter required similar social responses whenever the child wished to play with it.

The foregoing analysis of shaping illustrates several key elements of the procedure:

1. *The reinforcement is immediate.* Reinforcement acts most strongly on the behavior that immediately precedes it. If a delay intervenes between the desired response and reinforcement, a response incompatible, or in conflict, with the desired one may intervene and be conditioned instead. In other words, a "superstition" may form. Tokens represented instant reinforcement for social responses, even though the child ate candy several seconds later. (We will analyze the reasons for the effectiveness of the tokens later in our discussion of conditioned reinforcement.)

2. *The subject is active.* At each step in the program, the child makes a response and receives reinforcement. The shaper does not physically force the response to appear, or simply read off a set of instructions. The activity of the subject is gradually guided to the appropriate response.

3. *The steps are gradual.* When one response in the program has been established, the subject is in a better position to make the next response. Simply on a chance basis, the children were more likely to emit a recognizable syllable after they had emitted discrete sounds than after they had emitted coughs and sneezes. The reinforcement of successive approximations hastened the appearance of the final behavior.

OPERANT CONDITIONING: PRINCIPLES OF BEHAVIOR CHANGE

4. *The subject learns at his or her own rate.* The subject must acquire the responses early in the program before the shaper proceeds to later responses. As acquisition may come rapidly for some subjects, slowly for others, the shaper must be prepared to proceed at different rates for different subjects.

Mechanical tutors   It has occurred to many psychologists that the ideal educational environment may be one that incorporates these elements of the shaping procedure. In the standard classroom, students often listen passively as the instructor presents material and never really discover whether they have learned the material until they take an exam days or weeks later. Moreover, the instructor may jump from one topic to another without providing an adequate transition for the student, and may spend too little time on each topic to enable the student to fill in the gap. For some students, the choice of topics and the rate of presentation may be ideal, while for others the instructor may be proceeding too slowly and becoming a bore. How can the teacher be all things to all students? Unless the teacher individually tutors the students, many students are likely to experience frustration. As a remedy, Skinner (e.g., 1958) and colleagues (e.g., Holland, 1960) have advocated the use of "teaching machines" to shape verbal knowledge on an individual basis. One device developed by Skinner presents material to the student several sentences at a time. Associated with each small unit of material is a fill-in-the-blank question which the student must answer correctly before he or she can proceed to the next unit. Each unit, called a **frame,** differs only slightly from the one before it so that the student is always in a good position to answer the question correctly. Holland (1960) has presented some sample frames from a program designed to teach the principles with which we are concerned in this chapter:

1. Performing animals are sometimes trained with "rewards." The behavior of a hungry animal can be "rewarded" with _____. (FOOD)
2. A technical term for "reward" is reinforcement. To "reward" an organism with food is to _____ it with food. (REINFORCE)
3. *Technically* speaking, a thirsty organism can be _____ with water. (REINFORCED) (Holland, 1960, p. 280)

The student beginning the program sees the first frame in a window of the machine and writes his or her response in a separate window. Then the student operates a device that places a transparent cover over the just-written answer so that it cannot be changed, and exposes the correct answer. If the answer given by the student is correct, the student rotates the first frame out of view and presents the second frame. If it is wrong, the student covers the correct answer and attempts the question again. The steps are so gradual that errors are rarely made and progress through the program is rapid. All of the elements of shaping are present: the immediate reinforcement of being correct and moving to the next frame; the active involvement of the student in each step of the program; the gradual progression from one frame to the next; and the opportunity for a student to progress at his or her own rate, repeating questions that are missed to get a firm foundation for later material.

RESPONSE SHAPING: THE PSYCHOLOGIST AS SCULPTOR

Teaching-machine programs become increasingly complex as they more closely approximate the behavior of a live tutor. The **linear program,** above, is a relatively simple method of presentation in which all students encounter all the frames in the same sequence. Students who are making many errors receive the same instruction as students who make none. A **branching program** incorporates subprograms that provide remedial instruction to students who miss particular questions, and they may be equipped to enable students who make no errors to skip ahead. To diagnose the reasons for an error so that remedial instruction may be provided, the branching program typically employs multiple-choice questions rather than the fill-in-the-blank type. The incorrect alternatives may be written so that their selection would probably arise from a specific type of mistake. The student could then be detoured into a series of frames designed to correct that mistake. Because branching programs are more complex than linear programs, they usually require the use of computers, and much technological research has been performed in the field of computer-assisted instruction or CAI (Suppes and Morningstar, 1969). But teaching effectiveness is not a simple function of electronic complexity. Teaching effectiveness depends on the manner in which principles of learning are applied. Indeed, machines are only one vehicle for programmed instruction and much can be accomplished without them. Many textbooks, written on a variety of subjects and at varied educational levels, use the programmed format. Most programmed texts employ the linear program but branching programs also exist. A sample of a branching program from an advanced text on body-fluid metabolism appears in Fig. 3.6. You can acquire a feeling for the program by reading the material in the first frame and then answering the associated multiple-choice question. Each of the three alternatives will direct you to another frame, which will either advance you to new material if you were correct, or help you understand your error if you were wrong. Note how the program immediately reinforces an appropriate choice with the statement, "You are correct." If you find this statement reinforcing (in the sense that you read the subsequent material and would like to see the next frame), then you would probably have no difficulty working your way through the 610 frames that comprise the program!

SCHEDULES OF REINFORCEMENT: "IF AT FIRST YOU DON'T SUCCEED . . ."

Whether we are seeking a job, attempting to make a sale, or pursuing a potential mate, we should not be surprised to encounter an occasional setback before achieving our goal. The familiar adage advises us to try, try again, because success commonly follows a series of failures. Yet, despite the advisability of persevering in the face of failure, some people do not, and others who do may sometimes pursue a goal vigorously and at other times pursue it sluggishly. When we observe such variations in performance, the temptation to commit the nominal fallacy is strong. A person who has given up is an easy target for the

1

Many chemical processes supporting life in man take place primarily in the aqueous solutions of his body, and an understanding of the distribution, composition, and regulation of the body liquids is fundamental to a working knowledge of human physiology.

If we exclude from consideration fat, which incorporates virtually no water, the tissues in man, including the skeleton, average overall about 73% water by weight. On this basis, what per cent of the weight of a normally nourished, normally developed male adult would you expect to be water?

About 73%	item ③	
More than 73%	item ⑤	
Less than 73%	item ⑩	

3   (from item 1)

YOUR ANSWER: In the normal adult male, water would account for about 73% of the body weight.

We said that the tissue *excluding* fat average about 73% water. However, in the total body weight we would have to consider some fat. Fat as such contains practically no water. Intact fatty tissue contains only 15% to 30% water, which is much less than the overall average for the other tissues. The presence of fat, then will bring the proportion of water in the body below the 73% found in the nonfat tissues.

Now turn to item 1 and choose the correct answer.

5   (from item 1)

YOUR ANSWER: In the normal adult male, water could account for more than 73% of the body weight.

We said that the tissue, excluding fat, averaged about 73% water. However, in the total body weight we would have to consider some fat. Fat as such contains practically no water. Intact fatty tissue contains only 15% to 30% water, which is much less than the overall average for the other tissue. The presence of fat, then, will bring the proportion of water in the body below the 73% found in nonfat tissue, not above it, as your answer would have it.

Return to item 1 and choose the correct answer.

10   (from item 1)

YOUR ANSWER: In the normal adult male, water could account for less than 73% of the body weight.

You are correct. While the nonfat tissues average about 73% water, the presence of fatty tissue, which is relatively dry, lowers the proportion of body weight due to water. In the normal adult male, water is about 60% of the body weight. It is higher in youth and lower in old age.

Intact fatty tissue, because of its content of essentially water-free fat, contains only between 15% and 30% water. Variations in amount of fat account for most of the variations in water content among different mammalian species.

Would you expect the percentage of water in a normal woman to be greater or less than in the normal male?

About the same	item 4
Less in the woman	item 6
Greater in the woman	item 8

Fig. 3.6   Excerpts from a textbook on body fluid metabolism which uses the strategy of a branching program to present concepts. (From Wolf and Crowder, 1964)

SCHEDULES OF REINFORCEMENT: "IF AT FIRST YOU DON'T SUCCEED . . ."

label "quitter," but as our analysis of Robbie (the disruptive student) has shown, a search for concrete causes is likely to be a more useful approach than the simple invention of labels. Researchers in operant conditioning have long sought to understand how a series of successes and failures may influence an organism's actions. A framework for this analysis was introduced by Skinner (1938) but it was greatly elaborated later in a book entitled *Schedules of Reinforcement*, by Ferster and Skinner (1957).

A **schedule of reinforcement** is a rule specifying the conditions under which a response will be reinforced. The rat that receives a food pellet every time it presses the lever responds according to a very simple rule called a schedule of **continuous reinforcement** (abbreviated CRF). A simple extension of the CRF schedule is the **fixed ratio** schedule (FR) which provides reinforcement following a specified number of responses. Piecework pay is an FR schedule in the sense that a worker must always produce a given number of articles to receive payment. The number of responses required for reinforcement represents the size of the schedule; a requirement of five responses constitutes an FR 5 schedule. On a **variable ratio** (VR) schedule the number of responses required for reinforcement varies in an unpredictable manner from one reinforcement to the next. Gamblers who play slot machines respond on VR schedules in that they must pull the handle an unpredictable number of times before the machine releases any coins. The average number of responses required per reinforcement represents the size of the schedule; on a VR 100 schedule, the average requirement is 100 although the individual requirements may range from 1 to 1000.

On the FR and VR schedules, then, reinforcement depends upon the number of responses made. On so-called "interval" schedules, the passage of time is of primary importance. A **fixed interval** (FI) schedule delivers reinforcement for the first response after some period has elapsed since the last reinforcement. Responses during this period go unreinforced. For example, we may start a clock after giving reinforcement for a rat's lever press and refrain from giving additional reinforcement for the next minute. After one minute had elapsed, we would reinforce the next response and then repeat the procedure by timing another one-minute interval (this would thus constitute an FI one-minute schedule). A rough analogy could be drawn to a situation in which a student receives examinations at one-week intervals. Reading behavior would earn a passing grade (reinforcement) only after the week had passed and the test was administered.

On a **variable interval** (VI) schedule, the intervals between reinforcements vary in an unpredictable manner. A VI one-minute schedule would deliver reinforcement for the first response after an average of one minute had elapsed since the last reinforcement, but occasionally a response could produce reinforcement after as little as a second or as much as several minutes. When we attempt to reach someone by telephone but get a "busy" signal, we commonly hang up and try again later. We are responding on a kind of VI schedule in which the reinforcement is the sound of the other person's voice and the response is our dialing of the telephone. The availability of the person's voice depends on the duration of his or her conversation with the other party, not on the number of times we dial; that is what distinguishes a VI schedule from a VR schedule.

Response patterns on reinforcement schedules

Interest in schedules of reinforcement has grown not simply because it is possible to define them and find analogies in the "real world." The interest stems from the fact that each schedule tends to produce a characteristic pattern of respond-ing. To the extent that reinforcement schedules produce consistent response pat-terns, they may offer a possible explanation for occasional changes in the vigor with which we pursue goals and even for changes in our moods. Research on a wide variety of species (including man) has revealed the typical response pat-terns illustrated in Fig. 3.7, which presents cumulative records of performance of FR, VR, FI, and VI schedules. The short diagonal lines intersecting the curves represent reinforcements. On the FI schedule, there tends to be little or no responding immediately after reinforcement, but as time passes, the rate of re-sponding accelerates and reaches a peak just prior to the next reinforcement. The pattern that emerges is a series of so-called FI scallops. The pause after reinforcement probably arises from the consistent failure of responses to produce reinforcement at that time. In other words, the period immediately after rein-

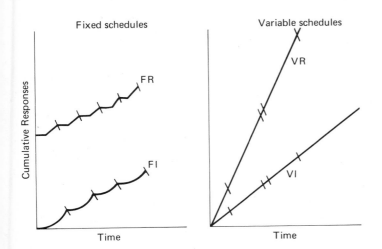

Fig. 3.7 Hypothetical cumulative records illustrating the typical performances produced by four basic schedules of reinforcement: fixed ratio (FR), fixed interval (FI), variable ratio (VR), and variable interval (VI). The short, oblique lines intersecting the functions represent reinforcements.

forcement resembles a period of extinction (Skinner, 1938). Of course, the remainder of the interval is also a period of extinction, but with the passage of time, this period becomes difficult to distinguish from the period of reinforcement (unless the subject has a clock).

Students commonly feel the effect of the FI scallop when they have recently taken an exam and must wait several days or weeks before the next one. Studying drops to a low level and then increases with the passage of time. This phenomenon has been demonstrated experimentally by Mawhinney, Bostow, Laws, Blumenfeld, and Hopkins (1971), who arranged to have college students do all of their studying for a course in a special room set aside for this purpose. Unknown to the students, the experimenters observed their behavior and recorded the amount of time actually spent studying. The students had the option of not studying at all by simply not showing up at the study room. When the experimenters administered tests daily, the students spent about the same amount of time studying every day. But later in the course, when the experimenters administered a single test after a three-week interval, the same students showed a dramatically different pattern of studying. Negligible studying occurred early in the interval, but as the days passed the pace quickened. Upon return to the daily exam schedule, studying again became uniform over days. The fact that the same students showed both patterns of studying is particularly important. Had an observer unfamiliar with the experiment viewed one of the students during the FI phase of the study (one test after three weeks), he or she might have taken the lack of studying early in the interval as a sign of "laziness." Similarly, had the uninformed observer viewed the student solely during the period of daily exams, he or she might have taken the consistent pattern of studying as a sign of diligence or self-discipline. The observer might then be surprised to learn that the two sets of labels applied equally well to the same student under different conditions. The finding is not surprising, however, to an individual who resists the temptation of the nominal fallacy and seeks to understand behavior in relation to its consequences.

As on the FI schedule, a pause after reinforcement also occurs on an FR schedule (Fig. 3.7) provided that the response requirement is relatively high. However, the pause usually ends with an abrupt transition to a high response rate rather than with a scallop. Once a response occurs on an FR schedule, it tends to lead quickly to another response, and responding usually continues until reinforcement is obtained. Skinner (1974) notes that workers on piece-rate pay systems also work very vigorously, sometimes reaching dangerous levels of activity. Because of this hazard, the piece-rate system commonly meets with opposition on humanitarian grounds and it is encountered today quite rarely.

The pause after reinforcement of FR schedules probably occurs for much the same reason as the pause on FI schedules. As the subject responds on an FR schedule, time necessarily passes. Since reinforcement never occurs immediately after the preceding reinforcement, the period following reinforcement resembles a period of extinction. Where FR schedules exist in "real-world" settings, pauses after reinforcement are common. For example, writers of short stories or articles often find it difficult to begin a new piece after recently completing one (Skinner, 1974). Their inability to start work could be characterized as a condition of **abulia,** a state in which a person lacks the will power to achieve an aim. However, Skinner (1974) believes the concept of will power to be unnecessary to explain this inactivity. If we view the completion of an article as analogous to the completion of an FR requirement, the writer's abulia may simply represent the post-reinforcement pause that FR schedules typically generate.

The effects of unpredictability   Unlike the FI and FR schedules, the VI and VR schedules maintain constant rates of responding without pauses after reinforcement (Fig. 3.7). The steady rate of responding reflects the unpredictable nature of the schedules: responses may produce reinforcement at any time and so the organism responds persistently. However, the effects of VI and VR schedules differ in that VR schedules typically maintain higher response rates. The reason lies partly in the fact that the faster an organism responds on a VR schedule, the sooner it will obtain reinforcement. On a VI schedule, there is no comparable advantage since the availability of reinforcement depends on the passage of time, not the number of responses made.

Intuitively, we might expect a person to respond less vigorously on a VI or VR schedule than on a CRF schedule. The larger number of reinforcements provided by the CRF schedule should produce stronger behavior. Actually, the picture is quite complex, the CRF schedule producing stronger behavior in some cases (e.g., Weiss, Buchanan, Alstatt, and Lombardo, 1971) and the intermittent schedules producing stronger behavior in others (e.g., Ince, 1968). A complicating factor is the possibility that an organism on CRF may soon have its fill, or become satiated, on the reinforcer and cease responding, while the organism on an intermittent reinforcement schedule may take longer to satiate and thus continue to respond (Ayllon and Azrin, 1968). As a general rule, the rate of responding decreases as the time between reinforcements increases (e.g., Catania and Reynolds, 1968), but we must remember that the reverse may hold if satiation becomes a factor.

Intermittent reinforcement in natural settings

Intermittent reinforcement tends to be a more efficient way of maintaining behavior than continuous reinforcement; the organism will respond more times before satiating when reinforcers come less frequently. Ince (1968) demonstrated the facilitative effects of VI schedules in a study designed to condition the speech of college students in an interview setting. The students had volunteered to meet with the experimenter six days a week to discuss the changes college had made in their attitudes, feelings, and goals. Ince selected for reinforcement any positive self-reference statement, that is, any statement that began with "I"

and lacked words involving negation (e.g., no, not, nothing) and words expressing doubt (such as maybe, perhaps, I think). Whenever the subject uttered a
positive self-reference statement, the interviewer responded by paraphrasing the
statement or by saying "good" or "mmhmm." Continuous reinforcement for
every statement increased the frequency of statements substantially above the
operant level recorded during a baseline condition (no reinforcement). But intermittent reinforcement was even more effective. The interviewer watched a small
red bulb located inconspicuously behind the subject. When the bulb lit up, the
interviewer knew that the required interval had elapsed and he reinforced the
next positive self-reference statement. The result of using the VI schedule was a
further dramatic increase in the frequency of these statements; a VI three-minute
schedule yielded approximately twice as many statements as the CRF schedule.
Ince's results imply that in any interview setting the interviewer must be alert to
the possibility that his or her reactions may influence the speech of the person
interviewed.

Increasing worker productivity Satiation may have been responsible for
Ince's (1968) finding that VI schedules maintained a higher response frequency
than a CRF schedule. The relatively large number of "mmhmm"s and "good"s
earned on the CRF schedule may have sapped their value. In other situations
where intermittent schedules have had facilitative effects, it is difficult to imagine
that satiation has played a role since the reinforcer was money. Yukl, Wexley,
and Seymour (1972) hired subjects on a part-time basis to process scores
obtained on a college examination. Students had marked their answers on IBM
cards and the workers were asked to score each card and enter the value on a
computer printout. During the first week of the study, the workers were paid on
a regular hourly schedule, but during the second week an incentive system was
added. In one condition, the worker received an additional 25¢ for every computer printout completed (each printout contained a number of IBM card
entries). We may label this condition CRF 25¢. In another condition, the worker
brought the completed printout to a supervisor in the room, who flipped a coin
and paid the worker 25¢ if the outcome was favorable. Since there was a
50-50 chance of winning, a worker would have to complete two printouts, on
the average, to obtain a quarter (VR 2 25¢). Finally, in a third condition, a coin
was flipped just as in the second condition, but the worker received 50¢ if he or
she won (VR 2 50¢). At this point, before reading the results of the study, you
may wish to stop and try to predict the outcome. Which of the three schedules—CRF 25¢, VR 2 25¢, or VR 2 50¢—would increase worker productivity
the most? Which the least? (Ties are permitted.)

To measure the effect of the schedules, the number of cards produced during the second week (with the incentive added) was compared with the number
of cards produced during the first week (with no incentive). The gain in production for each condition was calculated by subtracting the first-week score from
the second-week score. You can see the effects of the schedules in Fig. 3.8.

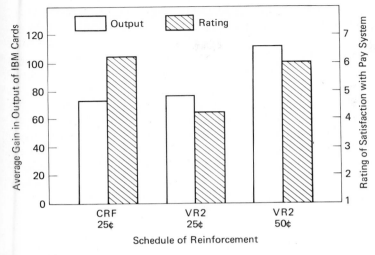

Fig. 3.8 How three pay schedules affected rate of work and job satisfaction in study of worker productivity. (After Yukl, Wexley, and Seymour, 1972)

The open bars in the figure represent the gain scores and the findings are quite remarkable. The highest production was achieved with the VR 2 50¢ schedule. It yielded substantially more output than the VR 2 25¢ schedule (not very surprising because VR 2 25¢ paid half as much), but it also yielded more output than the CRF 25¢ schedule, even though the two schedules had the same dollar value! In other words, as the employer, you would pay your workers just as much by giving them 25¢ for every printout as you would by giving them 50¢ for every other printout (on the average). But you would not receive an equal output from your workers; you would receive more with the VR schedule. Perhaps even more surprising than this finding was the discovery that paying workers 25¢ half the time on a VR 2 schedule yielded the *same* production as paying workers 25¢ every time on the CRF schedule. The facilitative effect of the VR schedule apparently compensated for the reduction in pay!

How did the workers feel about these incentive systems? After the study was completed, the workers rated the particular system they had experienced on a seven-point scale, giving a value of "1" if they were "very dissatisfied" with the system or "7" if they were "completely satisfied." The bars with diagonal lines in Fig. 3.8 show their reactions. Satisfaction closely matched the dollar value of the system. Job satisfaction was the same with CRF 25¢ as it was with VR 2 50¢ (the highest paying system), and it was lowest with VR 2 25¢ (the lowest paying system). Clearly, how a person acts may be quite unrelated to how a person feels.

SCHEDULES OF REINFORCEMENT: "IF AT FIRST YOU DON'T SUCCEED . . ."

The partial reinforcement effect   In summary, the results of the studies on speech conditioning and worker productivity show that intermittent reinforcement is capable of maintaining as many or more responses during a session than continuous reinforcement. Decades of research have also demonstrated that a history of intermittent reinforcement will cause an organism to make more responses during a period of extinction than will continuous reinforcement. In other words, intermittent reinforcement results in greater "perseverance." This **partial reinforcement effect** is at least partly explained by the fact that the transition from partial reinforcement to extinction can be very difficult to detect. For example, it might take a gambler all night to discover that the slot machine he or she has been playing is out of order and will not pay off. The transition from a lean VR schedule to extinction becomes detectable only after an unusually large number of responses fails to produce reinforcement. On the other hand, it should take this individual no more than one or two lost coins to discover that the nearby soft-drink machine is out of order, since such machines ordinarily pay off on a schedule of continuous reinforcement. The partial reinforcement effect has been found to occur under a wide variety of conditions. Lewis (1960) has provided an extensive review of studies of this phenomenon.

COMBINING REINFORCEMENT SCHEDULES

The five schedules of reinforcement discussed thus far—CRF, FR, VR, FI, and VI—can be viewed as psychological building blocks. They can be arranged in numerous ways both in the laboratory and the natural world, and each method of combination has a characteristic effect on behavior. In this section we will consider two important methods of combining reinforcement schedules: the **multiple** schedule and the **chained** schedule.

Multiple schedules: The processes of discrimination and generalization

On a multiple schedule, two or more simple schedules are presented in alternation, each associated with a distinctive cue. In a laboratory setting, we could establish a multiple schedule by reinforcing a rat in a Skinner box according to one schedule when a light was on and according to a different schedule when the light was off. For example, when the light was on, bar pressing might produce food on an FI schedule. When the light was off, bar pressing might produce food on a VI schedule. Eventually the rat would exhibit typical FI scallops in the presence of the light and a constant response rate in the absence of the light. The patterns of responding would be appropriate to whatever schedule was in force. In the language of operant conditioning, the presence and absence of the lights would be called **discriminative stimuli** (abbreviated S^ds and pronounced S-dees), stimuli that set the occasion for reinforcement and maintain an appropriate pattern of responding. As a general rule, an organism is said to

discriminate between two stimuli if it responds differently in the presence of each. A common sort of discrimination in everyday life is that between a stimulus associated with reinforcement (S^d) and a stimulus associated with extinction (S^Δ —pronounced S-delta). We stop for gasoline at a station where attendants are present (S^d), not at a station that appears deserted (S^Δ). A child may beg its parents for toys when the grandparents (S^d) are present because grandparents usually take the child's side and see that the child gets its way. When the grandparents are absent (S^Δ), the child does not beg for toys because without the additional pressure the parents never give in. Operant discrimination training involving S^ds and S^Δs closely resembles discrimination training in classical conditioning (Chapter 2). In both cases, reinforcement occurs in the presence of one stimulus but not in the presence of another stimulus. However, the two procedures differ in an important way. In operant conditioning, the subject must respond to get the reinforcer. In classical conditioning, the reinforcer is presented after the CS regardless of what the subject is doing.

Human vigilance Holland (1958) has provided a striking demonstration of the effect that S^ds may have on human behavior. His concern was with human vigilance—why are we alert on some occasions and inattentive on others? The problem has important practical relevance because many monotonous tasks require the continuous attention of observers. Radar operators may watch their scopes for long periods without sighting an enemy target. Firespotters may scan a forest from a mountain post for days or weeks without sighting smoke. Such uneventful routines often result in a reduction in vigilance and an increased likelihood that the target will go undetected. What causes this decline in attentiveness? Holland suggested that paying attention, or observing, is, in a sense, behavior, and that for observing behavior to be maintained it must be reinforced by the detection of targets. If a blip never appeared on the radar screen, the operator's observing behavior might decrease for much the same reason that a rat's lever pressing decreases when food pellets are withheld. To assess the validity of this idea, Holland devised a task that permitted precise measurement of observing behavior and allowed reinforcers (detections) to be scheduled in various ways. The subjects, Navy enlisted men, were to report the deflections of a pointer on a dial. Because they worked in the dark, the subjects were unable to see the pointer unless they pressed a key, which illuminated the dial briefly (.07 seconds). To light the dial again, it was necessary to release the key and press it once more. When the subject observed a deflection, he reported the event by pressing another key, and in so doing, he reset the pointer for another trial.

If we viewed Holland's situation from the standpoint of a Skinner box, the pressing of the illumination key (that is, the observing response) would correspond to the pressing of the lever; pointer deflections would correspond to food pellets (they are the events for which the subject is pressing the key); and the pressing of the other key used to report detections would correspond to the rat's eating from the food tray (since both rat and human do something with the reinforcer after obtaining it). Does this sound farfetched? If so, then you may find the results surprising. In one phase of the study, pointer deflections (reinforcers) were programmed on an FI four-minute schedule; four minutes after the previous deflection, the next observing response deflected the pointer. After several such sessions, Holland witheld pointer deflections entirely (extinction). Figure 3.9 presents a cumulative record of extinction for one subject. The session began with three reinforcements on the FI four-minute schedule (indicated by the diagonal lines intersecting the curve). The remainder of the session consisted of extinction and the graph shows that the observing behavior gradually tapered off. The extinction curve for human vigilance closely resembles the extinction curve for rats' lever pressing in Fig. 3.3, and supports Holland's notion that vigilance is maintained only if it is reinforced. But the analogy to lever pressing becomes even more compelling when we consider the results of another phase of the study in which a multiple schedule was introduced. When a red light was on, an FI three-minute schedule was in effect and when a green light was on an FR 40 schedule was in effect (that is, the pointer moved after the observer had made 40 observing responses). The red and green lights alternated during the session and eventually they acquired control over the pattern of responding. Figure 3.10 illustrates the effects of the multiple schedule. The segments of the cumulative record labeled "I" show responding on the FI schedule, while the segments of the graph labelled "R" show responding on the FR schedule.

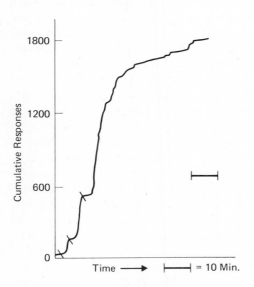

Fig. 3.9 Cumulative record showing extinction of a person's "observing responses" when they no longer resulted in detections of a target. The last three detections are represented by the short, oblique lines intersecting the function. (From Holland, 1958)

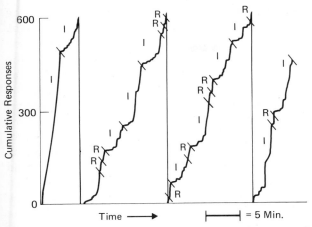

Fig. 3.10 Cumulative record of observing responses reinforced on a multiple schedule by detections of a target. In segments of the function labeled, "I," a fixed-interval three-minute schedule was in effect. In segments labeled, "R," the subjects responded on a fixed-ratio schedule with a requirement of 40 responses. (From Holland, 1958)

Figure 3.10 indicates that the red light produced FI scallops while the FR schedule produced rapid bursts of responding (apparently the ratio was too short to give a post-reinforcement pause). The practical implication of Holland's results is that dummy signals should occasionally be presented to observers to provide intermittent reinforcement for their vigilance. More broadly, these results suggest that in at least some cases, mental states may be analyzed and understood in the same terms as outward behavior.

Generalization   Suppose that Holland (1958) had employed a different kind of multiple schedule. When a red light was on, observing responses were intermittently reinforced on a VI schedule. When the red light was off, no responses were reinforced. Eventually the subject would probably make observing responses at a high rate when the red light was on (S^d) but not when the light was off (S^Δ). Now, following establishment of this discrimination, imagine that we discontinued reinforcement altogether, and instead of simply showing a red light, we showed a series of differently colored lights. For example, an orange light might appear for a minute, then a blue light, then a yellow light, then the original red light (without reinforcement), and so on. When the red light was on, we should not be surprised to find that the subject still responded; the VI schedule used to condition the behavior normally produces many responses in extinction. But what do you suppose the subject would do when the orange light was on? And the yellow? And the remaining colors of the spectrum? Comparable studies performed with lower animals (e.g., Guttman and Kalish, 1956) suggest that the subject would continue to respond to the new colors, but would

COMBINING REINFORCEMENT SCHEDULES

respond more to the orange than to the yellow, more in the yellow than in the green, and so on. In other words, the more similar the new color was to the original one (red), the more responses the color should produce. This is the phenomenon of **generalization,** which was first discovered by Pavlov in the context of classical conditioning. Without the ability to generalize, life would be difficult indeed. The individual who learned to drive in a Ford would be lost in a Chevrolet. The child who learned to read in one classroom would become an illiterate in another classroom. In clinical settings where the objective is to change behavior, the hope is that the effects of treatment will generalize from the training situation to novel situations. The shaping of social responses in the schizophrenic children, discussed earlier, was successful in this respect. The child who said "ba" and touched his father when he wished to play with a garden hose generalized behavior from the treatment room to the outside world. Once the behavior occurred, the father was able to reinforce it (by giving the child the hose) and thereby increase the future likelihood of the behavior at home.

Of course, generalization may not be appropriate in every circumstance. The child who learns to say "dada" in the presence of his or her father may generalize the response to other adults. Sailor (1971) encountered a similar problem in his attempts to teach retarded children the plural form of words. If you held up two spoons and asked these children what they saw, they would say "spoon," not "spoons." The rules for pluralization in English are quite complex and involve generalization within certain classes of words as well as discrimination between different classes. Words with unvoiced endings, such as "cup," "belt," and "truck," require a hissing sound for pluralization, while words with voiced endings, such as "pen," "card," and "ring," require a "zzz" sound. Sailor started with one type of word and successively presented different pairs of objects in this class, for example, two cups, two belts, etc. He asked, "What do you see?" and if a child gave the correct plural form within 15 seconds, the experimenter delivered reinforcement (a bite of ice cream or a sip of a fruit-flavored drink). If the child gave a singular response or failed to respond in time, the experimenter said "No," took the objects away for a few moments, and then presented them again for a new trial. The experimenter continued to present objects until a correct response was made, and then he presented a new pair of objects. After the child had mastered a class of words, members of the other class ("probes") were occasionally introduced for a few seconds without giving the child any feedback. At this point in training, the child was correctly *generalizing* the plural ending to one class of words. Would the child correctly *discriminate* between this class and the probe? Sailor found that the subject consistently generalized an inappropriate ending to the probe even though the subject may have learned the correct ending in past sessions. Whatever ending the child currently was being trained to use, he or she generalized to the probe. The results indicated that the training procedure did not effectively teach the rule for pluralization and that another procedure would be necessary to produce discrimination between response classes. The processes of generalization and discrimination play key roles in the learning of concepts generally, and we shall consider their contribution in more detail when we take up the subject of concept formation in Chapter 7.

Response chains and conditioned reinforcement

On a chained schedule, an organism receives reinforcement after completing two or more schedules in succession. Each schedule is identified with a distinctive cue that informs the organism of its position in the chain. In a laboratory setting, we normally establish a response chain by first teaching the organism a discrimination. For example, the rat in the Skinner box could be given reinforcement for lever pressing when a light was on (S^d) but not when the light was off ($S^\triangle$). Eventually, the rat would quickly respond when the light went on and would cease responding when the light went off. Having produced this discrimination, we would be in a position to observe a phenomenon with far-reaching implications: It would now be possible to establish and reinforce a new response by simply turning on the light. Imagine that we turned on the light when the rat happened to stand up on its hind legs. When the light went on, the rat would press the lever as before and receive food. After reinforcement, if we turned off the light, we would probably find that the rat again stood up for us, as if begging us to turn the light on. By quickly turning on the light and inducing the rat to press the lever, we could create a smooth sequence of responses in which the rat first stood up and then pressed the lever. The "glue" that holds this response chain together is the light, which has two important functions. First, the light serves as an S^d for pressing the lever; whenever the light is on, the rat presses the lever to obtain food. Second, the light serves a reinforcer for standing up; the rat "wants" to turn the light on. Not all rats will stand up to turn on lights, of course. Only rats with particular histories will do so. In general, whenever an organism repeatedly experiences reinforcement in the presence of a stimulus, the stimulus will acquire the power to reinforce new behavior; it will become a **conditioned reinforcer.** A **primary reinforcer** such as food requires no such training to be effective as its reinforcing value is innate.

In a sense, the light has the same significance for the rat as money has for us. The rat must earn the stimulus and have it "in hand" when it goes to the lever for food. The analogy between conditioned reinforcement and money was made highly explicit in a classic study by Wolfe (1936). Wolfe trained chimpanzees to insert a poker chip into a kind of vending machine to obtain a grape. Once the chimps learned to do this, they would work to earn poker chips by pressing a lever or pulling a string. The chimps had learned a response chain in which the token acted as a conditioned reinforcer for pressing the lever and as an S^d for operating the vending machine. Now, when a human earns money, his or her goal often lies in the distant future. There may be a substantial delay between payday and a trip to the mountains or a visit to the supermarket.

Chimps also show an ability to tolerate a delay of reinforcement. In one phase of Wolfe's study, the chimps continued to work for tokens even though they had to wait before inserting the coin into the vending machine. However, if they could insert the token as soon as they earned it, but had to wait before the grape came out, their working decreased. The behavior remained strong when something tangible filled the interval of delay; it deteriorated in the absence of a signal that reinforcement would be forthcoming.

The "token economy"   Wolfe's (1936) study suggests an important principle for strengthening behavior: If the consequences of behavior are distant in time, present a conditioned reinforcer immediately. This conditioned reinforcer should be physically available during the interval of delay and should be required in exchange for the ultimate reinforcer. While simple in concept, this principle has found an important application in modern psychotherapy. It plays a central role in the rehabilitation programs of a wide variety of institutions, including institutions for the multiply disabled, for psychotics, for the retarded, and for juvenile delinquents. The pioneer work was performed by Teodoro Ayllon and Nathan Azrin at Anna State Hospital in Illinois; they published the results of their work in a book entitled *The Token Economy: A Motivational System for Therapy and Rehabilitation* (1968). Working with psychotic patients, many of whom had been hospitalized for more than 25 years, Ayllon and Azrin undertook to establish behaviors that would make the patients once again acceptable to the community—useful behaviors such as completing a job that has been undertaken, asking questions when in need of help, following instructions, being prompt for appointments, and so forth. Of course, while acquiring such behavior the patient would also learn to get along with others and develop social skills. Ayllon and Azrin reasoned that once these social skills and job-related behaviors had been established in the hospital, the community would continue to reinforce and maintain them because they had value.

The project was an ambitious one; it entailed the design of a total environment capable of motivating behavior change. One of the first tasks was to discover reinforcers for each patient that could later serve to strengthen desirable behavior. To find reinforcers, Ayllon and Azrin applied an important principle developed previously by Premack (1959): Activities in which an individual engages frequently may be used to reinforce behavior in which an individual engages infrequently. Premack (1959) demonstrated this principle with elementary school children who were allowed to alternate freely between two activities—they could play a pinball machine or they could help themselves to bits of chocolate. During a 15-minute observation period, some children were more likely to play the pinball machine than to eat (manipulators), while others were more likely to eat than play the pinball machine (eaters). Several days later, during a second session, the manipulators were required to eat one piece of candy to earn one play at the pinball machine. Their consumption of candy increased substantially over the amount they ate in the first session (the operant level), demonstrating that pinball playing was a reinforcer for eating. Similarly, eaters who were required to play pinball to earn one piece of candy played pinball considerably more than they did during the first session, indicating that eating was a reinforcer for pinball playing. By carefully observing their patients, Ayllon and Azrin discovered many potential reinforcers in the sense that Premack had defined them—behaviors that occurred more frequently than the behaviors to be conditioned. For example, some patients frequently hoarded objects under their mattresses; others frequently sat in a particular chair; some patients frequently sought privacy by concealing themselves in various locations on the ward. All such activities were given a price tag in the new motivating environment. To hoard an object in a locked cabinet, to use a favorite chair, or to acquire a screen to put in front of one's bed, a patient now had to perform some socially useful behavior.

Many kinds of jobs existed, some of which contributed to the maintenance of the ward (commisary clerk, recreational assistant, grooming assistant, etc.), while others contributed directly to the patients' well-being (exercising, toothbrushing, bathing, etc.) A listing of the jobs appeared in a central location and patients typically made their own choices. The job requirements were specific so that it was clear both to the patient and the staff that the required behavior had been performed. For example, a recreational assistant might occasionally serve as a movie assistant, the requirements for which stated that the patient "sets up movie projector and shows movie to patients; Changes reels and rewinds tape" (Ayllon and Azrin, 1968, p. 249).

Now, a movie projectionist who completes the job Thursday evening may not have occasion to sit in a favorite chair until Friday afternoon. A delay of reinforcement that large could render the chair ineffective as a reinforcer. To bridge the delay, Ayllon and Azrin used tokens much as Wolfe (1936) had done. Immediately upon completion of the job, the patient received an appropriate number of tokens, which the patient later exchanged for reinforcement. Different reinforcers required different numbers of tokens, and different jobs paid different amounts. Living in this token economy, the patients showed dramatic changes in behavior. Instead of sitting off by themselves or pacing the halls all day as they had previously done, the patients now spent many hours working on socially useful behavior. The token economy system appears to hold great promise even for those once considered hopeless.

FROM CARROT TO STICK: AVERSIVE TECHNIQUES OF CONTROL

In all of the studies discussed thus far, the subjects have acted to produce some stimulus or event. Skinner's (1938) rats pressed a lever to produce food pellets; Robbie, the disruptive student, created disturbances and later studied to attract the attention of the teacher; the hospitalized retarded children injured themselves to secure the attention of the attendants; Holland's (1958) observers pressed a button to illuminate a dial. Any condition that an organism acts to produce is termed a **positive reinforcer.** Frequently an organism acts to terminate or **escape** a condition, and in these circumstances the organism obtains a different form of reinforcement. Any condition that disappears after a response is made, and leads to an increase in the future likelihood of the response, is known as a **negative reinforcer,** or an **aversive stimulus.** Note that both positive and negative reinforcement increase the probability of a response. The difference between them lies in what happens after the response is made: A stimulus is presented in the former case and terminated in the latter case.

Negative reinforcement is as much a part of daily life as positive reinforcement, and frequently the two types of reinforcement work together. For example, an individual turns down the volume of the radio to escape a particularly annoying commercial and in so doing receives negative reinforcement: He or she is more likely to turn off the same or similar commercials in the future. A minute or so after turning down the volume, he or she turns the knob in the opposite direction because the resumption of the program offers positive reinforcement. Similarly, the child who habitually whines for toys may do so because he or she often gets them. Those individuals around the child receive negative reinforcement when the nagging stops, and make future nagging more likely by positively reinforcing the behavior with the toys.

Punishment: Does it work? Aversive stimuli commonly influence behavior by encouraging us to escape them, as discussed above. Another common influence of aversive stimuli comes through the use of **punishment.** In punishment, a response produces, rather than removes, an aversive stimulus. The result of punishment is usually a quick reduction in responding, in contrast to the gradual reduction in responding that characterizes extinction. Note that punishment and negative reinforcement have opposite effects on behavior. Negative reinforcement increases response probability. Punishment decreases response probability. For years, psychologists have debated the effectiveness of punishment as a technique of control. Skinner, a long-standing opponent of punishment, has argued that punishment may temporarily suppress a response but it will not make the response weaker. In one of his studies (Skinner, 1938), two groups of rats received reinforcement for lever pressing and then underwent extinction. One group underwent extinction in the usual way—the reinforcement was simply withheld and their responses gradually decreased in frequency. By the end of the second extinction session, responses rarely occurred. The second group of rats was punished during the first few minutes of extinction by having their paws slapped when they pressed the lever. Responding virtually ceased, creating the impression that punishment plus extinction was more effective than extinction alone. But then punishment was discontinued; any future responses would simply not receive reinforcement. Eventually, a response occurred and another response quickly followed. Responding accelerated, and by the end of the second extinction session, the punished group had made as many responses as the unpunished group. Skinner argued that the punishment had temporarily suppressed the response by making the rats emotional, but it did not reduce the rats' disposition to respond. In subjective terms, although the rats were frightened, they still "wanted" to press the lever. According to Skinner, the response emerged in full strength following punishment because extinction was necessary to make it weaker. Having undergone extinction, the rat no longer sees any use in the activity. The warning is clear: Although punishment reduces the frequency of a response quickly, and offers the user quick negative reinforcement, we should not yield to the temptation. It is better to wait the additional time required by extinction to eliminate the response permanently.

But is this criticism of punishment fair? When punishment was discontinued, responding increased. But if extinction were discontinued (by resuming reinforcement) would not responding increase as well? Azrin and Holz (1966), comparing the effectiveness of a variety of procedures for reducing behavior, concluded that extinction reduced responding only while the procedure was in effect; resuming reinforcement increased responding. Moreover, if punishment were made sufficiently severe, responding would not recover after punishment was discontinued, in contrast to Skinner's (1938) finding with milder punishment. Therefore, a distinction between punishment and extinction on the grounds of reversibility would give punishment, not extinction, the advantage.

Punishment certainly carries serious risks. The initial introduction of punishment may generate much emotionality, which may suppresss all behavior, not just the punished response (Azrin and Holz, 1966). Moreover, punishment may disrupt social relationships by making the punitive agent an object of aggression or fear. Indeed, the entire situation in which an organism experiences an aversive stimulus may arouse fear and motivate the organism to escape. In a classic demonstration, Miller (1948) shocked rats in one compartment of a device and permitted the rats to escape to another compartment. He found that even after shock was discontinued, the rats would work to escape the first compartment by pressing a lever or turning a wheel. Initially, pain had motivated the rats to escape, but now, with shock discontinued, fear motivated them to escape. By analogy, we might imagine that a student who repeatedly experiences punishment at school by being humiliated or being required to stay after school, might eventually become a truancy case, or drop out of school altogether (Azrin and Holz, 1966).

Fortunately, punishment need not be severe to be effective. When an organism has an alternate means of securing reinforcement, even the mildest punishment may eliminate a response. Holz, Azrin, and Ayllon (1963) demonstrated the power of mild punishment by giving psychotic patients at a hospital a chance to earn cigarettes. They could obtain cigarettes on a VI schedule by either pulling a plunger or pushing a button on a vending machine. The patients showed a preference for pulling the plunger and so the experimenters decided to eliminate this response. After every ten responses on the plunger, the experimenters punished the response by turning off the machine for 30 seconds.

When the machine was turned off, the lights on the machine went out and neither the plunger nor the button would produce cigarettes. This method of punishment is known as **time-out** from positive reinforcement; it consists of the removal of a stimulus associated with positive reinforcement, rather than the introduction of an aversive stimulus as discussed earlier. It was found that if the button was made inoperative and the only means of obtaining cigarettes was pulling the plunger, the time-out treatment reduced the number of responses but did not eliminate them. However, if the button also became operative, the patients switched to it and stopped pulling the plunger entirely. The alternative means of obtaining reinforcement enhanced the effect of punishment. Parents commonly employ the time-out procedure when they prohibit a child who has been naughty from going outside to play. Dennis the Menace, the well-known cartoon character, finds himself in such a position when he must sit quietly in the corner of a room holding his Teddy bear. The study by Holz, Azrin, and Ayllon (1963) suggests that parents would find this procedure more effective if they gave the child an alternative way of getting what he or she wants. We might expect mild punishment to deter a child from stealing change at home if, by performing chores, he or she could earn a comparable amount of money.

Avoiding aversive stimuli When an aversive stimulus is impending, we commonly take steps to avoid it. If the engine of our car has begun to "shake, rattle, and roll," we are inclined to have the engine examined, lest we leave it behind one day on the road. In the laboratory, **avoidance** behavior is often studied by presenting a signal, such as a tone, and letting the signal terminate with an aversive stimulus, such as electric shock. If the organism makes an appropriate response, the signal goes off and the shock is witheld. The offset of the signal tells the organism that it is safe until the next presentation of the signal. Avoidance behavior can develop without turning off the signal, but the immediate feedback appears to facilitate learning (Kamin, 1956). In fact, avoidance behavior can develop in the absence of a warning cue. A rat may receive a shock every 20 seconds if it fails to respond, but if it responds, it can postpone the shock for another 20 seconds (timed from the response). Rats acquire avoidance behavior under such conditions, despite the absence of warning cues or safety signals (Sidman, 1953). Apparently, avoidance behavior is so basic to survival that nature provides organisms with the ability to protect themselves under the most difficult conditions. We shall be looking more closely at the factors influencing avoidance learning in Chapter 4.

An intriguing application of the avoidance procedure was made in the construction of a portable apparatus for improving posture (Azrin, O'Brien, Ayllon, and Roll, 1968). Beneath the subject's clothes was a sensing device capable of detecting slouching. An elastic cord was connected to a shoulder harness and stretched across the subject's back. At the other end, the cord was connected to a switch, so that if the subject rounded his shoulders, tension on the cord would increase and trigger the switch. When triggered, the switch made an audible "click" and the subject then had three seconds in which to resume normal posture. If he continued to slouch, another device (also concealed) sounded a loud, aversive tone. In addition to this avoidance procedure, the posture apparatus also incorporated an escape procedure. To get the tone off, it was necessary to stop slouching. Of course, implicit in the avoidance procedure was a punishment procedure since slouching produced an aversive stimulus if it continued for three seconds. With so many procedures focused on a single objective, it will perhaps come as no surprise that the apparatus virtually eliminated slouching. However, if the tone was disconnected, the subject resumed slouching, suggesting that extended training may be necessary to make the effect durable. Nevertheless, the development of the portable posture device raises the interesting possibility that for some behavioral problems machines may be able to give treatment in the field (Azrin and his colleagues explicitly expressed this hope). We have already seen that machines may serve as "mechanical tutors." Is it conceivable that we shall some day see "mechanical therapists"?

SUMMARY

In attempting to explain an individual's actions, people often commit the "nominal fallacy," attaching a label to the person rather than looking for concrete causes. Operant conditioning emphasizes the role that the consequences of actions play in determining future actions. Some events that follow an organism's actions increase the probability that the action will be repeated; these events are called "reinforcers." Withdrawal of a reinforcer (extinction) results in a gradual decrease in the frequency of the response. Whether we seek to condition a rat to press a lever, or induce a child to study, several rules are likely to make our efforts more fruitful:

1. Define the behavior as specifically as possible.
2. Develop a procedure for recording the behavior and counting its frequency.
3. Identify a reinforcer.
4. Make the desired behavior necessary for obtaining the reinforcer.

Often, the behavior we wish to strengthen exists in some strength prior to conditioning. When it does, we may wait until the response occurs and then reinforce it. Other times, the strength of a response prior to conditioning is very low and we must shape the behavior to hasten its appearance. Shaping involves the reinforcement of successive approximations to the desired response, and it incorporates four elements:

1. The reinforcement immediately follows the response.
2. The subject is always active.

88

3. The steps that are successively introduced are gradual, so that the subject is always in a good position to respond correctly.
4. The subject proceeds at his or her own rate.

"Schedules of reinforcement" are work requirements, rules specifying the conditions under which a response will be reinforced. "Fixed-ratio" and "variable-ratio" schedules require some number of responses for reinforcement; "fixed-interval" and "variable-interval" schedules reinforce a response after a period of time has elapsed. Each schedule maintains a characteristic pattern of responding, and to that extent they may offer a possible explanation for changes in the vigor with which we pursue goals. Intermittent reinforcement is capable of maintaining as many or more responses over a period of time than continuous reinforcement and is therefore a more efficient way of maintaining behavior. A history of intermittent reinforcement will also cause an organism to make more responses during a period of extinction than will a history of continuous reinforcement (partial reinforcement effect).

On a multiple schedule, two or more simple schedules alternate, each associated with a distinctive cue. Eventually, the cues produce the same response patterns as the schedules normally maintain in isolation; each cue thus becomes a discriminative stimulus, setting the occasion for reinforcement and maintaining an appropriate response pattern. Because the organism responds differently in the presence of the stimuli, it is said to discriminate between them. When a response conditioned to one discriminative stimulus occurs in the presence of other, similar stimuli, the organism exhibits generalization.

Through repeated pairing or association with a reinforcer, a previously neutral stimulus becomes a conditioned reinforcer. Conditioned reinforcement is an essential element of response chains, in which an organism satisfies the requirements of two or more reinforcement schedules in succession, each associated with a distinctive cue. Working for money is an example of a response chain in which money provides conditioned reinforcement for working, and becomes a discriminative stimulus for some subsequent action, such as going to the store.

Responses may not only be reinforced when they produce an event (positive reinforcement) but when they remove an event (negative reinforcement). Negative reinforcers, or aversive stimuli, maintain escape behavior when they are removed following a response. Punishment occurs when a response produces, rather than removes, an aversive stimulus, and the result is usually an immediate reduction in response frequency. The removal of a stimulus associated with positive reinforcement may also serve as punishment (Time out).

A third way in which aversive stimuli influence behavior is by producing and maintaining "avoidance" responding. A signal that warns of an impending aversive stimulus can be used to condition avoidance behavior. When the avoidance response occurs, the aversive stimulus is withheld, and the signal may then be turned off to inform the organism that it is safe. However, avoidance behavior develops even in the absence of warning signals and feedback.

STUDY QUESTIONS

1. What is the nominal fallacy? Using the example of the disruptive pupil and the label "lazy," show how the circularity of the nominal fallacy can be revealed by asking two questions.

2. What is an operant? How does the bar press response fit this definition? How do operants differ from respondents?

3. Define "operant level." How is the operant level of a response used to assess the effectiveness of conditioning procedures?

4. Labeling both axes of the graph, draw a cumulative record to illustrate three performances: a relatively high response rate, a relatively low response rate, and zero responding.

5. Define and distinguish from one another the following terms: "reinforcement," "reinforcer," "reward."

6. How did Skinner produce "superstitious" behavior in pigeons? What important feature of reinforcement does this phenomenon illustrate?

7. Why does operant conditioning also carry the title, "instrumental conditioning"? How does this aspect of the procedure make operant conditioning different from classical conditioning?

8. Draw a hypothetical extinction curve on a cumulative record. Describe the changes that take place in responding as a function of time.

9. State the four basic rules for strengthening behavior through operant conditioning. Using the example of "Robbie," the disruptive pupil, illustrate each rule.

10. What is an "ABA" experimental design? What is meant by the term "reversibility"?

11. Define "shaping." Under what circumstances is shaping used?

12. State the four basic features of the shaping procedure. Illustrate each feature using the study on the shaping of vocal and cooperative responses in schizophrenic children.

13. How do teaching machines incorporate the four features of shaping?

14. What is a "schedule of reinforcement"?

15. Define and give examples of the following schedules: CRF, FR, VR, FI, VI.

16. Draw cumulative records to illustrate the typical performances produced by FR, VR, FI, and VI schedules. Describe these performances.

17. Discuss the relationship between performances maintained by CRF and intermittent reinforcement schedules with specific reference to: (a) the factor of satiation; (b) the factor of time between reinforcements.

18. Describe the procedure and results of the experiment on worker productivity by Yukl, Wexley, and Seymour. Emphasize the difference in results obtained with the output measure vs. the ratings of the incentive systems given by the workers.

19. Define and give an example of the "partial reinforcement effect."

20. Define and give an example of a "multiple schedule."

21. Define and give examples of "discriminative stimulus" (S^d, $S^\triangle$).

22. How does operant discrimination training involving S^ds and $S^\triangle$s differ from discrimination training in classical conditioning?

23. Describe the procedure Holland used to study human vigilance. What features of the procedure corresponded to the following features of a conventional Skinner box situation: pressing the lever, food pellets, eating from the food dish? How did Holland's extinction curve compare with those observed by Skinner in rats?

24. Give an example of "generalization" in the context of operant conditioning.

25. What are the two functions of a stimulus in a response chain? Illustrate these functions using the example of the rat which stands up to turn on a light and then presses a bar for food.

26. How can tokens be used to fill the interval between a response and reinforcement? Illustrate using Wolfe's experiment with chimps. How did Ayllon and Azrin apply this principle in the treatment of psychotic patients at Anna State Hospital?

27. State and give an example of Premack's principle for discovering reinforcers.

28. Define, distinguish, and give examples of: "positive reinforcement," "negative reinforcement" (aversive stimulus), "punishment".

29. State Skinner's position on the effects of punishment. What counterargument was advanced by Azrin and Holz?

30. How can mild punishment, such as a "time out," be made more effective?

31. How is "signalled avoidance" studied in the laboratory. How can avoidance behavior be produced without a signal?

OPERANT CONDITIONING: PRINCIPLES OF BEHAVIOR CHANGE

CHAPTER 4
Learning and Motivation

Like the concept of "learning," the concept of "motivation" is difficult to define. Nevertheless, everyone has a strong intuitive sense of what motivation is, and examples of it are usually easy to recognize. I encountered a striking illustration of motivation one day when administering an examination to a large class in introductory psychology. Several minutes after the exams were distributed, I decided to reposition a microphone on the podium. The mike was attached to a long, adjustable tube, and it appeared that the mike was off because the signal light on the podium was out. Unfortunately, the light had blown out; the mike was on at its normal volume. The movement of the tube broke the silence with a sharp, grating noise, much like the sound you would make if you rubbed your hand over the surface of a balloon. Reactions were instantaneous. Many students gasped. Some literally jumped off their seats. All eyes turned towards the podium. "Sorry," I said, "the mike was on." It hardly seemed necessary to point that out, but what was one to say? Several minutes passed before the situation returned to normal.

The intensity of the reactions was surprising, for while the noise came unexpectedly, it was not especially loud. The gasps, the jumps, the prolonged disruption in performance—these reactions seemed exaggerated in relation to the intensity of the stimulus. Some additional factor must have contributed to the effect. Quite likely, the students were tense; they were eager to do well on the exam and were concentrating hard. This heightened state of arousal had apparently magnified the effect of the noise. That was my theory at the time of the incident. Several weeks later, this interpretation was supported by the results of an informal experiment conducted during a lecture. It was my impression from casual observation that my lectures were less arousing than my exams. If that were indeed the case, then introduction of the noise during a lecture should produce a milder startle reaction than the one which occurred during the exam. To divert attention from the microphone, a slide was projected on a large screen as an illustration of the lecture material. While the students watched the slide, I quickly reached over and jarred the microphone, producing the same sharp, grating noise the students had heard before. No one gasped. No one jumped. Mostly there were looks of puzzlement and curiosity. "What do you think you're doing?" was the message written on almost every face. I hope that the explanation that followed was sufficient justification for the interruption.

Motivation is commonly conceptualized as an internal state having two kinds of effects on behavior. One effect is general in nature. Whatever an organism happens to be doing, for whatever reason, it will tend to do more vigorously. This effect represents the "energizing" function of motivation. Unexpected noises often elicit startle reactions no matter what an individual happens to be doing at the moment the stimulus occurs. If the individual is in a strong motivational state, as apparently the students were when taking the exam, the startle reaction will be stronger than usual. The other effect of motivation is specific in nature. The organism's behavior becomes organized around a particular goal related to the motivational state. The goal of the introductory psychology students was to achieve a score on the exam that they would be satisfied with. Coming to class that day, sitting at the desk, reading the questions, contemplating the possible answers—all of these activities had a common objective. This effect of motivation represents its "directing" function.

Conceptualized as an internal state, motivation is not directly observable; it must be inferred from something the organism does. Judson Brown (1961, pp. 29-33) has identified three kinds of situations which often lead people to assume that an individual is in some sort of motivational state:

1. *"Evocation of vigorous responses by weak stimuli."* The vigorous startle reaction elicited by the noise during the exam would fall in this category. A diner who takes an unusually vigorous swat at a fly after spilling food on himself displays another motivational state—anger.

2. *"Variability of response in the presence of constant stimulating conditions."* You are offered a roast beef sandwich at 2:00 p.m. but decline. At 4:00 p.m. you accept a second offer and eat the sandwich heartily. In the second case, you were in a motivational state of hunger; in the first case, you were not. Similarly, the difference in startle reactions of the students during the exam and the lecture could be taken to signify different degrees of motivational arousal.

3. *"Equality or constancy of behavior in the presence of normally effective changes in the external stimulus situation."* An individual steps into the street. Suddenly a car appears. The person freezes. Normally, the appearance of an oncoming car would cause the person to take protective action. Under the present circumstances, a state of intense fear had a paralytic effect.

In each situation, it was assumed that the individual had the capacity to perform some response—to become startled, to eat, to swat flies, or to avoid oncoming cars. The vigor with which the response occurred, if it occurred at all, depended on the intensity of the motivational state. In conceptualizing the conditions responsible for motivational states, psychologists have traditionally distinguished between two classes of variables: those that "push" and those that "pull" the individual. "Pull" variables are characteristics of the goal for which the individual works. The term **incentive** refers to the motivational state created by characteristics of the goal. You may have difficulty motivating a child to mow the lawn for 50¢, but raising the pay to $5.00 may create sufficient incentive. It is known that a rat will press a bar to receive a few drops of sugar water. By raising the concentration of the sugar, you can induce the rat to press faster; the rat will have more incentive to work. "Push" variables impel action whether or not a goal subject is present or available. This is often accomplished by creating a condition of need. Deprivation of food creates a need for food, causing the individual to become tense and restless (energizing function of motivation), and to concentrate his or her efforts on obtaining that goal (directing function of motivation). A cut or burn impels action by producing pain; the individual seeks relief (directing function) and feels tense and restless until the pain subsides (energizing function). In many situations where the objective is to motivate behavior, one has a choice between employing a push variable or a pull variable. To motivate the rat to press faster, you could raise the concentration of the sugar (pull) or raise the number of hours of food deprivation (push). To motivate the child to mow the lawn, you could raise the monetary reward (pull) or deprive the child of money from other sources, such as his or her allowance (push). In the first part of the present chapter we shall examine some of the effects of motivating organisms by pushing. Our focus in the second part will be on the effects of motivating by pulling.

MOTIVATING BY "PUSHING"

Need vs. drive

The term "need" has sometimes been used interchangeably with the term "drive," but a distinction between the two seems advisable (Brown, 1961). "Drive" refers to a general state of arousal in the body; it corresponds to the energizing function of motivation. "Need" is a condition in which some requirement for normal functioning is unfulfilled. As such, need is a potential source of drive but it is not equivalent to it. It can be shown that to some extent the two conditions vary independently of one another. For example, to measure the level of drive in animals, psychologists have often employed a device called a stabilimeter. It is essentially a platform that tilts whenever the animal moves from one location on the platform to another. The number of tilts is taken as a measure of restlessness, or random activity. As the number of hours of food deprivation increases, so does random activity—up to a point. It then decreases, for the intense need weakens the animal. Under extreme deprivation, need and drive vary in opposite directions.

Precisely how drive activates behavior is a controversial question. The traditional view has been that drive is an internal force, one that instigates activity from within the organism. Campbell and Sheffield (1953) presented evidence that drive operates not by energizing activity from within, but by making the organism more sensitive to stimuli in the external environment. Rats were placed in stabilimeters and tested in a dark room where only the constant hum of a fan could be heard. Random activity was recorded in two kinds of conditions, one preceded by a change in the environment (the fan was turned off and the lights turned on), and one not preceded by a change in the environment. It may be supposed that change would tend to elicit exploratory reactions, such as sniffing at various places in the chamber. The more sensitive the rat was to external stimuli, the greater might be the tendency to explore. Campbell and Sheffield found that only in the stimulus-change condition did random activity increase with hours of food deprivation. Random activity remained constant in the monotonous, no-change condition. While this finding contradicts a longstanding theory of how deprivation increases activity, it is consistent with the basic generalization that has been made about motivation. Under normal environmental conditions, motivation enhances the vigor of behavior.

Drive and learning: The Yerkes-Dodson Law

Thus far, we have been concerned with how motivation affects the performance of a response already in the subject's repertoire. It is equally important to consider how motivation affects the acquisition of new responses. According to a well-known generalization about motivation and learning, increasing the level of drive will increase the rate of learning up to a point. After that point, the rate of learning will decrease. The optimal (best) level of motivation for learning depends on the difficulty of the task: The greater the difficulty, the *lower* will be the optimal level of motivation. These relationships were discovered in an early experiment with mice by Yerkes and Dodson (1908), and have since been repeated so many times by other researchers that they are now collectively designated the "Yerkes-Dodson Law."

Broadhurst (1957) tested the Yerkes-Dodson Law in an unusual situation—the level of drive was manipulated by depriving animals of air. Rats were trained to swim under water through the Y-shaped maze illustrated in panel (a) of Fig. 4.1. A roof was attached beneath the water level in the start box and stem of the maze to prevent the subjects from obtaining air in those sections. Relief was obtainable only by entering the arm of the maze which contained a platform above the water level. A door blocked the entrance to each arm, one door lit more brightly than the other. To reach the platform, the rat had to push against the brighter door; the other door was always locked. Broadhurst created three levels of task difficulty by adjusting the illumination of the locked door. With very dim illumination, the discrimination task was expected to be easy. With illumination just below that of the open door, the task was considered difficult. An intermediate degree of illumination was regarded as a moderately difficult task. Drive level was manipulated by detaining the subjects in the start box for varying periods of time. To ensure that the periods he selected would indeed produce different drive levels, Broadhurst conducted a preliminary experiment. Swimming speeds in a four-foot straight alley were measured following delay times ranging from 0 to 25 seconds, the assumption being that higher speeds would reflect higher drive levels. Swimming speeds were found to increase as delay times were increased up to 10 seconds—panel (b) of

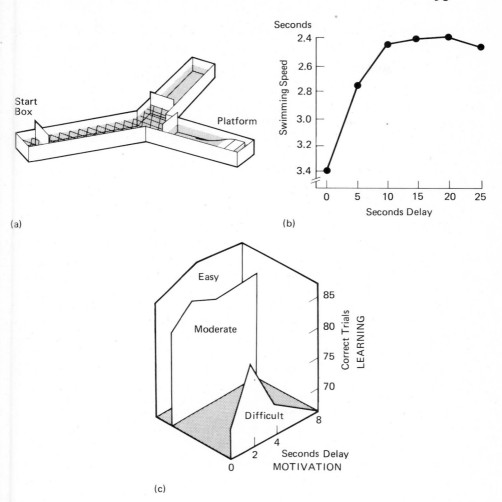

Fig. 4.1 (a) Y-maze apparatus used by Broadhurst in test of the Yerkes-Dodson Law. Rats learn to swim under water from the start box to the arm of the maze with the more brightly lit door. Upon opening the door, the rats gain access to a platform above the water level. A roof below the water level in the start box and stem of the maze (crossed lines) prevents the rats from escaping. (b) Results of a preliminary experiment in which rats swam under water in a straight alley to obtain air after varying periods of air deprivation. Swimming speed was taken as a measure of motivation level. (c) Relationship between level of motivation produced by air deprivation and number of correct responses on easy, moderate, and difficult discrimination problems in Y-maze. (Panels (b) and (c) from Broadhurst, 1957)

Fig. 4.1—but then they leveled off. Thus, there was theoretical justification only for selecting times in the 0 to 10-second range. Four times were studied: 0, 2, 4, and 8 seconds.

Panel (c) of Fig. 4.1 presents the learning scores on the three tasks as a function of delay time. A total of 100 trials was administered, and the learning scores were simply the number of trials in which no error was made. You can see that the three levels of task difficulty had the anticipated effects on learning. The number of correct trials was highest with the easy task, lowest with the difficult task, and intermediate with the moderate task. Consistent with the Yerkes-Dodson Law, learning scores rose to a peak and then decreased as the delay period was lengthened. The optimal level of motivation for learning tended to decrease as the difficulty of the tasks increased. On the easy task, the optimal level occurred with the four-second delay, while on the moderate and easy tasks the optimal level was the two-second delay.

Most tests of the Yerkes-Dodson Law have employed tasks requiring subjects to avoid a noxious condition. Ordinarily, this condition is electric shock. It appears that the foregoing generalizations about motivation and learning may not apply to tasks in which subjects learn to approach a goal (like food) rather than avoid a noxious condition. Fantino, Kasdon, and Stringer (1970) deprived pigeons of food until the animals were at 85, 75, or 65 percent of normal weight (low, medium, and high drive, respectively). The pigeons were then presented with one of three problems illustrated in Fig. 4.2. Each was a version of the well-known "umweg" or "detour" problem. A cup of food was placed in full view of a pigeon on the opposite side of a wire mesh barrier. The bird could obtain food by going around the barrier, a response in direct conflict with the pigeon's natural tendency to move directly toward the screen. In the simplest version of the problem, only the screen was present. In the moderate problem, additional barriers were placed on either side of the screen, thus forcing the animal to move further away from the goal in order to obtain it. In the complex problem, the barriers were extended. Each bird was tested seven times, one trial per day. The measure of mastery was the number of seconds that elapsed from the moment that the bird was placed in front of the screen to the moment the bird made contact with the food. Figure 4.3 presents the results expressed in terms of speed (1/time). As expected, the simple problem gave the fastest solutions, the complex problem the slowest, and the moderate problem an intermediate solution time. Note that on each problem the speeds increased consistently with the degree of hunger. There was no evidence that the optimal level of motivation varied with the difficulty of the task. While the Yerkes-Dodson Law can be applied with confidence to situations involving defensive motivation, we must be cautious when applying it to situations which lack the element of threat.

Anxiety, personality, and learning

The Yerkes-Dodson Law was originally intended as a statement about the effects of transient, situationally-created drive. But it is also possible to think of drive as a stable personality characteristic. For example, some people seem to be chronically

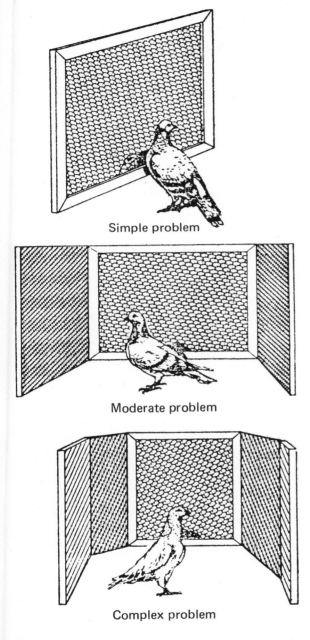

Simple problem

Moderate problem

Complex problem

Fig. 4.2 Simple, moderate, and complex versions of the "Umweg" (detour) problem used in test of the Yerkes-Dodson Law with hungry subjects. In each problem, a dish containing grain is located on the other side of the screen in full view of the pigeon. (From Fantino, Kasdon, and Stringer, 1970)

MOTIVATING BY "PUSHING"

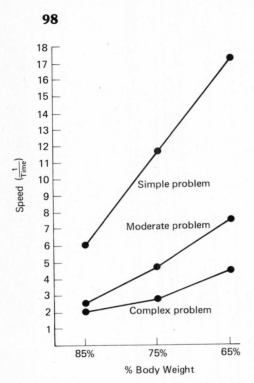

Fig. 4.3 Time required to solve each of the three Umweg problems illustrated in Fig. 4.2 as a function of hunger. Lower percentage body weights signify higher levels of hunger. (From Fantino, Kasdon, and Stringer, 1970)

anxious; they worry much of the time and are generally tense. Assuming that these traits were signs of heightened arousal, and that the arousal was of the same nature as that produced by noxious stimuli, the Yerkes-Dodson Law should provide useful information about how such individuals would perform in certain learning tasks. Suppose that we placed an anxious individual in a learning situation that contained an element of threat, perhaps punishment for incorrect responses. The drive generated by the chronic anxiety should combine with the drive generated by the noxious stimulus. If the task were relatively simple, the extra drive should facilitate learning. If the task were relatively complex, the extra drive should interfere with learning.

The simplest tasks are those in which the subject initially has a stronger tendency to make a correct response than an incorrect one. If the tendency to make the incorrect response were stronger, errors would be more frequent and learning would be slower. One theory of how drive affects learning states that raising the level of drive affects the higher-probability response differently than it affects the lower-probability response. The strength of the higher-probability response will increase more than will the strength of the lower-probability response, with the result that learning in a simple task will be faster while learning in a difficult task will be slower. To investigate the effects of chronic anxiety on learning, Taylor (1951) employed a simple task in the sense just discussed so that the prediction of the Yerkes-Dodson Law would be clear. Subjects acquired a response through classical conditioning. The unconditioned stimulus was a puff of air directed at the subject's eyeball. The subject reacted to the air puff as if a speck of dirt had entered the eye—by blinking. A light served as the conditioned stimulus, coming on just a moment before the air puff was delivered. Because the eyeblink response was the strongest one in the situation, chronic anxiety should have facilitated its acquisition. To identify anxious and nonanxious individuals, Taylor developed a self-report test, the "Manifest Anxiety Scale," consisting of statements descriptive of anxiety symptoms, for example, "I sweat easily even on cool days," and "I worry more than other people." Subjects were to answer "Yes" or "No" to each item. In a poll of clinical psychologists, at least 80% had indicated that the test items were accurate descriptions of anxiety symptoms. Subjects who scored very high (upper 12%) and those who scored very low (lower 12%) were designated "anxious" and "nonanxious," respectively. Figure 4.4 shows the rates at which the two groups acquired the eyeblink response. Consistent with the Yerkes-Dodson Law, the anxious subjects learned faster. Subsequent studies have shown that individuals with high scores on the Manifest Anxiety Scale do poorer than low scorers in more complex tasks (e.g., Matazarro, Ulett, and Saslow, 1955).

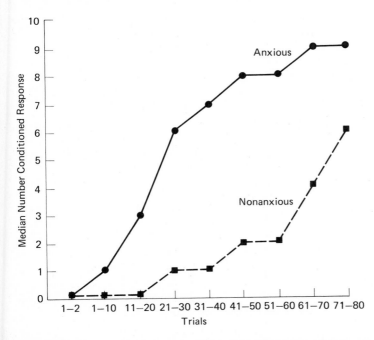

Fig. 4.4 Rate of acquisition of a classically conditioned eyeblink response in "anxious" and "nonanxious" subjects. Subjects were classified on the basis of score on a personality test, the "Manifest Anxiety Scale." (From Taylor, 1951)

MOTIVATING BY "PUSHING"

Many psychologists have challenged the concept of anxiety as a personality trait. The assumption behind the Manifest Anxiety Scale was that individuals carry with them a roughly constant level of anxiety from one situation to another. This anxiety combines with whatever additional anxiety the current situation produces. An alternative view, originally advanced by Mandler and Sarason (1952) and since developed further by others, is that the level of anxiety depends totally on the situation. A person can be highly anxious in one situation and free of anxiety in another. Further, it is asserted that anxiety does not energize behavior; it evokes reactions which may be relevant or irrelevant to the demands of the situation. Examples of such reactions would be feelings of inadequacy, a desire to quit, and extreme cautiousness. According to the situational view, the complexity of a task does not determine whether anxiety will facilitate or retard learning. Rather, it is the appropriateness of the anxiety reactions brought to the situation.

Because they believed that test anxiety had to be considered in the context of a specific situation, Mandler and Sarason decided to select one type of situation for intensive study. Test-taking was regarded as especially significant socially, so it was selected. The first step was to develop a technique for measuring test anxiety. The strategy adopted was to ask subjects to indicate by their responses to written items what kinds of experiences they had before and during exams. Among the experiences asked about were uneasiness, perspiration, accelerated heartbeat, emotional interference, and "worry." Mandler and Sarason found that subjects who scored high in test anxiety tended to solve problems from an IQ test more slowly than subjects low in test anxiety. This finding reflected favorably on the measuring technique, for the test anxiety scores correlated with actual performance. However, the results did not clearly distinguish between the trait and situational views of anxiety, as both can readily explain the longer solution times in anxious subjects. The trait explanation would be that incorrect responses were energized by the heightened level of arousal. The situational explanation would be that some reaction to anxiety, perhaps excessive cautiousness, was responsible for the longer times. What would constitute a strong case for the situational view of anxiety would be a demonstration that subjects with high test anxiety performed *better* in a complex task than subjects low in test anxiety. Only the situational view allows for this possibility.

Facilitation of problem-solving performance in high test-anxiety subjects was reported in a study by Ruebush (1960). Sixth-grade children performed a series of embedded-figures tasks resembling the familiar game in which one tries to find a hidden animal in a picture. After inspecting a simple figure, a child was shown a complicated one. The problem was to identify the embedded simple figure, and trace its outline, in the shortest possible time. A maximum of five minutes was permitted. When the child thought he or she had discovered the figure, he or she informed the experimenter, who noted the elapsed time. While the child attempted to trace the figure, the clock continued to run. If the child was correct, the additional time was excluded from the score. If the child was incorrect, he or she could try again, but the time spent tracing the incorrect figure was added to the score. Thus, while there was no limit on the number of attempted solutions, an abortive attempt was costly in time. At any point, the child could ask to see the simple figure to refresh his or her memory. The clock did not run while the child inspected the figure, so there was an advantage to doing so if there was any doubt about the shape of the figure. As noted earlier, a common reaction to anxiety is excessive cautiousness, and we might expect children with high anxiety to check the simple figures more often than children with low anxiety. Under the present circumstances, such a cautious approach should improve the child's time score because the additional exposures to the simple figure would probably reduce the number of unsuccessful attempts at solution. That is precisely what Ruebush found. The high anxiety children did check the simple figure more often than the low anxiety children, and as a result, they achieved lower time scores and a greater number of correct attempts. While these findings do not invalidate the trait view of anxiety, they show that the effect of anxiety on learning depends at least partly on the individual's reactions to anxiety.

Acquired drive: The role of anxiety in avoidance learning

The capacity to avoid injury is fundamental to the survival of species. Although the basic procedures for studying avoidance learning are relatively simple (Chapter 3), the processes responsible for avoidance learning have eluded precise description. Probably the most widely held theory is one that assigns a central role to anxiety, or fear, in the development of the avoidance response. Known as the "two-process" theory of avoidance conditioning, it has engendered controversy for decades (Mowrer and Lamoreaux, 1942; Mowrer, 1960). Figure 4.5 illustrates the basic concepts of the theory. Let us imagine that a rat has been placed in a chamber with a floor constructed of grid bars. We can electrify the bars in either half of the chamber without electrifying the bars in the other half. At various times during the session we sound a tone. If the rat remains where it is, the tone continues for five seconds and then we turn on the shock, keeping it on until the rat runs to the other side of the chamber. This type of trial in which the rat escapes the shock is diagrammed in the top portion of Fig. 4.5. If the rat runs to the other side of the chamber within five seconds, we immediately turn off the tone and withhold the shock. This type of avoidance trial is diagrammed in the bottom portion of Fig. 4.5. Eventually, the rat learns to avoid the shocks regularly, but how? According to the two-process theory, each type of trial represents a distinct learning process. Escape trials involve classical conditioning. Because the tone (CS) is temporally contiguous with the shock (UCS), the tone comes to elicit a fear reaction. Early in training, many of the trials are of this kind, and the frequent pairings of tone and shock make the CS a powerful source of drive. The initial avoidance trials are said to occur by chance. The running response happens to move up in time and precede the UCS. The immediate termination of the CS acts as negative reinforcement for the running response, increasing the likelihood of its occurrence on future trials. Avoidance behavior is thus acquired through instrumental conditioning. Note that the rat

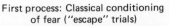

First process: Classical conditioning
of fear ("escape" trials)

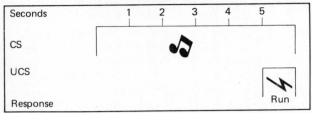

Second process: Instrumental conditioning
of avoidance response ("avoidance" trials)

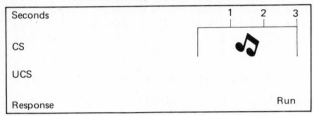

Fig. 4.5 How organisms acquire avoidance behavior, according to the two-process theory of avoidance conditioning. In the situation illustrated, the CS is a tone and the UCS is shock. To avoid the shock, a rate must run from one end of a chamber to the other during the five-second period when the tone is on. Failure to do so results in presentation of the shock, which can only be terminated by running ("escape trial," top panel). Repeated failures to avoid are said to make the tone a CS for fear, since the tone is temporally contiguous with shock. If, by chance, the rat runs before delivery of shock, the tone is immediately turned off and the shock is witheld ("avoidance trial," bottom panel). Termination of the tone, and the consequent reduction in fear, is said to reinforce the avoidance response.

is said to respond to get the tone off, not to avoid the shock. Avoidance is seen as a fortuitous consequence of an organism's basic tendency to keep anxiety to a minimum.

Why do the two-process theorists exclude the possibility that the subject responds to avoid the shock? Partly for philosophical reasons. It is said that to detect the omission of shock at the end of a trial, a subject would have to have acquired some anticipation of shock from earlier trials. As we saw in Chapter 2, "anticipation" was a concept rejected by Pavlov in his early studies of "psychic secretion." It was regarded as an unsupportable assumption about the mental life of animals, and like other mentalistic concepts, it had no place in scientific research. That attitude toward mental processes was one of Pavlov's legacies to "behaviorism," and the two-process theorists seek to explain avoidance learning within the behavioristic framework. Of course, there are also experimental findings supportive of the two-process view, but the evidence is not compelling. While it is well established that turning off the CS immediately after the avoidance response facilitates learning, there is no evidence that this is *essential* for learning. An important experiment by Kamin (1956) illustrates the kind of evidence that has been brought to bear on the issue.

Kamin's general procedure was like the one previously described in reference to Fig. 4.5. His experimental design is diagrammed in the left side of Fig. 4.6. Four groups were employed for which the two-process theory seemed to have straightforward predictions. The group labeled "Normal" performed in the standard procedure; a running response immediately terminated the CS and avoided the shock. The "Classical conditioning" group should not have acquired a substantial response, for the tone always terminated with shock regardless of what the subject did. In the "Avoid-UCS" group, the CS stayed on for five seconds on every trial, but if the rats ran to the other side of the chamber within five seconds, they avoided the shock. According to two-process theory, rats in the Avoid-UCS group should have done as poorly as the rats in the classical conditioning group because in neither group did the avoidance response terminate the CS. Finally, in the Terminate-CS group, rats could terminate the CS immediately by running to the other side of the chamber, but they always got shocked anyway. These rats should have learned as readily as the rats in the normal condition, for in both conditions the avoidance response terminated the CS. In sum, the two groups for which the CS

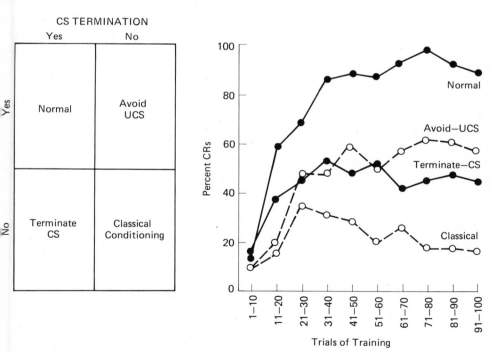

Fig. 4.6 Experimental design and results of study which tested predictions of the two-process theory of avoidance conditioning. (Graph from Kamin, 1956)

was terminated should have done equally well, while the two groups for which the CS was not terminated should have done equally poorly. The graph shown at the right in Fig. 4.6 presents the percentage of trials on which avoidance responses occurred in each group during training. The two-process theory was not supported; the Avoid-UCS group did too well (they should have been with the Classical group) and the Terminate-CS group did too poorly (they should have been with the Normal group). It appeared that the factor of UCS avoidance influenced learning, for with the factor of CS termination held constant, the group that avoided the UCS did better than the group that did not. Similarly, the factor of CS termination had apparently influenced learning, for with the factor of UCS avoidance held constant, the group that turned off the CS did better than the group that did not. Although alternative interpretations of the findings could be devised based on technical details of the procedure, the failure of the two-process theory to *predict* the results is a serious problem. Herrnstein (1969) has provided an outstanding review of the vast avoidance literature from an historical and philosophical perspective; it is highly recommended to the reader who wishes to pursue the two-process issue further.

MOTIVATING BY "PULLING"

In general, organisms respond more vigorously for larger rewards than for smaller ones (Crespi, 1942; Guttman, 1954). They also respond more vigorously for rewards presented immediately than for rewards presented after a delay (Chung and Herrnstein, 1967). Now, if you gave an organism a choice between an immediate small reward and a delayed large reward, which would it select? Which option would exert the greater pull? Such a choice has long been regarded as having particularly significant psychological implications. Freud interpreted the selection of an immediate small reward over a delayed large reward as a sign of impulsiveness. The pleasure-seeking part of the personality, the *id,* was said to dominate the part of the personality most in touch with reality, the *ego.* On the other hand, choice of the delayed large reward has often been construed as evidence for maturity and self-control. Because of the practical and theoretical significance of the capacity for delay-of-gratification, it has attracted the attention of researchers in diverse fields. Studies in the field of animal learning have shown that pigeons will almost always select the small reward (Ainslie, 1975). In psychoanalytic terms, you might say that a pigeon was essentially a feathered "id" demanding immediate gratification of its needs. Studies in developmental psychology have shown that young children, too, often choose the small reward (Mischel, 1974). Let us see how psychologists working in these disparate fields have approached a common problem.

Nisan and Koriat (1977) performed a clever study with kindergarten children to test two competing interpretations of impulsiveness. One was the psychoanalytic model, mentioned above, which views impulsiveness as a victory of the irrational side of human nature over the rational side. The other interpretation, called the "value-expectancy" model (Rotter, 1954; Mischell, 1966), can be seen as an affirmation of rationality in the face of apparent maladaptive behavior. The model assumes that an individual will choose that course of action judged to be most advantageous. The advantage of choosing one reward over another depends on two factors: (1) the individual's estimate of the probability that he or she will actually obtain the reward; and (2) the value, or desirability, of the reward. Delaying a reward could be interpreted as lowering the individual's estimate of the probability that he or she will ever get the reward. Therefore, selecting the immediate reward would be more advantageous, a more rational choice. Nissan and Koriat attribute the implication to the psychoanalytic model that an individual might choose a course of action knowing it to be disadvantageous because the ego, the rational side of the personality, can be dominated by the id, the irrational side.

The experimental procedure enabled Nisan and Koriat to compare a child's choice with his or her conception of the wiser choice. Choice of the wiser course of action would be consistent with the expectancy-value model, while choice of the unwise course of action would be consistent with the psychoanalytic model. At the start of the experiment, the children were asked to draw a series of figures. Then, the experimenter complimented the children on their performance and offered them a choice between an immediate small reward and a delayed large reward. The children were asked two questions. One pertained to the child's own preference:

> I have here a bag of candies. You may either have one candy now, or you may have two candies tomorrow. I'll be back tomorrow and will bring with me the bag of candies. So what would you rather have, one candy now or two candies tomorrow? (p. 490)

The other question asked some children to guess the preference of a fictional child described as "smart." Other children were asked to state the preference of a child described as "stupid." (For technical reasons, the same child could not be asked both questions.) Presumably, if the children stated that the "smart" child would pick the delayed reward, that would be their conception of the wise choice. Roughly 80% of the children made this guess; about 50% said that the "stupid" child would take the delayed reward. Interestingly, about 50% of the the children selected the immediate reward for themselves, suggesting that they were not always making what they considered to be the wise choice. The results were regarded as consistent with the psychoanalytic model.

Self-control in pigeons

Rachlin (1970), working within a behavioristic framework, developed a theory of self-control which in some respects resembles the expectancy-value model. It is well established that the longer the delay between a response and a reinforcer, the less effectively that reinforcer will maintain the response. This progressive decline in the value of a reinforcer is called a "temporal gradient." It is analogous to the decline in the value of a reward assumed to occur by the expectancy-value model when a subject's expectation of reward decreases. Rachlin's model of self-control is based on the concept of temporal gradients. Since it is a behavioristic model, there is no implication that the organism expects anything. But the model does assume, along with the expectancy-value model, that organisms choose the reward that has the higher value. In this limited sense, we can think of even lower animals as behaving rationally.

The unique feature of Rachlin's model is that it predicts an intriguing phenomenon, one that has been experimentally demonstrated in lower animals (pigeons) and that intuition suggests is pervasive in human affairs. Rachlin calls the phenomenon "commitment." It is a way of achieving self-control by avoiding the circumstances that lead to impulsiveness. A person recognizes that at some future time there will be a choice between an immediate small reward and a delayed large reward. When that time arrives, the individual will surely select the immediate small reward. To prevent an impulsive act, the individual makes a commitment in advance to avoid the situation entirely. Instead of having two courses of action, the individual has just one—to take the large reward. Such is the nature of the commitment workers make on a payroll savings plan. Let's say that at the end of every month, on payday, a certain worker finds that he has a choice between spending $10 immediately or spending $120 11 months later. He can obtain the $120 only by saving the $10 he now has and $10 per month for the next 11 months. Invariably, impulse prevails and he spends the money. To avoid impulsive acts in the future, he signs up at the beginning of the month to have $10 deducted from his paycheck for one year. In that manner he can obtain the delayed large reward.

Rachlin notes that the commitment strategy involves a reversal of preferences over time. Faced with the choice between $10 immediately and $120 a year from now, the worker prefers $10 immediately. Thirty days prior to that choice, at the beginning of the month, the worker prefers the large reward. Rachlin's model of self-control predicts this reversal of preferences without making any assumptions about the nature of personality. It assumes only the existence of gradients of reinforcer value like the ones depicted in Fig. 4.7. The symbols, A_S and A_L, represent a small amount and a large amount of reward, respectively. The symbols, X and Y, are choice points. The curves show the value of the rewards at varying temporal distances from the moment the rewards are presented. At choice point Y (payday), the organism can have A_S immediately, but must wait for A_L. Note that the value of A_S is higher than the value of A_L at choice point Y. This means that the organism should choose the immediate small reward. But at choice point X (beginning of the month) the organism must wait for both A_S and A_L. Note that the value of A_L is now higher than the value of A_S. The organism should prefer the delayed large reward and be willing to "sign up for payroll savings."

"Imitation of life" To test this "reinforcement-gradient model" of self-control, Rachlin and Green (1972) developed an ingenious procedure that simulated in the laboratory the trials and tribulations of everyday life. The subjects in the experiment, pigeons, performed in a small chamber. The pigeons were hungry and could

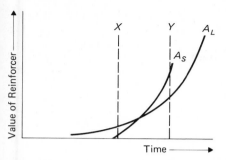

Fig. 4.7 The reinforcement-gradient theory of self-control proposed by Rachlin. The graph depicts the value of a large amount of reward (A_L) and a small amount of reward (A_S) as a function of how long a subject must wait before the rewards are delivered. The moments of delivery are the points on the horizontal axis directly beneath the letters A_L and A_S. The vertical dashed lines labeled X and Y signify times when the subject chooses between A_S and A_L. It is assumed that the subject prefers the reward with the higher gradient at the moment of choice. (From Navarick and Fantino, 1976)

obtain limited access to a grain hopper by pecking at discs on the wall. Experimental conditions were symbolized for the pigeons by illuminating the discs with different colors. You can see how this was accomplished by referring to the diagram of the procedure in Fig. 4.8. Part (a) of this figure gives the general plan of the experiment. The large reward, A_L, was four seconds access to grain while the small reward, A_S, was two seconds access to grain. At choice point Y, the pigeon had two options: to take A_S immediately or A_L after a four-second delay. It may be noted here that the pigeons almost always took A_S. They couldn't even wait four seconds! At choice point X, the pigeon was given the opportunity to make a "commitment" to the large reward, to "sign up for payroll savings." This opportunity came at various times, T, before choice Y, much as there might be various opportunities to sign up for the payroll plan during the month. If the pigeon made the commitment of A_L, then at the end of T the four-second delay started; there was no option to take A_S at that point. After four seconds elapsed, the pigeon received A_L.

Figure 4.8 (b) shows how this complicated procedure was communicated to the pigeon. Choice point Y was symbolized by red and green lights. A peck on the green disc produced A_L after a four-second delay. A peck at the red disc produced A_S immediately. Choice point X was represented by two white discs. Pecking the right disc led to choice Y. Pecking the left key constituted a commitment to the large reward. Each day the pigeon cycled through the procedure 50 times. By comparing the number of pecks on the two white discs, one could measure the pigeon's tendency to use the commitment strategy. The theory requires that the further in advance one presents the opportunity for commitment—the longer the duration of T—the stronger should be the tendency to make the commitment. The results confirmed this prediction, demonstrating that the theory was

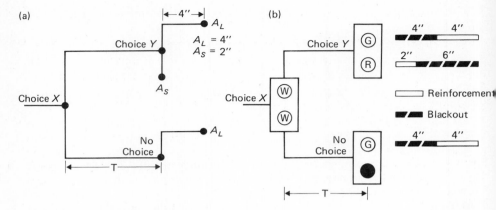

Fig. 4.8 Procedure used to study the phenomenon of "commitment" in pigeons. Diagram (a) presents the general features of the procedure. Diagram (b) presents more detailed information about the duration of experimental conditions and how the conditions were represented to pigeons by colors on the discs. (From Rachlin and Green, 1976)

indeed a viable one—at least for pigeons. Subsequent research developed a mathematical rule for making precise predictions of what the subjects would do (Navarick and Fantino, 1976). The theory is ripe for testing with human subjects, and appears to be very promising.

Miserliness: Conditioned reinforcement, "functional autonomy," or "instinctive drift"?

Let us conclude this chapter with a puzzle. Suppose that someone—an anonymous benefactor—gave you one million dollars to do with as you pleased. How would you spend the money? Would you buy a car? A house? A boat? Make donations to charity? Probably there are many things you would like to do. For some people, though, there is just one thing they would like to do—hoard it; put the green stuff in the bank and let it grow. These are the misers of the world, and they constitute something of a challenge to established principles of learning. We know that some goal objects create incentive motivation without a person's requiring any special training. These are the so-called "primary reinforcers," such as food and water. We also know that stimuli can acquire the power to create incentive motivation. In Chapter 3, we explored the principle of conditioned reinforcement, which stated that any stimulus could become reinforcing if it were repeatedly paired with a reinforcer. The tokens used by Ayllon and Azrin to create motivation for therapy and rehabitation became reinforcers through repeated pairing with reinforcing activities. Money has been assumed to become reinforcing for the same reason. Now, if the miser never exchanged money for reinforcers, should not the money lose its value?

The hoarding of money seems to be a contradiction of the principle of reinforcement.

Of course, the miser must buy a few things—sustenance, shelter. One possibility is that the few expenditures the miser must make are sufficient to maintain the value of the money. But this interpretation cannot tell the whole story. While it is true that the value of money should be maintained at some level, why should it be maintained at so high a level?

Another interpretation might appeal to the concept of **functional autonomy** introduced by Gordon Allport (Allport, 1937). Functional autonomy refers to the persistence of activities once necessary for achieving a goal after the goal has been removed. The persistence of vocational activities during retirement is often cited as an example. So, too, is the miser, who is imagined to have come from a background of material privation in which frugal habits were essential. The problem with the functional autonomy concept is that it lacks experimental support. This is not to say that it is wrong, only that its validity remains to be demonstrated under rigorously controlled conditions. One study purported to show that mice who had learned to dig through sand to reach food continued to dig even after they were no longer hungry. Subsequently, however, Fantino and Cole (1968) demonstrated that mice that were fully fed would dig through many pounds of sand even though they had never done so previously to reach food. Sand-digging was simply a common activity for the mice.

A more plausible interpretation of the miser's habits appears to be one based on the concept of **instinctive drift.** It was introduced by Breland and Breland (1961) as a way of summarizing some peculiar phenomena they observed in the course of their work in animal training. The Brelands operated a commercial enterprise which provided animals for TV shows and for displays at conventions, fairs, and stores. For many years they were successful in applying operant conditioning principles to the training of a wide variety of species, including reindeer, cockatoos, raccoons, porpoises, and whales. But as the tasks they devised became more and more unlike those used in laboratory settings, the Brelands encountered an increasing number of setbacks. Instinctive behavior would appear during the act and interfere with the performance of the learned behavior. For example, in one act, pigs were trained to pick up large wooden coins and carry them several feet to a "piggy bank," where they were to deposit the coins for a food reward. At first, they had to carry just one token for each reward, but gradually the requirement was increased to four or five. Although the pigs performed the routine speedily and flawlessly for several weeks, the behavior eventually began to deteriorate. On their way to the bank, they would repeatedly drop the token, root it, pick it up and carry it further, drop the coin again, root it, and so on. Raccoons performing in a similar task exhibited similar disruptions, except that they "washed" the token instead of "rooting" it as the pigs did. As raccoons and pigs naturally exhibit washing and rooting behavior in the course of food-getting, it appeared that the genetic histories of the animals had come into conflict with their conditioning histories. The Brelands held

MOTIVATING BY "PULLING"

the view that in such confrontations between nature and nuture, nature would prevail—"learned behavior drifts toward instinctive behavior." Perhaps the miser is one who has had an extensive history of exchanging money for food, drink, shelter, and little else due to economic hardship. Repeated use of the tokens to purchase biologically significant reinforcers may promote instinctive drift: Conventional, learned behavior toward the tokens gives way to instinctive behavior associated with the primary reinforcers. This is not to say that the miser actually eats the money but, rather, attaches the same value to money as he or she would attach to food. Whatever the answer to the puzzle of the miser, it is evident that we have just begun to understand the complex processes of learning and motivation.

SUMMARY

Psychologists have often conceptualized motivation as an internal state having two kinds of effects on behavior. One effect is energization; whatever an organism happens to be doing, for whatever reason, it will tend to do more vigorously. The other effect of motivation is directive; the organism's behavior becomes organized around a particular goal related to the motivational state. Judson Brown has identified three kinds of situations which often lead people to assume that an individual is in a motivational state: (1) Evocation of vigorous responses by weak stimuli; (2) Variability of response in the presence of constant stimulating conditions; (3) Equality or constancy of behavior in the presence of normally effective changes in the external stimulus situation. Two kinds of variables influence motivation. "Pull" variables are characteristics of the goal for which an organism works. The motivational state created by the goal object is called "incentive." "Push" variables produce motivation whether or not a goal object is present. This is often accomplished by creating a condition of need.

It is useful to distinguish between the terms "need" and "drive." Drive is a general state of arousal that energizes behavior. Need is a condition in which a requirement for normal functioning is unfulfilled. Need is a potential source of drive, but is not equivalent to drive, for under extreme deprivation it can be shown that drive may decrease while need increases. Drive has been measured in terms of an organism's level of random activity. By this criterion, a longstanding conceptualization of drive as an internal force appears to be inadequate. Ordinarily, the level of random activity increases under deprivation. However, it has been shown that an increase occurs only if there are changes in environmental stimuli. This suggests that drive increases an organism's sensitivity to stimuli in the environment which, for one reason or other, tend to elicit movements. Whichever view of drive is correct, however, it is generally the case that motivation enhances the vigor of behavior.

The Yerkes-Dodson Law is a statement about how drive affects the speed of learning. The Law has two parts: (1) As drive increases, the rate of learning first increases then decreases; (2) the optimal level of motivation for learning decreases as the difficulty of the task increases. The Yerkes-Dodson Law generally holds when the source of motivation constitutes an immediate threat to the organism, for example, the motivation to avoid pain. The Law is not generally applicable to situations that lack the element of threat, for example, situations in which the subject works for food reward.

The original intent of the Yerkes-Dodson Law was to describe the effects of drive created by the learning task. Attempts have been made to extend the Law to drive conceptualized as a personality trait. The notion is that the level of drive tends to be higher in some individuals than others. Drive generated by the personality trait is said to combine with that created by the task. The additional drive generated by the trait should facilitate learning in simple tasks and slow learning in complex tasks. Consistent with the expectation about simple tasks is the finding that anxious individuals acquire classically-conditioned responses faster than nonanxious individuals. There is also evidence that chronic anxiety can retard learning in complex tasks.

Opposing the concept of anxiety as a trait is the situational view of anxiety introduced by Mandler and Sarason. It states that: (1) The level of anxiety depends totally on the situation; (2) rather than energizing behavior, anxiety evokes responses that may be relevant or irrelevant to the task; (3) the complexity of the task does not determine the effect of anxiety on learning; it is the appropriateness to the task of the anxiety-produced responses. Consistent with the situation view are findings that individuals with high test anxiety can in some situations outperform individuals with low test anxiety. The trait view always requires high-anxiety persons to perform more poorly in complex tasks.

Anxiety, or fear, has been regarded by many psychologists as a critical factor in the acquisition of avoidance behavior. In a prototypical case of avoidance, a signal terminates with shock unless the subject makes a designated response prior to the shock. This response immediately terminates the signal and causes the shock to be omitted. According to the "two-process" theory of avoidance, both classical and instrumental conditioning contribute to acquisition of the avoidance response. The signal becomes a conditioned stimulus for fear by being paired with shock on those trials in which the subject fails to make the avoidance response (classical conditioning). On trials in which the subject does respond, the immediate termination of the signal serves as negative reinforcement for the response (instrumental conditioning). The two-process theory assumes that subjects respond only to reduce the drive created by fear; avoidance of the shock itself is not a factor in learning. There is strong evidence, however, that both CS termination and shock avoidance are important factors in avoidance conditioning.

Two major variables influencing an organism's degree of incentive are the amount and the delay of reinforcement. Organisms respond more vigorously for large rewards than for small, and for rewards presented immediately after the response than for rewards presented after a delay. There has been considerable interest in studying an organism's choice between an immediate small reward and a delayed large reward. Selection of the former is often taken as a sign of impulsiveness, while selection of the latter is taken as evidence for self-control. Young

SUMMARY

children often select the immediate reward. Lower animals (pigeons) almost always do so.

Freud conceptualized choice of the immediate reward as an irrational act imposed on the individual by an immature part of the personality. An alternative view, called the "value-expectancy" model, assumes that an individual always acts rationally in the sense that he or she always chooses the course of action seen to have the greater advantage. Results of a study with kindergarteners were inconsistent with the value-expectancy model. Although the children generally considered the delayed reward a wiser choice, they often selected the immediate reward.

Rachlin has developed a model of self-control based on the principle that the value of a reinforcer decreases as the time to reinforcement increases. This relationship between reinforcer value and time is called a "temporal gradient." The model attributes a particular form to the temporal gradients generated by the large and small rewards, and assumes that at any given moment an organism will select the reward which has the higher value. One advantage of the model is that it can account for the phenomenon of commitment, in which an organism achieves self-control by not allowing itself to choose between an immediate small reward and a delayed large reward. In advance of the choice, the organism ensures that only the large reward will be available. The commitment strategy has been demonstrated in pigeons and it appears to be a common strategy employed by people (e.g., the payroll savings plan).

Primary reinforcers create incentive naturally; one need not give an organism any special training to make the stimulus effective. Conditioned reinforcers create incentive motivation as a result of being paired with stimuli that are already reinforcing. When the association is broken, the conditioned reinforcer normally loses its value. Two major limitations on this principle have been proposed: (1) "Functional autonomy": It is said that activities once necessary for achieving a goal may eventually become self-sustaining after the goal is removed. There is no substantial evidence for such an effect. (2) "Instinctive drift": In animals, when learned behavior conflicts with instinctive behavior, the instinctive behavior tends to prevail. Repeatedly exchanging a token for food may lead an animal to exhibit behavior toward the token that it normally exhibits for food (e.g., washing). The animal may retain and manipulate the token instead of exchanging it for the primary reinforcer.

STUDY QUESTIONS

1. Describe the "energizing" and "directing" functions of motivation. Give examples of each function.

2. Describe the kinds of situations which often lead people to assume that a person is in a motivational state. Give an example of each kind of situation.

3. Motivational variables are often thought of as either "pushing" or "pulling" the organism. What is meant by these expressions?

4. Define "incentive."

5. A child who receives $5.00/week allowance refuses to mow the lawn for 50¢. State one way of increasing the child's motivation by manipulating a "push" variable and one way by manipulating a "pull" variable.

6. Define "need," "drive." What is the rationale for making a distinction between the two concepts?

7. What is a "stabilimeter"?

8. State the two views of how drives activate behavior. Describe the procedure used by Campbell and Sheffield to test the adequacy of these views. What were the results and conclusions of the experiment?

9. State the "Yerkes-Dodson Law" (two parts).

10. Referring to the specific points listed below, describe the procedure, results, and conclusion of Broadhurst's experiment on the Yerkes-Dodson Law:
    a) How the stem and two arms of the Y-maze were constructed; the nature of the rats' response.
    b) How the difficulty of the task was manipulated.
    c) How drive level was manipulated.
    d) The nature of the evidence that the delay times selected produced different levels of drive.
    e) The measure of learning.
    f) The relationship between rate of learning and drive level on each task.
    g) The relationship between the optimal level of motivation and the difficulty of the task.

11. Referring to the specific points listed below, describe the procedure, results, and conclusion of the study by Fantino et al. on the Yerkes-Dodson Law:
    a) The nature of an "umweg" problem in general.
    b) The nature of the three tasks employed in the experiment and why they were expected to differ in difficulty.
    c) How drive level was manipulated.
    d) How learning was measured.
    e) The relationship between rate of learning and drive level.
    f) The relationship between the optimal level of motivation and task difficulty.
    g) The general limitation which the results suggest must be placed on the generality of the Yerkes-Dodson Law.

12. State the trait view of anxiety. What would be the expected effect of trait anxiety on learning in a: (a) simple task; (b) complex task?

13. What feature characterizes the simplest learning tasks? More complex tasks? What processes are thought responsible for the effect of drive on learning in each type of task?

14. Referring to the specific points listed below, describe the rationale, procedure, and results of Taylor's experiment on anxiety and learning:

    a) The nature of the task and why it was considered to be "simple" in the sense described in Question 13.

    b) The measure of trait anxiety; give an example of an item from the test.

    c) The measure of learning.

    d) How the two groups differed in rate of learning.

    e) The conclusion of the study.

15. State the situational view of anxiety advanced by Mandler and Sarason. What factor is said to determine the effect of anxiety on learning? What is the role of task complexity?

16. Referring to the specific points listed below, describe the procedure, results, and conclusion of the experiment by Ruebush on anxiety and learning:

    a) The nature of the problem the children were asked to solve.

    b) When the clock ran; when it was stopped; under what condition would time accumulated on the clock be excluded from the time score?

    c) The type of reaction to anxiety that could influence performance in the task. How might this reaction benefit high-anxiety children?

    d) Comparison of time scores and number of problems solved for children high and low in anxiety.

    e) The general conclusion of the study.

17. State the two-process theory of avoidance conditioning. Do this by describing: (a) a prototypical case of signalled avoidance conditioning, indicating the nature of the signal, type of aversive stimulus, and type of avoidance response; (b) the events that characterize "escape trials" and the processes assumed to occur; (c) the events that characterize "avoidance" trials and the processes assumed to occur; (d) what the reinforcer for avoidance is assumed to be, and the "philosophical" rationale for this view.

18. Describe the procedure of Kamin's experiment on avoidance conditioning by fully labeling and filling in the cells of the diagram below:

CS Termination

	?	?
?	?	?
?	?	?

UCS Avoidance

What were the specific predictions of the two-process theory? What was found (consider effect of UCS avoidance with CS termination held constant, and of CS termination with UCS avoidance held constant)? What is the general conclusion?

19. What are the effects of magnitude and delay of reward on the vigor of performance?

20. What sort of choice task has been used to assess an organism's degree of self-control?

LEARNING AND MOTIVATION

21. How would Freud interpret a lack of self-control in the choice task, above? How would the value-expectancy model interpret it? In what sense does the value-expectancy model interpret an impulsive choice as rational?

22. How did Nissan and Koriat show that children did not always make the choice they considered to be wise? What are the implications of the results for the psychoanalytic and value-expectancy models?

23. What is meant by a "temporal gradient" of reinforcer value?

24. What does Rachlin mean by the term "commitment"? Illustrate using the example of the payroll savings plan.

25. In what sense does the commitment strategy imply a reversal of preferences over time?

26. Labeling both axes of the graph, draw the temporal gradients Rachlin assumes to underlie impulsiveness and self-control. Show two choice points, one at which the organism should make the impulsive choice, and one at which the organism should exhibit self-control. Explain why the organism should select the reward in each case.

27. Referring to the specific points listed below, describe the procedure and results of Rachlin and Green's study on commitment in pigeons:
    a) The nature of the alternatives at choice point Y (state amount of reward and duration of delay).
    b) The effect of pecking each key at choice point X.
    c) Which key represented the commitment, and why.
    d) The nature of the variable, T.
    e) How the likelihood of making a commitment varied as a function of T.
    f) How the results would be explained by the model described in Question 26.

28. Define: "functional autonomy," "instinctive behavior." Give an example of each. What flaw has been found in evidence frequently cited in support of functional autonomy? In what ways does the instinctive drift phenomenon limit the principle of conditioned reinforcement?

CHAPTER 5

Learning Through Observation

The patient, an adolescent boy, is diagnosed as "schizophrenic." His world is a solitary and bizarre one. He rarely speaks to anyone, and he devotes much of his time to a strange, mystical religion that he has apparently created. One reflection of his preoccupation with religion is his appearance; his long hair and beard make him look like the "Messiah." The boy's room is a privileged sanctuary that only a select few may enter. It is an incredibly messy place, and he can usually be found there, almost naked, sitting on the toilet studying stock quotations. To the dismay of the therapist, a stock portfolio that the boy selected for him has risen 40% in value in one year. Clearly, the boy possesses a keen understanding of the business world. A study of the family reveals striking similarities between father and son. The father, a successful business man, rules the home with absolute authority, which he justifies on the grounds of divine sanction. God's will, he believes, has been revealed through the small mystical cult of which he is a member. At home, he spends almost all his time in the bedroom, where he sits in his underwear reading religious books. Only the wife and governess may enter to attend his needs. (Fleck, 1960)

Jim, age six, and his brother Bobby, age three, are about to play a game with their father. While the children wait outside the living room, the father hides a piece of candy for each child. He puts one piece under the couch and another beside a cabinet. The father then gives a signal and the children enter the room to search for the candy. Jim, the older child, comes in first followed immediately by Bobby. Jim looks in the fireplace. Bobby looks there, too. Jim looks inside the piano bench. So does Bobby. Finally, Jim looks under the pillow and finds his candy. He now stops looking and Bobby is helpless. Bobby checks under the pillow but of course he finds nothing. Eventually, Bobby's candy is simply given to him. Later, the children play the game again and Bobby exhibits the same maladaptive behavior, always looking in the places that his brother has just checked. (Miller and Dollard, 1941)

Imitation is a common phenomenon, but the influence of those we imitate is often unrecognized. With a moment's reflection you can probably discover numerous similarities between your behavior and the behavior of loved ones and friends. Perhaps you make frequent use of the same pet phrase as a friend; possibly you share a brother or sister's enthusiasm for a sport; maybe you resemble a parent in being particularly outgoing or quiet. We often reproduce the behavior of others without any specific instructions or inducements to do so. Indeed, as the case reports, above, illustrate, imitative behavior can be very maladaptive and lead to undesirable consequences. What, then, impels us to imitate? In the early part of this century theorists commonly attributed imitation to instinct. Later, with the rise of behaviorism, many theorists rejected instinct as an explanation and turned to the principles of learning. The same factors that led Pavlov's dogs to salivate in response to bells, or Skinner's rats to press bars, led us to imitate. The initial attempts to incorporate imitation into the framework of learning theory adopted classical conditioning principles (e.g., Holt, 1931). Subsequently, in a major book entitled *Social Learning and Imitation* (1941), Neil Miller and John Dollard used the principles of instrumental conditioning to develop a more comprehensive theory. Although their approach has many limitations, it has been very influential and has stimulated the development of new approaches and insights. In essence, Miller and Dollard say this: We imitate because we have been rewarded for imitating. Now, at first blush, that may seem to be a direct contradiction of the facts. For example, how can reward account for Bobby's strange behavior, in the second case report, of repeatedly looking for candy in places that his older brother had just checked? These imitative acts never produced reward. The strength of Miller and Dollard's theory lies in its ability to explain just such cases in which there is no reward. Here is how the contradiction is resolved.

LEARNING TO IMITATE: WHY BOBBY FOLLOWS JIM

A year before the game in the living room, an unusual incident occurred involving the two brothers and their father. Customarily, the father brought home candy for each child when he returned from work in the evening. Jim, the older child, had learned to tell when his father had come home by the sound of his footsteps on the back stairway leading to the kitchen. When Jim heard this signal, he ran to the kitchen to greet his father as he entered the house, and there Jim received his candy. Bobby had not learned to identify this signal and never ran to the kitchen. Thus, it was surprising when one evening both boys ran to the kitchen. Bobby had still not identified the cue, but for one reason or other, he happened to be running behind Jim. Upon reaching the kitchen, both boys immediately received their candy, and from that day on, Bobby followed Jim to the kitchen with increasing regularity. Eventually, Bobby started to run whenever he saw Jim run, not only in this situation but in other places and at other times. Miller and Dollard reasoned that Bobby's running had "generalized" from the situation in which it was originally rewarded to the other situations. Apparently, Bobby's maladaptive behavior when playing the game in the living room was also the result of generalization. Miller and Dollard thought that Bobby's was a "pattern case" for much of our imitative behavior and they proceeded to analyze it in greater detail.

Four factors were regarded as essential to learning in any situation: drive, cue, response, and reward. The concept of "drive" was similar to that discussed in Chapter 4 and had a special relationship to the concept of "reward." "Drive" referred to any strong internal or external stimulus that impelled action. For example, the blare of a neighbor's radio, an external stimulus, would motivate one to eliminate the noise or seek refuge from it. The thirst produced by several hours in the sun was an internal stimulus that motivated one to seek fluid. Some drives were "primary" or innate, such as those for food and water, while others were "secondary," or acquired, such as an appetite for a particular food, or a desire for money. For Miller and Dollard, a reward was an event that followed the response and produced drive reduction. The reduction in drive strengthened the connection between the response that produced the reward and cues in the immediate situation. When the same or similar cues were encountered subsequently, the response was more likely to occur. Thus stuffing cotton in one's ears could become an habitual response to the blare of a neighbor's radio if the cotton sufficiently attentuated the noise. A person might search for a soft drink machine rather than a water fountain after several hours in the sun if he or she customarily drank soft drinks with meals. The drink might be preferred because of its more frequent associations with thirst reduction. The notion that reward is based on drive reduction was once very popular in the psychology of learning but is no longer regarded as being particularly useful. (We shall consider this development in greater detail in Chapter 6.) While Miller and Dollard employed the concepts of drive and drive reduction in their analysis of imitation, it will soon soon be evident that those concepts are not essential to it.

Important relationships between a leader and imitator were thought to be revealed by analyzing the behavior of each into the four elements of learning. An analysis of the behavior of Bobby and Jim when running to meet their father yields the following relationships (Miller and Dollard, 1941, p. 96):

	Jim (leader)	Bobby (imitator)
Drive	Appetite for candy	Appetite for candy
Cue	Father's footfall DEPENDENT →	Leg-movement of Jim
Response	Running ⟵ MATCHED →	Running
Reward	Eating candy	Eating candy

First, the response of the imitator "matches" the response of the leader. Both Jim and Bobby run. Second, the cue that triggers the leader's response differs from the cue that triggers the imitator's response. Jim responds to the sound of his father's footsteps on the back stairs. Bobby responds to the sight of Jim running. Thus the imitator's behavior is "dependent" on the leader's behavior. Miller and Dollard referred to imitation in which these two relationships were present as **matched-dependent behavior.** Note that one need not assume the existence of a physiological drive for this sort of analysis to make sense. For Jim and Bobby, the reward for running could simply be a cheery "Hello" from the father or a big hug. What is central to the analysis is the relationship between the cue and response of the leader and the cue and response of the imitator.

Everyday experiences are a rich source of ideas and often serve as the starting point for psychological theory. But in "real life" so much goes on at once that it is often hard to know what factors have been influential. Jim and Bobby's behavior suggested a way in which imitation might develop. Now experiments were needed to demonstrate that matched-dependent behavior would develop under the specified conditions, and further, that it would generalize to new situations. Recognizing this need, Miller and Dollard performed a series of experimental tests. In one study with first-grade children, a "game" was devised in which the object was to choose which of two boxes contained some candy. The boxes rested on chairs placed about 10 feet apart. On each trial, two children stood 10 feet from the boxes and took turns walking to the boxes and making a selection. One child, designated the "leader," always went first. Unknown to the second child, the leader was directed to go to a particular box while the second child was out of the room. The leader always found candy, and the second child, waiting his or her turn, observed the leader's success. The second child was designated a "dependent" subject, as the outcome of his or her choice depended upon the leader's choice. Some dependent subjects always found candy in the same box that the leaders chose. These subjects should have learned to imitate the leader. The other dependent subjects always found candy in the box *not* chosen by the leader. These subjects should have become "nonconformists" and learned to do the opposite of the leader. The box to which the leader went varied randomly from trial to trial so that his or her choice was the only reliable cue that the dependent children could use. In terms of the four elements of learning, we might conceptualize the conditions for imitation as follows:

	Leader	*Imitator*
Drive	Appetite for candy	Appetite for candy
Cue	Experimenter's signal	Leader's choice
Response	Walk to appropriate box, open lid, take candy	Walk to same box as leader, open lid, take candy
Reward	Candy	Candy

As in Bobby and Jim's case, the imitator's behavior matches the leader's (going to the same box) and the imitator and leader respond to different cues. The leader responds to the experimenter's directions; the imitator takes his or her cue from the leader's behavior. Figure 5.1 (a) shows the results of the experiment. The left side of the graph gives the percentage of dependent children who followed the leader on the first trial, before training. If at the outset of the experiment, the leader had no influence, we would expect half the children to choose the same box and half the other box. You can see that relatively few of the children later trained to imitate and nonimitate followed the leader—just 20 to 25%. The children came into the experiment as nonconformists. The right side of the graph presents the results on a test trial administered after the dependent children had made the

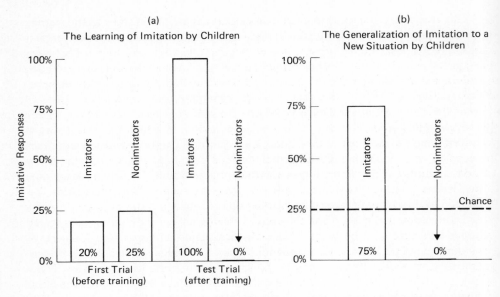

Fig. 5.1 Matched-dependent behavior: Acquisition (a) and generalization (b). (From Miller and Dollard, 1941)

appropriate choice on two successive trials. All of the children trained to imitate responded appropriately, and so did all of the children trained to nonimitate. But do these dependent relationships generalize to new situations, as Miller and Dollard's theory requires? To test the degree of generalization, a situation was devised that was similar to, but not identical with, the first one. Four boxes were placed on chairs at the corners of an imaginary square. The start position was in the center of the square and the object was again to choose the box containing candy. As before, the leader took his or her cue from the experimenter and made the first selection. The dependent subject, who had stood beside the leader and watched the choice, then took his or her turn.

Figure 5.1 (b) shows the percentage of imitators and nonimitators who chose the same box as the leader on the first trial of the generalization test. Please keep in mind that no rewards had been given as yet. Any influence of the leader would have to be the result of generalization. If the leader had no influence at all, there would be a 1-in-4 chance that the dependent subject would choose the same box. You can see that all of the nonimitators continued to act differently from the leader. However, fewer imitators followed the leader in the generalization test (75%) than during training (100%). Imitation was at a better-than-chance level, but the strength of the behavior had decreased. From studies of generalization in more conventional situations (Chapters 2 and 3), we know that generalization occurs to the extent that the new situation resembles the one in which the response was learned. Miller and Dollard's use of four boxes instead of two did change the stimulus conditions, so that a decrease in response strength should not be surprising. The results are clear evidence that matched-dependent behavior can be acquired and can generalize.

OF PUPPETS AND PARROTS:
SUBTLER INFLUENCES OF REINFORCEMENT

The principle of generalization can explain why a person may repeatedly imitate a model without reinforcement. In terms of the foregoing analysis, the imitative response had at one time been rewarded in another situation and it then generalized to the present one. But another sort of explanation is possible based upon the same principle. Miller and Dollard (1941) showed that when a person is rewarded for imitating one response of a model, the person will be more likely to imitate another response. The tendency to imitate generalizes from one aspect of the model's behavior to other aspects. Thus if you observed a person imitating a model without reinforcement, the reason could be that the person had received reinforcement for reproducing *something else* that the model did. This phenomenon is especially marked when a person is reinforced for imitating a variety of different responses of a model, not just one. The person then acquires a broad tendency to do whatever the model does, even imitating actions that do not resemble the ones associated with reinforcement. Such behavior is called **generalized imitation.** For example, recall the case of the schizophrenic boy who spent hours alone in his hospital room. His father exhibited similar behavior at home and had apparently served as a model. Generalized imitation may well have been responsible for this maladaptive behavior. The father required family members to participate in religious rituals and he probably presented himself as a model of proper behavior. In this and other situations, the boy probably received praise for acting like his father. Perhaps the boy came to imitate his father's solitary behavior because so many others of his imitative acts were rewarded.

Baer and Sherman (1964) presented a striking demonstration of generalized imitation in preschool children. The model was a "talking" puppet (Fig. 5.2) that "spoke" to each child from a stage (Baer, 1962). The puppet, dressed as a cowboy, sat in a chair with his hand on a lever. The child sat in front of the stage beside a similar lever. The experimenter introduced the child to the puppet saying, "This is Jimmy the puppet. He wants to talk to you. And this is your bar. See, it's just like Jimmy's bar, only bigger." The experimenter pressed the lever to show the child how it worked, and then the "show" began. First, the puppet pressed his lever a few times, the object being to see whether the child had a tendency to imitate the response initially. No child imitated. Then the puppet asked the child to imitate several other kinds of responses—mouthing (opening and closing the mouth without talking), nodding, and nonsense speech (e.g., "Red robbins run rapidly"). The puppet reinforced imitation with praise and soon imitative responses increased in frequency. Eventually, it became unnecessary to ask the child to imitate. At this point, the puppet pressed the lever without providing reinforcement for imitation of

Fig. 5.2 Puppet displays lever-pressing behavior to child in study of generalized imitation. (From Baer, 1962)

this response. Periods of lever pressing alternated frequently with periods of reinforcement for nodding, mouthing, and nonsense speech. If generalized imitation occurred, the child should have continued to lever press despite the lack of reinforcement for lever pressing. Baer and Sherman found that the majority of children did acquire generalized imitation and that the puppet exerted a powerful influence over their behavior. Figure 5.3 illustrates the behavior of two children in relation to the behavior of the puppet. The graph is a cumulative record and is read in the same way as the cumulative records we encountered in Chapter 3. The horizontal axis represents time, the vertical axis cumulative responses. On a cumulative record, the steeper the slope of the line, the higher is the frequency of responding. Each child's performance is illustrated just below the puppet's. Note that before reinforcement, neither child pressed the lever when the puppet did; the operant level of the response was zero. But when the puppet gave reinforcement for nodding, mouthing, and nonsense speech, imitative bar pressing increased. Witholding reinforcement from all imitative responses resulted in a typical extinc-

LEARNING THROUGH OBSERVATION

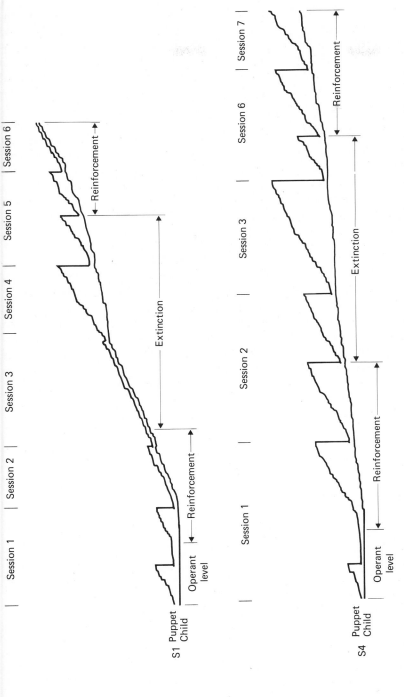

Fig. 5.3 Cumulative records of lever pressing by puppet and two subjects in study of generalized imitation. At no time was lever pressing reinforced. In the reinforcement conditions, the puppet complimented the children when they imitated responses other than lever pressing. In the extinction condition, this reinforcement was withdrawn. The children's lever pressing represents generalized imitation. (From Baer and Sherman, 1964)

OF PUPPETS AND PARROTS: SUBTLER INFLUENCES OF REINFORCEMENT

tion curve for bar pressing—a gradual slowing down of the response. When rein-forcement was resumed, generalized imitation reappeared. Here, in simplified form, is a process that undoubtedly plays a significant role in human social develop-ment. Parents often make themselves an example to their children and reward them for imitation. The parents of an infant reward the child with expressions of pleasure when he or she repeats the sounds "Dada" and "Mama." They praise the older child when he or she successfully imitates the use of knife and fork. Parents often fail to recognize that the child who has received reward for imitation will come to imitate other things that they do, so that the parents set an example whether or not it is their intention to do so. Occasionally, a parent's example conflicts with something the parent wishes to teach. Bandura and Huston (1961) describe a pos-sible case in which a parent spanks a child for hitting one of his friends. The parent's intention is to prevent future attacks, but by this example, the parent teaches the child that aggression is proper.

"Identification" in people and parrots

In the course of growing up, children naturally **identify** with their parents, internal-izing their values, attitudes, and moral standards. Identification occurs through observation of the parents in a variety of settings and the process appears to be similar to imitation. However, many psychologists (e.g., Mussen 1966) believe that imitation and identification are different processes. One distinction they make per-tains to the range of behaviors acquired. In imitation, a person acquires just one or a few specific actions he or she sees the model perform. In identification, a person acquires general behavior patterns and durable personality traits. Another distinc-tion that has been made pertains to the presence or absence of a model when the behavior is reproduced. In imitation, the model is physically present when his or her behaviors are reproduced (for example, Bobby's following Jim during the living room game), while in identification, the model is physically absent when his or her behavior is reproduced (for example, the schizophrenic boy's habit of staying in his room as his father had done). Other psychologists (e.g., Bandura and Walters, 1963) suggest that a distinction between imitation and identification is unneces-sary. They apply the term "imitation" to any case in which one person's behavior matches another's. The present chapter adopts this approach as it is a useful way of illustrating principles of learning. However, you should keep in mind that these principles may not tell the whole story of identification. One principle that seems to be particularly important to our understanding of identification is conditioned rein-forcement, the principle that any stimulus repeatedly paired with a reinforcer will become reinforcing. In Chapter 3, the conditioned reinforcers we examined were external stimuli such as tokens and lights. In the present case, the conditioned rein-forcers are internal stimuli and they are self-administered.

Sigmund Freud and the psychology of talking birds   Identification was a central concept in Freud's theory of personality. He maintained that identification begins in about the fourth year of life with the onset of the "phallic" phase of personality development. During the phallic phase, the child discovers the pleasure of genital stimulation and the genital zone becomes the focus of intense interest. The young boy develops a sexual desire for his mother and comes to perceive the father as a rival and a threat. The child fears that if the father found out about his secret wish to possess the mother, the father would castrate him. To reduce his anxiety over castration, the child decides to be as much like the father as possible. The child feels safe with this identity because he is sure that the father would never castrate himself. For the little boy, the prime motive for identification is anxiety, and Freud called the process **defensive identification.** For the girl, identification with the mother occurs for a different reason—love. The child discovers that she lacks the male organ and resents her mother for sending her into the world without one. In anger, and at great psychological cost, the girl rejects her mother's love. Loss of the mother creates a void in the child's life, as the mother has always been the major source of love. To fill the void, the girl strives to become the mother, because by acting like her, the child can again experience the good feelings the mother used to create. Freud called this type of identification springing from the child's original love of the mother **anaclitic identification.**

Although Freud's concepts of anaclitic and defensive identification were integral parts of a broader theory of personality, it is possible to assess the validity of these concepts apart from the rest of the theory. What Freud is basically saying is that one's emotional reaction to a model is a major factor in identification. Identification will occur to the extent that the model creates feelings of fear or affection. This hypothesis could be correct even if the specific rationale behind it based on psychosexual considerations is wrong. In a review of studies of identification, Mussen (1966) concluded that Freud's identification hypothesis was at least partly correct. While there is only weak evidence that fear of a model facilitates identification, there is very strong evidence that affection facilitates identification. Indeed, Mowrer (1952) discovered a remarkable counterpart to anaclitic identification in talking birds, suggesting that the underlying process may be a fundamental one in animals generally. From studies of parrots, Mynah birds, parakeets, and other species, Mowrer came to the conclusion that birds best learn to talk when the trainer becomes a "love object." In teaching a bird to talk, one must isolate the animal from other birds and make it a pet—tame it, tend to its needs, "baby" it. Because the bird is totally dependent on the trainer for food, water, and social stimulation, it develops an emotional attachment to him or her. While caring for the bird, the trainer must vocalize certain words repeatedly. Words consistently paired with satisfaction of needs become conditioned reinforcers and "good sounds." In the course of random vocalization, the bird may accidentally make a sound resembling the trainer's and it will repeat the sound. The accuracy of the imitation eventually increases because the more closely the bird approximates the trainer's sound, the stronger will be its conditioned reinforcement. Mowrer believes that human infants babble and acquire new words for similar reasons. The mother often speaks to the infant when caring and spending leisure time with it. After the mother leaves, the

OF PUPPETS AND PARROTS: SUBTLER INFLUENCES OF REINFORCEMENT

infant may continue to feel comfort and reassurance by making the sounds associated with the mother. This theory readily explains the fact that infants born deaf initially babble like normal infants but eventually stop. From Mowrer's standpoint, vocalization does not produce the rewarding stimulation necessary to maintain the behavior.

Although Mowrer (1960) acknowledges the possibility of identification based on fear of a model, he emphasizes the role of love and nurturance. Numerous studies in clinical and laboratory settings support such a view. For example, Bandura and Huston (1961) tested the effects of nurturance in a situation resembling the one employed by Miller and Dollard (1941). Nursery school children were asked to play a game in which they were to decide which of two boxes contained a reward. Each child played the game with an adult, who always went first and acted as the leader. The children consistently found a reward in the box chosen by the leader and they were expected to learn to imitate the leader's choice. This much was similar to Miller and Dollard's study. Bandura and Huston's study differed in that the children had previously met with the adult in two short sessions. With some children, the adult behaved in a "nurturant" manner. During the preliminary sessions, the adult and child played together with some toys on the floor. The adult stayed close to the child, expressed warmth, and quickly responded to bids for help. With other children, the adult maintained a nonnurturant relationship, staying busy at a desk while the child played alone on the floor. Mowrer's theory suggests that the children who experienced a rewarding relationship with the model would have a stronger motivation to imitate the model than would children who had experienced an unrewarding relationship. Reproducing the nurturant model's actions would be a source of conditioned reinforcement, even if those actions were not instrumental to obtaining a reward. To see whether children in the nurturant group did have a stronger tendency to imitate, Bandura and Huston had the model engage in irrelevant actions during the game with the two boxes. For example, the model did not simply walk to the boxes and choose, but first announced "Here I go," then marched slowly to the boxes, repeating "March, march, march." More than twice as many children were found to imitate these irrelevant behaviors in the nurturant group than in the nonnurturant group, supporting the conditioned-reinforcement concept. This finding is remarkable when we consider that the nurturant relationship consisted simply of two short encounters. Two brief doses of "caring" were sufficient to make imitation of the model rewarding in itself. Imagine how much stronger must be the motivation to imitate a parent! Bandura and Huston suggest that identification is basically a process of **incidental learning,** wherein the child imitates activities without any inducements or intentions to do so. Thus, social training is in progress whenever the parents are present, and they must be ever careful to practice what they preach.

LATENT LEARNING REVISITED

In Chapter 1 we saw that there is a distinction between "learning" and "performance." What an organism is able to do as the result of practice or experience (learning) may differ considerably from what the organism actually does (performance). The latent-learning experiments of Tolman and Honzik (1930) dramatically illustrated this distinction. Hungry rats that ran a maze without receiving food in the goal box made numerous errors and showed little improvement from day to day. Rats that received reward showed rapid improvement and eventually made few errors; they seemed to have learned more than the unrewarded rats. However, Tolman and Honzik demonstrated that the unrewarded rats had learned as much about the maze as the rewarded ones. Immediately after food was introduced, the previously unrewarded rats exhibited a sharp drop in errors and performed at the same level as the rats rewarded from the beginning. Learning had been latent, or hidden. Bandura and Walters (1963) suggest that a similar process of latent learning may take place when we observe a model make responses that are new to us. Simply by watching these novel responses we may acquire the ability to perform them, an effect Bandura and Walters call **modeling.** We need not practice the responses while watching the model, and reinforcers need not be delivered; the learning process is purely a "cognitive" or mental one. In the absence of incentives to make a response acquired through observation, it will probably remain latent within us. But if reinforcement is offered for the response, it may appear.

Strong evidence for latent learning through observation comes from a study by Bandura (1965). His subjects were nursery school children—boys and girls—and the model that they observed displayed novel aggressive responses. Previously, it had been shown (Bandura, Ross, and Ross, 1963) that children were more likely to imitate a model that was rewarded for aggression than a model that was punished. Had the children who exhibited more aggression learned more about how to be aggressive? Or had all the children learned just as much, but differed in the motivation to be aggressive? Bandura's (1965) experiment suggests that the difference was probably due to motivation, not learning. All of the children in his study observed the same sequence of aggressive responses. The children watched the model on a TV monitor much as they might watch a violent TV program at home. First, the model walked up to a Bobo doll and ordered it to clear the way. Seeing that the doll held its ground, the model tossed it over, sat on it, and began punching its nose, exclaiming, "Pow, right in the nose, boom, boom." Then the model raised the doll and beat it on the head with a mallet, saying, "Sacheroo . . . stay down." After that, the model said "fly away" and kicked the doll around the room. Finally, the model threw rubber balls at the doll and shouted "Bang" with each hit.

For some children, the "program" ended at this point. For others, positive or negative consequences for aggression were also displayed. In the reward condition, an adult gave the model candy and soft drinks and proclaimed the model a "strong champion." In the punishment condition, the adult shook his finger at the model and said, "Hey there you big bully. You quit picking on that clown. I won't tolerate it." Drawing back, the model "accidentally" fell, and the program ended with the model getting spanked with a rolled-up magazine.

Immediately after watching the program, the children were taken to a room filled with toys: a pegboard, a doll house, some plastic farm animals, cars, a dart gun—and a Bobo doll, a mallet, and rubber balls. The children were left alone for

LATENT LEARNING REVISITED

awhile and a count was made of the number of different aggressive responses they reproduced. As the model had displayed four distinct aggressive acts, the maximum score would be four. The lined bars in Fig. 5.4 show the number of aggressive responses at this point in the study. The results for boys and girls are shown separately, and you can see that whether the model was rewarded, punished, or given no consequences, boys were more aggressive than girls. This sex difference is consistent with findings in other kinds of settings showing that boys tend to be more physically aggressive than girls. However, both sexes responded to the models in essentially the same way: They reproduced more aggressive responses of the model who was rewarded, or given no consequences, than of the model who was punished. Now, had the children who observed the punished model learned less than the other children, and had the girls generally learned less than the boys? Or had latent learning taken place—were all the differences in aggressive behavior due to motivation?

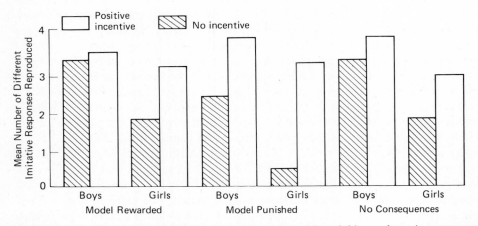

Fig. 5.4 Number of aggressive responses reproduced by children after observing an aggressive model. The children saw the model rewarded, punished, or administered no consequences for performing violent acts. Children were tested twice, once without incentive from the experimenter for reproducing the violent acts, and once with incentive. (From Bandura, 1965)

The answer became clear in the next phase of the study. The experimenter returned to the room carrying fruit juices and sticker pictures, and offered the children a picture and some juice for each aggressive response that they reproduced. Now, all the children had a strong incentive to show aggression, and if latent learning had occurred, differences in aggressive responding should have been eliminated. The solid bars in Fig. 5.4 present the results when this incentive was added, and it is clear that all the groups performed at about the same level. Latent learning had occurred. Bandura's theoretical point that latent learning occurs without reinforcement is debatable, since the children probably entered the situation with a generalized tendency to imitate, which we know is acquired through reinforcement. But the practical message is clear. Children who watch violence on TV may become aggressive. They are more likely to exhibit aggression when the violent model is a "hero" who earns rewards for aggression than a "villain" who incurs punishment. However, whatever the consequences to the model, the children will learn the techniques of aggression very well. With incentive, they may exercise some of these techniques and create a dangerous situation for themselves and others.

Why boys are generally more physically aggressive than girls also becomes clearer in the light of the present findings. Boys in our culture have more incentive for being aggressive than girls. Particularly in young children, physical strength is likely to be taken to indicate manliness, and an exhibition of brute force can be a very convincing demonstration of manliness to a little boy's peers. In contrast, an exhibition of brute force by a little girl could mean a loss of respect from her peers as such behavior is widely regarded as unfeminine. The general point is that one need not, and indeed should not, assume that sex differences in aggression are genetic in origin. They are more plausibly interpreted in terms of principles of learning.

IMITATION IN CLINICAL SETTINGS

Under appropriate conditions, imitation can have significant therapeutic benefits. Psychotherapists have successfully used imitative techniques to treat a variety of behavioral and emotional problems. Under uncontrolled conditions, however, the tendency to imitate can have disruptive effects and make therapy more difficult. In this section, we shall first see how imitation could become a disruptive influence in therapy, and then we shall see how proper control of imitation can be beneficial.

Aggression in the institutionalized retarded

Violent behavior can be a particularly serious problem in institutionalized retardates. Much of their aggressive behavior seems to arise from frustration over not being able to express needs and to communicate with others. Talkington, Hall, and Altman (1971) compared two groups of retardates in aggressiveness, one group judged by a language development staff as having no understandable language, and the other group judged as being able to communicate. Supervisory ward staff judged the noncommunicating retardates significantly more likely to destroy property, to tear their own clothes, to break windows, and to require restraints than the communicating retardates. Such behavior impedes treatment and its disruptive effects can extend beyond the individual who commits the violent act. Those retardates who observe the violent behavior may imitate it, and in turn may become aggressive models for others. The problem is particularly acute because many retarded individuals are dependent on others for guidance in how to behave. In proper circumstances, their dependency can be used to improve social and cognitive skills, but in a peer-dominated institution, their imitativeness can also be a source of antisocial behavior. Talkington and Altman (1973), who were concerned with this problem, demonstrated that retardates with IQs as low as 30 were highly susceptible to the influence of aggressive models. Some subjects viewed a three-minute silent film of a model kicking, hitting, and throwing a Bobo doll. Other subjects viewed a model engaging in affectual behavior—for example, kissing and petting the doll. A control group simply spoke with the experimenter for three minutes. Immediately following these experiences, the subjects were taken individually to a room where they found a Bobo doll. The experimenter asked the subject to wait in the room while he left to get a game. For the next three minutes a count was made of the number of aggressive and affectual responses. It was found that retardates who viewed the aggressive model made about three times as many aggressive responses as the other subjects, and made about one third as many affectual responses. In other words, not only did the observation of violence increase aggressiveness, it apparently inhibited displays of affection. Interestingly, the observation of an affectual model had no effects—it neither heightened affectual behavior nor inhibited aggression. Retardates are thus particularly likely to imitate aggressive behavior, so that any factors in the institutional environment that create hostility will probably have a magnified effect. These results underscore the urgency of identifying and eliminating such factors. We have already discussed one of them—a retardate's difficulty in communicating. Talkington and Altman also suggest that aggression may result from a lack of opportunities for self-direction and from impositions associated with group living. Building a therapeutic environment that fosters both social and intellectual development is truly a challenge to the therapist's ingenuity.

Teaching language to speechless children

In Chapter 3 we saw how the reinforcement procedure called "shaping" could be used to teach speechless children language. The therapist reinforced successive approximations to English syllables, reinforcing first any sound, then only short, discrete sounds, and eventually actual syllables. At no time did the therapist provide an example of the sound required for reinforcement. Rather, the therapist waited for the child to make an appropriate sound on his own. O. I. Lovaas and his colleagues (Lovaas, Berberich, Perloff, and Schaeffer, 1966) have shown that the shaping procedure can be effectively combined with imitative techniques. To a certain extent, normal children naturally acquire language through imitation (Chapter 9). Lovaas observed that the schizophrenic children with whom he worked lacked imitative behavior and thus could not experience the natural process of language acquisition. Lovaas wished to employ this process in his language training program, but first he had to teach the children to imitate. A four-step procedure proved to be highly effective. First, the experimenter rewarded the child either for making any sound or for looking at the experimenter's mouth. When the child vocalized at a rate of at least one sound per five seconds, and was looking at the experimenter's mouth at least half the time, the second step was instituted. The experimenter pronounced the word "baby" once every 10 seconds, and rewarded the child for making any sound (not necessarily "baby") within six seconds of the experimenter. The third step was begun after the child's responding rose substantially. The child now had to match the word "baby" within six seconds of the experimenter. If the child was unable to pronounce the word, the experimenter helped the child with a variety of techniques, such as breaking the word down into syllables. The fourth step involved the introduction of a new word. The experimenter returned to Step 3 and required reproduction of the new word within six seconds. Intermittently, the experimenter presented old words to check on the durability of the behavior changes. Lovaas reported large increases in vocabulary using this imitative technique; clearly, it is a valuable therapeutic tool.

Treatment of phobias: Modeling vs. systematic desensitization

What makes a horror movie horrifying? The character who suddenly encounters a hideous monster usually reacts with horror. We, in turn, may share some of that experience if we imagine ourselves to be in the character's place. The character is a stand-in for us, and our emotional experience occurs **vicariously** because of the character's actions. The arousal of vicarious experiences is an effective cinematic technique; appropriately arranged, vicarious experiences can also have therapeutic value. Albert Bandura (1969) has been a pioneer in the development of therapeutic films for eliminating fears, and his strategy is just the reverse of that found in a horror film: A person who fears an object sees a model interact with the object without fear and without adverse consequences. The model consequently transmits the experience of calmness to the viewer. Of course, the effectiveness of the film depends upon how it is constructed. Bandura suggests that therapeutic displays will have greatest impact when the model performs hazardous actions in a variety of threatening situations. Vicarious extinction of the fear response will occur provided that the level of emotional arousal does not become extreme. To minimize distress, Bandura typically shows the model in a graduated series of activities, starting with the least threatening and ending with the most. Extinction of fear to activities having low arousal value is thought to generalize to activities having higher arousal value. In this way, the aversiveness of modeled activities is reduced before the viewer sees them.

Bandura's strategy may seem familiar to you. Systematic desensitization, an application of classical conditioning principles (Chapter 2), also employs the strategy of stimulus graduation. Recall that in systematic desensitization the patient constructs a "fear hierarchy" of imagined scenes, ranging from scenes causing little fear to scenes causing intense fear. Then the patient imagines each scene in turn, starting with the least threatening, while remaining in a relaxed state. The assumption is that relaxation will generalize from scenes the patient currently imagines to scenes he or she has yet to imagine. The question naturally arises whether systematic desensitization and modeling are equally effective. Bandura and his colleagues (Bandura, Blanchard, and Ritter, 1969) sought to find out. Their subjects (mostly women) were volunteers who had an intense fear of snakes. The subjects wished to eliminate this fear because it interfered with everyday living. Some avoided recreational activities such as camping, hiking, and hunting because of the possibility of seeing a snake. Others avoided buying homes in rural areas. Some subjects experienced great distress when they came upon snakes unexpectedly in social or occupational situations.

To assess the effectiveness of the therapies, Bandura gave the subjects behavioral and attitudinal tests before and after treatment. The behavioral test measured avoidance of snakes. The subjects attempted to perform a series of 29 tasks involving a four-foot king snake. The entire sequence consisted of the subject's approaching the snake, which was kept in a glass cage, looking down at it, touching it, taking it out of the cage and letting it loose, returning it to the cage, picking up the snake again and holding it five inches from their face, and finally allowing the snake to crawl in their lap while letting their arms hang passively. The subjects could stop at any time, so that the fewer acts they were willing to perform, the higher would be their tendency to avoid snakes. In a test of attitudes, the subjects rated six possible encounters with snakes on a seven-point scale, ranging from strong enjoyment ($+3$) through indifference (0) to strong dislike (-3). Examples of encounters were visiting a reptile exhibit, coming across a snake on a hike, and handling snakes.

Each subject was assigned randomly to a method of treatment. The modeling treatment consisted of a 35-minute color film showing children, adolescents, and adults interacting with snakes. The scenes were initially mild but became increasingly threatening. The models first handled only a plastic snake, then they handled a large king snake, and eventually they let the snake crawl over their bodies. At no time did the models express fear or suffer any adverse consequences. To make the treatment more effective, Bandura instituted two additional features. First, before the subjects saw the film, they were given instruction in muscular relaxation and in the use of visual imagery to reduce arousal. This instruction was like that typically used in systematic desensitization (Chapter 2). The subjects were told to maintain the relaxed state throughout the film. The second additional feature of the procedure made relaxation easier to sustain. The subjects could regulate the duration and frequency of the scenes by stopping the film, running it in reverse, or running it forward. Consequently, if subjects felt anxious in the presence of a scene, they could reverse the film to a less threatening scene.

In the systematic desensitization procedure, subjects constructed a fear hierarchy of 34 scenes. They received instruction in how to achieve deep relaxation, and then imagined the scenes while trying to maintain the relaxed state. If, in working their way up the fear hierarchy, the subjects experienced anxiety, the scene was withdrawn until they again felt relaxed. The scene was presented repeatedly until the anxiety was extinguished.

Bandura also tested a variation of the modeling procedure that combined demonstration with actual participation. The model was present **(live modeling)** rather than displayed on film **(symbolic modeling).** The subject and model were in different rooms, and as the subject watched through a one-way mirror, the model displayed increasingly threatening interactions with the snake. During this observation period, which lasted 15 minutes, no relaxation procedures were used. The model then led the subject into progressively closer contact with the snake— first touching the snake, then stroking it, and eventually holding the snake at the midsection with gloved, followed by bare hands. Whenever the subject felt anxious about performing one of these acts, the subject placed her hand on the model's, and moved her hand down until she touched the snake. During this phase of guided participation, interactions with the snake were increasingly threatening and the assistance of the model was gradually withdrawn.

In all of the groups, treatment continued until the specified terminal performance was achieved, or until the subject had spent about five hours in treatment, whichever came first. Subjects in a control group took the same "before" and "after" assessment tests as the other subjects but did not participate in treatment during the intervening period. Later, these control subjects were administered a symbolic modeling treatment without relaxation training.

All of the treatments succeeded in reducing fear, but they were not equally effective. Of the three methods, live modeling with participation gave consistently superior results. Figure 5.5 (a) shows subjects' scores on the behavioral avoidance test before and after treatment. The nontreated control group did no better on the second test than on the first; this indicates that mere repetition of the test leaves fear unchanged. But the three treatment groups improved dramatically. Subjects who experienced live modeling with participation now performed almost the entire sequence of approach tasks. Subjects who experienced symbolic modeling and systematic desensitization performed fewer tasks, but did many more than they had before treatment. These two groups improved by approximately equal amounts. Figure 5.5 (b) shows that live modeling also produced superior results on the test of attitudes toward snakes. On this test, symbolic modeling had stronger effects than systematic desensitization.

The beneficial effects of treatment were not limited to snakes. Fear of other animals also decreased, and in some cases, the effects of treatment generalized to aspects of living unrelated to snakes. Generalization was tested by giving subjects a questionnaire before and after treatment that measured fear proneness in five threat categories: animals, tissue damage, social relationships, classical phobias, and miscellaneous events. In each category, subjects rated the fearfulness of items on a scale ranging from 0 to 4, and the sum of the ratings was taken. Figure 5.6 presents the changes in ratings following treatment. Post-test scores were subtracted from pretest scores, so that negative values on the graph would represent a reduction in fear. The control group, as you might expect, showed no reliable changes in ratings. In contrast, all of the treatments produced reliable reductions in the animal category. Symbolic modeling also reduced fear in the social events category, and live modeling had the most widespread effects, reducing fear of animals,

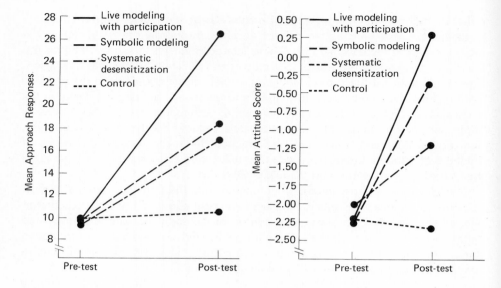

Fig. 5.5 Effects of three therapeutic treatments for snake phobia. Subjects in the control group received no treatment. Panel (a) shows results of behavioral test in which subjects attempted to approach and pick up snake. Panel (b) shows subjects' ratings of attitudes in several hypothetical encounters with snakes. (From Bandura et al., 1969)

physical injury, social relationships, and miscellaneous threats. Generalization is a dividend of each of the treatments, but most markedly of the modeling procedure with participation.

Why should modeling with participation be so effective? Bandura suggests that live and symbolic modeling extinguish much of a person's fear but do not eliminate it. They reduce fear sufficiently to enable the person to approach the actual fear object. Direct contact with the object is then necessary to extinguish the remaining fear. A lack of complete extinction with modeling really should not be surprising in light of what we know about the generalization of extinction effects. Recall from Chapter 2 Bass and Hull's (1932) finding that the presentation of a CS without a UCS results in a gradient of extinction extending from the CS to stimuli similar to the CS. The greater the similarity to the CS, the greater is the inhibition of the CR. The experience of seeing and touching an object is considerably different from the experience of seeing the object without touching it. One might therefore expect less than complete generalization from the latter experience to the former.

There was some direct evidence for the first phase of the therapeutic process, vicarious extinction. Remember that extinction is a gradual process. If the process responsible for fear reduction during the modeling phase is extinction, then fear should be decreasing gradually. On a 10-point scale, subjects in the symbolic

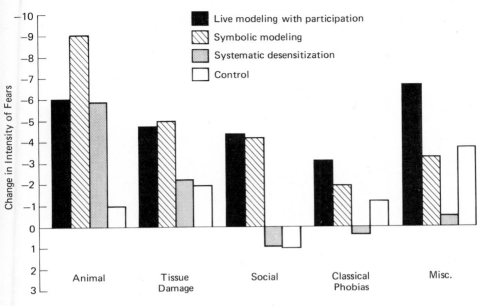

Fig. 5.6 Subjects' ratings of fear of several hypothetical situations following treatment for snake phobia. Ratings have been compared to ones given before treatment. On the graph, a change in the negative direction signifies a reduction in fear. (From Bandura et al., 1969)

modeling group rated the level of fear aroused by the scenes they saw. Since the subjects regulated the presentation of the film, they saw many scenes more than once. Theoretically, as the number of exposures to a scene increased, the ratings of fear should have decreased. The solid line in Fig. 5.7 depicts the ratings for this group. It is evident that fear did decrease gradually, a finding consistent with the supposition that vicarious extinction was occurring. But these subjects had first received relaxation training and had been instructed to maintain the relaxed state while watching the film. Is relaxation training necessary for vicarious extinction? The dashed line in Fig. 5.7 represents the ratings given by the control group, which ultimately experienced symbolic modeling without relaxation training. Their ratings also decreased gradually, indicating that mere exposure to the display was sufficient to extinguish fear. Also, upon retaking the behavioral avoidance test, the control subjects achieved about the same score as the subjects who experienced symbolic modeling without relaxation training. Thus, modeling without relaxation training reduces fear sufficiently to allow the patient to make physical contact with the fear object, whereupon the remaining fear can be extinguished.

How threatening should the display be? Recall that in Bandura's view, vicarious extinction will not occur if the modeling display arouses too much fear. To minimize the risk of excessive fear, Bandura's displays depict the model as calm

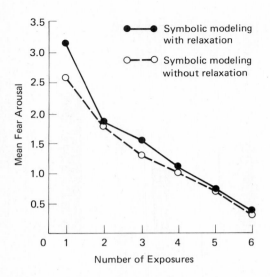

Fig. 5.7 Vicarious extinction of snake phobia in two varieties of symbolic modeling treatments. During each exposure to the therapeutic film, subjects rated their degree of fear. (From Bandura et al., 1969)

and as suffering no adverse consequences. But this strategy does not always work. At least one type of problem seems to require a more threatening display—the problem of anxiety in test-taking situations. Focusing on test anxiety, Jaffee and Carlson (1972) studied separately two components of modeling displays—the appearance of the model (calm or anxious), and the consequences to the model (positive or negative). Before treatment, the subjects took several subtests of an individually administered IQ test and rated themselves on anxiety. Then they watched a one-hour tape of a model taking the same tests. For some subjects, the model appeared calm, business-like, and organized, while for others, the model appeared nervous, fidgeting, and expressing great concern over performance. The consequences to each type of model could be positive or negative. If the consequences were positive, the tester told the model that his or her performance was above average. If the consequences were negative, the tester told the model that his or her performance was below average, that it was remarkable to find such a person in college, and that the subject might want to consider alternative careers that did not require a college education. It was found that negative consequences to a model, calm or anxious, reduced self-reports of anxiety when the subjects retook the same type of IQ test. The subjects who saw the calm model with positive consequences (the kind of model in Bandura's procedure) did not significantly improve. Why should this display have been ineffective? Jaffee and Carlson suggest that it may have been too artificial. The displays with negative consequences perhaps more closely resembled situations which subjects encountered and thus readily aroused fear. Since nothing actually happened to the subjects while watch-

LEARNING THROUGH OBSERVATION

ing the display, their fear rapidly extinguished. Apparently, there is no simple formula to guide the therapist in constructing modeling displays.

CREATIVITY THROUGH IMITATION

Imitative behavior hardly seems creative. After all, the imitator simply does what the model does. But imitation can be creative if it is creativity that the model exhibits. Zimmerman and Dialessi (1973) increased the creativity of fifth-grade children using an imitative technique, but the model had some unexpected effects. The test of creativity was simple: The children were asked to name as many uses as they could for a tin can. First, however, they watched an "expert" play the "game" with a different object, a cardboard box. Different groups saw models display different levels of creativity. One dimension of creativity was the number of uses named (fluency factor). For example, a cardboard box could serve as a doghouse, a hamsterhouse, or a chickenhouse. A second dimension of creativity was the number of different categories into which the uses fell (flexibility factor). For example, a cardboard box not only could be used to build a type of house, but to make a wash tub for different kinds of animals, and to make various sorts of cut-outs. Logically, fluency and flexibility are independent dimensions. A person could name many uses (high fluency) but they might all fall in the same category (low flexibility). Or, a person could name a variety of different categories (high flexibility) but overall give a small number of uses (low fluency). Two groups of children saw the model display low flexibility (one category), one group also seeing the model exhibit low fluency (six items) and one seeing high fluency (18 items). Another two groups observed the model display high flexibility (six categories), one group additionally observing the model display low fluency (one item per category) and one observing high fluency (three items per category).

Zimmerman and Dialessi's findings were surprising. The model's fluency and flexibility influenced the children in opposite ways. With flexibility held constant, increasing the fluency of the model *increased both* the fluency and the flexibility of the children. That fluency and flexibility were correlated in the children's performance suggests that the model conveyed a unitary message: "Use your imagination." Improvements in creativity were not simply cases of mimicry. Rarely did the children copy the model's words. The ideas they expressed were truly novel ones. With fluency held constant, increasing the model's flexibility *decreased both* the fluency and flexibility of the children. Possibly it was difficult for the children to grasp the relationships among the many different categories used by the model, and the model's message simply did not get through. The technique of increasing the model's flexibility might be better suited for use with older children. In any event, the present findings underscore the complexity of imitative learning. The effects of a model on an observer can be quite inconsistent with expectations based on common sense. One cannot safely assume that an observer will passively reproduce whatever a model does. Research on the many factors influencing imitation offers opportunities for making significant contributions to psychotherapy, education, and the psychology of learning.

SUMMARY

People often reproduce the actions of models without being reinforced for doing so. Nevertheless, a history of reinforcement could be responsible for the acquisition of imitative behavior even when there is no reinforcement in the immediate situation. An early conceptualization of imitative behavior based on reinforcement principles was developed by Miller and Dollard and called "matched-dependent" learning. The key features of matched-dependent learning were: (1) The behavior of the imitator matched the behavior of the leader. (2) The cues that initiated the responses of the leader and imitator were different. The cue for the imitator's response was the sight of the leader's response. In this sense, the imitator's behavior was dependent on the leader's. The leader responded to a cue that was independent of the imitator's behavior. (3) Both the leader and the imitator received reinforcement after responding to their respective cues. Studies by Miller and Dollard with children and rats showed that an imitator's response to a leader would generalize to settings similar to the one in which the imitative response was acquired. Thus imitation occurred in the absence of reinforcement in the immediate situation but was traceable to a history of reinforcement.

Another facet of imitation identified by Miller and Dollard was generalization from one action of a model to another action. An extreme form of this tendency, called "generalized imitation," arises when an individual receives reinforcement for imitating many different actions of a model. The individual then tends to do whatever the model does, even imitating actions which do not resemble the ones originally associated with reinforcement. Generalized imitation probably accounts for much of a parent's influence over a child.

Imitation closely resembles identification, the internalization of a model's values, attitudes, and moral standards. While some psychologists assert that the processes underlying imitation and identification are different, analyses of identification in terms of principles of learning have yielded important insights. Freud distinguished between two kinds of identification, one motivated by fear of the model ("defensive identification"), and one motivated by affection ("anaclitic identification"). Evidence for the latter type is much stronger than evidence for the former. An apparent counterpart to anaclitic identification in talking birds led Mowrer to propose a theory of identification in terms of self-administered conditioned reinforcement. The importance of affectional motivation has been underscored by the finding that brief exposure to a nurturant model will produce more imitation in children than will exposure to a non-nurturant model.

In their formulation of matched-dependent learning, Miller and Dollard assumed that in order for an imitative resoponse to be acquired, it first had to occur by chance and be reinforced. Bandura and Walters took issue with this assumption, asserting that a person could acquire totally new responses through observation alone. To demonstrate this modeling effect, Bandura arranged to have a model exhibit four novel aggressive responses to children. The children did not perform any of these responses while watching the model. Nevertheless, they reproduced most of the responses when later offered an incentive for exhibiting what they had seen. This study also showed that the consequences to a model influence the degree of imitation. In the absence of additional incentives to the imitator, an aggressive model who has been rewarded will produce more imitation by children than a model who has been punished or received no consequences.

The capacity for imitation has important implications for psychotherapy. When not taken into account, imitation can become a disruptive influence in therapy, as in the case of the institutionalized retarded who readily imitate the aggressive acts of their peers. When properly controlled, imitation can be a source of significant therapeutic benefits, as in the teaching of language to speechless children, and in the treatment of phobias. Bandura has developed a symbolic-modeling treatment for phobias in which the patient observes a film of a model making contact with the fear object in a variety of threatening situations. Because the model remains calm and suffers no adverse consequence, the observer is assumed to maintain a degree of calmness while watching the display. If the observer can keep the level of arousal low, some vicarious extinction of the fear eventually develops. More complete extinction is possible if the individual actually makes physical contact with the fear object under a procedure called "live modeling with participation." Bandura's strategy of displaying a calm model who suffers no adverse consequences is not equally effective for all phobias, so that a therapist cannot always rely on this formula when constructing modeling displays.

Imitation does not always involve direct reproduction of a model's behavior. Under appropriate conditions, a model can produce general behavior changes, such as an enhancement of creativity. The possibility of facilitating intellectual functioning through modeling makes this strategy a promising one for education.

STUDY QUESTIONS

1. Why might one be tempted to attribute imitative behavior to instinct?

2. What do Miller and Dollard mean by the terms "drive" and "reward"? Give examples.

3. Apply Miller and Dollard's conceptualization of "matched-dependent learning" to the case in which Bobby learns to follow Jim. For each child, identify the drive, cue, response, and reward. What relationships between Bobby and Jim do Miller and Dollard refer to when they use the terms "matched" and "dependent"? State these relationships in general terms, substituting the terms "imitator" and "leader," for Bobby and Jim.

4. How can matched-dependent learning explain imitative behavior in a situation where the behavior does not produce reward? Illustrate this process by describing the procedure and results of the experiment in which children, acting as imitators and leaders, first made choices between two boxes and then made choices between four boxes.

5. Define "generalized imitation." Illustrate by describing the procedure and results of Baer and Sherman's experiment involving the puppet who acted as a model for children. Using the aggression example mentioned in the text, state how generalized imitation could result in a parent's unintentionally teaching a child to do something which the parent has forbidden.

140

6. What is "identification"? State two criteria by which some psychologists distinguish identification from imitation.

7. In Freud's theory, what emotions are said to underlie defensive and anaclitic identification? For which type of identification is the evidence stronger?

8. Describe Mowrer's theory of identification using the example of the talking birds.

9. State the procedure and results of the experiment by Bandura and Huston which investigates the effects of nuturant and non-nurturant models.

10. What do Bandura and Walters mean by the term "modeling"? How does this conceptualization of imitative learning differ from Miller and Dollard's discussed in question 3?

11. Using the format given below, describe the procedure, results, and conclusions of the experiment by Bandura on the modeling effect:
    a) By what medium was the modeling display presented?
    b) Give two examples of the novel aggressive acts displayed by the model. What was the total number of acts displayed?
    c) Describe the modeling displays used to portray reward and punishment of the model. What did children in the control group see?
    d) How was aggression tested?
    e) Compare the levels of aggression under the reward, punishment, and control conditions prior to the introduction of the incentive. Also, compare the levels of aggression exhibited by boys and girls.
    f) State the results obtained after introduction of the incentive.
    g) In what sense do the results demonstrate latent learning? Why can one not completely rule out the possibility that reinforcement was a factor in the results?

12. Describe the procedure and results of the experiment by Talkington and Altman on the imitation of aggression and affectual behavior by the institutionalized retarded. In what sense might factors in the institutional environment which create hostility have a magnified effect?

13. Using the "baby" example discussed in the text, illustrate the four steps followed by Lovaas in teaching schizophrenic children vocabulary (the specific numbers of seconds given in the text can be excluded).

14. What is a "vicarious experience"?

15. Describe Bandura's general method of constructing modeling displays for psychotherapy. In what way does it resemble systematic desensitization?

16. Describe the procedure, results, and conclusion of the experiment by Bandura, Blanchard, and Ritter on the relative effectiveness of symbolic modeling, live modeling with participation, and systematic desensitization. Include the following points in your discussion:
    a) The behavioral test of avoidance—what it generally involved and some specific examples of the steps.
    b) The nature of the attitude test.

LEARNING THROUGH OBSERVATION

c) The modeling display in the symbolic modeling treatment, and the "two additional features" of the procedure.

d) The nature of the systematic desensitization treatment.

e) The nature of the treatment involving live modeling with participation—what the patient first saw the model do, and what the patient herself subsequently did. What happened when a patient felt anxiety?

f) The nature of the control condition.

g) A comparison of the results (behavioral and attitudinal) between the control condition and the three treatments, and a comparison of results among the three treatments.

h) The method and resuts of the generalization test.

17. What is Bandura's interpretation of the effects of modeling and participation (direct contact with the fear object)?

18. Describe the procedure and results of the part of Bandura's experiment dealing with vicarious extinction. What specific feature of the results suggests that the process actually was vicarious extinction?

19. What two components of modeling displays were studied in the experiment by Jaffee and Carlson on test anxiety? What feature of the displays produced the therapeutic gains? Was this outcome consistent or inconsistent with Bandura's formula for constructing modeling displays?

20. Define and give examples of the "fluency" and "flexibility" dimensions of creativity.

21. In the experiment by Zimmerman and Dialessi, how did the fluency and flexibility of the model influence the fluency and flexibility of the children?

CHAPTER 6

Theories of Learning in Historical Perspective

"Give me a dozen healthy infants, well-formed, and my own specified world to bring them up in," declared John B. Watson in 1924, "and I'll guarantee to take any one at random and train him to become any type of specialist I might select— doctor, lawyer, artist, merchant-chief, and, yes, even beggar-man and thief . . ." (p. 82). With this challenge, Watson expressed a fundamental tenet of the burgeoning behavioristic movement. Human actions were to be understood not as the products of instincts, as many psychologists of the day supposed, but as the products of learning. Therefore, by proper application of principles of learning, one should be able to mold a human personality to any specifications. Although Watson did not profess to have knowledge of all the necessary principles, he was unequivocal about the method by which they would eventually be discovered and the general form they would take. The principles would be those governing the formation, maintenance, and elimination of conditioned reflexes. The method of investigation would involve experimentation with muscle movements and the secretions of glands. Consideration of a person's thoughts, feelings, or sensations was unnecessary and counterproductive, Watson warned. Psychologists could predict and control human behavior without talking about mental activities.

Now, more than 50 years after Watson issued his famous challenge, are we any closer to developing a technology capable of engineering a human personality to specifications? That methods of prediction and control have improved is evident from our discussions in previous chapters. The trend toward greater precision is consistent with Watson's vision of what psychology could some day achieve. But the theoretical climate today is quite unlike the one Watson had anticipated. While behaviorism has remained a vigorous movement in the psychology of learning, interest in mental processes, which was declining when Watson wrote, has since undergone a revival. Today, many specialists in learning, perhaps the majority, have a mentalistic, or cognitive, orientation. "Cognition" refers literally to the act or process of knowing. Learning psychologists with a cognitive orientation seek to identify and explore the mental processes responsible for the acquisition of knowledge. Although no single theory exists to which all cognitivists would subscribe, there does seem to exist a general cognitive perspective on learning, a predisposition to view certain kinds of experimental variables and issues as more significant than others. Similarly, there is no single behavioristic theory of learning, but it is possible to talk about a general behavioristic perspective, one that is quite distinct from the cognitive.

THREE CLASSIC EXPERIMENTS

These core assumptions of cognitivism and behaviorism are not very unlike the views people commonly hold about the processes of learning. Of course, a layman's theory of learning is likely to be much simpler than the psychologist's. Indeed, the individual may not even know that he or she has a theory. One way to reveal it is to describe an experimental situation and ask for a prediction. Assuming the person is not already familiar with the experiment or with similar ones, and assuming that the prediction is not simply a guess, one should be able to deduce the theory from the prediction. Certain experiments are particularly interesting in this regard because historically they have served as tests of the two major traditions in learning theory. Although none of the experiments proved to be decisive, many have become classics because they effectively transformed abstract issues into concrete questions. You may wish to assess your own theory of learning. Briefly described below are three experiments, each bearing on an issue which historically has divided the behavioristic and cognitive traditions. The procedures will be given without discussion of the rationales which lay behind them, or the positions taken by psychologists of the day. After an experimental procedure is described, possible outcomes will be listed and you will be asked to make a prediction. A full discussion of the experiments will appear later in the chapter, at which time you will be able to check your accuracy.

Experiment 1: To obtain food, a chimpanzee must discriminate between two shades of gray. On each trial during the training phase of the experiment, the chimp sees two boxes. Attached to one box is a light gray card; attached to the other is a medium gray card. Only the box with the medium gray card has food inside, and the chimp learns to select this box consistently, making just one error in 75 trials. Upon mastering the task, the chimp encounters a new discrimination involving the medium gray card from the previous trials and a dark gray card. Although both boxes now contain food, the chimp selects one of the boxes on 18 of 20 trials, an aftereffect of the previous training. Which box does the chimp select?

The box with the medium gray card _____

The box with the dark gray card _____

Experiment 2: Two groups of rats run in a maze like the one illustrated in Fig. 6.1. The maze has no walls or ceiling so that the rats have a full view of the objects in the experimental room (e.g., a door, a lamp). There are two start boxes and two goal boxes. The rats are placed in start box 1 on a random half of the trials and in start box 2 on the other half of the trials. Rats in Group A always find food in goal

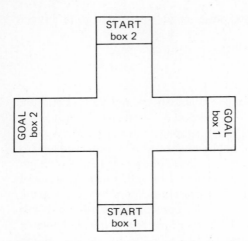

Fig. 6.1 Cross-maze used in "Experiment 2," a classic test of behavioristic and cognitive interpretations of learning. (After Tolman, Ritchie, and Kalish, 1946)

box 1, regardless of the start box from which they start. In other words, when the rats run from start box 1, a right turn at the choice point leads to food, and when the rats run from start box 2, a left turn at the choice point leads to food. Rats in Group B have a different problem. When they run from start box 1, they find food in goal box 1, but when they run from start box 2, they find food in goal box 2. In other words, rats in Group B always obtain food by turning right at the choice point. One of the two groups masters the task very quickly; the rats take just eight trials to reach a criterion of 10 trials without an error. The other group does poorly. Some rats never learn to go to the correct goal box and those rats that do learn take about 70 trials to reach criterion. Which group learns faster?

Group A learns faster _____
Group B learns faster _____

Experiment 3: This experiment is unusual in that it presents to the subjects a problem that cannot be solved. To obtain food, rats must traverse the four-component runway diagrammed in Fig. 6.2. Each compartment has two exits, one open and one blocked. As a rat enters a compartment, it cannot see which exit is open and so must choose an exit path on some other basis. Now, in other experiments that have employed the four-compartment runway, the rats have received a reliable cue to follow. For example, a hurdle might be placed in whichever path is open, left or right; or the correct path might be lit brighter than the incorrect path. Not so in the present experiment. Here, the rats are given a cue to follow, but it is totally worthless. Sometimes the brighter path is open and sometimes it is closed. There are no other consistent patterns, either. Occasionally the left path is open and occasionally it is closed. Occasionally the left path is brighter and occasionally it

Fig. 6.2 The four-compartment runway used in third classic test of behavioristic and cognitive views of learning. (From Krechevsky, 1932a)

is darker. The rat runs through the four compartments 168 times, and 168 times it encounters random conditions. The question is this: Will a given rat make random choices as it traverses the runway, or will it show a consistent pattern, like always choosing the left path or the path that is brighter?

The rat will make random choices _____

The rat will show a consistent pattern _____

On the basis of the predictions you have made for the three experiments, you may discover that you have a clear-cut theoretical orientation, at least as it pertains to animal behavior. The field of animal learning has been our "testing grounds" because it was in this area that the early theorists fought their classic battles. As you learn the outcomes of the experiments, you may find yourself reacting in much the same way as the original combatants. Should an outcome prove to be contrary to your prediction, you may decide to modify your theory to fit the conditions of the experiment rather than give up the theory entirely. And the inevitable result will be a more complicated theory than the one you started with. This process of testing and revision is the essence of theory building, and we shall witness many examples of it on our tour through the history of theories of learning.

THE MANY FACES OF BEHAVIORISM

Watson, Guthrie, Thorndike, Hull, Spence, Skinner, Mowrer—these major theorists in the behavioristic tradition have presented widely divergent views of the processes of learning. Ironically, Watson's theory, the one that has probably had the greatest impact on the psychology of learning, was the least developed. His role in the history of learning theory was more that of a publicist for behaviorism than that of a theoretician. Many psychologists were growing dissatisfied with the prevailing mentalistic approach, which, with its emphasis on the use of introspection to study consciousness, had yielded a mass of conflicting reports. With his vigorous attacks on mentalism, Watson gave vent to widespread frustration over the inability of psychology to make progress as a science. With his calls for viewing behavior as a bundle of conditioned reflexes, he offered hope that psychologists could establish principles as credible as those to be found in biology, physics, and chemistry. Because of Watson's central role in the development of behaviorism—he gave the movement its name and for years served as its leading spokesman—his theory deserves our close attention.

Watson and the conditioned reflex

Watson did not totally reject the notion that genetic factors influence human behavior. He maintained that organisms possessed a small repertoire of unconditioned reflexes that served as the starting point for learning. The manner in which learning came about was essentially the one Pavlov had demonstrated (Chapter 2). If the unconditioned stimulus for a reaction was repeatedly paired with some event, that event would acquire the capacity to elicit the reaction. Conditioned reflexes established in this simple way could be linked in many complex arrangements and were responsible for all the complexity we saw in human behavior.

At the time Watson wrote, it was fashionable for psychologists to draw up long lists of instincts to explain different kinds of behavior. A list proposed by William James particularly roused Watson's ire, probably because of James's preeminence among theorists. Sociability, pugnacity, acquisitiveness, cleanliness, shyness, parental love, jealousy, curiosity, imitation, rivalry, and more—24 instincts in all—comprised James's list. Like other lists, James's was essentially a set of labels. The tendency of people to congregate was labeled with the sociability instinct, the tendency to fight was labeled with the pugnacity instinct, the tendency to collect material goods was labeled with the acquisitiveness instinct, and so on. Because psychologists used their labels as explanations of behavior, they were committing the "nominal fallacy," which as we know from Chapter 3 is a fruitless practice. Watson accused psychologists engaged in the search for instincts of substituting mere words for facts. More productive, he asserted, would be a close examination of the behavior of young infants, who, having undergone relatively little conditioning, reveal man's genetic heritage quite clearly. What one would find is a limited number of unconditioned reflexes, not a trace of sociability, pugnacity, acquisitiveness, or any other instinct on James's list.

On the basis of available data on infant behavior, Watson compiled a list of reflexes he presumed to be unconditioned. Among the reflexes were: sneezing, hiccoughing, crying, erection of the penis, urination and defecation, eye movements, smiling, movements of the head, neck, limbs, and appendages, feeding responses, vocalization, and blinking. For each unconditioned response, Watson tentatively identified one or more unconditioned stimuli. For example, sneezing could be elicited by various internal conditions, by moving the infant from a cool room to a warm room, and in some cases, by exposure to sunshine. Hiccoughing was produced by pressure on the diaphragm from a full stomach. Hunger and noxious stimuli produced crying. Watson also proposed that human beings possessed three unconditioned emotional reactions: fear, rage, and love. Of course, he used these terms in a strictly behavioral sense; there was no reference to subjective feelings. Thus fear consisted in part of a momentary halt in breathing and a stiffening of the body, followed by crying. Rage involved a more prolonged halt in breathing and crying with the mouth open more widely than in fear. Gurgling, cooing, smiling, and erection were characteristic of love. As with the nonemotional reactions, Watson identified stimuli that seemed to call out the emotional responses innately. A loud sound, or a loss of support, elicited fear; restricting the infant's movements produced rage; various forms of gentle contact, like stroking and rocking, elicited love.

For Watson, an adequate analysis of any behavior, not just the inborn reflexes of infants, always consisted of two parts, a precise description of the response and a precise description of the stimulus. All psychological questions were of two kinds. In one case you observed a stimulus and were called upon to predict the response. In the other case you observed the response and were called upon to deduce the stimulus. Watson was optimistic that these objectives could be achieved, and to a generation of psychologists grown weary of debate over conflicting introspective reports, the behavioristic program was very appealing. Today, it is generally recognized that Watson's goals were unrealistic. His own analysis of infant behavior points to one difficulty. Recall that some of infants' reflexes could be elicited by more than one stimulus. Now, if you observed the reactions characteristic of fear, would you deduce the stimulus of a loud sound or the stimulus of loss of support? You can imagine that the problem would be multiplied many times in an adult, who has had an extensive history of conditioning. To deduce a stimulus from a response in the simple manner envisioned by Watson may well be an impossibility. To predict an exact response from a stimulus may also be an impossibility, for not one but many stimuli are usually involved. Few modern behaviorists, if any, would regard exact prediction as an attainable goal, except perhaps under strictly controlled laboratory conditions (Skinner, 1977, p. 1008). What remains of Watson's prescription for research is the general framework, the conceptualization of psychological problems in terms of stimulus and response. Over the years, "behaviorism" and "stimulus-response psychology" have become almost synonymous terms.

It's learning, but is it classical conditioning? There is little doubt that classical conditioning produces a portion of our learned behavior. Little Albert, the infant who Watson conditioned to fear furry objects (Chapter 2), is a prototypical case. Whenever Albert inspected a tame rat, Watson struck a steel bar behind Albert's head. Initially, only the sudden loud sound elicited a fear reaction, but after several pairings of the rat and the sound, the rat produced a similar reaction. While some of our learning probably takes place in the way that Albert learned to fear the rat, it is by no means clear that *all* of our learning takes place in this way.

Now, here is another instance of learning that Watson attributes to classical conditioning (Watson, 1924; republished 1970, pp. 226-227). See if you agree. A six-month-old infant was taught to say "da" in response to the sight of a bottle. There was one training trial a day during the initial three-week phase of the experiment. On each trial, the infant was allowed to nurse awhile from the bottle and then the bottle was removed and held in front of the infant. This procedure caused the infant to squirm and kick, and as he did so Watson pronounced the sound, "da." If the infant started to whine, he was immediately given the bottle. Eventually, the infant repeated "da" in response to the verbal prompt and he was quickly given the bottle. Watson repeated the procedure three times, on each occasion giving the bottle as soon as the infant responded to the prompt. Then, Watson omitted the prompt while still holding the bottle in front of the infant. On five successive occasions, the infant said "dada" in response to the bottle alone. Obviously, learning had occurred, but was it classical conditioning?

On a superficial level, the verbal prompt, "da," may seem to function as an unconditioned stimulus and the bottle may seem to function as a conditioned stimulus. The experimenter pairs the bottle with the prompt and eventually the child's response to the prompt gets attached to the bottle. One problem with this interpretation is that the verbal prompt could not have been an unconditioned stimulus in the strict sense. Certainly it does not elicit an imitative response in all infants in the way that a loud sound elicits fear; and it did not produce a response in Watson's subject for several weeks. It is possible that the prompt came to elicit an imitative response through accidental pairings with some internal unconditioned stimulus for "da." But this takes us out of the realm of demonstration and into the realm of speculation.

A second, still more serious objection to Watson's demonstration concerns the use of reward. After each imitative response, and subsequently after each response to the bottle alone, Watson gave the bottle to the infant as a reward. The use of reward is problematical because it is a procedure characteristic of operant conditioning, not classical conditioning. Pavlov trained dogs to salivate to a bell by ringing the bell and then quickly presenting the food. He did not withhold the food until the dog made a conditioned response to the bell. Watson does not explain why he used reward in a training procedure intended to demonstrate the pervasiveness of conditioned reflexes. However, in the context of another demonstration we get some notion of Watson's rationale.

When is a reward not a reward?   While a three-year-old child watched, Watson placed a piece of candy in a specially designed wooden box and then closed the lid. The only way to open the box was to push in a small button, and the child was told he could have the candy if he found a way to open the box. On the first trial, the child made many fruitless responses, like hitting the box with his fist and banging the box against objects. Eventually, he pushed the button and got his candy. On the second trial, the child made fewer useless responses and got the candy sooner. On subsequent trials, performance progressively improved, until on the tenth trial the child pushed the button immediately. Common sense tells us that the candy served as a reward for making the correct response, but precisely how did the reward lead to learning?

Watson suggested two principles. First, he noted that the box was built in such a manner that the button-pushing response was likely to occur more frequently than any other response. For example, while the child might pound the box with his fist on one trial, he might not repeat that response on the next trial. In contrast, button pushing occurred on every trial because that was the only way to get the candy. From these observations, Watson deduced a principle of **frequency** which essentially says that the more often you make a response to a particular stimulus, the more likely you are to repeat the response when you encounter the stimulus again. Watson also suggested a principle of **recency**. He noted that the last response the child made on every trial was button-pushing. It seemed reasonable to suppose that button-pushing became stronger as training progressed partly because it was always the response the child had made most recently when a trial began.

This interpretation of learning in terms of frequency and recency is not illogical, and you may be inclined to accept it. However, if you do, you should know that you are adopting a truly radical theory, one that is completely contrary to common sense. Essentially, you would be saying that there is no such thing as "reward"; the child does not learn to push the button because he wants the candy. Learning occurs because when the box opens, a series of movements is interrupted. You should get similar results by interrupting the series in ways that are not rewarding, for example, by quickly taking the box away or distracting the child with the words, "Hey! Look at that!" If the interruptions occurred just when the child touched the button, he should eventually make that response first at the start of every trial. Watson did not conduct this test, but as we shall soon see, similar experiments have been performed.

What Watson is emphasizing here is learning by contiguity, contiguity between a stimulus (the box) and a response (pushing the button). He could have applied the same concepts of frequency and recency to the verbal learning experiment discussed earlier. When Watson gave the bottle to the infant, he ensured that the response, "da," was the last verbal response the child made while looking at the bottle from a distance (recency). He also increased the chances that "da" would be uttered more often than any other sound (frequency). Watson did not explicitly relate his idea of stimulus-response contiguity to Pavlov's concept of contiguity between a conditioned stimulus and an unconditioned stimulus. This is one reason why the theory is considered to be inadequately developed. However, Watson did accomplish his major purpose of explaining learning without recourse to the concepts of thought and feeling. While subsequent behaviorists have disagreed with many details of Watson's theory, they have retained this basic objective. It is Watson's most enduring legacy to the psychology of learning.

Edwin R. Guthrie: In theory-building, simpler is better

To support his metaphysical and theological arguments, a well-known philosopher of the Middle Ages, William of Ockham, advanced a general rule for devising explanations of events. Because of its relevance and intuitive appeal, the rule has become an important consideration in the development of scientific theories. Ockham asserted that explanations should always be as simple as possible; in his

150

own words, "a plurality is not to be posited without necessity," This rule is known as "Occam's Razor" (in the more common spelling), and its relevance to science is very straightforward. Scientific knowledge is knowledge based on observed facts. If the facts do not necessitate including a principle in one's theory, on what basis can that principle be justified? Scientifically, no justification exists. Occam's Razor is a scientist's protection against biases, prejudices, and preconceptions acquired during a lifetime of experience outside the laboratory.

Watson applied Occam's Razor with a vengeance, cutting from his theory every last vestige of the human mind. Although the removal of the mind from psychological theory met with widespread approval, many behaviorists felt that Watson had gone too far in asserting that learning was reducible to just two principles, frequency and recency. However, in the view of one influential theorist, Watson had not gone far enough; he had one principle too many. Edwin R. Guthrie (1886–1959) independently developed a theory of learning based exclusively on the concept of recency. The basic principle was simply this:

> A combination of stimuli which has accompanied a movement will on its recurrence tend to be followed by that movement. (Guthrie, 1952)

In other words, your last or most recent response in a given situation will be the one you will probably make should that situation again arise. Guthrie believed that the bond between a stimulus and a response reached full strength on the first occasion that they were paired. Additional pairings did not increase the strength of the bond. Thus the three-year-old child in Watson's experiment with the puzzle box learned to push the button because this response was the last one to occur while the box was closed. It did not matter that button-pushing had occurred more frequently than any other response.

Why, then, did the child take 10 trials to master the task? If Guthrie was right, should not the child have mastered the task on the second trial? The response of pushing the button was the last one to occur on Trial 1 and it should therefore have been the first response to occur on Trial 2. That would have to be Guthrie's prediction except for one critical word in the principle he stated, the word, "tend." Guthrie asserts that a combination of stimuli which has accompanied a movement will "tend" to produce that movement in the future. "Tend" implies a weak expectation that the response will occur, not a firm prediction. There are two reasons why a firm prediction is not possible. First, Guthrie points out that we cannot record a stimulus pattern in its totality. The stimulus of a closed box is just one component of a pattern whose other features would have to be ascertained from questions like these: From what angle does the child view the box? Where is the experimenter standing? What is the noise level in the room? What is the temperature? What is the precise position of the child's body? (Stimuli also arise from one's muscles.) Innumerable stimuli contribute to the total pattern, and a conditioned response will only be made if the original stimuli are all in place. Because stimulus patterns are variable, we should expect to find variability in behavior.

Guthrie would also say that the response of button-pushing has a complex structure. In fact, it is misleading to call button-pushing a response for it is really the outcome of many finely coordinated muscle movements, each of which constitutes a response. You hand the child the box. He takes it in one hand and raises the other, positioning his fingers as they draw near the button. For the final act to occur, all of the movements must be executed in the proper sequence. One reason why improvement is gradual from trial to trial is that so many stimulus-response connections must be established in the context of a changing stimulus situation. Thus, gradual improvements in performance can be explained in terms of one-trial learning, but only by increasing the complexity of the theory.

How to break a habit Guthrie sought simplicity in theory not because he thought psychological processes were simple, but because he thought a simple theory would be easier to communicate than a complicated theory. In a paper written shortly before his death (Guthrie, 1959), Guthrie emphasized the importance of transmitting scientific principles to succeeding generations; unless a person could use a principle to make a prediction, to influence others, or to guide his own actions, that principle might as well not exist. This concern for communication reflects the strong professional commitment Guthrie had made to undergraduate teaching. Spanning a period of 42 years, his academic career was devoted mainly to instruction; in comparison to other major theorists, he produced little experimental research to support his ideas. Yet Guthrie was very persuasive. The evidence he presented in support of his theory consisted mainly of informal accounts of real and hypothetical incidents in the areas of child-rearing and animal training. What made these anecdotes so persuasive was the ease with which one could relate to them and the straightforward manner in which they could be interpreted within Guthrie's framework. It is truly remarkable that he managed to take a single principle of learning as far as he did. Let us consider some of its practical applications.

One implication of the principle is that every time a response is learned another response is unlearned. Unlearning occurs because a response can only get attached to a stimulus by replacing the previous response to that stimulus. This process of response elimination through conditioning Guthrie called **associative inhibition,** and we can turn this process to our advantage whenever our goal is to break a habit. The basic strategy is to identify the stimulus that evokes the unwanted response and to perform a different response in the presence of that stimulus. Here are three techniques Guthrie recommends for eliminating responses through associative inhibition:

1. Present the stimulus for an unwanted response in a situation where a different response is likely to occur. We might call this the procedure the "method of conflict." To some extent it resembles systematic desensitization (Chapters 2, 5), the therapeutic procedure in which a stimulus that normally produces fear (a scene from the fear hierarchy) is presented in a situation likely to evoke a different feel-

ing—relaxation. For Guthrie, though, the emphasis was on behavior, not feelings. One example he gives is that of a dog which habitually chases and eats chickens. The cure is to tie a dead chicken around its neck. The dog will make vigorous movements to get rid of the chicken, and on future occasions when a chicken appears, the dog is likely to flee instead of chasing the bird.

2. Present the stimulus for an unwanted response over and over until the response disappears through fatigue. Whatever behavior occurs during the fatigue state will then replace the unwanted response. Guthrie illustrates this method of fatigue with the example of a disobedient child who habitually lit matches in defiance of her mother. Scoldings and punishment did not stop her. Eventually, the mother found a technique that worked. She had the child light match after match until the child protested vigorously and pushed the matchbox away. That broke the habit because—in theory—the response of pushing the box away was the last one to be made to the stimulus of the box.

3. Present the stimulus for the unwanted response in gradual steps, starting with a level of intensity so low that the response is not made. If the unwanted response does not occur as the intensity is increased, the response should be unlearned, since the individual will always be doing something else when the stimulus is present. Suppose that a student had difficulty studying when her roommate played the radio. Instead of reading, the student constantly stared into space or looked blankly at the page. Using the method of gradual introduction, the student could unlearn this unproductive habit. When her roommate was away, the student might turn the radio on at a level sufficiently low that reading was possible. On successive occasions, the intensity would be increased until the student could read at the intensity normally used by the roommate.

Guthrie did not rule out punishment as a means for breaking habits, but he emphasized the importance of using punishment in a way that would produce associative inhibition. Inflicting pain or causing a "bad" feeling would not necessarily change behavior. For punishment to be effective, two conditions had to be met: (1) It had to be used in the presence of the stimulus that produced the unwanted response. (2) It had to generate behavior that was incompatible with the unwanted response. Suppose that a young child who is jealous of the attention received by the family dog habitually pulls the dog's tail while it lies sleeping on the floor. Slapping the child after the dog jumps up and barks will not solve the problem because the stimulus for the unwanted response is no longer present. Instead, the parent should administer the slap (or interrupt the child in some other way) as the child menacingly approaches the sleeping dog.

Lessons from the laboratory   As mentioned earlier, Guthrie did not produce a large body of experimental research to substantiate his views. One major study (Guthrie and Horton, 1946) did support the notion that the last response to a stimulus would tend to be repeated. However, the study did not bear directly on the question of how rewards lead to learning. Cats were placed in a small box from which they could escape only by moving a stick mounted in the center of the floor. At the moment the escape door opened, a camera photographed the position of the cat. Because the stick could be moved in any direction, the cat could be in many possible positions when the door opened. However, according to theory, the cat should have been in only one position: the position it was in on the previous trial. The cat could hit the stick with its tail, with the side of its body, or with its paw; it could be looking up, down, or straight ahead; it could be facing north, south, east, or west. Whatever the exact combination of movements when the stimulus situation changed, that combination should have been repeated on the next trial. There was, in fact, remarkable consistency from trial to trial in the way the cat moved the stick. At least in this comparatively simple experimental situation, the factor of recency appeared to be a powerful determinant of what was learned.

Nevertheless, the experiment leaves unanswered the fundamental question of how escape from the box led to learning. Was escape effective because it was a reward, or because it merely interrupted a series of movements and changed the stimulus situation? An experiment by Seward (1942) suggests that the latter inter-pretation—the core assumption of the theory—could not be entirely correct. Two groups of food-deprived rats performed in a standard bar-pressing apparatus, mak-ing one response per day for three weeks. In one group, the rats were given a food pellet upon pressing the bar and were then quickly removed from the box. In the other group, the rats were removed from the box without being given a food pellet. One measure of learning was the number of seconds that elapsed before the rats pressed the bar. By the simplest interpretation of the theory, we would expect the two groups to show equal decreases in the time to respond, for in both groups the stimulus situation changed immediately after the rats pressed the bar. Although decreases occurred in both groups as training progressed, the rats that received food showed much greater learning. The rewarded rats also made more responses during an extinction phase of the experiment in which responses were permitted continuously for an extended period without any consequences.

It is important to emphasize that the results were inconsistent only with the simplest version of the theory. Seward (1942) discusses two other explanations of the findings within the framework of Guthrie's theory, each involving additional assumptions. These explanations point up an intriguing feature of the theory. On the one hand, it offers simple rules of thumb for dealing with everyday behavior problems. On the other hand, it contains the germ of a complicated formulation, one amenable to mathematical treatment (Estes, 1959). Both the casual reader and the professional experimental psychologist can find much of value in Guthrie's works. His theory truly stands as a monument to communication.

Edward L. Thorndike and the Law of Effect

Although the contiguity theories of Watson and Guthrie contradicted common sense, they had behind them a long and respected philosophical tradition. The Associationist philosophers of the 17th, 18th, and 19th centuries had maintained that all knowledge was the product of associations formed between sense impressions, and that the factor primarily responsible for the development of associations was temporal contiguity. If two sense impressions were experienced at the same time, they would be linked in the mind (Chapter 2). Watson and Guthrie advanced essentially the same principle except that they substituted objective events—stimulus and response—for sensations. In addition to this tradition of associationism, many behavioristic theories have incorporated features of another centuries-old philosophy called "hedonism," which asserts that each individual strives to maximize pleasure and minimize pain. So commonsensical is this view of human nature that one might expect psychologists to have adopted it unanimously. Yet it gained influence among early behaviorists only over intense opposition, and largely through the pioneering research efforts of one psychologist, Edward L. Thorndike (1874–1949).

Thorndike's earliest experiments were in the field of animal psychology and are today regarded as classics. His apparatus appears in Fig. 6.3. You may have some difficulty seeing it as the handiwork of a pioneer, but in the context of the times, Thorndike's experiments were immensely innovative. Methodologically, his studies served as a model for many subsequent experiments on learning, and conceptually, the positions he took became a reference point which other investigators used to characterize their own ideas. We have already encountered two examples of Thorndike's influence: Watson and Guthrie. Watson's study with the child who learned to open a box for candy, and Guthrie's study with the cats who learned to escape from a box, were extensions of Thorndike's methods and were undertaken to dispute Thorndike's positions on the role of reward and punishment in learning.

As in Guthrie's more refined version of the procedure, Thorndike placed cats in a box and required them to make a response to escape; for example, they had to depress a pedal or pull down on a loop of string. Outside the box the cats found

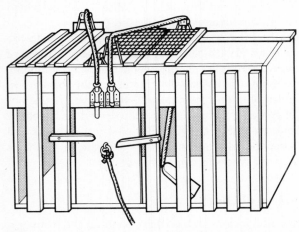

Fig. 6.3 One of Thorndike's "problem boxes." By stepping on pedal, cat can open door and escape. (From Thorndike, 1898)

THEORIES OF LEARNING IN HISTORICAL PERSPECTIVE

food. On the early trials, the cats made numerous unproductive responses before they made the correct one. As training progressed, the correct response occurred sooner and sooner until the cats escaped almost immediately after being placed in the box. What impressed Thorndike was the "stupidity" of the cats' behavior. Had they "understood" the solution to the problem, they would have repeated on the second trial the response that permitted them to escape on the first trial. (Perhaps because Guthrie's box included a number of refinements, his cats learned faster.) The need for many trials was surprising to students of animal behavior because at that time lower animals were assumed to think and reason much as people did. This assumption reflected the growing popularity of Charles Darwin's theory of evolution. Darwin had established many similarities in the anatomy and behavior of species, and argued that each species originated from some earlier one. Attributing thought and reason to lower animals was consistent with this concept of continuity across species. Thorndike did not dispute the theory of evolution, but he did object vigorously to the attribution of higher mental processes to lower animals. Anecdotes, not experiments, were responsible for the belief that animals solved problems intelligently, Thorndike said; and it was only the rare, intelligent solution that storytellers talked about. Most often, animals solved problems in a mechanical, trial-and-error fashion. Whenever they encountered an obstacle, they would make one random response after another until the obstacle was overcome. The correct response would increase in strength while the incorrect responses would decrease in strength, so that on future occasions the correct response would occur sooner than before. Thorndike was the first investigator to measure an animal's progress on successive exposures to a problem, and he believed that he had demonstrated that the learning process was mechanical rather than insightful. Moreover, examination of human performance in problem-solving situations convinced Thorndike that people, too, solved problems by trial and error.

On the basis of his studies with lower animals, Thorndike formulated a general principle of learning he called the "Law of Effect." It consisted of two parts. First, it stated that if a stimulus was followed by a response and then by a "satisfying state of affairs," the connection between the stimulus and the response would increase in strength. Second, if a stimulus was followed by a response and then by an "annoying state of affairs," the connection between stimulus and response would decrease in strength. Of course, there was nothing new in the assertion that organisms learned to repeat responses that produced pleasure and to withhold responses that produced pain; that was the old hedonistic philosophy. What was new was the emphasis upon automaticity in learning, the notion that learning took place without reasoning or understanding. Watson subsequently made this view of learning in terms of stimulus-response connections a core assumption of behaviorism, but it was Thorndike who originated the concept.

Some behaviorists objected to the Law of Effect on the grounds that "satisfying" and "annoying" states were subjective in nature and could not be observed. Their criticism was unwarranted, for Thorndike gave objective definitions of these terms: "By a satisfying state of affairs is meant one which the animal does nothing

156

to avoid, often doing things which maintain or renew it. By an annoying state of affairs is meant one which the animal does nothing to preserve, often doing things that put an end to it (Thorndike, 1913, p. 2)." The hypersensitivity of the behaviorists to Thorndike's mentalistic language caused them to miss the meaning of his words. The definitions were in terms of behavior, not feelings.

Although Thorndike enunciated a number of laws of learning, including a Law of Exercise similar to Watson's principle of frequency, the Law of Effect remained paramount in his writings. He did eventually modify the Law of Effect, however. Experiments had suggested to him that punishment did not weaken the bond between a stimulus and response. Instead, it seemed to increase the variability of behavior and led to the emergence of a response that brought about a satisfying state of affairs. The organism then performed this new response without actually unlearning the punished response. This view of punishment anticipated Skinner's criticisms of punishment as a technique of behavioral control (Chapter 3). With the exclusion of punishment, the Law of Effect essentially became a statement about positive reinforcement, and it was in this form that the principle had its major impact on behavioristic theories.

Clark L. Hull: Discovery through deduction

Imagine, if you will, a theory of behavior so precise and so broad in scope that it could predict exactly what you would do in any situation. The organization of the theory is formal and logical, very much like that of Euclidean geometry. It begins with a set of definitions. It then proceeds to state a few broad principles, or **postulates,** comparable in generality to the geometric axiom, "A straight line is the shortest distance between two points." Unlike axioms, however, the postulates are not given as self-evident truths but as generalizations based on scientific observation. From these postulates, a larger number of **theorems** have been deduced that are sufficiently specific to permit exact predictions in a variety of common settings. Behavior in any other setting can be predicted by selecting the postulates relevant to the problem and making the proper deductions.

Of course, we have no such theory, nor are we on the verge of producing one. There was a time, though, when a formal and logical theory, global in scope, seemed within reach, and psychologists worked tirelessly to make it a reality. It was Clark L. Hull (1884-1952), an engineer turned psychologist, who sketched the broad outlines of the theory in a book boldly entitled *Principles of Behavior* (Hull, 1943). What happened to the theory in the years that followed is reflected in the titles of Hull's subsequent books. After *Principles of Behavior* came the more conservatively titled, *Essentials of Behavior* (1951), and the final book, published posthumously, bore the humble title, *A Behavior System* (1952). It was the steady accumulation of experimental facts that forced retrenchment, a process that Hull himself encouraged. He assumed at the outset that revisions would be necessary, and he sought to facilitate the process of revision by making the theory's predictions precise. Because the theory could often be pinned down on one side or the other of an experimental question, it generated numerous tests, and in the period from about 1940 to 1970 Hull was the most frequently cited theorist in the literature of learning. Thus, as a stimulus for research, Hull's theory was immensely successful. As a model for theory-building, however, its effect was just the opposite of what Hull intended. Instead of encouraging the development of similarly ambitious projects, it convinced many psychologists that a global theory of behavior was not yet attainable. Today, theories of learning are much narrower in scope, each focusing on behavior in a particular kind of setting rather than seeking to explain behavior in all possible settings.

Speaking with numbers Precision is a goal of all scientific theories, and in striving for precision a theorist tries to speak with numbers whenever possible. To predict that using reinforcement in a particular setting will increase a child's study behavior may be useful. To predict that reinforcement will increase study behavior by a factor of three is far more useful. Rules, or laws, that will permit such precise predictions are what the psychological theorist seeks. Sometimes numerical rules are implicit in the words we use to interpret behavior, and if we make the effort to extract the rules we can greatly increase the precision of our interpretation. Generating numerical rules may yield an additional benefit, too: they may lead us to anticipate phenomena we would not have expected otherwise. By rearranging the rules and making appropriate deductions, one conceivably could discover a phenomena without actually observing it! Isaac Newton made major discoveries in the field of physics by deducing phenomena from quantitative laws. It was Clark Hull's hope that a theory could be developed that would do the same for psychology.

Although we all think about behavior and its causes, seldom do people think about it in quantitative terms, like a Newton or a Hull. To illustrate the process of developing a quantitative theory, you may wish to try your hand at the following problem. Several plausible assumptions about behavior will be stated, assumptions actually made by Hull. Your objective is to write a numerical rule, or equation, that expresses all of these ideas. Do not look for complicated solutions; the equation is a very simple one. In fact, it is so simple, that it may be the last one you consider. Following the last assumption, a solid line has been drawn across the page. The answer appears below that line, so if you are tackling the problem, you may wish to cover that portion of the page. Here are the assumptions:

1. Learning establishes connections between stimuli and responses. The strength of a connection between a stimulus and a response will be called "habit strength" and will be symbolized, $_sH_R$.

2. Physiological needs create a general state of activation in the body called "drive" (D).

3. A response will occur only if two conditions are met: (a) There must be a connection between the response and some stimulus in the situation, and (b) the organism must possess drive. In other words, if there is no connection, or if there is no drive, there will be no response.

4. The overall tendency to make a response will be called "reaction potential," and will be symbolized $_sE_R$. Reaction potential increases as habit strength $(_sH_R)$ and drive (D) increase.

   The equation is: $_sE_R = ?$

To combine habit strength with drive, you have a choice of four basic numerical rules. One is the additive rule, $_sE_R = {_sH_R} + D$. The additive rule will not work here because it violates the assumption that both drive and habit strength must be present for a response to occur. If we let $D = 0$ or $_sH_R = 0$, while the other factor had a value greater than 0, we would have to predict that a response would still occur. Subtraction will not work, either: $_sE_R = {_sH_R} - D$, or $D - {_sH_R}$. In the first case, increasing the level of D decreases reaction potential, while in the second case increasing the level of $_sH_R$ decreases reaction potential. Reaction potential should increase as these factors increase. Division involves a similar problem: $_sE_R = {_sH_R}/D$, or $D/{_sH_R}$; reaction potential decreases rather than increases as D and $_sH_R$ increase. It is the multiplication rule that encompasses all of the necessary ideas: $_sE_R = {_sH_R} \times D$. As $_sH_R$ and D increase, $_sE_R$ increases; and if either $_sH_R$ or D is 0, then $_sE_R$ is 0. Hull made this multiplicative relationship between habit strength and drive a central tenet of his theory, stating it in the form of a postulate:

> Any effective habit strength is sensitized into reaction potential by all primary drives active within an organism at a given time, the magnitude of this potentiality being a product obtained by multiplying an increasing function of $_sH_R$ by an increasing function of D. (Hull, 1943, p. 253, Postulate 7)

This postulate leads to an interesting prediction. Suppose that we had two subjects differing in the habit strength of a response. For Subject A, $_sH_R = 5$ units; for Subject B, $_sH_R = 20$ units. We test each subject's reaction potential twice, once under high drive (10 units) and once under low drive (2 units). We now calculate reaction potential using Hull's equation, as follows:

	$_sH_R$	$\times$	D	$=$	$_sE_R$
Subject A	5	$\times$	10	$=$	50
	5	$\times$	2	$=$	10
Subject B	20	$\times$	10	$=$	200
	20	$\times$	2	$=$	40

For Subject A, the difference between the reaction potentials is 40 units. For Subject B, the difference is 160 units. Increasing the level of drive makes more of a difference in behavior when a subject's habit strength is high than when it is low. If we could demonstrate this phenomenon experimentally, our multiplicative view of behavior would gain strong support. But how do we set about performing an experiment when the theory is so abstract? "Habit strength," "drive," and "reaction potential" are concepts, words on a page. They have no existence apart from the theory.

The solution, of course, is to devise **operational definitions** for the concepts. For experimental purposes, Hull defined habit strength as the number of reinforcements a subject had received for a response. Drive was defined as the number of hours an animal had been without food. Reaction potential had several operational definitions, for example, the number of responses a subject made during extinction, and the magnitude or intensity of a response. Hull expressed all of his postulates in broad, conceptual terms. His concepts of an organism's internal processes had physical reality only after he attached operational definitions to them, and there was always a risk that the experimental procedures he chose as definitions would be inappropriate. This is a risk inherent in all theories that seek to explain behavior in terms of so-called "intervening variables."

In the present case, Hull's operational definitions were well chosen, for they led to an important insight. In classic experiments that became cornerstones of the theory, Perin (1942) and Williams (1938) deprived rats of food for 23 hours and gave them five to 90 reinforcements in a bar-pressing apparatus. The different numbers of reinforcements defined different levels of habit strength. After bar-press training, the rats were placed on extinction, half under 23 hours deprivation (high drive) and half under three hours deprivation (low drive). The number of responses the rats made before they extinguished was the operational definition of reaction potential. The results are presented in Fig. 6.4. You can see that at higher levels of habit strength, increasing the level of drive made more of a difference in behavior

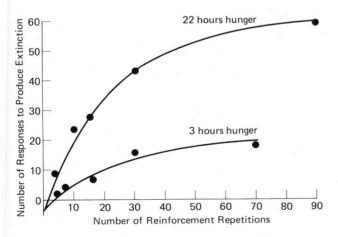

Fig. 6.4 Results of study on the relationship between "drive" and "habit strength." The vertical axis represents the number of responses rats made before they stopped responding during an extinction session. The horizontal axis represents the number of times responses had been reinforced during training. Subjects were tested under 22 and 3 hours food deprivation. (From Perin, 1942)

THE MANY FACES OF BEHAVIORISM

than it did at lower levels of habit strength. This need not have happened. The invigorating effects of drive could have been the same at all levels of training.

Unfortunately, research findings did not always fit so neatly into Hull's system. Perhaps the theory's most serious shortcoming was its view of the processes responsible for habit formation. Hull adopted a special form of Thorndike's Law of Effect, which stated that if a stimulus was followed by a response and then by a *reduction in need or drive,* the connection between the stimulus and response would grow stronger. Need, or drive, reduction replaced Thorndike's concept of a "satisfying state of affairs." The theory suffered a serious setback when Sheffield and Roby (1950) demonstrated that learning could take place in the absence of need reduction. Hungry rats acquired a response for which the reinforcement was saccharin, a sweet substance with no nutritive or caloric content. Subsequently, experiments demonstrated that undeprived animals would learn responses for which the reinforcement was simply to look at interesting objects or to explore a miniature environment. Again, no need reduction was involved. The theory could explain learning in the absence of need reduction by making some additional assumptions about the nature of drive and its relationship to needs (e.g. Brown, 1961). But the damage was done. The theory lost much of its credibility and enthusiasm for it waned.

Neo-Hullian theory

Although Hull's theory is no longer regarded as viable, many of its core assumptions have survived in theories of smaller scope developed by psychologists sympathetic to Hull's approach. Probably the most influential of these neo-Hullian theories was that of Kenneth W. Spence (1907-1967), who achieved recognition early in his career when he successfully defended behavioristic theory against a serious challenge from the cognitivists. The subject of the controversy was the nature of discrimination learning. The cognitivists presented findings which strongly suggested that lower animals solved discrimination problems intelligently rather than mechanically through a process of stimulus-response learning. The behaviorists seemed to have no choice but to concede the issue until Spence advanced an ingenious theory of discrimination learning based on Hullian concepts (Spence, 1936). Spence's theory won the day against the cognitivists and established him as a leading figure in the behavioristic movement. We shall be looking at the theory in detail later. For the present, it may be noted that the prediction you made at the beginning of the chapter for Experiment 1 places you on one side or the other of this controversy.

After Hull's death, Spence continued to develop the conceptual underpinnings of the system, and his efforts led him to propose several major changes. These changes revolved around the concept of "incentive." For Hull, "incentive" was an internal state (symbolized by the letter K) that contributed to the reaction potential of a response in the same way as did habit strength and drive; it acted as a psychological multiplier: $_sE_R = {}_sH_R \times D \times K$. The degree of incentive was related to the size of the reward the organism received for a response. If you had been giving a subject a small reward for a response and then suddenly shifted to a large reward, K would increase and cause a sudden increase in response strength. This concept of incentive helped Hull explain the results of experiments on latent learning (Chapter 1). Recall that the rats that had never found food in the maze showed an immediate drop in errors after food was introduced. Before the introduction of food, said Hull, simply removing the rat from the maze constituted a small reward and was sufficient to build up the habit strength for correct turns. That errors decreased slightly from day to day in this group supported the contention that learning was taking place. When food was placed in the goal box, K increased; this magnified the effects of previous training.

Spence had two major objections to Hull's concept of incentive. First, he questioned the idea that magnitude of reinforcement had a big effect on incentive without having any effect on habit strength. Was it plausible that habit strength was sensitive to the difference between no reward and a tiny reward, but was insensitive to the difference between a tiny reward and a huge reward? Spence did not think so. Second, the concept of incentive in Hull's system had no clear physiological representation. Habit strength conceivably was represented by neural connections beween sensory impulses and motor impulses. Drive apparently had its representation in the reticular formation of the brain stem; studies had shown that the reticular formation was capable of producing a general state of arousal in the brain. But where in the body was incentive?

To resolve these difficulties, Spence decided to give greater prominence to a concept that Hull had introduced but had not fully developed, the concept of the "fractional anticipatory goal response." As imposing as that title may sound, the basic idea was really quite simple. Let us say (just for illustrative purposes) that you are an orthodox behaviorist. You do an experiment in which rats must traverse a runway for food. After administering a number of trials, you note that the rats are running faster than they did at first. What reason would you give for the increase in running speed? You may be inclined to say, "The rats expect to find food in the goal box." But if you are an orthodox behaviorist, the word "expect" is not part of your vocabulary, for "expectations" are mental events. What you need is a mechanism that captures the sense of anticipation without assuming the existence of a mind. Here was Hull's solution:

Let us call the behavior of eating the food a "goal response" (R_g). Just before the rat enters the goal box, it notices a portion of the runway. Because the stimulus of the wall occurs just before the stimulus of food, we have a classical conditioning situation: The wall acts as a conditioned stimulus and comes to elicit goal behavior. Only a fraction of R_g can be elicited, however, because the rat does not have food in its mouth. Salivation, chewing, licking—these components of R_g are all reduced in magnitude. The goal behavior elicited outside the goal box thus constitutes a fractional anticipatory goal response, and to distinguish it from the "big" R_g we designated it as r_g ("little" RG). It is reasonable to assume that r_g has a sensory or

162

stimulus component, s_g, since organisms presumably can detect salivation, chewing, and licking that is going on inside their own mouths. Let us represent the learning that has taken place thus far in the following manner:

$$S_{Runway} - r_g - s_g$$

Since movement toward the goal is occurring, this behavior should become associated with s_g. The complete sequence would then be:

$$S_{Runway} - r_g - s_g - R_{Run}$$

Now, one part of the runway looks very much like any other part. Consequently, as training proceeds, stimulus generalization should become a factor, and $r_g - s_g$ should occur at points progressively closer to the start box. As $r_g - s_g$ "moves back," the rat runs sooner and sooner after leaving the start box. From small chewing and licking movements, one may have the impression that the rat is thinking about the food. But, says Hull, we need not assume that rats think. It is sufficient to say that the runway elicits an r_g.

Spence elevated the status of the $r_g - s_g$ mechansim by equating it with the concept of incentive. An organism's degree of incentive was said to depend on how strong the r_g was in a given situation. This gave incentive an anatomical location, a feature Hull's theory lacked. In addition, Spence revised Hull's famous multiplicative equation to give incentive itself a more prominent role:

$$E = H(D + K) \quad \text{(Spence omitted the subscripts)}$$

Recall that in Hulls' equation, if habit strength or drive were 0, reaction potential would be 0, no matter how high the organism's degree of incentive. Spence's equation implies that if habit strength were greater than 0, then all that would be necessary to activate reaction potential would be some degree of incentive; there need not be any drive. To demonstrate this implication, simply substitute numbers for the letters; for example, $K = 5$, $D = 0$, $H = 5$. What would such an effect be like in the "real world"? Suppose that you had regularly eaten at a restaurant and developed a strong r_g to the mere sight of the building (high incentive). You are now walking past the restaurant. Even if you have just eaten elsewhere (zero drive), you should have some inclination to stop at the restaurant and go inside.

The most radical change in Hull's theory introduced by Spence was the elimination of the Law of Effect in instrumental conditioning. Habit strength was said to depend simply on the number of times a response had been made to a stimulus (frequency principle). No longer was there a need to make the implausible distinctions mentioned earlier between zero rewards, tiny rewards, and large rewards.

Overall, perhaps the most enduring of Spence's contributions has been the advancement of the $r_g - s_g$ mechanism. It has played a major role in the development of neo-Hullian theory and has taken a wide variety of forms. For example, Amsel (1958; 1967) has employed a variation of $r_g - s_g$ in his very influential theory of frustration; he calls the mechanism the "fractional anticipatory frustration response" $(r_f - s_f)$. Kendler and Kendler (1962) used a variation of $r_g - s_g$ to explain differences in conceptual ability between children and adults. We shall be looking at their theory in detail in Chapter 8. All such theories based on the $r_g - s_g$ concept have two general features in common: (1) They distinguish between external behavior, which one can see, and internal behavior, which one ordinarily cannot see but must infer in some way. The internal behavior is said to **mediate,** or act as a bridge between, external stimuli and external responses: The external stimulus triggers an internal response (like r_g) with a stimulus component (like s_g) that produces the external response. (2) Internal mediating responses are governed by the same behavioral laws as external responses. This means that we can explain internal states and processes like "frustration" and "thinking" without inventing new principles. William of Ockham (the medieval philosopher who brandished the "razor") would surely have found that feature of the mediational approach appealing. By focusing attention on the $r_g - s_g$ mechanism, Spence did much to promote the extension of behavior theory to new areas of inquiry.

B. F. Skinner and radical behaviorism

Are theories of learning necessary? That question may have occurred to you at some point during the chapter. B. F. Skinner, whose work on operant conditioning we examined in Chapter 3, posed the same question to the entire field of psychology in a well-known paper (Skinner, 1950) and suggested that the answer was "No." Theories of learning were not necessary for doing research on learning. By a "theory," Skinner meant any explanation of behavior that appealed to processes inside the individual—be they processes of a mental, physiological, or conceptual nature. The latter category included intervening variables of all kinds, so that the argument applied with full force to behavioristic theories like those of Spence and Hull. The premise of the argument was that in the final analysis it was always necessary to specify the environmental conditions that had initiated an internal process. Anger does not explain hostile behavior; one must specify how the anger arose. "Habit" does not explain the rapid execution of routine acts; one must specify how the habit developed. Having specified the environmental conditions responsible for an internal state, why continue to refer to the internal state? One should not, says Skinner, if it is possible to predict and control the behavior on the basis of the environmental analysis alone.

Skinner's approach is truly a "radical behaviorism" (Skinner, 1974, pp. 16-18). It is radical in the sense that it makes behavior the exclusive focus of psychological research. This is not to say that it denies the existence of feelings or thoughts. Rather, it defines those processes as forms of behavior and insists that they be analyzed like any other behavior—in relation to the environment. That research can proceed along the lines Skinner suggested is evident from the many contributions of operant conditioning. How far such research can go before "theories" become necessary to predict and control behavior is an experimental question.

THE MANY FACES OF BEHAVIORISM

164

How many kinds of learning?

To reduce bookkeeping costs, a factory owner decides to institute a new, simplified system of paying workers. No longer will the owner keep records on workers' attendance. Instead, paychecks will be sent out at the end of the month regardless of who shows up for work. In all likelihood, this employer will end up saving not only on bookkeeping, but probably also on materials, utility bills, and rent, for with this new pay system he or she should not be in business very long. Obviously, a pay system that does not require work is bound to be ineffectual. We know from experience that rewards are effective precisely because we must do something to get them. Lower animals behave similarly. Skinner's operant conditioning apparatus (Chapter 3) released pellets into a dish only after the rats pressed the bar. Had the pellets been delivered every minute regardless of performance, the rats would have shown up punctually at the dish for their pellets but would have done very little bar pressing.

In the context of such observations, the phenomenon of conditioned reflexes seems incongruous. Consider the means by which Pavlov trained dogs to salivate in response to a bell. After ringing the bell, Pavlov gave the dogs food whether or not they reacted to the bell. Although salivation was not instrumental in producing food, the response was nevertheless conditioned. Or, consider the experiment by Bass and Hull (1934) discussed in Chapter 2, in which human subjects were shocked on one hand and their Galvanic Skin Response (GSR) was recorded on the other. You may recall that the GSR measures the extent to which a person sweats in response to an aversive stimulus. Just before the shock was administered, the experimenter applied a vibratory stimulus to a part of the body. After several pairings with the shock, the vibratory stimulus came to elicit the GSR, even though this response did not help the subjects avoid the shocks.

Classical conditioning and operant (instrumental) conditioning differ in another significant way. Suppose that we conducted discrimination training with a rat in a bar-pressing apparatus. A bell was our S^d, and training was carried out to a point that the rat pressed the bar at the instant we rang the bell. If the bell was off, the rat never pressed the bar. Superficially, the bar press resembles the conditioned salivary reaction of Pavlov's dogs. But look at the two situations more closely. In both cases, the food was an unconditioned stimulus; it elicited unconditioned responses involving salivation and chewing. In both cases, too, the bell acquired the power to evoke a new reaction. But what were the conditioned responses in the two situations? With classical conditioning, the conditioned response was the same as the unconditioned response, salivation. With operant conditioning, the conditioned response, bar pressing, was not the same as the unconditioned response.

Despite these fundamental differences between classical and operant conditioning, most of the theorists we've discussed so far have maintained that the processes of learning underlying the two procedures are identical. They have not proposed one set of laws for classical conditioning and another set of laws for operant conditioning. To support the position that there is only one kind of learning, a theorist could point out that classical and operant conditioning show many similar phenomena: extinction, spontaneous recovery, generalization, discrimination. Nevertheless, the procedures are so different that many psychologists, including Skinner, have adopted the view that there are two processes in learning, one represented by classical conditioning and the other by operant conditioning (Rescorla and Solomon, 1967). Learning in classical situations is said to be governed by the temporal relationship between the conditioned stimulus and the unconditioned stimulus. Learning in operant situations is said to be governed by the relationship between a conditioned response and its consequences.

Within the Hullian framework, O. H. Mowrer (b. 1907) has been the leading spokesman for a two-process view of learning. He expressed his concept of the relationship between classical and operant conditioning in the context of avoidance learning (Chapter 4). Classical conditioning was thought to be responsible for making the danger signal an aversive stimulus. The danger signal became aversive through repeated pairings with a painful stimulus, which initiated a powerful state of drive. For Mowrer, "drive *induction*," rather than "drive *reduction*," underlay acquisition of the fear response. The avoidance response itself was said to be the product of instrumental conditioning and drive reduction. When the subject responded in advance of the painful stimulus, the danger signal went off, reducing the subject's fear and reinforcing the response. Hull, of course, would say that drive reduction was the basis of learning in both classical and instrumental conditioning.

Historically, two-process theorists have also distinguished between classical and operant conditioning on the basis of the kinds of behavior with which the two procedures are effective. Operant conditioning has been said to be effective only with "skeletal" responses, the responses thought to be under voluntary control. Waving your arms, walking, talking, and turning your head are all skeletal responses. In contrast, responses of the interior organs like the salivary and sweat glands, heart, stomach, kidneys, and intestines have been regarded as modifiable only through classical conditioning. Such visceral activities are regulated by the primitive autonomic nervous system and are difficult to bring under voluntary control. Trying to salivate is a good illustration. This is not an activity you can perform simply by willing it, although you may be able to increase salivation by recalling a delicious meal you have had. However, this indirect strategy would essentially be an application of classical conditioning, for you would be administering to yourself a conditioned stimulus that in one way or another had become associated with food.

To say that visceral activities are modifiable only through classical conditioning is basically to say that they are insensitive to reward. Performing an experiment to see whether an organ can acquire a response through reward is more difficult methodologically than may be apparent. Suppose, for example, that an experimenter unfamiliar with the methodological pitfalls decided to pay you $10 every time your heart rate increased. The experimenter would lose a bundle of cash without resolving the issue because all you would have to do is perform a few deep-knee bends or push-ups. These skeletal responses are under voluntary control and directly influence heart rate. Although heart rate would increase, the change would not be due to direct reinforcement of visceral activity.

To do a credible study, one must ensure that the subject is unable to perform skeletal responses that influence the visceral activity being reinforced. There is a procedure one could use to selectively eliminate an organism's skeletal responses, but it creates another technical problem. By injecting an animal with the drug curare, one could paralyze all the voluntary muscles without affecting visceral activities. Since curarized animals cannot breathe on their own, it would be necessary to employ a mechanical respirator, but keeping the subject alive is not the major difficulty. The problem is this: If the animal were paralyzed, how could it obtain reinforcement? An ingenious solution to the problem was developed by Neil Miller (b. 1909) and his colleagues in an extensive series of studies on the operant conditioning of visceral responses (Miller, 1969).

Miller has had a long-standing interest in the question of whether classical and operant conditioning represent different learning processes. For many years he has played an active role in extending Hullian concepts to a wide variety of phenomena, although much less formally than was characteristic of Hull himself. His analysis of imitation in terms of drive, cue, response, and reward discussed in Chapter 5 is one example. Over the years, Miller has taken both one- and two-process positions, a reflection of the unsettled nature of the issue. However, the results of his visceral learning experiments were consistent with the one-process view. Miller used curarized rats as subjects, and for reinforcement stimulated parts of their brains sometimes referred to as "pleasure centers." It is known that stimulation of the pleasure centers will reinforce conventional operant responses such as bar presses. Miller's results indicated that stimulation of the pleasure centers could also reinforce many different kinds of visceral responses.

The experimental arrangement in Fig. 6.5 was designed for conditioning changes in heart rate. In a typical experiment, the heart rate is measured in successive observation intervals lasting several seconds. The operant level, or unconditioned rate, of response is first measured. Then, reinforcement is administered at the end of any observation interval in which heart rate increases by a certain percentage of the base rate. Initially the criterion for reinforcement is low, lying within the normal range of fluctuation. When this criterion is being met consistently, the experimenter raises the requirement for reinforcement. By reinforcing progressively higher responses rates, Miller indicated that he could achieve response levels as high as 13 percent above normal. Comparable reductions in heart rate were also shaped.

Miller anticipated the possible objection that changes in the behavior of a particular organ may simply reflect a general state of excitation or depression in physiological activity. To meet that objection, he recorded the behavior of organs other than the ones being reinforced, and reported that only the organs undergoing conditioning were affected. In the heart-rate experiment, for example, intestinal contractions underwent no systematic changes as heart rate increased or decreased.

THEORIES OF LEARNING IN HISTORICAL PERSPECTIVE

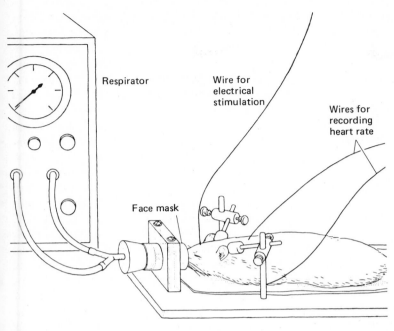

Fig. 6.5 Experimental arrangement for studying instrumental conditioning of heart rate in rats paralyzed by curare. Electrical stimulation of "pleasure center" in brain serves as reinforcement for appropriate changes in heart rate. Paralysis of muscles involved in breathing necessitates use of mechanical respirator. (From DiCara, 1970)

Other visceral activities Miller reported to be sensitive to reinforcement included salivary secretion, intestinal contractions, urine formation, blood pressure, and changes in blood-vessel diameter. How would the body benefit from the capacity of organs to learn through reinforcement? DiCara (1970) notes that the environment inside one's body must be finely regulated to maintain the individual's survival. Deviations from the norm quickly trigger mechanisms that restore the optimal environment. Shivering when the body temperature drops and sweating when the body temperature rises are familiar examples. Perhaps if an organ "accidentally" makes a response that corrects an internal disturbance, that response is reinforced and becomes more likely to occur in the future.

Since the original publication of the visceral learning experiments, Miller has had difficulty reproducing some of the results. The reasons for the discrepancies are not known and the problem is currently under investigation. Recent findings from other laboratories suggest that changes in heart rate can be reinforced provided that an appropriate shaping procedure is used (Black, Osborne, and Ristow, 1977). But the extent to which visceral learning through reward takes place without skeletal mediation remains to be documented (Miller, 1978).

THE MANY FACES OF BEHAVIORISM

On the practical side, Miller's studies have important implications for our understanding of psychosomatic disease. We should always be alert to the possibility that we can reinforce physiological disturbances by reacting to them inappropriately. The child who repeatedly stays home from school because of mild stomach upsets and receives lavish parental attention may acquire the stomach disorder as an attention-getting response. In the future, the condition may erupt whenever the child cannot obtain sufficient attention through other means.

Sometimes it is useful to be able to produce a physiological state. Individuals suffering from a variety of ailments have found that they can realize significant benefits by learning to increase their control of certain functions, and a strategy for learning called **biofeedback** is becoming increasingly popular as a form of clinical treatment for psychosomatic problems (Fuller, 1978). For example, by learning to increase the temperature of a finger relative to the temperature of the forehead, one can reduce the frequency, intensity, and duration of migraine headaches. Relief from tension headaches has been achieved by reducing tension in the frontalis muscle located in the forehead. In all biofeedback applications, the therapist presents a signal whenever the individual manages to produce a physiological change in the desired direction. This feedback acts as reinforcement for the physiological change and makes larger changes possible. Of course, no curare is administered and the individual is free to use any technique that works. Although we do not yet fully understand the learning processes underlying biofeedback, it is clear that we have only begun to exploit our powers of self-regulation.

THE GREAT BATTLES

So fundamental are the disagreements among the theorists we have considered that you may be wondering whether a single behavioristic perspective on learning really exists. Notwithstanding the many differences in viewpoints, several common features can be identified as characteristics of a behavioristic approach. First, the goal of all of the theories has been to explain what organisms *do*. Not all theories of learning have that objective. Traditionally, cognitive theorists have been less concerned with what organisms do than with what organisms *think*. Although objective experimentation eventually replaced introspection as the cognitivists' chief method of investigation, the study of behavior has never been an end in itself. For cognitive theorists, the end has been to advance our understanding of mental processes, and behavior has served as a means of making inferences about these processes. This difference between the objectives of cognitive and behavioristic theories has strongly influenced the kinds of behavior psychologists have selected for study. Cognitivists have always had a predilection for confronting subjects with complex problems which require them to think. Behaviorists have traditionally focused on behavior in simpler situations with the hope of clarifying the elementary processes assumed to be responsible for all learning, simple and complex.

Another common feature of theories we have considered is the belief that organisms learn responses to stimuli. The principles of frequency and recency, the

Law of Effect, the concept of habit strength—all were essentially statements about connections between stimuli and responses. Cognitive psychologists have traditionally taken the view that learning brings about changes in mental processes; these precede and are responsible for any changes in behavior.

A third feature of the behavioristic approach relates to the role of the subject in determining the course of learning. Behaviorists characteristically trace a subject's progress to the conditions of practice arranged by the experimenter. Cognitivists do not ignore these conditions but they tend to place greater emphasis on strategies for learning which the subject invents. It is sometimes said that behaviorists view the learner as a passive responder to events while cognitivists view the learner as an active contributor. This distinction is misleading. Nothing a subject does "just happens." Some combination of factors is always responsible for the adoption of a strategy, and one could argue that the strategy itself was a passive response to those factors. The distinction between cognitive and behavioristic perspectives on the role of the learner is best seen as a difference of opinion about what kinds of factors a theory of learning should emphasize.

Earlier in the chapter, three classic experiments were presented to illustrate the contrast between the behavioristic and cognitive perspectives on learning. If you have not yet attempted to predict the outcomes of the experiments, you may wish to do so before continuing. In this section we shall see what the outcomes were and how they were interpreted.

The problem of transposition (Experiment 1)

The pattern of dots below demonstrates a well-known perceptual phenomenon:

Instead of perceiving a row of 10 dots, we naturally organize the dots according to their proximity to one another and perceive them in groups of two. Another well-known perceptual effect is demonstrated by the following pattern:

Because of a tendency to group similar items, we perceive the open and closed dots in columns rather than in rows or in an unordered array. Proximity, similarity, and many other familiar principles of perceptual organization were the contributions of **gestalt psychology,** a movement founded during the early part of the century by Max Wertheimer (1880–1943) as an alternative to the prevailing "structuralist" school. Wertheimer's views on perception helped shape what we have called the "cognitive" perspective on learning.

THE GREAT BATTLES

It was the structuralists who aroused the ire of John B. Watson with their efforts to study consciousness. Wertheimer, too, sought to explore the nature of consciousness but he rejected the structuralist strategy of analyzing consciousness into its constituent sensations, feelings, and thoughts. In Wertheimer's view, what one experienced could only be understood by examining the relationships prevailing among the constituents. In other words, one had to do more than examine the parts; it was also necessary to consider how the parts were put together. Dots on a page were parts of your perceptual experience a moment ago, and you put those parts together on the basis of proximity and similarity. Without considering how the parts were related, we could not have understood the nature of the experience. Wertheimer used the German term "gestalt" (rough translation: "configuration," "form") in reference to such impressions of wholeness in a stimulus array.

Wolfgang Kohler (1887-1967) was an early colleague of Wertheimer who helped extend gestalt principles beyond the realm of perception. Kohler initiated a classic confrontation with the behaviorists on the question of automaticity in learning. His observations of problem solving in wild chimpanzees convinced him that Thorndike's conceptualization of learning as a "blind," trial-and-error process was grossly inadequate. Kohler argued that animals also had a capacity for **insight.** After surveying the relevant attributes of a problem, an animal eventually might discover how all the parts were related. The animal would then carry out the complete sequence of actions necessary for obtaining the goal without having been rewarded for the individual steps. One of Kohler's problems involved hanging a banana beyond reach of the chimps and placing a box nearby which could be used as a platform. Here is a description of the performance of Kohler's smartest chimp, Sultan:

> The objective was nailed to the roof in a corner, about two and a half metres distant from the box. All six apes vainly endeavored to reach the fruit by leaping up from the ground. Sultan soon relinquished this attempt, paced restlessly up and down, suddenly stood still in front of the box, seized it, tipped it hastily straight towards the objective, but began to climb upon it at a (horizontal) distance of half a metre, and springing upwards with all his force, tore down the banana. About five minutes had elapsed since the fastening of the fruit; from the momentary pause before the box to the first bite into the banana, only a few seconds elapsed, a perfectly continuous action after the first hesitation. (Kohler, 1925, pp. 39-40)

The pause in front of the box was important because it could have been the moment when Sultan discovered the relationship between the box and the banana. In analogous circumstances, we might imagine a human being thinking, "Aha, now I see!" That Sultan quickly proceeded to grab the fruit strengthens the impression that the pause was a period of discovery. Kohler found that animals that attained a solution through such insight also characteristically repeated the solution quickly on subsequent presentations of the problem. This was in marked contrast to the "stupidity" of Thorndike's cats, which required many trials to reach perfect performance.

Even more striking than the insight experiments were Kohler's experiments on discrimination learning (Kohler, 1918). "Experiment 1," at the beginning of this chapter, was an example. After being rewarded for choosing the medium gray card over the light gray card, the chimps were given a choice between the medium gray card and a dark gray card. From the behavioristic perspective, it seemed obvious that the chimps would select the medium gray card, since responses to that stimulus had previously been reinforced. Kohler made the opposite prediction—the chimps would choose the dark gray card. What was learned during the original training was not a connection between a stimulus and a response, but a relationship: the *darker* of the two stimuli was correct. Since the dark gray card was the darker stimulus on the test trial, that was the stimulus the chimps should have picked. Kohler was right; the chimps picked the darker card. They appeared to have learned a relationship rather than a connection. This sort of phenomenon has since been found many times under diverse conditions (e.g., Zeiler, 1963). It is called **transposition:** The subject transposes the relationship between the original pair of stimuli to a new pair of stimuli. The behaviorists wished to avoid the notion that animals perceived relationships because it seemed incompatible with the concept of stimulus-response learning. With just a few reasonable assumptions about the processes underlying discrimination learning, Spence (1936; 1937) showed how the dilemma could be resolved.

Spence's discrimination theory According to Spence the solution to the problem of transposition lay in the principle of stimulus generalization. In our discussion of Bass and Hull's (1934) experiment in Chapter 2 we saw that one could produce a gradient of stimulus generalization in two ways—by pairing the CS with the UCS (reinforcement gradient) and by presenting the CS without the UCS (extinction gradient). (See Fig. 2.4.) The reinforcement gradient endowed stimuli other than the CS with the power to elicit the response. The extinction gradient endowed stimuli other than the CS with the power to inhibit the response. Now, in discrimination training there is both reinforcement and extinction. Kohler's chimps received reinforcement for choosing the medium gray card and received no reinforcement for choosing the light gray card. Therefore, we should expect discrimination training to produce both excitatory and inhibitory gradients across the dimension of brightness. Spence asks us to imagine gradients like those in Fig. 6.6, and to assume that the net tendency to choose a card depends on how much higher the excitatory gradient is at that point on the dimension than the inhibitory gradient. You can see that on the test trial, the tendency to choose the dark gray card would be greater than the net tendency to choose the medium gray card. Thus, says Spence, there is no need to attribute to animals an ability to perceive relationships. Basic stimulus-response concepts can explain transposition.

Spence's theory of discrimination training became a frame of reference for decades of research on discrimination learning. Unfortunately, not all the facts fit this theory so neatly as did those of transposition. A major discrepancy is the phenomenon of **behavioral contrast** (Reynolds, 1961b). Suppose that pigeons

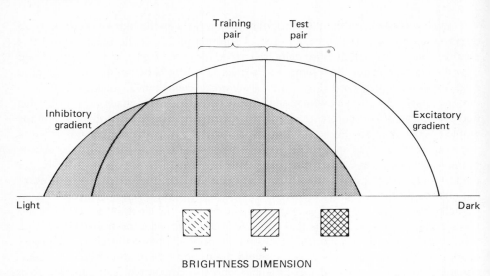

Fig. 6.6 How Spence explained the phenomenon of transposition without assuming that animals could perceive relationships. The stimuli used in training and test phases of procedure differ in brightness, as indicated by their locations on horizontal axis. During training, subject is reinforced for choosing medium gray card (+) but not for choosing light gray card (−). Reinforcement is said to create a tendency to approach stimuli resembling the medium gray card (excitatory gradient), while lack of reinforcement creates a tendency to avoid stimuli resembling the light gray card (inhibitory gradient). Wherever the two gradients overlap, there are tendencies to both approach and avoid the stimulus. Subjects' behavior depends on the difference between the excitatory and inhibitory gradients. When two stimuli are presented, that stimulus is chosen whose excitatory gradient exceeds its inhibitory gradient by the greater amount. Thus, by the end of training, subject consistently chooses medium gray card over light gray card. For the same reason, the subject subsequently chooses dark gray card over medium gray card during test, when selection of either stimulus produces reinforcement. (After Spence, 1937)

received reinforcement intermittently for pecking at a disc. Occasionally the disc was medium gray and occasionally it was light gray. After responding became stable, reinforcement was withheld in the presence of the light gray disc to build up an inhibitory gradient. What should happen to the response rate in the presence of the medium gray disc? Spence would expect response rate to decrease due to the spread of inhibition from the light gray disc. In actuality, response rate increases, a reflection of the contrast between the positive and negative stimuli. No theory incorporates all of the facts of discrimination learning, and it turns out that the reasons for transposition are more complex than either Spence or Kohler had assumed (Zeiler, 1963). The controversy over transposition demonstrates the advisability of retaining a healthy skepticism toward all theoretical positions, however appealing they may be.

THEORIES OF LEARNING IN HISTORICAL PERSPECTIVE

Where does learning take place? (Experiment 2)

During the great theoretical battles, the headquarters of the opposing camps were located at opposite ends of the country. For the behaviorists, the headquarters were at Yale University in Connecticut, where Clark Hull was a professor. The center of cognitive theory and research was at the University of California at Berkeley, where Edward C. Tolman (1886–1959) and his colleagues devised many ingenious tests of the competing viewpoints (Tolman, 1932; 1948; 1959).

Tolman was a unique figure, a blend of cognitive and behavioristic inclinations. His attitude toward methodology was indistinguishable from that of the behaviorists. He shared their concern for objectivity, and based his theoretical positions on careful measurements of behavior in experimental settings. Mental processes in Tolman's theory had the status of intervening variables, just as did habit strength, drive, and incentive in Hull's theory. What Tolman disputed was the premise that learning involved a direct modification of behavior. Learning took place in the mind, not in behavior. His studies of latent learning discussed in Chapter 1 were intended as demonstrations that learning could occur in the absence of behavior modification. The effect of learning was to produce certain expectations about the environment. For example, imagine a person driving to the supermarket along a familiar route. At an intersection with a large, lighted billboard, the driver "expects" that a right turn will bring him or her to another intersection with a gas station on the corner. Proceeding past the gas station, the driver expects to come eventually to a shopping center. Just beyond the shopping center will be the supermarket. Experience has taught the driver relationships among the various locations; he or she has a kind of cognitive map of the area. Experience has *not* taught him or her to make right turns and left turns.

"Experiment 2," described at the beginning of this chapter, was conducted by Tolman, Ritchie, and Kalish (1946) to assess the adequacy of the cognitive-map concept. The question they posed was this: Do rats learn the *location* of the goal box in a maze, or do they learn the specific sequence of *movements* leading to the goal box? In other words, does experience in the maze result in "place learning" or in "response learning"? Recall that the maze they used was cross-shaped, with two start boxes at opposite ends of one alley and two goal boxes at opposite ends of the other alley (Fig. 6.1). Rats were placed in start box 1 on a random half of the trials and in start box 2 on the other half of the trials. Group A always found food in goal box 1. Rats in Group B found food in goal box 1 when they ran from start box 1, and found food in goal box 2 when they ran from start box 2. In other words, a right turn at the choice point led to food on every trial. Tolman expected Group A to learn faster. Having food in one location throughout the experiment should have facilitated the acquisition of a "cognitive map," an organism's natural mode of learning. From the perspective of stimulus-response theory, Group B should have learned faster. Making a right turn at the choice point on every trial would be expected to facilitate acquisition of a series of movements. Tolman was right; Group A learned faster. Apparently, experience in a maze resulted in place learning rather than response learning.

Because of its theoretical importance, the experiment was later repeated by other investigators with various modifications in the procedure. It was discovered that under certain conditions the results were just the opposite of what Tolman had found. Place learning was slower than response learning if cues outside the maze did not permit an adequate discrimination between left and right. Performance in the cross-maze did not clearly favor the cognitive or the behavioristic interpretation. Nevertheless, as the problem was originally formulated, it did reveal Tolman's approach to learning very well. Like Kohler, Tolman conceptualized learning as a change in the organism's mental representation of a problem. The effect of experience was to teach the organism how relevant features of the problem were related. This emphasis on relational learning remains a hallmark of the cognitive perspective in learning theory.

The role of the learner (Experiment 3)

For Tolman, the rat in a maze was a kind of scientist. Learning the relationships necessary for attaining the goal was a matter of devising hypotheses about the correct path and testing them out against experience. Thorndike had emphasized the random appearance of behavior during the period preceding solution of a problem. Tolman believed that the appearance of randomness was more a result of how one observed the behavior than of how learning took place. When observed closely, behavior during the presolution period was not random but systematic.

"Experiment 3," described at the beginning of this chapter, provided the first clear evidence for "hypothesis-testing" in lower animals. It was conducted by Krechevsky (1932b), a colleague of Tolman at the University of California. Recall that the rats traversed a runway consisting of four compartments (Fig. 6.2). Each compartment had two exit paths, only one of which was open on any given trial. There was no way that the rat could learn the correct path to the goal, for the positions of the open paths varied from trial to trial in an unpredictable manner. To add to the complexity, one of the paths in each compartment was lit brighter than the other, the position of the brighter path varying randomly across trials independently of the open path. Despite the random nature of the problem, each of nine subjects performed in a systematic way. On one day, a rat might choose the left path consistently (i.e., more than would be expected by chance). On another day, the same rat might choose the darker path consistently. Choice of a particular route seemed to reflect an "hypothesis" about the way to reach the goal. When one hypothesis was disconfirmed by experience, that hypothesis was rejected in favor of another. Only by observing the performances of individual subjects could the patterns be detected. Looking at the averages for the entire group was uninformative. In a related study, Krechevsky (1932a) found that such hypothesis-testing was also characteristic of rats during the presolution period of solvable problems.

The conceptualization of learners as inventors of hypotheses and strategies continues to be a hallmark of cognitivism, although modern cognitive theorists have a very different frame of reference than did Krechevsky, Tolman, and Kohler. In the days of the "great battles," animal behavior, particularly the behavior of rats, was the focus of attention. What an animal did under the influence of an experimental variable was assumed to represent in a simplified way what a human being would do in analogous circumstances. Today, the computer has replaced the rat as a model of human learning in cognitive theories. The processes by which computers convert inputs into outputs are assumed to represent in a general way the mental processes responsible for learning. Cognitivists borrow freely from the terminology and concepts of computer science, and their theories often have the appearance of computer flow charts. This orientation toward learning theory is known as the **information processing** approach, and we shall see many examples of it in later chapters, particularly Chapters 10 and 11 on the topic of memory. While information processing is the predominant framework for modern cognitive theory, to equate information processing with cognitivism would be a mistake. The computer is the current vehicle for expression of cognitive principles, but it, like the rat, can be replaced. Some time in the future a better model of learning may materialize. What is most enduring in cognitivism, and behaviorism as well, is to be found in the views of the early theorists. That is why we have taken this tour through the history of theories of learning.

INSTINCT: THE PENDULUM SWINGS BACK (A LITTLE)

Rejection of mental processes as explanations for behavior was one tenet of John B. Watson's behaviorism. Another tenet was the rejection of instincts. He expressed his contempt for heredity and his boundless faith in humankind's potential for learning with the famous challenge, "Give me a dozen healthy infants . . ." For decades, the behavioristic attitudes toward instincts and the mind dominated psychological theory. Discussion of these topics was widely regarded as unproductive. The rapid growth of the cognitive psychology movement during recent years has restored to the human mind the status it had before the advent of behaviorism. Paralleling this development, the subject of instinct has again become a focal point of interest and controversy. There is growing concern among behaviorists about the adequacy of traditional conceptualizations of the processes of learning. In previous chapters we have encountered several cases in which biological factors have set limits on the generality of behavioral principles. Studies on the conditioning of taste aversions discussed in Chapter 2 revealed important exceptions to the principle of temporal contiguity. The phenomenon of "instinctive drift" described by the Brelands (Chapter 4) placed a limitation on the principle of reinforcement. As the list of anomalies has grown longer, calls for reformulation of behavioral principles have grown louder (e.g., Seligman, 1970; Herrnstein, 1977. For a cogent reply to Herrnstein, see Skinner, 1977).

Watson would not necessarily have objected to the revival of interest in instinct. His attack on instinct was directed primarily at the practice of explaining behavior by inventing labels. No one has suggested a return to that practice. Indeed, as a consequence of the controversy, experimental research on biological factors has accelerated and many important new facts have been established. There is a danger, however, that the pendulum will swing too far, that psychologists will attach more importance to the exceptions than to the rules. We should be alert to that danger, for it is as undesirable to abandon a principle prematurely as it is to push a principle beyond its limits.

SUMMARY

Two general orientations characterize research in the psychology of learning: the behavioristic and the cognitive. These orientations are reflected in the kinds of variables and issues a researcher chooses to emphasize. They are not unitary theories, as within each approach there is a great diversity of viewpoints. The primary feature distinguishing behaviorism from cognitivism is the researcher's attitude toward mental processes. Cognitivists attribute learning to mental processes and make them the focus of study. Behaviorists attribute learning to environmental influences and generally avoid reference to the mind. During the first half of the century, experiments often were designed with the objective of testing the validity of the two approaches. These experiments were not decisive, but they did serve the useful purpose of clarifying the differing expectations of cognitivists and behaviorists concerning the course of learning in a variety of situations. Today the two approaches are better seen as complementary than as competitive, as together they have encouraged a more comprehensive investigation of learning than would have been possible with either approach alone.

Watson invented the term "behaviorism" and for years was the leading spokesman for the movement. He criticized two common practices of the day: (1) the use of introspection to study consciousness—data from this technique often were inconsistent and it was impossible to check the accuracy of observers' reports; (2) the explanation of behavior in terms of instincts—it was customary to apply labels to behavior and regard the labels as explanations. Watson objected that the practice discouraged investigation of the factors that had actually produced the behavior. From these methodological issues, Watson developed substantive ones. He rejected not just introspection but the concept of mind; and he rejected not just the practice of labeling, but the notion that biological heritage was a major determinant of behavior. His theory of learning was based on the conditioned reflex concept, and emphasized two principles: (1) *frequency*—the more a response is made to a stimulus, the more likely it is that the response will be repeated if the stimulus is presented again; (2) *recency*—other factors equal, the last response to a stimulus will be the one most likely to occur if the stimulus is presented again. Watson rejected the concept of reward as an explanatory principle, focusing on the temporal contiguity between stimuli and responses.

Guthrie's theory of learning also rejected the principle of reward. It relied on a kind of recency principle to explain all learning: "a combination of stimuli which has been accompanied by a movement will on its recurrence tend to be followed by that movement." Theoretically, the bond between a stimulus and a response emerged at full strength on the first occasion that the stimulus and response were paired. However, it was not usually possible to predict the occurrence of a response with certainty for two reasons: (1) the stimulus situations on two occasions were rarely identical; (2) the behavior one saw consisted of many finely coordinated movements, each of which had to be executed at the proper time. An important corollary of Guthrie's principle of learning was that of "associative inhibition," which stated that every time a response was learned, another response was unlearned. Associative inhibition has practical implications for the development of procedures to eliminate unwanted behavior.

"Hedonism" is a centuries-old philosophy which asserts that each individual strives to maximize pleasure and minimize pain. Thorndike injected hedonism into behavior theory with his Law of Effect. Originally, it consisted of two parts: (1) If a stimulus is followed by a response and then by a satisfying state of affairs, the connection between stimulus and response increased in strength. (2) If a stimulus is followed by a response and then by an annoying state of affairs, the connection between stimulus and response decreased in strength. "Satisfiers" and "annoyers" were defined in terms of their effects on behavior, not in terms of feelings. Organisms acted to maintain or renew satisfiers, and to remove annoyers. In the revised Law of Effect, Thorndike dropped the second part pertaining to the effect of annoyers. What made the Law of Effect theoretically innovative was its implication that learning was a mechanical process in which connections between stimulus and response were gradually stamped in or stamped out. Thorndike advanced the view that problem-solving was reducible to trial-and-error learning and did not involve reasoning or understanding.

The most formal of behavioristic theories was that of Hull, who adopted a plan similar to that of Euclidean geometry. The theory started with a few broad postulates about behavior, and from these deduced a larger number of theorems which were sufficiently specific to predict behavior in given settings. The goal of the theory was to express laws of behavior as equations so that predictions would be quantitatively precise. The terms in Hull's equations represented "intervening variables," conceptualized internal states assumed to underlie the effects of independent variables on dependent variables. The three major intervening variables were: *reaction potential* ($_sE_R$—the net tendency to respond), *habit strength* ($_sH_R$—the strength of the connection between a stimulus and response), and *drive* (D—a general activating force). Each intervening variable was operationally defined in terms of experimental procedures or aspects of performance. The equation relating these variables to one another was: $_sE_R = _sH_R \times D$, which implied that both habit strength and drive were necessary for a response to occur. Although the theory accumulated considerable experimental support, it fared poorly on a central assumption—that a reduction in need or drive following a response was necessary for learning. It was largely on account of this issue that Hull's theory lost its appeal.

Many contemporary behavior theories incorporate elements of Hull's formulation but are much narrower in scope. These are the so-called "neo-Hullian" theories. Spence's theory was particularly important because it did much to pro-

SUMMARY

178

mote the extension of Hullian concepts to new areas of inquiry, for example, the areas of thinking and frustration. It did this by giving greater prominence to a concept which Hull introduced but did not fully develop—the fractional anticipatory goal response (r_g). Intended as an alternative to the cognitive concept of expectancy, the r_g concept has had a broad range of applications. Theories based on r_g have two general features in common: (1) they distinguish between external behavior and internal behavior; the latter is inferred from the former; (2) the theories assume that internal mediating behavior is governed by the same laws as external behavior.

B. F. Skinner is a proponent of a radical form of behaviorism which rejects any explanation of behavior that appeals to processes going on inside the organism. The rationale is that such processes must in turn be explained in terms of the conditions which produced them. Having done that, one need no longer refer to the internal process, for the analysis at the environmental level would be sufficient to predict and control behavior.

Another source of disagreement among behaviorists is the question of whether classical and instrumental conditioning represent two learning processes or one. Two-process theorists have long assumed that operant conditioning is effective only with skeletal responses, those actions under voluntary control. Visceral responses—responses of interior organs—have been considered to be modifiable only through classical conditioning. To demonstrate operant conditioning of visceral responses is technically difficult because of the possibility that subjects may acquire skeletal responses that can influence the visceral responses under study. Miller and his colleagues solved the problem by paralyzing the skeletal system of rats and administering reinforcement in the form of electrical stimulation of the brain. Initial reports indicated successful operant conditioning of visceral responses, results supporting the one-process view. However, subsequent studies have generally failed to reproduce these findings and the visceral learning issue remains unresolved.

Despite their differences, the major behavioristic theories have several basic features in common: (1) the goal of the theories has been to explain what organisms *do;* (2) the theories have assumed that learning brings about a change in an organism's response to the environment; (3) the theories have traced a subject's progress during an experiment to conditions of practice arranged by the experimenter. In contrast, cognitive theories: (1) have as their primary objective the study of thinking; (2) assume that learning brings about a change in mental process; these precede and are responsible for any changes in behavior; (3) emphasize the strategies for learning invented by the subject. Tolman's formulation was the most influential of early cognitive theories, and was the one most often pitted against behavioristic theories. Another major figure was Kohler, who applied gestalt principles of perception to problems in learning, and vigorously opposed Thorndike's conceptualization of problem-solving as a blind, trial-and-error process. Kohler suggested that animals had the capacity for insight. After surveying the relevant parts of a problem, an animal might suddenly discover how the parts were related and execute the entire sequence of movements necessary for obtaining the goal without having been reinforced for them.

Three classic experiments were described to illustrate the contrasting views of cognitivists and behaviorists. The experiments together with the issues involved were: (1) *Transposition:* relational (cognitive) learning vs. stimulus-response learning; (2) *Place vs. response learning:* does learning bring about a change in behavior or a change in mental processes?; (3) *Hypothesis-testing in rats:* To what extent does the subject contribute to the course of learning by inventing strategies?

Just as there has been a revival of interest in mental processes in recent years, so has there been a revival of interest in instinct. However, the methods of investigation today differ greatly from those in the past. Experimentation has replaced introspection in the case of mental processes, and has replaced the circular practice of labeling in the case of instinct. The result has been an enrichment of knowledge about the processes of learning.

STUDY QUESTIONS

1. "Give me a dozen healthy infants. . . ." What basic tenet of behaviorism was Watson expressing in this famous challenge?

2. Define "cognition." What is the objective of a specialist in learning who has a cognitive orientation?

3. Why might it be said that Watson's role in the history of learning theory was more that of a publicist for behaviorism than that of a theorist?

4. How did many psychologists of Watson's day commit the "nominal fallacy" when attempting to explain behavior in terms of instincts? Give an example.

5. According to Watson, what were the two requirements for an adequate analysis of behavior? Give an example from Watson's analysis of reflexes in infants. What two sorts of questions should psychologists be able to answer? Why are these goals now considered unrealistic?

6. Describe the procedure Watson used to teach an infant to say "da." How does the procedure resemble classical conditioning? In what two ways does it differ?

7. State Watson's principles of recency and frequency. Illustrate using the example of the child and the problem box. Explain how this analysis of the child's behavior eliminates the concept of reward as an explanatory principle. What unusual prediction would Watson have to make?

8. State the rule known as "Occam's Razor." How is it applied in developing explanations in science?

9. State Guthrie's principle of learning.

10. How would Guthrie explain the fact that in Watson's experiment the child did not master the task on the second trial? (Answer has two parts, one related to the nature of a stimulus, the other related to the nature of a response.)

11. State Guthrie's principle of associative inhibition. Describe the three techniques Guthrie recommends for breaking unwanted habits. Give an example of each technique. According to Guthrie, how should punishment be used to maximize its effectiveness? Give an example.

12. How did Guthrie's experiment with cats in a puzzle box support his theory. In what way was Seward's experiment with rats in a bar-pressing apparatus inconsistent with the theory?

13. In what sense were Watson and Guthrie "contiguity" theorists?

14. What is the basic principle of the philosophy of hedonism?

15. In Thorndike's experiments with cats in a puzzle box, what aspects of performances suggested that the cats learned in a "stupid" manner? How would the cats have performed if they had truly understood the solution to the problem? Why were the results surprising at that time?

16. State Thorndike's original Law of Effect (two parts). How were "satisfying" and "annoying" states of affairs defined? Why did many behaviorists of the day reject the Law of Effect? How did Thorndike later modify the Law?

17. In what way did the plan of Hull's theory resemble that of Euclidean geometry?

18. How does the scope of theories today compare with that of Hull's theory?

19. How did Hull generally define: "habit strength," "drive," "reaction potential"? What two conditions had to exist for a response to occur? As habit strength or drive increased, what was the expected effect on reaction potential? Explain how the formula, $_sE_R = {_s}H_R \times D$, expresses these relationships. Illustrate by substituting numbers for the letters.

20. How did Hull *operationally* define "habit strength," "drive," and "reaction potential"? Explain how the results of the Perin-Williams experiment supported Hull's multiplicative rule. Do this by: (a) substituting numbers into the equation to illustrate the expected relationship between drive and habit strength; (b) stating the procedure and results of the experiment; (c) indicating another relationship that could have been found.

21. What central assumption of the theory was not generally supported by experimental findings?

22. What are "neo-Hullian" theories?

23. How did Hull define "incentive" and relate it to drive and habit strength? How did he use this conceptualization to explain the results of latent learning experiments?

24. What were Spence's two objections to Hull's concept of incentive?

25. Describe Hull's concept of the "fractional anticipatory goal response" (r_g). Indicate how he would use the r_g concept to explain a rat's running from the start box of a runway to the goal box. Why would Hull be reluctant to say that the rat runs "because it expects to find food in the goal box"?

26. How did Spence use r_g to solve one of the problems he saw in Hull's theory? How did he solve the other problem? How did Spence's behavior equation differ from Hull's?

27. State the two features of mediational theories. In what sense are they consistent with Occam's Razor?

28. What does Skinner mean by the term "theory"? What is his view on the question of whether such theories are necessary for doing research in learning? In his view, how should thoughts and feelings be analyzed? In what sense is his approach a radical form of behaviorism?

29. State two procedural differences between classical and instrumental conditioning. What are the "one-process" and "two-process" theories of learning?

30. What distinction have two-process theorists made concerning the kinds of behavior with which classical and instrumental conditioning are effective?

31. What technical problem arises in attempting to demonstrate instrumental conditioning of visceral responses? How did Miller solve the problem? What were Miller's initial findings? What is the current status of research on instrumental conditioning of visceral responses?

32. What is "biofeedback"? Give an example of how the technique might be used to reduce tension in the frontalis muscle of the forehead. How does the biofeedback procedure resemble operant conditioning? How does biofeedback research differ from research designed to test operant conditioning of visceral responses?

33. State three features of the behavioristic and cognitive approaches to learning.

34. How did the gestalt approach to the study of perception differ from the structuralist approach? Illustrate the gestalt approach using the example of the principles of proximity and similarity.

35. According to Kohler, what are the characteristics of problem-solving through insight? What does Kohler's conceptualization of insight have in common with the gestalt conceptualization of perception? How does Kohler's view of problem-solving differ from Thorndike's?

36. Describe the procedure and results of the transposition experiment involving the chimpanzee. Why did these results suggest that relational learning occurred rather than stimulus-response learning?

37. Describe Spence's behavioristic solution to the problem of transposition. Do this by: (a) defining "excitatory" and "inhibitory" gradients. Illustrate these concepts by referring to the procedures used by Bass and Hull discussed in Chapter 2; (b) drawing the excitatory and inhibitory gradients assumed to be generated during training. Label the horizontal axis and indicate the positions of the positive and negative stimuli on this dimension. Also show the position of the third stimulus used in the test of transposition; (c) stating what factor causes the subject to choose one card over another; (d) explaining why the chimps should choose the darker stimulus in the test.

38. Define "behavioral contrast." How is this phenomenon inconsistent with Spence's theory of discriminating learning?

182

39. In what ways was Tolman's theory of learning behavioristic? What assumption of behaviorism did Tolman reject?

40. Describe the procedure used in the experiment on response learning vs. place learning. State the cognitive and behavioristic predictions, and the rationales behind them. What were the results of the experiment? How must the conclusions be qualified?

41. Describe the procedure used by Krechevsky to study hypothesis-testing in rats. What was the nature of the evidence from which hypothesis-testing was inferred? What sort of performance would be expected from a behavioristic point of view?

42. What is the "information-processing" approach to learning? What is the distinction between information processing and cognitivism?

43. How is the method of studying instinct today different from that which Watson criticized?

CHAPTER 7
Verbal Learning

Your ability to read this sentence is the product of many years of development. It is one of your most important accomplishments, and yet perhaps the accomplishment which you least recognize as such. To extract meaning from a sequence of visual patterns, as you are now doing, requires skills of intricate complexity. You can readily grasp their complexity when you consider the relatively simple skills with which you started. In your early stages of development, "reading" consisted simply of word recognition. When you saw the letters C-A-T on the chalkboard or the flashcard, you responded with the sound "cat." When you saw D-O-G, you responded with "dog." Associations between visual patterns and sounds grew, and eventually your primitive vocabulary enabled you to read short sentences. These sentences, in turn, opened the way to comprehension of passages and books.

For many children, recognizing words is a difficult and frustrating task. These difficulties create a serious educational problem because word recognition skills must be mastered before any further development can occur. Consequently, educators have worked intensively with a wide variety of techniques to find the most efficient way of teaching word recognition skills. You probably can recall some of the techniques you experienced. "Sounding the word out" is the **phonics** approach. The child learns that individual letters and various groups of letters stand for specific sounds. Word recognition involves stringing together the constituent sounds of the word. The **sight-word** approach teaches the child to recognize words as complete visual patterns. In one sight-word technique, the child studies the word on a flashcard while the teacher pronounces the word. The child links the sound to the entire pattern without attempting to break the word down. In another technique, the teacher displays pictures of objects together with their names conspicuously about the classroom. All such methods of teaching word recognition skills have a common objective—the formation of links between sounds and visual patterns. These methods represent some of our earliest verbal learning experiences. Later, verbal learning takes the form of reading comprehension—the extraction of meaning from passages. In the present chapter we investigate the processes that underlie both forms of verbal learning.

LEARNING WORDS THROUGH PICTURES: HOW MUCH IS A PICTURE REALLY WORTH?

For adults, a picture may be worth a thousand words, but for some children a picture may not be worth even one word. Intuitively, we might expect pictures to be helpful in teaching word recognition skills. For example, a teacher employing the sight-word approach might consider adding pictures to flashcards. Seeing the picture should prompt the child to say the word, and thereby increase his or her involvement in the learning process. However, experiments that have focused on this question have shown that the inclusion of pictures on flashcards may actually hinder learning. These studies demonstrate more generally that the attachment of verbal responses to stimuli is a complex process, one that requires a close, detailed analysis.

Samuels (1967) tested three teaching methods with pre-first graders. With each method the words "boy," "bed," "man," and "car" were typed on separate index cards. Some children saw these words without any additional visual aids. Other children, who served in a "simple picture" condition, saw on the card a black-and-white line drawing of the object to which the word referred. Children in the "complex picture" condition saw a full-color picture taken from a reading primer. This picture was complex in that it depicted several objects in addition to the one represented by the word. For example, the picture for "boy" showed a boy holding a dog and pointing to a horse in the distance. There were two kinds of trials. On "learning trials," the experimenter presented each card for four seconds during which the child was to say the word. At the end of the interval the experimenter pronounced the word. Immediately following a learning trial the experimenter conducted a "test trial" in which the words were presented individually for four seconds *without pictures*. The child was required to say the word as on learning trials, but no feedback was given at the end of the interval. Samuels found that over the 10 learning trials the cards with pictures produced more correct responses than those without pictures; the pictures were effective prompts. But over the 10 test trials—in which no pictures were present—children who had seen pictures on learning trials made fewer correct responses than children who had not seen pictures. Apparently, the pictures diverted attention from the words, so that the child often failed to associate the word he or she pronounced with the word on the card.

A similar problem arises in reading instruction at a more advanced level. Reading primers often contain pictures to motivate interest, but the presence of pictures may be a distraction for some children. Samuels (1967) compared the effectiveness of illustrated and nonillustrated reading primers with first graders. The story, entitled "Fun at Blue Lake," was 106 words long and included 50 different words. Since the children had been in the first grade for seven months, they should have been familiar with some of the words, and so a pretest was conducted. The 50 words comprising the story were each shown for 10 seconds, during which the child was to say the word if possible. Groups receiving illustrated and nonillustrated stories were equated for familiarity with the words on the basis of these pretest scores. The illustrated materials consisted of printed text on the right-hand page and a complex picture on the left. The picture showed a family with their dog beside a lake. In the background was a cabin in a wooded area. The nonillustrated materials substituted a blank page for this picture. The teacher conducted a standard reading lesson, first discussing the background of the story to create interest, then introducing periods of silent and oral reading. Assistance with words was provided when children asked for help. Immediately after the lesson, recognition of the 50 words was again tested. Samuels found that "good" readers—those children above the median on the pretest—were unaffected by the pictures; good readers who saw pictures recognized as many words as good readers who did not see pictures. On the other hand, poor readers who saw pictures did worse than poor readers who did not see pictures. For these children the pictures were distracting. Thus, while pictures may be useful for motivating children, teachers who use them in remedial instruction may be defeating their purpose. Not all visual techniques have this disadvantage, however. Certain techniques do appear to assist verbal learning in children with a minimum of distraction. In addition to being useful educationally, they are significant from a theoretical standpoint, for they are an application of a principle of fundamental significance for the psychology of learning. This principle serves to broaden our understanding of a concept discussed many times in previous chapters, the concept of an "association."

The nature of an association

To recognize a word, one must associate a visual pattern with a verbal response. But what, precisely, is an association? For behaviorists, the term "association" is almost synonymous with the term "contiguity"; if two events are experienced together in space or time, a connection will form between them. Thus the conditioned stimulus which has occurred contiguously with the unconditioned stimulus comes to elicit a conditioned response; the lever-press response which has occurred contiguously with reinforcement increases in probability. With the revival of cognitive psychology, however, the concept of association has undergone some redefinition. Solomon Asch (1969) has proposed that contiguity is just one of many conditions that promote associations. Indeed, in Asch's view, contiguity is the least important condition.

In the "real world" we seldom experience events in a condition of sheer contiguity. Events usually stand in some more complex relation to one another. The cat sits *on* the chair; the refrigerator appears *larger* than the dishwasher; the bat *hits* the ball. Contiguity does exist between these objects, but the relations between them are more conspicuous. According to Asch, the effects of relations are not reducible to contiguity, and to fully understand the associative process we must focus directly upon relations.

Asch's emphasis on relations, as contrasted with contiguity, is not without precedent. Recall from Chapter 6 that the debate between behaviorists and cognitivists on the question of transposition also involved relations. An animal would learn to discriminate between a dark stimulus, X, and a lighter stimulus, Y, approaching X while avoiding Y. Cognitivists maintained that the animal learned to choose the *darker* of the two stimuli—a relation. Behaviorists maintained that the animal learned to approach X and avoid Y without seeing the relationship between them. By making a few simple assumptions, Spence (1937) showed how the behavioristic view could explain the results of transposition experiments involving different sets of stimuli. Now, in the context of verbal learning, we see a revival of the cognitive position. Indeed, throughout this book, as we encounter new and diverse research areas we shall be able to recognize extensions of the older behavioristic and cognitive positions. While the research areas of interest to psychologists have changed markedly over the years, the older theoretical orientations have retained their identities.

What evidence is there that relationships between stimuli promote associations between them? Asch (1969) reported a series of experiments indicating that people more readily associate stimuli that are related than stimuli that are simply contiguous, or paired. The visual patterns shown in Fig. 7.1 provide an example of this phenomenon. On the right side of the figure are sets of paired patterns. The "squiggly" line in the top row is paired with the short, vertical stroke; the "step-ladder" pattern in the center row is paired with the curved line; and the "backwards S" in the bottom row is paired with the column of circles. The only relationship between the elements of a pair is contiguity. On the left side of the figure the stimulus elements "come together" to form a unitary pattern. In addition to being contiguous to one another, the elements bear a more complex relationship—they are parts of a whole. Asch asked one group of subjects to study a series of paired patterns and another group to study a series of unitary patterns. The subjects saw each unit or pair for four seconds and then attempted to draw them all from memory in any

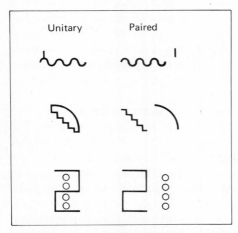

Fig. 7.1 Examples of "unitary" and "paired" designs presented to subjects in study of associative learning. (From Asch, 1969)

order. Asch found that subjects who saw the elements in a unit produced almost twice as many of the elements than subjects who saw the stimuli in pairs. The quality of relatedness greatly facilitated learning.

Perhaps you already see the application to teaching word recognition. Instead of presenting the picture and word separately on the flashcard, why not tie the picture and letters together in some way? In other words, try to *relate* the two patterns physically. This technique, called **accentuation,** is indeed effective. Some examples of it appear in Fig. 7.2. They are from a study by Lippman and Shanahan (1973), which employed third-grade children as subjects. Since these children already had sizable vocabularies, Lippman and Shanahan tested the accentuation technique in an indirect way. The words to which the children responded were not actually words, but *paralogs*, meaningless, two-syllable units. For example, DELPHIN stood for "pail," SAGROLE stood for "clock," and VOLVAP stood for "candy." In the accentuation technique, one or more letters of a word are modified to look like the object referred to. This can be done in three ways. Paralog A in Fig. 7.2 represents the "superimposition" procedure; the letters D-E-L-P-H-I-N are placed inside a picture of a pail. Paralog B uses the "one-letter" procedure; the "O" in SAGROLE looks like a clock. Paralog C is an example of the "inclusion" procedure; all of the letters in VOLVAP include stripes, a feature associated with candy canes. In each procedure—superimposition, one-letter, and inclusion—the word and the picture form a unitary pattern, much as the stimulus elements did in Asch's experiment.

Fig. 7.2 Three types of "accentuation" evaluated in study of word-recognition learning: A, superimposition; B, one-letter; C, inclusion. Subjects' task was to associate the paralogs in each case with the words represented by the pictures. DELPIN was to be associated with PAIL, SAGROLE with CLOCK, and VOLVAP with CANDY. (From Lippman and Shanahan, 1973)

Lippman and Shanahan compared the effectiveness of the accentuation technique with the effectiveness of simple line drawings and of "words" without visual aids. The children saw a series of nine cards, three of which presented paralogs without visual aids, three of which showed pictures plus paralogs, and three of which employed accentuation. The procedure included two types of trials. On "study trials" the experimenter presented the card and simultaneously pronounced the word for which the paralog stood. Immediately following a study trial, the experimenter conducted a multiple-choice "test trial." The nine paralogs appeared on a list together with the nine possible words, and the children circled their choices. Lippman and Shanahan found that over five test trials, paralogs accentuated by inclusion (such as VOLVAP in Fig. 7.2) gave more correct responses than paralogs presented in any other manner. In fact, the inclusion procedure was the only effective one. Paralogs accentuated by superimposition or one-letter designs, and paralogs presented with a line drawing, gave no more correct responses than paralogs without visual aids. We see then that appropriate use of the principle of relatedness can assist the learning process. Later in the chapter we shall explore other dimensions of this principle.

METHODS IN THE STUDY OF VERBAL LEARNING

How rapidly a subject learns verbal responses depends critically on how the experimenter presents material. Methods of presentation take many forms but they generally fall into two categories: the **paired-associate procedure** and the **serial-anticipation procedure.**

Paired-associate learning

Most of the experiments discussed thus far have employed the paired-associate procedure. The subjects have encountered stimuli two at a time and attempted to link one stimulus with the other. To measure the degree of learning, the experimenter has presented the first stimulus alone for a period of time during which the subject has tried to respond with the second stimulus. For example, in the experiment by Lippman and Shanahan (1973) on accentuation, the stimulus items were printed paralogs and the response items were words spoken by the experimenter. Stimulus and response items were presented together during a study trial, after which the stimulus items appeared alone during a test trial.

As an alternative to this "study-test" method of presentation, one could use an "anticipation" method (this is different from the serial-anticipation procedure which we shall soon examine). Unlike the study-test method, the anticipation method involves only one type of trial. The experimenter presents the stimulus item alone for several seconds during which the subject tries to anticipate the response item. At the end of the interval, the response item appears, giving the subject feedback on his or her response and an opportunity to examine the complete pair. Figure 7.3, left and middle columns, illustrates the distinction between the anticipation and study-test methods.

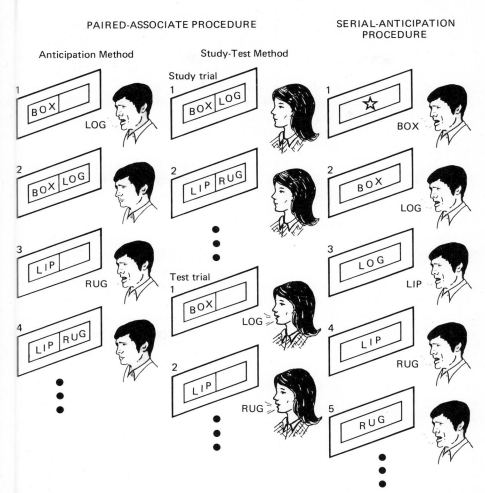

Fig. 7.3 How items are presented to subjects using the paired-associate and serial anticipation procedures. In the examples illustrated, it is assumed that the subject is already familiar with the list. The paired-associate procedure has two versions, the anticipation method (left column) and the study-test method (center column). In the former, the stimulus item of a pair initially appears by itself and the subject attempts to state the associated response item (frame 1). Then the response item appears, giving the subject an opportunity to study the two items together (frame 2). Following this study period, the stimulus item of the next pair appears by itself (frame 3), then the complete pair appears (frame 4), and so on until the list is completed. In the study-test method, the subject sees each complete pair, one after the other, during a study trial. Then, during a test trial, the stimulus items are successively presented and the subject attempts to state the associated response items. A trial of the serial anticipation procedure (right column) begins with the presentation of an arbitrary symbol, which cues the subject to state the first item in the list (frame 1). The first item then appears (frame 2), giving the subject feedback on his or her response to the symbol and serving as a cue to state the next item in the list. The remaining items are presented in the same fashion (frames 3 through 5).

METHODS IN THE STUDY OF VERBAL LEARNING

While these methods may seem to differ very little, they can have very different effects on learning. The study-test method tends to make learning easier. For example, Winters, Attlee, and Harvey (1974) compared the two methods with normal and retarded children. The retarded children, some of whom were institutionalized, were about 13 years of age and had IQs of about 60. The normal children, with IQs of about 100, were younger than the retardates (about eight years old) but had about the same **mental age.** That is, the normal and retarded children could perform intellectual tasks of approximately equal difficulty on an intelligence test. However, the normal children had attained this level of ability at an earlier chronological age than the retarded children. The stimulus and response items in the experiment were pictures of common objects: onion-shoe, pig-thumb, cake-boat, etc. In the study-test method, each pair of pictures appeared on a screen for five seconds (study trial), after which the first pictures appeared alone for five seconds (test trial). In the anticipation procedure, the first picture of a pair appeared for five seconds and then the second picture for five seconds. It was found that both the normal and retarded children made more correct responses with the study-test method. Interestingly, with this method the normal and retarded children differed very little in their performance. But with the anticipation method the institutionalized children did worse than the other children, who did not differ among themselves. We see, then, that an intellectual deficit does not mean intellectual inferiority on every task. Much depends on how the conditions for learning are arranged.

The serial-anticipation procedure

Often the material we learn consists of several parts that must go together in a certain order. The alphabet is a familiar example. Pupils in elementary school are commonly taught the alphabet not as a random collection of letters but as a serial list in which every letter has its proper place. According to one theory of serial learning (which, as we shall see, is not entirely adequate), the result of such instruction should be to create a response chain in which the letter A acts as a stimulus for saying "B," B acts as a stimulus for saying "C," and so on. That the response-chain theory is a plausible one can be demonstrated by seeing how long it takes to answer the following two questions: (1) What letter comes after H? (2) What letter comes *before* H? Chances are you took less time to answer the first question than the second. The letter H acts as a stimulus for saying "I," so you responded quickly. The letter H is at best a weak stimulus for saying "G," so you took longer to respond. Indeed, you may have arrived at the answer by going to a letter further back in the alphabet and proceeding in the forward direction until you reached G. Spelling is another example of serial learning. It usually takes much less time to spell a word in the forward direction than in the backward direction.

The serial anticipation procedure, illustrated in the right column of Fig. 7.3, allows us to analyze the processes responsible for sequential learning. The subject's task is simply to memorize a list of items. Prior to the appearance of the first item, the subject sees the word, "start," or some arbitrary symbol. This is the cue for giving the first item in the list. Several seconds later, the first item appears, giving the subject feedback on whether the response to the initial cue was correct, and providing a cue for saying the next item. After a few seconds, the second item appears, providing feedback on the response to the first item and acting as a stimulus for saying the third item. The procedure continues until the subject finishes the list. Like the paired-associate procedure, the serial-anticipation procedure can be of great value in investigating processes relevant to instruction.

SERIAL LEARNING IN THE CLASSROOM

As mentioned earlier, learning to spell is a form of serial learning. If the serial-anticipation procedure truly reveals processes at work outside the laboratory, it should tell us something about this academic skill. Psychologists have long known that some items in a serial list are easier to learn than others. Subjects usually make fewer errors on items at the beginning and end of the list than on items in the middle. In laboratory situations, this pattern occurs under a wide variety of conditions and with many different kinds of material. Outside the laboratory, the same pattern is characteristic of the spelling errors people make. In an experiment by Jensen (1962), students in a 10th grade class were read a list of eight 9-letter words by their regular teacher. After the teacher pronounced each word, the students wrote down the letters on an answer sheet. The solid line in Fig. 7.4 shows the pattern of errors in the students' responses. All of the spelling errors have been pooled, and the graph shows the percentage of errors involving the first letter of a word, the second letter, etc. It is clear that the students more frequently missed the letters in the middle of a word than the letters at either end.

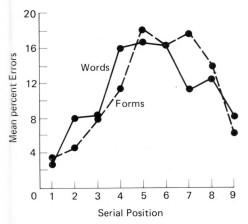

Fig. 7.4 Serial position curves showing pattern of errors in a spelling task (solid line) and a serial anticipation task (dashed line). In each task, the number of errors at a given serial position was divided by the total number of errors for all serial positions. (From Jensen, 1962)

For comparison, Jensen asked a group of college students to learn a list of items by the serial-anticipation method. The items were geometric forms—triangles, squares, and circles—each of which could be red, yellow, or blue. The experimenter presented the list until the subject reached a criterion of one trial without an error. The dashed line in Fig. 7.4 shows the pattern of errors; it is almost identical to the pattern of spelling errors. The equivalence of these two **serial-position curves** does not mean that spelling and serial-anticipation learning result from identical processes. Words have structural features that are usually absent in serial lists—prefixes, suffixes, syllables—and these features undoubtedly influence performance. But when we average over different types of words, as in Jensen's study, we see very clearly the effects of serial position. Whatever produces this pattern in the laboratory probably also plays a role in the classroom.

The serial-position curve also characterizes the learning of ideas from lectures. Holen and Olster (1976) presented a 15-minute tape-recorded lecture to a class of graduate students. After the lecture, the students took a 28-item multiple-choice test, with nine questions based on material in the first five minutes of the lecture, 10 questions on material in the second five minutes, and nine questions on material in the last five minutes. Errors on the exam followed the usual serial-position pattern. The students missed 41 percent of questions on the beginning material, 50 percent on the middle material, and 47 percent on the end material. Apparently, the beginning and end periods of a lecture are the best times for learning.

Modifying the serial-position curve

Can we speed up the learning of sequential material? Common sense suggests a simple technique. Suppose that an elementary school class was having difficulty learning to spell the word "necessary." Rarely did the children miss the two letters at the beginning or end of the word, but they frequently missed the letters in the middle, especially the letter "c." The teacher wishes to reduce the number of times the children must practice the word before they can spell it without errors. Since the letter "c" is missed most often, the teacher could emphasize this letter by pronouncing it more loudly than the others, or by writing it larger on the chalkboard. The technique is certainly simple, and intuitively we might expect it to work. Unfortunately, such an **isolation** procedure is likely to fail. Emphasizing the "c" may reduce the number of times the children miss this letter, but it probably will not reduce the number of times the teacher must present the word.

That is the basic conclusion of experiments which have examined the effects of isolation in the serial-anticipation procedure. In one experiment, Newman and Saltz (1958) presented a group of subjects (adults) with a list of 13 two-syllable words. Another group received the same list except for item 7, which was a two-syllable paralog. In the context of 12 words, the paralog would "stand out" as an isolated item. The subjects practiced the lists until they reached a criterion of one errorless trial. Figure 7.5 presents the serial position curves for the isolated and nonisolated lists. For subjects who received the isolated lists (circles), item 7 could

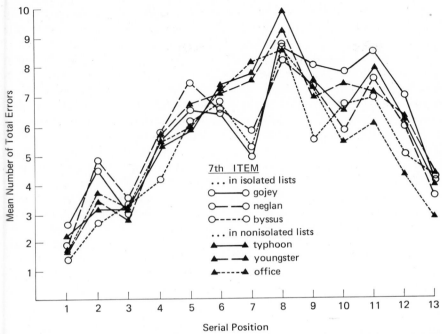

Fig. 7.5 Serial position curves illustrating the "von Restorff effect." Curves marked by triangles show pattern of errors when all items in the list were words. Curves marked by circles show effect of "isolating" the seventh item by making it a paralog instead of a word. (From Newman and Saltz, 1958)

be any one of three paralogs; for subjects who received nonisolated lists, item 7 could be any one of three words. As you can see, item 7 was missed less often when it was isolated than when it was not isolated, regardless of the specific paralog or word in the 7th position. This effect of isolation is known as the **von Restorff effect,** after its discoverer. Errors at position 8 (which was not isolated) also tended to be lower in the isolated condition than in the nonisolated condition. Overall, however, the effects of isolation were confined to the isolated item, and the number of trials to reach the criterion of mastery was the same in the two conditions. Obviously, there are no simple remedies for learning problems in sequential tasks. A fuller understanding of the processes underlying serial learning is essential for improvements in educational methods.

Processes in serial learning

It is reasonable to assume that if we understood the processes underlying serial learning, we could deduce the reasons for the serial-position curve. For many years there was a consensus on the nature of these processes, but as research accumu-

194

lated, the prevailing interpretation came under serious question. The controversy has continued until the present time, and as a result we do not have a generally accepted explanation of the serial-position curve.

The original interpretation of serial verbal learning was that of Hermann Ebbinghaus (1885), whose pioneering work on memory we shall examine in Chapter 10. According to this view, when one learns to recite a series of items, each item becomes associated with others in the list. Figure 7.6 illustrates the associative network which would result from learning five items in the sequence A, B, C, D, E. Horizontal lines represent direct connections between adjacent items. Curved lines represent connections between items separated by one or more intervening items. After we have mastered the list, saying the first item, A, prompts us to say the second item, B, which prompts us to say the third item, C, and so on. During practice, however, we also acquired **remote associations** linking each item with nonadjacent ones. For example, item A has links to items C, D, and E. In theory, remote associations are largely responsible for the errors we make while learning the list. Instead of giving item B as the response to A, we might give C, D, or E. Backward associations, both direct and remote, could also produce errors. After saying "C," we might say "B" or "A." Mastery of the list requires that direct associations in the forward direction be substantially stronger than all other associations.

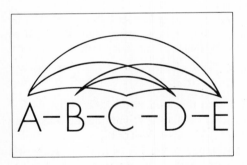

Fig. 7.6 Pattern of associations that develops when learning a serial list, according to Ebbinghaus. Horizontal lines represent direct associations between adjacent items. Arcing lines represent "remote" associations between nonadjacent items.

Although the associative theory of serial learning has been very influential over the years, many of its assumptions are without clear support. Consider the assumption of remote associations. One implication of this concept is that mastery of the original list should help the subject learn other versions of the list. For example, a subject might learn nine items in the sequence ABCDEFGHI. The concept of remote associations implies that the subject would have a head start on the sequence ACEGIBDFH, since in learning the original list, the subject acquired remote associations between A and C, C and E, E and G, etc. This was the kind of evidence that led Ebbinghaus (1885) to propose the existence of remote associations. However, Slamecka (1964) has shown that subjects often learn the sequence ACE . . . no faster than a randomly jumbled sequence. Faster learning of the ordered sequence only occurs if the subjects see its relationship to the original sequence. The nature of the items to be learned and the instructions subjects receive are crucial factors for this reason. According to the associative theory, faster learning of the ordered series should be automatic and independent of the perception of a relationship. Theorists have marshaled other kinds of evidence in support of remote associations, but this evidence also has shortcomings (Slamecka, 1964).

What of direct associations? The heart of the theory is that the pronunciation of an item serves as a stimulus for saying the next item. This view has a straightforward implication. Suppose that a subject learns the series ABCDEF, and then encounters a paired-associate list comprised of the same items: A-B, C-D, E-F. In theory, the serial list should establish the associations needed to learn the paired-associate list, and thus give the subject a head start. Similarly, a subject who first learns the paired-associate list should have a head start on the serial list. Such effects usually do not occur, however, and where positive results are reported, other interpretations are possible (e.g., Jensen and Rohwer, 1965). Few, if any, theorists would argue that associative processes play no role in serial learning. But there appears to be a growing consensus that the concept of an associative network cannot by itself explain the facts. One's perception of relationships, and the strategies one employs during learning, are also important factors.

MORE ABOUT PICTURES

Earlier in the chapter we saw that experimental facts established with the paired-associate procedure had direct implications for instruction in reading. It may have occurred to you that the paired-associate procedure was also relevant to learning a second language. In first learning to read, the child must associate the sounds of words he or she already understands with unfamiliar visual patterns. In learning a foreign language, one begins by associating unfamiliar sounds with English words. Studies of paired-associate learning have suggested ways of increasing the efficiency of vocabulary training for a second language. As in vocabulary training for a first language, pictures can be used with considerable advantage.

Imagine that you have before you a page of foreign words whose English equivalents you must memorize. Is there anything the publisher could do to speed up the learning process? A study by Kopstein and Roshall (1954) suggests that you would learn the words efficiently if a picture appeared next to each word illustrating the English meaning. In their study, adult subjects learned the English equivalents of eight Russian nouns. English spellings of the Russian words appeared together with the English words having the same meaning or with pictures of the objects to which the Russian words referred. After three study trials, the subjects received a test in which they attempted to write the Russian words in response to the English words or in response to the pictures. Altogether three tests were interspersed among nine study trials. Kopstein and Roshall found that with pictures as stimuli on the tests, the use of pictures during study trials gave more correct responses than the use of English words. This was true on all three tests. With English words as stimuli on the tests, the effectiveness of pictures on study trials was somewhat less; subjects who received pictures on study trials made more correct responses on two of the three tests. Thus foreign vocabulary was acquired better with pictures as stimuli instead of words, but the value of pictures depended on the method of testing.

Recall that pictures do not always facilitate learning. Young children learn to recognize words faster when they see the printed words alone than when they see the words together with a picture (Samuels, 1967). But note the differences between the word recognition procedure and the present one. In the word recognition procedure, the child attaches his or her verbal response to a printed word, not a picture. The picture already elicits the correct verbal response and simply acts as a prompt. In the Kopstein and Roshall study, the subjects attached a new verbal response to the picture (a Russian word). Here we see that a picture is a more effective stimulus than a printed word. Studies have shown that children as well as adults learn responses to pictures faster than responses to words.

In a study by Dilley and Paivio (1968), children at the nursery school, kindergarten, and first-grade levels learned one of four paired-associate lists. In one list, pictures served as both stimulus and response items; in another list, words served as stimulus and response items; in a third list, pictures served as stimulus items and words as response items; and in a fourth list, words served as stimulus items and pictures as response items. If an item was a picture, the child saw a simple line drawing of an object, such as an airplane, bird, or shoe. If an item was a word, the experimenter pronounced the name of the object without showing a picture. Interestingly, Dilley and Paivio found that while pictures assisted learning when they served as stimuli, they hindered learning when they served as response items. The left side of Fig. 7.7 (Panel A) illustrates this phenomenon. As the various age groups did not differ in rate of learning, their scores have been combined. You can see that whether pictures served as response items (solid line) or words served as response items (dashed line), the children gave more correct responses when the stimulus items were pictures. However, with each type of stimulus item, the children gave fewer correct responses when the response items were pictures.

Adults, unlike children, do not show impaired learning when pictures serve as response items. The right side of Fig. 7.7 (Panel B) presents results from an experiment by Paivio and Yarmey (1966) with adults as subjects. Pictures assisted learning as stimulus items, as they did for children, but they had no consistent effect on learning as response items. Dilley and Paivio suggested that the use of pictures as response items required intellectual skills which the children had not fully developed. The children had difficulty converting their memory of a picture into a verbal response; they could not "find the right word." Apparently, children who heard the experimenter pronounce the response items had little or no difficulty converting the remembered sounds into verbal responses.

Why did pictures assist learning when they served as stimulus items? Paivio and his colleagues have developed the following sort of explanation.

VERBAL LEARNING

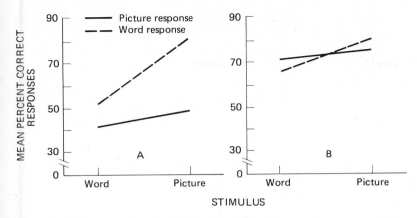

Fig. 7.7 Effects of substituting pictures for words in a paired-associate task with children (left panel) and adults (right panel). Dashed lines show results when response items were pictures. Solid lines show results when response items were words. Under each condition, stimulus items could be either pictures or words, as indicated on horizontal axis. (From Dilley and Paivio, 1968)

The invisible chain

Suppose that the stimulus item in a paired-associate list was a picture of an airplane and the response item was the printed word "fork." After sufficient repetitions of the list, the picture and the word would eventually become associated through contiguity. But a subject need not rely on sheer contiguity to learn the response. The picture of an airplane naturally evokes images of things that "go along" with airplanes. One of these images might already have a tendency to elicit the verbal response "fork," and the subject could learn the response faster by using the image as a prompt. Figure 7.8 illustrates a possible case. The picture of the airplane evokes images of a cloud, a suitcase, a dinner tray, and a passenger seat. Because the tray carries utensils, it tends to elicit the verbal responses "fork," "knife," and "spoon." The weak association between the mental image and the response "fork" becomes strong after a few repetitions of the list, and the subject says "fork" when the picture of the airplane appears. If we had used the *word* "airplane" as the stimulus item instead of the picture, the subject might have formed fewer images and missed the crucial one, the tray. Possibly, pictures assist learning because they stimulate the imagination.

The experimenter, of course, observes only the stimulus item and the word the subject utters in response to it. In theory, however, an "invisible" chain links the stimulus to the overt response, with the image of a tray in the present case serving as the intermediate link, or "mediator." This concept of mediation has a long history. You may recall from Chapter 6 the concept of the fractional anticipatory goal response, which also served as a mediator between a stimulus and a response. The context was quite different, though; the subject was a rat, the stimulus was a runway, and the response was simply running. The behaviorists who developed this

Stimulus   Mediators   Response

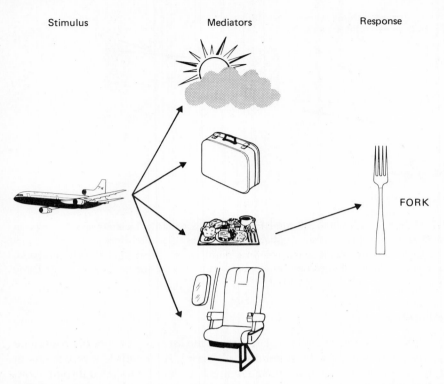

FORK

Fig. 7.8 How learning could be facilitated in a paired-associate task by presenting a picture as the stimulus item. The subject's objective is to associate the picture of an airplane with the word "fork." It is assumed that associations already exist between the airplane and several images, one of which is a fork on a tray. The image of the fork prompts the subject say "fork," and thus serves as a link, or mediator, between the stimulus item and the response item.

notion would certainly have frowned on the idea of mental images. But the concept of mediation is an extremely useful one for theory construction, and we shall encounter many more applications of it in subsequent chapters.

Airplanes for dinner

Earlier we saw that one readily forms an association between stimuli which bear some relation to one another. For example, in the experiment by Asch (1969), subjects readily learned to associate two nonsense figures which were parts of a whole. When the experimenter presented the same figures side by side, subjects learned fewer associations. Now, an airplane and a fork bear no obvious relation in reality, but with a little imagination one could invent a relation. Supplying a physical relation between two ideas, even one that is absurd and impossible in reality, can greatly facilitate learning. Consider, for example, the relation depicted in Fig. 7.9. Here

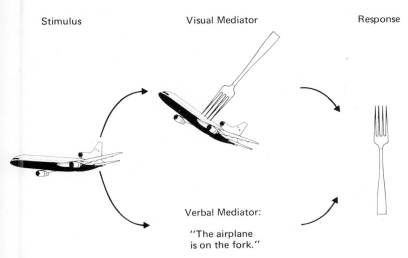

Stimulus   Visual Mediator   Response

Verbal Mediator:

"The airplane
is on the fork."

Fig. 7.9 How paired-associate learning can be facilitated by inventing a relationship between stimulus and response items. Here, pictures of an airplane and fork serve as stimulus and response items, respectively. The center panel of the figure shows how the plane and fork can be "put together" in a relationship—either by visualizing a plane on a fork (visual mediator) or by saying to oneself, "The airplane is on the fork" (verbal mediator).

we imagine that we are having airplanes for dinner and that we have just placed one piping hot plane on the tip of our fork. In the upper half of the figure we let a mental image of the relation be a mediator between the stimulus and the response. In the lower half, we express the same relation verbally by saying to ourselves, "The airplane is on the fork." In a classroom setting, the invention of relations could be a useful instructional technique. Suppose that an elementary school teacher wished to inform pupils about the various kinds of commercial products we derive from different animals. To convey the idea that wool came from sheep, the teacher might display a picture of a sheep wearing a sweater. Or, to convey the idea that beef comes from steers, the teacher might show a picture of a steer eating a hamburger.

All relations are not equally effective as mediators for children. Relations that involve action are usually more effective in building associations than relations that are static; and relations expressed visually are more effective than those expressed verbally. Differences in the instructional value of various relations emerged clearly in a study by Rowher, Lynch, Suzuki, and Levin (1967). Children in the first, third, and sixth grades viewed pictures of 24 pairs of objects. A narrator described each pair as it appeared on the screen according to a prearranged grammatical rule. One rule made use of conjunctions. If a towel and a plate appeared, the narrator would say, "the towel *and* the plate." Another rule inserted a preposition between the nouns: "the towel *across* the plate." A third rule inserted a verb: "the towel *wipes* the plate." These word strings differed in the information they conveyed about the relation between the objects. The conjunction expressed no relation; it simply indicated that two objects were present. The preposition expressed a spatial relationship, and the verb an active relationship. In a control condition, the narrator omitted grammatical mediators and simply named the objects: "the towel . . . the plate."

The experiment had an intriguing feature. At the same time that the children heard the narrator, they saw a visual translation of one of the three grammatical mediators. This procedure enabled the experimenters to assess the relative effectiveness of the visual and verbal modes of expression. In the visual translation of conjunctions, the children saw the two objects of a pair lying side by side. In the translation of prepositions, they viewed the objects in the same spatial orientation that the narrator described when using the preposition for that pair; for example, the towel would lie draped across the plate. In the translation of verbs, the children watched a brief movie depicting the same action described by the narrator when using a verb for that pair. Each group heard one type of narrative and saw one type of depiction. Thus a particular child might hear verbs but "see" prepositions, or hear conjunctions but "see" verbs. Altogether there were four study trials and four test trials.

At all three grade levels, the children proved to be more sensitive to the visual mode of expression than to the verbal. Only the verbs in the narrations facilitated learning; prepositions and conjunctions produced no more correct responses over the four trials than the control condition which omitted grammatical mediators. On the other hand, the children showed clear differences in their responsiveness to the different visual methods of presentation. The visual translations of verbs produced the most correct responses, the translations of conjunctions the fewest number, and the translations of prepositions an intermediate number. These results suggest that what a teacher shows a child will have greater impact on learning than what a teacher says. However, there are still many unanswered questions about imagery and children's learning despite extensive research on the subject. Pressley (1977) has provided a thorough review of studies in this area.

THE MEANING OF NONSENSE

What makes a word meaningful? In studies of verbal learning, psychologists have found it useful to define the meaningfulness of a word by its tendency to bring other words to mind. One method of measuring meaningfulness involves presenting an item to a group of subjects and counting the number of subjects who respond with another word within a short period. Another method involves counting the number of words that subjects think of in a limited period. With both methods of measurement, studies have shown that subjects will learn a list of words high in meaningfulness faster than they will learn a list of words low in meaningfulness. It is not hard to see why. If a word brought to mind many additional words, at least one of them should function as a link to the next word in the list. In other words, the subject should be more likely to find an effective mediator for learning if the words are high in meaningfulness.

This "associative-probability" interpretation of verbal learning (Underwood and Schulz, 1960) has practical implications. It suggests that you can increase your rate of learning by generating as many associations as possible from the material. Here, your imagination can be a valuable asset, as the following example will illustrate. Harry is an ambitious young man who likes to remember the name of every lady he meets. One evening, Harry attends a party and meets Bernice, who has striking red hair, and Eve, a brunette. Knowing about the associative-probability theory of verbal learning, Harry puts his imagination to work and comes up with the following associations to remember the names:

BERNICE→ FIRE→ GIRL WITH RED HAIR

EVE→ NIGHT→ DARK→ GIRL WITH BLACK HAIR

Bernice, for her part, wishes to remember Harry's name, but also the name of another young man, Joel. Focusing on Harry's beard and moustache, Bernice invents the following associations:

HARRY→ HAIRY→ GUY WITH BEARD AND MOUSTACHE

Noting that Joel has an unusually large chin, Bernice invents the following mediator:

JOEL→ JOWL (meaning "jaw")→ GUY WITH BIG CHIN

One need not have a "photographic memory" to learn things quickly. Simply a willingness to use your imagination in an uninhibited way can take you far.

Of BEKs and XMBs

In his pioneering studies of verbal learning and memory, Hermann Ebbinghaus recognized that people often attached surplus meanings to words. These idiosyncratic associations seemed to him an obstacle to a scientific study of learning. Like the early British philosophers, Ebbinghaus believed that learning was essentially a process of associating one idea with another. If, at the outset of an experiment, a tendency already existed to associate the words in a list, one could not observe the learning process in its earliest stages.

To reduce idiosyncratic associations, Ebbinghaus created an artificial vocabulary. Instead of using words in his experiments, he used **nonsense syllables,** each consisting of one vowel between two consonants. One sign of the impact Ebbinghaus has had on the psychology of learning is the prevalence of nonsense syllables during nearly a century of research on verbal learning. Many studies have used the original consonant-vowel-consonant (CVC) type of nonsense syllable, while others have used nonsense syllables consisting of three consonants (CCC type). Earlier, in the experiment on accentuation techniques (Lippman and Shanahan, 1973), we encountered still another type of artificial vocabulary—the *paralog*, which consisted of two nonsense syllables "stuck together," such as DELPIN and SAGROLE.

THE MEANING OF NONSENSE

The popularity of nonsense syllables testifies to their usefulness, but can one really say that they are meaningless? Here is a simple test that should provide the answer. Listed below are two nonsense syllables and two words. You can compare the meaningfulness of these items by simply counting the number of words each item brings to mind in a period of 30 seconds:

1. BEK   2. COG   3. XMB   4. CAT

To say that BEK and XMB were meaningless, you would have had to experienced no associations at all during the 30-second test period. While XMB may have left you cold (CCC nonsense syllables usually produce very few associations), it is likely that BEK elicited at least one reaction—perhaps "pen" (because of "Bic" pens), or "beak," or "beckon." Perhaps you also found that the two words COG and CAT differed in meaningfulness; CAT, being a more common word (unless you are a mechanic who works with gears), should have acquired more associations. In general, words as well as nonsense syllables vary in meaningfulness, and psychologists routinely consult published norms to select materials for their experiments (e.g., Archer, 1960; Noble, 1952).

Meaningfulness, or . . . ?   Verbal units that are similar in meaningfulness are usually similar in other ways. For example, Underwood and Schulz (1960) discovered that if a nonsense syllable ranked high on meaningfulness, it was also likely to rank high on pronunciability. In other words, not only is BEK more meaningful than XMB, BEK is easier to pronounce. The correlation of meaningfulness with other dimensions raises a question of logic: Is it meaningfulness which facilitates learning, or is it one of the other dimensions? After an intensive study of paired-associate learning, Underwood and Schulz (1960) concluded that meaningfulness was important, but so, too, was another dimension: the frequency with which a person had previously uttered the sound of an item. To illustrate, suppose that BEK was a response item in a paired-associate list. Before you could associate BEK with the stimulus item, you would have to learn to say the letters B-E-K. According to Underwood and Schulz, that should be an easier task than learning the letters X-M-B; in the past, it is more likely that you have uttered the sound BEK (as in "beckon") than the sound XMB. Frequency of pronunciation is important during this early phase of learning when you must learn a new sequence of letters. Learning to spell words of a foreign language would be a comparable task. Following the response-learning phase, meaningfulness becomes important in helping you to "hook up" the response with a stimulus. The more "hooks" you can pull out of the response, the more likely it is that one of them will "catch" the stimulus.

Which helps more, I or M?

When you hear the word "democracy" what do you see? While many words may come to mind, you may find it difficult to form an image of anything. Abstract words like "democracy," which refer to general ideas rather than specific objects, do not readily evoke images. In contrast, one easily forms images in response to concrete words like "apple," "lion," and "airplane." The capacity of a word to evoke images (symbolized by I) is independent of the meaningfulness of the word (M), and studies suggest that I assists learning more than M.

In one experiment, Paivio and Yuille (1967) constructed paired-associate lists using a pool of words for which measures of I and M were already available. The values of M had been obtained by counting the number of associations the words produced in a 30-second period. The values of I were obtained by asking subjects to rate the ease with which they could form images in response to the words. In one list, the words were approximately equal in M, but half the pairs were high in I and half were low. In another list, the words were approximately equal in I, with half the pairs high in M and half low. Because the methods of measuring I and M were different, a high value of of I did not mean exactly the same thing as a high value of M. However, there was a basis for comparison. In terms of a statistical index ("standard scores"), words high in I were as far above the average rating of I as words high in M were above the average value of M.

Paivio and Yuille found that a high value of I gave subjects more of an advantage than a high value of M. Word pairs high in I produced about two more correct responses per trial than did word pairs low in I. In contrast, word pairs high in M gave an advantage of only about one response per trial in comparison with word pairs low in M. These findings extend the results with children discussed earlier, which indicated that children are better able to use visual mediators than verbal ones (Rohwer et al., 1967). It seems that adults, too, learn better with visual mediators.

WITHOUT THIS, YOU MIGHT AS WELL CLOSE THE BOOK

Hopefully, the paragraph you just read made sense to you. It is perhaps an obvious observation—but nevertheless an important one—that your comprehension of the preceding paragraph did not result from reading that section alone. Information which you acquired from earlier sections was also important. Without the ability to **transfer** knowledge from one page to the next (or, indeed, from one sentence to the next), nothing you read would make much sense. Suppose that you had transferred no knowledge at all to the preceding paragraph. You would not know what I and M meant, and would probably have only a vague understanding of the terms "word pairs," "visual mediators," and "verbal mediators." Not only does transfer of learning make reading possible; to a large extent it makes reading worthwhile. Often we read a book or article with the explicit purpose of using the information afterward. Textbooks such as this one should, at a minimum, facilitate the learning of concepts in class. Ideally, the information in the book would be transferable to settings beyond the classroom.

Transfer of learning is a benefit attributed to education generally. We often hear that math courses help us to think logically. Courses in English literature and composition are said to improve our ability to read and write. Some of the claims naturally arouse suspicion because the relationship between course content and "real life" may seem very remote. Does knowing the Pythagorean theorem or being able to solve simultaneous equations really give you an edge in business, or help you to manage your home life? In 1700, the philosopher John Locke offered the following opinion (cited in Eriksen, 1969, p. 329):

> Would you have a man reason well, you must use him to it betimes, exercise his mind in observing the connection of ideas and following them in train. Nothing does this better than mathematics, which therefore I think should be taught to all those who have the time and the opportunity, not so much to make them mathematicians as to make them reasonable creatures . . . that having got the way of reasoning, which that study necessarily brings the mind to, they might be able to *transfer* [italics added] it to other parts of knowledge as they shall have occasion.

Locke was expressing an age-old view of transfer known as the **Doctrine of Formal Discipline.** It likened the mind to a muscle which one could strengthen through exercise. The mental work required to master a subject strengthened the mind, and was therefore of greater importance than the specific content of the subject.

Eriksen (1969) traces the Doctrine of Formal Discipline to the ancient Greeks, who practiced oratory to develop a quick and logical mind. In the Middle Ages, monks believed they could develop the soul through hard work, self-denial, and meditation. Formal discipline remained a guiding principle of education until recent times. Experiments during the present century, especially those of Edward L. Thorndike, persuaded many educators that the content of a task strongly influenced the degree of transfer to other tasks. In one experiment by Thorndike and R. S. Woodworth, subjects were asked to judge the area of pieces of paper of various shapes. Practice in judging the size of rectangles helped subjects more on another set of rectangles than on a set of papers with different shapes. From such results, Thorndike developed the theory that transfer would occur to the extent that the original task had "elements" in common with the transfer task. This **theory of identical elements** suggested that courses taught in school should emphasize those skills and concepts that students were likely to use outside the classroom.

Thorndike's theory stimulated decades of research on transfer. The times were ready for an approach that would emphasize the importance of task variables. Behaviorism was on the rise, and many psychologists saw in the theory of identical elements an opportunity to study a complex subject without reference to the mind. It was easy to translate the concept of identical elements into the language of behaviorism. In mastering a task, one formed associations between stimuli and responses. Transfer should therefore occur to the extent that one task resembled another along the dimensions of stimulus similarity and response similarity. Experiments on transfer supported the major premise of the associationistic approach: Transfer did depend heavily upon stimulus and response features of the tasks. But the relationship between transfer and the dimensions of stimulus and response similarity was not a simple one.

Most experiments on transfer include at least two groups (Fig. 7.10). In Phase 1 of the procedure, an experimental group learns some task while a control group rests or performs an activity unrelated to the task. In Phase 2, the experimental group learns a second task, which the control group also learns. The experimenter can now determine whether practice on the first task influenced the rate at which experimental subjects learned the second task. If the experimental group takes less time to master task 2 than the control group, **positive transfer** has occurred. If the experimental group takes more time to master task 2, **negative transfer** has occurred. There is zero transfer if the experimental and control groups learn task 2 at equal rates.

	Phase 1	Phase 2
Experimental Group	Learn task 1	Learn task 2
Control Group	Rest or unrelated activity	Learn task 2

Fig. 7.10 General procedure for studying transfer of learning. Comparison of Experimental and Control groups' rates of learning on Task 2 reveals whether Experimental group was helped, hindered, or unaffected by Task 1.

Many experiments have let paired-associate lists serve as tasks 1 and 2 in order to study the effects of stimulus and response similarity. With paired-associate lists, the experimenter can manipulate the similarity of the tasks along one dimension while holding constant the degree of similarity on the other. For example, as part of the first list, the experimenter might include the nonsense syllables BOL (stimulus item) and FID (response item). In the second list, the same stimulus might appear together with an entirely different response (BOL-XOG), or the same response might appear together with a different stimulus (SUZ-FID). The experimenter could study degrees of similarity by changing one or two letters of a nonsense syllable instead of all three. The use of words is also possible since they can vary in similarity along the dimension of meaning. For example, the word SURF is more similar to the word WAVE than to the word DESK.

Figure 7.11 summarizes some of the major conclusions which have been drawn from studies of transfer. For convenience, we may symbolize the content of a paired-associate list with a pair of letters. All of the subjects will first encounter a list consisting of "A-B" pairs. Studies have shown that positive transfer to the

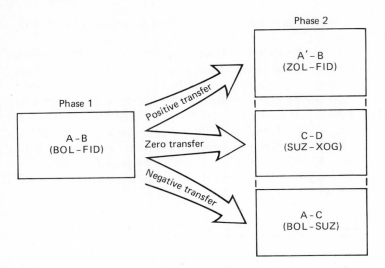

Fig. 7.11 Relationships between tasks which are likely to produce positive, negative, and zero transfer. The stimulus and response features of the task in Phase 1 are labeled A and B, respectively. After learning this task, the subject encounters one of three tasks in Phase 2 whose stimulus and response features bear the indicated relationships to those in List 1: similar stimuli, identical responses (A′-B), different stimuli, different responses (C-D), and identical stimuli, different responses (A-C). Nonsense syllables illustrate how these relationships would apply to paired-associate tasks.

second list is likely to occur if the stimulus items resemble those given in the first list (A′) and the response items are identical. You might recognize this A-B, A′-B arrangement as the condition that leads to stimulus generalization. Just as Little Albert generalized the fear response from a rat to a dog (Chapter 2), so we might expect a subject to generalize the verbal response FID from BOL to ZOL. Because of generalization, the subject has a head start on the second task, and finds it easier to learn than a subject who has not had the first list. For much the same reason, a knowledge of English can give us a head start when learning the meaning of certain foreign words. For example, the French word "exclure" means "exclude," and "excentrique" means "eccentric." It is easy to learn the meanings of these words because their similarity to English words enables us to generalize from the English to the French.

Negative transfer is likely to occur if the stimulus items of the second task are identical to those of the first, but the response items are different (A-B, A-C). Here, the subject begins the second list with a strong tendency to say the wrong response (B). To learn the correct response (C), the subject must overcome the tendency to say the wrong one. You would probably experience similar conflict if your instructor insisted that the A-B, A-C arrangement resulted in positive transfer rather than negative. From the preceding sentences, you have learned the response "negative," and would have to overcome this tendency to learn the new response.

When two tasks are completely different (A-B, C-D), we normally expect zero transfer; practice on the first list teaches the subject nothing about the content of the second. However, under certain conditions there could be positive transfer. The subject may never before have served in an experiment involving paired-associate learning. Practice on the first list could teach the subject how to work efficiently in this unusual setting. If that happened, positive transfer would result simply from the subject's *learning how to learn.* The content of the course for which you are reading this book has little in common with the content of a chemistry course. Although positive transfer to the chemistry course is unlikely as a consequence of course content, there could be some positive transfer due to the acquisition of better study habits. We shall return to this important phenomenon shortly.

There are many additional ways in which researchers have varied the similarity of the two lists (for a classic review, see Osgood, 1949). The major conclusion to be drawn from associative studies of transfer is that one must consider both stimulus and response features of the tasks to predict the direction and degree of transfer.

And to push the point a step further . . .

Thus far we have examined only the relatively simple situation in which a subject transfers learning from one task to another. Surely, the human organism must be capable of greater feats! At a higher level of complexity, one can easily imagine that transfer of learning might extend over several tasks. Not only may reading Chapter 1 of a text aid in the comprehension of Chapter 2, Chapters 1 and 2 *together* may aid in the comprehension of Chapter 3. Transfer of this sort, in which the learner puts 1 and 2 together does take place, and an associative analysis of the tasks can help us understand why.

Horton and Kjeldergaard (1961) performed an elaborate series of experiments with the three-step procedures illustrated in Fig. 7.12. They identified three kinds of arrangements between tasks in the first two phases which lead to positive transfer in the third phase. In the "chaining arrangement" (top), the subject learns to associate A with B in Phase 1 and B with C in Phase 2. Putting Phases 1 and 2 together, the subject forms a chain—A to B to C—which provides a head start on learning the A-C association in Phase 3. The "stimulus-equivalence" arrangement in Phases 1 and 2 (middle) also assists the subject on the A-C association in Phase 3. From Phase 1 the subject learns A-B, and from Phase 2, C-B. Because A and C evoke the same response, A tends to evoke C. The "response-equivalence" arrangement is similar. Here, the subject learns in Phases 1 and 2 that one stimulus evokes two different responses: B-A, B-C. In Phase 3, A tends to evoke C because of the common association to B. These transfer effects are certainly complex. But within the associative framework, they are not difficult to interpret. In each case, the item B acts as a mediator between A and C due to the unique experiences of the subjects in Phases 1 and 2. From the associative standpoint, mediated transfer is one of the hallmarks of higher learning.

WITHOUT THIS, YOU MIGHT AS WELL CLOSE THE BOOK

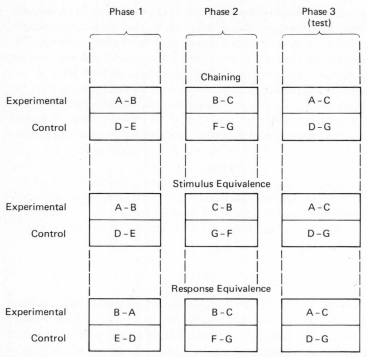

	Phase 1	Phase 2	Phase 3 (test)
		Chaining	
Experimental	A – B	B – C	A – C
Control	D – E	F – G	D – G
		Stimulus Equivalence	
Experimental	A – B	C – B	A – C
Control	D – E	G – F	D – G
		Response Equivalence	
Experimental	B – A	B – C	A – C
Control	E – D	F – G	D – G

Fig. 7.12   Three-step procedures used by Horton and Kjeldergaard (1961) in study of "mediated" transfer. Subjects learned paired-associate lists with the indicated relationships between stimuli and responses. In each variety of mediated transfer—chaining, stimulus equivalence, and response equivalence—the Experimental group is found to learn faster in Phase 3 than the Control group. The reason is that in the Experimental group subjects have acquired a mediator (item B) that helps them link the stimulus to the response.

Warning: Do NOT understand and remember what you read next

Is transfer automatic? When the opportunity arises to apply something you know, will you? From the standpoint of associationistic theory, transfer should be automatic if the stimulus and response features of the tasks are appropriately arranged. We have already encountered one example of this implicit assumption of associationistic theory. In testing Ebbinghaus's theory of serial learning, psychologists drew the implication that a subject who mastered the serial list, A-B-C-D-E-F, would automatically have an easier time learning the paired associate list, A-B, C-D, E-F. This expectation of positive transfer was not confirmed; subjects exhibited positive transfer only if they perceived the relationship between the lists and adopted an appropriate strategy for learning. Wittrock (1963) has demonstrated a similar phenomenon in a classroom setting. His results also suggest that the instructor can play a significant role in creating the proper climate for positive transfer to occur.

VERBAL LEARNING

College students read a 2500-word passage on Buddhism, a topic with which most students were unfamiliar. Prior to reading the passage, some of the students were asked simply to understand and remember what they were about to read. Other students were given more specific instructions designed to create a strategy for learning. Essentially, the strategy involved relating the material on Buddhism to the knowledge that students already had about Judeo-Christian beliefs. In one condition, the experimenter instructed the students to note *similarities* between Buddhism and Judeo-Christian beliefs: "As you read this selection, try to note and remember the many similarities which exist between the Buddhist religion and the religions of the Judeo-Christian tradition with which you are familiar. The main purpose of the study is to determine how well you learn and remember similarities . . ." (Wittrock, 1963, p. 86). In another condition, the experimenter asked students to note *differences* between the religions, and in a third condition both *similarities and differences.*

The orientation, or **set,** created by the instructions clearly influenced learning. Asking students to understand and remember the material gave the lowest scores on a multiple-choice test administered immediately after the students read the passage. Asking them to note differences, or similarities plus differences, resulted in appreciably higher scores—about 15% higher. Simply noting the similarities between religions also seemed to help, but the effect was not statistically reliable. The advantages of a proper set were lasting; the higher scores also showed up on a retention test three weeks later. Thus, having relevant knowledge does not guarantee that one will use it to best advantage. One must know *how* to use it.

Experiments by Harlow (1949) suggest that one learns how to learn through extensive experience with problems of a particular type. Harlow gave monkeys a simple discrimination problem which enabled them to earn rewards by making a correct choice between two stimuli. The stimuli were objects of various shapes, such as a cylinder and a cube, and each appeared on a random half of the trials on the left and right. On the first occasion that the monkeys encountered a discrimination problem, they spent many trials learning to ignore the position of the objects and to focus instead on the shapes. After hundreds of problems of the same general type—each one employing a new pair of objects—the monkeys became "experts." They discovered that they could solve a problem in at most two trials by adopting a simple strategy. If the first choice was correct, they continued to choose that object on subsequent trials. If the first choice was incorrect, they switched to the other object on the second trial, and stayed with it thereafter. Learning this strategy was a gradual process, not a flash of insight. As a monkey encountered more and more problems of this type, the number of trials required to master the problem decreased, until the animals reached the point of being able to solve the problem in one or two trials.

Harlow's monkeys obviously benefited from positive transfer. But the source of transfer could not have been the specific content of a problem, since no two problems were alike. The transfer was of a general sort, and transcended the individual problems. This seems rather like the benefits of practice envisioned by John Locke and other advocates of the theory of formal discipline. The major dif-

WITHOUT THIS, YOU MIGHT AS WELL CLOSE THE BOOK

210

ference was that Harlow's monkeys did not become "logical thinkers" on all types of problems. They were "specialists" on the particular type of problem which they had practiced. Thus neither the theory of formal discipline nor the theory of identical elements seems entirely correct. Transfer is more specific to the conditions of practice than Locke imagined, but more general than Thorndike imagined. As in so many areas of psychology in which we find extreme points of view, the "truth" apparently lies somewhere in between.

SUMMARY

The term, "verbal learning," has traditionally encompassed two broad areas of investigation: the formation of associations between verbal responses and visual patterns, and the extraction of meaning from passages. Both areas have direct implications for education—the first bears on the teaching of word recognition skills (among other applications), and the second bears on instruction in reading comprehension. Theories of verbal learning thus potentially have practical as well as scientific significance.

An example of a theory with direct educational relevance is Solomon Asch's conceptualization of the nature of an association. Behaviorists have traditionally maintained that an association will develop between two events if the events occur at about the same time, that is, if the events occur contiguously. Asch, a cognitivist, argued that temporal contiguity is just one of many factors that promote associations—and the least important factor at that. According to Asch, the relationship between two events contributes more to the formation of an association than does contiguity. He illustrated the importance of relationships by asking subjects to memorize sets of nonsense figures. Some subjects saw the figures in each set side-by-side (contiguous) while other subjects saw the figures as parts of a single pattern (related). The latter subjects recalled many more figures, a result suggesting that the relationship between figures was more important than the factor of contiguity alone.

This theory led to the development of a technique for teaching word recognition skills called "accentuation." The teacher presents vocabulary words on flash cards in a manner that relates the letters to pictures of the objects referred to. One or more letters are modified to look like the object so that the child sees a unitary pattern. Accentuated words promote faster learning than does the presentation of words without pictures, or the presentation of words and pictures next to one another (i.e., contiguously). There is evidence that the latter strategy actually retards learning.

Two ways of presenting verbal material to subjects in the laboratory are the paired-associate procedure and the serial-anticipation procedure. Paired-associate presentation is analogous to instruction in word recognition, and can be accomplished with a study-test technique or an anticipation technique. Although both techniques require the subject to remember items in pairs, the study-test technique sometimes promotes faster learning. The serial anticipation procedure requires subjects to remember items in sequence and is analogous to instruction in spelling. Serial learning resembles the formation of a response chain in which each item acts as a stimulus for saying the next item in the list.

It is well established that some items in a serial list are more difficult to learn than others. Subjects usually make more errors on items in the middle of a list than on items at the beginning or end. This pattern of errors is often depicted on a graph showing the number of errors on the vertical axis and the serial position of each item on the horizontal axis. The resulting function, an inverted "U," is known as the "serial-position curve." Intuitively, one might expect that making items in the middle of the list stand out from the others would make those items easier to learn and lead to faster learning of the list as a whole. This expectation is only partly borne out by the facts. Isolating a middle item by making it appear different from the others results in fewer errors on that item ("von Restorff effect"). However, the number of trials required to master the entire list is unaffected.

The first theory of serial verbal learning was developed by Hermann Ebbinghaus during the late 19th century. It stated that practice on a list produced two kinds of associations: direct associations between adjacent items, and "remote" associations between nonadjacent items. Mastery of a list required that direct associations in the forward direction be stronger than all other associations. Ebbinghaus' interpretation of serial learning prevailed for many years. However, certain findings eventually raised doubts that the concepts of direct and remote associations could explain all the facts of serial learning. While associative processes undoubtedly contribute to serial learning, one apparently must also consider the strategies for learning invented by the subject, a factor long emphasized by cognitive theorists.

In the paired-associate procedure, pictures can facilitate learning when substituted for words on the stimulus side. This effect occurs in both children and adults. When pictures are substituted for words on the response side, adults are unaffected while childred learn more slowly. To explain the facilitative effects of pictures, Paivio suggested that pictures naturally evoke many mental images of objects, some which may have preexisting associations to the response item. The subject can learn a paired-associate list faster by using such mental images as links, or mediators, between stimulus items and response items. To explain the detrimental effects of pictures in children, Paivio suggested that children, unlike adults, have difficulty converting the memory of a picture into the appropriate word at the time of recall.

Another type of mediation in paired-associate learning involves the invention of a picture or phrase that relates the stimulus item to the response item. With children, active relations are more effective in facilitating learning than static relations, and relations expressed visually are more effective than relations expressed verbally.

Two features of words strongly influence the rate of paired-associate learning: "meaningfulness" (M) and "imagery value" (I). Meaningfulness is measured by the number of words subjects give in response to an item on a free-association basis, or by the percentage of subjects who respond within a limited period. The imagery

SUMMARY

value of a word can be measured by asking subjects to rate the ease with which they form images in response to the word. Meaningfulness and imagery value are thought to assist paired-associate learning by providing mediators between stimulus items and response items. Imagery appears to be a more potent aid in this regard than meaningfulness. To limit the number of word associations to an item, psychologists often use lists of nonsense syllables, verbal units which do not form words. Nonsense syllables usually rate lower in meaningfulness than words but still may elicit a substantial number of associations.

Fundamental to learning is a capacity to transfer, or apply knowledge acquired in one context to the process of acquiring knowledge in another context. Transfer of learning is a major concern of the field of education. Ideally, students would be able to transfer what they have learned in the classroom to situations that arise in everyday life. The question of how to maximize transfer has been discussed for centuries. An early view of transfer, called the "Doctrine of Formal Discipline," assumed that the mind could be strengthened through mental exercise much as a muscle could be strengthened through physical exercise. The implication was that the mental work required to master a subject was more important than what was learned. During the 20th century, Thorndike developed a contrary view of transfer known as the "Theory of Identical Elements." It stated that transfer would occur to the extent that the original task had elements in common with the transfer task. Academic subjects should therefore provide skills that students will use outside the classroom.

Research inspired by Thorndike's theory has shown that transfer depends importantly upon the specific features of the original and transfer tasks. A standard procedure for studying these features involves presentation of paired-associate lists to two groups of subjects. The experimental group learns Lists 1 and 2 while the control group learns only List 2. Positive transfer from List 1 to List 2 has occurred if the experimental group learns List 2 faster than does the control group. Negative transfer has occurred if the experimental group learns List 2 more slowly; and zero transfer has occurred if the two groups learn List 2 at equal rates. The direction and degree of transfer depends in a complex way on the similarity between stimulus items and between response items in Lists 1 and 2. A more complex form of transfer has been investigated with a three-step procedure in which paired-associate lists presented in the first two steps assist learning of a paired-associate list in the third step. Three varieties of transfer in the three-step procedure have been established: "chaining" (A-B, B-C . . . A-C), "stimulus equivalence" (A-B, C-B . . . A-C), and "response equivalence" (B-A, B-C . . . A-C).

According to behavioristic theories, positive and negative transfer should be automatic when the stimulus and response features of the tasks are appropriately arranged. However, there is evidence that transfer will occur only if the subject perceives the relationship between the original task and the transfer task. In educational settings, teachers can facilitate positive transfer by providing students with explicit instructions as to how they should relate previously acquired knowledge to new material. Such instructions are said to create a "set," or orientation to the material. It is to a student's advantage to know how to approach new material without having to depend on teachers' instructions. Studies by Harlow with monkeys suggest that organisms acquire suitable strategies for learning through extensive experience with problems of a particular type. This phenomenon is called "learning how to learn." It arises from the fact that positive transfer can occur from one task to another even if the tasks differ significantly. From a theoretical stand-point, "learning how to learn" supports a compromise position between the Doctrine of Formal Discipline and the Theory of Identical Elements.

STUDY QUESTIONS

1. Describe the procedure and results of Samuels' experiment on the effects of including pictures on flashcards. In stating the results, compare the performances of the three groups on learning trials and on test trials. Interpret this discrepancy. What similar problem arises in reading instruction at a more advanced level?

2. What factor have behaviorists traditionally considered to be most important in pro-moting associations between events? What factor does Solomon Asch consider to be most important? Give two examples of Asch's conceptualization from everyday life.

3. Describe the rationale, procedure, and results of Asch's experiment with the nonsense figures. Use a specific set of figures from the experiment to illustrate how the two groups differed. State how Asch's results bear on the theoretical issue discussed in Question 2.

4. In general terms, what is the basic strategy of the "accentuation" technique for teaching word recognition skills? Describe the three varieties of accentuation and state how they illustrate Asch's view of associative learning. Which type of accentuation did Lippman and Shanahan find effective?

5. State how you would present the word-pairs BOX-LOG, LIP-RUG, and LAMP-PAINT using the study-test method of the paired-associate procedure. State how you would present the word-pairs using the anticipation method. Which method tends to produce faster learning? Cite evidence.

6. State how you would present the words, BOX, LOG, LIP, and RUG using the serial anticipation procedure. In what way does serial learning resemble the formation of a response chain? Give an example.

7. Labeling the vertical and horizontal axes, make a graph showing a typical serial posi-tion curve for a nine-item list. Describe this pattern in words. How did Jensen demon-strate the serial position curve in a spelling task?

8. What is the von Restorff effect? What effect does isolating a middle item have on mastery of the entire list? Cite evidence.

9. Assume that the letters A, B, C, D, E are items in a serial list. Draw the pattern of asso-ciations which Ebbinghaus assumes would develop during the learning of such a list. Identify the direct and the remote associations. According to Ebbinghaus, what con-dition must be satisfied for a serial list to be mastered?

10. Again using the letters A-E to represent a serial list, cite two kinds of evidence suggesting that Ebbinghaus's interpretation of serial learning is not entirely adequate.

11. How can pictures be used to facilitate the learning of foreign language vocabulary? Cite evidence.

12. In the study by Dilley and Paivio, which examined paired-associate learning in children and adults, what was the effect on children's learning of substituting pictures for words on the stimulus side? Of substituting pictures for words on the response side? What effect did these substitutions have on adults' learning? How did Paivio explain the facilitative and detrimental effects of pictures?

13. To associate the word "airplane" with the word "fork," a subject creates a mental picture of an airplane on the tip of a fork. Another subject makes up the sentence, "The airplane is on the fork." What principle of learning do these strategies illustrate?

14. Referring to the specific points outlined below, summarize the procedure and results of the study by Rohwer et al. on mediational effects in children's paired-associate learning:
    a) How the narrator used conjunctions, prepositions, and verbs when describing pairs of objects? (Illustrate using the objects "towel" and "plate.")
    b) How the three grammatical mediators were visually translated—illustrate each type using "towel" and "plate."
    c) Two examples of how a child might see one type of mediator but hear another type.
    d) The method of paired-associate presentation (study-test or anticipation), and the number of trials.
    e) Comparison of the effects of prepositions, conjunctions, and verbs used in the narrations.
    f) Comparison of the effects of prepositions, conjunctions, and verbs in the visual presentations.
    g) Overall effects of visual presentation vs. auditory presentation.

15. State two methods of measuring the meaningfulness of a verbal item.

16. State the associative-probability theory of verbal learning.

17. What is a nonsense syllable? Give an example of a nonsense syllable that is relatively high in meaningfulness and an example of one that is relatively low.

18. According to Underwood and Schulz, what are the two major phases of paired-associate learning? What factor most influences learning in each phase?

19. How is the imagery value of a word measured? Which factor appears to affect paired-associate learning more strongly, meaningfulness or imagery value?

20. What is meant by the term, "transfer of learning"?

21. State the Doctrine of Formal Discipline.

22. State Thorndike's Theory of Identical Elements. How would an educational program

based on Thorndike's theory differ from one based on the Doctrine of Formal Discipline?

23. Describe the two-step procedure for studying transfer of learning. What are the criteria for positive, negative, and zero transfer?

24. With paired-associate lists as the original and transfer tasks, what conditions are most likely to produce positive, negative, and zero transfer. Illustrate using nonsense syllables and examples from educational settings.

25. Using paired-associate lists and the two-step transfer procedure, how would you go about demonstrating the phenomenon called "learning how to learn?"

26. Using the letters A-G to symbolize stimulus and response items in paired-associate lists, state the three varieties of mediated transfer identified by Horton and Kjeldergaard. In the three-step procedure for studying mediated transfer, what would be the experimental and control conditions for each type of transfer?

27. What implication of associative interpretations of transfer is not generally valid? Support this conclusion by referring back to your answer to Question 10.

28. Describe the procedure and results of Wittrock's experiment which provided students with different "sets" for reading an unfamiliar passage. What general conclusion about transfer do these results suggest?

29. Describe the type of discrimination problem Harlow used to investigate "learning how to learn" in monkeys. What was the nature of this learning process? How do the results relate to the two major theories of transfer: The Doctrine of Formal Discipline and the Theory of Identical Elements?

CHAPTER 8

Concept Formation

The aim of education is to foster intellectual growth, but intellectual growth does not begin with formal education. Learning takes place during the earliest years of life, and what a young child learns can influence his or her responsiveness to classroom instruction. Prior to the twentieth century, the intellectual growth of young children was left largely to chance. Little effort was made to structure their intellectual experiences. The present century has seen a dramatic increase in the number of institutions devoted to "preschool" education. Children from two to four years of age encounter a wide variety of experiences designed to stimulate and guide intellectual development. One objective of these educational programs has been to convey the meaning of comparatively simple but fundamental concepts like "height," "length," and "number," with the expectation that they will help lay the foundation for later learning. In the first part of the chapter we shall examine the processes underlying the acquisition of such concepts. Later sections of the chapter will focus on the acquisition of complex concepts.

MARIA MONTESSORI: THE SENSES ARE
THE AVENUE TO DISCOVERY

One of the earliest advocates of intellectual guidance for young children was Maria Montessori, an Italian educator. Montessori first achieved recognition by earning a degree in medicine, a field not previously entered by women in Italy. After graduating in 1896, Montessori spent two years in a psychiatric clinic teaching mentally defective children to read and write. During this period she developed techniques that proved remarkably effective. A number of the children were administered an exam usually taken by school children of normal intelligence. The children passed the exam, an unprecedented and widely heralded event. To Montessori, however, the accomplishment was a source of concern. Why should normal children perform at a level comparable to that of mental defectives? Surely, if the children had received adequate training, they would have performed at a much higher level. Montessori believed that the techniques she had used with mental defectives could also serve the needs of normal children. In 1907, to test her approach, Montessori became director of a day-care center in a slum section of San Lorenzo, Italy. The results of the project were impressive. The children showed a higher degree of concentration on exercises than had the mental defectives. They would commonly repeat an exercise many times on their own before they would set it aside, and when they were through, they seemed rested and happy. One child repeated an exercise 42 times and was so absorbed in the activity that she apparently did not notice being moved in her chair to another part of the room (Lillard, 1972). Following San Lorenzo, additional schools using the "Montessori Method" opened in Italy, and eventually the approach spread throughout the world. In the United States alone, there are currently more than 1000 Montessori schools.

The Montessori Method (Montessori, 1912; 1914) relies heavily on sensory experiences to teach children fundamental concepts. The child has available a wide assortment of instructional materials and is free to select any exercise he or she finds appealing. Typically, the child works independently of other children (although cooperative work is encouraged), and is free to devote as much time to the exercise as he or she desires. Figure 8.1 shows a set of materials designed to teach the concepts of height and thickness to children as young as two and one-half years of age (Montessori, 1914). Panel A pictures a case containing a series of cylinders varying in diameter, or thickness. The button on top of the cylinders serves as a handle and enables the child to remove or insert the cylinders into the correct holes. Panel B shows a case in which the cylinders vary in height, and Panel C depicts a case in which the cylinders vary in both height and diameter. To introduce a child to these materials, the teacher might first take the case in which the cylinders vary in diameter (Panel A) and remove the cylinders from the case. The teacher mixes up the cylinders and asks the child to put them back in their proper holes. The material naturally gives the child quick feedback on his or her decisions. If an attempt is made to place a wide cylinder into a narrow hole (a common error), the cylinder will obviously not fit and the child would have to select a smaller cylinder. If a small cylinder were placed in a large hole, the error would soon be discovered since there would be no hole for at least one other cylinder. The objective in requiring the child to make comparisons among cylinders is to teach not only the specific concept of thickness, but the general concept of a *dimension,* the idea that objects can exhibit varying degrees of a property. When the child has completed the exercise, he or she may repeat it or work with another case. The case in which the cylinders vary in height (Panel B) not only teaches the concept of height, but demonstrates that height may vary independently of thickness, that these are separable dimensions. The third case (Panel C) shows the child how objects look when the two dimensions vary together, thus providing a basis for contrast with the situations in which only a single dimension varies. Logically, the third case is more complex than either of the preceding ones, but psychologically it is not the most difficult exercise to perform. The children find the case in Panel A easiest, the case in Panel C more difficult, and the case in Panel B most difficult, and the teacher is likely to introduce the child to the materials in this order. This unusual finding demonstrates that we must distinguish between the logical complexity of a concept and the level of difficulty it presents to a learner. We shall examine the relationship between complexity and difficulty in greater detail when we turn to the acquisition of complex concepts.

MARIA MONTESSORI: THE SENSES ARE THE AVENUE TO DISCOVERY

A Cylinders decreasing in diameter only.

B Cylinders decreasing in height only.

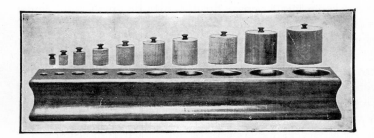

C Cylinders decreasing in diameter and height.

Fig. 8.1 Materials designed by Montessori to teach preschool children the concepts of height and thickness. In panel A, cylinders differ only in diameter; in panel B, cylinders differ only in height; in panel C, cylinders differ in both diameter and height. (Montessori, 1914)

The cylinders are only one of many sets of materials used to enhance sensory awareness. After the child masters the cylinders, he or she may encounter the "tower," a series of 10 wooden cubes that vary in size. The tower will stand only if the child uses the biggest cube as the foundation, places the next largest cube on top of that one, and so on. Since the cubes are alike in every respect but one (for

CONCEPT FORMATION

example, they are all the same color), the dimension of size naturally attracts the child's attention without distraction. According to Montessori (1914), if the child is responsive to the exercise, he or she will repeat it by knocking down the blocks and rebuilding the structure.

Other materials familiarize the child with such dimensions as length, hue, and shade. After the child has mastered a variety of dimensions, the teacher introduces their names. For example, the teacher might take two cylinders varying greatly in diameter and name the distinguishing aspects: "This is thick. This is thin." He or she may then test the child's ability to recognize the named objects by placing them on a table and asking the child to "Give me the thick; give me the thin." Finally, the teacher may have the child pronounce a word by holding up one of the cylinders and asking, "What is this (Montessori, 1914)?" Thus, in the Montessori method, sensory training becomes the foundation for higher forms of learning. The importance of early sensory experience in intellectual development is widely recognized. Jean Piaget, the pioneering developmental psychologist, theorized that "Sensorimotor intelligence lies as the source of thought and continues to affect it throughout life . . . (1950, p. 119)"

The Montessori Method is an excellent example of a technological contribution that has preceded, rather than evolved from, basic research. In Chapter 1 we noted that basic research may serve the needs of society by suggesting new procedures and new ways of looking at problems. But important technological advances may also occur without guidance from the laboratory. Montessori developed practical procedures in a practical setting to meet an urgent need. She did not structure her exercises to meet the demands of experimental design. Basic research has since established facts that help to clarify the psychological effects of some of Montessori's procedures. It should be kept in mind that the research we shall examine was not designed to test the effectiveness of preschool practices. The objective of the research was to learn more about the basic processes underlying concept learning. Still, the procedures of the laboratory and the practices of the preschool have sometimes been quite similar, and the relevance of the laboratory work we shall consider will be very evident.

CONCEPT LEARNING IN THE LABORATORY: INTELLECTUALLY, YOUNG CHILDREN ARE NOT QUITE "HUMAN"

The study of concept formation in laboratory settings usually involves the presentation of a problem to the subject. One type of problem, called a **solution shift,** has been widely used. It is unique in that it allows the investigator to study the conceptual behavior of lower animals such as rats as well as the conceptual behavior of children and adults. By observing how different species solve the problem, we can gain insights into the evolutionary development of intelligence. By observing how human beings of different ages solve the problem, we can make inferences about the course of intellectual development in one individual. Before we look at the solution shift problem, a word of caution is in order. It is notoriously difficult to draw any conclusions about the relative intelligence of different species. How an animal performs in any learning task depends critically on the technical details of the procedure. Factors unrelated to intelligence, such as sensory capacities, could easily influence performance and distort our picture of how the species compare intellectually. In the present case, though, the results from lower animals, children, and adults form a pattern too provocative to be taken lightly.

Figure 8.2 illustrates a solution-shift problem used by Kendler and Kendler (1959) with kindergartners and by Tighe (1965) with first-graders. The stimuli were cylindrical tumblers that varied along two dimensions—height and brightness. Each subject encountered two problems involving these stimuli. In both problems, the experimenter presented the tumblers in pairs: the short black tumbler together with the tall white one, and the short white tumbler together with the tall black one. The experiment was represented as a game in which the object was to accumulate marbles that could later be exchanged for prizes. There was a marble beneath one tumbler in each pair, and the child's task was to choose the tumbler that led to reward. Figure 8.2 illustrates a situation in which the correct choice for Problem I was the smaller of the two tumblers, regardless of whether the tumbler was white or black. In other words, the dimension of size was relevant to the solution but the dimension of brightness was irrelevant. For simplicity, the figure shows the two smaller tumblers on the left side, but in practice the positions of the tumblers were varied from trial to trial. The child could not obtain a marble consistently by simply choosing the tumbler on the left side. It was assumed that the problem was solved when the child made a total of nine correct choices in 10 successive trials.

After the child mastered the problem, the experimenter changed the "rules of the game." If the child next encountered a **reversal shift,** the correct choice became the larger, rather than the smaller, of the two tumblers. The dimension of size was still relevant to the solution, but the correct value on this dimension was now the reverse of the correct value in Problem I. If the child encountered a **nonreversal shift,** the correct choice became the darker of the two tumblers. Only by choosing the short black tumbler or the the tall black one could the child be consistently correct. Thus the dimension of size was now irrelevant to the solution and the dimension of brightness was relevant. The experimenters continued to present pairs of stimuli until the child mastered the problem, recording the number of trials to criterion. The question was this: Which of the two shift problems would be easier for these kindergartners and first-graders to solve? Would the reversal shift be learned more rapidly, would the nonreversal shift, or would the two problems be learned at an equal rate? Perhaps would like to hazard a guess before reading the answer. But first, so that you have some scientific basis for a prediction, consider the following facts. When similar problems are given to college students (in a more sophisticated form, of course), they learn the reversal shift more rapidly than the nonreversal shift (Kendler and D'Amato, 1955). When solution shifts are given to nursery school children, they learn the nonreversal shift more rapidly than the reversal shift, just the opposite result (Kendler, Kendler, and Wells, 1960). This type of problem has also been presented to rats, using food reward (Kelleher,

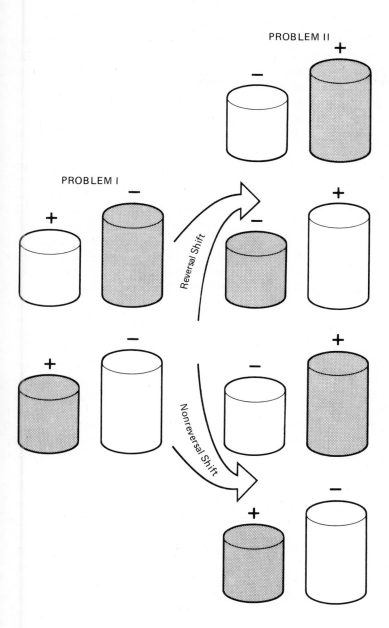

Fig. 8.2 A solution shift problem presented to young children. In each phase of procedure, subjects made choices at various times between a small white and a tall black tumbler, and between a small black and a tall white tumbler. Correct and incorrect choices are represented by " + " and " − " respectively. The first problem was given to all subjects, after which some subjects encountered the "reversal shift" while others encountered the "nonreversal shift."

CONCEPT LEARNING IN THE LABORATORY

1956), and the results are consistent with those for preschoolers—the rats learn the nonreversal shift more rapidly than the reversal shift. Now, against that background of contradiction, what might you expect? Both Kendler and Kendler (1959) and Tighe (1965) found that their subjects learned the reversal and nonreversal shifts at equal rates. In other words, the kindergartners and first-graders were neither like the rats and preschoolers on the one hand, nor were they like the college students on the other. They were "in between," in a kind of transition period between two distinct modes of response.

The implications are far-reaching. Possibly, the same ability that distinguishes adults from rats also distinguishes adults from young children. If so, intellectual growth may be a kind of evolution in which the child gradually acquires some distinctly human trait. Our understanding of intellectual development would surely benefit from a satisfactory explanation of these findings. Explanations vary considerably, but the major theoretical accounts tend to agree on some points, which we may summarize as follows. There are two ways in which a subject can consistently obtain rewards in Problem 1. In one approach, the subject forms a concept of the solution. This entails seeing a relationship between the big and small tumblers, recognizing that they are points on a continuum. The subject separates the dimension of size from the dimension of brightness, and generalizes that tumblers having the property of smallness are correct choices regardless of the brightness. Concept formation always has this characteristic. It always involves generalization across a class of stimuli that have something in common. In addition, concept formation requires discrimination between this class and stimuli that lack the common feature. Thus the subject rejects the two tumblers that lack the quality of smallness. The other approach to Problem I is less "intelligent." There is no concept formation. The subject does not see dimensions but rather four unrelated stimuli. What the individual learns is to approach the small black tumbler and avoid the tall white one when they appear, and to approach the small white tumbler and avoid the tall black one when they appear.

By examining performance on the reversal and nonreversal shifts, we can infer the approach that the subject has adopted in Problem I. A subject who forms a concept of the solution in Problem I should learn a reversal shift more rapidly than a nonreversal shift. In the reversal shift, the subject is already responsive to the relevant dimension (size), and needs only to switch from the small tumbler to the large one. But in the nonreversal shift, the subject has two tasks: he or she must become responsive to a new dimension (brightness) and then learn to choose the appropriate value on this dimension (black). Because there are fewer tasks in the reversal shift than in the nonreversal shift, the subject should learn the reversal shift more rapidly. Now, consider the subject who fails to form a concept of the solution in Problem I. By examining Fig. 8.2, you will see that this individual should learn the nonreversal shift more rapidly than the reversal shift. When the nonreversal shift is presented, two of the four responses that were appropriate in Problem I remain appropriate—the choice of the small black tumbler and the avoidance of the tall white one. Only two of the original four responses must be changed; the subject must now approach the tall black and avoid the small white tumblers. In other words, after Problem I, the individual has a head start on the nonreversal shift. In contrast, when the reversal shift is encountered, all four of the original responses are inappropriate and must be changed. Because fewer responses must be changed in the nonreversal shift than in the reversal shift, the nonreversal shift should be learned more rapidly.

That may sound like the whole story, but something important is missing. In fact, without this missing ingredient the story really tells us very little. In order to form a concept of the solution, it was necessary for a subject to see that height and brightness were separable dimensions. This enabled the subject to conceptualize a small tumbler and ignore the irrelevant aspects of whiteness and blackness. Why is one subject able to separate the two dimensions and another one not? If we knew the answer, not only could we complete the story, we might also be in a better position to accelerate the intellectual development of children. Two theories have been influential. One theory states that the subject who forms a concept has had greater opportunity for "perceptual learning" (Tighe and Tighe, 1966). The other states that the subject is better able to use language to guide his or her behavior (Kendler and Kendler, 1962). Both theories have experimental support, and both are useful sources of ideas for education. We turn now to an examination of these theories.

Forming simple concepts

Perceptual learning Recall that Montessori's approach to early education emphasized sensory training. Many of her exercises sought to demonstrate the existence of dimensions and to show that objects could differ along one dimension while being identical on another (Fig. 8.1). Montessori believed that one's sensitivity to features of the physical world depended heavily on such experiences. The trained eye registered information that the untrained eye ignored. For example, a botanist, trained in the structure of plants, and a layman might be given two varieties of ferns and asked to describe their differences. We would probably receive a longer description from the botanist, since he or she is prepared to see more independent dimensions along which the two plants might differ. Similarly, one might be quite able to distinguish a poodle from a terrier, but have great difficulty distinguishing one's own poodle from a friend's. The dogs could be virtually identical on the more obvious dimensions of size, weight, and color. But on less conspicuous dimensions the dogs might differ considerably. After comparing the two poodles a number of times, one might finally see that the eyes of one's own poodle were set more widely apart or that the snout was narrower. Through practice, the poodle owner and the botanist increase their ability to extract information from the physical world. They have experienced **perceptual learning** (Gibson, 1969, p. 3).

As the Montessori exercises demonstrate to children the nature of physical dimensions, they might conceivably influence a child's behavior on the solution-shift problem. Theoretically, if a child could be taught to perceive dimensions rather than isolated stimuli, he or she would be able to form a concept of the solution in

Problem I. Tighe (1965), using the materials in Fig. 8.2, gave first-grade children an exercise that closely resembled the Montessori exercise with cylinders (Fig. 8.1). However, Tighe's study was not directly a test of the effectiveness of Montessori techniques. It was a test of a general theory of perceptual learning advanced by Gibson and Gibson (1955) and further developed by Tighe and Tighe (1966) and Gibson (1969, especially Ch. 5). The theory states, in part, that perceptual learning takes place without external reinforcement for improvement. Repeated exposure to the environment will alone result in greater sensitivity to detail. To test this idea, Tighe developed an exercise that lacked a feature present in Montessori's exercise with the cylinders—Tighe gave the children no feedback on whether their comparative judgments were correct. Before starting Problem I, the children received sensory training with tumblers of various heights and brightnesses (white, grey, and black). The experimenter presented one tumbler for a moment, the Standard, then removed it and presented another, the Comparison. The children, imagining the Standard to be theirs, were asked, "Is this object exactly like yours?" The children responded "Yes" or "No" without receiving information about whether the response was correct. After the children responded, the experimenter presented another Comparison tumbler and continued to do so until a total of four Comparison tumblers was presented. Then the experimenter repeated the series or started a new one.

The training took place in two stages. In Stage 1, the Comparison tumblers of a series differed from the Standard in height or brightness, but not both. This part of training therefore resembled Panels A and B in Fig. 8.1, in which the cylinders differed in height or thickness. The experimenter employed a number of different Standards for each kind of series, height and brightness, and repeated the series several times to increase exposure to the stimuli. In Stage 2 of training, the Comparison tumblers of a series differed from the Standard in *both* height and brightness, a situation resembling that in Panel C in Fig. 8.1. As in Stage 1, the experimenter employed a number of Standards and repeated the various series to increase exposure. After this sensory training, the children started Problem I of the solution shift.

Now, we know that a group of children in Tighe's (1965) study who lacked sensory training learned the reversal and nonreversal shifts at approximately equal rates. They were in transition between a primitive rat-like performance and an "intelligent" adult performance based on concept formation. How will children perform who have had sensory training? Tighe found that these children performed much as an adult would; they learned the reversal shift three times faster than the nonreversal shift, suggesting that they had formed a concept in Problem I. These results reflect favorably on the Montessori exercises. At least in the context of the solution-shift problem, sensory training accelerates intellectual development.

The role of language in concept formation   Not only has the adult had more opportunity for perceptual learning than the preschool child, the adult has acquired a far greater ability to use language. One aspect of this superiority is obvious—the adult has a richer, more extensive vocabulary than the child and has a firmer grasp of grammatical rules. Another aspect is more subtle—the adult is better able to use speech or thought to guide his or her behavior. Luria's studies (1961), discussed in Chapter 2, revealed several stages through which young children passed in acquiring this capacity. His studies showed that while children might be able to issue commands to themselves, they might not be able to obey. The children spoke, but did not necessarily "listen." According to Kendler and Kendler (1962), both aspects of language ability play a central role in solution shift performance. Sensory training such as that used by Tighe (1965) can be effective only to the extent that children possess appropriate vocabulary and can "listen" to what they say. Figure 8.3 illustrates the theory. When an adult or older child encounters a pair of stimuli, the theory assumes that the stimuli trigger an internal response that identifies the relevant dimension. This internal response, symbolized "r," would be the word "size" in Fig. 8.3 (a). The internal response has a stimulus component ("s") which eventually evokes the external response of choosing the correct stimulus—a small tumbler. In essence, the theory asserts that mature subjects think before they act. Only after internally stating the relevant dimension do the subjects make a choice.

In a reversal shift (b), subjects retain the internal response, "size," but must change the external response and choose a large tumbler instead of a small one. In a nonreversal shift (c), the subjects must change both the internal and external response, since a new dimension becomes relevant (brightness) and the subjects must choose a black tumbler instead of a small one. Because the reversal shift requires fewer new responses than the nonreversal shift, the reversal shift is learned more rapidly. It is important to remember that there is more to this process than an understanding of the words "size" and "brightness." A young child may be fully able to attach these labels to the appropriate dimensions, but still not perform in the manner of an adult. The child might first choose a tumbler and then state the relevant dimension, or make the two responses simultaneously. The adult first labels the relevant dimension, then chooses.

The theory of Kendler and Kendler is a "mediational" one. The internal response, $r - s$, acts as a bridge between visible stimuli, the tumblers, and a visible response, the act of choosing. Recall that a similar mechanism was proposed years ago by Hull (1930; 1931) in a different context. Early learning theorists had sought to explain the simple, but theoretically important, fact that a hungry rat would run a maze for food (Chapter 6). Cognitive psychologists such as Tolman maintained that the rat ran because it "expected" food. Behaviorists, wishing to avoid any reference to mental activity, maintained that the maze elicited a fractional goal response, r_g, consisting of chewing movements, salivation, etc. This "little" goal response had a stimulus component, s_g, that had become conditioned to running. Although we did not observe $r_g - s_g$ directly, it nevertheless served as mediator between the stimulus of the maze and the response of running. Many behaviorists felt that the $r_g - s_g$ mechanism could explain intelligent, goal-directed behavior and that we did not need to assume that rats could "think." Now, in the theory of Kendler and Kendler, we see a revival of the $r_g - s_g$ mechanism in a context that

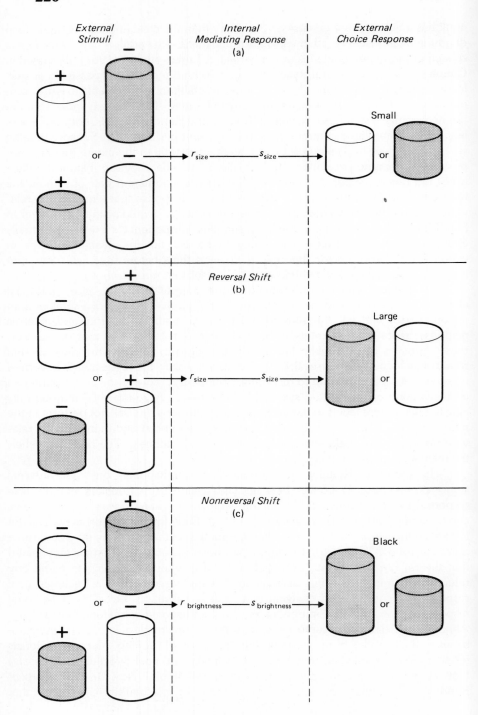

CONCEPT FORMATION

explicitly recognizes the existence of thought. The $r_g - s_g$ mechanism is attractive to many behaviorists today not because it is a substitute for thought, but because it seems to be a useful way of explaining thought. All the principles of learning established with lower animals are assumed to apply to these internal responses as well. For example, the principle of extinction would explain why it takes the adult so long to stop paying attention to the dimension of size in the reversal shift and to start paying attention to brightness. Extinction is a gradual process, not an instantaneous one (Chapter 3). Later, in Chapter 9, we will encounter still another version of the $r_g - s_g$ mechanism, one with far greater scope than any discussed thus far. This version forms the basis of a general theory of language and meaning (Mowrer, 1960).

The theory of Kendler and Kendler suggests that language training, appropriately designed, might make reversal shifts easier for young children to perform than nonreversal shifts. However, Kendler, Kendler, and Wells (1960) found no effect of language training on the performance of nursery school children. After reaching a criterion of mastery on Problem (a), but before going on to Problem (b), the children were given 10 additional trials on Problem (a). On these trials, the children attached labels to both the positive and negative stimuli, so that if the relevant dimension was size, the children might indicate that the "big" one was right and the "small" one was wrong. After making the verbal responses, the children chose a stimulus and received reward if correct. Children who received the language training performed in much the same manner as children who did not; they learned the nonreversal shift faster than the reversal shift. The problem may have been that nursery school children are incapable of performing like adults (subjects in Tighe's successful study with sensory training were somewhat older), but it is also possible that they had simply received too little training. Kendler, Kendler, and Wells observed that some children occasionally stated the correct solution but made the wrong choice. Perhaps the connection between verbalization and choosing was weak and would have become stronger with additional practice.

That four-year-olds can acquire verbal labels and use them in a solution shift situation has been shown by Kendler and Kendler (1962). Their procedure, which differed from that of Kendler, Kendler, and Wells (1960) in several ways, is illustrated in Fig. 8.4. In Problem I, the children were rewarded for choosing a large black square over a small white square. In addition, some children were required to

Fig. 8.3 How older children and adults solve solution shift problems, according to Kendler and Kendler. In each row of panels, the panel on left shows the stimuli presented for choice, the center panel shows the internal response produced by these stimuli, and the panel on right shows the response that the experimenter sees—the subject selects one or the other tumbler depending on which pair of tumblers was presented for choice. All subjects acquire an internal response labeling the dimension of size in (a). For subjects who encounter the reversal shift (b), this response continues to be appropriate and is maintained. For subjects who encounter the nonreversal shift (c), a new internal response must be learned which labels the dimension of brightness. Because the internal response must be changed in the nonreversal shift, this type of problem is harder to solve than the reversal shift.

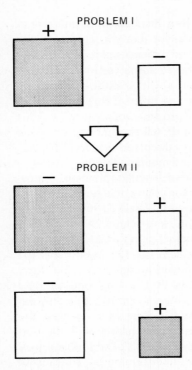

Fig. 8.4 Stimuli used by Kendler and Kendler (1962) in variation of solution shift problem presented to young children.

name the stimulus that they chose. One group learned to say "large" when they chose the large black square while another group learned to say "black." Of course, both labels were correct and appropriate at this point. In Problem II, two pairs of squares were presented: large black together with small white, and large white together with small black. The appropriate choice was always the smaller of the two, regardless of brightness. Now, children who had learned to say "large" in Problem I were verbalizing the relevant dimension in Problem II (although the precise value that they stated was incorrect), but children who learned to say "black" in Problem I were verbalizing an irrelevant dimension. On the basis of the mediational theory, we would expect the relevant verbalization to produce faster learning than the irrelevant. In the relevant case, the children possessed the appropriate mediator and only had to change the choice response. In the irrelevant case, the children had to learn a new mediator and a new choice response. The results were consistent with the mediational theory. Children in the irrelevant verbalization condition required almost twice as many trials to master Problem II as children in the relevant

CONCEPT FORMATION

verbalization condition. Children who were not required to verbalize the solution in Problem I mastered the problem at an intermediate rate. Thus, depending on the type of label a child has available, language can either facilitate or hinder concept formation.

Concept formation and mental retardation

Our discussion of concept formation thus far has emphasized learning in young children with normal intelligence. But what of children with mental deficits? For example, does the learning process of normal children resemble that of mentally retarded individuals of comparable mental age but higher chronological age? Let us briefly review what has been said about normal children. Young children have difficulty perceiving dimensions. They do not readily see that a big object and a small object are points on a continuum, but instead they tend to see two isolated objects. To form a concept of "large," the child must be able to perceive the relationship between large and small and to ignore the irrelevant dimensions at the same time, such as the brightness of the objects. The sensory training procedure of Tighe (1965) and the language training procedure of Kendler and Kendler (1962) were designed to help the child place objects on dimensions and to see that different dimensions were separable. Studies of concept formation in retarded individuals (Zeaman and House, 1963) suggest that retardates have a different problem. Retardates are not necessarily unable to perceive dimensions; they seem to have difficulty paying attention to the appropriate ones.

Zeaman and House (1963) formulated this theory after examining the performance of retardates on simple discrimination tasks. The subjects had mental ages from two to six years, but of course they were chronologically much older. In a typical experiment, the subjects were presented with a triangle and a circle, the positions of which were varied randomly from trial to trial. The subject's task was to choose the triangle on every trial regardless of whether the triangle appeared on the left side or the right side. Mastery of the problem came slowly, but progress was not always slow. For many sessions the subjects performed at a chance level, choosing the triangle on about 50 percent of the trials. But then, rather abruptly, the subjects improved and they soon mastered the problem completely. "Fast" learners—those retardates who required just a few sessions to master the problem—showed the same pattern as "slow" learners. The main difference between fast and slow learners was the number of sessions in which performance remained at a chance level. There were more such sessions for slow learners, but once the slow learners began to improve, they improved at the same rate as fast learners.

Zeaman and House theorized that the two segments of the learning curve were related to the acquisition of two kinds of response. First, the subject had to learn to pay attention to the relevant dimension—form. Only after the subject had learned to attend to form did it become possible to learn the response of choosing the triangle. If, on a particular trial, the subject attended to position, the irrelevant dimension, he or she could learn something about the left side or the right side, but that was all. On this assumption, we would expect progress to be slow until the subject "looked" at the form of the objects. The most that a subject would learn by attending to position would be that each side yielded reward on 50 percent of the trials. While attending to position, the subject might respond all the time on one side or alternate randomly, since there would be no advantage to adopting either strategy. In both cases, the subject would end up with a record of about 50 percent correct responses. But once the subject observed the form of the objects, it would soon become apparent that the triangle yielded reward on 100 percent of the trials and the circle on 0 percent. The result would be an abrupt transition from performance at a chance level to rapid learning, the pattern actually observed. According to Zeaman and House, one of the major obstacles that retardates generally face when solving problems is the one they believed to be present here—learning to pay attention to the relevant features of the situation.

Selective attention   Is the theory plausible? Could a person see an object on the left or right side without noticing its form? "Tuning in" one feature of a situation while "tuning out" another is really a very familiar phenomenon. Cherry (1953) has called it the "cocktail party" effect—the kind of effect in which we listen to one conversation in a crowded room while ignoring other conversations nearby. In a classic study, Cherry (1953) simulated the cocktail party effect by playing two recorded messages to subjects through headphones, one message to the left ear and one to the right. When subjects were asked to repeat the message in one ear as it played, they could do so. But they usually could not say much about the message presented to the other ear. While they might know that sounds were present, they were ignorant of the content. Their attention was highly selective in nature, "tuning in" one source of information while "tuning out" another. **Selective attention** is a basic psychological process, appearing in lower animals such as pigeons (Reynolds, 1961a) and rats (Mackintosh, 1965) as well as humans. For example, in Reynolds' (1961a) study, one pigeon "tuned in" a triangle but "tuned out" the color of the background on which the triangle was projected. With selective attention so prevalant, it is not hard to imagine that it may be a significant factor in retardate learning.

Zeaman and House (1963) assume, then, that retardates are capable of recognizing dimensions when they see them, but they take a long time to shift their attention from irrelevant dimensions to relevant dimensions. The performance of retardates on reversal and nonreversal shifts supports that view. The subjects in a solution-shift experiment by Zeaman and House had mental ages comparable to those of young children with average intelligence. As we have already seen, young children of normal intelligence usually learn a nonreversal shift faster than a reversal shift, or learn the two problems at equal rates. The retardates in Zeaman and House's experiment learned the reversal shift faster than the nonreversal shift, and to this extent they performed in much the same manner as would a normal individual who could perceive dimensions. This suggests that remedial instruction for the retarded should concentrate on ways of directing attention specifically to the relevant features of a problem rather than on teaching what dimensions are. For example, Tighe's (1965) sensory training procedure taught children the independence of height and brightness by having the children make comparative judgments on each dimension separately. Tighe did not direct attention specifically to the dimension that would later be relevant in the problem situation. Retardates apparently require this kind of direction (cf. Lobb and Childs, 1973).

One instructional technique evaluated by Żeaman and House (1963) and found effective helps retardates form concepts of two-dimensional patterns. As we have seen, retardates usually find pattern discriminations difficult. Before attempting a discrimination, the subject practices with three-dimensional objects that correspond to the two-dimensional patterns. Experience with the three-dimensional figures appears to heighten sensitivity to the distinctive features of the two-dimensional ones. In other words, the child generalizes his or her concept of the figures. Interestingly, a similar approach has long been used in Montessori preschools with normal children (Montessori, 1914). Young children, like older retardates, often require assistance in making pattern discriminations. Montessori's method, like the one tested by Zeaman and House, relies on prior experience with three-dimensional objects, but it includes additional refinements to make the transition to patterns easier. To illustrate, let us use the Montessori materials to teach a child to distinguish rectangles from triangles. First, we present the child with the materials shown in Fig. 8.5, a set of rectangular objects and a set of triangular objects. The figures are held in frames, which, like the figures themselves, have an instructional purpose. Each figure is colored blue and the surface of the frame beneath the figure is also blue. Because the colors are the same, the surface produces an image of the object when the child lifts the object out of the frame. At once, the child notices the correspondence between the three-dimensional figure and the two-dimensional one. The child now handles and inspects the figure, extracting information about its distinctive features through the sense of touch as well as the visual sense.

After the child has fully explored the objects, we give him or her a set of cards designed to bridge the gap between object and pattern. These cards are illustrated in Fig. 8.6. In addition to the cards associated with rectangles and triangles, cards are shown for a variety of other figures such as a pentagon, trapezoid, and circle. A given figure requires three cards, one depicting the figure in blue, one showing a thick blue outline of the figure, and one giving only a thin black outline of the figure. Since our goal is to familiarize the child with rectangles and triangles, we might select the three rectangles shown in Column 1, Rows A, B, and C, and the three right triangles shown in Column 2. The child begins by resting the appropriate three-dimensional objects on the solid blue two-dimensional figures in Row A. The child is prepared to do this because he or she has previously observed a similar correspondence between these objects and the surface of the frame. Next, the child places the objects on the cards showing a blue outline of the figures, and finally the child places the objects on the cards showing the black outline. Using this series of gradual steps, we keep the child attentive to the relevant features of the figures. The

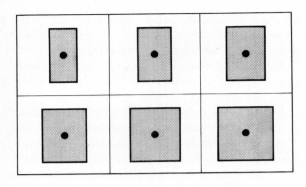

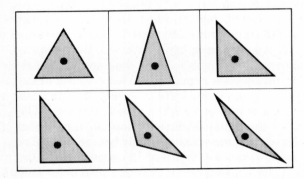

Fig. 8.5 Three dimensional forms developed by Montessori to teach children the concepts of rectangle and triangle. Upon lifting a form, the child notices that it is of the same color as the bottom surface of the frame (blue). This correspondence draws attention to the relationship between three-dimensional and two-dimensional figures. (From Montessori, 1914)

physical changes from one step to another are not distracting because the child is always prepared for them. As the final step in our procedure, we might teach the child the name of each figure so that he or she may apply it to objects and patterns in his or her everyday experience. Montessori (1914) observes that young children are eager to learn even the most exotic terms and use the terms happily and spontaneously. For example, Montessori (1914, p. 35) relates the following story of a disadvantaged child who had used her exercises:

> In one of the people's dwellings at Milan, a mother, preparing the dinner in the kitchen, took from a packet a slice of bread and butter. Her little four-year-old boy who was with her said, "Rectangle." The woman going on with her work cut off a large corner of the slice of bread, and the child cried out, "Triangle." She put this bit into the saucepan, and the child, looking at the piece that was left, called out more loudly than before, "And now it is a trapezium."

CONCEPT FORMATION

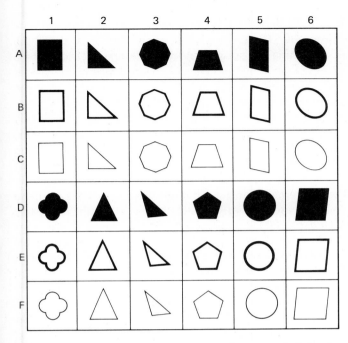

Fig. 8.6 Cards designed by Montessori for use with three-dimensional forms like those in Fig. 8.5. Purpose of cards is to help child perceive relationship between three-dimensional and two-dimensional figures. Some cards display figures in solid blue color (rows A and D), the same color as the three-dimensional forms. Other cards display figures in heavy blue outlines (rows B and E), while a third set of cards displays figures in thin black outlines (rows C and F). Child places the appropriate three-dimensional form on each type of card, going from the first type to the third. (From Montessori, 1914)

The father, a working man, who was present, was much impressed with the incident. He went straight to look for the teacher and asked for an explanation. Much moved, he said, "If I had been educated in that way I should not now be just an ordinary workman."

ACCELERATING INTELLECTUAL DEVELOPMENT: WHAT ARE THE LIMITS?

If you have access to a five-year-old child, a pair of scissors, and a piece of paper, you may wish to perform a revealing experiment. First, cut out eight male figures and separate them into two groups, four figures per group. Then, tell the child that all the figures on one side are fathers and all the figures on the other side doctors. Relate the story that one of the fathers is a doctor and gets up early in the morning to join the other doctors at work. Here you should move one of the figures from the fathers' group to the doctors' group. Now, referring to the doll that you have just moved, ask the child, "Is he still a father?" The question may seem absurd, but the answer will probably surprise you. There is a good chance that the child will say "No." In the child's eyes, by joining the group of doctors, the man ceases to be a father. That was the typical response of five-year-old children to this and similar problems studied by Sigel, Saltz, and Roskind (1967). An equivalent problem employed female figures, one group of which were mothers and the other group schoolteachers. When a mother joined the group of schoolteachers, she usually shared the fate of the father who joined the doctors: She ceased to be a mother. The likelihood that children would give such answers decreased with age, reaching a very low probability by the age of eight years. Children of five may appear to understand the concepts of "mother" and "father," but the results of this study indicate that their concepts are extremely narrow. That narrowness extends to many more concepts besides "mother" and "father." You can demonstrate the generality of the phenomenon by asking the child to play another game. Take three glasses— two tall slender ones and a short broad one—and fill the two tall glasses with equal amounts of water. Ask the child if he agrees that the amounts are equal, making whatever adjustments are necessary to secure his agreement. Then, pour all of the water from one tall glass into the short glass. Ask the child, "Do you think that this glass (the tall one) has more water, do the glasses have the same amount, or does this one (the short glass) have more water?" You may be surprised to hear the child say, "The tall one has more." The irrelevant change in water level is likely to distort the child's judgment of volume much as the irrelevant feature of occupation distorted his judgments of "mother" and "father." If you have managed to maintain the child's attentiveness thus far, you might try one more experiment. Take 14 objects—pennies, poker chips, bottle caps, or whatever you can find—and arrange them in two horizontal rows, seven objects to a row. Arrange the objects so that the rows are equally long and the objects within each row are at equal distances from one another. Ask the child to confirm that there are as many objects in one row as in the other. If he can do this, then extend one row so that it is twice the length of the other, keeping the distances beween objects equal. Now, ask the child, "Do you think there are more pennies in this row (the longer one), the same number of pennies, or does this row (the short one) have more?" The child may reply that the long row has more pennies, the change in length distorting his judgment of number.

This pattern of distortions was first reported by the developmental psychologist Jean Piaget (1950; 1952), and it has become the focal point of a vigorous debate on whether we can truly accelerate intellectual development. At about the age of seven, children begin to recognize that "volume," "number," "length," and other dimensions remain constant despite irrelevant changes in appearance. Piaget called this ability **conservation** to capture the idea that children preserved the integrity of a concept in the face of irrelevant changes. As we have seen, the ability to conserve qualitative concepts such as "mother" tends to follow the same chronological course as the ability to conserve quantitative ones. This suggests that conservation is a fundamental ability, its development underlying the acquisition of a wide variety of concepts. Many psychologists and educators have wondered whether we must wait for conservation to develop naturally. Perhaps there is a way to make conservation emerge at an earlier age and thereby enable us to accelerate intellectual development. In Chapter 6 we saw that the behavioristic tradition, beginning with John B. Watson, has always held an optimistic view of human potential. The ability to learn was great at any age, and with appropriate educational technology, we could expect remarkable achievements. From the behavioristic standpoint, it should be possible to teach young children to conserve concepts. Piaget, a cognitive psychologist, has a somewhat different view. He believes that conservation naturally emerges as part of a general reorganization of mental structure. It is not an isolated ability and could not emerge without appropriate supporting abilities. This view implies that we could teach conservation only by inducing the development of a complex mental structure. That is a far more difficult task than the one envisioned by behaviorists, who typically have a narrower focus. To the behaviorist, conservation may depend on other skills, but producing conservation should not require a massive change in intellectual capacity.

There have been many attempts to teach conservation, but they have been on a much smaller scale than would be ideal from Piaget's perspective. The studies have usually been performed over a short period of time, and they have focused on the immediate goal of teaching conservation, rather than the broader objective of inducing a new phase of mental development. Nevertheless, on the basis of an extensive review of conservation training experiments, Brainerd and Allen (1971) concluded that conservation could be artificially induced. We must qualify that conclusion, however, for as Kuhn (1974) points out, different studies have used different indexes of conservation attainment, and there is no general agreement on what constitutes a valid index. Although the weight of evidence supports the view that training accelerates development of conservation, the issue remains controversial.

Teaching conservation: The Piagetian approach

The experimenter's choice of a teaching method in a conservation training study reflects his or her ideas about the nature of the learning process. If the method is found to be effective, the experimenter's theory is supported. But equally important, the discovery of an effective method for teaching conservation leads to a quick practical application, since conservation is an important educational goal. To illustrate the relationship between theory and practice, let us examine Piaget's approach to learning in general, and then the method for teaching conservation that follows from his approach.

Piaget's theory   According to Piaget, every organism, at every stage of life, has a basic goal—to adapt to the environment, to function effectively in the world. In pursuit of adaptation, the human organism constructs ways of behaving and thinking that are highly organized. Organization can be seen in the simple behavior of an infant grasping a rattle. Grasping requires coordination of several actions. To reach for the rattle, the infant must look at it and coordinate looking with arm movement. To hold the rattle, the infant must coordinate arm movement with the action of its fingers. For Piaget, psychological development involves the progressive modification and bringing together of different activities. Piaget (1952) illustrates the process of development with observations of his infant daughter, Jacqueline. At the age of one month, Jacqueline would cease crying upon hearing a voice or a sound, but she showed no special recognition of the sound, nor did she attempt to locate the source visually. After several days, she smiled when she heard a pleasing sound, showing development of her ability to listen, but Jacqueline did not yet know that sounds had sources that might be visible. Several days later, Piaget noted that when he spoke, Jacqueline moved her head in the direction of his voice. Subsequently, she simply moved her eyes and was able to localize the source of the sound precisely. Jacqueline possibly did not know that the visual object directly caused the sound, but she had succeeded in coordinating two psychological "structures"—listening and looking. Together, listening and looking formed a new structure that enhanced Jacqueline's adaptation to the environment.

In Piaget's theory, the process of adaptation has two aspects, **assimilation** and **accommodation.** Once a psychological structure has been established, there is a tendency to apply it to new situations, to "assimilate" new realities into the structure. An infant may originally have learned to grasp things by clasping its fingers around narrow objects such as people's fingers and utensils. Subsequently, the infant may attempt to grasp a large pillow in the same manner and fail because it has not sufficiently opened its hand. The child's first tendency is to assimilate the pillow into the existing structure. Not succeeding, the infant perhaps reaches for the pillow again with fingers spread more widely apart. It now seeks to "accommodate" the existing structure to a new reality by changing a part of the structure. If the child manages to grasp the pillow, the newly modified structure will have enhanced adaptation and will be preserved until new objects are encountered requiring further accommodation. Piaget maintains that there is a basic tendency to construct psychological structures that are stable, needing very few changes. Such a structure would be sufficiently developed that a person could readily assimilate new events into it and could easily accommodate the structure to new demands. Structures that achieve this sort of balance between assimilation and accommodation are said to be in a state of **equilibrium.**

Thus far we have focused on the simple behavioral structures of the infant. As the individual matures, not only do behavioral structures increase in complexity, but mental structures emerge. Piaget (1952) sees the beginning of true mental activity occurring between the ages of 18 months and two years, toward the end of the **sensorimotor** phase of development. To illustrate the emergence of mental processes, he relates observations of his daughter, Lucienne, at this developmental stage. Piaget and Lucienne played a game in which the goal was to remove a chain from a matchbox. They had played the game on several previous occasions, and Lucienne had acquired two strategies for retrieving the chain. Either she would turn the matchbox over, causing the chain to drop out, or she would slide her fingers

CONCEPT FORMATION

through the opening on top and pick the chain out. Piaget now made the opening smaller than before so that neither strategy would work. A child younger than Lucienne would probably have responded to the dilemma by physically manipulating the box in a trial-and-error fashion. Lucienne's search for an appropriate strategy was internal (mental) rather than external (behavioral). She paused awhile and focused all her attention on the box. Then she quickly slid the match cover open and picked out the chain. This pattern of problem-solving—a pause followed by rapid execution of the movements necessary for reaching the goal—is reminiscent of the pattern Kohler identified as characteristic of insight (Chapter 6). We can almost hear Lucienne say, "Aha," as she perceives the relationship between the matchbox cover and the size of the opening. Piaget believed that the capacity for insight emerged toward the end of the sensorimotor phase when the child developed an ability to substitute mental activity for physical activity.

Mental activity later undergoes three successive stages of development, according to Piaget. After the sensorimotor phase, the child enters the **preoperational phase,** which lasts until the age of about seven years. The child in the preoperational stage has only a primitive grasp of logical operations and generally thinks on an intuitive level. The failure to grasp logical operations is revealed, in part, by violations of the conservation principle. For example, when water is poured from a tall thin glass into a small broad glass, the child fails to see that the increase in width compensates for the decrease in height. The child does not coordinate the two dimensions. In addition, the child fails to see that if the water were poured back into the tall glass, it would reach the original level. The child cannot reverse operations. The **concrete operational phase** of development, beginning at about seven years, continues until the age of about 11 and involves the development of logical operations lacking in previous stages. It is in the concrete operational phase that children come to grasp the principle of conservation; they can coordinate two or more dimensions and can reverse operations. However, the capacity for abstract thought is limited and logical operations are applied mainly to objects in the children's immediate experience. The children can solve conservation problems because they deal with concrete objects that are physically present. It is in the **formal operational stage** of development that children achieve the ability to think abstractly, to manipulate symbols, and to reason by deduction. These three stages of mental development reflect qualitatively different ways of thinking, according to Piaget—the child does more than simply accumulate facts—but the basic process by which thought changes from one stage to the next is always the same. It is always a process of assimilation and accomodation, an attempt to apply existing structures to new situations, and to change structures to account for discrepant facts.

Application to conservation Piaget's view of thought has straightforward implications for education. To correct a deficiency in thinking, we must find a way to induce **cognitive conflict.** We must confront the existing mental structure with facts that cannot possibly be assimilated into the structure. To accommodate these facts, the mental structure would have to change. Gruen (1965) devised a procedure for teaching conservation based on the principle of cognitive conflict. For comparison, Gruen also devised a procedure based upon the familiar principle of reinforcement. Conservation of number was the focus of the study. The subjects were about five years of age and were screened to ensure that they did not show conservation prior to training, and could also count to nine, a skill essential to solving the problem that Gruen used. Two rows of corks, nine per row, were arranged in parallel fashion on a table. When the distances between corks in the two rows were equal, the children recognized that they contained an equal number of corks. But when the distances between corks in one row were increased or decreased, making that row longer or shorter than the other, the children usually changed their judgments. If the row was longer, they said it had more corks and if it was shorter, they said it had less. The object of training was to teach the children that the number did not change with changes in the length of the row. Two training sessions were conducted, each consisting of 16 trials in which the width of one row was varied. After each change in width the experimenter asked the standard conservation question: "Do you think there are more corks in this row, the same number of corks in each row, or more corks in that row?" The procedures that followed the child's response defined the teaching method. In the reinforcement method, the child counted the number of corks in each row and thereby received feedback on whether his or her response was right or wrong. Reinforcement theory would suggest that correct (conservation) responses would increase in strength through reinforcement while incorrect responses would decrease through extinction. In the cognitive conflict method, the child did not count the corks but rather the experimenter subtracted a cork from whichever row the child thought had more. Corks were always subtracted from the center of the row to keep the width of the row constant. After removing the cork, the experimenter asked, "Now, which row has more corks, this row or that row?" If the child made another wrong response, the experimenter removed a second cork and then repeated the question. After every wrong response, the experimenter subtracted another cork, continuing to remove corks until the child changed his or her response. The intent of the subtraction procedure was to remove so many corks from the longer row that it would become obvious that it had fewer corks. We might imagine that up to the point when the children changed their minds, they experienced progressively greater conflict. Their use of length as a measure of number was in conflict with the actual number of corks on the table. Initially, the children would attempt to assimilate the shrinking number of corks into a faulty mental structure, but eventually the discrepancy between number and length would become too large to assimilate and accommodation would occur. The children would eventually ignore length when determining number.

After training, the reinforcement and cognitive conflict groups were retested on the number conservation problem initially used to determine that they lacked conservation. This test problem resembled the training problem but it was not a carbon copy. Poker chips were used rather than corks: seven white chips in one row and seven blue chips in the other. Upon retesting the children, Gruen found that the cognitive conflict group gave more conservation responses than the reinforcement group. The reinforcement group gave about the same number of conservation responses as a control group which received no conservation training, but rather performed an irrelevant task with the experimenter. These results support Piaget's principle of cognitive conflict, but they do not mean that reinforcement was an unimportant factor. Presumably, the children in the cognitive conflict group received reinforcement when they made correct responses, and underwent extinction when they made incorrect responses. Reinforcement plus cognitive conflict was apparently more effective than reinforcement alone. In other words, the effectiveness of reinforcement depended on how it was used.

It should be emphasized that while the results were consistent with a Piagetian principle, Piaget himself would not favor a procedure such as Gruen's unless the child was developmentally ready for it. If conservation training were administered prematurely, he would expect the effects to be temporary and highly task-specific. To evaluate Piaget's position, more complicated research strategies will be needed. Children will have to be tested and retested over longer periods of time, and in a greater diversity of settings, than has been customary.

COMPLEX CONCEPTS: FOOD FOR THOUGHT

The next page contains the solution to a conceptual problem, which you may wish to solve before turning this page. The problem is this. The author has a friend who has strong opinions about the kinds of foods people should eat. He finds only a restricted range of foods acceptable and refuses to eat many foods that others might consider nutritious. Listed below are 11 foods together with his judgments of whether the foods are acceptable or unacceptable. As you go through the list, see if you can construct a general statement about this person's dietary values:

	Food	Acceptable?
1.	Sardines	No
2.	Raisins	Yes
3.	Potato (baked)	No
4.	Carrots	Yes
5.	Chicken	No
6.	Lettuce	Yes
7.	Zucchini (steamed)	No
8.	Celery	Yes
9.	Hamburger	No
10.	Apples	Yes
11.	Tomatoes (stewed)	No

If you have correctly conceptualized his values, then you should be able to utilize the concept to predict his judgment of the following food: 100% whole wheat bread. If you said "acceptable," you are wrong. The author's friend frowns on whole wheat bread, or any bread for that matter. His idea of a good food is any "raw fruit or vegetable." Since bread is baked (like the potato on line 3), it would be judged unacceptable.

The concept "raw fruit or vegetable" is more complex than may be apparent. We can see its complexity best when we analyze the concept in logical terms. To begin this analysis, let us focus on the first half of the concept, the part about the "raw fruit." We can say that this part of the concept has two **attributes,** the quality of rawness, and the quality of fruit. We can also say that the idea of "raw fruit" contains a rule relating one attribute to the other. The requirement that a food must be both raw and a fruit is an example of a rule known as **conjunction.** A food satisfies our definition only if both attributes are present. A convenient shorthand method for writing and analyzing concepts is to represent attributes by letters, for example, R could stand for "raw" and F for "fruit." By convention, the symbol •, a centered dot, represents the conjunctive rule, so that the idea of a "raw fruit" would become:

R • F

Similarly, the idea of a "raw vegetable" could be represented as:

R • V

These ideas would be quite different if their attributes were tied together by another rule called **disjunction.** (symbolized "v"). The disjunctive rule states that a stimulus is an instance of a concept if one or both attributes of the concept are present. Thus, to fit the category, (R v F), a food would have to be raw, or a fruit, or a raw fruit. You can see that such a diet would be ridiculous. Using the disjunctive rule, the author's friend would be willing to eat raw hamburgers but not cooked hamburgers! It is evident that a seemingly small change in a conceptual rule can make for a big change in the concept.

Actually, disjunction is involved here but in a complex way. A food would be considered acceptable if it fell in the category (R • F) *or* (R • V). The disjunctive element, "or," relates one category to the other. Thus, we have the following representation of the concept:

(R • F) v (R • V)

From the foregoing analysis, you may have gotten the impression that the author's friend is a rabbit. This is not so; by all accounts he is fully human. To do him justice, it should be said that his diet is somewhat broader than the one we have discussed. In addition to eating raw fruits and raw vegetables, he often eats cultured milk products such as cheese and yogurt. As an exercise, you may wish to add "cultured milk product" to our formal representation of the concept, above.

Concepts, then, can become quite complex, even concepts of everyday things such as what people eat. Our concept of the diet contrasts markedly with the simple concepts studied in the solution shift problem. In solution shifts, concepts are defined by the simple presence of a single attribute, for example, "smaller" or "darker." When the simple presence of an attribute defines a concept, the rule is called **affirmation.** When the simple absence of an attribute defines a concept, the rule is called **negation.** For example, a "coward" is a person who lacks the attribute of courage.

Which concepts are the most difficult to learn?

All concepts involve rules, and some rules tax the intellect more than others. As one might expect, the rules that are the most difficult to learn are the ones that are logically most complex. Neisser and Weene (1962) distinguished three levels of logical complexity and showed that they correspond to three levels of psychological difficulty. Table 8.1 summarizes this hierarchy of rules. On the lowest level of complexity, Level 1, are the simple rules of affirmation and negation, the simple presence or absence of a single attribute. On Level 2 are rules involving the presence or absence of two attributes. Conjunction and disjunction fall into this category as well as several variations of these rules. Whereas conjunction and disjunction specify that one or more attributes must be present, most other rules on Level 2 specify that one or more attributes must be absent. Thus "conjunctive absence" refers to a concept in which two specific attributes are missing. (In conjunction, two specific attributes must be present.) A possible example of conjunctive absence would be a doctor's concept of a nonallergenic food, one which contains neither strawberries nor tomatoes. Letting the symbol -, a short dash, represent the idea "not," we could symbolize this concept as $(-S \cdot -T)$. "Disjunctive absence" refers to a concept in which one or both attributes are missing. (In disjunction, one or both attributes are present.) A possible example of disjunctive absence would be one's concept of a "poor quality product," one which lacks superior materials (M), superior workmanship (W), or both $(-S \vee -M)$. All the rules on Level 2 have one feature in common: They specify combinations of two attributes, each of which may be either present or absent. In that sense, Level 2 rules are built from Level 1 rules, which refer to the presence or absence of a single attribute. Level 3 rules are built from Level 2 rules and are thus the most complex. The components of Level 3 rules are pairs of attributes rather than single attributes. For example, the "either/or" rule states that A must be present and B absent $(A \cdot -B)$ or B must be present and A absent $(-A \cdot B)$. In other words, you must have either A or B but not both. This is the rule for negative numbers in multiplication. The number 5×-2 gives a negative product, -5×2 gives a negative product, but -5×-2 gives a positive product. Either the 5 or the 2 must be negative, but not both.

To test the psychological difficulty of these rules, Neisser and Weene presented subjects with strings of four letters, each printed on a separate card. In each of the four positions of the card, the subject might see any one of the letters J, Q, V, X, or Z. Altogether, there were 625 possible combinations of these five letters taken four at a time: JJJJ, JJJQ, JJJV, QJQZ, . . . ZZZZ. Subjects were instructed to

242

Table 8.1 Types of concepts which can be defined by presence or absence of two features (from Neisser and Weene, 1962.)

Name and symbolic designation	Description of positive instance	Example
Level 1		
Presence (A)	A must be present	Vertebrate: must have a backbone
Absence (−A)	A must not be present (complement of presence)	Invertebrate: must not have a backbone
Level 2		
Conjunction (A·B)	Both A and B must be present	Good quality: both material and workmanship must be first class
Disjunction (AvB)	Either A or B or both must be present	Allergenic: a food which contains either tomatoes or strawberries (for example)
Exclusion (A·−B)	A must be present and B not present	Eligible for driver's license: must have passed test and not have committed felony
Disjunctive absence (−Av−B)	Either A or B, or both, must be absent (complement of conjunction)	Poor quality: either material or workmanship is not first class
Conjunctive absence (−A·−B)	A and B must both be absent (complement of disjunction)	Nonallergenic: a food which contains neither tomatoes nor strawberries (for example)
Implication (−AvB)	A may be absent, but if A is present then B must be also; thus A implies B (complement of exclusion)	Ineligible for driver's license: must either have not passed test or have committed felony
Level 3		
Either/or (A·−B)v(−A·B)	Either A or B must be present, but not both together	Negative product: either factor negative, but not both
Both/neither (A·B)v(−A·−B)	Both A and B must be present, unless neither is (complement of either/or)	Positive product: both factors may be negative, or neither, but not just one

CONCEPT FORMATION

look for the presence or absence of particular letters and to ignore the serial position of letters. They were also told that not more than two letters would be relevant in any one problem. Thus, if the concept were "presence of X," the following cases could be examples of the concept: XJJJ, JJXJ, QVXZ, XXXQ. If the concept were "conjunctive absence of X and Z" (both X and Z missing), the following cases could be examples of the concept: JJJJ, JVQJ, VQJV, VJJV. The concept "either X or Z but not both" could appear as XJVQ, JVVX, ZZZZ, XXVV. From these examples, you may be able to sense the difficulty a subject would encounter who received no advance knowledge about the rule.

On a given trial, the experimenter presented a card that either exemplified or did not exemplify the concept. When a card was shown, the subject flipped a switch up if he or she thought the card was an example of the concept, and down if he or she thought the card was not an example. After the subject responded, the experimenter informed him or her of the correct answer. The experimenter continued to present cards until the subject satisfied a criterion of mastery: 25 consecutive trials with at least 24 correct responses. The experimenter simply terminated the problem if the subject failed to satisfy the criterion in 100 trials. All subjects were presented with all of the concepts shown in Table 8.1 (in a random order).

Neisser and Weene found that the number of trials required to reach criterion was lowest for Level 1 concepts, highest for Level 3 concepts, and intermediate for Level 2 concepts. There was no overlap between levels. All Level 2 rules required more trials than all Level 1 rules, and all Level 3 rules required more trials than all Level 2 rules. Within a level, however, there was considerable variation in the difficulty of rules. For example, on Level 1, affirmation was more difficult than negation. On level 2, conjunction was more difficult than conjunctive absense. The reasons for such differences are not clear; we have not yet found the rule that ties all of the findings together. At present, we can say that logical complexity correlates with psychological difficulty, but the relationship is not perfect.

ADDITIONAL FACTORS INFLUENCING CONCEPT FORMATION

Knowing what the concept isn't

When we are in the process of learning a concept, we often find that an example of the concept helps to make the idea clearer. But how much clearer would the idea be after we saw a nonexample? Does knowing what something is *not* help us to understand what something is? Hovland and Weiss (1953), in a classic experiment, sought to answer that question by giving subjects the following sort of problem. Imagine that you are being shown a series of figures, each drawn on a separate card. The figures differ from one another along three dimensions—shape, size, and color—and there are three values on each dimension—three shapes, three sizes, and three colors. The various possibilities are listed below:

	Dimensions	
Size	*Color*	*Shape*
Small	Red	Circle
Medium	Green	Square
Large	Yellow	Triangle

On a given card, you might see a small red circle, a small red square, a large yellow square, etc. The concept that you are to discover involves only two of these dimensions. One value will be selected from each dimension and the two values will be presented together on the card. Try to state the concept by naming the two values that define the concept. Both of the following cards, below, are "positive instances" of the concept; they depict the two key values:

Card 1: Small red square

Card 2: Small yellow square

What is the concept? Clearly, the concept is a small square. When you are shown examples of what the concept *is*, you require very few cards to learn the concept. Now let us change the procedure so that cards you will see are "negative instances" of the concept. Hovland and Weiss determined that to solve the problem you would need at least 10 cards:

Card 1:	Medium green circle	Card 6:	Medium yellow square
Card 2:	Small red square	Card 7:	Medium red circle
Card 3:	Large red circle	Card 8:	Large green square
Card 4:	Small green triangle	Card 9:	Large yellow triangle
Card 5:	Large red triangle	Card 10:	Small yellow circle

The answer is "medium triangle." If you found these ten cards less instructive than the two cards in the first experiment, you shared the experience of the subjects in Hovland and Weiss's study. Almost all subjects formed the correct concept when given the minimum number of positive instances to make a deduction (2). Very few subjects formed the correct concept when given the minimum number of negative instances. The simple difference in number of instances was not the sole reason for the difference in performance. Hovland and Weiss also gave problems in which the number of positive instances equalled the number of negative instances. The difference in performance remained substantial, although it did decrease. Inexperience in using negative instances played a significant role in the study. The more practice subjects received with negative instances of the concept, the better their performance became. The effects of practice were later examined more fully in a study by Freibergs and Tulving (1961). Freibergs and Tulving gave half their subjects the minimum number of positive instances to form a concept (four) and the other half the minimum number of negative instances (also four). On the first

CONCEPT FORMATION

problem, none of the subjects receiving negative instances solved the problem in the 3.5 minute time limit, while subjects receiving positive instances solved the problem in less than three minutes. However, as additional problems were presented, the time required to form concepts decreased in both groups, and the difference between them eventually disappeared. These results suggest that we may find positive instances more helpful in learning concepts than negative instances because positive instances are more familiar. Teachers and textbooks commonly use positive instances to convey concepts, and we are accustomed to learning in that manner. But with sufficient practice we would probably be able to use positive and negative instances equally well. We might be able to form a concept as readily from 10 negative instances as from two positive ones.

Abstract concepts: Why are they difficult to learn?

If you asked a five-year-old child what money was, he or she might show you a penny or a dime. If you asked an economist the same question, you would probably get a very different kind of answer. The economist might say that money was a "commodity" that people accepted in exchange for things. Both answers would be correct, but the economist's answer would have far greater generality. Young children think in concrete, physical terms. Their concept of money is linked to a limited class of objects. Economists think in *abstract* terms. Their concept of money is linked to features that exist in many different kinds of objects. "Money" for them could be an ounce of sea salt as well as an ounce of gold, depending upon what the population accepted as a medium of exchange. Trying to explain this concept to a five-year-old would probably be a frustrating experience. Young children primarily learn concrete concepts, and later, after they have developed intellectually, they begin to learn abstract concepts. Piaget (1952) describes this advance as a transition from the "concrete operational phase" of intellectual development to the "formal operational phase." But even in the formal operational phase, abstraction continues to be a significant source of difficulty in concept learning. Adults as well as young children find abstract concepts more difficult to learn than concrete concepts. For example, Heidbreder (1947) gave college students a paired-associate task in which the stimuli were pictures and the responses were nonsense syllables. When the picture appeared, the subjects tried to anticipate the associated nonsense syllable before it was presented. An unusual feature of the task was that the picture associated with each nonsense syllable was changed from trial to trial. For example, on Trial 1, a picture of a man might be associated with the response RELK, on Trial 2 a picture of a woman might be associated with RELK, and on Trial 3 a picture of a young boy. The subject could show improvement across trials only by discovering what the pictures had in common and associating the common feature with RELK. If the subject learned to anticipate RELK when a picture appeared, we could say that he or she had formed a concept of the "human face."

A more abstract concept in Heidbreder's experiment was "number." On Trial 1, two shoes might be associated with the response "LING"; on Trial 2, two ducks;

on Trial 3, two socks. The common feature, "twoness," was abstract in that it could be present in many different kinds of objects. In contrast, the feature "human face" could be present in only one kind of object. Heidbreder found that subjects learned concrete concepts more rapidly than abstract concepts, a result that she interpreted in biological terms. Her position was that people, by nature, learned concepts with "thing-character" more readily than concepts without clear physical roots.

But other interpretations are possible. For example, the difficulty we experience when learning abstract concepts could result from other things we have learned; the problem is not necessarily biological. An important experiment by Underwood and Richardson (1956) shows how verbal habits could hinder concept learning. Subjects were given the names of four objects and were required to discover their common feature. For example, the words "barrel," "doughnut," "knob," and "balloon" might be assigned the common feature "round." The word would appear, and if the subject said "round" the experimenter would say "right." If the subject said anything else, the experimenter would say "wrong." Underwood and Richardson theorized that the ease with which a subject discovered the common feature would depend on his or her verbal habits. If subjects went into the situation with a tendency to think "round" when they saw the words individually, they would be more likely to think of "round" as the common feature. On the other hand, if each word tended to bring different ideas to mind, it would be more difficult to discover the common feature. The tendency to give a response such as "round" when presented with a stimulus such as "barrel" is called the **dominance level** of the response.

To study the effects of dominance level, Underwood and Richardson gave subjects a free-association test before conducting the concept-learning experiment. Words were flashed on a screen, and the subjects wrote down the first sense impression that came to mind. The percentage of subjects who responded with the same sense impression determined the dominance level of that response. For example, many subjects wrote "round" in response to barrel, doughnut, knob, and balloon, and so the dominance level of "round" for these words was high. But very few subjects wrote "round" in response to snail, cherry, grapefruit, or skull, and so the dominance level of "round" for these words was low. In the concept-learning experiment, some subjects were required to learn the concept "round" with the first set of words (high dominance) and some subjects were required to learn the concept "round" with the second set (low dominance). Another group had the task of learning "round" when the dominance level was "medium." Figure 8.7 shows the results for this and other concepts. Each subject encountered a list of 24 words, which were divided into sets of four words. Associated with each set was a concept for which the appropriate descriptive response had a high, medium, or low dominance level. The list was presented 20 times, so that the maximum number of correct responses a subject could give for a particular concept was 80. The graph shows that for every concept studied, the number of correct responses increased with dominance level. In other words, subjects soon discovered the common fea-

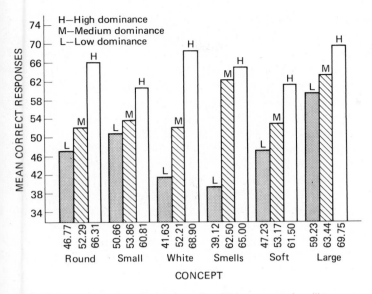

Fig. 8.7 Results of study on the role of "dominance level" in concept formation. Subjects learned to respond with each word listed on the horizontal axis to four words in a paired-associate list. Vertical axis shows number of correct response summed across the four stimulus words in a given set for 20 trials. The dominance level of a concept word in relation to the stimulus words could be "high" (open bars), "medium" (lined bars), or "low" (shaded bars). (From Underwood and Richardson, 1956)

ture of a four-word set if they already tended to think of that feature when the words were shown individually.

These results may explain why Heidbreder's subjects had difficulty learning the concept of number. On Trial 1, the subjects might see two shoes, but the dominance level of "two" would probably be low. In a free-association test, the subjects would more likely have given the response "socks" or "feet" than the response "two." Similarly, on Trial 2, the subjects might see two ducks, but the likelihood of thinking of "two" also seems low; "quack" or "water" seem more likely. If subjects thought of "socks" in the first case and "water" in the second, how could they discover that the items had something in common? The subjects' verbal habits would make concept learning very difficult. Perhaps the same principle applies to the differences we observe among people in the rate at which they learn abstract concepts. It would be easy to "explain" differences in learning by saying that they reflected differences in inherited intelligence. From an educational standpoint, that would be a pessimistic view because we cannot change a person's genetic history. But a closer analysis of a person's history of learning may reveal factors, such as verbal habits, that interfere with learning. To the extent that we can identify such factors, we are in a good position to help people learn.

248

Strategies for discovering concepts

We have now examined a wide variety of procedures for studying concept formation: solution shifts, conservation tests, the presentation of positive and negative instances of a concept, and the paired-associate procedure. These procedures differ in many ways but they do have a common feature. The experimenter, not the subject, has determined the sequence of conditions from which the concept could be inferred. For example, in the solution-shift situation, the experimenter might present a large dark cylinder together with a small white cylinder on two successive trials. On Trial 1, the large cylinder might be on the left and on Trial 2 it might be on the right. This sequence of conditions could tell the subject something about the relevance of position. If the subject chose the large cylinder on both trials and was correct both times, he or she could infer that position was irrelevant. The opportunity to make this inference was provided by the experimenter; the subject did not create the opportunity as part of a plan or strategy. Similarly, in the study by Neisser and Weene (1962) on rule learning, the experimenter arranged the order in which cards depicting letters were presented. The subject did not personally select cards from the deck to test a possible idea about the concept or to pursue an approach to the problem. When the experimenter arranges the sequence of conditions, we have what is known as a **reception procedure.** When the subject arranges the sequence, we have a **selection procedure.** The selection procedure is a relatively recent development, growing largely out of the work of Bruner, Goodnow, and Austin (1956) It is used whenever our main interest is the strategy a subject adopts when solving a conceptual problem.

The study of strategies is directly relevant to real-world problems calling for diagnosis or troubleshooting. If you went to a doctor complaining of dizziness, he would perform a series of diagnostic tests to discover the cause of the problem. If the doctor chose an appropriate sequence of tests, he would quickly discover the cause of the problem. If he chose an inappropriate sequence, he would take longer and would perhaps never develop a diagnosis. By gaining insight into how people map strategies in such situations, we may be able to make them more efficient problem-solvers. Of course, we cannot wait around in doctors' offices until a particularly revealing case walks through the door. A more realistic approach is to construct revealing problems in the laboratory and to ask people to make a diagnosis. That was essentially the approach of Bruner, Goodnow, and Austin (1956). They set out an array of 81 cards varying in four dimensions: the shapes of figures, the number of figures, the color of the figures, and the number of borders around the card. The subject was told that he or she was to discover a concept defined by the presence of one or more attributes, e.g., "All cards containing two borders," or "All cards containing red squares and two borders." These cards were positive instances of the concept. The cards that lacked one or more of the relevant attributes were negative instances. The experimenters began by showing the subject a positive instance of the concept. Thereafter, the subject chose cards, one at a time, and the experimenter told the subject whether each card was a positive or a negative

CONCEPT FORMATION

instance of the concept. After the selection of any card, the subject could state an hypothesis about the nature of the concept.

Bruner and his associates were able to distinguish four kinds of strategies based on the selections of subjects, and some strategies were more efficient than others. For example, suppose that the experimenter showed the following card: three red circles with two borders. This card is a positive instance of the concept; it contains all of the relevant attributes. In one type of strategy, the subject uses this card as a "focus" and systematically tests the attributes for their relevance. The way in which the subject tests for relevance reveals something about his disposition to gamble. Listed below are two cards, either of which a subject might select next:

Card A: Two red circles with two borders

Card B: Three green crosses with one border

Which card would you take next? If you picked Card A, then you adopted a strategy called **conservative focusing.** You are testing the relevance of one attribute at a time. If Card A turned out to be a positive instance, then you would know that "three figures" was irrelevant to the concept. If Card A turned out to be a negative instance, then you would know that the number of figures was relevant. Conservative focusing has the advantage of always imparting some information about the concept when you select a card. It has the disadvantage of being a slow procedure. After determining that the number of figures was irrelevant, you would have to test the relevance of another attribute. A strategy that could solve the problem in a single stroke, but also carries the risk that the card selected will tell you little or nothing, is called **focus gambling.** That would be your strategy if you chose Card B, above. You would be gambling that "three figures" was the concept. If Card B turned out to be a positive instance of the concept, you would know that "three figures" defined the concept, since that was the only attribute shared by the focus card and Card B. But if Card B was a negative instance, you would be back at square one. You could infer that one or more of the attributes that changed was relevant, but which one or ones? You would also have the problem of not being able to assess the relevance of the common attribute "three figures." Logically, it may or may not be relevant to the concept based on the information given by Card B. Focusing gambling is best suited for situations in which a concept must be formed quickly. Unlike conservative focusing, focus gambling offers the possibility of a quick solution.

Another type of strategy observed by Bruner and his associates was **scanning.** Here, subjects constructed one or more hypotheses about the concept and chose cards to test the hypotheses. For example, an hypothesis might be "red figures with one border" and the subjects would then successively choose all the possible instances of this concept. Positive instances would support the hypothesis but a single negative instance would refute it. Encountering a negative instance after several positive instances could be quite disappointing, as all the previous selections would, in a sense, have been unnecessary. That is the risk subjects take with a **successive scanning** strategy. They test only one hypothesis at a time. On the other hand, with a **simultaneous scanning** strategy, these prior cards could be very useful, as several hypotheses are entertained at the same time. Scanning strategies are difficult to use. They require us to remember all the hypotheses we have tested, and the potential for confusion can be great. Of the four strategies, the most realistic one is probably conservative focusing.

Bruner's work illustrates well a basic feature of the cognitive approach to learning. In Chapter 6 we saw that one difference between the cognitve and behavioristic approaches pertained to the role of the subject in determining the course of learning. Behaviorists have traditionally traced the course of learning to the conditions of practice arranged by the experimenter. Cognitivists have traditionally emphasized the ways in which the subject modifies experimental conditions through the invention of strategies and hypotheses. It is evident that both orientations are necessary to give us a complete picture of the processes underlying concept formation. This is the sort of relationship that one commonly finds between the behavioristic and cognitive approaches. While the theoretical interpretations of learning given by behaviorists and cognitivists can differ in fundamental ways, the facts they emphasize are often complementary.

SUMMARY

Fundamental to intellectual development is a grasp of the concept of a "dimension," the idea that objects can exhibit varying degrees of a property. A grasp of this concept entails recognition that objects can differ on one dimension (such as height) while not differing on another dimension (such as thickness). In other words, the individual recognizes that dimensions are separable and independent.

The extent to which a human being or lower animal distinguishes one dimension from another can be assessed by administering a solution-shift problem. In the first phase of the experiment, the subject learns to discriminate between pairs of stimuli that differ on at least two dimensions. One dimension is relevant to the solution of the problem while the other dimension is irrelevant. The problem can be solved conceptually by isolating that value of the relevant dimension which is consistently associated with reinforcement. Alternatively, the problem can be solved in a nonconceptual fashion by learning separate approach and avoidance reactions to the stimuli without grasping the relationships between them. The approach taken by subjects can be inferred from how they perform when the solution to the problem is shifted. In a reversal shift, the dimension that was relevant in the first problem remains relevant but the correct choice becomes the other value on this dimension. In the nonreversal shift, the dimension that was relevant on the first problem is made irrelevant and the other dimension becomes relevant. The correct choice is a particular value on the newly relevant dimension. If the reversal shift is learned faster than the nonreversal shift, concept formation on the original problem is indicated. If the nonreversal shift is learned faster, the nonconceptual approach to the original problem is indicated. Rats and preschoolers generally learn the nonreversal shift faster, while older children and adults learn the reversal shift faster. Kindergartners and first graders learn the two shifts at about equal rates.

Theoretical controversy centers on the question of why some subjects apparently form a concept of the solution on the original problem while others do not. One theory, advocated by Tighe and Tighe, emphasizes "perceptual learning." The premise of the theory is that organisms learn to perceive independent dimensions through repeated exposure to the environment. Reinforcement need not be given for improvements in performance. The competing theory, developed within a behavioristic mediational framework by Kendler and Kendler, emphasizes linguistic abilities. To form a concept of the solution, the individual must attach a label to the relevant dimension and use that label when making choices. Both the perceptual learning and the linguistic-mediational theories remain viable interpretations of simple concept learning in normal subjects. Zeaman and House proposed a theory with a different emphasis to account for simple concept learning in retardates. It is known the both human beings and lower animals have the capacity for "selective attention." At any given moment, an organism could be receptive to only part of a complex stimulus. On the basis of discrimination-learning experiments, Zeaman and House suggested that retardates have difficulty not in perceiving independent dimensions but in paying attention to the appropriate ones. Concept formation was said to be a two-stage process in which the subject first learned to pay attention to the relevant dimension of the problem and then learned to choose the appropriate stimulus on that dimension.

In addition to exhibiting conceptual deficits on the solution shift problem, young children generally fail to grasp a conceptual principle called "conservation." They do not recognize that a dimension can remain constant in magnitude despite changes in its appearance. Piaget discovered this phenomenon and interpreted it within the context of a theory which asserted that intelligence develops in four stages: sensorimotor, preoperational, concrete operational, and formal operational. Advances in intellectual development were said to result from an experience of cognitive conflict: A person encountered a fact that was inconsistent with his or her customary way of thinking about a subject. Although attempts to teach conservation based on the principle of cognitive conflict have given promising results, further research is needed to assess the durability and generality of the effects.

All concepts consist of attributes and rules. Attributes are features of stimuli which must be taken into account when deciding whether a stimulus is an example of a concept. Rules are statements about which features must be present in the stimulus and which features must be absent. Neisser and Weene divided conceptual rules into three levels of logical complexity and found a strong but imperfect correlation between the complexity of a rule and the difficulty of learning it.

In general, it is easier to deduce a concept from a series of positive instances (examples of what the concept *is*) than from a series of negative instances (examples of what a concept is *not*). There is evidence that we can reduce this advantage of positive instances through practice with negative instances. Another major factor that influences the rate of concept formation is the level of abstractness

SUMMARY

of a concept. Abstract concepts contain attributes that exist in many kinds of objects (e.g., round, tall). Concrete concepts contain attributes that exist in limited classes of objects (e.g., dog, penny). Abstract concepts are generally harder to learn than concrete concepts, possibly because of our linguistic habits. Each instance of an abstract concept is likely to suggest a different word, thereby reducing the chances that we will discover the attributes which all the instances have in common.

There are two general procedures for studying concept formation. In the "reception" procedure, the experimenter arranges the sequence of stimuli from which subjects are supposed to deduce the concept. In the "selection" procedure, the subjects arrange the sequence of stimuli. By examining the choices of subjects it is possible to infer the kinds of strategies being used to solve the problem. Bruner, Goodnow, and Austin identified four major strategies: conservative focusing, focus gambling, successive scanning, and simultaneous scanning. Each was shown to have advantages and disadvantages in problem-solving situations.

STUDY QUESTIONS

1. What is a "stimulus dimension"?

2. Describe Montessori's exercise which uses three sets of cylinders to teach children the concepts of height and thickness. Why are three sets of cylinders used instead of one?

3. What is the purpose of comparing the performances of different species on the solution-shift problem? What is the purpose of comparing the performances of human beings of different ages?

4. Assume that you are using tumblers with the following characteristics to present a solution-shift problem to children:

    tall black vs. short white

    tall white vs. short black

On the original problem, tall black and short black are the correct choices. State the correct choices that you would use for a: (a) reversal shift; (b) nonreversal shift.

5. Within each of the following groups of subjects, compare the rates at which the subjects learn reversal and nonreversal shift problems: college students, preschoolers, first-graders, rats, kindergartners.

6. What inference is made when a subject learns a reversal shift faster than a nonreversal shift? A nonreversal shift faster than a reversal shift? State the rationale behind these inferences. What "missing ingredient" in this rationale has become a source of theoretical controversy?

7. State Tighe and Tighe's perceptual learning theory of solution-shift performance.

8. Addressing the specific points stated below, describe the method and results of Tighe's study dealing with the effects of perceptual training on solution shift performance:

    a) The nature of the stimuli used in the solution shift problem.

    b) How the general procedures for the experimental and control groups differed.

CONCEPT FORMATION

c)   The nature of the stimuli used during perceptual training.

d)   The perceptual training procedure—what the experimenter asked to get compara- tive judgments, and how the experimenter reacted to the child's responses; how Stage 1 training differed from Stage 2 training.

e)   How performance of the experimental and control groups on the solution shift problem differed.

f)   How the results bear on the theory advocated by Tighe and Tighe (Question 7).

g)   What the results suggest about the Montessori exercise described in Question 2.

9.   In what two general ways are adults' linguistic abilities superior to young children's?

10.   Using the example of the tumblers, describe Kendler and Kendler's interpretation of why reversal shifts are learned faster than nonreversal shifts. In what sense is this a mediational theory? (Your answer should show how the Kendlers' mediational mechanism is analogous to the $r_g - s_g$ mechanism discussed in Chapter 6.)

11.   What was the general strategy used by Kendler, Kendler, and Wells to test mediational theory with nursery school children? How did it differ from Tighe's with first-graders? What was the outcome of the experiment?

12.   Describe the nature of the evidence favorable to the mediational theory reported by Kendler and Kendler.

13.   Define and give an example of "selective attention."

14.   According to Zeaman and House, what two processes are involved in retardate dis- crimination learning? Describe the evidence which led to this theory.

15.   Describe the Montessori exercise that uses three-dimensional and two-dimensional figures to teach children to recognize shapes.

16.   Define "conservation." Give two examples of violations of conservation, one involving a quantitative concept (like volume), the other a qualitative concept (like doctor).

17.   Contrast the views of Piaget and the behaviorists on the question of whether conser- vation can be taught. Where does the weight of evidence presently lie? What qualifica- tions must be made?

18.   Define and give examples of: "assimilation," "accommodation," "equilibrium."

19.   Using the example of Lucienne playing the matchbox game, illustrate Piaget's view of mental activity during the latter part of the sensorimotor phase of development. What two features of Lucienne's behavior suggested that she solved the problem by insight (in Kohler's sense of the word)?

20.   What two logical operations necessary for conservation are missing during the pre- operational phase of development?

21.   In what major way does thinking during the concrete operational phase differ from thinking during the formal operational phase?

22.   What is "cognitive conflict?" In Gruen's experiment, how did the procedures for the cognitive conflict and reinforcement groups differ? How did the task in the test phase

of the experiment differ from the task in the training phase? What were the results and conclusions of the experiment?

23. Define each of the following conceptual rules in general terms using both words and logical symbols. Also, for each rule, give one "real-world" example: "disjunctive absence," "either/or," "affirmation," "conjunctive absence," "conjunction," "negation," "disjunction."

24. On what general basis did Neisser and Weene assign conceptual rules to three levels of logical complexity? State the level of each rule in Question 23. What relationship was found between logical complexity and psychological difficulty?

25. What is meant by "positive" and "negative" instances of a concept? From which type is it easier to deduce concepts? How can this difference be modified?

26. Define and give examples of "abstract" and "concrete" concepts.

27. Describe Heidbreder's procedure for studying the learning of abstract and concrete concepts. What were the results of her experiment and her conclusion?

28. State the alternative interpretation of Heidbreder's results based on Underwood and Richardson's ideas concerning the dominance level of responses.

29. How do the reception and selection procedures for studying concept learning differ?

30. Define and give examples of the following strategies for concept learning: "conservative focusing," "focus gambling," "successive scanning," "simultaneous scanning." Which strategy is probably the most suitable for general use? Why?

CHAPTER 9

The Learning of Language

The experience of walking into a dark theater from bright sunlight can be startling. Suddenly, our visual sense is gone, and we find ourselves groping blindly for an empty seat. Several unsuccessful attempts later, we may lapse into a state of frustrated immobility, patiently waiting for our eyes to adapt to the dark. At last the faint outlines of seats and people begin to emerge, and we proceed cautiously. It is an unnerving thought, but imagine for a moment the consequences of living continuously in a world of such darkness. Imagine, too, the experience of also being unable to hear, and you will have some appreciation of the obstacles overcome by the famous author, Helen Keller (1880-1968).

Deprived of sight and hearing at the age of nine months by a severe illness, Helen Keller lived a significant part of her childhood in a state of intellectual as well as visual darkness. She communicated with others through a few simple signs, and had only the vaguest understanding of the world. Through the efforts of her teacher, Anne Sullivan, and through her own perseverance, Helen Keller mastered the English language. She communicated in a variety of ways: by spelling words into people's hands with her fingers, by writing messages on a special braille typewriter, and, most remarkably, by speaking! These accomplishments were only the beginning. Helen Keller was an avid reader. Her insatiable curiosity about the world drove her to acquire the knowledge and skills necessary to attend college. After a period of intensive preparation, she succeeded in gaining admission to Radcliffe College in Cambridge, Massachusetts, a difficult task even under normal conditions. With the help of Anne Sullivan, who acted as a translator during classes, Helen Keller performed exceptionally well. In 1904, she graduated *with honors.*

These unique accomplishments have become a source of inspiration to many persons deprived of sight or hearing. Yet, in a sense, Helen Keller's mastery of language was not entirely unique, as she underwent much the same learning process as the normal individual. Indeed, normal children, who typically master the basic rules of language by the age of three years, can also lay claim to a remarkable accomplishment. Although they have the advantages of sight and hearing, rarely do children receive the kind of careful tutoring that Helen Keller was fortunate to have. Many psychologists believe that for a child to overcome the difficulties inherent in language learning, a natural inclination to use language must already be present. It is testimony to the strength of this human inclination that language

256

learning should be possible under the unusual circumstances of Helen Keller's life. We begin our study of language learning with a glimpse of this rare individual's early life.*

A CHILD DISCOVERS LANGUAGE: THE WELL-HOUSE INCIDENT

Anne Sullivan arrived at the Keller home in rural Alabama when Helen was nearly seven years old. Helen had as yet received no instruction in language and communicated only with primitive signs. Sullivan, herself partially blind, had come to live with the family so that she could devote her full attention to the task of educating the child. While helping her teacher unpack, Helen found a doll that some blind children had sent to her as a gift. Sullivan noted Helen's keen interest in the doll and decided to demonstrate a signing technique by spelling "d-o-l-l" into Helen's hand. Helen readily imitated the letters, but when Sullivan took away the doll, intending to return it after Helen spelled the word again, the child threw a tantrum. The object meant far more to her than the word.

That continued to be Helen's attitude for several weeks. She readily imitated the names of objects that she touched, but Sullivan felt that Helen had not yet grasped the purpose of learning the words. She did not seem to understand that the words "stood for" objects, and that every object had a name. One April day, Helen discovered the meaning of language. She had recently been having difficulty with two words that Sullivan was persistently trying to teach her—the words "mug" and "milk." Helen would point to a mug when spelling "milk" and would make a sign that represented pouring or drinking when spelling "mug." Sullivan thought of a new approach to the problem on this day after Helen happened to ask the name for water while she was washing. Sullivan led Helen outside to the well-house, and had Helen hold her mug beneath the spout. While Sullivan pumped the well, she spelled "w-a-t-e-r" into Helen's hand. She describes Helen's reaction in graphic detail (in Keller, 1954, p. 257):

> The word coming so close upon the sensation of cold water rushing over her hand seemed to startle her. She dropped the mug and stood as one transfixed. A new light came into her face. She spelled "water" several times. Then she dropped on the ground and asked for its name and pointed to the pump and the trellis, and suddenly turning round she asked for my name. I spelled "Teacher." Just then the nurse brought Helen's little sister into the pump-house, and Helen spelled "baby" and pointed to the nurse. All the way back to the house she was highly excited, and learned the name of every object she touched, so that in a few hours she had added thirty new words to her vocabulary.

Helen Keller, writing many years later, remembered this incident as one of great personal significance (Keller, 1954, p. 36):

*Biographical information from H. Keller, *The Story of My Life.* New York: Doubleday, 1954.

Suddenly I felt a misty consciousness as of something forgotten—a thrill of returning thought; and somehow the mystery of language was revealed to me. I knew then that "w-a-t-e-r" meant the wonderful cool something that was flowing over my hand. That living word awakened my soul, gave it light, hope, joy, set it free! There were barriers still, it is true, but barriers that could in time be swept away.

The process by which Helen learned the names of objects was the familiar one of association by contiguity. As she held a doll, petted a dog, or ate a piece of cake, she would "listen" to Sullivan spell the name of the object. But how would Sullivan know when to introduce such words as "sweet," "think," and "love"? She could not directly observe the child's sensations, thoughts or emotions. The solution, of course, was to observe these private events indirectly. For example, Helen was once trying to string beads of various sizes according to the pattern, two large beads, three small beads, and so on. Despite Sullivan's best efforts to teach this rule, Helen continued to make many errors. Suddenly, she became motionless and her face assumed an expression of deep thought. Sullivan quickly touched Helen's forehead and at the same time spelled into her hand the letters, "t-h-i-n-k." Looking back on the incident, Keller (1954, p. 41) wrote, "In a flash I knew that the word was the name of the process that was going on in my head. This was my first conscious perception of an abstract idea."

It was possible to teach the names of emotions and sensations by a similar strategy of commonsense deduction. "Love" was the name for the emotion that Helen must have felt when being gently carressed. "Sweet" was the name for the sensation when she ate candy, smiling and smacking her lips. But mastery of language obviously requires more than an ability to understand and use names. Our speech is not simply a series of disconnected nouns. We speak in phrases and sentences composed of many different kinds of words. Moreover, these phrases and sentences are not simply repetitions of utterances we have heard before. To express our individual thoughts and feelings, we must speak *creatively;* we must produce new combinations of words. Of course, these combinations cannot be so new as to leave people baffled. To be comprehensible, our phrases and sentences must conform to grammatical rules, and it is this creative use of grammatical rules that is the essence of language.

OUT OF DARKNESS

Helen's mastery of language came gradually. Her first lesson on grammar dealt with the meaning of prepositions, words that express spatial relationships among objects (Chapter 7). To convey the meanings of "in" and "on," Sullivan spelled the words while putting a dress *in* a trunk and then *on* the trunk. Helen often acted out these place relations, for example, by standing *on* a chair or stepping *into* the closet that held her clothes. Although Helen seemed to understand these words, she seldom used them in sentences. Her early utterances typically consisted of nouns, verbs, and adjectives. For example, just three months after learning her first word, she managed to write a letter on a braille slate. It described the birth of some puppies that she had witnessed, and the oppressivley hot June weather. She brought the letter to Sullivan and asked her to put it into an envelope. When Sullivan asked Helen what was in the letter, she replied:

> Much words. Puppy motherdog—five. Baby—cry. Hot. Helen walk—no. Sunfire—bad. Frank—come. Helen—kiss Frank. Strawberries—very good. (Keller, 1954, p. 265).

Although she omitted certain words, Helen demonstrated that she had grasped some basic grammatical rules. She understood that nouns precede verbs (Baby—cry, Helen walk, etc.), that adjectives precede nouns (Much words) or follow verbs (Strawberries—very good; the verb "are" is implied), and that direct objects follow the subject and predicate (Helen—kiss Frank). To draw attention to missing words, Sullivan would repeat Helen's sentences and fill in the gaps. On one occasion, Helen asked for milk with the words, "Helen milk." Sullivan got the milk to show Helen that she had used the correct noun, but would not let her drink it until she repeated the grammatically correct sentence, "Give Helen some milk to drink." To demonstrate the creative aspect of grammar, Sullivan would often state a single idea in several ways. When Helen was eating candy, Sullivan might ask, "Will Helen please give teacher some candy?" or, "Teacher would like to eat some of Helen's candy." Within three months, Helen started to communicate in complete sentences and to vary the words she used to express an idea, for example, "Helen wants to go to bed," or, "Helen is sleepy, and Helen will go to bed." (Keller, 1954, p. 299)

Several weeks after her arrival at the Keller home, Sullivan decided upon a major change in strategy. Her original plan called for formal lessons on vocabulary, grammar, and reading. However, it soon became evident that Helen was most responsive to instruction when some incident prompted her to "speak" or to request information. Sullivan came to believe that the best approach to instruction was to converse with Helen spontaneously while sharing experiences of interest to the child. In other words, the most effective motivation for learning language seemed to be the child's natural curiosity about the world. Thus Sullivan relied on the kind of verbal interchange that naturally arises between a parent and child. That this approach works superbly is obvious not only from Helen's mastery of language, but from the mastery that every normal child exhibits. Why it works is only now becoming clear as psychologists increasingly seek to understand the processes responsible for language acquisition.

WHAT EVERYBODY KNOWS, BUT DOESN'T KNOW

All speakers of a language have a vast store of knowledge about its most intricate details. Yet few people realize that they are linguistic "experts." To be sure, it is not the kind of knowledge that most people can readily state, or even give in response to prompting. The knowledge is implicit in their speech and in their reactions to other speakers. "Linguists," who are concerned with the nature of language, and "psycholinguists," who are concerned with the processes governing its acquisition and use, have developed methods of demonstrating this knowledge indirectly. To appreciate the depth of the information we all possess, we must consider not only the meaning of our words, but the sounds.

"Phonemes": Our elementary concepts of speech

The production of speech sounds   To utter even a single word requires skills of extraordinary complexity. Fortunately, we need not think about these skills while exercising them. If we had to plan the formation of every speech sound, we would have great difficulty keeping track of the message we wished to communicate. We usually speak as we exhale. Air from the lungs flows upward through the windpipe and passes between the vocal cords located inside the "voicebox," or **larynx.** If we adjust the position of the vocal cords appropriately, they will vibrate and generate a sound. However, the sound will not yet be recognizable as an element of speech. Further processing of the air stream must be performed by structures of the **vocal tract,** the region encompassing the throat, the mouth, and the nose. By changing the shape of the vocal tract in various ways, we can **articulate** a wide variety of speech sounds.

Some speech sounds do not require vibration of the vocal cords. If we constrict the vocal tract in certain ways while we exhale, the turbulence in the air stream will create a "hissing" sound. This is the means by which we produce sounds like, "s," "sh," and "f." Alternatively, we may briefly block the flow of air with our tongue or lips. When air pressure inside the vocal tract rises sufficiently, we quickly release the air. The result is a sound like "p" or "t." Such speech sounds, produced without vocal cord vibration, are said to be **unvoiced.** Sounds that are produced with vocal cord vibration, are said to be **voiced.**

To form a speech sound, we must precisely coordinate the movements of the vocal cords, mouth, tongue, and lips. Figure 9.1 illustrates the various shapes of the vocal tract during the pronunciation of four vowels. One way to appreciate the complexity of articulation is to compare the shapes of the vocal tract for any two vowels. You will see that the diagrams differ in many ways. For example, during the pronunciation of "e" and "ee" the positions of the lips differ, and the tongue assumes different contours. Remember, we are considering here the articulation of isolated sounds. To articulate the series of sounds comprising a word, we must make rapid changes in vocal tract configurations.

The articulation of consonants involves further complications. While all vowels are voiced, some consonants are voiced and others are not. The presence or absence of vocal cord vibration is the major feature that allows us to distinguish among some speech sounds. For example, we form all of the following sounds with the "blocking" method of articulation discussed earlier: "p-b," "t-d," "k-g." What makes the two members of each pair distinguishable is the unvoiced quality of the

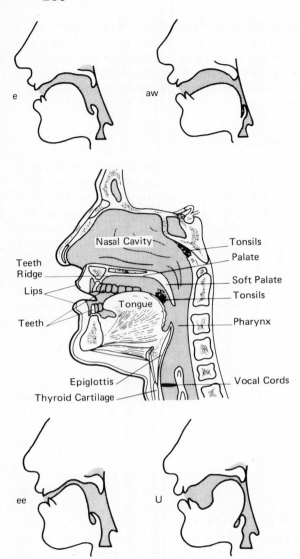

Fig. 9.1 Configuration of the vocal tract during production of four vowel sounds (From Denes and Pinson, 1973)

first member and the voiced quality of the second member. Another feature that complicates the articulation of consonants is the presence of a nasal quality in some sounds ("m," "n," "ng") and its absence in others ("b," "d," "g"). To produce the nasal quality, we make use of the "soft palate" at the back of the mouth near the throat (Fig. 9.1). When we lower the soft palate, some of the air traveling up the windpipe can escape through the nasal cavity. When we raise the soft palate, all of the air flows through the mouth.

In summary, all articulatory movements have the effect of changing the shape of the vocal tract, and each configuration creates a distinctive sound. The pattern of vibrations set up in the vocal tract leaves a physical "signature" that can be analyzed visually. A device called the **sound spectrograph** performs this feat, and the record it produces is called a **spectrogram.** Figure 9.2 shows a spectrogram of the sentence, "I can see you." Letters symbolizing the sounds which comprise the sentence appear at the top of the record. The horizontal line at the bottom represents the passage of time. For example, the initial sound, "I," begins 0.1 second after the signal to speak, and lasts an additional 0.3 second. This sound, like the others, is actually a composite of different frequencies. (In general, the higher the frequency of vibration, the higher is our sensation of pitch.) The vertical axis on the spectrogram represents the frequencies that potentially make up a sound. You have probably observed that several dark bands run across the record. These bands, or **formants,** are the frequencies of a sound with the greatest intensities; they make the biggest contribution to our perception of the sound. Note that the formants often undergo changes over time. For example, two of the formants of the sound, "I," run parallel for a brief period, and then diverge. Seemingly small changes in a formant can produce dramatic changes in perception. To decipher a person's speech, we must "tune in" to these subtle changes in frequency in relation to the overall pattern.

"Categorical perception" of speech   If a friend said to you, "Excuse me, I have to take a pill," you might assume that he was taking medication for a cold. If he said, "Excuse me, I have to take a spill," you might find yourself reaching out to break his fall. The meaning of the sentence depends critically upon the presence or absence of a single sound—"s." But the words "pill" and "spill" also differ in a way

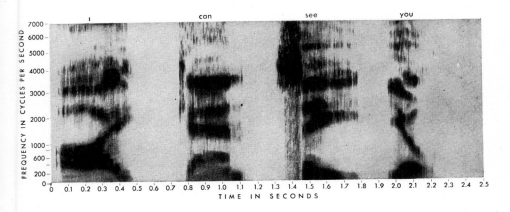

Fig. 9.2   Spectrogram of the sentence, "I can see you." (From Denes and Pinson, 1973)

WHAT EVERYBODY KNOWS, BUT DOESN'T KNOW

that few people notice. The puff of air that accompanies the pronunciation of "p" in "pill" is considerably stronger than the puff that accompanies the pronunciation of "p" in "spill." To fully describe the articulation of the two words, we would have to point out that the "p"s differ **phonetically,** that is, in sound. However, since most people do not detect this difference during normal conversation, linguists consider the two sounds to be instances of a single sound category, or **phoneme.** Similarly, the sound of "r" in the word "red," differs phonetically from the sound of "r" in the word "tree." The first "r" is voiced while the second is unvoiced. Since most people do not detect this difference, the two "r"s are equivalent phonemically. In general, the use of a single letter to represent phonetically different sounds indicates that the sounds belong to the same category.

To say that two sounds belong to different categories, we must show that they permit us to discriminate between utterances. That the sounds, "s" and "p," belong to different categories is obvious from the contrast between words like "sit" and "pit," and "gas" and "gap." We would symbolize these two sound classes, /s/ and /p/. All of the vowels and consonants of English represent distinct sound classes, but there are about 14 additional phonemes. For example, the sentence, "The mouse chased the cat," could be a declarative statement of fact, or a question, depending upon the emphasis we give to the last word. If the pitch in our voice rises when we pronounce "cat," the declarative statement becomes a question. Consequently, an increase in pitch would be a phoneme.

Our inclination to perceive categories rather than individual sounds is very strong. It is so strong, in fact, that we sometimes cannot tell the difference between two distinct sounds that belong to the same category. Yet if two equally different sounds happen to fall into different categories, we can tell them apart readily. This remarkable fact was demonstrated in an ingenious study by Liberman, Harris, Hoffman, and Griffith (1957). They studied the perceptual effects of three phonemes produced by the "blocking" method of articulation: /b/, /d/, and /g/. Phonemes produced in this way are called **stops.** Because /b/, /d/, and /g/ are pronounced with vocal cord vibration, they would be further classified as "voiced stops." We discriminate one voiced stop from another by a very subtle cue. To illustrate this cue, consider the spectrograms in the top panel of Fig. 9.3. The figure depicts 14 different stimuli, each consisting of two formants. The spectrograms are clearer than the one in Fig. 9.2 because they were created artificially and translated into sounds by a device called a **pattern playback.** Note that the lower, or "first," formant is identical in the 14 stimuli; it is the "second" formant that carries the relevant cue for discrimination. To tell apart /b/, /d/, and /g/ we must "tune in" to the brief early segment of the second formant, which rises or falls in varying degrees. The 14 stimuli were played in a random order, and subjects were asked to label each with the letter "b," "d," and "g." As you can see in panel (b) of Fig. 9.3, which gives the results for one subject, the physical boundaries separating the categories were very sharp.

Could the subject tell that the sounds comprising a phoneme category were slightly different? Or did the psychological boundaries between phonemes erase these differences? The ability to discriminate sounds was tested with a simple proce-

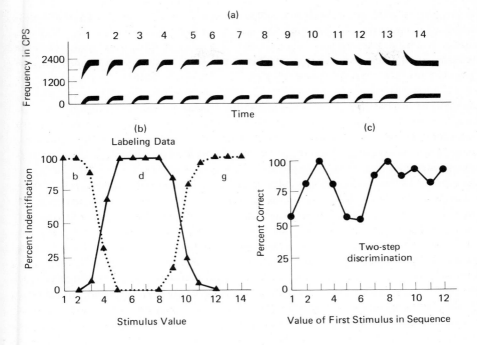

Fig. 9.3 Results of study on the discrimination of speech sounds. (a) Spectrograms numbered 1 to 14 differed only in early segment of second formant. (b) Labels used by one subject to categorize each of 14 sounds illustrated in top panel. (c) Accuracy of subjects' judgments in discrimination task. Subjects first heard one of the stimuli indicated on the horizontal axis, and then another stimulus two steps higher. Task required subjects to say whether third stimulus in sequence matched the first or the second. A correct response meant that the subject could discriminate between the first two speech sounds. (From Liberman, Harris, Hoffman, and Griffin, 1957)

dure. The subjects heard three sounds in succession. The initial two sounds differed; the second of the two was one, two, or three steps higher than the first. For example, in a two-step discrimination, the subject might hear sound #1 then sound #3, or sound #2 then sound #4. The third sound in the sequence matched the first or the second. The subjects would indicate that they could discriminate between the first and second sounds by responding with a correct match. Panel (c) in Fig. 9.3 presents results for the two-step discrimination. The value of the first stimulus in the sequence appears on the abscissa; the second stimulus was always two steps higher. Perfect discrimination between the first and second sounds would be indicated by 100% correct matches; a complete inability to discriminate the sounds would be indicated by 50% correct matches (chance performance). You can see that discriminative ability varied greatly across the physical scale. Often, if the first and second stimuli fell in the same category (e.g., 1 vs. 3, 6 vs. 8), discrimination was poor; if the stimuli lay on opposite sides of a phoneme boundary (e.g., 3 vs. 5, 8 vs. 10), discrimination was better. Thus it appears that when listening to another person speak, we wear perceptual "blinders." We tend to ignore variations in speech sounds that are not essential for recognizing a phoneme.

Nature or nurture? The subjects in the foregoing experiment were adults. Would children have given similar results? Possibly a person must have many years of experience with a language before these subtle perceptual categories emerge. Surprisingly, infants just one month old have been shown to perceive some speech sounds categorically (Eimas, Siqueland, Jusczyk, and Vigorito, 1971). This provocative finding suggests that the categorical perception of these sounds may not be acquired at all! We may have a natural tendency to "tune in" some features of speech sounds and "tune out" other features. The implication would be that certain phoneme categories of languages might have a genetic basis.

The adult subjects in the previous study of categorical perception performed according to verbal instructions. Eimas and his colleagues had the feeling that the one- and four-month-old infants in their study might prefer a different approach. Consequently, instead of verbal instructions, the experimenters used an operant conditioning procedure. The infants could generate a speech sound, and maintain it continuously, by sucking on a non-nutritive nipple. The speech sound was the voiced stop /b/ or the unvoiced stop /p/. After several minutes, the infants typically "habituated" to the sound (Chapter 1), and their rate of responding decreased. At that point, the experimenters introduced a slightly different stimulus. If the infants could detect this change, we would expect their response rate to increase.

To discriminate voiced stops (/b/, /d/, /g/) from unvoiced stops (/p/, /t/, /k/) we listen to a relationship between the first formant of the sound (low frequency component) and the second formant (higher frequency component). You can demonstrate this relationship by pronouncing the sounds, "ba" and "pa." With "ba," you will hear the consonant (second formant) and the vowel (first formant) at about the same time. With "pa," you will hear the first formant a moment after the second formant starts. This lag in the onset time of the first formant is the cue we use to discriminate unvoiced stops from voiced stops.

How sensitive is the infant to this cue? In one experimental condition (labeled 20D), the infants were habituated to a sound in which the first formant came 20 milliseconds (20 thousandths of a second) after the second formant started. Adults perceived this sound as /b/. After the infants' response rate had declined considerably, the experimenters introduced a slightly different sound—the first formant came 40 milliseconds after the second formant started. Adults perceived this sound as /p/. Thus, to adults, the two sounds were members of *different* phoneme categories. Could the infants discriminate the change from 20 to 40 milliseconds?

You can see the answer in panel (a) of Fig. 9.4. The data are for four-month-old infants; data for one-month-old infants gave similar results. The isolated dot above the "B" on the abscissa is the "Baseline" response rate without reinforcement. The connected dots to the left of the vertical line show the response rate

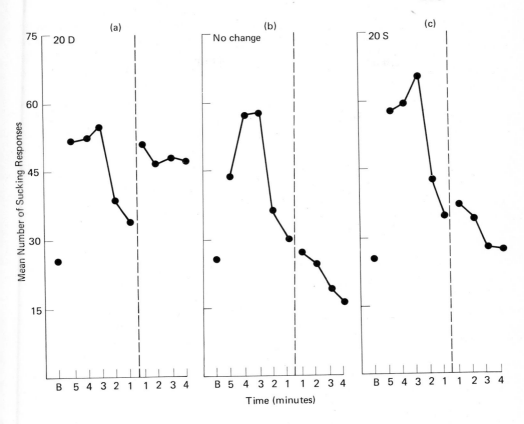

Fig. 9.4 Results of study on the perception of phonemic categories by infants. Vertical axes of the three graphs show number of responses infants made to maintain a speech sound. Habituation to the sound is displayed in those portions of graphs to the left of the vertical lines. These data are from the final five minutes of the first phase of the experimental procedure. Data from the next four minutes are displayed to the right of the vertical lines. In graph (a), a new sound was introduced that adults said belonged to a different phoneme category. In graph (c), a sound was introduced that was said to belong to the same phoneme category. Physically, this sound differed from its predecessor by the same amount as the sound used in the leftmost graph. In graph (b), the same stimulus was used throughout the experiment. An increase in sucking responses in the period following introduction of a new sound implied that the infants detected the change. The isolated dots represent response rates during a baseline period ("B" on horizontal axis) when responses produced no sounds. (from Eimas, Siqueland, Jusczyk, and Vigorito, 1971)

when sucking responses produced the first sound. Habituation to the stimulus is evident from the large decrease in response rate. Upon introduction of the second sound after the vertical line, response rate rose sharply. This increase indicates that the infants could discriminate the sounds. Had there been no change in sounds (panel b), response rate would have continued to decrease.

WHAT EVERYBODY KNOWS, BUT DOESN'T KNOW

Could the infants discriminate a 20-millisecond change when the two sounds lay within the same category (condition 20S)? For example, suppose they were habituated to a sound in which the second formant came 60 milliseconds after the first formant started, and then heard a sound with delay of 80 milliseconds. To adults, both sounds seem like instances of /p/. Panel (c) in Fig. 9.4 shows that the second sound produced no substantial change in response rate. The infants failed to discriminate the two sounds even though the sounds were just as different as those that lay in the categories, /p/ and /b/. Thus the infants perceived voiced and unvoiced stops categorically, much as adults do. As we shall see, many psychologists believe that we are genetically "tuned" to many aspects of language in addition to sounds.

Making sounds meaningful

From phonemes to sentences   The sounds we generate as we speak must follow certain patterns to be meaningful. Linguists describe the speech patterns of a population in the form of rules, but psychologists disagree about whether people actually use rules to generate speech. The rules developed by linguists are essentially summaries of the conventions that speakers of a language tend to follow. Discovering the processes responsible for these speech patterns is a primary aim of psycholinguistic research.

Linguistic rules state relationships among the elements that make up a sentence. These elements vary in size, with smaller units combining to form larger units. The smallest units of speech are phonemes. As an illustration of how phonemes combine to form larger units, consider the phonemes one produces when saying the words, "The wily weasel wagered the watchful warbler":

Th + e + w + i + l + y + w + ea + s + e + l + w + a + g + er + ed +

th + e + w + a + tch + f + u + l + wh + a + r + b + l + er

Obviously, one does not pause between these sounds when pronouncing the sentence, but they are nevertheless independent phonemes. In appropriate combinations, phonemes form elementary units of meaning called **morphemes.** In the foregoing sentence, there are 10 morphemes:

The—wil + y—weasel—wager + ed—the—watch + ful—warbler

Note that some morphemes are words, but other morphemes are fragments of words. For example, the morpheme "y" means "characterized by." By adding "y" to "wile," we create a word meaning "characterized by trickery." In combining the two morphemes, we must follow a rule which states that "y" always comes after the root word; it is a suffix. Similarly, "ful" and "ed" are suffixes. If we ignored this rule, and combined suffixes with root words at random, our speech would at best be puzzling, and would probably be unintelligible.

THE LEARNING OF LANGUAGE

Each word in a sentence belongs to a grammatical class. "Nouns" are words which refer to people, places, or things; "verbs" are words which refer to actions; and so on. In the foregoing sentence, the words belong to four different categories:

Article	Adjective	Noun	Verb	Article	Adjective	Noun
The	wily	weasel	wagered	the	watchful	warbler.

Words, in turn, combine to form linguistic segments called **phrases.** The combination of a noun with an adjective or article constitutes a noun phrase, and the combination of a noun phrase with a verb constitutes a verb phrase:

			Verb phrase			
Noun phrase				Noun phrase		
The	wily	weasel	wagered	the	watchful	warbler.

Finally, the combination of a noun phrase and a verb phrase forms a complete sentence.

Is grammar for real?   One could reasonably ask whether the rules developed by linguists really represent people's speech patterns. Even the most fluent speakers violate the rules occasionally with false starts and "um"s and "uh"s. And average speakers, who make many more errors, are frequently unable to state grammatical rules explicitly even when they have followed the rules to the last letter. Of course, linguists recognize that the average person is not a grammarian, and that no one adheres to the rules all the time. Linguists seek to represent the speech patterns of the "ideal speaker," a fictional person who exhibits only those speech patterns which most members of a population have the potential to produce, or could recognize as being grammatical. The ideal speaker does not exhibit idiosyncratic speech patterns, and never makes mistakes. But psychologists must confront real people. To what extent do linguistic concepts make contact with real psychological processes?

An important experiment by Fodor and Bever (1965) stimulated much interest in this problem of the psychological reality of linguistic concepts. Their findings, and the findings of subsequent experiments, indicate that people are sensitive to the phrase structure of sentences. One might expect people to ignore phrases when listening to speech, and to concentrate on the individual words. For example, do you perceive the phrases that make up the following sentence?

That he was happy was evident from the way he smiled.

This sentence consists of two major phrases, "That he was happy," and "was evident from the way he smiled." You may have "felt" the break between "was happy—" and "was evident." However, even if you did not have this feeling, as a subject in Fodor and Bever's experiment you might have shown indirectly that you did perceive the break. Subjects in their experiment listened through headphones to a number of sentences presented to one ear. At some point in each sentence, the subjects heard a click in the other ear. Following the presentation of a sentence, the subjects' task was to write down the sentence and to indicate the precise location of the click. The clicks were presented either at the major break between phrases, or at various distances from the break. Thus, in the sentence discussed above, the subjects heard clicks in the locations designated by Xs:

$$\text{X X X X X X X X X}$$

That he was happy was evident from the way he smiled.

Because the points were very close together, the subjects made many errors (80 percent of responses). But the errors were not random. Most of the erroneous indications of click locations (66 percent) lay in the direction of the break between phrases. If the click occurred at the same time that the speaker pronounced "hap" in "happy," it was more likely that subjects would indicate a location to the right of this point (toward the break) than to the left. The break appeared to "stand out" and to attract the subjects' responses. It is possible that the break influenced the subjects' memory of the click location rather than their perception of it. In either case, these and subsequent findings strongly suggest that such basic linguistic concepts as the phrase are psychologically important.

The deep In composing an essay, have you ever rewritten a sentence several times to perfect it? Although the sentences differed from one another, they expressed essentially the same idea. Or, have you ever had the experience of knowing what you wanted to say without quite knowing how to say it? These are common experiences, and they illustrate a fundamental concept of modern linguistic theory: The idea expressed by a sentence exists independently of that sentence. Consequently, it is possible to have an idea without a sentence, or to express a single idea in several different ways. To illustrate the latter possibility, consider the following two sentences, which differ grammatically but carry precisely the same meaning:

Low grades worry serious students.
Serious students are worried by low grades.

The first sentence expresses the underlying idea in the "active voice," while the second sentence expresses the idea in the "passive voice." Both sentences are reducible to three distinct propositions. First, there is the proposition that "grades worry students." Second, we qualify "grades" with the proposition that "grades are low." Third, we qualify "students" with the proposition that "students are serious." In linguistic theory, we recognize these propositions and their relationships intuitively. The phrase structures of the two sentences serve to bring the propositions together and relate them in an explicit way. The implication is that there are two levels of linguistic analysis. On one level, one analyzes the **surface structure** of a sentence into its constituent phrases. On a more general level, one analyzes the

deep structure of the sentence into its underlying propositions and their relationships.

The concepts of deep and surface structure originated centuries ago. The appeal of such a distinction waxed and waned over the centuries, and during the first half of the present century other approaches to linguistic analysis prevailed. Then, in 1957, the linguist Noam Chomsky published a major book entitled *Syntactic Structures*, in which he revived the concepts of surface structure and deep structure and developed the concepts further than earlier linguists had done. Chomsky's approach emphasizes rules which permit us to transform general propositions into grammatical sentences. Many psycholinguists attach particular significance to Chomsky's rules of **grammatical transformation** because they potentially explain a person's ability to produce novel sentences. If you wished to communicate an idea, you would select a set of transformation rules to bring your propositions to the surface. You might apply the rules in succession, and after each operation your propositions would come a bit closer to a recognizable sentence. Completion of all of the operations would result in a sentence of a certain type, such as a declarative statement in the active voice. With the same rules you could produce an infinite variety of sentences; you would simply apply them to new propositions. Thus, in Chomsky's framework, we have a limited number of transformation rules with unlimited potential.

Figure 9.5 illustrates the deep structure of a simple sentence—"A wise man is honest"—and the changes in this structure resulting from application of several transformation rules. Chomsky (1968, pp. 25-26) notes that the deep structure consists of two propositions "a man is honest" and "man is wise." Panel I of Fig. 9.5 shows the relationship between the two propositions, with S representing the complete sentence, NP representing a noun phrase, and VP representing a verb phrase. According to Chomsky, four transformation rules are necessary to produce the surface structure diagrammed in the last panel. You can trace the effects of each rule as you go from Panel I to Panel IV.

Chomsky's conceptualization of transformational grammar has proven especially useful as a framework for investigating possible genetic influences on language learning. We have seen that there is evidence for genetic tuning in the perception of phonemes. Many psychologists suspect that there is also a genetic disposition to learn the grammatical rules of a language. The apparent ease with which children overcome obstacles to language learning suggests that children already have some conceptualization of what features of a language are important and how these features should be related. This does not mean that French children are born with a knowledge of French grammar, and Chinese children are born with a knowledge of Chinese. The grammatical rules which enable one speaker of a language to communicate with another obviously must be learned. In the context of Chomsky's formulation, these are the rules of transformation, the rules which enable us to comprehend and produce the surface structure of sentences. What all children possess innately, says Chomsky, is a knowledge of the deep structure of their language. While different languages have different vocabularies, all languages

I. Assign "wh–" marker to most deeply imbedded NP ("man").

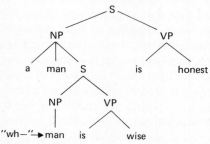

II. Replace the NP so marked by "who."

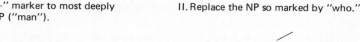
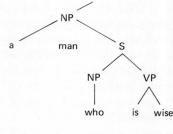

III. Delete "who is."

IV. Reverse "man" and "wise."

Fig. 9.5 Deep structure of the sentence, "A wise man is honest" (panel I), and the transformations considered necessary to generate the surface structure of the sentence (panels II through IV). (After Chomsky, 1968)

are said to put words together in the same way at the level of deep structure. In exploring innate sensitivities to grammar, many psychologists have adopted Chomsky's distinction between surface structure and deep structure, and looked to the deep structures of languages for evidence of a genetic contribution to language learning. We shall see an example of this approach later in the chapter when we take up the problem of how children learn the grammatical rules of languages.

EARLY LANGUAGE LEARNING: WHAT'S IN A NAME?

The foregoing section examined the kinds of knowledge we must possess to speak intelligibly and to understand the speech of other people. Our depth of knowledge is impressive; it encompasses both the sound structure and the grammatical structure of language. Precise knowledge of the sound structure enables us to perceive speech sounds categorically. With this capacity we can listen to the important details of speech sounds while ignoring the unimportant details. In addition to being able to perceive phonemes, we can articulate them. The articulation of speech sounds is made possible by complex motor skills involving precise coordination of structures of the vocal tract. We have seen that phonemes combine to make up morphemes, the elementary units of meaning, and that morphemes are the constituents of words. To extract meaning from sound, we must have a firm grasp of these sound combinations. But perhaps our most striking linguistic achievements are the abilities to comprehend and produce grammatical strings of words which are new to us. These are the abilities which make language creative. Having explored the kinds of linguistic knowledge we possess, our next objective shall be to investigate the processes by which we acquired them.

Origins of the first word

Speech perception in young infants is surprisingly well developed. We have seen that infants just one month old were able to perceive a subtle cue that distinguished the voiced stop /b/ from the unvoiced stop /p/ (Eimas, et al., 1971). In contrast to speech perception, speech production in early life is highly primitive. According to Lenneberg (1967, pp. 276-280), infants exhibit no coordination of articulatory organs for several months after birth, and the level of coordination they attain by the end of the first year is very low by adult standards. The earliest form of vocalization is crying, which is present at birth. Crying cannot be considered a speech sound, however, because it entails no articulation, except for the infant's simply opening and closing his mouth. In Lenneberg's (1967, p. 276) words, "the infant simply blows his horn without operating the keys." Toward the end of the second month, another form of vocalization develops. The infant makes short (approximately half-second) cooing sounds in response to social stimulation. Although the cooing sounds resemble vowels, and involve some articulation by the tongue, they are not yet speech sounds. Neither the articulatory movements nor the resulting spectrograms are like those associated with vowels. With the development of new articulatory skills during the next few months, cooing sounds become differentiated into vowel-like and consonant-like elements. Still, articulatory movements are erratic and the infant's vocalizations are highly variable.

From this pool of varied sounds emerges the infant's first words between the ages of 12 and 18 months. Associative theories of learning emphasize the role of reinforcement in this important development. In our study of imitation in Chapter 5, we examined Mowrer's (1952) interpretation of word learning, which attaches special significance to the concepts of conditioned reinforcement and self-stimulation. Mowrer theorized that speech sounds made by adults as they care for and play with the child become associated with reward. In the course of babbling, the infant happens to produce sounds which resemble those associated with gratification. Because these sounds are pleasurable, the infant repeats them, and seeks to approximate the sounds which adults have modeled as closely as possible.

In support of his "autism" (self-stimulation) theory of word learning, Mowrer cites studies of word learning in talking birds. He reports that birds learn words best when the trainer speaks to the birds while feeding and caring for them. It seems reasonable to assume that a similar process of self-stimulation may play a role in human language development. That feedback from vocalization is important is suggested by the common observation that deaf infants rarely babble. Since they would not have had an opportunity to associate sounds with rewards, they would not have an incentive for babbling.

Another source of reinforcement for infant vocalization is the reactions it may elicit in adults. If the child happens to utter a recognizable syllable such as "da" or "ma," adults are likely to react by smiling, vocalizing, or caressing the infant. The rewarding effects of such reactions were demonstrated in a well-known study by Rheingold, Gewitz, and Ross (1959). An experimenter stood by the infants' crib and reinforced vocalizations by first smiling, then making three "tsk" sounds, and finally touching the infants' abdomen. Only discrete voiced sounds (similar to cooing) could produce reinforcement; the experimenter ignored other noises such as coughs, whistles, and snorts. Prior to the introduction of reinforcement, the infants vocalized at a rate of about four sounds per minute. After two days of reinforcement, the rate of vocalization rose sharply to eight sounds per minute. Subsequent removal of reinforcement brought about a gradual decline in vocalization much as one would expect from conventional studies of extinction.

Although infants respond to direct reinforcement, reinforcement through self-stimulation probably plays a more important role in word learning. Few parents provide reinforcement according to a deliberate plan, and it is hard to imagine how infants could learn the subtle features of speech sounds without consistent feedback. The process of reinforcement through self-stimulation provides some measure of consistency because only those sounds which adults have modeled would be reinforcing. Still, children often make errors when they pronounce words, and certain types of errors are quite common (Oller, Wieman, Doyle, and Ross, 1976). For example, young children tend to omit the final consonant of a word, and say "bi-" or "do-" instead of "big" and "dog." They also tend to delete a consonant which should be pronounced together with another consonant. The child might say "-top" instead of "stop." Since adults rarely make such errors, it is unlikely that the errors result from imitation. The children probably have a natural tendency to articulate these speech patterns.

Evidence for a genetic influence on articulation comes from an observational study by Oller, Wieman, Doyle, and Ross (1976). These investigators taped the babbled utterances of children ranging in age from four to thirteen months. The objective was to see if sound patterns considered to be "errors" in later speech occurred with relatively high frequencies in babbled utterances. Errors in child speech which have a natural basis should be foreshadowed in early vocalizations. In the analysis, only those sounds were counted which consisted of at least one vowel and at least one consonant. Within this restriction, infants exhibited clear phonetic preferences. For example, they were three times more likely to utter a consonant before a vowel than they were to utter a vowel before a consonant (foreshadowing the "do-" vs. "dog" error). And the infants were nine times more likely to join a single consonant to a vowel than they were to join consecutive consonants to a vowel (foreshadowing the "-top" vs. "stop" error). Such phonetic preferences in early life suggest that word learning is the product of an interplay between natural dispositions and imitative processes.

Back to the well-house

A parrot proudly announces, "Big Mac! Big Mac!" You look about, but there is not a hamburger in sight. Has the bird mistaken a bag of french fries for a hamburger? No, there are no french fries either. Of course, trying to guess the meaning of a parrot's words is a fruitless endeavor, for the words have no meaning. The parrot utters them without reference to anything.

The imitative process Mowrer described would also lead an infant to utter words without reference to things. The words would simply be a source of self-gratification. Psychologically, words become elements of language when the child recognizes that they are symbols. That insight was the turning point in Helen Keller's intellectual development. Her early words were mere repetitions of the letters which Anne Sullivan spelled into her hand. Sullivan surmised, and Helen Keller later confirmed, that the words had no symbolic content. It was the experience at the well-house that taught Helen the purpose of using words. The temporal contiguity between the letters w-a-t-e-r and the sensation of water flowing over her hand impressed on her that the letters stood for the object.

Recognition that words stand for things may not come with such dramatic suddenness for most children. But the process of association by contiguity has long been regarded as the means by which people learn the referents of words. As we saw in Chapter 2, Pavlov believed that words functioned in much the same way as conditioned stimuli. By pairing the sound of a bell with food, one created a kind of symbol for food. The sound stood for the object in the sense that it and the object elicited similar reactions. Subsequently, investigators reported evidence that supported Pavlov's view more directly. They showed that it was possible to attach physiological reactions to words through classical conditioning, and that the conditioned reactions would generalize to other words on the basis of meaning (Riess, 1940; 1946; Razran, 1949).

Mowrer (1954; 1960) saw in Pavlov's approach a way of answering a fundamental question about language: How can we acquire knowledge about objects through words alone? If you heard that your tap water had been contaminated and might make you sick, you would probably refrain from drinking the water. You would exhibit an avoidance reaction even though the water had never actually made you sick. How is this possible?

Fig. 9.6 illustrates the kinds of processes which, in Mowrer's view, enable us to learn about the world through words. Let us imagine that you meet a fellow named "Cecil" one evening at a party. After some casual conversation, Cecil leaves to make a phone call, and a friend tells you, "Cecil is a surgeon." When Cecil returns, you change the topic of conversation to medicine, indicating that you have learned something about the person from the words spoken earlier. The first panel of Fig.

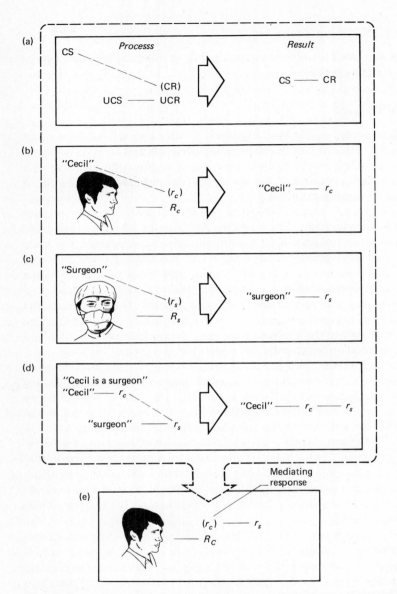

Fig. 9.6 Learning about the world through words—a Pavlovian interpretation. Panel (a) presents the general features of classical conditioning, with the solid lines representing established associations and the dashed line representing an association in the formative stage. Succeeding panels apply this general scheme to a problem in sentence comprehension—a person acquires information about a recent acquaintance from the sentence, "Cecil is a surgeon." It is assumed that with Cecil physically present, the person associates the word, "Cecil," with an image of Cecil (r_c) that can be retained after Cecil leaves (panel b). Previously, the word, "surgeon," became associated with the image of a surgeon (r_s) in a similar manner (panel c). When, with Cecil out of the room, the person hears that "Cecil is a surgeon," an association forms between r_c and r_s (panel d). Upon returning, Cecil evokes the image, r_c, which elicits r_s (panel e). Elicitation of r_s means that the person recognizes that Cecil-the-person is a surgeon, even though the idea of a surgeon had previously been associated only with "Cecil"-the-word.

9.6 gives a diagram of the general process of learning through classical conditioning and the nature of the association acquired. The solid lines represent established associations. The dashed line represents the association that is strengthened.

We shall assume that you have a perceptual response to Cecil-the-person (R_C), and that a theoretical fragment of this response (r_C) gets connected to the name "Cecil." Previously, you learned the meaning of the word "surgeon" through a similar process. You may have observed an image of a surgeon in a photograph or movie (R_s), and a fragment of this response (r_s) became associated with the word "surgeon" when that word happened to be spoken. The sentence, "Cecil is a surgeon," serves as a conditioning device. Your conditioned response to "surgeon" (r_s) gets connected to your conditioned response to "Cecil" (r_C). When Cecil-the-person reappears, he produces in you the large perceptual response, R_C, which contains the fragment r_C. This fractional response triggers r_s, and you realize that Cecil-the-person is a surgeon. The critical link in the chain is r_C. It acts as a "mediator" between the person and your idea of a surgeon. Without the mediator, you would learn nothing about the person from the words.

Does the theory seem plausible? It does push Pavlovian principles rather far, but a central assumption of the theory has found support in a provocative study by Staats, Staats, and Heard (1959). The theory asserts that the "meanings" of two words can be joined through classical conditioning. To test that idea, Staats, Staats, and Heard visually presented each of six words for a five-second period. A second after a word appeared, the experimenter pronounced another word. The subjects thought that the purpose of the study was to memorize the visually and orally presented words as separate lists. The real objective of the experiment was to establish associations among the meanings of some visual words (conditioned stimuli, CSs) and the meanings of some oral words (unconditioned stimuli, UCSs). One CS word was CARPET. It was linked on successive trials to positively valued words like BEAUTY and SWEET. Another CS word was ROCK. It was linked to negatively valued words like BITTER and CRIMINAL. After 14 conditioning trials, the subjects rated synonyms of the CS words (RUG in place of CARPET; STONE in place of ROCK) on a scale ranging from extreme "pleasantness" to extreme "unpleasantness." Although the subjects indicated no awareness that they were rating synonyms, they judged RUG to be a more pleasant word than STONE. From the standpoint of mediational theory, the CS words and their synonyms had produced similar internal responses that carried the meanings of the words (r_m). During conditioning, an evaluative reaction was attached to the meaning response, r_m, associated with the CS. Since the synonym produced a similar r_m, the evaluative reaction "generalized" from the CS.

Just how far one can push a Pavlovian interpretation of sentence comprehension is a matter for further research to determine. Intuitively, though, we can see that an extension of Pavlovian principles beyond the type of sentence which Mowrer considered is likely to be difficult. Learning through contiguity is a credible interpretation of sentence comprehension when one word in a sentence acquires meaning from a subsequent word, as in "Cecil is a surgeon." But it is not clear how temporal contiguity would explain our comprehension of sentences in which there is no such relationship between words, for example, "Cecil *knows* a surgeon." A more fruitful Pavlovian approach to sentence comprehension would appear to be one initiated by Razran (1949), in which the entire sentence, rather than a single word, is conceptualized as a conditioned stimulus. This approach was briefly discussed in Chapter 2. You may recall that Razran conditioned subjects' salivary responses to sentences like "Poverty is degrading," and then tested generalization to sentences whose meanings were either consistent or inconsistent with the meaning of the CS. Generalization was stronger to sentences whose meanings were consistent with the CS ("Wealth is uplifting") than to sentences whose meanings were inconsistent ("Poverty is not degrading"). That meaning was the dominant factor in generalization is particularly significant from the standpoint of Chomsky's distinction between surface structure and deep structure. Using an entire sentence as a CS, one could test generalization to sentences which, on the basis of a purely linguistic analysis, had deep structures similar to that of the CS but surface structures that were different. Strong generalization to such sentences would provide striking evidence for the psychological reality of linguistic relationships. This is just one way in which Pavlovian principles could be used to investigate the processes underlying sentence comprehension.

THE CHILD'S ACQUISITION OF GRAMMAR

Developmental changes in speech patterns

The babbling phase of language development ends gradually. Before children say their first words, and for some time afterward, they produce utterances that resemble babbling in some ways and words in other ways (Dore, Franklin, Miller, and Ramer, 1976). The utterances do not sound like words. However, they occur frequently in the child's speech, are phonetically consistent, and are partly correlated with environmental conditions. One child uttered a particular sound in the following situations: when she looked out a window while playing, when she looked back at a bathroom which she had just left, when she looked at herself in the mirror, and when she looked at some plastic beads in a sink. The utterance seemed to be an expression of interest in certain aspects of the environment which had little, if anything, in common. Dore et al. (1976) suggest that such utterances do not actually refer to things, but rather contain the "germ" of reference.

As the child's vocabulary grows, a peculiar feature of his or her linguistic development becomes evident. The child rarely combines words in a single utterance. The words are spoken in isolation even though the child may have a vocabulary of some 50 words from which to produce combinations (Lenneberg, 1967, p. 283). Some psycholinguists believe that the isolated words may actually be primitive sentences that express complete propositions. If a child said "Mommy" while observing his or her mother walking up the street, the child might mean, "Mommy is coming home." Or, if the child entered the kitchen, approached the refrigerator, and said "milk," the child might be asking, "May I have some milk to drink?" The "one-word" phase of language development ends when the child begins to produce combinations of two words. In the ensuing months, the number of different two-word combinations increases slowly at first, but then very rapidly. Braine (1963) reported that one child produced 14 different word combinations during the first month in which a two-word utterance was noted. During subsequent months, the child exhibited 24, 54, 89, 350, 1400, and 2500+ different combinations. What is most significant about the "two-word" phase of development is that the child does not combine words haphazardly. Regularities are present which strongly suggest that the child has acquired primitive grammatical rules. However, even though the combinations consist of only two words, deducing the child's rules has not been easy. It now appears that initial conceptions of children's grammar may have been a "false start" (Brown, 1973).

Pivot grammar   When analyzing records of children's speech, Braine (1963) noted many two-word combinations of the following sort: BYEBYE PLANE, BYEBYE MAN, BYEBYE HAT, ALLGONE SHOE, ALLGONE VITAMINS, ALLGONE DIRTY, ALLGONE EGG. The children seemed to select words from two distinct classes, and to combine them according to a simple rule. One class contained a few **pivot words** like ALLGONE and BYEBYE. The other, **X-class** contained a much larger number of words, primarily nouns. The child apparently combined one pivot word with one word from the X-class, usually letting the pivot word occupy the first position. The child seemed to treat the two classes of words very differently. Both children in Braine's study uttered words from the X-class alone as well as in combination with pivot words. However, they tended to avoid using pivot words alone; the pivot words went before X-words. Another difference between the classes was that pivot words could occur together with many different X-words, but a given X-word occurred with only one or two pivot words. That pivot constructions were not merely imitations of adult speech was suggested by the occurrence of expressions which adults probably never used, such as ALLGONE DIRTY. The children seemed to have acquired a **generative rule** which enabled them to produce novel expressions.

During the early months of the two-word phase, there was a large increase in the number of words in the children's X-classes. As the children discovered a new pivot word, they tended to use it quickly. One child used the pivot word SEE for the first time in the expression SEE HAT. The child's next three pivot constructions were SEE SOCK, SEE HORSIE, and SEE BOY. Approximately five or six months after they produced their first word-combinations, the children entered a significant new phase of development: they began to produce constructions with X-words in *both* positions. Braine considered the new constructions to be primitive sentences. For example, MAN CAR apparently meant, "The man is in the car," and CAR BRIDGE seemed to mean, "The car is under the bridge."

Brown and Bellugi (1964) reported another significant elaboration of pivotal constructions in a study of how children learn to use noun phrases. Early noun phrases consisted of one pivot word followed by a noun—for example, A DIRT, A

BECKY, MORE COFFEE, MORE NUT. Subsequently, the children produced noun phrases with two pivot words preceding the noun. The order of the pivot words suggested that the children had acquired important new rules. The pivot class had apparently been subdivided so that certain pivot words would always go before others. The children produced phrases like A BLUE FLOWER and A NICE NAP, but never BLUE A FLOWER or NICE A NAP. The rule was: articles go before nouns. Brown and Bellugi suggested that a basic dimension of language development was a differentiation of "privileges" within the pivot class, a recognition that some words went before others.

But what does it all mean?   When a child says BYEBYE SHOE, precisely what does he or she mean? The pivot word, BYEBYE, could refer to the complete disappearance of the shoe; it could refer to the movement of the shoe away from the child; it could refer to a desire to get rid of the shoe; it could refer to many possible events. Obviously, to ascertain its meaning, we would need a description of the situation which prompted the child to speak. Unfortunately, little or no information about the context of children's utterances was included in early reports on pivot grammar. The oversight was a serious one, for when we consider pivot constructions in context, we see them in a different light.

Bloom (1970) first drew attention to the importance of context in interpreting pivot constructions. She obtained speech samples from several children in three kinds of situations: while the children played with selected toys, while they played with peers, and while they engaged in self-care activities (dressing, eating, toileting). By carefully observing the situations in which the children spoke, Bloom could make reasonable inferences about what the children were trying to say. She found that many of the utterances were in the mold of pivot constructions, but they did not seem to be the product of the generative rule assumed to underlie pivot constructions: "Select first one word from the pivot class and select second one word from the X-class." Instead, the children apparently were trying to represent in their speech relationships which they perceived in the environment. For each type of relationship, the children selected two key words and put them together in a particular order. One type of relationship which the children sought to represent was a subject-object relationship. Here, a person or thing performed an action that influenced another person or thing. Bloom noted that one child said "Mommy sock" while the mother helped the child put on a sock. The child was expressing a relationship in which the mother (subject) performed an action which influenced the sock (object). On another occasion, the child said "Mommy sock" while the child picked up her mother's sock. Here the child was expressing a genitive relationship, or relationship of possession, in which the mother was the possessor of the sock. Had the child (whose name was Kathryn) said, "Kathryn sock," she would have been stating the subject-object relationship.

According to Brown (1973), children reach a milestone in their development when they learn to put two relationships together in a single utterance. Suppose that a child watched his or her father hit a baseball. In an earlier phase of development, the child might simply say "Daddy hit" to express the subject-action relationship, or "Hit ball" to represent the action-object relationship. The more advanced child would put the two relationships together ("Daddy hit" + "Hit ball"), remove one of the repeated words ("hit"), and say, "Daddy hit ball."

The studies of Bloom (1970) and Brown (1973) do more than shake the validity of pivot grammar. They help to clarify the fundamental question that studies of language development must eventually answer: How do children learn to represent relationships in words? Few questions pose as serious a challenge to established principles of learning.

Imitation, production, and comprehension

Lenneberg (1962) described the case of a child with a rare language disorder. In most ways, the child seemed normal—he was alert, had an adequate attention span, and responded quickly to verbal instructions. What the child could not do was speak. Although he was capable of emotional vocalizations—crying, laughing, grunting—he had never uttered a word, and totally lacked voluntary control over his voice. Once he was asked to make the pointer of a sound meter in a tape recorder jump by vocalizing into the microphone. The child found the task impossible. He would move his head and lips toward the microphone as if to speak, but then, in frustration, he would simply clap his hands or put the microphone to the examiner's mouth. That the child could comprehend speech was evident from the fact that he would follow instructions, such as, "Take the block and put it on the bottle." The child did not simply respond to facial expressions or other inadvertent cues that the examiner may have given, as he responded equally well to instructions played through a tape recorder.

Lenneberg was able to discount two possible causes of the speech deficit—deafness and emotional disturbance. The child's IQ was below normal (72–83), but that problem alone would not explain the speech deficit. Lenneberg notes that patients with IQs as low as 25–35 are capable of limited speech. Whatever the cause, this child's case demonstrated clearly that the comprehension of speech and the production of speech are different capacities. That comprehension was present without production was theoretically significant. Lenneberg took the phenomenon as evidence that a child need not imitate adult sentences to learn what they mean.

Actually, the presence of comprehension without production is not unusual. Parents often have the impression that children have a better understanding of language than their speech suggests. Fraser, Bellugi, and Brown (1963) were able to substantiate this impression in a study testing children's ability to imitate, produce, and comprehend sentences. As an illustration of the procedure, consider the sentences, "The sheep are jumping" and "The sheep is jumping." The sentences are equivalent except for the verbs. In the first sentence, the verb "are" implies that "sheep" is plural, while in the second sentence the verb "is" implies that "sheep" is singular. How sensitive is a child to the is-are distinction? Fraser, Bellugi, and Brown tested the children's comprehension by presenting two pictures, one with two sheep jumping a fence, the other with one sheep jumping while a companion watched. The experimenter initially pronounced both sentences, then presented one sentence and asked the child to point to the corresponding picture. After the child responded, the experimenter presented the other sentence and again asked the child to point to a picture. The procedure for testing production was similar to that for testing comprehension. The major difference was that after pronouncing the two sentences, the experimenter pointed to each picture in turn and asked the child to name it. To be correct, the child had to produce the key grammatical feature—"is" or "are." In the procedure for testing imitation, the experimenter initially pronounced both sentences, then asked the child to repeat each sentence in turn after the experimenter pronounced it a second time. No pictures were present. The child merely had to imitate the key grammatical feature to be correct.

Fraser, Bellugi, and Brown studied a total of 10 grammatical contrasts. The children were approximately 3½ years old. With all but one contrast, the children achieved their highest scores on the imitation task, somewhat lower scores on the comprehension task, and by far their lowest scores on the production task. A possible inference from these findings is that imitation is a source of progress in the child's acquisition of grammar. Imitation seemingly precedes comprehension and production. With sufficient repetition of grammatical features, children may come to comprehend what they are saying, and subsequently, to produce grammatical features without prompting. This conception has appeal because imitation probably plays a major role in another area of language development—the acquisition of words (Mowrer, 1960).

But children have apparently opted for more complex principles. Whatever role imitation may play in the acquisition of grammar, it is neither simple nor direct. That was the strong suggestion of findings reported by Ervin-Tripp (1964). She reasoned that if imitation were a source of progress in the acquisition of grammar, we might expect children's imitative utterances to be grammatically more complex than their spontaneous utterances. However, Ervin-Tripp found no evidence that imitative and spontaneous utterances differed in complexity; they exhibited grammatical patterns that were virtually identical. The implication was that the children imitated a grammatical pattern only if they could *already* produce that pattern on their own. Together with Lenneberg's (1962) observations, Ervin-Tripp's data suggest that the acquisition of grammar does not result from the mere "parroting" of adult speech.

Adults as language teachers

How, then, do children learn language? Adults must influence children's speech in some way. Anne Sullivan's work with Helen Keller provides some possible clues. You may recall that Sullivan used two methods to teach sentence structure. One method involved encouraging Helen to express a single thought in several different ways. Once Sullivan requested candy by asking, "Will Helen please give Teacher some candy?" On another occasion, she said, "Teacher would like to eat some of

Helen's candy." The other method of teaching sentence structure involved the addition of words to Helen's grammatically incomplete sentences. In her early stages of development, Helen typically produced content words like nouns, main verbs, and adjectives, and omitted grammatical elements such as auxiliary verbs and articles. Once Helen spelled the words, "Helen milk." Sullivan expanded on Helen's words with the sentence, "Give Helen some milk to drink."

Interestingly, the expansion technique seems to be one which parents often use. Brown and Bellugi (1964) found many examples of expansions in taped conversations between children and adults. On one occasion a child said "Mommy eggnog," and the mother replied, "Mommy had her eggnog." On another occasion the child said, "Baby highchair," and the mother responded, "Baby is in the highchair."

But do adult reactions such as those described by Brown and Bellugi actually influence children's speech? A revealing experiment by Nelson, Carskaddon, and Bonvillan (1973) clarifies the effects of adult speech patterns. Children who were about 3½ years of age engaged in conversation with an adult while looking through a picture book. The experimenter reacted to each new sentence spoken by the child in one of two ways. In the "recast sentence" condition, the experimenter repeated the child's words in a new grammatical context. The objective was to present new grammatical relationships while maintaining the exact meaning of the child's utterance. In the "new sentence" condition, the experimenter presented new grammatical relationships but specifically excluded nouns, verbs, adjectives, and other content words used by the child. The adult's sentences were short and grammatically complete. Sessions lasted 20 minutes and were conducted for a period of 11 weeks. The evaluation of the procedures was based on a subsequent conversation with the children. Their utterances were evaluated on several measures of language development, and the levels of performance compared with those of children who had not undergone language training.

The recast-sentence procedure resulted in significantly higher performance on several measures in comparison to the control procedure. However, the new-sentence procedure did not significantly accelerate development. Recasting the children's sentences raised performance on such dimensions as the number of words per utterance, and the number of auxiliary verbs per verb construction. These findings do not actually reveal the nature of the learning process, but they do show that verbal interaction with adults plays an important role.

A role for Mother Nature?

Learning through interaction with the environment is a recurrent theme in behavioristic theories. In the present case we see that utterances of the child influence utterances of adults, which in turn influence future utterances of the child. Superficially, at least, some sort of feedback or reinforcement process seems to be operating, but it is not at all clear that traditional associative principles are adequate to explain the many subtleties of linguistic behavior. Cognitive approaches to language development emphasize the extraordinary obstacles children face and the apparent ease with which they overcome them. Few parents provide feedback according to a plan. From the cognitive perspective, inconsistent feedback would make language acquisition vitually impossible if associative processes were the only ones operating. Children must have an innate disposition to learn language, a disposition to sift through the welter of sounds and extract regularities.

Chomsky (1965), McNeill (1966; 1970), and others have begun to develop the notion of an innate "Language Acquisition Device" (LAD). It is said that children analyze linguistic data according to a genetic plan. This plan makes children sensitive to basic features of their language, features which are present in all languages. Precisely what these "universal features" of languages are remain to be worked out through cross-cultural studies, but it is nevertheless possible to imagine ways in which LAD might use the features. McNeill (1966) suggested a plan of analysis consisting of two tasks. One task requires the child to categorize words. In a sense, the child has "preconceived ideas" about what distinctions among words should be made to speak intelligibly. Categories might include: animate nouns, inanimate nouns, transitive verbs, intransitive verbs, and so on. The child realizes intuitively that the positions of words in a sentence depends in part on the categories to which the words belong. Having learned which words are animate nouns and which words are inanimate nouns, the child would recognize that the sentence, "John likes chocolate" is more grammatical than "Chocolate likes John." While LAD performs the task of categorization, it performs a second task: it seeks ways of expressing basic grammatical relationships within the limits of its categories. The genetic plan assumes that the language has ways of expressing relationships between subject and predicate, verb and object, noun and modifier, and so on. These grammatical relationships presumably make up the deep structures of all languages; they are universal features. But the transformation rules required to bring the grammatical relations to the surface differ among languages and must be learned. Thus, having learned to categorize certain words as nouns and other words as adjectives, the child would proceed to discover the word order. Should adjectives precede the noun or follow the noun?

LAD makes the child a "scientist." The child is constantly forming hypotheses about the language and testing them out. But how does the child learn from tests of his or her hypotheses? We have come full circle to the question that prompted the invention of LAD in the first place, the question of how children learn language.

Speculation will not provide the answer. Facts are needed. To the extent that LAD leads to the discovery of facts about language learning, it will have made a valuable contribution. But we must be alert to the danger that LAD, and other theories that emphasize innate dispositions, may discourage—not encourage—the search for facts. We know from previous chapters that the concept of instinct was once used to explain virtually all forms of behavior. The maternal instinct was the reason mothers cared for children. The pugnacity instinct started fights. The herding instinct led people to congregate. With such simple "explanations" available, psychologists had little incentive to explore relationships between behavior and environment. If we assume that an aspect of linguistic behavior is innate, might we not fail to pursue possible environmental influences? We can minimize this danger by keeping an open mind about language, so that we will feel free to follow leads that may eventually contradict our assumptions.

OF CHILDREN AND CHIMPANZEES

Language is the cornerstone of intellectual growth. By enabling us to learn from the experience of other people, language frees us from the constraints of our own experience. It exposes us to new facts, new points of view, new values, new ways of life. That is why the human species has continually sought to expand its means of communication. Radio, television, space satellites—all have the purpose of expanding our range of communication. What are the limits? For years, science-fiction writers have contemplated the idea of communicating with creatures from other worlds. Those fantasies have gained a measure of credibility as scientists now explore the possibility of contacting alien civilizations through radio transmissions The efforts of the scientists may well fail, and the stories of the science-fiction writers remain fantasies. But there are undeniably creatures on this planet whose life experiences are very different from our own. Consider the cat down the street. Are not its experiences different from yours? You may feel that cats and dogs have little to offer intellectually, and perhaps that is so. But what about "higher" animals—dolphins, gorillas, orangutans, and chimpanzees?

Just conversing with an animal would have immense philosophical implications. It is widely believed that only the human species has the ability to use language. This view rests on the fact that lower animals do not communicate in the way that people do. The vocalizations of lower animals are instinctive reactions: all members of the species generally produce the same sounds. In contrast, people produce invented sounds, and they use the sounds *creatively*. That is, people generate sounds in novel sequences and react appropriately to the sequences produced by other people. Because our ability to use language is apparently unique in the animal kingdom, it is said that the human species is unique. Lower species differ from one another in degree. All of them differ from the human species in kind. Consequently, there are principles of human behavior that are not discoverable in the behavior of lower animals. Such views were expressed centuries ago by the philosopher Descartes, who considered language to be the best evidence that an organism could think. Since people possessed language, and lower animals did not, only people could think.

The belief that lower animals are unable to use language is now under heavy attack. Reports emanating from laboratories throughout the country indicate significant progress in training animals to converse with people. The subjects of these studies have been chimpanzees. None of the chimps shows promise of becoming a second Shakespeare. But many give evidence of having mastered the rudiments of language.

Early attempts to train chimps to vocalize words were not successful. Since the first major study of chimp communication was published in 1932, chimps have managed to produce just three words: "mama," "papa," and "cup" (Kellogg, 1968). Why chimps are unable to mimic words is not known. The vocal apparatus of chimps differs from that of humans, but biologists disagree about whether it is capable of producing words. Behaviorally, chimps tend to be silent except when aroused. Also, they do not undergo an extended period of babbling in early life. Chimps are not natural vocalizers. However, they are natural manipulators, and they have made significant progress in communicating with their hands.

One means of manual communication which chimps have begun to master is sign language. Several chimps have acquired sizeable vocabularies of signs. Perhaps the most advanced chimp is a protege of Gardner and Gardner (1969; 1974) named Washoe. Two systems of signs are in current use by the deaf. One system, the method of finger spelling employed by Helen Keller and Anne Sullivan, would have been too difficult to train. Gardner and Gardner adopted instead a system in which each sign represents an entire word: American Sign Language (ASL). To focus Washoe's attention on the signs, Gardner and Gardner prohibited trainers from speaking in the presence of the chimp. All communication had to be through signs. The most productive procedure for training Washoe to use signs was the "method of guidance," in which the trainer simply made the signs with Washoe's hands. Prompting the chimp to imitate signs was also effective. The trainer would make a sign in connection with a situation, and repeat the sign until Washoe produced it. "Shaping" signs through the reinforcement of successive approximations was effective but slow. In one application, Washoe learned to produce an accurate version of the ASL sign for "more." The proper ASL sign consists of tapering the hands and bringing them together repeatedly, with the tips of the fingers on one hand touching those on the other hand. Gardner and Gardner noted that Washoe made a rough approximation to this sign when she was being tickled. The chimp typically covered the tickled area of her body with her arms, and if the trainer pulled her arms apart, she would tend to bring them together again. Just as the hands came together, the trainer resumed tickling in an effort to reinforce the behavior. Subsequently, the trainer deliberately interrupted play and required the chimp to make a response resembling the ASL sign to obtain more tickling. Progressively closer approximations to the sign were required, and eventually Washoe reproduced it accurately.

What suggested that Washoe had acquired symbols, rather than mere motor reactions, was her tendency to transfer signs to new situations. For example, after Washoe acquired the "more" sign in connection with tickling, the trainer required her to make this sign to be pushed again across the floor in a laundry basket. Thereafter, Washoe used the "more" sign appropriately in all of her activities. Further evidence that she had acquired rudiments of language was her tendency to combine signs. The combinations were often of her own invention, and resembled pivot constructions, for example, "go in," "go out," "go sweet."

A chimp named Sarah has achieved notoriety with another means of communication (Premack and Premack, 1972). She communicates with plastic chips displayed on a board in the manner illustrated in Fig. 9.7. The message on the board reads, "Sarah insert apple pail banana dish." To demonstrate comprehension of this sentence, Sarah had to put the apple in the pail and the banana in the dish, a task which she performed accurately. Sarah was also able to produce novel sequences of chips. For example, to establish that a particular chip meant "raisin," the trainer presented the chip next to a real raisin, and inserted between the symbol and the object another chip meaning "name of." Sarah had previously learned to react appropriately to the "name of" chip in connection with an apple and a banana. Some time after being taught the name for raisins, she requested a raisin with the sentence, "Mary give raisin Sarah."

The achievements of Sarah, Washoe, and other tutored chimps generally support behavioristic interpretations of language. Although behavioristic accounts differ in many ways (Skinner, 1957; Mowrer, 1960), they work from a common premise: the basic processes underlying human behavior exist to some degree in lower animals. To the extent that chimps master the fundamentals of language, they add credibility to the behaviorists' faith in the continuity of species.

Fig. 9.7 Sarah follows "written" instructions to "insert apple pail" and "banana dish." (From Premack and Premack, 1972)

Language in chimps: How inventive?

After reviewing the literature on language in chimpanzees, Limber (1977) has concluded that chimps have yet to exhibit true inventiveness in their use of language. By inventiveness, Limber does not mean the creative genius of a Shakespeare. He means the kinds of everyday inventiveness we display when we name things. Few people realize that they are being inventive when they refer to objects for which they lack conventional names. You are being inventive when you produce phrases like "the man who sold us the lemon," or "the house without a roof." The "man" and the "house" are identified by the descriptions which follow them. According to Limber, no one has yet demonstrated that chimps can refer to objects or actions by inventing novel descriptions of them. In contrast, Limber reports that he has observed this ability in children as young as 2½ years of age. One child produced the sentences, "Do it the way I say," and "I cook it the way Mommy makes a cake." The child evidently discovered that she could identify ways of performing actions by saying the word "way" and attaching to it a short descriptive sentence ("I say" in the first case; "Mommy makes a cake" in the second case).

Of course, the most remarkable evidence of human linguistic inventiveness is the invention of language itself. The first grunts of our ancestors were monumental achievements. Is that primieval spark which created language still in us? Evidence that it has remained comes from an intriguing study of deaf children by Goldin-Meadow and Feldman (1977). Their observations strongly suggest that a child need not experience language to produce language.

Due to their deafness, the children, who ranged in age from 17 to 49 months, had not acquired oral language. Neither had they learned a formal system of signs, for their parents had planned to enroll them in oral education programs that discouraged instruction in signing. Nevertheless, the children exhibited sophisticated sign systems of their own. The signs adopted by each child were idiosyncratic. But, surprisingly, all of the children tended to combine the signs according to the same grammatical rule! The rule determined the order of signs in two-sign phrases, and applied to the following categories of words: the "patient" of an action (the person or object acted upon), the "act," and the "recipient" of the action (the person or location towards which the patient moves). For example, to request that a shoe be put on a table, one child pointed at the shoe (patient) and then at the table (recipient). Another time, the child used a two-sign phrase to draw attention to the mother's having twisted open a jar. The sequence consisted of pointing to the jar (patient) and then making a twisting motion (act).

The grammatical rule specified that signs had to be made in the order, patient, act, recipient. Note how the rule was applied in the foregoing examples: "shoe" (patient) preceded "table" (recipient), and "jar" (patient) preceded "twisting open" (act). Fig. 9.8 shows the frequency with which the children produced two-sign sequences according to this grammatical rule. The rule specifies three possible orders of categories: patient-act, act-recipient, and patient-recipient. In a number of cases the children exhibited no tendency to order a pair of categories. For example, Kathy and Chris produced as many patient-act phrases as they did act-patient

THE LEARNING OF LANGUAGE

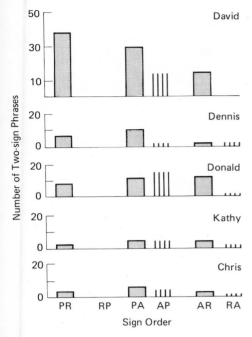

Fig. 9.8 Number of times each of five deaf children produced two-sign phrases in which the order of signs was consistent with a grammatical rule (solid bars) or inconsistent (lined bars). P, patient; A, act; R, recipient. (From Goldin-Meadow and Feldman, 1977)

phrases. However, you can see that if a child ordered categories at all, he or she used the order prescribed by the rule.

The children were not simply imitating the gestures of the mothers. There was little similarity between the signs of mother and child, and where similarity existed, it was usually the mother who imitated the child. The sign systems of these deaf children dramatically illustrate how inventive our species can be. While the linguistic abilities of chimps are striking, we must always keep in mind who is training whom.

SUMMARY

Children normally master the basic rules of language by the age of three years. To achieve this feat, many psychologists believe that human beings must have a natural inclination to learn language. That Helen Keller was able to master language despite the seemingly insurmountable obstacles of deafness and blindness lends support to the view that nature gives children a "head start."

To produce and comprehend speech requires a vast store of knowledge about the most intricate details of the language. Motor learning, perceptual learning, vocabulary learning, and the learning of grammatical rules all contribute to one's

288

ability to communicate. The motor skills involved in the production of speech sounds are exceedingly complex. What sound will be heard as air flows upward from the lungs is determined by two factors: (1) the shape of the "vocal tract" (the region encompassing the throat, mouth, and nose); and (2) the presence or absence of vocal cord vibration. Sounds produced with vocal cord vibration are said to be "voiced" (for example, b, d, g), while sounds produced without vocal cord vibration are said to be "unvoiced" (such as, p, t, k). Patterns of vibration set up in the vocal tract can be precisely analyzed with a device called a "sound spectrograph." The product of the analysis is a "spectrogram" showing the frequencies that make up a sound (vertical axis) at different times (horizontal axis). Dark bands on the spectrogram represent the frequencies which contribute most to the sound, and are called "formants." Small changes in a format can correlate with large changes in the perception of speech sounds.

Under conditions of normal conversation, speech sounds are perceived "categorically." Minor "phonetic" differences among sounds are ignored even though the differences are potentially detectable. Linguists consider two sounds to be instances of a single sound category, or "phoneme," if listeners typically do not use the difference to discriminate between utterances. Categorical perception markedly influences discriminative capacity. The ability to discriminate two sounds which have a minor physical difference is much greater if the sounds belong to different phoneme categories than if the sounds belong to the same phoneme category. Learning may not be completely responsible for this effect. Infants just 1 to 4 months old have been shown to perceive some phonemes (/b/, /d/) in much the same way as adults perceive them.

Linguists describe the speech patterns of a population in terms of a hierarchy of rules. At the most elementary level of analysis are rules for combining phonemes to form units of meaning called "morphemes." At progressively higher levels of analysis are rules for combining morphemes to form words, rules for combining words to form phrases, and rules for combining phrases to form sentences. Recognizing that no one adheres to all the rules all the time, linguists assume that they are describing the speech patterns of an "ideal speaker." This is a hypothetical person who is said to exhibit speech patterns that most members of a population have the potential to produce or recognize as being grammatical. There is evidence that real speakers are at least partially sensitive to relationships within a sentence identified through a purely linguistic analysis.

Noam Chomsky, probably the most influential of modern linguists, introduced a framework for the analysis of sentence structure and meaning that is widely used. Every sentence is said to have a "surface structure" and a "deep structure." The surface structure is the arrangement of phrases explicitly stated in the sentence. The deep structure is a set of propositions implicit in the sentence and sensed intuitively by the speaker. Deep structure is related to surface structure by "rules of grammatical transformation," which can be conceptualized as a succession of operations upon the deep structure which creates progressively closer approximations to the sentence actually expressed. Many psychologists have adopted Chomsky's view that the deep structures of all languages are essentially alike and only the rules of transformation differ. The implication is that while knowledge of transformational rules must be acquired, knowledge of deep structure is innate. This gives children a "head start" in acquiring language.

Although speech perception during the first year of life is well developed in certain respects, speech production is highly primitive. Vocalizations toward the end of the first year begin to resemble vowels and consonants, but the sounds are quite variable. The infant's first words emerge when the infant is between the ages of 12 and 18 months. Mowrer's theory of imitation based on the concepts of secondary reinforcement and self-stimulation provides a plausible interpretation of early word learning. That there is an interplay between imitative learning and genetic factors is suggested by an analysis of babbled utterances in infants. This analysis revealed that certain patterns of sounds in babbling "foreshadow" or anticipate the errors children commonly make when pronouncing words.

The mechanism of self-stimulation proposed by Mowrer could explain the acquisition of sound patterns, but it does not explain how words come to act as symbols. Words may acquire meaning through the sort of process described by Pavlov in connection with the "second signaling system": Through temporal contiguity with an event, a word comes to elicit a reaction similar to that elicited by the event itself. Mowrer has attempted to extend the contiguity principle to the comprehension of sentences, suggesting that one word in a sentence can take on meaning from a subsequent word. While the analysis is plausible in certain kinds of sentences, it would be difficult to extend the analysis to all possible kinds.

A peculiar feature of the period in which children produce their first words is that the words are usually uttered in isolation from one another rather than in combination with other words. It is possible that in this "one-word" phase of development, children use single words to represent entire sentences. The first clear evidence that children can produce grammatical utterances appears in the "two-word" phase. Early analyses of the two-word phase suggested that children constructed utterances by combining words from two distinct categories: A large "X-class," consisting primarily of nouns, and a smaller "pivot class." Pivot constructions were seen as highly significant because they were not mere imitations of adult speech. Instead, the constructions seemed to be products of a "generative rule," the kind of mechanism which in adults is widely thought to be responsible for the production of novel sentences. This ability to produce sentences one has not heard before is a fundamental characteristic of human language. Subsequent analyses of the two-word phase have called earlier interpretations into question on the grounds that the meaning, or semantic content, of the utterances was not considered. Current theory assumes that children use various word orders in their speech to represent various kinds of relationships perceived in the environment. It is important to note that the foregoing description of phases in the acquisition of grammar applies to speech production, not necessarily to speech comprehension. Studies have shown (e.g., Lenneberg; Fraser, Bellugi, and Brown) that children comprehend grammar before they can produce it.

SUMMARY

The processes underlying the acquisition of grammar are poorly understood. That imitation probably plays a minor role, if any at all, is suggested by findings (Ervin-Tripp) that children imitate a grammatical pattern only if they can already produce that pattern on their own. Adults' reactions to children's speech seem to be very important in language development. Typically, young children produce utterances containing content words (e.g., nouns, adjectives) but not grammatical words (e.g., articles, auxiliary verbs). Parents often "expand" on children's utterances, filling in the missing grammatical elements, and experimental data indicate that "expansions" can increase the grammatical complexity of children's speech. Further research is needed to clarify the processes responsible for this effect.

From the cognitive perspective, the principle of reinforcement is not adequate to explain the acquisition of grammar because children do not receive consistent feedback on the accuracy of their efforts. Cognitivists see the learning process as one in which the child extracts regularities from adult speech according to a genetic plan. Chomsky and McNeill developed one conceptualization of a genetic plan called the "Language Acquisition Device." It generally asserts that children have an inborn disposition to categorize words (e.g., animate and inanimate nouns, transitive and intransitive verbs) and to put the categories together in ways characteristic of the deep structure of the language. These innate relationships among categories are said to be "universal" features of all languages. Children must learn the transformation rules necessary for producing and comprehending the surface structure of the language. Supporting the notion of universal features is a study by Goldin-Meadow and Feldman showing that deaf children who have invented signs for communication put the signs together in similar ways.

Behaviorists assume that the processes responsible for the acquisition of grammar are no different from the processes responsible for other forms of complex behavior. On the belief that there is continuity across species, behaviorists have attempted to teach language to chimpanzees using principles of learning developed with lower animals. Evidence that chimps have mastered the rudiments of grammar is sufficiently strong to make the behavioristic position credible. However, doubts have been raised that chimps can match human beings in certain linguistic functions indicative of "inventiveness."

STUDY QUESTIONS

1. Describe the incident at the well-house in which Helen Keller discovers the meaning of the word "water." What principle of learning does this incident illustrate? How did Anne Sullivan teach Helen the names for internal events such as "love" and "sweet?"

2. In what sense is language creative?

3. What kinds of words did Helen include in her early utterances, and what kinds did she omit? How did Sullivan correct this deficiency? Give an example.

4. What was Sullivan's original plan for teaching vocabulary, grammar, and reading? How and why did she change this plan? In what way was Sullivan's strategy similar to that used by parents of normal children?

THE LEARNING OF LANGUAGE

5. Define "larynx," "vocal tract," "voiced sound," "unvoiced sound."

6. Describe the means by which we articulate the sounds "t," "d," "s."

7. What is a "spectrogram?" What does a spectrogram show on the vertical and horizontal axes? How does a formant relate the variable on one axis with the variable on the other axis?

8. Define "phoneme." Give two examples, one of which involves a letter of the alphabet and one of which does not. In what sense do phonemes entail categorical perception of speech sounds?

9. Referring to the procedure and results of the experiment by Liberman et al., explain how categorical perception can influence one's ability to discriminate speech sounds.

10. How did Eimas et al. use "habituation" to study speech perception in infants? What were the results and conclusion of the study?

11. Define "morpheme," "noun phrase," "verb phrase." Give examples.

12. In linguistic theory, what is meant by an "ideal speaker"? Referring to the procedure and results of the experiment by Fodor and Bever, discuss the issue of whether real speakers are sensitive to the relationships within a sentence identified through linguistic analysis.

13. Define "surface structure," "deep structure." Use sentences in the active and passive voice to illustrate these concepts. What does Chomsky mean by "rules of grammatical transformation"? What aspects of linguistic knowledge does he consider to be innate? What aspects acquired?

14. What are the two possible sources of reinforcement for early word learning? Which source is more likely to play a significant role? Why?

15. Referring to the study by Oller et al., discuss the possibility of a genetic influence on early word learning. Give an example of a speech pattern in infancy that foreshadows a speech error in later life.

16. In what sense does Mowrer's interpretation of word learning through rewarding self-stimulation fail to account for the symbolic meaning of words? What additional principle must be included?

17. Using the sentence, "Bobby is a burglar," as an illustration, describe Mowrer's theory of Pavlovian conditioning within sentences. How do the results reported by Staats, Staats, and Heard support this theory? Give an example of a sentence that the theory cannot readily explain.

18. What is peculiar about the "one-word" phase of language development?

19. What is a "generative rule?"

20. Describe the "pivot grammar" characteristic of the "two-word" phase of development. Include the following points in your discussion: (a) definitions and examples of X-words and pivot words; (b) the different ways in which children use pivot words and X-words; (c) the reasons why pivot grammar was thought to represent a generative rule.

21. On what grounds did Bloom object to the foregoing conception of pivot grammar? What type of analysis did she propose as a substitute? Illustrate using the utterance, "Mommy sock," and the cases of "subject-object" and "genitive" relationships.

22. Describe the strategy used by Fraser, Bellugi, and Brown to study imitation, production, and comprehension of speech by children. Illustrate using the sentences "The sheep are jumping," and "The sheep is jumping." What was the rank order of performances on the imitation, production, and comprehension tasks? What is a possible inference from these findings?

23. What is the "expansion" technique of teaching grammar identified by Brown and Bellugi in observations of conversations between parents and children? What experimental evidence is there that expansions actually increase the complexity of children's speech?

24. Why do many psycholinguists believe that the principle of reinforcement cannot explain the child's acquisition of grammar?

25. Describe the "Language Acquisition Device" proposed by Chomsky and McNeill. What knowledge of grammar is assumed to be innate, and what knowledge learned? Illustrate using the example of adjectives and nouns.

26. How does human language differ from vocalization in animals? What would be the theoretical significance of teaching language to chimpanzees?

27. What two methods of training chimpanzees did Gardner and Garder find effective? What method was "slow"? Illustrate the latter method using the example of the ASL sign for "more."

28. What evidence suggested that Washoe acquired symbols? What evidence suggested that Washoe had acquired a generative rule?

29. According to Limber, what feature of human language is missing in chimpanzee language? Give an example.

30. In the study by Goldin-Meadow and Feldman on sign language in deaf children, how were the categories "patient," "act," and "recipient" defined? What grammatical rule did the children generally follow when they combined signs? How do these findings relate to Chomsky's theory of innate grammatical knowledge?

CHAPTER 10

Memory:
An Introduction

Korsakoff's syndrome is a memory disorder occasionally found in chronic alcoholics and individuals suffering from encephalitis and brain tumors. Although it is a bizarre disorder and is relatively rare, studies of this syndrome have provided important insights into the normal processes of memory. Briefly, a person with Korsakoff's syndrome has great difficulty remembering events that have just occurred, but has normal recall of events that transpired before onset of the disease. For example, the individual may be unable to recognize recent acquaintances despite numerous introductions, while readily recalling parents, relatives, and old friends. A similar disorder has been found in some individuals who have undergone brain surgery for relief of epileptic seizures. One such patient, "H. M.," has been studied particularly closely (e.g., Scoville and Milner, 1957; Milner, 1966; Milner, Corkin, and Teuber, 1968) because his case has not been complicated by the disorders of perception, conceptual ability, and personality often accompanying Korsakoff's syndrome. We shall examine H. M.'s case in some detail and then consider the general view of memory which it and similar cases suggest.

CASE H. M.: "EVERY DAY IS ALONE IN ITSELF . . ."

H. M.'s difficulties apparently began when, at the age of seven, he fell off a bicycle and suffered a minor head injury. A year later he experienced minor seizures and they worsened over time. Major convulsions appeared when H. M. was 16, and eventually he was suffering about one major convulsion per week and numerous minor attacks each day. Massive doses of anticonvulsive drugs failed to help, and so, in desperation, extensive brain surgery was undertaken. Technically, the operation involved "bilateral destruction of medial parts of the temporal lobe," including a structure called the "hippocampus" (Milner, 1968). Following the operation the convulsions decreased dramatically, but an unanticipated side-effect soon appeared. H. M. could not recognize hospital staff members whom he had recently met, although he did remember the surgeon whom he had known for years. Simple tasks such as finding his way to the bathroom were impossible to remember or relearn. After leaving the hospital, H. M. required constant assistance in meeting the demands of everyday life. Once his family moved to a new address a few blocks

294

from their old one. H. M. was not permitted to find his own way home because he would constantly go to the old address. H. M. also could not be left at home alone. Not being able to recognize friends of the family he had met since the operation, he would invite total strangers into the house to wait for his mother, thinking they were friends he had not recognized. H. M. was not totally helpless, however. For example, he had no difficulty mowing the lawn, something he learned to do before the operation. But he always had to be shown where to find the lawn mower.

Patients who have had less extensive surgery than H. M. can usually remember emotionally-toned events better than neutral events (Milner, 1966). H. M. had equally poor recall of both kinds of experience. For example, when his mother entered the hospital for a minor operation, he had only the dimmest awareness of her absence, even though she normally cared for him and accompanied him everywhere. During her absence, H. M. went on a trip to a research institute. Ordinarily his mother would have helped him prepare for the journey, but now his father took over, assisting him with his bags and taking him to the doctor supervising the trip. En route to the institute, H. M. remembered none of this, although he did feel uneasy and thought there might be something wrong with his mother or father. When asked who helped him pack his bags, H. M. said "seems like it was my mother. But then that's what I'm not sure about. If there's something wrong with my mother, then it could have been my father (Milner, Corkin, and Teuber, 1968, p. 216)." Although his mother's illness was explained to him repeatedly, H. M. never retained the information and he still felt uneasy upon reaching the institute. But these feelings gradually subsided. When asked again who had helped him pack his bags, he replied that it must have been his mother as she always tended to such matters. For H. M. there was never any yesterday, only the present moment. "Every day is alone in itself," he once said, "whatever enjoyment I've had and whatever sorrow I've had (Milner, Corkin, and Teuber, 1968, p. 217)."

What H. M. could learn

Although H. M.'s memory deficit was severe, he could acquire and retain information under certain conditions. For example, Milner (1965) presented H. M. with the experimental task illustrated in Fig. 10.1. The dots represent boltheads which were used to create a kind of maze. H. M. was asked to discover a preselected sequence of bolts leading from the "Start" position in the lower left-hand corner to the "Finish" position in the upper right. The correct route, shown by the lines interconnecting the dots, involved 28 steps. H. M. indicated his choice of a bolt by touching it with a metal rod. Errors caused a loud click which served as a signal to go back to the preceding bolt and make another choice. Normal subjects whose ages and IQs were similar to H. M.'s solved the problem in less than 25 trials, but H. M. did not improve in 215 trials. The maze was subsequently shortened by covering up all of the bolts outside the dotted lines in Fig. 10.1 (Milner, Corkin, and Teuber, 1968). With the bolt labeled S as the start position and the bolt labeled F_a as the finish position, there were now only 10 choices to learn, but in 125 trials

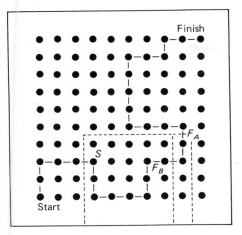

Fig. 10.1 Maze problem presented to H. M., an individual with Korsakoff's syndrome. Large dots represent bolt-heads, which were analogous to stepping-stones. The initial task was discover and remember the path from the point labeled "Start" to the point labeled "Finish." H. M. went from bolt-head to bolt-head, touching each with a pointer. Clicks from an error counter signalled incorrect choices. After H. M. failed to solve the original problem, the path was shortened; the bolt-head labeled "S" became the starting point and the bolt-head labeled "F_A" became the finish point. Because he failed to make substantial progress, the path was shortened further, with "S" serving as the starting point and "F_B" as the finish point. H. M. eventually mastered this task. (After Milner, 1965)

H. M. gave little evidence of improvement. Once again the maze was shortened, with F_b serving as the finish position and eight choices required for solution. Under these conditions H. M. did solve the problem, although the process was painfully slow. Figure 10.2 shows the number of errors H. M. made in successive blocks of five trials. Errors decreased slowly, but the criterion of mastery (three successive trials without an error) was finally attained on Day two after 155 trials. On Days 3, 5, 8, and 14, retention was tested by having H. M. relearn the task to the same criterion. Note that he made fewer errors at the start of each session than he had originally, and that he reduced his error score very rapidly. H. M. did have the ability to learn and retain information provided that it was sufficiently short and that it was repeated sufficiently often.

It is striking how sensitive H. M. was to the number of steps he had to master. The eight-step maze was within his capability but the 10-step maze apparently was not. Why should a difference of just two steps be so important? Milner, Corkin, and Teuber (1968) suggest that eight choices was within H. M.'s **span of immediate memory.** This intellectual capacity is commonly measured by presenting a person with a series of digits or letters and having the person immediately repeat the series in the forward or backward direction. The maximum number of items that can be given without error defines the memory span for that particular type of material.

CASE H.M.: "EVERY DAY IS ALONE IN ITSELF . . ."

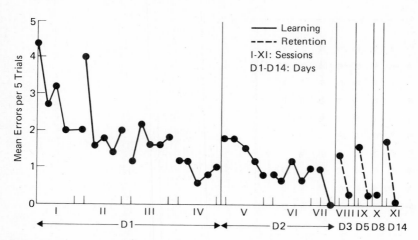

Fig. 10.2 Number of errors H. M. made while learning shortest maze path illustrated in Fig. 10.1 (*S* to F_B), and while performing in tests of retention after mastery of the task. (From Milner, Corkin, and Teuber, 1968)

For most people the memory span is seven items plus or minus two (Miller, 1956), and H. M.'s memory span was in this normal range. His ability to learn material within the memory span is not hard to understand when viewed from a particular theoretical perspective. Let us see how this view of memory would interpret H. M.'s case.

MULTIPLE MEMORIES

People customarily think of memory as a single capacity with one set of characteristics. That is the implication, for example, when a person claims to have a poor memory or a good one; an evaluation is being made of a single system. But many psychologists believe that we possess several memories, each with its own set of characteristics, and that the acquisition of information entails a complex interplay among these systems. The concept of multiple memories belongs to the "human information processing" tradition in learning theory (Chapter 6). An analogy is drawn between the processes computers employ in information systems and the processes people employ in acquiring and remembering information. Theories of memory in the human information processing tradition sometimes resemble computer flow-charts, with boxes representing different storage units and arrows representing movements of information between the units. Perhaps the most influential such theory is that proposed by Atkinson and Shiffrin (1968). It takes most of its details from standard laboratory experiments, but the theory relies on studies of patients like H. M. for support of its main assumption—multiple memories.

The major features of the theory are diagrammed in the top portion of Fig. 10.3. There are three storage units, the "sensory register," the "short-term store"

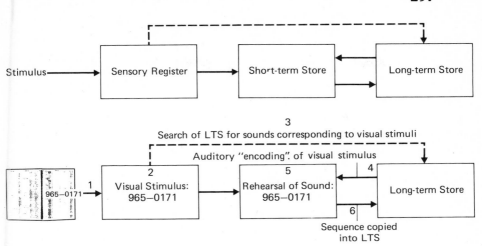

Fig. 10.3 Atkinson and Shiffrin's multistore model of memory. The diagram at the top illustrates the general features of the model. The diagram at the bottom depicts the sequence of steps one theoretically would go through to memorize a telephone number. (After Atkinson and Shiffrin, 1968)

(STS) and the "long-term store" (LTS). The LTS is the repository of all knowledge that we retain on a permanent basis. Once information enters LTS, it persists indefinitely; it rarely decays or drops out of storage. When forgetting takes place, the difficulty is usually that one is unable to locate or retrieve the information. In theory, all such information is potentially recoverable, whereas information that has decayed is not recoverable. Another feature of LTS is its huge capacity—no known limit exists on the amount of information LTS can hold. Before information can enter LTS it must pass through the sensory register and STS. The sensory register provides a momentary copy of external stimuli after they are removed. For example, as you read these words, your eyes are making brief stops at various positions on the line. When your eyes leave a position, the visual stimulus terminates but a copy of what you saw persists. During the period that your eyes are moving to the next position, your sensory register enables you to continue processing information from the last position. Information in the sensory register is rapidly scanned and the important features are passed along to STS. The information might go directly to STS, but usually the route is indirect. One reason is that STS typically takes inputs in a particular form, a form that we can "hear." If the information in the sensory register is visual (as when you read), the information must be converted to an acoustic form. This process of representing, or **encoding,** information acoustically is accomplished by quickly searching through LTS for the "sounds" corresponding to the visual stimuli. Theoretically, you are doing this now as you "listen" to the words on this line. From LTS, the acoustic information goes directly to STS where it awaits further processing.

If our goal is to remember the information permanently, it must be copied back into LTS. Repetition or rehearsal of the sounds in STS increases the likelihood that a copy will be made. Associating the material with information already in LTS also makes permanent storage more likely. Information can be held in STS indefinitely provided that rehearsal continues. If rehearsal stops, the information decays and drops out of STS within 30 seconds. For example, consider a situation in which you have looked up a number in the phone book intending to dial at that moment. You have read the number just once and it is crystal clear in your mind. Suddenly, someone calls you away and engages you in conversation for a minute. When you return to the phone to dial, you find that the phone number is gone. Theoretically, the information has dropped out of STS, and because the number was never repeated, no copy of it was made in LTS.

The STS has another limitation: it can hold very few items. The capacity of STS depends upon how fast items decay and how fast items can be rehearsed. If it took one second to rehearse an item and an item decayed in eight seconds, then the maximum capacity of the STS would be eight items. Rehearsal of Item 1 would bring it to maximal strength. Rehearsal of the next seven items would take seven seconds, leaving one second to "get back" to Item 1. A common measure of STS capacity is the immediate memory span—seven items plus or minus two. Theoretically, if a person could repeat eight digits in the proper order but could not repeat nine, there was a problem in "getting back" to an early item before it decayed.

As a summary of the theory it would be useful to consider the complete sequence of steps one would go through to memorize some information. The bottom portion of Fig. 10.3 illustrates the processes you theoretically would employ in memorizing a phone number. In the first step, you look at the number in the phone book. The visual stimuli produce a copy in your sensory register (step 2) which you then seek to encode in an acoustic form. You search LTS for the sounds corresponding to each digit in the phone number (step 3) and then enter these acoustic codes into STS (step 4). Note that the input to LTS from the sensory register does not establish a permanent visual trace of the number in LTS. According to Atkinson and Shiffrin, it is conceivable that a permanent trace could be set up under certain conditions, but typically permanent traces must come through STS. You now silently rehearse the acoustic information which has entered STS (step 5); in a sense, you can "hear" yourself repeating the digits and there may even be minute articulatory movements in your vocal muscles. Finally, if you have held the information in LTS long enough, a permanent copy will be set up in LTS (step 6).

Atkinson and Shiffrin viewed their theory as a conceptual framework for research of memory; it was not an attempt to guess the facts. The need for a conceptual framework is strong in any field. A single experiment necessarily has limited objectives and addresses relatively narrow issues. Without some general theoretical perspective, relationships between experimental findings would be more difficult to see and a mass of isolated, disconnected facts could accumulate. By tentatively assigning an experimental fact on memory to a particular box or arrow in Fig. 10.3, we might better appreciate how that finding fits into the "big picture."

MEMORY: AN INTRODUCTION

H. M.'s memory deficit fits well into Atkinson and Shiffrin's framework. Viewing his problem from their perspective, we might say that his STS was unimpaired since his immediate memory span—a measure of STS capacity—was normal. Additional evidence is that H. M. could maintain information in STS indefinitely through rehearsal. For example, he could remember a number like 584 if he continually repeated it, although he would quickly lose the number if distracted (Milner, 1966). We might also say that much of H. M.'s LTS was unimpaired since he had no difficulty recalling information from before the operation. Milner, who has studied H. M. and similar cases extensively, believes that the memory deficit consists in being unable to transfer information from STS to LTS. In terms of our sequence of steps for memorizing a telephone number (Fig. 10.3), it is as if the arrow representing step 6 had been partially erased. This view suggests a possible reason why H. M. could learn an eight-step maze but not a 10-step maze. After reaching the finish position in the eight-step maze, H. M. might still have held the previous seven steps in STS. He maintained the full sequence of steps in STS through rehearsal, and after sufficient repetitions, the information finally "got through" to LTS. But 10 steps was beyond the capacity of STS and some of the information always had to be sacrificed during a trial. In contrast, normal subjects readily acquired permanent traces of various parts of the maze and did not have to hold the full sequence in STS.

Warrington and Weiskrantz (1972) have proposed an entirely different view of the memory defect. In contrast to Milner, they suggest that information held in STS is copied into LTS normally. However, retrieval of information from LTS is greatly impaired by interference from other information in LTS. Warrington and Weiskrantz devised a special retention test showing that subjects with memory defects remember more than conventional tests indicate, and that the information they retain is a powerful source of interference during recall. Further research will be needed to clarify the mechanisms underlying the memory defect. But having a conceptual framework such as Atkinson and Shiffrin's helps make relationships between the different viewpoints easier to see, and research should thus be facilitated.

HOW THE FURIES WERE UNLEASHED

The notion that we possess more than one memory has a long history, but only recently has the idea aroused the interest of researchers. In the late 19th century, the philosopher and pioneering psychologist William James (1890, Volume I; reprinted 1950) distinguished between two memories, **primary** and **secondary,** roughly corresponding to Atkinson and Shiffrin's STS and LTS. James believed that a distinction between the two memories was necessary because they gave rise to different mental experiences. An object in primary memory had never left consciousness and was always easy to recall. We experienced it as belonging to the "rearward portion of the present space of time, and not to the genuine past." An object in secondary memory differed in that it had previously dropped from con-

300

sciousness and had to be "fished up," often with great difficulty. When the object entered consciousness it always brought with it the feeling that "we have thought or experienced it before" (1950, Vol. I, pp. 646-648). These introspective observations stimulated little interest in succeeding years. Behaviorism was on the rise and introspection ran counter to the growing emphasis on precise measurement of external responses. Also, in keeping with William of Ockham's admonition about "parsimony" (Chapter 6), many researchers hoped to discover a single set of principles that would apply to memory in all its aspects.

In the late 1950s, Brown (1958) and Peterson and Peterson (1959) reported results of similar experiments which appeared inconsistent with prevailing views of memory. Previous studies of memory had typically presented subjects with a list of items for a number of trials and then tested retention after a period ranging from several minutes to several days. Peterson and Peterson presented subjects with a single item (a set of three letters) just once, and tested retention immediately or after delays of three to 18 seconds. During the delays, the subjects counted backward from a number to prevent rehearsal of the item. There was no evidence that this task caused any confusion at the time of recall. Although retention was very high immediately after presentation of an item, it dropped sharply with several seconds delay and was negligible after 18 seconds. This result was surprising considering the simplicity of the material subjects were asked to remember. It suggested that a principle of decay might apply in certain kinds of memory tasks, namely, tasks in which there was a single exposure to the material and the opportunity for rehearsal was minimal. As we shall see in Chapter 11, the decay concept had generally been rejected as an explanatory principle in conventional studies of memory, and the prospect of its revival was to many a psychologist like a red flag to a bull. The question of whether performance in short-term situations required a different set of principles than performance in long-term situations triggered a dramatic upsurge in research. The question has not been definitively answered, but the controversy has given us a wealth of information about short-term retention.

WHY SOME SAY THAT TWO MEMORIES ARE BETTER THAN ONE

In addition to studies of the memory defect, three lines of evidence from normal subjects have been used to support a distinction between short-term and long-term storage. These findings not only make important theoretical contributions, but are helpful in interpreting a variety of intellectual disorders.

1. Serial position effects in free recall

Suppose that we presented a group of subjects with a long list of unrelated words, one item at a time, and immediately afterwards asked the subjects to recall the words in any order they wished. This is known as a "free recall procedure." Does it seem likely that so simple a procedure would tell us anything significant about the structure of memory? Despite its simplicity, this procedure yields an intriguing pattern of recall scores, a pattern which strongly suggests the operation of two distinct

MEMORY: AN INTRODUCTION

memory systems. The results of a typical experiment by Rundus (1971) appear in Fig. 10.4. The solid function represents the proportion of times that the subjects recalled items at each serial position in the list. As in many other experiments of this type, a clear U-shaped curve emerged: recall of items toward either end of the list exceeded recall of items in the middle. The initial descending segment of the U has become known as the **primacy effect** and the terminal "ascending" segment has become known as the **recency effect.**

Primacy and recency seem to come about for different reasons. Rundus provided an important clue to the origin of primacy and recency by asking subjects to repeat items aloud during the five seconds that each item appeared. He placed no restrictions on which items subjects could rehearse at any point in the list. Thus, item 3 might be rehearsed a few times during its presentation and then again during the presentations of items 4, 5, 6, etc. The dashed function in Fig. 10.4 represents the average number of rehearsals given each item. Note the initial descending segment; it closely corresponds to the descending segment of the recall function (primacy). Apparently, the early items were remembered better than the middle items because the early items were rehearsed more frequently. But no terminal ascending segment exists on the rehearsal function corresponding to the terminal segment of the recall function (recency). Why were the final items remembered better than the middle items? There is a simple explanation: the final items were retrieved from short-term storage (STS) and required no rehearsal. Since the recall test was administered immediately after presentation of the last item, the last item under-

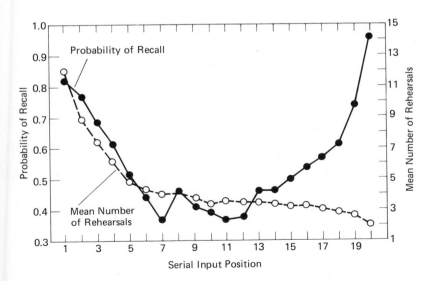

Fig. 10.4 Solid line: The probability of recalling each item from a list as a function of the serial position of the item. In this "free recall" test, subjects could give items in any order. Dashed line: Number of times subjects rehearsed each item aloud as the list was presented. (From Rundus, 1971)

WHY SOME SAY THAT TWO MEMORIES ARE BETTER THAN ONE

went very little decay and was readily given. The next-to-last item underwent more decay due to the longer interval preceding the test, making recall lower. Eventually, a point was reached at which decay was complete (perhaps by item 10), and the probability of recalling an item depended solely on the chance that it was in the other storage system, LTS. The implication is that primacy was an LTS phenomenon. As early items were rehearsed more often than middle items, the early items were more likely to be in LTS.

It is a neat explanation, and all the more persuasive in the light of certain other facts about serial position effects. If the terminal items are retrieved mainly from STS, then introducing a delay of several seconds before the recall test should reduce recall of these items. Provided that no rehearsal occurred, the delay would permit the terminal items to decay. In contrast, if the initial items are retrieved mainly from LTS, they should be unaffected by the delay. Items in LTS theoretically resist decay and a few seconds would hardly be sufficient time for erosion to occur. Glanzer and Cunitz (1966) tested these predictions using delays of 0, 10, and 30 seconds. During the 10- and 30-second delays the subjects counted aloud from a number so that rehearsal was difficult. The results appear in Fig. 10.5 and are clearly consistent with the predictions. The immediate recall test (0-second delay) produced a strong recency effect. The 10-second delay reduced the recency effect, and the 30-second delay eliminated it. No reliable differences in recall occurred among any but the terminal items.

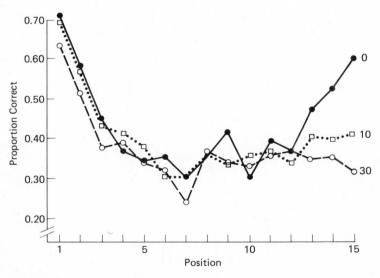

Fig. 10.5 Serial position curves of subjects administered free-recall test immediately after presentation of the last item (solid line), after a 10-second delay (dotted line), or after a 30-second delay (dashed line). (From Glanzer and Cunitz, 1966)

MEMORY: AN INTRODUCTION

Serial position effects have been studied primarily for theoretical reasons, but they also appear to be useful for diagnosis of memory disorders. Baddeley and Warrington (1970) used the serial position curve to evaluate two groups of patients, one group consisting of alcoholics with Korsakoff's syndrome (except for one patient, who like H. M. had undergone brain surgery), and the other a control group consisting of patients with nerve damage not involving the brain. The two groups were similar in intelligence, age, and occupation, and apparently differed only in memory function. As we have seen, Korsakoff's syndrome usually is interpreted as leaving STS intact while making storage or retrieval of information from LTS difficult. The effect of Korsakoff's syndrome on the serial position curve should therefore be selective. Recall of the terminal items should be normal since they theoretically are retrieved mainly from STS, but recall of initial and middle items should be abnormally low due to their dependence on LTS. Figure 10.6 presents the serial position curves for the amnesic patients and for the controls. Consistent with theory, the amnesics were far below controls in retention of the initial and middle items and were equal to controls in retention of the terminal items. Closer analysis reveals that despite the severity of their deficit, the amnesics did exhibit a small primacy effect, from which we may infer that some information had entered and had been retrieved from LTS. Baddeley and Warrington's findings demonstrate that the serial position curve is useful for analyzing memory in both clinical and laboratory settings.

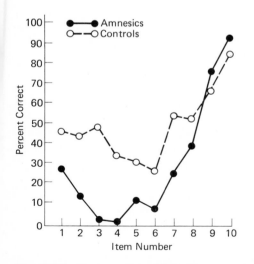

Fig. 10.6 Free-recall, serial position curves of subjects with Korsakoff's syndrome (solid line), and of subjects with normal memory (dashed line). (From Baddeley and Warrington, 1970)

WHY SOME SAY THAT TWO MEMORIES ARE BETTER THAN ONE

2. The capacity of STS

Another line of evidence supporting a distinction between STS and LTS pertains to their apparent difference in capacity. As mentioned earlier, there is no known limit to the amount of information that we can retain on a permanent basis, information presumably held in LTS. But a sharp limit does exist on the span of immediate memory, which theoretically reflects the capacity of STS. Precisely how the memory span relates to STS is a complex matter. For any particular individual, the memory span will vary with the type of material tested and with the sensory system through which the material is perceived (e.g., visual vs. auditory systems). Moreover, for any particular type of material and sensory system, the memory span will vary with overall intelligence and chronological age. The memory span apparently reflects more than the structural or physical limit of STS; it also seems to reveal one's general ability to process incoming information.

A study by Baumeister (1974) illustrates some of the foregoing relationships. The subjects were normal and retarded children matched either for mental age or chronological age. The retarded children (whose average IQ was 71) had an average mental age of 7.8 years and an average chronological age of 11 years. One group of normal children consisted of second graders who had roughly the same mental age as the retarded children (7.9 years), while another group consisted of sixth graders who had approximately the same chronological age as the retarded children (11.9 years). The second and sixth graders had similar IQs and differed only in chronological age. Seven types of materials were presented: digits, letters, animal names (tiger, monkey, sheep, etc.), simple three-letter words (car, pot, egg, etc.), colors, letters plus digits in a random sequence, and letters tied to digits in paired-associate fashion (Z-5, P-3, etc.). Two manners of presentation were employed for each type of material: visual by means of a slide projector, and spoken. For example, in the visual presentation of colors, colored tapes were projected on clear slides, while in the auditory presentation of colors, the experimenter pronounced the words "red," "orange," etc. The number of items in the sequence was gradually increased until the child was no longer able to repeat the sequence correctly. The longest sequence a child could repeat correctly twice in succession constituted the memory span "threshold."

Figure 10.7 presents the memory span thresholds for the seven types of material. Open bars represent visual presentation and shaded bars represent auditory presentation. You can see that sixth graders consistently exhibited longer memory spans than second graders, who in turn exhibited longer memory spans than the retarded children. The rank order of the groups probably reflects the extent to which children possessed skills for handling incoming information, such as rehearsal. You can also see in Fig. 10.7 that auditory presentation often yielded longer memory spans than visual presentation, a finding with important theoretical implications which we shall consider in the next section.

The intellectual deficits responsible for the short memory spans of retarded children are at least partly correctable. Wambold, Jellinski, and Brown (1976)

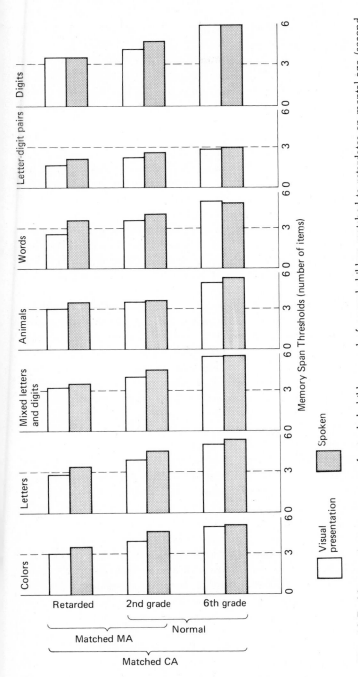

Fig. 10.7 Maximum memory spans of retarded children, and of normal children matched to retardates on mental age (second graders) or on chronological age (sixth graders). Subjects either saw the items indicated in the panels (open bars) or heard the items named (shaded bars). (After Baumeister, 1974)

WHY SOME SAY THAT TWO MEMORIES ARE BETTER THAN ONE

demonstrated that instruction in how to rehearse material increased the memory span of children with IQs of only 43 to 58. A piece of orange paper served as a "playing area" and had two rows of rectangles drawn on it, the upper row to display stimuli and the lower row to display the children's responses. The stimuli were cards depicting objects that the children had learned to name. During a trial, two to five cards were arranged in the top row. The teacher, holding the same cards, displayed a different order by showing the cards one by one at five-second intervals. The children then moved the cards from the top row of the playing area to the bottom row in the same order they thought they had just seen.

The objective of the rehearsal training was to teach the children to repeat the name of each object during the period that it was visible, plus the names of all the preceding ones. For example, when card A was presented, the child was to repeat A over and over; when card B was presented, the child was to repeat A-B; when card C was presented, the child was to rehearse the sequence A-B-C, and so on. The children were thus being trained to employ a skill that adult subjects in Rundus' (1971) free recall experiment used spontaneously. Training started with a two-item sequence and proceeded in steps to a five-item sequence. The teacher gave the child a hard-coated chocolate candy or a bit of cereal whenever the child correctly reproduced a sequence. If the child was incorrect, the teacher demonstrated the rehearsal technique and showed the child the proper arrangement of the cards. Another attempt at the same sequence followed these demonstrations, with praise being given for a correct reproduction of the series. Three successive correct choices were required before the teacher added another stimulus. After each stage of training was completed, the teacher assessed performance on sequences of two, three, four, and five items, administering reward only for correct performance of the sequence length just taught.

The effects of this teaching program are shown in Fig. 10.8. The data are percentages of correct responses at each serial position rather than memory span thresholds as in the preceding figure. The numbers next to the curves indicate the sequence lengths just taught. During the assessment phase, a particular serial position could occur in sequences of several lengths. For example, serial position 1 occurred in all the sequences, serial position 3 occurred in sequences of three, four, and five items, and serial position 5 occurred only in a sequence of five items. It is important to know whether the effects of training with a particular sequence length generalized to the same number of items in other sequence lengths. If generalization occurred, the curve labeled "2" would show virtually perfect performance on serial positions 1 and 2 even though these positions occurred in sequences of several lengths. Similarly, after training on the three-item sequence, performance would be consistently high on serial positions 1, 2, and 3. Figure 10.8 indicates that performance broke down when sequence lengths other than the one used in training were introduced. For example, the curve labeled "3" shows less than 60% correct responses at serial positions 1, 2, and 3 despite the child's just having mastered the three-item sequence. However, after training on the five-item sequence, performance became perfect on all five positions. The necessity for careful and thorough training is clear (as well as patience on the part of the teacher), but it is

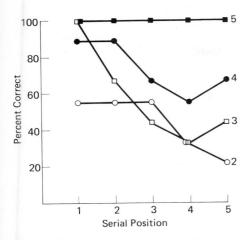

Fig. 10.8 The effects of rehearsal training on immediate memory of highly retarded children. Sequences presented to subjects were from three to five items in length. Graph shows percentage of times that children correctly recalled items in each serial position, whether that position was in a sequence of three, four, or five items. Numbers next to functions indicate the lengths of sequences which children had mastered before being tested. (From Wambold, Jellinski, and Brown, 1976)

encouraging to see than even highly retarded individuals can acquire fundamental cognitive skills.

The memory span can hold more information than may be apparent. Although the memory span encompasses relatively few items, each item can represent a great deal of information. How much information we can apprehend at once depends on the kind of item we attempt to remember. Sometimes we can convert incoming stimuli into a form that will increase the information encompassed by the memory span. Telegraph operators are able to apprehend long sequences of *dits* and *dahs* because they organize the individual sounds into larger units, such as words and phrases. Someone unfamiliar with Morse Code would listen to each dit and dah and consequently would apprehend a much shorter sequence (Miller, 1956). With a little practice, one can perform a feat almost as impressive as the telegraph operator's. Most people would be unable to repeat the following sequence of digits after hearing it read to them: 1-0-1-1-1-0-0-1-0-1-0-0-1-1-1-0-0-1. The average memory span for such "binary" digits is only 9 (Miller, 1956), as compared with 18 digits in the sequence. But one can readily repeat any sequence of 18 binary digits by appropriately reorganizing them. The strategy to follow involves converting groups of binary digits into regular base-10 numbers, a process that reduces the amount of material to be remembered. Figure 10.9 illustrates the conversion process, with the left side showing how to convert binary numbers into base-10 numbers and the right side showing how to apply these rules to the memory span task (Miller, 1956). Imagine a series of boxes, each having a potential numerical value. The box furthest to the right has a potential value of 1, the box

WHY SOME SAY THAT TWO MEMORIES ARE BETTER THAN ONE

308

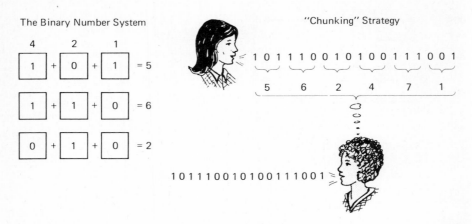

The Binary Number System

"Chunking" Strategy

Fig. 10.9 Use of a "chunking" strategy to increase the amount of information encompassed by the memory span. In this example, the objective is to repeat a long series of binary digits immediately after they are presented. The left panel shows how to chunk the digits into units of three by converting the digits into base-10 numbers. The right panel illustrates this strategy in action. As the binary digits are presented, the listener quickly chunks them and remembers the base-10 equivalents (not the binary digits *per se*). At time of recall, the base-10 numbers are decoded into the binary digits.

to its immediate left a potential value of 2, the box to its left a potential value of 4, and so on. If the digit "0" appears in a box, the box loses its value; if the digit "1" appears, the box gains its value. To convert a binary number into a base-10 number, one simply adds up the values of the boxes. For example, 1-0-1 sums to 5 and 0-1-0 sums to 2.

In the memory span task (right side of Fig. 10.9), the objective is to convert groups, or "chunks" (Miller, 1956), of binary digits as they are being read to you into their base-10 equivalents, and to remember the base-10 numbers instead of the binary digits. If you were given the sequence 1-0-1-1-1-0-0-1-0, you would think "5-6-2." The encoding process must be rapid to avoid losing any of the binary digits. After the sequence has been presented, you simply decode the base-10 numbers into the binary digits. To spectators unaware of what you are doing, the perfect reproduction of 18 digits will probably seem like a superhuman feat. Of course, the fact is that you are not remembering 18 items but six. By learning to encode bigger chunks of binary digits into base-10 numbers, you can apprehend even greater amounts of information. Miller (1956) cites the case of a person who could successfully repeat a string of 40 binary digits!

The chunking strategy is more than a cute trick. It simulates a natural learning process of fundamental importance. How much information we can apprehend at one time during a conversation or while we read depends on the size of the chunks that we encode. As we become more familiar with a certain type of information, we learn to encode larger chunks, and the speed with which we process information increases. For example, try to repeat the following sequence of syllables: "is-a-sci-art-psy-o-an-ence-and-gy-chol." It is likely that you find the task difficult, if not impossible, but perhaps the following sequence of words is less troublesome: "science-an-psychology-a-art-and-is." Finally, consider the same words arranged in a more natural sequence: "psychology-is-a-science-and-an-art." The same sounds comprise each sequence, but in one form they are easy to remember and in another form they are difficult. The difference lies in chunking. Through experience with the English language, we have converted elementary sounds into chunks such as words, word sequences, and phrases. All of the sounds comprising a chunk are remembered as a single unit. In the sentence, "psychology is a science and an art," the word "psychology" probably constitutes one chunk, the familiar word sequence "is-a" may constitute another chunk, and so on. It is possible that entire sentences could function as chunks if they were sufficiently familiar: "the-pen-is-mightier-than-the-sword-action-speaks-louder-than-words-birds-of-a-feather-flock-together." Chunking is a subtle and inconspicuous process, but it is one of the cornerstones of intellectual growth.

3. Acoustic coding in STS

A third line of evidence supporting a distinction between STS and LTS pertains to the form in which each system is said to hold information. Semantic meaning is held to be most important in LTS while sound qualities or acoustic features are held to be most important in STS. As we shall see in Chapter 11, one's verbal knowledge (which is theoretically a part of LTS) seems to be sorted into categories. For example, Collins and Quillian (1969) have presented striking evidence for a sorting system consisting of broad categories, each subdivided into progressively narrower categories. The general category "animal" contains the narrower categories "birds" and "fish," which in turn contain still narrower categories. Information concerning "birds" is sorted into the categories "canary" and "ostrich" while information concerning "fish" is sorted into the categories "shark" and "salmon." The basis for these subdivisions is obviously semantic. But verbal information to which we have just been exposed seems to have much less semantic significance. Conrad (1964) was the first to demonstrate the paramount significance of acoustic features. He gave subjects strings of six letters and asked for immediate recall in the original order. Occasionally, subjects mistakenly substituted one letter for another, but these errors were not random. Conrad discovered that the wrong letter usually sounded like the correct one. For example, "B" frequently occurred in place of "P" and "V" but rarely in place of "N" or "S". Conrad's findings were remarkable because the presentation of letters was *visual,* not spoken. It appeared that the subjects had actively transformed the visual information into an acoustic form. Subsequently, Baddeley (1966) showed that acoustic similarity among words produced more errors in immediate recall than semantic similarity. The sequences were presented orally and consisted of five words. Some sequences had words with similar sounds (e.g., cap, can, cat) and some had words with similar meanings (e.g., big, long, broad). For each type of sequence there were control sequences matched for the frequency with which the words appeared in print, but lacking the feature of similarity. Baddeley found that only 9.6% of the acoustically similar sequences were recalled correctly as compared with 82.1% of control sequences. In contrast, 64.7% of the semantically similar sequences were recalled correctly versus 71% of the matched control sequences. Apparently, in the early stages of processing, the sounds of words have more significance to us than the meanings.

Our tendency to encode incoming information acoustically may be a factor in a peculiar learning disability called **dyslexia.** Some children of average to high intelligence have great difficulty learning to read and spell. Spring and Capps (1974) suggested that these dyslexic children may be particularly slow in converting visual information into speech-motor patterns, which are closely associated with acoustic features of stimuli. From a theoretical standpoint, it is easy to see how difficulty in encoding visual information might interfere with reading. Information contained in the written word must pass through STS before it enters LTS. Since STS typically "handles" acoustic (or speech-motor) information, difficulty in transforming the visual stimuli would slow the normal processing sequence. An alternative view of dyslexia proposes that STS itself is defective. Dyslexics typically score low on digit-span tests, which may mean that the capacity of their STS is greatly reduced. Spring and Capps attribute the low digit-span scores to slow speech-motor encoding rather than to reduced STS capacity. Normal individuals often employ rehearsal during the presentation of the digits to enhance retention. For dyslexic children, however, such rehearsal is difficult. Rehearsal requires encoding, and by the time dyslexics encode one digit, they may have received another. Little time, if any, is left for rehearsal. Perhaps the dyslexics have the same feeling we might have when first trying to convert binary digits to base-10 numbers (Fig. 10.9). It is hard to keep up with the digits.

To test their interpretation of dyslexic children's low digit-span performance, Spring and Capps needed some means of measuring encoding speed. They employed a task in which subjects (dyslexics and normal children) scanned a row of 50 digits and attempted to name the digits as rapidly as possible. It was assumed that the more quickly subjects completed the naming task, the faster they had encoded the visual stimuli. For comparison, the subjects also performed similar tasks with colors and drawings of common objects. In the test of sequential memory, the experimenter presented eight cards, each showing a digit from 1 to 8. A particular card was displayed for 1.5 seconds and then placed face down on a table. Following presentation of the eighth card, the experimenter introduced a "probe digit" and the child tried to point to the card having the same digit on the reverse side.

The dyslexics proved to be slower than normals on all three naming tasks. This supported the hypothesis that dyslexics encode visual stimuli at an abnormally low rate. The dyslexics also scored lower than normals on the memory test, thus establishing the correlation between digit span and encoding speed. Interestingly, it was only on items 1 to 6 that recall by dyslexics was deficient; recall of items 7 and 8 was normal. We might draw an analogy to the serial position effects discussed earlier in which the terminal items of a sequence seemed to be recalled from STS and the initial and middle items from LTS. The implication would be that the dyslexic child's STS functioned normally but that information failed to enter LTS. Failure to store information in LTS would be the natural consequence of inadequate rehearsal. Spring and Capps's findings suggest that dyslexic children might benefit from training designed to increase encoding speed.

Looking back now at the memory span thresholds illustrated in Fig. 10.7, we are in a good position to appreciate why visual presentation often produced shorter memory spans than auditory presentation. The visual stimuli were probably transformed into an acoustic form, a process that necessarily took time. The auditory stimuli were already in a suitable form for processing and required less transformation. Consequently, auditory presentation may have allowed more time for rehearsal, and this additional processing may have produced the longer memory spans. It is always encouraging to find such consistency in the results from different experimental procedures.

ARE TWO MEMORIES NECESSARY?

Psychologists do not unanimously favor a distinction between STS and LTS. Theorists in both the associative and cognitive traditions have presented strong arguments against it, and while the issue remains unresolved, opponents of a distinction have at least succeeded in demonstrating that there is more than one way to view the facts.

Melton (1963) has eloquently summarized associative viewpoint, drawing upon a theory of forgetting we shall consider in detail in Chapter 11—the "interference theory" of forgetting. The central tenet of interference theory is that information to which we are exposed is retained indefinitely; there is no decay. Forgetting results from interference caused by other information we have acquired. Melton took the position that performance in short-term memory experiments differs quantitatively, not qualitatively, from performance in long-term memory experiments. We can make perfect sense out of short-term memory findings, Melton asserted, by inserting new numbers into the established formulas. Melton was particularly concerned with Peterson and Peterson's (1959) experiment, the one discussed earlier in which retention of three consonants was negligible just 18 seconds after presentation of the letters. Since there seemed to be no substantial source of interference in the situation, the extraordinarily rapid forgetting suggested to many psychologists that the memory trace had decayed. But Melton pointed out that one source of interference had been overlooked—the letters themselves. It was possible that each letter interfered with recall of the other two, and that recall was simply a function of the number of letters to be remembered. Consistent with the interference interpretation, Melton showed that retention of one consonant was nearly perfect. As more letters were added to the item, retention progressively decreased, an apparent reflection of the build-up of intra-item interference.

In standard long-term memory experiments, intra-item interference and interference among the different items comprising a list presumably decrease as the

312

number of exposures to the list increases. Since Peterson and Peterson presented their single item just once, we might expect intra-item interference to be very high. That leads to an important prediction. If long-term and short-term performance are points on a continuum, as Melton suggested, increasing the number of exposures to a single item should reduce intra-item interference and increase recall. Hellyer (1962) examined recall after one, two, four, and eight repetitions. At various retention intervals up to 27 seconds, Hellyer found that recall did increase as the number of exposures increased. More support for the interference interpretation came from an experiment by Keppel and Underwood (1962). They noted that the Petersons had tested each subject many times with different items. In an earlier survey of long-term memory experiments, Underwood (1957; discussed in Chapter 11) had found that experiments that tested subjects many times with different *lists* usually reported lower recall scores than experiments that tested subjects fewer times. It appeared that each previous list to which the subjects had been exposed became a source of interference when they attempted to recall the current list. If long-term and short-term retention obeyed the same principles, a similar phenomenon should be present in the Petersons' situation. Keppel and Underwood examined recall of the very first item to which subjects were exposed, recall of the second, recall of the third, and so on. At a retention interval of 18 seconds (the same as the Petersons' had used), Keppel and Underwood found almost perfect retention of the first item and progressively lower retention on succeeding tests. It appeared that interference was as much a factor in short-term situations as in long-term ones.

The span of immediate memory, serial position effects, and many other provocative findings are also susceptible to analysis in terms of associative principles. Why, then, does the controversy persist? In large part, the issue is difficult to resolve because information could theoretically be in STS and LTS at the same time (Waugh and Norman, 1965). Both systems could contribute to recall probability, so that when interference is found to be a factor, one could say that LTS is playing a significant role. If the history of learning theory is any guide, no single experiment is likely to be decisive. Resolution of the issue, if it comes at all, will likely be the cumulative effect of many experiments. Perhaps the issue is unresolvable, and like numerous issues of the past it will eventually cease to stimulate research and discussion.

Levels of processing

One can view the individual as an information processing system without representing memory as a series of boxes. Craik and Lockhart (1972) have developed a conceptual framework that retains the information processing perspective but rejects the concept of multiple memories. They believe that the "boxes" approach has numerous problems which undermine its usefulness. One problem arises from the assumption that STS has a structural capacity limiting the number of items the box can hold at one time. Measurement of this physical limit is a difficult, if not impossible, task. Part of the difficulty is that cognitive skills contribute heavily to the chief estimate of STS capacity, the immediate memory span. As we know, visual-to-acoustic encoding and rehearsal can be influential factors in memory span performance. How, then, should we interpret a digit-span of five items? To what extent does it reflect proficiency at encoding and rehearsal, and to what extent does it reflect the structural limits of STS? It is hard to separate these factors. Another reason that the measurement of STS capacity is difficult pertains to the necessity for counting the number of chunks in a sequence. The assumption has been that several items in a sequence may comprise a single unit, and that it is this unit, not the individual items, that one remembers. Since each subject sets the boundaries of chunks on the basis of personal experience, the experimenter cannot know with certainty how many chunks the subject has created. The experimenter must estimate the number, and there is a preexisting tendency to view the memory span as encompassing about seven chunks. The number "7" could easily be read into the subject's performance and the prevailing view of STS capacity could be perpetuated erroneously. According to Craik and Lockhart, some method is needed for counting the number of chunks independently of the subject's memory span performance. Other bases for distinguishing between different boxes also have problems. For example, STS supposedly holds information mainly in an acoustic form while LTS mainly holds information in a semantic form. However, as Craik and Lockhart point out, there is some evidence for semantic encoding in STS and it may be that the nature of the task, rather than any special property of STS, determines how subjects represent information.

Craik and Lockhart's alternative to boxes is the concept of "levels of processing." Exposure to information triggers a series of processes of progressively greater complexity and subtlety. First there is a sensory analysis that extracts important features from the input. Later, an encoding process alters the form of these features, perhaps converting them to another sense modality. Deeper levels of processing relate semantic features of the information to information already in storage. The further the processing goes, the more persistent will be the memory. Thus a levels-of-processing interpretation of memory always considers what the individual has done with the information but never seeks to discover the box in which these operations have been performed. Craik and Lockhart reexamine past data from the levels-of-processing perspective and show that new issues emerge from such an analysis. Whether the levels-of-processing approach will facilitate research better than the multistore approach is a question that research itself must answer.

As a practical matter . . .

Although the theoretical controversy continues, we should keep in mind that much is now known about short-term retention. Practical application of established principles need not, and should not, await resolution of the broader issues. Individuals with deficiencies in short-term retention can benefit from remedial instruction guided by insights from the laboratory. Perhaps the most significant insight is that short-term retention depends heavily on cognitive skills. Abnormally short memory spans and accelerated rates of forgetting are potentially correctable by developing cognitive skills that normal individuals employ routinely. Winschel and Lawrence (1975) have called for the inclusion of short-term retention training in remedial programs for the retarded. In principle, they state, the goal of the remedial programs is to develop intelligence, but in practice they have sought to communicate content from regular school programs. The real goal has evolved into one of helping the child "to know more rather than to think better (p. 395)." The first priority should be to improve thought processes, and since short-term retention is essential to intellectual functioning, that would be an appropriate focus for remedial instruction. Winschel and Lawrence propose several additions to the remedial curriculum, including the following:

1. *Practice in labeling.* It is important to develop the habit of attaching names to stimuli. Labels in themselves are not necessarily helpful, but they are the basis of other skills, such as rehearsal. Special education classrooms often display lettered signs near objects as an aid to the reading program. Short-term retention training requires intensive drill in labeling to increase the accuracy and speed of responses. Equally important, the children need practice at inventing labels for objects without common names. The goal is not to communicate the proper names for things but to encourage the child to name things spontaneously.

2. *Practice in grouping.* The memory span may encompass large or small amounts of information depending on the size of the encoded chunks. Retarded children would benefit from practice at grouping or chunking a variety of materials. The teacher might first present groups of familiar objects and ask the child to reproduce them. Later, the objective would be to have the child reproduce the groups without being asked to do so. The ultimate goal would be to have the child spontaneously create novel groupings.

3. *Practice in intersensory processing.* In our examination of dyslexia, we saw that slowness in encoding visual information probably shortened the memory span. Practice at converting visual information to an acoustic (speech-motor) form therefore seemed advisable for dyslexics. Winschell and Lawrence make a similar proposal for retarded children but they also suggest practice in other kinds of intersensory processing. For example, the children could listen to stimuli and then try to recognize them visually, or look at stimuli and try to identify them through the sense of touch (cf. the instructional strategies of Montessori and Zeaman and House discussed in Chapter 7).

Winschell and Lawrence note that retarded children have an "exaggerated deficiency" in short-term retention tasks. We can see this deficiency very clearly in Fig. 10.7, which shows that the memory spans of retarded children are shorter than those of normal children of equal mental age. Retarded children seem to lack specific skills which normal children possess, a deficiency that should be remediable.

MEMORY: AN INTRODUCTION

THE SENSORY REGISTER

In Atkinson and Shiffrin's (1968) multistore framework (Fig. 10.3), information must pass through a "sensory register" before it enters STS or LTS. Theoretically, the sensory register assists processing by providing a literal copy of stimuli which no longer activate the sense organs. Atkinson and Shiffrin propose that the copy decays very quickly (within 0.2 seconds for visual stimuli), and that it cannot be preserved through rehearsal or any other means. They posited only a visual register because at the time they wrote there was insufficient evidence for registers in other sense modalities. Subsequent experiments have suggested the presence of auditory, olfactory, and tactile sensory registers.

Evidence for the visual register emerged dramatically from similar (and independently conducted) experiments by Sperling (1960) and Averbach and Coriell (1961). In Averbach and Coriell's procedure, an array of 16 letters appeared on a white field for 50 milliseconds (50 thousandths of a second). A typical array might be:

X T J L V S A Z
Z Q C M W P D O

Following termination of the array, the screen stayed blank for a period ranging from 50 to 200 milliseconds. Then a small vertical bar was projected briefly above one of the positions in which a letter had appeared earlier. Over trials, the bar was shifted from one position to another, and the subject's task was to name the letter that had filled the designated position. Recall was relatively high immediately after presentation of the array—from 8 to 11 letters. This degree of accuracy suggested that the subjects had preserved a literal copy of the letters since the memory span would only have encompassed five to nine letters. But recall dropped sharply as the delay preceding presentation of the bar marker increased. Performance reached its lowest level with delays of just 100–200 milliseconds, leveling off at 25 to 35% accuracy. Averbach and Coriell inferred that the sharp drop in recall resulted from decay, while the final level of performance resulted from entry of information into LTS. However, the decay process—if it really existed—would create a practical problem. Suppose that while reading these lines you fixated one point less than 200 milliseconds after fixating the previous point. Would not the copy of the first segment merge with your visual impression of the second and make the words impossible to read? If we truly retain brief copies of visual inputs, there must be some mechanism in addition to decay that prevents run-on images. In fact, one seems to exist. Averbach and Coriell discovered an erasure phenomenon when instead of using bar markers to designate positions for recall, they projected circles around the positions. Recall was much lower with the circle than with the bar marker. Apparently, the circle had functioned like the letter "O" and had "erased" the copy of the letter in that position.

Although provocative, the foregoing evidence does not prove that a sensory register box exists. Craik and Lockhart (1972), the advocates of the levels-of-processing view, note that sometimes people preserve literal copies of visual impressions for long periods. We shall encounter some striking examples of this in Chapter 11. Indeed, Averbach and Coriell's own subjects seemed to retain about 35% of letters idefinitely. If literal visual copies are the product of a box with a rapid decay feature, we should not find long-term copies. Of course, one could say that there is a direct link between the sensory register and LTS which permits permanent storage of copies. But is it not simpler to say that visual traces vary in persistence and omit the sensory register? Whatever the ultimate status of this box, it is clear that even simple acts such as looking at things trigger processes of remarkably intricate complexity.

SUMMARY

A memory disorder called "Korsakoff's Syndrome" has provided significant insights into the normal processes of memory. In Korsakoff's Syndrome, the individual is unable to retain recent events but has normal recall of events which transpired before onset of the disease. Although retention of recent events is impaired, the span of immediate memory is intact. The memory span is measured by presenting a person with a series of digits or letters and immediately thereafter having the person repeat the items in the original order. The maximum number of items the person can give defines the memory span; the limit is usually five to nine items.

Korsakoff's Syndrome has been cited as evidence supporting a conceptual framework for research on memory developed by Atkinson and Shiffrin. Referred to as a "multistore model," it distinguishes three memory systems: a sensory register, a short-term store (STS), and a long-term store (LTS). The LTS holds information indefinitely and has a very large capacity. Although information in LTS may be forgotten, the problem is usually one of retrieval rather than of storage. The information is present, and potentially recoverable, but it cannot be located. Before information can enter LTS it must pass through the sensory register and STS. The sensory register enables us to retain a momentary copy of stimuli that have been removed. This copy is scanned and the significant features are passed along to STS. Visual inputs must be converted, or encoded, into an auditory form with the assistance of LTS. The LTS can hold information only as long as it is rehearsed. If rehearsal stops, the information decays and drops out of STS within 30 seconds. Another limitation of STS is its small capacity, which is roughly equal to the memory span, five to nine items. One interpretation of Korsakoff's Syndrome is that STS and LTS are intact, but information cannot pass from STS to LTS. A more recent interpretation is that information enters LTS normally but cannot be retrieved due to excessive interference from other information in LTS.

The distinction between STS and LTS was made at the turn of the century by William James, who called them "primary memory" and "secondary memory," respectively. For decades, the notion of dual memories was resisted because many psychologists sought to develop a single set of principles that would apply to all memory tasks. In the late 1950s, a phenomenon was reported which was difficult to incorporate into existing theory. Subjects were presented with a set of three letters and were asked to recall the letters after 0 to 18 seconds without rehearsal. The rate of forgetting over 18 seconds was extremely fast, suggesting that the material had been lost through decay. Since the concept of decay had been rejected as an explanatory principle in conventional studies of memory, a debate ensued on the question of whether this principle was applicable to short-term memory tasks.

Three lines of evidence support a distinction between STS and LTS: (1) *Serial position effect in free recall:* Subjects are presented with a serial list just once and are asked to recall the items in any order. Recall of the initial items and the last items is usually superior to recall of the middle items (primacy effect and recency effect, respectively). Studies suggest that the initial items are retrieved from LTS while the terminal items are retrieved from STS. (2) *Capacity limits on STS:* Theoretically, the memory span reflects the capacity of STS. Since the memory span is severely limited, it is asserted that the capacity of STS is severely limited. However, the relationship between STS capacity and the memory span is a complex one and is not fully understood. The memory span varies considerably with age, intelligence, type of material, sense modality, and skill at handling incoming information. Also, it is possible to increase the amount of information encompassed by the memory span by increasing the amount of information contained in each item. This strategy is called "chunking." (3) *Acoustic coding in STS:* In contrast to LTS, STS is said to be more sensitive to the sounds of words than to the meanings. When a serial list is presented visually and subjects are asked to recall the items in the original order, confusions are most likely to arise between words with similar sounds rather than between words with similar meanings.

Objections to a distinction between STS and LTS have come from psychologists with both behavioristic (or associative) and cognitive orientations. The associative argument draws on principles of the interference theory of forgetting, which rejects decay as an explanatory concept. It focuses instead on the effects of interference from other information the individual has acquired. Efforts to extend interference principles to short-term memory tasks have been successful in some cases. However, the decay issue remains unresolved because when interference can be demonstrated in a short-term memory task, one can argue that subjects retrieved information from LTS rather than STS. Within the cognitive tradition, an alternative to the multistore model has been proposed as a framework for memory research. Called the "levels-of-processing" approach, it assumes that incoming information can initiate mental processes of varying degrees of complexity. The greater the degree of processing, the better the information will be retained. The emphasis of this approach is on studying what the individual does with information rather than on defining the limitations of hypothetical memory systems. Whatever the outcome of the theoretical controversies, it is clear that performance in short-term memory situations is modifiable by appropriate training procedures. Possible remedial techniques have been proposed for retarded individuals, who are usually deficient in short-term retention.

SUMMARY

318

The concept of a sensory register, like the concept of a short-term store, is controversial. Sensory registers have been proposed for the visual, auditory, olfactory, and tactile sense modalities. The capacity of the sensory registers is said to be greater than that of the short-term store, but the time for which information is said to be retained is much shorter—just a fraction of a second. From the perspective of the levels-of-processing approach, such rapid forgetting should be attributed to minimal processing of the information rather than to any inherent limitation of a hypothetical memory system.

STUDY QUESTIONS

1. What memory deficit characterizes Korsakoff's Syndrome? Give three examples of this deficit from the case history of H. M.

2. How is the span of immediate memory measured? What is the effect of Korsakoff's Syndrome on the memory span?

3. According to Atkinson and Shiffrin's multistore model of memory, what sorts of processes are responsible for forgetting in STS and LTS? What are the capacity characteristics of STS and LTS? What is the function of the sensory register?

4. Describe the dynamic features of the multistore model by outlining the steps one would go through to memorize a telephone number from a phone book. Include in your answer the concepts of "encoding" and "rehearsal."

5. State two interpretations of Korsakoff's Syndrome from the perspective of the multistore model.

6. What characteristics did William James attribute to primary and secondary memory? Why was James's notion of dual memories resisted by many psychologists (two reasons)?

7. Describe the nature of the evidence presented by Peterson and Peterson to support the concept of short-term memory.

8. What is the "free-recall" procedure?

9. Labeling both axes, draw a graph to illustrate the "serial-position effect" in free recall. Indicate those portions of the curve which represent the "primacy" and "recency" effects. Translate these patterns into a verbal description.

10. Referring to the procedure and results of the study by Rundus, interpret the primacy effect in term of the process of rehearsal.

11. Referring to the procedure and results of the study by Glanzer and Cunitz, interpret the recency effect in terms of the process of decay.

12. In theory, how should the serial position curve for individuals with Korsakoff's Syndrome differ from the curve for normal individuals? How should the curves be similar? What are the reasons for these expectations? What was the outcome of Baddley and Warrington's experiment?

13. The memory span appears to reflect more than a structural limitation of STS. What additional factor seems to be involved?

14. For each of the following pairs of conditions, indicate whether the memory spans are equal or unequal. If unequal, state the condition under which the memory span is higher: (a) visual presentation vs. auditory presentation; (b) normal children in the second grade vs. normal children in the sixth grade; (c) normal children vs. retarded children of equal mental age; (d) normal children vs. retarded children of equal chronological age.

15. What cognitive skill did Wambold et al. seek to develop in retarded children to increase memory span? What was the general strategy of the training procedure?

16. What is "chunking"? By what means does it affect the amount of information that can be held in short-term memory? Illustrate by describing the procedure for converting binary numbers to base-10 numbers. What is the role of chunking in intellectual functioning?

17. Referring to the studies by Conrad and by Baddeley, summarize the evidence for acoustic coding in STS.

18. What is "dyslexia"?

19. According to Spring and Capps, what deficit in intellectual functioning is responsible for dyslexia? What is the alternative view which they considered? Describe the experimental procedure Spring and Capps used to assess the two views. What were the results and the conclusion?

20. According to Melton, how should one view the results of short-term memory experiments? What was Melton's interpretation of Peterson and Peterson's experiment in particular? Describe the evidence on which he based this interpretation. How do the results of studies by Hellyer and by Underwood and Keppel support Melton's position?

21. Why are the issues raised by Melton difficult to resolve?

22. State two reasons why Craik and Lockhardt object to the multistore model of memory. How does the "levels-of-processing" approach differ from the multistore approach? What basic factor is said to influence the degree of retention?

23. Describe three features of the short-term memory training program for retarded children proposed by Winschel and Lawrence. Give an example of each technique.

24. How did Averbach and Coriell determine the capacity of the sensory register? Instead of using the probe technique, why did they not simply ask subjects to state all of the letters they could after the visual display was turned off? How does the capacity of sensory register compare with that of STS?

25. Describe the "erasure" phenomenon discovered by Averbach and Coriell. How might erasure assist us during ordinary reading?

26. On what grounds do Craik and Lockhardt object to the concept of the sensory register?

CHAPTER 11

Long-Term Memory

Here is one person's recollection of a typical day in California many years ago. The description was given to the psychologist, G. M. Stratton (1919), who was investigating the ability of people to recall various kinds of experiences:

> The 22nd (of August) dawned clear in the San Joaquin valley. I arose early and remember wearing a pink gingham dress which was difficult to fasten and of having called upon my cousin to fasten it for me. I remember being rather tired that day and being vexed when asked to run a few errands for my grandmother. We were sitting at the luncheon table when she asked me to go on these errands and her eyes never seemed to me to be so vividly blue as then. There was a canary in the window, too, and I remember his having sung until it was necessary for us to remove his cage. . . . (p. 479)

The recollection is almost "photographic" in its vivid description of moods (being "tired" and "vexed"), minor events (moving the canary's cage, arising early) and physical details (wearing a pink gingham dress). This person's memory of other days was not nearly as accurate, and yet there appears to be nothing unusual about the day she describes. What accounts for this? The answer lies in events that transpired that evening. Returning from a theater outing, the family suffered an auto accident:

> About seven o'clock in the evening my aunt, uncle, their two-year-old baby, my two young lady cousins and myself went to Stockton to the theater. It was a motion picture and we started home at half-past nine because the baby was fretting . . . There is a crossroad about three miles from Stockton where we turned off to go to our home. I shall draw a diagram to show the exact position of the cars, and where the accident occurred. (p. 479)

The ability to recall the fine details of an experience is called **hypermnesia.** When a person suffers an accident or undergoes stress, as did Stratton's subject, the experience may live on in memory for years. But the person may also have a vivid memory of events that occurred as much as 24 hours before the shock, and this **retroactive hypermnesia** is even more remarkable than the memory of the shock itself. In some stressful circumstances, a person may pay more attention to the details of the situation than he or she otherwise would. This greater attention to detail could be responsible for the greater memory. But 24 hours before the shock, a person would have no way of knowing what was to come, and would be paying no more attention to things around him or her than usual. The existence of retroactive hypermnesia suggests that even the most incidental experiences can make a permanent imprint on our minds. From the perspective of the multistore model of memory (Chapter 10), it appears that information can pass from the sensory register and short-term store to the long-term store without our actively trying to make this happen.

Hypermnesia can be triggered by positive experiences as well as traumas. As one of Stratton's subjects relates, simply making friends may be enough to revive the past:

> About a year and a half ago I met casually at the dedication of a service flag in Oakland a man. We spoke of various trivial things and I did not once think of him as one whom I should ever see again. He was almost forgotten by me and indeed when I met him six months later a reintroduction was necessary. This time, however, we became very good friends, and with the development of our friendship there came back to me suddenly one day the picture of this meeting, the people present, the ceremony, the trivial conversation in all its detail, almost with all the little by-play of motion, etc. . . . (p. 475)

Consider the practical implications of these cases. If information can pass into long-term memory without deliberate efforts at memorization, how much more information must be there which you have actively studied? Everyone knows the experience of being unable to recall a bit of information after having studied it. The phenomenon of hypermnesia suggests that on many such occasions the information we seek is still in storage—it has not decayed—but conditions are simply not conducive to retrieval. As we shall see in this and the next chapter, there is much one can do when studying to make retrieval of information from long-term memory easier.

THE ABILITY TO REMEMBER VS. THE ABILITY TO LEARN

It is obvious that some people learn more rapidly than others, but it does not follow that fast learners have better memories than slow learners. As Underwood (1964) has pointed out, the degree to which material is retained depends partly on the degree to which material is learned. When fast learners show better retention than slow learners, they may do so because they have learned the material more thoroughly. If we took steps to ensure that fast and slow learners learned material to the same degree, we might find equal retention. Shuell and Keppel (1970) performed a study to test the possibility with fifth-grade children. The material subjects were asked to learn was a list of 30 simple nouns. In a preliminary experiment, Shuell and Keppel developed a procedure for equating fast and slow learners on degree of learning. First, of course, a definition of "fast" and "slow" learners was needed. Shuell and Keppel projected each of the 30 words on a screen at a two-second rate, and immediately afterward, they asked the subjects to give back the items in any order. The upper third of the subjects—those who gave the most items—were designated fast learners, and the lower third—those who gave the fewest items—were designated slow learners. The number of items given would represent the strength of the trace left by a single learning trial. This is the raw material of memory. The next step was to see how much material fast and slow learners acquired at different rates of presentation. Perhaps if slow learners were given more time to study the material than fast learners, the two groups would learn the same amount. Shuell and Keppel found that the two groups both learned about 10 of the 30 items when the fast learners saw each item for one second and the slow learners saw each item for five seconds. In the main experiment, new fast and slow learners were given 30-item lists at one- and five-second rates. Tests of retention after 24 and 48 hours showed that the two groups recalled an equal number of items. The ability to remember was unrelated to the ability to learn when the degree of learning was held constant. These results suggest that it may be useful to think of memory as a kind of resource that all people possess in equal amounts. To develop that resource, one must find ways of storing information in a manner that permits easy retrieval. Some people have developed their resources more than others, and they realize advantages in accuracy of recall and speed of learning. In the present chapter and the one to follow, we shall examine principles that anyone can use to develop his or her memory. The emphasis of Chapter 11 is on the nature of the processes responsible for retention and forgetting. Chapter 12 focuses on memory training techniques.

WHAT CAUSES FORGETTING?

Memories fade with time. That basic fact is familiar to everyone. Material studied 24 hours before an exam may seem crystal clear at the time, but during the exam key ideas have vanished, connections between some of the remembered ideas are missing, and much of the material is jumbled. A month later, the material has practically vanished. Such experiences pose the central question that any theory of forgetting must answer: Why does retention decrease over time?

The first step in answering this question requires a restatement of the question in numerical terms. We must know *how much* material is lost over a period of time and we must require a prospective theory to explain this loss precisely. Precision is necessary because on a general level several competing theories may make the same prediction, so that it would be impossible to say which theory was correct. On a quantitative level the competing theories may differ considerably, and with exact measurements of forgetting available we would have the means of distinguishing among them. Hermann Ebbinghaus, in 1885, recognized the importance of exact measurement in the study of memory. He introduced techniques of measurement that are still in use, and that have stimulated the development of many new techniques. From previous chapters we are already familiar with one of Ebbinghaus's contributions—the nonsense syllable. Ebbinghaus believed that the material to be memorized in a study of memory had to be uniform and devoid of personal significance to the subject. If the material were meaningful (for example, the lines of a poem), some of the material might attract the attention of the subject more than other parts. The greater attention paid to the interesting parts might lead to greater retention, and thereby make the subject's performance variable and inconsistent. In place of meaningful material, Ebbinghaus used three-letter units consisting of two consonants separated by a vowel. Although these units did not form words, it is clear that such units may have meaning. For example, the nonsense syllable TAJ means nothing in English but it may bring to mind a majestic edifice. Similarly, the syllable WOM is not a word, but it certainly suggests a word. Nonsense syllables may reduce meaningfulness but they do not eliminate it (Underwood and Schulz, 1960).

Ebbinghaus's dedication to the task at hand was surely a standard of perseverance for us all. He arranged hundreds of lists of nonsense syllables, some as long as 36 units, and then memorized them all himself. He served as both subject and experimenter. Experiments took place throughout the day and were performed according to rigid rules. Ebbinghaus would read a series of nonsense syllables at the precise rate of .41 seconds per syllable, concentrating as carefully as he could. He always read a series from beginning to end without stopping, but occasionally, after a run through the list, he would stop to see whether he could recite the material by heart. If he could, he took 15 seconds to record his data, and then proceeded to another list in the set. In one experiment, Ebbinghaus examined the effect of number of repetitions of a list on subsequent retention, varying the number from 8 to 64. Why, you may ask, did he stop at 64? Why not 65, 75, or 100? Ebbinghaus (1885) explains, ". . . with this number each test required about three-fourths of an hour, and toward the end of this time, exhaustion, headache, and other symptoms were often felt which would have complicated the conditions of the test if the number of repetitions had been increased (p. 55)." Now that is dedication.

Ebbinghaus assumed that he had learned the material when he could give at least one perfect recitation of it by heart. To measure retention, Ebbinghaus waited a period of time and then relearned the list to the same criterion. His measure of retention was a relative one: The amount of effort required to relearn the material relative to the amount of effort required to learn the material originally. The less effort required to relearn the material, the greater would be the "savings" due to retention. This **savings score** has become a standard measure of retention, and it may be calculated by the following formula:

$$\frac{(\text{Number of trials to learn}) - (\text{Number of trials to relearn})}{(\text{Number of trials to learn})} \times 100.$$

WHAT CAUSES FORGETTING?

For example, suppose that Ebbinghaus required 30 trials to learn a list of items originally, but required only 20 trials to relearn the list one day later. His savings due to retention of the material would be $30 - 20$ trials $= 10$ trials. In relation to the original number of trials, Ebbinghaus would have reduced his effort by $^{10}\!/_{30}$ trials $= 33$ percent.

In perhaps the most famous experiment on memory ever performed, Ebbinghaus learned lists of 13 nonsense syllables to a criterion of two perfect recitations. He then tested his retention at intervals of 19 minutes, 63 minutes, 8¾ hours, 1 day, 2 days, 6 days and 31 days. His results are shown in Fig. 11.1, which presents the savings scores at each of these retention intervals. A 100-percent savings score would mean perfect retention—no additional trials necessary to recite the list perfectly. The graph shows that after only 19 minutes, retention had dropped to 58 percent. After one day, retention was down to 36 percent, reflecting a loss of 64 percent of the material. Thereafter, retention decreased slowly with a further loss of only 13 percent over the next 30 days. This pattern of results—rapid forgetting at first, followed by slower forgetting—has been reproduced many times by other investigators. It is a basic fact of forgetting.

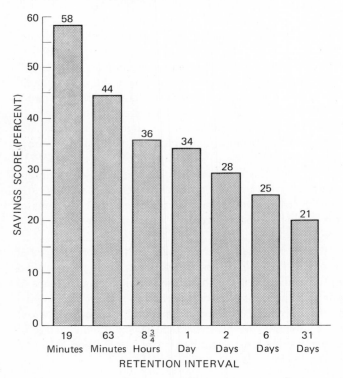

Fig. 11.1 Classic view of how retention decreases with the passage of time. (After Ebbinghaus, 1885)

The Bartlett tradition in memory research

Ebbinghaus's approach to the study of memory dominated American psychology during the first half of the century. With its emphasis on rigorous experimental control and precise measurement of responses, it fit well within the behavioristic framework. In 1932, F. C. Bartlett published a book setting forth an entirely different approach. He was particularly critical of Ebbinghaus's desire to rid research of the subject's attitudes and cultural background. Bartlett argued that in using nonsense syllables to erase the effects of prior learning, Ebbinghaus had erased from his experiments any sense of reality. One could not separate memory from other aspects of psychological life. Memory was not a simple reexcitation of fixed, lifeless traces but rather an active reconstruction of the past, an act of imagination colored by one's attitudes and background. To do justice to the complexity of human thought, one had to study memory in context, and Bartlett introduced techniques of his own to show how this could be done.

In Bartlett's *method of reproduction*, subjects were presented with a complex story entitled "The War of the Ghosts." At various times after reading the story, the subjects returned to write down as much of the story as they could remember. Bartlett found that most changes in memory occurred early in the experiment, and in this respect his results resembled Ebbinghaus's discovery that most nonsense syllables were forgotten within the first 24 hours. But Bartlett was not so much interested in the quantity of the material reproduced as in the nature of the material reproduced. Subjects tended to preserve the general form or outline of the story in their reproductions, but they rarely preserved the style or rhythm. Details of incidents were often omitted too, especially when subjects gave infrequent reproductions. Those events that were remembered were simplified, and if the events were strange, they were often transformed to something more familiar. Long-term reproductions were grossly distorted, preserving just one or two striking details of the original story. In general, the nature of the reproductions reflected the personality and interests of the individual, and for Bartlett this was the fundamental fact of memory to be explored. Indeed, the method of reproduction is now undergoing a revival and it has become a useful tool for studying memory for passages.

In the *method of picture writing*, Bartlett sought evidence for social influences on visual memory. Subjects studied a series of cards, each of which displayed a sign and a word. Fifteen minutes later, Bartlett read a story which included some of these words, and the subjects were asked to draw the associated signs. After two weeks, subjects returned for another dictation. Bartlett found that the first signs to be omitted were the ones that did not "look like" the things they represented. For example, the signs for eye, head, and sword shown in Fig. 11.2 were rarely omitted, but the signs for word, wind, and back often were dropped. Thus one's personal history influences visual memory as well as memory for written material.

Bartlett's willingness to confront the full complexity of human memory reflects the cognitive orientation to research on learning (Chapter 6). Cognitivists have traditionally preferred experimental procedures in which subjects are called upon to

WHAT CAUSES FORGETTING?

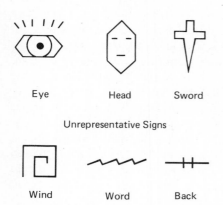

Representative Signs

Eye　　　　Head　　　　Sword

Unrepresentative Signs

Wind　　　　Word　　　　Back

Fig. 11.2 Examples of signs used by Bartlett to study visual memory. "Representative" signs resembled the objects they symbolized; "unrepresentative" signs did not. (After Bartlett, 1932)

solve difficult problems, problems that will make the subjects "think." Kohler's experiments on insight in chimpanzees is a classic example. Behaviorists have traditionally assumed that complex learning arises from elementary processes, and that we are in a better position to understand the complex forms of learning after studying the simpler forms. Research in the Ebbinghaus tradition could thus be seen as laying the foundation for the sort of research that Bartlett favored. Although the two approaches have been competitive over the years, each striving to attract adherents, in a more important way they have been complementary. Psychologists working in both traditions have pursued interesting and productive issues, and our knowledge of memory has been made more comprehensive as a result.

The interference theory of forgetting

Ebbinghaus (1885) did not propose a theory of forgetting; his objective was to introduce scientific method into the study of memory and to establish some basic facts. But he did summarize several important theories of the day, theories that have continued to be influential in one form or other. These theories generally fall into two categories. One view assumes that forgetting results from the gradual destruction of the memory trace. As time passes without rehearsal of the material, the material breaks into parts and decays. Once the material is forgotten, it can never again be retrieved, as the memory trace no longer exists. Thorndike, who initiated the reinforcement tradition in behavior theory with his Law of Effect (Chapter 6), formalized the decay theory of memory with another law: the Law of Disuse. This principle stated that "When a modifiable connection is not made between a situation and a response during a length of time, that connection's strength is decreased (Thorndike, 1914, p. 4)." Forgetting was thus viewed as a passive process of erosion that increased with time.

The other view of forgetting assumes that the memory trace is not destroyed by time, but rather gets "covered over" by subsequent experiences. For example, Aristotle believed that sense impressions left behind "pale images" that came in conflict with later sense impressions. If these stronger sense impressions could somehow be prevented from occurring, the pale image of the earlier experience would easily be remembered.

Common experience tells us that the decay theory could not be completely correct. In general, forgetting increases with the passage of time, but we can some- times remember information that we have not used for many years. Hypermnesia is an extreme case, but there are many other, less dramatic instances. For example, can you recall the name of your first-grade teacher? What was your address when you were eight years old? You may be able to recall such information although you have not used it for many years. The ability to recall unused information after 10 or 15 years would surely be inconsistent with the spirit of decay theory, which suggests that the memory trace would have deteriorated greatly. In a classic theoretical paper, J. A. McGeoch (1932) argued vigorously against the decay theory (or the Law of Disuse), and encouraged further development of the competing theory— what has since become known as the "interference theory of forgetting."

McGeoch attacked the Law of Disuse on both logical and factual grounds. Logically, McGeoch maintained, it makes no sense to say that time destroys the memory trace. "Time, in and of itself, does nothing (p. 359)." Unused iron rusts with time, but oxidation, not time, is the cause. People grow old with time, but bio- chemical processes, not time, cause aging. The causes of forgetting are events that take place in time, and our objective must be to discover these events.

On factual grounds, McGeoch criticized the Law of Disuse because one of its main predictions had been shown to be untrue. Suppose that a person acquired some information and waited a period of time before recalling it. Provided that no further rehearsal took place, the nature of events that filled this interval should have no effect on forgetting. Time alone should be important. That prediction did not fare well in a fascinating study by Jenkins and Dallenbach (1924) on retention fol- lowing a period of sleep vs. retention following a period of wakefulness. Normal waking activity introduces many events that could potentially interfere with memory. We talk; we listen; we think; we read. Such activities could place new verbal habits in competition with the old, so that at the time of recall some of this new material might incorrectly be given. In contrast, sleep is a kind of "vacuum" in which mental activity is minimal. Obviously, our brain continues to function during sleep, but except for occasional dreams, words and ideas do not cross our mind. From the standpoint of interference theory, retention may be substantially higher after a period of sleep than after a period of wakefulness. Sleep should protect material from interference. From the standpoint of decay theory, there should be no difference in retention because the nature of events that fill a period of time is irrelevant. Jenkins and Dallenbach had two college seniors learn lists consisting of

10 nonsense syllables to a criterion of one perfect trial. The subjects then attempted to recall the items after different periods of sleep or wakefulness. If the subject was to recall the material after sleep, he learned the material just before going to bed, between 11:30 P.M. and 1:00 A.M. If he was to recall the material after waking activity, he learned the material between 8 and 10 A.M. and went about his normal activities. The results are shown in Fig. 11.3. The graph presents the average recall of both subjects after one, two, four, or eight hours of sleep or waking activity. It is evident that recall was much higher after sleep than after wakefulness at all retention intervals. The difference was greatest eight hours after the material was learned, where recall was about six times higher with sleep than with wakefulness. Another aspect of the results damaging to the decay theory was the lack of any forgetting after the first two hours of sleep. Between the second and eighth hours, retention remained constant at about five and one-half items. Almost all of the forgetting took place during the first two hours of sleep, when the subjects had just gone to bed and probably lay awake for awhile. In contrast, forgetting continued at a high rate during all eight hours of wakefulness. Thus the passage of time does not always cause forgetting, as the decay theory assumes. Forgetting takes place to the extent that experiences accumulate that interfere with retention. That is an important point practically as well as theoretically. If you were studying for an exam tomorrow, these results suggest you should do most of your studying just before going to bed. The interval between your studying and your exam would then be filled with a maximum amount of sleep, which should help to protect the material from interference.

Interference in the laboratory   In his attack on the Law of Disuse, McGeoch (1932) drew upon many studies in addition to that by Jenkins and Dallenbach. Research under more conventional laboratory conditions had already established that material learned now could interfere with the retention of material learned before,

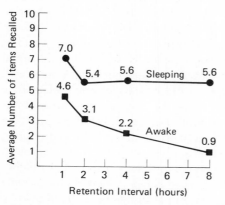

Fig. 11.3   Recall of verbal information following periods of sleep and periods of waking activity. (After Jenkins and Dallenbach, 1924)

LONG-TERM MEMORY

an effect known as **retroactive inhibition** (RI). By showing the flaws of disuse as an explanation of forgetting, McGeoch did much to stimulate further research on RI. The basic experimental procedure for investigating RI is diagrammed in the upper portion of Fig. 11.4. The procedure calls for an experimental group and a control group. Both groups initially learn some material, A. Then the experimental group learns some additional material, X, while the control group rests or performs an activity unrelated to the learning of A. Finally, both groups attempt to recall A. If the experimental group recalls fewer items than the control group, RI has occurred. We would attribute this RI to the learning of X, since that would be the only factor distinguishing the two groups. It is also possible that the material, X, might help the subject recall A. If the experimental group recalls *more* items than the control group, **retroactive facilitation** (RF) has occurred.

Whether or not material X causes RI depends mainly on the relationship of items in X to items in A (the first-learned material). In general, the more similar X is to A, the more likely it is that RI will occur. However, as we saw in Chapter 7, "similarity" is a complex concept. Two paired-associate lists could be similar on the stimulus side, on the response side, or on both sides. To make a prediction about a subject's retention of material A, we can employ the same rules that helped us predict the direction of transfer in Chapter 7. The type of similarity most likely to cause RI when the subject recalls A is the same type most likely to cause negative transfer

RETROACTIVE INHIBITION

	Phase 1	Phase 2	Phase 3
Experimental Group	Learn A	Learn X	Recall A
Control Group	Learn A	Rest or unrelated activity	Recall A

PROACTIVE INHIBITION

	Phase 1	Phase 2	Phase 3
Experimental Group	Learn X	Learn A	Recall A
Control Group	Rest or unrelated activity	Learn A	Recall A

Fig. 11.4 Basic experimental procedures for studying retroactive inhibition (top) and proactive inhibition (bottom).

WHAT CAUSES FORGETTING?

when the subject learns X—identical stimuli in the two lists and different responses. Retroactive facilitation—improved retention of material A—is most likely to occur when responses in the two lists are identical and stimuli are similar. This is also the condition most likely to produce positive transfer when the subject learns X. The condition in which the two lists have different stimuli and different responses is neutral; it has negligible effects on transfer and retention. The condition in which the two lists have the same stimuli and the same responses gives maximum positive transfer and maximum RF. Here we do not have two lists at all, but repeated presentations of the same list—ordinary practice. These rules were derived exclusively from artificial rote learning tasks, but as we shall see, they are also useful for making predictions about retention of regular school materials.

Retroactive inhibition was the basis of McGeoch's (1932) rejection of the Law of Disuse, but in recent years, the interference theory of forgetting has come to place greater emphasis on another type of interference. **Proactive inhibition** (PI) occurs when material learned now interferes with retention of material learned later. This is precisely the opposite of RI, in which material learned later interferes with retention of material learned now. The basic experimental procedure of investigating PI is diagrammed in the bottom portion of Fig. 11.4. As in the procedure for studying RI, the procedure for studying PI calls for an experimental group and a control group. The experimental group initially learns some potentially interfering material, X, while the control group rests or performs an unrelated activity. Then, both groups learn a different material, A. Finally, both groups attempt to recall A, and if the experimental group recalls fewer items than the control group, we may say that PI has occurred. The material X, which the experimental group learned before it learned A, will have reduced retention of A. The material X may also be designed to improve retention of A. If the experimental group recalls *more* items than the control group, **proactive facilitation** (PF) has occurred. In general, the same rules used for determining whether RI or RF will occur are useful for determining whether PI or PF will occur.

Interference in the classroom   Retroactive inhibition can substantially reduce retention of typical educational materials. The extent to which RI occurs depends on two factors: the nature of the materials and the nature of the test. Myrow and Anderson (1972) showed how these two factors operate. On the first day of their experiment (in Fig. 11.5a), the experimental and control groups read a 2200-word passage on a fictional African tribe (Tribe A). On the second day, the experimental group read another 2200-word passage on a different fictional tribe (Tribe X), while the control group read an unrelated passage on Zen Buddhism. Finally, on the eighth day, both groups were given a test on Tribe A. Now, from that brief description, it may seem to you that the experimental group would recall fewer items than the control group. Retroactive inhibition should occur because the similarity of the passages on the two tribes would be a potential source of confusion. Basically, that is what happened, but only under certain conditions, which we shall now examine.

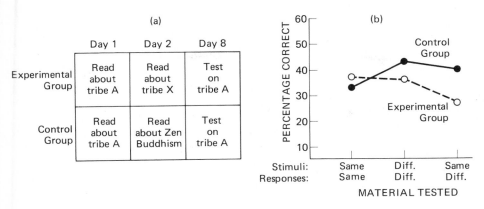

Fig. 11.5 (a) Conditions used to study retroactive inhibition and retroactive facilitation in memory for written passages. (b) Retention of passage on Tribe A by Experimental and Control groups. For Experimental group, passages on Tribes A and B were related in three ways, each simulating a common relationship between paired-associate lists in conventional studies of retention: same stimuli–same responses; different stimuli–different responses; same stimuli–different responses. The first arrangement ordinarily produces retroactive facilitation; the second, no effect on retention; the third, retroactive inhibition. The graph shows percentage of correct answers on questions which dealt with material falling in each category. If facilitation occurred, the Experimental group would score higher than the Control. If interference occurred, the Experimental group would score lower than the Control. (After Myrow and Anderson, 1972)

First, it is necessary to consider the content of the passages. We know from studies on RI using paired-associate lists that RI is most likely to occur when the stimuli in the two lists are the same and the responses are different. Myrow and Anderson attempted to create this condition in some of the material read by the Experimental group. For example, the passages stated that both Tribe A and Tribe X had a complex clan system, but one tribe's system was based on occupation while the other tribe's was based on the stars. The idea of a clan system–which is common to both tribes–can be viewed as a kind of stimulus. It is linked for one tribe to the idea of occupation (a response) and for the other tribe to the idea of the stars (a different response). Other material in the two passages was designed to facilitate retention (RF)—the stimuli and the responses in the two passages were identical. For example, both tribes had a religious practice (the stimulus) in which only the family of a deceased tribesman could prepare the body for cremation (the response). A third portion of the passages was designed to be neutral—both the stimuli and the responses were different. Thus retention of different parts of the first passage should have varied.

The second important factor in performance was the construction of the tests. Myrow and Anderson used both the multiple-choice and short-answer formats. The tests consisted of 34 questions, 14 testing retention of material subject to RI (same stimuli, different responses), 10 testing material subject to RF (same stimuli,

WHAT CAUSES FORGETTING?

same responses), and 10 testing neutral material (different stimuli, different responses). In the short-answer test, the "stems" of the questions were followed by blank spaces in which the subjects wrote their answers. In the multiple-choice test, the stems were followed by four alternatives—one correct response and three "distractors."

Now, every student knows that multiple-choice tests differ in difficulty. What makes one test harder than another is the nature of the distractors. A distractor is likely to give a student problems when it directly competes with the correct response. For example, suppose that a question began: "The clan system of Tribe A is based upon: . . ." and the correct response was "occupation." The clan system of the other tribe, as mentioned previously, was based upon the stars. If "stars" were included as a distractor, it might well be mistakenly chosen as an answer. In contrast, a nonspecific competitor which had never been mentioned as a basis for a clan system (e.g., "physical strength") should cause the student less difficulty. Myrow and Anderson tested that prediction. For questions on material subject to RI, they used three different sets of distractors. One set, labeled "specific-both," included the specific competitor to the correct response from the second passage, and two nonspecific competitors, one from the first passage and one from the second. The second set, called "nonspecific-both," lacked a specific competitor for the correct response. The distractors were nonspecific and were selected from both passages. The third set of distractors, labeled "original-learning-only," also lacked a specific competitor, but unlike the "nonspecific-both" set, the "original-learning-only" set included distractors solely from the first passage about Tribe A.

Now, considering both the nature of the material and the nature of the tests, under which condition should RI be most likely to occur? First, RI should occur with that portion of the first passage which had a stimulus in common with the second passage but a different response associated with the stimulus. Second, RI should occur with the multiple-choice test questions that included the specific competitor to the correct response. Myrow and Anderson found that this combination of conditions did, indeed, produce substantial RI. But it is interesting that RI also occurred with the short-answer test (which, of course, had no distractors). The graph in Fig. 11.5(b) shows the combined test scores for questions dealing with each of the three types of material. Note that the control group scored considerably higher than the experimental group when "stimuli were the same and responses were different": this is the expected RI. But the experimental group did not score higher than the control where RF was expected (same stimuli and same responses). Perhaps rereading this material just once in the second passage was insufficient. Additional repetitions of the second passage might have produced the expected facilitation. The neutral condition proved to be neutral; the two groups did not differ reliably when stimuli and responses were both different.

Do tests really show what you know? One thing is clear—tests do not agree on what you know. How well a person does on a test depends critically on how the test is constructed. Figure 11.6 shows how subjects did on the various exams dealing with the same material—that portion of the first passage subject to RI. The

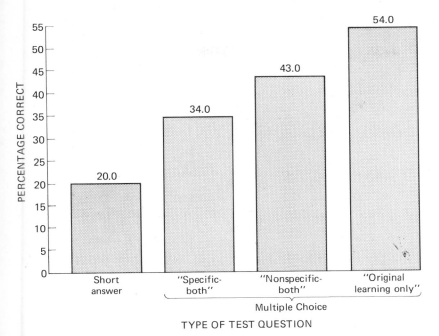

Fig. 11.6 How subjects scored on four types of exams designed to assess retention of passage on Tribe A. The multiple-choice tests differed in the kinds of distractors presented as alternatives to the correct answers. (After Myrow and Anderson, 1972)

short-answer test gave lower scores than any of the three multiple-choice tests. However, performance on the multiple-choice tests varied greatly depending on the nature of the distractors. As a general rule, multiple-choice (**recognition**) tests give higher scores than short-answer and essay (**recall**) tests, but the difficulty of an exam depends greatly on its make-up. Under special conditions, recall may even exceed recognition (Watkins, 1974).

Look before you leap to predictions The study by Myrow and Anderson (1972) shows that RI occurs in the "real world" only when conditions are right. This implies that in order to make predictions from interference theory in natural settings, we must take many details into account. The importance of exercising caution in making predictions is underscored by two studies which should have produced interference but gave unexpected results. Ausubel, Stager, and Gaite (1968) designed their study to produce RI (upper portion of Fig. 11.7). The experimental group first read a passage on Zen Buddhism and then several days later read a similar passage on Buddhism. The control subjects read about Zen but then read a completely unrelated passage about the causes and types of drug addiction. A multiple-choice test on Zen was given a week after the subjects read the material on Zen, and the experimental subjects should have scored lower than the control sub-

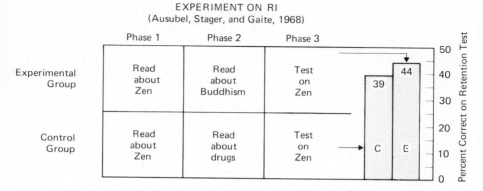

Fig. 11.7 Two experiments on interference which had unexpected results. One experiment was designed to produce retroactive inhibition (top), the other proactive inhibition (bottom). Each panel shows arrangement of conditions and scores of Experimental and Control groups on retention test. The passages on Buddhism, Zen, and drugs were identical in the two studies. (After Ausubel, Stager, and Gaite, 1968, 1969)

jects. But just the opposite happened. The experimental subjects scored reliably higher—retroactive facilitation occurred.

Subsequently, Ausubel, Stager, and Gaite (1969) used these readings in a study designed to produce PI (bottom portion of Fig. 11.7). The experimental group first read about Buddhism while the control group read about drugs. Then both groups read about Zen Buddhism and a week later received a multiple-choice test on this material. There were two reasonable predictions. First, interference theory would suggest that the experimental group would recall fewer items than the control group (PI) because of the similarity between the passages on Zen Buddhism and Buddhism. Alternatively, the previous study by Ausubel, Stager, and Gaite (1968) showing RF would suggest that PF would occur. Surprisingly, neither PI nor PF occurred; the two groups achieved the same scores on the retention test. To account for the results of these two studies, Ausubel, Stager, and Gaite (1969) distinguished between the learning of nonsense syllables and word lists on the one hand (from which the principles of interference theory are derived) and the learning of meaningful, connected discourse on the other. We usually relate the material we read in books or newspapers to things we already know. This serves to anchor the new material and protect it from interference. Nonsense syllables only exist in laboratories and subjects cannot anchor this material. Consequently, nonsense syllables are subject to much interference. Ausubel explains his results within this framework, but we know from Myrow and Anderson's (1972) experiment that interference does occur with meaningful discourse when conditions are right. The content of the passages and the nature of the test questions in Ausubel's studies may have been such as to minimize interference. The unexpected results of his studies suggests that in any complex educational setting, the application of interference theory will be equally complex.

The nature of interference   What actually happens when a person experiences interference? Imagine that you are a subject in an experiment on RI. First you learn a paired-associate list of nonsense syllables. Then you learn another list with the same stimuli as the first but different responses. Immediately after learning the second list, you get a recall test—you see the stimuli one by one and attempt to give the responses from the *first* list. What sort of difficulty would you expect to have? To some extent, you would have difficulty discriminating one list from the other and you would occasionally give some responses from the second list instead of responses from the first list. But you would also experience another, more serious difficulty. Often, when a stimulus appeared, you would not say *anything*. You would know the response from the second list that went with the stimulus, but you would not know the response from the first list. In the short time that it took you to learn the second list, the response from the first list would have vanished. For many years, this problem was unrecognized. When interference theory was in its early stages of development, theorists believed that RI was mostly due to a failure to discriminate lists, and to the resulting competition between responses. But Melton and Irwin (1940) showed that much more was going on besides response competition. Their subjects first learned one serial list and then received different numbers of trials on a second list. Afterward, the subjects attempted to recall the *first* list, and Melton and Irwin took the standard measure of RI. They recorded the number of correct responses given by these subjects (experimental) and the number given by subjects who do not get any trials on the second list—just the first list (control). The number of correct responses given by control subjects *minus* the number given by experimental subjects was the measure of RI. This difference was the deficit or loss caused by the different numbers of trials on the second list. As you might expect, the amount of RI increased as the number of trials on the second list increased. Basically, this meant that the better subjects learned the interfering material, the more interference it produced. This was not surprising. What was surprising was the kind of errors subjects made. With just a few trials on the second list, subjects sometimes gave responses from the second list in the recall test. These "intrusion errors" increased as subjects got more trials on the second list, but then they *decreased* with further trials. With many trials on the second list, there was a huge amount of RI but almost no intrusion errors! Something else besides intrusion errors was causing the RI, but what? Melton and Irwin called it "factor X."

What was factor X? Let us return for a moment to our imaginary experiment in which you were a subject. Recall that the two paired-associate lists had the same stimuli but different responses. You are on the early trials of your second list and are trying to attach new responses to the "old" stimuli. It is not easy. On the first few trials of List 2, your head is still "filled" with the List 1 responses. A stimulus appears, but you do not correctly anticipate the List 2 response. Instead, the response from List 1 trips out of your mouth. You discover your mistake when the experimenter presents the correct response. When the next stimulus appears, you again respond with the List 1 response. Time after time you respond with an item from List 1 and each time you experience the frustration of being wrong. Eventually, what should happen? Since List 1 responses never result in positive reinforcement (the feedback that you were right), they should decrease through extinction. Having undergone extinction, these responses should be unavailable to you in the recall test on List 1. That is indeed what happens. Barnes and Underwood (1959), using nonsense syllables as stimuli and adjectives as responses, did an experiment similar to that by Melton and Irwin. Barnes and Underwood specifically looked for errors of omission in the recall of List 1. They found that as the number of trials on List 2 increased, the number of responses subjects could give from List 1 decreased. In other words, as the List 2 responses were learned, the List 1 responses were unlearned. Retroactive inhibition is thus a product of two factors— extinction and (to a lesser extent) response competition.

A theoretical thicket   The best theories are the simplest theories, the ones that can explain many facts with very few principles. Unfortunately, theories often start simple, but as facts accumulate, the theories add new principles and increase in complexity. They get "messy." The two-factor theory of interference was neat. It apparently explained a complex phenomenon with simple, well-established associative principles—extinction and response competition. But these principles did not completely explain some other facts. When subjects learn two paired-associate lists (with identical stimuli, different responses), and then immediately attempt to recall both lists, they recall many more responses from List 2 than from List 1. This was understandable in terms of extinction and response competition. Having just learned List 2, List 1 had undergone extinction (RI). Since the responses of List 1 were unavailable, they could not compete and interfere with recall of List 2 (PI). Twenty-four hours later, recall from the two lists is the same; RI (interference with retention of List 1) equals PI (interference with retention of List 2). The twin principles of extinction and response competition *almost* explain this shift, but not quite; and here things start to get messy.

From studies of extinction in lower animals, it is known that an extinguished response may "spontaneously recover" strength over a period of time. For example, the bar pressing of a rat may have stopped entirely by the end of the first extinction session, but one day later, at the beginning of the second extinction session, the response temporarily reappears. Underwood (1948 a, b) suggested that such spontaneous recovery may explain the shift in RI and PI over time. List 1 responses, which had undergone extinction right after List 2 was learned, spontaneously recover over 24 hours and compete with List 2 responses. The increase in response competition causes the increase in PI. This is an elegant concept because it does not require the invention of a new principle or process. Spontaneous recovery naturally goes along with extinction, at least in lower animals, and behavioristic psychologists have long maintained that principles derived from lower animals also apply to human behavior (Chapters 2, 3, and 6). Now that basic faith appears to have borne fruit. Unfortunately, the principle of spontaneous recovery does not quite work. If List 1 responses recovered over a 24-hour period, then we should count more List 1 responses 24 hours after List 2 was learned than immediately after List 2 was learned. This often does not happen (e.g., Koppenaal, 1963). Recall of List 1 tends to remain constant or decrease slightly over 24 hours, while recall of List 2 decreases sharply. What interference theorists would like to see is a decrease in List 2 retention and an increase in List 1 retention. To explain this discrepancy, new principles have had to be added and much of the elegance of interference theory has been lost.

And the thicket thickens . . . For years, interference theory relied on RI to explain the facts of forgetting. Material learned *after* the material to be recalled was responsible for forgetting. But this reliance on RI created a thorny problem. In the many experiments on memory performed with nonsense syllables or word lists, there was too much forgetting. For example, if you look again at Fig. 11.1 showing Ebbinghaus's results, you will see that only 24 hours after he had learned a list, he could remember just 35 percent of it. Some experiments after Ebbinghaus showed even less retention after 24 hours. McGeoch's (1932) explanation would be that things learned outside the laboratory during the 24-hour period interfered with retention of materials learned in the laboratory. But, as Underwood (1957) pointed out, that assumption required a considerable stretch of interference theory. Materials encountered outside the laboratory were very unlike materials encountered in the laboratory. Is it plausible that a couple of chapters in a good novel, a casual reading of the daily newspaper, and some routine conversation could cause a person to forget as much as 88 percent of a list of nonsense syllables? The assumption was very implausible in the light of findings that similarity was necessary for interference.

In a masterpiece of theoretical detective work, Underwood (1957) apparently solved the problem, but in doing so he opened a veritable Pandora's box. Underwood noted that previous studies of memory typically used an experimental design in which the same subjects were tested many times under different conditions. A single subject might learn dozens of lists. (Remember how many lists Ebbinghaus learned!) This meant that another potential source of interference existed besides the materials learned outside the laboratory. It was possible that all the previous lists a subject had learned created PI, and that materials learned during the 24-hour retention interval created very little RI. Underwood tested this possibility by carefully examining the conditions under which the earlier experimenters had administered recall tests. His suspicions were confirmed. The more lists a subject had learned before the recall test, the lower was the retention. With 20 previous lists, retention was down to 20 percent, but with no previous lists, retention was about 75 percent. Methodological considerations suggested that the earlier experimenters had underestimated retention by at least 10 percent, which would raise the estimate of retention with no previous lists to 85 percent. It was thus necessary to account for only a 15 percent retention loss over 24 hours instead of approximately 75 percent as previously assumed.

A 15 percent loss could be caused by materials learned outside the laboratory during the 24-hour retention interval. But, as Underwood (1957) pointed out, it is more likely that materials learned outside the laboratory *before* the experiment began caused the forgetting. In the years before the experiment, there was far more opportunity to learn something that could cause interference than there was during the 24 hours before the retention test. In other words, natural linguistic habits were important, as earlier theorists had assumed, but not because they produced RI. *Proactive* inhibition from natural linguistic habits was responsible for the forgetting during the 24-hour retention interval. This idea also fit well with the logic of interference theory (Underwood and Postman, 1960). For example, suppose that a subject was presented with the nonsense syllable QAM. For years before the experiment the subject had repeatedly seen the letter Q followed by the letter U but never by the letter A. During the experiment, the natural association between Q and U would have to be unlearned to "make room" for the artificial association between Q and A. But over the next 24 hours, the Q-U association would spontaneously recover strength and compete with the Q-A association. Instead of saying QAM on the retention test, the subject would say QUM, and the experimenter would record a retention loss. It fits well, it is reasonable, but it does not happen. The evidence for any interplay between verbal habits established inside and outside the laboratory has ranged from weak (Underwood and Postman, 1960) to negative (Slamecka, 1966). In solving one problem for interference theory, Underwood (1957) had planted the seeds of an even thornier one. Together with the shaky results on spontaneous recovery, the results on PI from natural linguistic habits has reduced the credibility of interference theory. Interference theory has given us many important principles of forgetting, but it clearly does not tell the whole story.

Cue-dependent forgetting

The art of memory   The scene is ancient Greece. The nobleman, Scopas, is giving a banquet and has commissioned the reknowned poet, Simonides, to recite a poem in his honor. Simonides angers Scopas when he devotes half the poem to praise for two Greek gods, and in retaliation, Scopas refuses to pay the full amount agreed upon. He will pay half, and the gods to whom the passage was read can pay the other half. Soon a messenger appears to summon Simonides outside where two young men wish to speak to him. Simonides leaves and while he is gone the roof collapses and crushes everyone inside. The twin gods have repaid Simonides by saving his life. Simonides reaps another reward when a subsequent event gives him an important insight into human memory. Relatives of the dead who come to remove the bodies for burial cannot identify them. Simonides solves the problem by remembering the places around the table at which the guests sat. The mental image of each location brings to mind the face of the guest who sat there, and Simonides can make the identifications.

So goes the legend of how Simonides came to invent a powerful technique for improving memory (Yates, 1966). **The method of loci** (or locations) was one of the first **mnemonic devices.** Greek and Roman orators relied on the method of loci to remember their speeches. Paper had not yet been invented and the orators had to make mental notes to be sure that they discussed topics in the proper order. After they had composed a speech, the orators invented a mental image to symbolize the content of each topic. For example, if the topic was war, they might associate the subject with the image of a knife. To bring images to mind in the proper order, the orators imprinted on their memory a series of locations, or loci. Commonly, they would take a mental walk through a familiar building and note landmarks in their natural sequence, for example, the entrance, a court, a statue, a bedroom, a parlor, etc. The speakers deposited the images by which topics were to be recalled in these loci. It was important that the order of topics matched the order of loci. If the first topic was war, and the first locus was an entrance, the knife symbolizing war might be deposited at the threshold of the building. The second image might be deposited in the court, the third on top of the statue, etc. During the speech, the orators took another walk through the building, noting each locus in turn. The loci brought to mind the images, the images brought to mind the topics, and the audience heard an effective, well-organized speech.

The method of loci works on the principle of retrieval cues. Complex material is cut in pieces and set on "hooks." When it is time to remember the material, one thinks of the hooks and uses them to "pull up" the associated material. You do not have to be a Greek or Roman orator to use this principle. Ross and Lawrence (1968) showed what with just a little practice, college students could use the method of loci to perform remarkable feats of memory. In one experiment, a subject committed to memory 52 loci on the campus of a university. The experimenter then read a list of 50 concrete nouns (for example, bird, shoe, matchbox). As each word was read, the subject deposited an image of the word at a locus on campus and then nodded to indicate readiness for the next word. Immediately after the list was read, the subject performed a striking feat: she recited every other word in the list in the exact order. When the list was read again in a new order, the subject performed the same feat with just two errors. Then, the experimenter conducted a more difficult test. The subject was read a list of 20 nouns. Immediately afterwards, a second list was read and the subject was to pair each word from the second list with the corresponding word from the first list. In other words, the subject deposited pairs of words at loci rather than single words. Four days later, the subject recalled all 20 pairs with just one mistake—the order of words in the eighth pair was reversed.

Clearly, visual images, which form the basis of the method of loci, are powerful retrieval cues. In part, these cues seem to assist memory by protecting material from interference. In a second experiment, Ross and Lawrence (1968) asked inexperienced subjects to memorize 52 loci on the university campus and gave them a list of 40 nouns for practice in memorization. Several days later, a new list of 40 nouns was presented with the rate of presentation determined by each individual. On the following day, the subjects recalled the previous list and then memorized a second. On the third day, the subjects recalled the second list and memorized a third, and so on until four lists were memorized and recalled. Now, the principle of proactive inhibition (PI) would lead us to expect that retention would be lower on the second list than on the first, lower on the third than on the second, and lowest of all on the fourth list. The first list should interfere with recall of the second, the first and second should interfere with recall of the third, and so on. Ross and Lawrence found no reliable decrease in retention. Retention of List 1 after 24 hours was 96 percent; List 2, 78 percent; List 3, 76 percent; and List 4, 88 percent. The use of visual retrieval cues protected the material from PI.

Loss of retrieval cues   Suppose that an ancient orator did not fully grasp the method of loci and followed only half the procedure. For each topic in his speech he invented an image that readily brought the topic to mind, but he did not link these retrieval cues to loci. He stands now before his audience and has run through the first few topics in the correct order. But then he draws a blank; the retrieval cue for the next topic eludes him. Correct use of the method of loci would have prevented this problem. Had the orator attached his cues to loci, he would have been sure to bring each cue to mind when he took his mental walk. The use of loci prevents loss of the retrieval cues. This experience, in which one is unable to remember information due to loss of a retrieval cue, is called "cue-dependent forgetting" (Tulving, 1962).

Words as well as visual images may serve as retrieval cues. Tulving and Pearlstone (1966), using words as retrieval cues, demonstrated an important feature of cue-dependent forgetting: it is reversible. If a person has forgotten something because he or she cannot locate the retrieval cue, presentation of the cue brings the material back. In other words, the memory trace is available somewhere in the mind, but it is temporarily inaccessible. The retrieval cue provides access to the trace. Tulving and Pearlstone showed this by asking subjects to memorize lists of nouns constructed in a special way. The words were arranged in categories, for example:

ANIMALS—cow, rat

WEAPONS—bomb, cannon

CRIMES—treason, theft

LONG-TERM MEMORY

The subjects were instructed to remember the category entries (cow, bomb, etc.) but were not explicitly instructed to remember the category labels (animals, weapons, etc.). Although the subjects were given no instructions on how to memorize this material, Tulving and Pearlstone assumed that they would proceed in an organized fashion. The logical breaks between categories would probably lead subjects to memorize categories of items rather than isolated items. The cow and the rat would be stored together in memory, the bomb and cannon would be stored together and so on. With memory so organized, each category label would serve as a retrieval cue with which subjects could "pull up" the relevant items. Their strategy would be quite similar to that used by the Greek and Roman orators, who broke their speeches into topics and attached the material to mental symbols. Unlike the orators, however, the subjects in Tulving and Pearlstone's experiment would not have loci available to ensure recall of the retrieval cues. Without assistance, the subjects would probably forget some category labels and lose the items attached to them. Consequently, on the recall test, Tulving and Pearlstone "helped" some subjects by including the category labels. Other subjects received a test without cues. Both tests came immediately after one presentation of the list. As expected, recall was higher with the cues than without. Then a second test was given that included cues to those subjects who did not have cues the first time. Recall increased dramatically. These subjects "knew" as much as the others but the information was inaccessible due to loss of the retrieval cues. The subjects had experienced "cue-dependent forgetting."

In classroom settings, teachers may be able to reduce cue-dependent forgetting on exams by providing retrieval cues. For example, suppose that a teacher planned to give an objective exam (multiple choice, fill-in-the-blank, etc.) on several chapters of a textbook. To aid retention, the teacher could present questions according to chapters instead of presenting them in a random order. The names of chapters would appear as headings (category labels), and the questions would follow in the same order as the material was discussed in the book. The page numbers would also be included. Thus, for an exam in introductory psychology, the format might look as follows:

Chapter 1 Psychology as a Science

1. . . . (p. 3)
2. . . . (p. 8)

Chapter 2 Methods in Psychology

8. . . . (p. 29)
9. . . . (p. 32)

Chapter 3 Conditioning and Learning

16. . . . (p. 53)
17. . . . (p. 54)

This format does not assume that students have memorized every line and page number. The assumption is simply that in reading the material, a student usually notices the names of chapters and the general order in which topics are discussed. If these features became associated with the content, they could serve as retrieval cues.

Of course, students should not depend on teachers to provide retrieval cues; students can do much to provide retrieval cues for themselves (*legitimately*). Suppose that you are reading a chapter on Personality Theory and the discussion turns to Maslow's concept of the self-actualizing person. According to the text, Maslow believed that self-actualizers had a number of unique characteristics, for example, they were "spontaneous," "problem-centered," and "appreciative" of everyday natural occurrences, such as sunsets. Knowing your instructor's interests, you expect to get an essay question on Maslow's concept of self-actualizers, and you know that this instructor likes to see detailed answers to essay questions, not vague generalities. How should you study the material? One approach would be to make up cue words to represent the material on each characteristic; obvious ones would be "Spontaneous," "Problem," and "Appreciative." After reading the material on each topic, you would stop, state the cue word, and recite as much of the material as you could. You would repeat this procedure until you could produce, on cue, an adequate amount of material without looking at the book. Now you need some way to help you remember your retrieval cues; the more cues you have, the greater is the danger of forgetting one. Take the first letter of each word and make another word (either a real or invented one) out of these letters, such as SAP. On the exam, you would write down your **acronym** and quickly decode it:

S
Spontaneous

A
Appreciative

P
Problem

As you decoded the acronym, material associated with the retrieval cues might come to mind, and you would write it down as soon as possible. Other material might require additional time for retrieval. Finally, with the facts before you, you would be ready to compose your essay. In Chapter 12, we shall return to this mnemonic strategy with some additional illustrations and some passages with which to practice.

Organization and interference   The strategy for studying discussed above can be summarized in general terms as follows:

1. Divide the material to be remembered into topics.
2. Invent a cue word to represent the content of each topic.
3. State the cue word and recite the associated material.

LONG-TERM MEMORY

4. Construct an acronym from the first letters of the cue words.
5. At the time of recall, decode the acronym into the retrieval cues. Production of the retrieval cues should bring to mind the associated material.

Step 4—construction of an acronym—is extremely important. It serves much the same purpose as the "loci" served in the method of loci—it reduces the risk of forgetting retrieval cues. Earlier, we saw that the method of loci protects material from interference (Ross and Lawrence, 1968). The mnemonic above should provide similar protection provided that the retrieval cues are firmly linked to the acronym. Tulving and Psotka (1971) showed that when material is organized into categories, interference reduces recall by causing loss of retrieval cues; interference does not seem to break the association between retrieval cues and category content. Tulving and Psotka presented subjects a list of 24 words consisting of six categories of four words each. Some subjects recalled this list (in any order) immediately after three presentations. Other subjects recalled the list after receiving one, two, three, four, or five additional lists. Clearly subjects who received five additional lists were in considerable danger of experiencing retroactive inhibition (RI) when recalling the first. Subjects who received four additional lists were in less danger of RI, and so on.

Figure 11.8 shows the percentage of material recalled from the first list when zero, one, two, three, four, or five additional lists were presented before the recall test. As expected, the percentage of words recalled (filled dots) decreased as the number of additional lists increased—RI. The percentage of *categories* recalled also decreased (open circles). A category was said to have been recalled when at least one item from that category was given. But, remarkably, if a category was recalled, most of the category entries could be given, regardless of the number of additional lists presented. This is shown by a horizontal line labeled "items per category" (triangles). The reason that subjects recalled fewer words with more lists is now evident—they recalled fewer categories. Tulving and Psotka reasoned that if subjects were given the category labels on a retest, they would gain access to the lost category entries and RI would be eliminated. A few minutes after the noncued test, subjects received a cued test showing the names of categories. This did indeed eliminate RI. The percentage of *words* recalled was now just as high with five additional lists as with none. These results underscore the importance of making sure that retrieval cues are firmly implanted in memory when organizing material into categories.

Forgetting through repression

Sigmund Freud, founder of psychoanalysis, assigned a central role to memory in his theory of neurosis. According to Freud, everyone seeks to avoid the feeling of anxiety, and in our effort to minimize anxiety, we commonly banish from conscious awareness thoughts that are painful or threatening. These thoughts do not go away, however. The act of **repression** deposits them in the unconscious part of the mind where they remain psychologically active. There, without our awareness, they may induce physical symptoms or cause us to act in strange ways. Freud

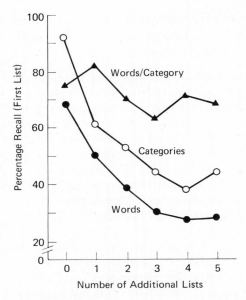

Fig. 11.8 Retroactive inhibition in retention of organized information. Curve marked "Words" shows recall of words from categorized list after subjects learned 0 to 5 additional lists. Curve marked "Categories" shows percentage of categories recalled from the initial list. To exhibit recall of a category, subject had to give at least one word from that category. The percentage of words recalled from such categories is shown in the "Words/Category" curve. (From Tulving and Psotka, 1971)

believed that only by becoming aware of these thoughts and experiencing the painful emotions associated with them could we free ourselves from their influence. One of the classic cases of repression was that of a woman who could not bear to drink any kind of fluid. Even on the hottest day of the year she refused water and had to eat melons and fruits to relieve her tormenting thirst. One of Freud's colleagues, Joseph Breuer, placed the woman under hypnosis, and during the trance she relived an event that had transpired years earlier. She told of walking into the room of her governess and there seeing the governess's little dog drink from a glass. The woman hated this dog and she felt rage at what she saw, but in keeping with good manners, she held the emotion in. Now, years later, she let the anger out, and when the experience was over asked for a glass of water. She awoke from hypnosis with the glass still at her lips, and thereafter the neurotic symptom never returned. As Freud was a very poor hypnotist, he used other techniques to help patients recall painful experiences—dream analysis and free-association. They continue to be the major techniques of psychoanalytic therapy.

Freud's evidence for repression came from clinical observations. Subsequently, experiments designed to produce repression (for example, by pairing verbal material with shock) have yielded conflicting results, perhaps because of the difficulty of making experimental procedures personally significant to the subjects. But everyday experience suggests that motivation must have something to do with forgetting. For example, have you ever intended to call a friend but forgotten about it until calling would be impossible? Perhaps you did not really want to make the call. Or have you ever lost a textbook? Perhaps it was for a course you regretted taking. Such "Freudian slips" should remind us that our true intentions may sometimes be very hard to acknowledge and accept.

The problem of consolidation

It is a perfect day for the beach. For Tom, age 17, each minute behind the wheel seems like an eternity. He can hardly bear the frustration: on his right, his girlfriend, May; ahead, a poke driver doing 25 in a 50 mile-per-hour zone; on his left, heavy oncoming traffic that makes passing impossible. For at least two miles, Tom honks and shouts, but to no avail. Suddenly, he sees his chance. He accelerates, pulls out, then. . . . Two years later he tells the court that he recalls swerving to avoid the crash, but cannot recall the moments just before impact or the crash itself. But the honking, the shouts, the attempt to pass—these are clear. The phenomenon is not uncommon. It is called **retrograde amnesia** and its effect is precisely the opposite of that of retrograde hypermnesia, the phenomenon considered at the beginning of the chapter. Some theorists (e.g., McGaugh, 1966) have interpreted retrograde amnesia as evidence for a **consolidation** process in memory. Experiences are said to leave behind traces that are initially fragile and easily destroyed. Before they can become permanent, traces require a period of time to consolidate or "solidify." During the consolidation period, a severe blow may be sufficient to erase the trace from memory forever. Retrograde amnesia is often studied in the laboratory by teaching a rat a response and then administering electro-convulsive shock (ECS). The ECS immediately throws the rat into an unconscious state, and when the rat awakens it may show amnesia for the response. As the consolidation theory predicts, the shorter the interval between the learning experience and the ECS, the greater is the behavioral deficit. Some theorists (e.g., Lewis and Maher, 1965) disagree that ECS destroys the memory trace and argue that the rat cannot retrieve the trace because of interference from a trace left by the ECS. Support for this position has come from studies showing that it is sometimes possible to recover the lost response. Consolidation theorists have objected to these demonstrations on technical grounds, and the reasons for retrograde amnesia remain to be determined.

THE STRUCTURE OF MEMORY

The method of loci and the acronym technique help us to organize material in a manner that greatly improves recall. But what of material that we have acquired without the use of mnemonic strategies? Is it disorganized? Evidence from a variety of sources suggests that human memory is intricately organized, although perhaps not as efficiently as it would be if all our information were learned with mnemonics. Let us look at some of the theoretical conceptions that have emerged from research on the structure of memory.

The tip of your tongue

Listed below are the definitions of four uncommon words, followed by several questions about the words. If you definitely know a word, or you definitely do not know a word, the questions will be quite meaningless and there will be no point in answering them. But if you feel that you know the word without actually being able to state it; if you feel that the word is about to come to you—that it is on the tip of your tongue—then you may find the questions very revealing. Here are the definitions:

1. Patronage bestowed by reason of family relationship and not of merit.
2. An opaque, ash-colored substance secreted by the sperm whale, found floating in tropical seas, and used in perfumes.
3. A small boat used in the rivers and harbors of China and Japan, propelled by a single oar at the rear, and equipped with a mat roofing.
4. A navigational instrument used to measure angular distances at sea, especially with respect to the sun, moon, and stars.

Now, here are the questions:

A. How many syllables does the word have?
B. What is the first letter of the word?
C. What words sound like the one you are searching for?
D. What words mean about the same thing as the one you are searching for?
E. On which syllable is the heaviest stress placed when pronouncing the word?

You may have found—to your surprise—that you could answer at least one of the above questions. It is not an unusual occurrence. This was also the experience of subjects in a study by Brown and McNeill (1966) on The "Tip-of-the-Tongue" Phenomenon (TOT) using similar definitions and questions. Brown and McNeill found that subjects guessed the number of syllables in the target word with impressive accuracy. For target words consisting of one, two, three, four, and five syllables, subjects guessed, on the average, 1.53, 2.33, 2.86, 3.36, and 3.50 syllables, respectively. The rank-order correlation was 1.00, although subjects did tend to underestimate the number of syllables in longer words. Subjects also guessed the first letter of the target word quite accurately—57 percent of the time, as contrasted with a chance performance of just one correct in 26 tries. With better-than-chance accuracy, too, they could guess the syllable of the target word on which the heaviest stress was placed. It was even possible for subjects to give words similar in sound and meaning to the target word, while recognizing that the target word was not among them. Now, the obvious question is: Why? If people in the

TOT state can provide so much information about the target word, why is the word itself so difficult to give? Brown and McNeill developed the following theory to account for this strange phenomenon. Incidentally, in case you are wondering, the words to which the definitions above correspond are: nepotism, ambergris, sampan, and sextant.

We are concerned here with **semantic memory**—memory for the meaning of words. As a cautionary note, it should be stated that the processes of semantic memory may differ in significant ways from those of **episodic memory** (Tulving, 1972)—memory for events with a clear beginning and end. For example, Tulving suggests that in the very act of recalling an incident we may change our memory of it. Memory for the meaning of words is far less subject to change. Brown and McNeill imagine that our semantic memory has a structure similar to that of a dictionary: Each word is represented together with a definition. But unlike a dictionary, semantic memory allows you to look up a word knowing the definition as well as to look up the definition knowing the word. In its flexibility, semantic memory more closely resembles a "keysort" card system than a dictionary. Figure 11.9 illustrates the analogy, as described by Brown and McNeill. On the left side of the figure we see the processes involved in correctly recalling a word given the definition, while on the right side we see the processes underlying the TOT state.

Let us first consider how a subject might correctly identify the target word SEXTANT when presented the definition, "A navigational instrument used in measuring angular distances, especially the altitude of the sun, moon, etc." The subject has thousands of cards on file giving a word and a definition. Key features of the definitions, such as "instrument" and "measurement," are represented at different locations at the top of the card. The words VIOLIN, PROTRACTOR, and SEXTANT are all instruments and for each card the location reserved for "instrument" has been broken. SEXTET is not an instrument and so the hole in this location remains intact. Similarly, for PROTRACTOR and SEXTANT the subject has coded the information that they are concerned with measurement by breaking the hole in the "measurement" location. A violin is an instrument not concerned with measurement and so the hole in the measurement location remains intact. With an actual keysort system, the subject would stick a rod through all the holes in the instrument location and through all the holes in the measurement location, and then lift. All the cards in the instrument-measurement category would remain behind as the cards not belonging to the category were raised. The subject would then read all the definitions of the category members and eventually would find one that matched the input definition. The word written on that card would be the one the experimenter obtained: SEXTANT. Such is the nature of the retrieval process assumed to underlie correct recall. First there is a search through memory for all definitions having in common one or more features related to the input definition. Obviously, the more features used to construct the category of possible definitions, the more restricted the category will be. Then the definitions of category members are scanned until one is found matching the input. As the definition and the word are stored at the same location, it is a simple matter to find the word.

THE STRUCTURE OF MEMORY

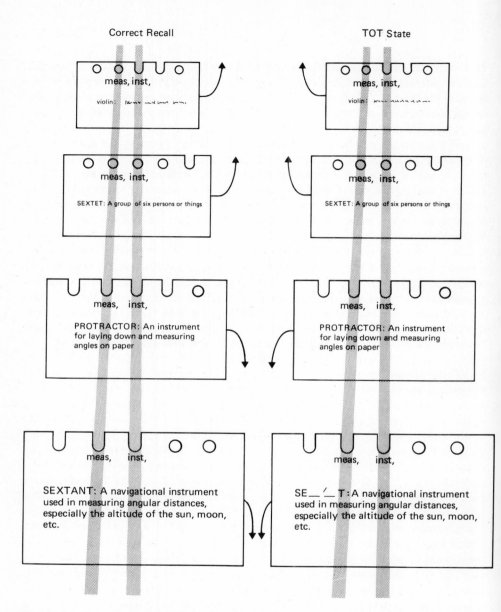

Fig. 11.9 Brown and McNeill's keysort model of retrieval processes in semantic memory. In this example, subject must locate the word "sextant" after being read the definition. Two concepts mentioned in the definition—measurement and instrument—are used to form a category of words whose definitions mention these concepts (protractor and sextant). By comparing the definition associated with each word to the input definition, the subject locates the "card" on which "sextant" is written. On the left side of the figure, the letters on the card are clear, so that subject can correctly state the word. On the right side, a correct response is not possible because several letters are missing. However, since the subject has located the card, he "feels" that he knows the word (tip-of-the-tongue state). Sufficient information is available on the card to allow subject to give the first and last letters of the word, the number of syllables, and the syllable on which stress is placed. These are common features of the TOT state.

The retrieval processes underlying the TOT state (right side of figure) are exactly the same as those responsible for correct recall, except that letters are missing in the word SEXTANT. The subject has the feeling he or she knows the word because the definition on the card matches the input, but with letters missing the subject cannot identify the word. All the subject can do is give the information that is available—possibly the first and last letters and the number of syllables. If we ask the subject to give us words similar in *sound* to the target word, he or she could do so by performing a second retrieval. We might imagine that the existing letters and the information about number of syllables were represented by broken holes. The subject would now insert three rods through the holes to search memory for words having three features: (1) first letter S; (2) last letter T; and (3) two syllables. After lifting the rods, the subject might come up with SEXTET and SECANT.

When reading the definitions earlier, you might have felt certain that you did not know one or more of the words. Brown and McNeill would explain your feeling by saying that you simply did not find a card which had a definition matching the input. The definitions on the cards you did have were sufficiently clear that you could discriminate them from the input. Perhaps you thought you knew a word, but then discovered you were wrong. Here, SEXTANT was not among your cards, but the definition that you found on another card, such as PROTRACTOR, may have been very imprecise. The vagueness made the definition difficult to discriminate from the input and so you responded with PROTRACTOR. If your memory were organized in the manner envisioned by Brown and McNeill, you would have great flexibility in how you retrieved information. The more features of words and definitions that you had coded, the more ways you would have of locating the information. You would decide on a category by defining the necessary features, and if that failed to turn up the information, you might create another category based on other features. If your memory were organized in the manner described by the next theorists, you would think in very different ways and with considerably less flexibility.

True or false? — A canary eats

The question is so simple that it may seem absurd, and yet it is not the easiest question that one could ask you. You would probably take less time to respond to the statement, "A canary flies," and less time than that to respond to the statement, "A canary sings." Collins and Quillian (1969) found such differences when they made precise measurements of subjects' reaction times to these and similar statements. The results are hard to fathom when considered out of theoretical context, but in the framework of the theory of memory structure developed by Collins and Quillian, the results make perfect sense.

Collins and Quillian envision broadly defined categories, in each of which information is further sorted into more specific categories. Figure 11.10 illustrates the manner in which information in the category "Animal" would be arranged. At the highest level of the category, the person stores information that is true of all

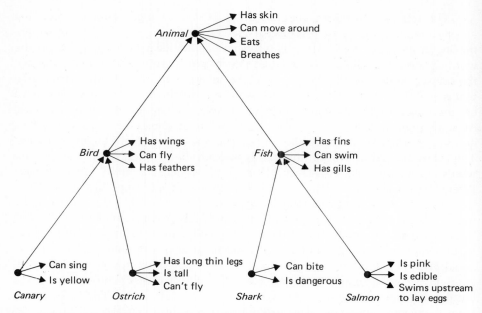

Fig. 11.10 How information about animals might be stored in memory. Facts are sorted into categories which are arranged as a kind of hierarchy, with the most general category ("animal") at the top, and the narrowest categories ("canary," "ostrich," "shark," "salmon") at the bottom. (From Collins and Quillian, 1969)

animals, for example, that they eat, have skin, etc. At a lower level, the person sets up categories representing different classes of animals such as birds and fish. Information that is usually true of all members of the class is stored at this level, so that for the category "Bird" we find such features as "has wings" and "can fly." Within a class, a separate category for each species stores information about the special features of that species. Thus in the category "Canary" the person has entered the facts that canaries can sing and are yellow, and in the category "Ostrich" he or she has entered the facts that ostriches have thin legs and are tall. A key assumption of the theory is that information stored at one level is not repeated at other levels. At the canary level, for example, there is no information on whether a canary eats.

This hierarchy of categories sets limits on the speed with which a person can retrieve information. Let us imagine, with Collins and Quillian, that to evaluate the statement "A canary eats" a person first searches memory for the "Canary" category and examines the contents of that category. Not finding any information about eating, the person must next go to the intermediate category, "Bird"; he or she cannot go directly to "Animal." Again, there is no information about eating and so the person moves up the hierarchy to the highest level, "Animal," and there discovers that animals eat. Since canaries are members of this category, the subject responds that the statement is true. Moving from one level to the next takes time, and if one must move up two levels to evaluate a statement, the evaluation should take longer than it would if one only had to move up one level (e.g., to "Bird"), or could stop at the "ground floor" ("Canary"). It should therefore take more time to find out whether a canary eats than to find out whether a canary flies, and it should take more time to find out whether a canary flies than to find out whether a canary sings.

Collins and Quillian projected the statements on a screen for two seconds and the subjects responded by pressing one button if the statement was true and another if it was false. Many different sentences from a variety of categories were tested, for example, "Seven-up is colorless" and "A birch has seeds." Collins and Quillian not only wished to test the basic assumptions of the theory, but to discover some additional facts about the retrieval process, such as: Was the amount of time required to go from one level to the next always the same, regardless of which levels were involved? And once a person reached a level, how much time would it take to retrieve the information stored there? Figure 11.11 presents the mean reaction times to true sentences at the various levels and it answers both of these questions.

The "Canary" category is at Level 0, the "Bird" category is at Level 1, and the "Animal" category is at Level 2. Reaction times clearly increased as the level of the sentences to be evaluated increased. This supports the basic assumptions of the theory. On closer examination, we see that the increase in reaction time resulting from the subjects' going from one level to the next is generally constant, about .075 second. With further analysis, we can determine how much time it takes a person to retrieve information from a particular category. Note that at Level 2, it takes the subject more time to respond to "A canary has skin" than to respond to "A canary is an animal." In terms of the theory, the subject can evaluate the latter statement immediately upon reaching the category "Animal" but must go into the category to evaluate the former statement. The subject must inspect the various properties to see whether animals have skin. The difference between the reaction times for these two statements is the extra time the subject spends retrieving the relevant property—about .225 second. Thus the theory provides a framework for making some very precise measurements of the processes underlying memory. Other interpretations of the data are possible (e.g., Rips, Shoben, and Smith, 1973), but in general the hierarchical approach remains influential and has taken many interesting new forms (e.g., Rumelhart, Lindsay, and Norman, 1972).

The difference that learning makes

Although the two theories of memory organization we have considered differ in many details, they do share two basic assumptions. Both assume that in order to retrieve information, one must first enter the category in which the information is located. For Brown and McNeill, the categories do not exist prior to retrieval but are created in the act of retrieval. For Collins and Quillian, categories exist prior to retrieval and have definite links to other categories. Both theories also assume that

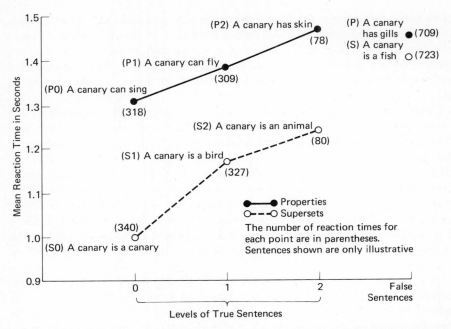

Fig. 11.11 Results of a test of the memory structure illustrated in Fig. 11.10. Subjects responded "True" or "False" to statements about facts stored at each level of the hierarchy. Graph shows reaction times to sentences that were true. Levels of sentences are indicated on horizontal axis, with Level 0 representing information drawn from the narrowest categories, and Level 2 representing information drawn from the most general category. Dashed-line function gives reaction times to sentences concerning category labels. Theoretically, subjects did not have to scan category entries to respond. Solid-line function gives reaction times to sentences concerning information contained within categories. These sentences theoretically required scanning of category entries. According to the theory, reaction times should increase with sentence level, and should be higher when category scanning is necessary than when it is not. Data points are based on sentences on a variety of subjects in addition to animals. (From Collins and Quillian, 1969)

in order to retrieve information, one must search the contents of a category for the appropriate member. For example, to determine that "sextant" was the navigation instrument described by the input definition, subjects in Brown and McNeill's study scanned all the entries in the "Navigation instrument" category until they found a definition that matched the input. To determine whether a canary could fly, subjects in the Collins and Quillian study scanned the contents of the "Bird" category until they found a statement about flying. Thus there is considerable agreement among cognitive theorists about what the basic structure of memory is like and how one goes about retrieving information from it.

LONG-TERM MEMORY

How long does it take to build a memory structure? Of course, the complexity of the structure has a lot to do with it, but it appears that categories begin to form upon one's first exposure to material. In a classic study that did much to stimulate interest in category formation, Bousefield (1953) presented subjects a list of 60 nouns drawn from four categories—animals, names, professions, and vegetables. Each category was represented by 15 items arranged *randomly* in the list; for example, part of the list was "Wallace, parsnip, milkman, druggist, leopard, wood-chuck, Adam. . . ." The experimenter read the list to the subjects and immediately afterward the subjects wrote down as many items as possible *in any order.* Bousefield was mainly interested in the order that subjects might impose on the material, and he found that they tended to cluster items in categories. If the subject had written a word from the "profession" category, the very next word he wrote tended to be from the same category. Through various means, Bousefield showed that the probability of a subject's giving two successive items from the same category was higher than we would expect by chance along. This finding suggests that as the list was read to them, the subjects started to construct categories and then deposited each new word into the appropriate one. During retrieval, they went to a particular category and retrieved several items at a time.

With additional repetitions, organization of material increases (Tulving, 1962). Indeed, one might go so far as to say that organization is one mark of the educated mind. Loftus and Loftus (1974) discovered that advanced students have apparently organized information far more thoroughly than beginning students. Their subjects were graduate students in a psychology program that divided the field into six areas—learning, perception, memory, personality, social, and developmental. We might expect that advanced graduate students would be more familiar with this division than beginning students and would categorize information accordingly. For example, the advanced students might sort the names of psychologists into these six categories while beginning students might not. The beginners might simply link names to ideas or discoveries without relating them to broad areas of investigation. If that is so, then beginning and advanced students should retrieve information about psychologists in very different ways, and Loftus and Loftus devised an ingenious procedure to reveal such differences. The students were asked to respond with the name of a psychologist when given one of the areas of investigation mentioned above and the first letter of a psychologist's last name. For example, if the area was "Memory" and the letter "M," the students could respond with "McGeoch." On some trials, the area was presented before the letter while on others the letter was presented before the area. If a student had sorted the psychologists into categories, then the order of presentation should have influenced his or her reaction time in a special way. When given the category first, the student would immediately go to the representation of that category in memory and would be ready to scan the category members as soon as the letter was given. With the category presented first, the reaction time should be very low. On the other hand, when given the letter first, the student would find the information useless since, in theory, it is necessary to enter a category before information can be scanned. This is

354

lost time. Now, when the category was given, the student would start the retrieval process, going to the category and then scanning the category members. The student's reaction time should be longer because he or she started the retrieval process later.

The beginners should retrieve information differently. Having had less exposure to the program and its division of psychologists into areas, the beginners should store names separately from one another rather than together in categories. Lacking categories, the beginners would probably respond with a name faster when given the letter first than when given the area first. If given the letter first, they would immediately scan their mental list of psychologists until they found an appropriate one. They would probably ignore the area because they would not yet have learned its significance. Right after the area was given, the beginners would respond with a name that might or might not be correct. On the other hand, getting the area first would simply delay the retrieval process; the beginners would wait for the letter before beginning their search and this would result in a longer reaction time. You can see the results of the experiment in Fig. 11.12. There were very striking differences between the beginning and advanced students. Consistent with theory, the advanced students gave shorter reaction times when they received the area first than when they received the letter first. The beginners gave just the opposite results. Not only did the advanced students know more about psychology than the beginners; they organized what they knew much more thoroughly than did beginners. Loftus and Loftus suggest that educators would do well to take note of this effect. Too often we assess the effectiveness of instruction by examining students on *how much* they know. Rarely do we seek to discover how well students have *organized* what they know. The reaction time technique holds promise as a means of assessing the degree of organization in memory. With further research and development, it could become a regular companion to the standard achievement test.

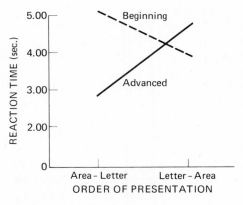

Fig. 11.12 Reaction times of beginning and advanced students in retrieval task designed to measure degree of organization in memory. (From Loftus and Loftus, 1974)

SUMMARY

Information is said to be in long-term memory if it persists for an indefinitely long period. Far more information enters long-term memory than one ordinarily supposes. Even incidental experiences to which one has paid little attention may be stored permanently, as evidenced by the phenomenon of hypermnesia in which a personally significant incident triggers vivid recall of an earlier event. Hypermnesia suggests that much of the information which one has actively committed to memory, but has since forgotten, is still available. The difficulty in such cases is that the information cannot be located or retrieved. There is evidence that everyone has roughly equal potential for developing a memory capable of reliable and accurate retrieval. The basic strategy for doing this is to store information in a suitable manner; a variety of memory aids is available for this purpose.

In 1885, Hermann Ebbinghaus introduced methods for measuirng retention that are still widely used. He also provided valuable information about the course of forgetting over time. Serving as both experimenter and subject, Ebbinghaus memorized lists of nonsense syllables and tested retention after intervals ranging from 19 minutes to 31 days. The measure of retention was a "savings score," which compared the number of trials necessary to learn a list with the number of trials necessary to relearn the list. The fewer the trials required for relearning, the greater would be the savings due to retention. Ebbinghaus found that most forgetting occurred within the first 24 hours of learning, with relatively little forgetting thereafter.

During the first half of the century, research on memory was generally in the Ebbinghaus tradition. Investigators presented subjects with lists of words or nonsense syllables under rigorously controlled experimental conditions, with the objective of making the measurement of retention as precise as possible. This concern for rigor and precision reflected the growing influence of behaviorism. In 1932, F. C. Bartlett criticized the Ebbinghaus approach as too artificial and proposed alternative procedures to take into account subjects' attitudes and cultural backgrounds. His "method of reproduction" and "method of picture writing" clearly demonstrated social influences on memory for written passages and visual stimuli. In his eagerness to investigate memory in its full complexity, Bartlett anticipated modern cognitive research on memory.

Two competing explanations of forgetting are the decay theory and the interference theory. The decay theory asserts that as time passes without rehearsal of information, the representation of that information in the brain deteriorates. Eventually, the information is irretrievably lost. The interference theory states that the passage of time per se has no effect on retention. Information is stored permanently, and it is interference from other information the individual has acquired that produces forgetting. Two forms of interference have been extensively documented in the laboratory—retroactive inhibition (RI) and proactive inhibition (PI). In RI, the source of interference is information acquired *after* the information to be remembered. In PI, the source of interference is information acquired *before* the information to be remembered. The experimental procedure for investigating interference calls for at least two groups. The experimental group learns two lists in succession, subsequently receiving a test on List 1 in a study of RI or a test on List 2 in a study of PI. The control group learns only the list on which the experimental group is tested and recalls the list after the same delay. If the control group recalls more items than the experimental group, then the experimental group has experienced interference. With paired-associate lists, interference is most likely to occur when the stimulus items in the lists are identical and the response items are different. If the stimulus items are similar and the response items are identical, the experimental group is likely to recall *more* items than the control (facilitation). Completely different lists tend to be a neutral condition. Attempts to extend these principles to written passages have met with limited success. There is evidence for RI in an educational setting under conditions analogous to those which produce it with paired-associate lists, but the effect is small. In general, the use of interference theory to predict retention in educational settings requires close attention to two conditions: the precise wording of the passages and the manner in which retention tests are constructed.

The nature of the processes underlying interference are not clear. An early interpretation of RI, advanced by Melton and Irwin, was that two factors were responsible for a subject's forgetting of List 1 after learning List 2—response competition and extinction. Extinction of List 1 responses occurred during the learning of List 2 and resulted in the omission of these responses on the recall test. Response competition arose from confusion as to which items belonged to List 1 and which items belonged to List 2. The result was intrusion errors on the recall test. The two-factor interpretation of interference implies that extinguished List 1 responses should spontaneously recover strength over time, but the evidence for spontaneous recovery is weak at best. Another theoretical problem relates to the effect of natural linguistic habits on the forgetting of nonsense syllables. To account for the amount of forgetting over a 24-hour period, Underwood found it necessary to assign a role to natural linguistic habits acquired prior to the experiment. However, there is no persuasive evidence for such an effect, and this gap in theory, together with the spontaneous recovery problem, has led investigators to pursue additional interpretations of forgetting.

Much attention has been given to the phenomenon of cue-dependent forgetting. Information that has been associated with some cue is said to be forgotten because the individual cannot retrieve that cue. In an important study, Tulving and Pearlstone demonstrated that they could induce subjects to recall forgotten information by presenting the cues with which the information was originally associated. The practical implication of this phenomenon is that one should be able to improve memory by developing techniques for maintaining ready access to retrieval cues. The method of loci, a memory aid developed by the ancient Greeks, has this effect. Another memory technique employs acronyms, words constructed from the first letters of other words. Information is sorted into categories and each category is associated with a word that acts as a retrieval cue. By constructing an acronym from these cue words, one can maintain ready access to the associated categories. Use of the acronym is crucial; without it, one is exposed to interference. There is evidence that RI operates by causing a loss of unprotected retrieval cues; it does not appear to break the association between the cues and category content (Tulving and Psotka).

Two controversial interpretations of forgetting are Freud's theory of repression and the consolidation theory. Freud maintained that people were motivated to forget ideas that posed a threat or created anxiety. These ideas were deposited in the unconscious mind, where they remained psychologically active. Efforts to produce repression in the laboratory have yielded conflicting results, perhaps because of the difficulty of making procedures personally meaningful to subjects. The consolidation theory asserts that experiences leave behind fragile traces that require a period of time to consolidate, or solidify. During the consolidation period, memory traces are subject to destruction by traumas. After the consolidation period, memory traces become permanent. Consolidation theory readily explains the phenomenon of retrograde amnesia, in which memory for experiences just prior to a trauma may be totally erased, while experiences more distant in time from the trauma are remembered progressively better. There is disagreement about the processes responsible for retrograde amnesia, however.

Researchers commonly distinguish between one's memory for words (semantic memory) and one's memory for events (episodic memory). Semantic memory is probably less subject to change than episodic memory, and it may not always be possible to generalize findings with one system to the other. Semantic memory appears to be highly organized. Conceptions of organization differ in many details but they generally emphasize the notion that information is retrieved from categories, each category containing bits of information that have certain features in common. An early theory of memory organization was developed by Brown and McNeill to explain the familiar tip-of-the-tongue (TOT) phenomenon. Given the definition of an uncommon word, an individual can sometimes provide information about various features of the word without being able to recall the word itself. The essence of Brown and McNeill's theory was that each word was stored together with information about its meaning, number of syllables, sound, etc. Categories of words having one or more of these features in common could be created as needed. Another conception of memory organization was developed by Collins and Quillian. They assumed that information about objects was stored in categories arranged in a hierarchical fashion. At the highest level of a hierarchy was a category containing information that was true of a broad class of objects. Additional information about the objects was further sorted in categories at lower levels. The time necessary to retrieve information about an object was said to be a function of two factors: (1) the time necessary to move from one level of the hierarchy to the next; (2) time necessary to scan the contents of a category. Using a reaction-time procedure, Collins and Quillian showed how these times could be measured individually.

There is evidence that the more thoroughly information is learned, the more highly organized it is. Loftus and Loftus developed a procedure for measuring the extent of categorical representation in memory, and showed that organization of information about psychology was greater in advanced psychology students than in beginning students. This procedure is a potentially valuable one for measuring achievement in educational settings.

STUDY QUESTIONS

1. Define "hypermnesia." What is the distinctive characteristic of retroactive hypermnesia? What are the practical and theoretical implications of these phenomena?

2. Shuell and Keppel conducted an experiment to study the relationship between learning ability and memory. Two groups of subjects were identified—fast and slow learners. How were these groups established? How did Shuell and Keppel equate the groups for degree of learning? With degree of learning held constant, how did the groups compare in retention after 24 and 48 hours? What conclusion does this finding suggest about the potential of people to develop their memories?

3. Why did Ebbinghaus recommend that investigators use nonsense syllables in studies of memory?

4. State the formula for calculating the "savings score." Explain the relationship between this formula and the degree of retention.

5. What pattern of forgetting did Ebbinghaus find as a function of time?

6. Why did Bartlett object to the use of nonsense syllables in memory research?

7. Describe Bartlett's "method of reproduction." In his experiment with the passage entitled "the War of the Ghosts," over how long a period did most memory changes take place? Relate this finding to Ebbinghaus's with nonsense syllables. State two qualitative changes in memory that took place in Bartlett's experiment.

8. Describe Bartlett's "method of picture writing." How did retention of signs that resembled their referents differ from retention of signs which did not resemble their referents?

9. State the "decay" theory of forgetting. Describe Thorndike's version of the theory and indicate the name he gave to it.

10. State the basic assumption of the "interference" theory of forgetting.

11. What logical argument did McGeoch advance against the decay theory?

12. Describe the procedure used by Jenkins and Dallenbach to assess the effects of sleep and waking activity on retention. What results would be expected on the basis of the decay theory? On the basis of the interference theory? Describe the results by: (a) comparing retention after a period of sleep with retention after an equivalent period of waking activity; (b) describing changes in retention after varying periods of waking activity. What are the theoretical implications of the findings?

13. Diagram the procedures for studying retroactive and proactive inhibition. What kind of outcome would be taken as evidence for interference? What kind of outcome would indicate facilitation?

LONG-TERM MEMORY

14. With paired-associate lists as the learning tasks, state the conditions most likely to produce interference and facilitation. What condition tends to be neutral?

15. Referring to the following points, describe the rationale, procedure, and results of the experiment by Myrow and Anderson on the application of interference principles to an educational setting:

    a) The times separating Phases 1, 2, and 3.

    b) The general topics of the passages read by the experimental and control groups in Phases 1 and 2. Indicate which passage each group was tested on in Phase 3.

    c) How passages for the experimental group were arranged to produce RI, RF, and zero effect. Relate these arrangements to your answer in question 14, and give examples from the passages.

    d) The general procedure for constructing the short-answer and multiple-choice tests. For the latter, describe the three sets of distractors (specific-both, nonspecific-both, and original learning only).

    e) Comparison of retention in the experimental group with retention in the control group under the RI, RF, and neutral conditions.

    f) Comparison of retention scores on the four exams described in part d above.

    g) The general conclusion regarding the application of interference theory to the "real world."

16. In the study by Melton and Irwin, what relationship was found between RI and the number of trials the experimental group received on the second (interfering) list? What was the relationship between the number of intrusion errors and the number of trials on the second list? What aspect of performance led Melton and Irwin to posit the existence of a factor X?

17. What process was factor X thought to be? What expectation about this process has not been confirmed by experiments?

18. It was long assumed by interference theorists that forgetting of a list of nonsense syllables over a 24-hour period was attributable to RI. Why did Underwood question this assumption? What evidence did he offer that PI was responsible for most of the forgetting?

19. Underwood suggested that natural linguistic habits contributed to the forgetting of nonsense syllables. Describe the process he considered to be responsible, illustrating it with the example of the letter sequences, Q-U and Q-A. What has been the general outcome of experiments on this problem?

20. Describe how Greek and Roman orators used the method of loci to remember the topics in their speeches. In what sense did the images used by the orators to symbolize topics act as retrieval cues? How did taking a mental walk generate recall of the retrieval cues?

21. Describe the procedure used by Ross and Lawrence to study the amount of PI in retention of word lists memorized with the method of loci. If PI occurred, what would be the pattern of results? What pattern was found?

22. Describe the nature of the word list used by Tulving and Pearlstone to study cue-dependent forgetting. What parts of the list were expected to act as retrieval cues?

STUDY QUESTIONS

What parts were subjects specifically asked to remember? How were the recall tests administered to the two groups? What two findings demonstrated cue-dependent forgetting? (One answer involves a comparison between groups, the other a comparison within the same group.)

23. State the five steps for using acronyms as a memory aid. How do the letters of the acronym resemble the loci in the method of loci?

24. Through what mechanism does RI produce forgetting when material is organized into categories? How was this effect demonstrated in the experiment by Tulving and Psotka? What principle of memory do the findings underscore?

25. Define "repression." Illustrate using the example of the woman who refused to drink fluids.

26. State the "consolidation" theory of memory.

27. Define and give an example of "retrograde amnesia." How does the consolidation theory explain this phenomenon? What alternative interpretation has been proposed based on studies with rats and electro-convulsive shock?

28. Define: semantic memory, episodic memory.

29. How did Brown and McNeill produce the "tip-of-the-tongue" (TOT) state in subjects? State three kinds of information the subjects could give about words they could not recall.

30. Describe Brown and McNeill's theory of retrieval from semantic memory. Do this by discussing the mental processes assumed to occur when a subject is given a definition and is asked to state the associated word. What are the two phases of information retrieval? What is the relationship between the number of features used to construct the category of possible definitions and the number of definitions in the category?

31. Within the framework outlined in question 30, discuss the processes assumed to be responsible for the TOT state. How might subjects retrieve words that sound like the target word?

32. Using the categories, ANIMAL, BIRD, FISH, CANARY, OSTRICH, SHARK, and SALMON, draw the hierarchical structure assumed by Collins and Quillian to relate one category to the others. What kinds of information are stored in each category? What is the key assumption of the theory regarding the storage of information in a particular category?

33. Using the framework outlined in Question 32, describe the processes involved when a subject tries to answer True or False to the following statements: (a) A canary has feathers; (b) A canary breathes; (c) A canary is an animal.

34. Describe the procedure used by Collins and Quillian to measure: (a) the time necessary to "move" from one level of the hierarchy to the next level; (b) the time necessary to scan the contents of a category. Using the sample statements provided in Question 33, illustrate the kinds of comparisons involved in measuring the duration of each process.

35. How did Loftus and Loftus measure the extent to which advanced and beginning students in psychology organized information in categories? Describe the retrieval processes assumed to occur in each group. What were the results of the experiment?

LONG-TERM MEMORY

CHAPTER 12

How to Improve Your Memory: A Short Course

This chapter will show you how to develop practical skills that can assist you every day for the rest of your life. Several previous chapters (7, 10, 11) have examined principles of memory, but the emphasis has been on basic processes. Our exclusive concern now is memory training. The practical advantages of having a trained memory are virtually unlimited. Perhaps the most obvious advantages are those to be found in educational settings, which often force students to rely upon their memories. When, for example, was the last time that you took an open-book examination? Like most students, you are probably painfully aware of the consequences of failing to remember material on a test. You may fully understand certain ideas and their relationships, but if you cannot remember key bits of information, your accomplishments are likely to go unrecognized. A trained memory is not a substitute for understanding, but it may help you get the academic recognition which you deserve.

In everyday life, many situations arise that provide an opportunity to use our memory but do not require us to do so. Most people do not take full advantage of these situations because their untrained memories are not equal to the task. Simply remembering the names of casual acquaintances can yield significant benefits. As the manager of a store, you might have opportunities to learn the names of customers when making out credit card receipts. You could show those customers that you appreciate their patronage by keeping their names in mind. If they happened to return to the store, you would be able to greet them personally, and you might transform a casual customer into a regular customer.

In social situations, remembering the names of acquaintances can promote the development of genuine friendships. Especially at parties, when names seem to fly at us from all directions, we may be reluctant to learn a name because we do not expect to meet the person again. Often, though, that individual reappears, and we regret that we cannot greet him or her in a personal way. To add to the awkwardness of the situation, the person may show that he or she cared enough about us to remember our name! The anonymity of our greeting may suggest that the feelings were not mutual, and further expressions of friendship from that person may be long in coming. By reducing the effort we must exert to remember names and faces, a trained memory can be an important social asset.

If you can remember additional information about a person, so much the better. Not only does this demonstrate interest, it provides a basis for conversation.

After saying, "Hi, Pete," you might ask about the hiking trip that Pete had planned to take, or about the history paper he was writing. Having information at your fingertips can also be a great professional asset. Politicians interviewed on TV and radio often cite statistics from memory to support their points. Not only do they add credibility to their views, they give the impression of being knowledgeable, of knowing what they are talking about. As a rule, it is usually far more effective to speak from memory than to speak from notes. The audience gets a sense of spontaneity and immediacy, and listens more attentively. The author can personally attest to the power of memory in public speaking. In my early, inexperienced days as a teacher, I would often consult notes when describing an experiment or summarizing key points. I could see from the expressions on students' faces that I might as well have held up a sign reading, "Intermission." Those periods became times to engage in a little pleasant daydreaming or to do a bit more studying for the exam in the next class. Now I commit all lecture material to memory. The class does not hang on every word, but there are noticeably fewer "intermissions" than before.

You can see, then, that a trained memory has uses in a virtually infinite variety of situations. This chapter will examine just a few applications of memory techniques, for it is a "short course." However, you should have no difficulty extending the techniques that you will learn to many more areas. Be prepared to invest some time after reading the chapter. Although the techniques are basically simple, they require considerable practice to be used effectively. You should not expect to produce a trained memory simply by reading this chapter any more than you would expect to produce a cake by reading a cookbook. Practicing the techniques will not be difficult, though, for you will soon find that using the techniques is fun as well as helpful.

STRATEGIES FOR IMPROVING MEMORY

Strategies for improving memory take many forms, but we can generally think of them as falling into three categories. One class of strategies involves the memorization of items in pairs. You are remembering items in pairs when you learn to connect names with faces or foreign vocabulary with English translations. Another class of strategies is useful for memorizing a series of items in a fixed order. Examples of a fixed series would be the topics in a speech, the numbers and letters of an automobile license, and the notes on a piano keyboard. Finally, there is a class of strategies designed to improve memory for groups of items when the order of the items is unimportant. Examples would be the items on a shopping list, the cards that have been removed from a deck, and the key points made by a textbook author when discussing a topic. We shall first examine each class of strategies in a general way, and then consider how they may be applied to a variety of everyday memory problems.

Memorizing items in pairs

Verbal mediation In laboratory experiments on paired-associate learning (Chapter 7), subjects are asked to inspect a list containing several pairs of items (words, nonsense syllables, pictures), and to associate the first item in each pair with the second item. Studies have shown that the associations are easiest to learn when one item already reminds the subject of the other item, for example, DAY-NIGHT, BOY-GIRL. If an association between the items does not exist at the outset of the experiment, or if the association is a weak one, subjects often will adopt a strategy of linking the items indirectly. The first item in the pair may suggest a word that brings to mind the second item. This word thus becomes a mediator or bridge between the items. In the word pair CAVITY-NAIL, the stimulus item, CAVITY, may bring to mind the word TOOTH, and TOOTH may remind the subject of the response item, NAIL (as in the phrase, "to fight tooth and nail"). Using mediators to join stimulus and response items can be an effective strategy provided you are willing to use your imagination without inhibition. Conventional associations, like that between day and night, are often not available to provide a mediator between items. You must be prepared to draw upon personal experiences to fill gaps, and the mediator that works best may be one that is somewhat embarrassing. For verbal mediation to be most useful, you must allow yourself to adopt any mediator if it is effective.

When searching for a mediator, it is sometimes better to focus on part of a word than it is to concentrate on the entire word. Suppose that you wished to remember that COPENHAGEN was the capital of DENMARK. The letters, P-E-N, in COPENHAGEN rhyme with and have a meaning similar to three letters in DENMARK, D-E-N. If you were given the name of the country and were asked to state the capital, you could use DEN to remind yourself of COPENHAGEN. Or if you were given the name of the city and were asked for the country, you could use PEN as the mediator.

Another approach to verbal mediation involves the insertion of a phrase or sentence between the items to be remembered. Conventional phrases can be effective mediators but they often are not relevant to the task at hand. You could quickly learn the word pair, COW-MOON, by recalling the familiar line, "the cow jumped over the moon." It is unlikely, though, that you would find many other uses for this line. As in the case of mediators consisting of a single word, you will usually find yourself drawing upon personal experiences to find suitable phrases. Possible sources of phrases are the lyrics of songs, the lines of poems you have read or written, book titles, and, of course, your imagination. Using your imagination to invent lines is especially likely to be effective if you can visualize the scene you have created. This brings us to another strategy for remembering items in pairs, one that is probably more effective than the strategy of verbal mediation.

Mediation by imagery   In Chapter 7 we examined evidence that mental imagery was a more effective aid to memory than words alone. The invention of mental images is also the strategy emphasized by the well-known memory trainer and performer, Harry Lorayne (Lorayne, 1975; Lorayne and Lucas, 1974). Lorayne believes that the invention of mental images aids memory by focusing attention on the information. He suggests that when people claim to have forgotten something, they usually have not forgotten it at all. They never learned the information in the first place due to inattention. On the next occasion that you cannot come up with the name of an acquaintance, you may take that as a sign that you paid too little attention to the name and the face when you were introduced to the person. You would have linked the name to the face permanently had you initially listened carefully to the name and associated it to some distinctive feature of the face.

For the purpose of focusing attention on information, Lorayne believes that the best images are ones that are ridiculous, impossible, and illogical. Plausible or logical images tend to be vague; they do not emphasize sufficiently the key features of the items to be remembered. Lorayne suggests four techniques for making images nonsensical (Lorayne and Lucas, 1974), which we may illustrate as follows. Let us say that you wish to purchase a bottle of WINE and a pair of SHOES one afternoon. It is important that you remember to do both, but there are so many other chores to do, that you fear you may accidentally buy one and forget the other. You would like to associate SHOES with WINE so that when you pass the shoe store, you will remember that you must also go for the wine. Lorayne's strategy for creating a link between SHOES and WINE is to invent a ridiculous image by applying one or more of the rules, below:

1. **Substitution:** Let one item take over the function that is normally performed by the other item. See yourself walking down the street wearing a pair of wine bottles instead of shoes, or imagine yourself at a dinner party pouring a bottle of shoes instead of wine.

2. **Out of proportion:** Try to make the objects ridiculously large. Picture yourself walking down the street wearing a pair of *huge* wine bottles, or pouring a bottle of shoes that is as big as you are.

3. **Exaggeration:** Take each object and multiply it by a "million." Rather than seeing just yourself wearing a pair of wine bottles, picture a crowd of pedestrians at a busy intersection clunking along in the same way. Instead of seeing a single pair of shoes come out of the wine bottle, picture a "million" pairs spilling over the table and onto the floor.

4. **Action:** Make things happen in your images. Create mental movies, not mental snapshots. Watch the *movement* of the crowd at the intersection; picture the shoes *pouring* from the bottle.

Would you feel comfortable making up such images? It may seem more like a children's game than a serious strategy for improving memory. Indeed, one does get the impression that the imagination of a child is far more vivid than that of an adult, and in this sense, Lorayne's approach may resemble a child's game. But Lorayne's performances are certainly not "child's play." How many adults do you know (not to mention children) who can walk onto a stage and recite the name of every individual in the audience after hearing the name just once? Lorayne claims that this and many more feats of memory are within reach of anyone willing to adopt the simple device of creating silly images.

HOW TO IMPROVE YOUR MEMORY: A SHORT COURSE

Concrete, meaningful words like WINE and SHOES are easy to picture, but many words are not. People's names are especially difficult to visualize. While some names do refer to things that can be visualized—BAKER, CARPENTER, GOLDSMITH, SILVER, KNOTT, FOX, etc.—most names have no obvious meaning. In such cases, Lorayne suggests that you make up a substitute word or phrase that reminds you of the name. Here are some examples:

PECORARO: peck a rare roe

SANCHEZ: sand chest

DIEDERICH: deed rich

STROUD: round, trout

ARDOLINO: our doll

Note that the substitute word or phrase need not be a literal translation of every sound in the name. It is sufficient to capture just the most distinctive sounds, for they will remind you of the rest of the name. With this substitute word technique, all words are potentially visualizable, no matter how abstract they are. There are many conventional symbols of abstract concepts that you could draw upon. LIBERTY, an abstract concept, can be remembered by visualizing a bell, PEACE by doves, KNOWLEDGE by books, and so on. Idiosyncratic associations are also common. ELECTRICITY may remind you of wires, WEALTH may bring to mind a mansion, SCIENCE may conjure up a test tube. Even numbers can be visualized as common objects, as we shall see in the next section.

Memorizing items in a fixed series

Both strategies for memorizing items in pairs—verbal mediation and imagery—are applicable to tasks that require the memorization of several items in a fixed order. In one verbal mediation technique, the first letters of words in a sentence represent the first letters of the items to be remembered. "Every Good Boy Deserves Fun," or some variation on this line, is a well-known device for remembering the order of notes on the music staff: E, G, B, D, F. The sentence "Ladies Prefer Men," can help you remember the order of three major streets on Manhattan Island in New York City. Going from east to west, the names of the streets are Lexington Avenue, Park Avenue, and Madison Avenue. Mediation by imagery can readily be extended to lists to items by picturing sequences of scenes. You can let one scene incorporate the first and second items, another scene incorporate the second and third items, and so on. You could remember the words, SHOES, WINE, and BREAD, in that order, by picturing first a crowd of pedestrians wearing wine bottles instead of shoes, and picturing second a view of the sidewalk showing that the people are walking on slices of bread. Although verbal and visual mediation can be extended to lists, additional strategies are available expressly designed for this purpose. These strategies have the advantage of allowing you to visualize numbers as well as words.

The number-consonant system Does the number 390 mean anything to you? To the author it has several meanings: a room full of MOPS, MOBS of people on the streets, MAPS piled high on a table. How about the number 953? To the author, it looks like a PLUM. And the number 312? It bears a marked resemblance to a MITTEN. Every number, in fact, is a picture, provided that you know how to make the conversion. With the assistance of the system you are about to learn, you will be able to visualize telephone numbers, statistics, credit card numbers, product style numbers, prices—virtually any sequence of digits. Having visualized the number, you can then relate it easily to other information by using the strategy of mediation by imagery.

Here is how the system works. There are ten digits in our numerical system: 1, 2, 3, 4, 5, 6, 7, 8, 9, and 0. Each digit corresponds to the sound of one or more consonants, so that by filling in appropriate vowels, you can convert the number into a word. For this system to be most effective, you must be able to "hear" the consonants at about the same time the digits are given to you. Although you could learn the associations between digits and sounds by sheer rote, memory aids are available that can minimize the amount of time spent on drill.

The digit 1 corresponds to the sound of "t" or the sound of "d." The memory aid for associating "t" with 1 is the fact that you write a "t" with a single downstroke. You can remember that "t" and "d" are interchangeable by the similarity in the ways you pronounce them. With both letters, you raise the tip of your tongue to the roof of your mouth just behind the teeth.

The digit 2 corresponds to "n." The memory aid here is that you write an "n" with two downstrokes.

By the same logic, you can remember that the digit 3 is represented by "m"; there are three downstrokes.

The digit 4 corresponds to "r." To remember that sound, think of the word "four," which ends with a strong "r."

For the digit 5 the sound to remember is "l." As a memory aid, consider the fact that you can form a capital "L" with your left hand by raising your index finger and lowering your thumb so that it is perpendicular to the index finger.

All of the remaining digits are represented by more than one sound based on similarity in manner of pronunciation. For the digit 6, one of the sounds is "j," which you can remember by noting that a 6 and a capital J look somewhat like mirror images: 6 J. The other sounds associated with 6 are "sh," "ch," and soft "g" (as in page). These sounds, like J, are all pronounced by raising the middle of the tongue to the roof of the mouth.

For the digit 7, the sounds to remember are "k," hard "g" (as in "gum"), and hard "c" (as in "cut"). The memory aid for associating "k" with 7 is that you can make a capital K out of two 7s, one right-side up and the other upside down. ($\mathcal{K}$).

The digit 8, corresponds to the sounds made by the letters "f," "ph," and "v." In associating "f" with 8, it may be helpful to remember that an italicized *f* has two small loops, one above the midline and one below. This pattern resembles the two "circles" that make up an 8.

The sounds representing the digit 9 are "p" and "b." As a memory aid, capital P and 9 look like mirror images.

For the digit 0, the sounds to remember are "z" and soft "c" (as in "center"). As a memory aid, you might keep in mind that the word "zero" starts with the letter "z."

The number-consonant system is summarized in the following chart:

1 — t or d	6 — j, sh, ch, soft g
2 — n	7 — k, hard g, hard c
3 — m	8 — f, ph, v
4 — r	9 — p, b
5 — l	0 — z, s

Can you recall the numbers mentioned at the outset of this section? The numbers probably made a much weaker impression that the words that were used to represent them. If you can remember those words, then it will be possible to decode them into the numbers. One of the words was "a room full of ____." This word (mops) translates as M = 3, O = no value, P = 9, S = 0, or 390. Another word was a type of fruit: ____. If you recalled "plum," then you could easily get the number: P = 9, L = 5, U = no value, M = 3, or 953. Do you recall the third word? It was a type of clothing. The word was "mitten," so: M = 3, I = no value, TT = 1 (if double letters sound alike, they translate into a single digit), E = no value, N = 2, or 312.

Once you have converted a number to a word, you can relate the word to other information by inventing a suitable image. For example, as a regular customer at a restaurant, you may wish to remember its phone number so that you can make reservations without having to check a phonebook. The restaurant specializes in Italian food, and the phone number is 761-5058. You could convert this number to the following words:

C a G e D - L o o S e L e a F
7   6   1   5   0   5   8

Now, to associate the "caged looseleaf" with the restaurant, you might picture a cage with tomato sauce dripping from the roof like raindrops. So ridiculous is this image that it is bound to make a lasting impression.

Another example: Let us assume that you are an avid baseball fan and have frequent discussions on the subject with friends. You would like to buttress your arguments with statistics, but it would hardly be practical to carry around a baseball fact book. One statistic you would like to remember is the batting average of a player named LANGE (fictional) in the year 1948. The average was .284. To create an image incorporating these bits of information, you might make the following translations:

1948 = T u B R o o F   Lange = LONG
.284 = N e V e R

Now, you could construct the phrase, "LONG TUBROOF, NEVER!" To remember it, imagine yourself at a store inspecting a bathtub with a long roof. You are shaking your head as if to say "Never," while in the distance stands another customer "longing" to buy the tub. The customer stands at a distance as a reminder that "LONG" represents a name, not a number, and should not be decoded in the same manner as the other elements in the picture.

Coming up with scenes that incorporate all the necessary information may be difficult when you first try the number-consonant system. But the invention of scenes will become easier with practice, and as you develop proficiency, you will discover more and more uses for this strategy.

The pegword system   In Chapter 10 we examined a centuries-old strategy for memorizing items in sequence called the "method of loci (locations)." Greek and Roman orators relied upon the method of loci to remember the order of topics in their speeches. Each topic was associated with a concrete word that reflected the content of that section of the speech. For example, a section on war might be symbolized by the word "knife," while a section on food might be symbolized by "fish." In preparation for the speech, the orator would take a mental walk through a familiar building, tying images of the words to the locations he passed. During the speech, the orator would take another mental walk. As he passed each location, the associated image would come to mind and remind the orator of the material he should discuss.

The pegword system resembles the method of loci in that it provides images which, like the locations, act as "receptacles" for words you want to remember. However, the pegword system, unlike the method of loci, does not require you to memorize locations or take mental walks. The pegword system also has a capability that the method of loci does not have. You can recall items in order, as in the method of loci, or you can recall items by position number. For example, in a 20-item list, you could quickly pick out item 14 without having to run through the first 13 items.

There are two versions of the pegword system, one of which may already be familiar to you. It is a simple poem that goes as follows:

One is a bun

Two is a shoe

Three is a tree

Four is a door

Five is a hive

Six is sticks

Seven is heaven

Eight is a gate

Nine is a line

Ten is a hen

"Bun," "shoe," "tree," and so on are pegwords in the sense that you can easily "peg" them to the words you want to remember. All you have to do is visualize them in some relationship to items from your list. "Heaven," unlike the other pegwords, is an abstract term, so you may want to use a substitute word like "angel" or "halo" that can more easily be visualized. After associating the pegwords to the items you want to remember, you will be able to perform two feats. Given the number, you could state the item; or, given the item, you could state the number. The pegwords serve as mediators. In the first case, the number reminds you of the pegword and the pegword produces an image of the appropriate item from the list. In the latter case, the item produces an image of the pegword and the pegword brings to mind the appropriate number.

Here are ten words with which to test the system. Before attempting to memorize them, be sure the associations between numbers and pegwords are strong. You should be able to state the pegword when given the number, and state the number when given the pegword. To check yourself: what pegword goes with 6? With 3? With 10? With 2? What number goes with "tree"? With "line"? With "house"? (Hope you caught that last one.)

Now, the list: BOOK, TABLE, CAT, APPLE, WINDOW, CAR, PAINT, FLOWER, CIGAR, UMBRELLA. Let us consider some possible ways of visualizing the items. It is important to keep in mind that you are associating the items with pegwords, not with other items. To ensure that you will focus your attention on the pegwords, we shall take the items in a random order.

Item 4 is APPLE and the pegword is DOOR. You could associate APPLE with DOOR by picturing a door that has an apple as a doorknob.

Item 8 is FLOWER and the pegword is GATE. Here, you might use Harry Lorayne's substitution technique and imagine that a flower has taken over the function of a gate. Picture a fence with a long-stemmed tulip growing sideways across the entrance.

Item 1 is BOOK. To associate BOOK with the pegword, BUN, you might imagine a book between two halves of a bun like a hamburger. By applying Lorayne's substitution technique, you can create an even more ridiculous image. Let the book serve as a bun and picture a steaming hamburger between the pages.

Item 7 is PAINT. Since the pegword, HEAVEN, is abstract, you could employ a substitute word that is concrete and easier to visualize, say ANGEL. Picture the angel with a can of paint above his head instead of halo.

Item 2 is TABLE and the pegword is SHOE. Here, you might imagine a table with a shoe under each of its legs. Harry Lorayne recommends that you put action into your images wherever possible, so let the table walk down the street in its new shoes.

Item 6, CAR, should be associated with the pegword STICKS. You could picture a car made out of toothpicks, or a huge car traveling across a tiny bridge made of twigs.

Remember, for the pegword system to work, you must visualize the descriptions or create images of your own. It is not sufficient simply to read the descriptions.

Item 5 is WINDOW and the pegword is HIVE. This is an easy one. There are windows all around a beehive and the bees are looking out at you.

Item 10 is UMBRELLA. To associate UMBRELLA with the pegword, HEN, imagine that eggs are falling from the sky like raindrops and a hen is walking down the street holding an umbrella.

Item 9 is CIGAR and the pegword is LINE. Here, a man could be seen smoking several cigars lined up end to end.

Last, item 3, CAT, is to be associated with the pegword TREE. An obvious image is one of a cat sitting in a tree, but that may be too ordinary to make much of an impression. Instead, picture hundreds of cats hanging by their tails from the branches like leaves.

If you have visualized the foregoing descriptions, or created your own images, you should now be able to do two things: you should be able to state the numbers when given the items, and state the items when given the numbers. Listed below are the numbers in a random order followed by blanks. See if you can fill in the items:

6. _____
2. _____
1. _____
7. _____
10. _____
5. _____
3. _____
8. _____
9. _____
4. _____

Working, now, in the reverse direction, can you supply the numbers when given the items:

PAINT   _____
TREE   _____
BOOK   _____
CIGAR   _____
CAR   _____
UMBRELLA _____
TABLE   _____
CAT   _____
FLOWER   _____
APPLE   _____

How did you do? The time-worn expression, "Practice makes perfect," is an apt principle in memory training. With practice, you will be able to achieve perfect performance with the pegword system, and will do so with a feeling of effortlessness.

Earlier it was mentioned that there are two versions of the Pegword System. The version we have just examined—based on rhymes—has the advantage of being easy to remember, but it has the disadvantage of applying to just 10 numbers. The other version of the system has complementary features: it is somewhat more difficult to memorize but it can be extended to any number of items. The pegwords are tied to the digits on the basis of the number-consonant system. Consonants that make up the pegwords have the numerical values indicated previously. Vowels have no value. Harry Lorayne (Lorayne and Lucas, 1974) has provided pegwords for numbers from 1 to 100, the first 16 of which appear below:

1. Tie	5. Law	9. Bee	13. ToMb
2. Noah	6. SHoe	10. ToeS	14. TiRe
3. Ma	7. Cow	11. ToT	15. ToweL
4. Rye	8. iVy	12. TiN	16. DiSH

Note that the pegwords corresponding to numbers 1–9 contain only one consonant from the number-consonant system. Pegwords for numbers consisting of two digits contain two consonants, the first representing the digit in the "tens" place and the second representing the digit in the "ones" place. You can look up the remaining digits in Lorayne and Lucas (1974) or make up words of your own. Even if you do not anticipate a need for using a large number of pegwords, it would be to your advantage to generate at least a few more on your own. In that way you can reinforce your knowledge of the number-consonant system while preparing for unexpected demands on your memory.

Memorizing lists when item order is unimportant

The method of loci and the pegword system—strategies for memorizing items in a fixed sequence—can also be used with lists in which the order of items is unimportant. In such cases the order that you learn will necessarily be arbitrary. Still, you will accomplish your objective of learning the material in a way that will allow you to retrieve items at will.

You also have the option of using two additional strategies, both of which were discussed at some length in Chapter 10. One strategy involves the invention of acronyms, words whose letters correspond to the first letters of the words you want to remember. In the example described in Chapter 11), the strategy was applied to the task of remembering three attributes of self-actualizing individuals. Since the order of the attributes did not have to be remembered, the first letters of traits were rearranged to spell the acronym, SAP. Of course, acronyms can also be used when the order of items matters. It is common practice for organizations to choose names that form acronyms so that people will have an easier time remem-

372

bering the organizations' goals. One group, an organization of prostitutes, came up with an impressive acronym—COYOTE, meaning "Call Off Your Old Tired Ethics." Although the acronym strategy applies to task involving fixed orders, it is most useful when you have the flexibility to rearrange the letters. Hence, it has been suggested for tasks not involving fixed orders.

The other strategy involves categorization, putting items together that belong together. An obvious application of this strategy is the categorization of items on a shopping list. It is usually a simple matter to organize supermarket items into groups like, "vegetables," "fruit," and "dairy products." If you can remember the number of items in each category (the number-consonant system would be useful here), then you should be able to retrieve all of the items when needed.

Applications of categorization of a more subtle nature have been suggested by Cermak (1975). He notes that there is a natural tendency to store information in categories. If you were asked the name of your fifth-grade teacher, you might start with your first-grade teacher and run through each of the succeeding grades until you reached the fifth. Or you might think of teachers' names more or less randomly and check the names against other information you had about your teachers. However you went about it, you surely would not consider the names of any United States presidents. Teachers and presidents are stored in different categories. Without this kind of natural categorization, information retrieval would be a terrible ordeal. We would search endlessly through a hodgepodge of facts and perhaps never locate the information we wanted.

Cermak recommends that we try to intensify this categorization process. Always make an effort to relate new information to something you already know. Your friend Tom introduces you to his cousin Fred. You try to associate this name with a distinctive feature of Fred's face so that you can address Fred by name in the future. Fine. But do not stop there. Relate the name to something you already know. Repeat to yourself the information that Fred is Tom's cousin. By putting the name in your "Tom" category, you will make it easier to remember the name. It is possible that on the next occasion that you meet Fred, the setting will be entirely different and the name may at first elude you. But the face will be familiar and you will probably say to yourself, "Who is that? Ah, yes. Tom's cousin. His name's Fred."

Additional information about Fred should be stored in the same way. If you heard that Fred was a biology major, you should think, "Okay, Tom's cousin Fred is a bio major." Has he been to Europe? Then tell yourself, "Tom's cousin Fred has been to Europe." If all this information is in the same "place"—in the same category—then recalling the information should be quite easy.

The same principle applies to information you get from textbooks and the media. Always relate the information to something you already know. Part of a course on personality may cover humanistic theories, and to introduce you to the subject, the instructor may discuss general features of humanism, features that characterize the theories of all humanistic psychologists. Use these features to construct a general "humanism" category. As you learn about each new theorist, remind yourself of the general features of humanism. This will serve as a review and give you an additional means of recalling details of the individual theories. On an exam you might be asked to discuss Carl Rodgers' theory of personality, but the details may elude you. Since you know that Rodgers is a humanist, you can start your essay by writing about the general features of humanism. Chances are that as you write, information about Rodgers that you have stored in this category will come to mind.

The bottom line: Keep your mental house in order. Put ideas in their proper places and you will find them easily.

HOW TO REMEMBER NAMES AND FACES

Conceptually, the strategy for linking names with faces is simple. Convert the name to a concrete word or phrase, pick out a distinctive feature of the face, and visualize the two elements together. But finding a way to practice this strategy may not be simple. How many new people do you meet in a typical day? Of those people, how many do you see again within a reasonable period so that you can test yourself? If you had to depend on chance, you might spend months polishing your technique. But you need not depend on chance. This section will introduce you to a number of people (through pictures) and give you an opportunity to meet them a second time.

What features of a person's face should you focus on when learning his or her name? In his book, "Remembering People," Harry Lorayne (1975) suggests that you scan the face, giving special attention to the following features:

FOREHEAD: Is it unusually high, wide or narrow? Are there lines on the forehead?

EYEBROWS: Are they arched? Bushy? Straight?

EYES: Do they seem unusually small or large? Note the spacing between the eyes. Are they set wide apart? Are they close-set?

NOSE: Noses are good features to focus on because you can often find something distinctive about them. Some noses are unusually large or small. Others have a "classic" shape. There are pug noses, ski-shaped noses, hooked noses, bulbous noses. Check the nostrils. Are they especially narrow or wide?

CHEEKS: Do they seem full? Sunken?

CHEEKBONES: Are they especially high? Wide?

LIPS OR MOUTH: Note whether the lips are full, thin, straight, arched.

LINES: Lorayne mentions several varieties of facial lines. You may notice lines running from the nostrils to the corners of the mouth, or "character" lines running horizontally across the forehead. Check for dimples, pimples, scars, and warts.

EARS: Do they seem especially small or large? Do they stick out? Are they pressed close to the side of the head?

Now, if you have a moment, I will introduce you to two friends and tell you a few things about them. You will be meeting these people again later, so make a special effort to remember what you hear. Some suggestions will be made for memorizing the information; but later, when you encounter additional people, you will be on your own.

To your left, sitting on the couch, is TIM COULSEN (Fig. 12.1). He is a COMPUTER PROGRAMMER and enjoys BACKPACKING and GOLF. Before scanning the face for a distinctive feature, be sure that you have really heard the name. Harry Lorayne (1975) suggests several ways of focusing attention on a name during a first meeting. When you hear the name, spell it silently to yourself or ask to have it spelled for you. This ensures that you will get the name right. If the name prompts you to make a remark, go ahead and make it. Perhaps the name will be similar to that of someone you already know, or will have an unusual sound. Repeat the name and then make your remark. Another technique: Use the name as much as possible during the conversation and when you say goodbye. The more often you say the name, the more likely it is to register with you. Now, if you have really heard the name, COULSEN, you should have no difficulty coming up with substitute words that are easy to visualize. One possibility is a COOL SON: a little boy is shivering outside in the cold. Another possibility is a COOL SUN; the sun has icicles shooting out from it instead of flames. Some such image should be created and associated with a distinctive feature of the face. What feature did you notice first? You should probably use that one as it will probably also be the one you notice first on future occasions. The author noticed two features: the long nose and the curvature of the upper eyelids. The nose could be seen as an icicle with a COOL SON beneath it on the upper lip. He is shivering as he walks across the lip, with a knapsack on his back (to represent BACKPACKING) and a set of golf clubs slung over his shoulder (symbolizing the interest in GOLF). Getting a computer into the picture to symbolize Coulsen's occupation will require a real leap of the imagination. Let the eyes, with the marked curvature of the upper lids, be reels of tape, and imagine them spinning rapidly as the computer executes a program to retrieve information. On the next occasion that you meet Tim Coulsen, his face should initiate the following associations. There beneath the icicle you will see the COOL SON trudging across the upper lip, with knapsack (symbolizing BACKPACKING) and GOLF clubs on his back. As he walks, the reels of tape will be spinning, a reminder that Coulsen is a COMPUTER PROGRAMMER.

To your right is GAIL MYERS (Fig. 12.2). She works for a public relations firm and enjoys playing the card game, bridge. My substitute word for MYERS is MIRES, and the image that it conveys to me is that of a swamp with thick, overhanging trees and vines. Several features of the face are outstanding. Ms. Myers has a full lower lip, full cheeks, high eyebrows, and a deep indentation running from the tip of the nose to the center of the upper lip. This sort of indentation is called a "philtrum." I find it easy to imagine that the philtrum is a MIRE. As a

Fig. 12.1 Meet Tim Coulsen. He's a computer programmer and enjoys back-packing and golf. (From Lorayne, 1975)

Fig. 12.2 This is Gail Myers. She's in public relations and enjoys playing bridge. (From Lorayne, 1975)

reminder that Gail Myers plays bridge, a rickety wooden bridge overhangs the mire. The term "public relations" is too abstract for me to visualize directly, so the word, "microphone," will be substituted for it. Probably the image of a microphone reminds me of public relations because microphones are used in public address systems. How can we get a microphone into the mire? Well, imagine that hundreds of leafy microphones, some tall and some short, are growing like trees out of the swamp. Adding Ms. Myers' first name, GAIL, is easy—a gale is blowing across the swamp and all the trees and microphones are shaking violently. While we are on the subject of first names: How might we include Mr. Coulsen's first name, TIM, in the picture of a little boy walking across the upper lip? For me, the name, TIM, brings to mind Dickens's character, Tiny Tim, from "A Christmas Carol." Since Tiny Tim walked with crutches, so, too, does the COOL SON on Tim Coulsen's lip.

The foregoing images may seem too complicated to be efficient cues for recall, but if you are acutally visualizing the descriptions, rather than simply reading them, you will realize that they are helpful. Certainly, they are more helpful than the words alone. You may have the feeling that inventing such pictures would take more time than learning the information by rote. That may be true when you first try the procedure. Unfortunately, as we grow older, we tend to lose the vivid imagination that children seem to exercise so effortlessly. Harry Lorayne's technique for remembering people should get the wheels turning again, and before long you will be creating pictures almost instantly.

See for yourself. On pages 376 and 377 you will meet 10 people (Fig. 12.3). Under each person's picture is a brief profile consisting of the name, occupation, and recreational interests of the person. After studying the faces and the profiles you can test your memory on pages 378 through 380, where you will find the same pictures (Fig. 12.4) in a different arrangement. Your task is to fill in the name, occupation, and interests. After practicing with these surrogate persons, you should note an improvement in your ability to invent and decode mental images.

NAME: Ms. Fegley
OCCUPATION: Lawyer
INTERESTS: Politics,
biking, camping

NAME: Mr. Williams
OCCUPATION: Owns TV/Radio Store
INTERESTS: Ham radio operator

NAME: Mr. Petrus
OCCUPATION: Construction worker
INTERESTS: Movie buff, CB

NAME: Mr. Bonning
OCCUPATION: Insurance salesman
INTERESTS: Tennis, cooking

NAME: Ms. Feher
OCCUPATION: Housewife, 2 children
INTERESTS: Golf, likes to read
mysteries by Agatha Christie

Note: Names and profiles are fictional.

Fig. 12.3 Here is an opportunity to practice techniques for remembering people. Try to associate the names, occupations, and interests with the faces.

NAME: Ms. Musgrove
OCCUPATION: Interior decorator
INTERESTS: Follows real estate
and the stockmarket

NAME: Mr. Wells
OCCUPATION: Owns hardware store
INTERESTS: Carpentry
stamp collecting

NAME: Ms. Douthitt
OCCUPATION: College student
INTERESTS: Majoring in
accounting; likes to ski

NAME: Ms. Wallach
OCCUPATION: Receptionist-secretary
INTERESTS: Cooking, travel

Note: Names and profiles are fictional.

Fig. 12.3 *(Continued)*

NAME: Mr. Hall
OCCUPATION: High school
biology teacher
INTERESTS: Has large aquarium
at home; reads extensively
on oceanography

HOW TO REMEMBER NAMES AND FACES

NAME: _____

OCCUPATION: _____

INTERESTS:_____

_____

_____

NAME: _____

OCCUPATION: _____

INTERESTS:_____

_____

_____

NAME: _____

OCCUPATION: _____

INTERESTS:_____

_____

_____

NAME: _____

OCCUPATION: _____

INTERESTS:_____

_____

_____

Fig. 12.4 These are the 10 people you just met (plus two old friends). See if you can fill in the names, occupations, and interest.

NAME: _____

OCCUPATION: _____

INTERESTS:_____

_____

_____

NAME: _____

OCCUPATION: _____

INTERESTS:_____

_____

_____

NAME: _____

OCCUPATION: _____

INTERESTS:_____

_____

_____

NAME: _____

OCCUPATION: _____

INTERESTS:_____

_____

_____

Fig. 12.4 (Continued)

HOW TO REMEMBER NAMES AND FACES

NAME: _____

OCCUPATION: _____

INTERESTS:_____

_____

_____

NAME: _____

OCCUPATION: _____

INTERESTS:_____

_____

_____

NAME: _____

OCCUPATION: _____

INTERESTS:_____

_____

_____

NAME: _____

OCCUPATION: _____

INTERESTS:_____

_____

_____

Fig. 12.4 (Continued)

HOW TO REMEMBER TEXTBOOK MATERIAL

Experiments discussed in Chapter 11 have shown, and you can probably testify from personal experience, that essay tests are harder than multiple-choice tests. On multiple-choice tests, the correct answers are already on the page and your task is basically to discriminate them from the incorrect answers. On essay tests, the page is blank and you must retrieve the information you need from memory, a task that can be enormously frustrating. You may know that the information is in your head, but somehow it eludes your best efforts to recall it. Our goal in this section is to end those frustrations. We shall explore techniques that should enable you to recall the information necessary for writing detailed, well-organized answers to essay questions.

How you study textbook material largely determines how well you will recall it. For the purpose of maximizing recall, it is not sufficient to read the chapter, underline the important points, and later reread those points. You must think about what you read. Organizing the information and stopping frequently to test retention provide the best insurance against memory failure on exams. To organize material is essentially to sort it into categories. Each category is labeled by a key word, and as you read material you constantly associate it to the key word. By taking the first letters of the key words and making an acronym out of them, you can greatly reduce the risk of forgetting the retrieval cues. On the test, you would recall the acronym and decode it into the key words. As you recall these words, they will call up the information with which they were previously associated.

To illustrate the strategy, a section from a book on personality has been reprinted below (Wiggins, Renner, Clore, and Rose, 1976, pp. 408–410). At its conclusion, we shall apply the categorization-acronym strategy. The subject of the section is the cognitive-developmental approach to personality, one of several approaches treated in the text. For purposes of comparison, you may wish to read the material as you normally would for a course, and note any similarities and differences between your approach and the approach to be described later.

A theory of personality necessarily assumes a certain model of the individual. Some underlying assumptions about human nature are implicit in the work of personality theorists, and the assumptions determine much of their theories, the type of behavioral phenomena to which they attend, the methods of inquiry that they use, and the forms of explanation that they offer.

The active person. According to the theories presented in the last two chapters, personality development is an essentially irrational, behavioristic process. For both psychoanalysts and early social learning theorists, the human organism responds in quite automatic ways to stimuli from the external environment. It does so as a consequence of its prior experiences, or it is unconsciously driven to behavior choices by instinctive drives. In either case, the emphasis is on the subject as passive responder to experience rather than initiator of it. By contrast, in this chapter and again in the next, we examine theoretical views of personality in which *the individual is regarded as consciously and rationally making behavior choices and seeking new roles.* In these conceptions, people are the active and initiating determinants of their own behavior choices.

Cognitive-development theorists argue that *individuals are less what their experience makes them than what they make of their experience* (Langer, 1969). Given such an active view of the individual, these theoretical perspectives imply that the self has a key organizing role in social development. Whereas self and phenomenological theories place primary emphasis on human social development, however, cognitive-developmental theories place primary emphasis on biological development as it occurs through continuing social experience.

Hierarchical growth. Cognitive-developmental theories reject the mechanistic philosophy inherent in behavior theory. Social learning views implicitly assume that personality development is *additive;* that is, personality arises through numerous discrete experiences that accumulate over time. But the research of Werner and Piaget suggests that distinctive behaviors are not merely additive; they are emergent. There are some sudden transformations or reconstructions of the behavior of the total organism that are not reducible to lower or earlier functions.

Interactionism. One can recognize three views of development: maturational, environmental, and cognitive-developmental. The maturational view suggests that development is largely an innate process in which stimulation may elicit or maintain but does not create development. Maturational theories stress the notion of unfolding maturational stages in which the order, timing, and patterning of their development is encoded into the genotype.

In contrast to the maturational assumption that mental structures result from innate patterning, environmental theories assume that mental structures result from the patterning of external events. On the other hand, the theoretical structure of cognitve-developmental theories is interactional: *personality results from the interaction of certain structuring tendencies within the organism with the structure of the external world.* The interaction leads to cognitive stages that represent the transformation of early cognitive structures as they are accommodated to or restructured by external experience.

Thus cognitive-developmental theory suggests that growth is self-directed through interaction with social experience. Cognitive theorists reject a strict maturational view because they believe that the structures which organize experience arise themselves through experience. And they reject a *tabula rasa* view because it leaves no room for the modification of experience produced by the structural processes, once acquired. Experience cannot act on the developing human infant without some constraint, because the infant has available only a small number of organized behavioral systems. These systems develop through experience and, once acquired, modify subsequent experiences (Hunt, 1969).

Cognitive relativity. Piaget's descriptions of the growth of reality in the child were based initially on observations of his own children when they were infants. From observations of the child's conception of causality, time, number, and space, Piaget concluded that there is a sequential development of formal thought. Further, for the developing child, thought directs perception. *The world that exists for the child is a function of the child's cognitive construction of it.*

At a higher level, cognitive-developmental theorists conclude that what is true for the child is true for us all. Cultural modes of thought and the formal logic invented for science change as the human construction of reality changes.

One can think of the above argument as a cognitive-relativity hypothesis: *thought directs perception so that reality is a function of our cognitive construction of it.* An even stronger version of this notion is known as the linguistic relativity hypothesis. Here the argument is that the structure and grammatical rules of the language one speaks affect one's perception of the world so as to alter one's knowledge of reality in a profound and pervasive way. And because the concepts symbolized by the constructions of one language are never exactly translatable into another, the thinking processes of those who speak different languages are not identical. In short, the structure of language profoundly affects thought processes. Thought may therefore be relative to the language in which it is conducted. The hypothesis of linguistic relativity finds some support in differences between languages (Whorf, 1956), but available experimental evidence suggests that commonalities among languages are far greater than their structural differences.

We can summarize the philosophical perspective of cognitive-developmental theory as follows: We are what we make ourselves by our own actions; development is a self-constructive process in which the individual is the active agent, not the passive recipient; we do not mirror our experience, we create it, and in the process we change ourselves (Langer, 1969). Reality is a function of our cognitive construction of it, and our cognitive constructions change through experience.

The material is already organized into categories with the category labels explicitly stated. Much textbook material lacks this kind of clear, definite structure and would have to be cast into an appropriate format. What was your acronym for remembering the key words? My own was HAIR: Hierarchy, Active, Interactionism, Relativity. Of course, you cannot always count on key words to form acronyms so conveniently. It is common, for example, to encounter situations where all of the keywords begin with consonants, thus making the creation of an acronym impossible. One approach to dealing with such cases is to add special features to the system. Suppose that you wished to form an acronym to remember the four elements of Miller and Dollard's (1941) theory of imitation (Chapter 5): Drive Cue, Response, Reward. The letters you are working with are D C R R. With the addition of a few vowels, you would have C a R R i e D. Since the consonants stand for key words and the vowels do not, you would need a way to remember that you should decode only the consonants. One approach would be to assume that vowels will be decoded only when the acronym has an "s" at the end. The final "s" would not actually represent a key word but simply the instructions for decoding. If you used this rule, then it would be necessary to change the acronym HAIR to HAIRs. Adding special codes to the system could complicate matters more than you would like. Another approach to inventing acronyms in difficult cases is to search for substitute words that remind you of the key words. For example, to remember the four elements of Miller and Dollard's theory, you could substitute "Act" for "Response" so that you would have the letters D C A R. These letters can be rearranged to spell CARD.

Once you have the key word for a category, you should extract from the test the basic idea for that category. For the section on personality theory, above, the basic ideas would be as follows:

HIERARCHY—New behaviors are emergent rather than additive.

ACTIVE—The individual consciously and actively makes choices.

INTERACTIONISM—The individual imposes organization on the environment; the environment, in turn, alters the individual's organizing tendencies.

RELATIVITY—The individual's perception of reality depends on his or her ways of thinking about it.

To solidify these ideas, you should test yourself on them periodically. Stop yourself at various points in the chapter, look away from the page, and see whether you can state the key words and the basic ideas that go with them. Do not tell yourself that you *know* the material until you can recite both the key words and the basic ideas. Being able to give the basic ideas may be adequate for your purposes, but essays are most impressive when they are rich in detail. It is likely that if you have read the material closely, the basic ideas will bring to mind some additional information. You can maximize the level of detail by making use of mediational techniques. A key word in your basic idea could be joined to a significant detail by creating an appropriate image. For example, a key word in the idea of INTERACTIONISM is "organization." A significant detail in this category is the view of maturational theories, which is directly contrasted with the view of cognitive-developmental theories. Maturational theories, according to the text, assert that people go through fixed stages of development that are genetically determined. You can represent the abstract word "organization" by the first four letters, ORGAN. And you can represent the abstract concept "maturational theory" by the key word STAGE. Now, imagine an organ on a stage and the word "organization" will be linked to maturational theory. On an exam, you could expect the following sequence of events. You write the key word INTERACTIONISM, and it prompts the basic idea, "The individual imposes organization on the environment. . . ." The word "organization" makes you think of an organ on a stage, and the image of the stage reminds you of maturational theory. You would now want to write about maturational theory in some detail. The text mentions that the "order, timing, and patterning" of the stages unfolds according to a genetic blueprint. Rearrange the letters to spell TOP, and picture a dozen tops spinning along the edge of the stage. When you picture the stage, you will also see the tops, and they will remind you that the stages referred to by maturational theory involve timing, order, and patterning.

These strategies may seem too elaborate to put into practice, but what is the alternative to them? Rote memorization of such complex ideas is likely to take considerably more time than the strategies of categorization and mediation, and the product will not be as dependable. Also, rote memorization is boring. Creating fanciful images can be fun. It is not often that we have the opportunity to do things that are both fun and useful, so why pass it up?

HOW TO REMEMBER FOREIGN VOCABULARY AND TECHNICAL TERMS

Much of the effort one puts into learning a foreign langauge consists of memorizing vocabulary. The formation of associations between foreign words and English translations occupies an especially large part of a person's time during the early phases of language learning. Even in the later phases, when grammatical rules become increasingly important, the development of vocabulary continues to be a major concern. Consequently, by applying appropriate strategies to the memorization of vocabulary, you should be able to cut the total effort you devote to acquiring a foreign language.

Atkinson and Raugh (1975) tested a strategy for learning foreign vocabulary that incorporated two techniques we have emphasized in this chapter. Suppose that you wished to remember that the Russian word, ZVONÓK (pronounced zvahn-oak, with the emphasis on "oak"), meant "bell." First, you would invent a substitute word or phrase that sounded like a part of ZVONÓK. "Oak" or "his van" would do. Then, you would picture the substitute word in some kind of relationship to the English translation of ZVONÓK. You might imagine a bell whose clapper was an oak tree, or a van—"his van"—swaying back and forth like a bell as it rode down the highway. The strategy, then, is to create an acoustic link between the foreign word and a substitute word, and a visual link between the substitute word and the English translation.

Atkinson and Raugh (1975) found that this approach was highly effective. They had college students memorize a list of 120 Russian words and English translations, 40 pairs of words on each of three successive days. Two groups of students were given instructions in how to use the keyword system before the word pairs were presented. The groups differed in the amount of assistance they received during the presentation of the material. The experimenter gave one of the groups the substitute words to be linked to the English translations. At the same time that these students heard a Russian word pronounced, they saw the substitute word and the English translation on a screen. The other group heard the Russian word and saw the English translation, but if they wished to use the substitute-word strategy they had to make up their own substitutes. Since the presentation time for each item was only 10 seconds, having the substitute word on the screen would make the system a lot easier to use.

During a session, there were three runs through the 40-item list. At the end of a run, the students took a recall test in which each of the 40 Russian words was pronounced and the students had to type the English translation into a computer within 15 seconds. To test long-term retention of the material, a comprehensive test based on all 120 items was administered six weeks after the last study session. Atkinson and Raugh found that on both the immediate and delayed tests, the students who had the substitute words available on the screen outperformed the students who had no substitutes. The scores were 72 percent vs. 46 percent on the immediate test, and 43 percent vs. 28 percent in the delayed test. You, or course, do not have to study under a 10-second time restriction. If it takes you 20 or 30 seconds to devise a substitute word, so be it. With proper use of this strategy, you should be able to achieve perfect retention.

To illustrate the strategy further, here are some examples of the items presented in Atkinson and Raugh's experiment.

For the Russian word, DÉLO, which means AFFAIR, the substitute word was "jello." Since AFFAIR is an abstract word and is difficult to visualize directly, it would be a good idea to use a concrete substitute that reminds you of this word. As in other applications of the substitute word technique, different people will have different preferences. For me, there is some linkage between AFFAIR and "kiss," so "kiss" will be the substitute word here. Can you picture two lumps of jello kissing in the shadows of a conveyor belt on which boxes of jello are moving? Sure, it's a ridiculous thought, but the technique works. Give it a try.

ZÁPAD in Russian means WEST. The substitute word given to the students was "zap it." As a substitute word for WEST, you could use "cowboy." Imagine a rowdy cowboy shooting up an Old West town. He is really "zapping it."

STRANÁ means COUNTRY. The substitute word for STRANÁ was "strawman." A possible substitute for COUNTRY would be "farm." You could picture a strawman baling hay on a farm.

Now that you know how the system works, you may want to try a few words on your own. Presented below are 10 Russian words and English translations from Atkinson and Raugh (1975). To use the system, make up substitutes for the Russian words on the basis of sound, and, if necessary, make up substitutes for the English terms. Then invent a picture relating the substitute for the Russian word to the English term (or to the substitute for the English term if one was adopted).

HOW TO IMPROVE YOUR MEMORY: A SHORT COURSE

Russian word	Substitute	English word	Substitute (if necessary)
TOLPÁ	_____	CROWD	_____
VNIMÁNIE	_____	ATTENTION	_____
ROT	_____	MOUTH	_____
GORÁ	_____	MOUNTAIN	_____
DURÁK	_____	FOOL	_____
ÓSEŃ	_____	AUTUMN	_____
SÉVER	_____	NORTH	_____
DYM	_____	SMOKE	_____
SELÓ	_____	VILLAGE	_____
USLÓVIE	_____	CONDITION	_____

The Russian words appear below in a new order. See how many English translations you have learned.

GORÁ	_____	SELÓ	_____
DYM	_____	VNIMÁNIE	_____
TOLPÁ	_____	USLÓVIE	_____
DURÁK	_____	ÓSEŃ	_____
ROT	_____	SÉVER	_____

Given the English words, can you remember the Russian words?

FOOL	_____	ATTENTION	_____
CROWD	_____	MOUTH	_____
CONDITION	_____	SMOKE	_____
VILLAGE	_____	AUTUMN	_____
NORTH	_____	MOUNTAIN	_____

The strategy may seem unduly complicated for so short a list. You would perhaps have taken less time to learn the list had you used rote memorization, since the substitute word approach is still new to you. But if you were learning a foreign language, you would have not 10 but hundreds of words to learn. Under those conditions, the advantages of using the system would soon become obvious.

Technical terms

Physicists, machinists, plumbers, lawyers, real estate agents, physicians, construction workers—each group speaks a language that is to some extent "foreign" to the other groups. Technical terms are short-cuts to communication. Instead of spelling out a basic concept all the time, a professional will refer to it by a technical term. To get along in your profession, you must speak the language.

388

Technical terms differ from foreign vocabulary in an important way. With foreign words, the English translations usually consist of a single word, while with technical terms the "English translations" usually consist of one or more sentences which describe the concept. As a result, your strategies for remembering foreign vocabulary and technical terms will differ. To remember foreign words, you can often relate the substitute words based upon sound directly to the English translations. To remember technical terms, you will find it necessary to represent the definition by one or more key words that bring to mind the important features of the definition. If the definition is a complex one, with several important aspects, your representation of it will also be complex. The complete strategy would be this: Invent a substitute word for the technical term on the basis of sound, invent a key word for each important aspect of the definition, and picture some relationship between the substitute word and the key words.

Here are some terms and definitions from the field of biology. The terms refer to parts of the nerve cell:

DENDRITES—short FIBERS extending from the cell body, which RECEIVE INFORMATION from other nerve cells. The first part of DENDRITES sounds like "dent." You can relate this substitute word to FIBERS by picturing strands of nylon fibers with dents in them. Instead of being straight fibers, they are bent this way and that. To get RECEIVE INFORMATION into the picture, you could imagine the fibers are antennas radiating from a wireless RECEIVER that is getting signals (INFORMATION) from a distant receiver.

MITOCHONDRION—a structure in the cell body that converts FOOD substances and OXYGEN to ENERGY. The first two syllables sound like "mighty con." Picture a muscular person wearing a striped prison suit—a "mighty con"—having a feast; he is eating loads of FOOD. After forking down each chunk of food, he takes a deep breath of OXYGEN then quickly forks down another chunk. It is obvious that the mighty con is eating very ENERGETICALLY.

GOLGI BODY—structures in the cell body that SECRETE substances, such as insulin. This one is easy. GOLGI sounds like "goalie." Picture a goalie SECRETING hockey pucks.

That is the system. Just get the wheels of imagination turning, and you will quickly learn to speak the language of any field.

HOW TO REMEMBER NUMERICAL INFORMATION

You park your car in section 9D of a gigantic parking lot. Because there are so many sections, each designated by a different number and letter, you decide to write down the location of your car. You reach into your pocket for a pen, but the pocket is empty. "Well," you think, "no matter. I can remember 9D." And sure enough, you do remember it—all the way to the store. Then an advertising display catches your eye, and your attention shifts from the parking lot to the big sale going on in the store. As you leave the store, weighted down with packages, your stomach sinks. Were you parked in section 6C? 3B? 19D?

HOW TO IMPROVE YOUR MEMORY: A SHORT COURSE

If you have not yet had such an experience, you may be due for one. But why tempt fate? You can ensure recall of the number and the letter by creating a mental picture that relates the two. Earlier, we examined two strategies for translating numbers to words, the number-consonant system and the pegword system. You can also translate letters to words with a little preparation. Make a list of all the letters of the alphabet and next to each letter write a word that sounds as much like that letter as possible. For example,

A = Ape
B = Bee
C = Sea
D = Deed
E = Eel
F = Effort
G = Jeep, etc.

These will be your symbols for letters. Try to use them only in pictures intended to represent letters so that you will know instantly how to decode the images.

To visualize 9D, the hypothetical section where you parked earlier, you could make use of the pegword system and represent 9 with LINE. The word we used to symbolize D was DEED, so picture a bunch of deeds waiting in line somewhere. A good place would be at the door of the store. When you leave the store, the door would bring to mind that ridiculous picture of the deeds waiting in line, and you will think, "Oh, I'm parked in section 9D."

Many other kinds of numerical codes incorporate letters and can be memorized in the same way as the parking lot location. License plates are a common example. By applying the number-consonant system, you could translate the license plate 820 G71 to the following words:

8 2 0   G   7   1
FiN S   Jeep D o G

These three words could be remembered by constructing two pictures, the first incorporating FINS and JEEP and the second incorporating JEEP and DOG. The first picture might show a JEEP with FINS swimming under water like a fish. The second picture might show a DOG behind the wheel of the JEEP. If you concentrate on the pictures and think about their order, the first picture should bring to mind the second.

Birthdays, anniversaries, historical dates—all can be remembered reliably by the strategy of converting numbers to words. For birthdays and anniversaries, the information one usually wants to retain is the month and day of the event. You can make use of the fact that every month already has a number. Just follow the rule that the first one or two digits of a sequence will always stand for the month. After the month will come the day, and it will always be represented by two digits (01 to

31). Thus, January 15 translates to 115, April 30 to 430, Novemeber 6 to 1106, and May 1 to 501. Do not forget to add the 0 when the day is a single digit. Without the 0, you would be unable to tell whether 116 was January 16 (1/16) or November 6 (11/6). You can picture January 15 (115) as a DooDLe. April 30 (430) is a herd of RaMS, November 6 (1106) is a DeaD SaSH, and May 1 (501) is LuST. Associate these code words with the person's name and you will know the birthday or anniversary forever.

When was the first psychological laboratory founded? Every psychology major should know: the year is 1879. To make sure that you remember that date, just translate 1879 to DoVeCooP—imagine a screened enclosure with lots of doves inside. What object does the term "psychology laboratory" bring to mind? Perhaps you think of a laboratory device, such as a "memory drum." Okay, imagine that the doves are walking on top of the memory drums for exercise.

Whatever it is you wish to remember, there is a strategy to suit your purpose. This is National Memory Training Week, so give the systems a try. You may find that they are the most valuable of all the principles of learning.

Glossary

ABA experimental design A procedure for studying the effect of an experimental variable on the behavior of an individual subject. In the simplest version of the procedure, the subject initially performs in the absence of the variable (condition A), then in its presence (condition B), and again in its absence (condition A). If the behavior change brought about by condition B is at least partially eliminated upon return to condition A, there is evidence that the experimental variable had a reliable effect.

Abulia Inability to perform a task due to a lack of "willpower."

Accentuation A technique for teaching word recognition in which the letters of a word are integrated with a picture of the word's referent.

Accommodation In Piaget's theory, the process by which a person changes a concept to take into account a fact that is inconsistent with the concept. (cf. **assimilation**)

Action rule A rule for constructing mental images to assist memory for pairs of words. The rule states that the representations of words in a mental picture should display movement so that they will attract maximal attention.

Anaclitic identification In Freudian theory, the process by which a young girl internalizes the personality characteristics of her mother. Once dependent upon the mother for affection, the child is said eventually to reject the mother's love. To maintain a sense of closeness, the child comes to act and think like the mother, thereby simulating the mother's presence. In behavior theory, a counterpart to anaclitic identification is the view that organisms tend to imitate those actions of a model that have been associated with reinforcement. (cf. **defensive identification**)

Anthropomorphism The attribution of human traits to lower animals.

Articulation The production of sound through manipulation of the speech organs. (See also, **vocal tract.**)

Assimilation In Piaget's theory, the tendency of a person to interpret a newly discovered fact within the context of a preexisting concept (cf. **accommodation**)

Associative inhibition In Guthrie's theory of learning, the elimination of one response upon acquisition of another response.

392

Attribute In the logical analysis of concepts, an attribute is any property of a stimulus. Every concept is defined by one or more attributes and by a logical rule. The rule specifies those attributes which a stimulus must possess, and/or those attributes which the stimulus must lack, to qualify as an instance of the concept.

Aversion therapy A form of classical conditioning designed to help people control activities considered harmful to them (for example, alcohol and cigarette consumption). Treatment involves the repeated pairing of a stimulus to which an individual is attracted with an aversive stimulus such as pain or nausea. The resulting association causes the person to reduce contact with the once attractive, but now aversive, stimulus.

Aversive stimulus See **negative reinforcer.**

Avoidance behavior Any action an organism must perform to prevent the occurrence of an aversive stimulus at some future time.

Backward conditioning A type of classical conditioning in which the onset of the unconditioned stimulus precedes, rather than follows, the onset of the conditioned stimulus.

Behavioral contrast A change in the rate of responding under one schedule of reinforcement as the rate of responding changes in the opposite direction under another schedule. A common form of contrast occurs when an organism is trained to discriminate between a stimulus associated with reinforcement and a stimulus associated with extinction. As response rate decreases during the extinction stimulus, response rate increases during the reinforcement stimulus.

Biofeedback A form of operant conditioning designed to increase an individual's control over bodily functions usually considered to be "involuntary." Ordinarily, slight changes in the activity of a gland, organ, or muscle are imperceptible. In biofeedback training, an instrument monitors the activity and delivers a signal whenever the individual succeeds in producing a change in the desired direction. This feedback reinforces the individual's efforts and makes further changes possible. Biofeedback training has proven useful as a treatment for a variety of ailments, including tension headaches, migraine headaches, and stress.

Branching program A plan of instruction in which the learner's performance partly determines the nature of the materials presented. (cf. **linear program**)

Chained schedules A plan for reinforcing operant behavior under which an organism obtains reinforcement only after satisfying the requirements of two or more reinforcement schedules in succession. A different stimulus accompanies each schedule, with a change in stimuli signaling passage from one component of the chain to the next. (cf. **multiple schedule**)

Classical conditioning A form of training, introduced by Pavlov, that has the effect of endowing a stimulus with the power to evoke a response on virtually every occasion that the stimulus occurs. This effect is ordinarily accomplished by repeatedly presenting the stimulus just prior to another stimulus that already elicits the response as an innate reflex. (same as **Pavlovian conditioning**)

Cognitive conflict An experience assumed to accompany the process of accommodation in intellectual development. Sufficiently intense conflict between a concept and a discrepant fact is said to induce appropriate changes in the concept.

Concrete operational phase In Piaget's theory, a phase of intellectual development, said to occur roughly between the ages of seven and 11 years, in which a child can perform certain logical operations on physical stimuli but not necessarily on abstract concepts.

Conditioned reinforcer A stimulus that has become a reinforcer through a conditioning procedure; commonly, the repeated pairing of the stimulus with one that is already a reinforcer.

Conditioned response (CR) In classical conditioning, the response to a conditioned stimulus (CS); a response arising from associative learning rather than from an innate connection, or a heightened sensitivity to stimuli in general.

Conditioned stimulus (CS) In classical conditioning, a stimulus that acquires the power to elicit a response through the formation of an association between that stimulus and one that already elicits the response.

Conjunction A logical rule that states that a stimulus must possess two or more specified attributes to qualify as an instance of a given concept.

Conservation In Piaget's theory, the recognition that a physical quantity can remain constant despite changes in its appearance. More generally, the recognition that a stimulus continues to be an instance of a concept despite the addition or deletion of irrelevant attributes.

Conservative focusing In concept formation problems, a strategy for determining the relevance of certain attributes to the definition of a concept. The main characteristic of conservative focusing is that the individual seeks information that bears on the relevance of just one attribute at a time. (cf. **focus gambling**)

Consolidation A hypothetical process said to be responsible for making the storage of information in memory permanent. Exposure to information is assumed to establish a neural trace that initially is in a fragile state and subject to destruction by traumatic events. With the passage of time, the neural trace becomes increasingly resistant to destruction (i.e., undergoes consolidation), and eventually the trace resists destruction entirely.

Continuous reinforcement schedule (CRF) A plan for reinforcing operant behavior under which every response produces reinforcement.

Counterconditioning A strategy for eliminating an undesired response by substituting for it an incompatible response. A well-known application of counterconditioning is the "systematic desensitization" treatment for phobias, in which individuals learn to respond to threatening situations with "relaxation" instead of fear.

Cumulative record In research on operant conditioning, a graph showing the total number of responses a subject has made since the start of a session as a function of time. The slope of the line on a cumulative record represents the subject's rate of responding. For example, a high response rate would contribute many responses to the total number within a given unit of time, resulting in a line with a steep slope across that interval. (See also, **cumulative recorder**)

Cumulative recorder In research on operant conditioning, an instrument that plots a subject's cumulative responses as a function of time while the session is in progress. A revolving drum on the cumulative recorder moves paper horizontally (right to left) at a constant speed. Each response causes a pen to move one small step vertically across the paper, producing a diagonal line whose slope represents the subject's rate of responding. (See also, **cumulative record**)

Deep structure In linguistic theory, the set of interrelated propositions implied by a sentence and sensed intuitively by a listener; the underlying meaning of a sentence, as opposed to the particular words and phrases a speaker uses to express that meaning. (cf. **surface structure**)

Defensive identification In Freudian theory, the process by which a young boy internalizes the personality characteristics of his father. Fearing retribution from the father for harboring a sexual wish to possess the mother, the child strives to become as much like the father as possible. By assuming the father's identity the child gains a sense of security because, from the child's perspective, the father would never deliberately harm "himself." (cf. **anaclitic identification**)

Delayed conditioning A type of classical conditioning in which the conditioned stimulus begins before the unconditioned stimulus and continues until the unconditioned stimulus is terminated.

Determinism The philosophy that human actions are caused by natural events. An opposing philosophy is that human actions occur spontaneously, the product of a "will" free of environmental or biological constraints.

Discrimination In classical conditioning, the tendency of an organism to respond to a conditioned stimulus which has been paired with an unconditioned stimulus, and to refrain from responding to other stimuli which have not been paired with the unconditioned stimulus. In operant conditioning, a difference between an organism's rates or patterns of responding in the presence of different stimuli.

Discriminative stimulus In operant conditioning, a stimulus that evokes a response because of the possibility that the response will produce reinforcement in the presence of that stimulus.

Disinhibition In classical conditioning, the reappearance of a conditioned response after it has undergone extinction, due to the sudden introduction of a novel stimulus. (cf. **external inhibition**)

Disjunction A logical rule stating that a stimulus must possess at least one, but not necessarily all, of the attributes in a set to qualify as an instance of a particular concept.

Doctrine of Formal Discipline A centuries-old philosophy which holds that transfer of learning from one task to another depends on the amount of mental work required by the original task rather than on the specific facts or skills the task provides. In education, the Doctrine of Formal Discipline has long served as a rationale for the practice of teaching certain courses with little apparent relevance to everyday life. (cf. **theory of identical elements**)

Dominance level The probability that a subject will make a particular verbal response to a particular verbal stimulus in a free-association test.

Dyslexia A condition in which an individual of normal intelligence experiences unusual difficulty in acquiring reading skills.

Encoding An operation performed on incoming information that causes the information to be remembered in a particular form, for example, the encoding of written (visual) information in an auditory form.

Episodic memory Memory for events with a clear beginning and end. (cf. **semantic memory**)

Equilibrium In Piaget's theory, a condition in which one's conceptualization of a phenomenon requires relatively minor changes, if any at all, as new facts about the phenomenon are encountered. More technically, a state of equilibrium represents a balance between the tendencies toward assimilation and accommodation.

Escape behavior Behavior maintained by negative reinforcement.

Exaggeration rule A rule for constructing mental images to aid memory for pairs of words. The rules states that the two words represented in a mental picture should appear many times so that they will attract maximal attention.

External inhibition In classical conditioning, the disappearance of a conditioned response during training due to the sudden introduction of a novel stimulus. (cf. **disinhibition**)

Extinction In classical conditioning, the procedure of eliminating a conditioned response by repeatedly presenting the conditioned stimulus without the unconditioned stimulus. In operant conditioning, the procedure of eliminating a response by permitting the response to occur without reinforcement. In both types of conditioning, the term "extinction" also refers to the decline in responding produced by the respective extinction procedures.

Fixed action pattern An inborn sequence of movements having the same form, and elicited by the same stimulus, in all members of a species or subgroup of a species (e.g., all males or all females).

Fixed interval schedule (FI) A plan for reinforcing operant behavior under which reinforcement is administered for the first response that occurs after a specified interval has elapsed (usually timed from the last reinforcement), the interval remaining constant throughout the experimental session. Responses that occur before expiration of the interval do not produce reinforcement.

Fixed ratio schedule (FR) A plan for reinforcing operant behavior under which reinforcement is administered upon completion of a specified number of responses, the number remaining constant throughout the experimental session.

Focus gambling In certain concept formation problems, a strategy for determining which attributes of a stimulus are relevant to the definition of a concept. A person who employs a focus gambling concept seeks information that bears on the relevance of two or more attributes at a time. The logic of the situation creates a risk that the information obtained may not permit a deduction concerning any of the attributes, whereas information designed to bear on just one attribute would necessarily allow for such a deduction. The individual thus "gambles" that seeking information on more than one attribute is the more efficient course of action. (cf. **conservative focusing**)

Formal operational phase In Piaget's theory, a phase of intellectual development, beginning at roughly 11 years of age and continuing into adulthood, in which a person can perform logical operations on abstract concepts that are not represented as physical entities. (cf. **concrete operational phase**)

Formant A dark band on the spectrogram of a speech sound representing a set of frequencies emitted with an especially high intensity. These frequencies contribute more to the physical pattern characterizing the sound than do frequencies not comprising the formant.

Frame The basic unit of information in programmed instruction, usually consisting of a few sentences followed by a question to test comprehension of this material.

Frequency principle In behavior theory, a principle stating that the more often a stimulus has evoked a response in the past, the more likely it is to evoke that response in the future, other factors being equal.

Functional autonomy The theory that an activity which has repeatedly served as a means to an end may eventually become an end in itself, i.e., the individual may engage in that activity even though it is no longer necessary for achieving the original goal.

Generalization In classical conditioning, the tendency of stimuli that are similar to the conditioned stimulus (but have not been paired with the unconditioned stimulus) to elicit the conditioned response, the strength of the response increasing with the degree of similarity. In operant conditioning, the tendency of stimuli that resemble the discriminative stimulus for a response to evoke that response, even though the response has never produced reinforcement in the presence of those stimuli. The strength of the response increases as the degree of similarity to the discriminative stimulus increases.

Generalized imitation The tendency of an organism to imitate a broad range of a model's activity as a result of having received reinforcement for imitating many other actions of the model.

Generative rule A hypothetical rule said to enable a person to produce sentences of a particular grammatical type even though the person has not previously heard or uttered those sentences.

Gestalt psychology A school which holds that psychological research should focus not on the individual elements that make up an experience or action, but on the relationships prevailing among those elements. The term "gestalt" refers to the pattern, or configuration, created by such relationships.

Grammatical transformation In linguistic theory, the process of creating a phrase or sentence from an unverbalized thought; more technically, the process of constructing the surface structure of a sentence from the set of interrelated propositions that constitute the deep structure.

Habituation A reduction in responsiveness to a stimulus produced by repeated presentations of the stimulus, or by continuous presentation for a prolonged period.

Hypermnesia Recall of an experience in unusually fine detail. (See also, **retroactive hypermnesia**)

Identification Acquisition of behavior patterns characteristic of another individual's personality. Although the learning takes place through observation of a model, some psychologists distinguish between the processes of identification and imitation. Two major reasons are that: (1) Identification is said to result in the acquisition of a broader range of the model's behavior than imitation; (2) Behavior acquired through identification may occur in the absence of the model, while behavior acquired through imitation is said to occur only in the presence of the model.

Imagery mediation Use of a mental picture to facilitate associative learning. Imagery mediation takes two forms: (1) The mediator depicts a relationship between the two items to be remembered; (2) The mediator occurs as a response to one item and tends to elicit the other item due to preexisting associations. In this role, the mediator does not express a relationship between the items, but rather functions as a link in a chain of stimuli and responses.

Incentive The motivational state created by a goal object.

Incidental learning Acquisition of behavior through observation of a model in the absence of any instructions or inducements to reproduce the behavior.

Information processing The prevailing framework for development of cognitive theories of learning. The information processing approach draws upon computer technology for many of its basic concepts and terms, the assumption being that cognitive processes resemble the processes by which computers receive, organize, store, and retrieve information.

Insight Discovery of a relationship among various elements of a problem. This discovery typically occurs suddenly after a period of close examination of the elements and results in immediate attainment of the solution.

Instinct An innate behavior pattern exhibited by all members of species or subgroup of a species (e.g., all males or all females). (cf. **reflex, tropism**)

Instinctive drift In operant conditioning with lower animals, the emergence of instinctive behavior that interferes with performance of the conditioned behavior, the severity of this conflict increasing as training progresses.

Instrumental conditioning The procedure of increasing the strength of a response by waiting until the response occurs and then presenting a reinforcer. The term "instrumental" derives from the fact that the response is instrumental, or necessary, for producing the reinforcer. (Alternate term: "operant conditioning")

Internal inhibition In classical conditioning, a process thought by Pavlov to be responsible for suppressing a conditioned response during extinction.

Introspection Examination of one's own thoughts, feelings, or sensations. During the late 19th and early 20th centuries, a refined version of introspection was used by psychologists of the "structuralist" school to study the contents of conscious experience.

Isolation In serial anticipation learning, a technique for facilitating acquisition of an item in the middle of a list by making it appear different from the other items in the list. (See also, **von Restorff effect**)

Korsakoff's syndrome A memory disorder in which an individual has great difficulty remembering information to which he or she has just been exposed, but has normal recall of information acquired before onset of the disease.

Larynx The "voice box"; the structure containing the vocal cords, located at the upper end of the windpipe.

Latent learning Learning not exhibited in behavior due to a lack of motivation.

Linear program A plan of instruction in which all of the learners receive identical information irrespective of their performance. (cf. **branching program**)

Live modeling Acquisition of a new form of behavior through observation of a model who is physically present rather than depicted in a film. (cf. **symbolic modeling**)

Matched-dependent behavior A form of imitation in which the behavior of the imitator is evoked by (is dependent on), and closely resembles (matches), the behavior of the model.

Mediation The formation of an indirect connection between an external stimulus and an external response through the action of an internal, intermediary event. This event is conceptualized as a response to the external stimulus, and as incorporating a stimulus component capable of developing an association with the external response. (See also, **imagery mediation** and **verbal mediation**)

Mental age A measure of intellectual development that compares an individual's performance on a battery of mental tests with that of individuals who have achieved similar scores. "Mental age" refers to the chronological age of this reference group. Thus, a 5-year-old child with a mental age of 10 years has attained a score comparable to that of the typical 10-year-old.

Method of loci A memory aid that relies on knowledge of locations ("loci") in an area to assist recall of items in a fixed sequence. Each location is assigned a serial position based on the order in which the locations would be encountered on a walk through the area. The items to be remembered are then associated with the locations in the corresponding serial positions by means of visual imagery: Mental pictures are created that depict the items and locations in some kind of relationship. At the time of recall, one imagines walking past the various locations, and as a given location is visualized it brings to mind the associated item. The method of loci is especially useful when each item has been associated with additional information, such as material from a speech.

Mnemonic device An aid to memory.

Modeling Acquisition of a new form of behavior after seeing that behavior performed by another person.

Morpheme A unit of meaning that cannot be divided into smaller units.

Multiple schedule A plan for reinforcing operant behavior by which reinforcement is administered according to two or more reinforcement schedules correlated with different stimuli and operating at different times. (cf. **chained schedules**)

Negation A logical rule stating that a stimulus must lack a specified attribute to qualify as an instance of a particular concept.

Negative reinforcer A stimulus which, if terminated after a response occurs, will tend to evoke that response in the future. (Same as **aversive stimulus**)

Negative transfer A phenomenon in which the information or skill acquired in one task slows the rate of learning in another task.

Nominal fallacy The presumption that a label descriptive of a response constitutes an explanation of that response (for example, the notion that "lazy" behavior arises from a trait of "laziness").

Nonreversal shift See **reversal shift**.

Nonsense syllable In research on verbal learning, a sequence of letters that does not form a word but that the subject attempts to learn as a complete verbal unit.

Operant The unit of analysis in research on operant conditioning. Those actions of an organism having a common effect on the environment are treated in an identical manner for purposes of administering reinforcement and recording response frequency. The term "operant" refers to this class of actions. Thus, reinforcement may be administered and a response may be recorded every time that a rat presses a lever, whether the rat presses with the left paw, the right paw, or with both paws.

Operant level In operant conditioning, an organism's rate of responding before introduction of reinforcement.

Operational definition Definition of a concept in terms of a procedure that will enable one to study the concept scientifically. For example, the meaningfulness of a verbal item is often operationally defined as the number of words the item evokes on a free-association basis during a specified period.

Out-of-proportion rule A rule for constructing visual images to aid memory for pairs of words. The rule states that the representations of words in a mental picture should be unusually large so that they will attract maximal attention.

Paired-associate procedure A procedure for studying the formation of associations between verbal or pictorial items presented in pairs. In one version of the procedure, the "study-test" method, subjects inspect the complete pairs during a study trial, and then, during a test trial, the subjects attempt to give the second item of each pair when the first item is presented. In the other version of the procedure, the "anticipation" method, each pair is presented in two phases. Subjects initially view the first item of a pair and attempt to give the second item. Both items then appear for a short period, after which the first item of the next pair is presented.

Partial reinforcement effect A phenomenon in which subjects who have received reinforcement for 100 percent of responses during training are found to make fewer responses in extinction than subjects who have received reinforcement for less than 100 percent of responses during training.

Pattern playback An instrument capable of producing a speech sound from an artificially created spectrogram. The sound has the same perceptual qualities as the one that would have produced the spectrogram naturally.

Pavlovian conditioning See **classical conditioning.**

Perceptual learning An increase in sensitivity to the features that distinguish one stimulus from another as a result of frequent or extended exposure to the stimuli.

Phone A speech sound.

Phoneme A class of speech sounds that has two major characteristics: (1) Differences among the sounds are not ordinarily perceived in normal conversation (for example, the voiceless "r" in "tree" versus the voiced "r" in "red"); (2) The sounds belonging to one phoneme category are readily distinguished from those belonging to any other category (for example, the "r" in "red" is readily distinguished from the "b" in "bed" and the "w" in "wed.")

Phonics A method for teaching word recognition in which the student learns to associate every letter of the alphabet and certain groups of letters with one or more sounds. The student identifies a word by pronouncing its constituent sounds in a serial fashion, i.e., by "sounding the word out."

Phrase In linguistic analysis, a sequence of words that are arranged according to a grammatical rule and function as a unit within a sentence.

Pivot grammar An early conceptualization of grammatical relationships in the speech of very young children. A child was said to form two- or three-word phrases by joining words from two distinct categories in a fixed order. The categories differed in size, with words from the smaller category ("pivot" words) typically coming first in the sequence. (See also, **pivot word, X-class**)

Pivot word In the pivot grammar of young children, a word drawn from the smaller of two hypothetical categories that the child was said typically to utter first in two-word sequences and to combine with any one of a large number of words from the other category. (See also, **pivot grammar, X-class**)

Positive reinforcer A stimulus which, when presented after a response occurs, increases the future probability of the response.

Positive transfer A phenomenon in which the information or skill acquired from one task accelerates the rate of learning in another task.

Postulate In some psychological theories, a general statement about behavior which, though too abstract to be tested directly, permits the derivation of statements that are sufficiently precise to be tested. (cf. **theorem**)

Preoperational phase In Piaget's theory, a period of intellectual development, occurring roughly between the ages of two and seven years, in which the child solves problems in a primitive intuitive fashion rather than through application of logical skills. A major deficiency of this stage is failure to solve problems in conservation.

Primacy effect The tendency to recall more words from the beginning of a list than from the middle when the order of recall is unconstrained.

Primary memory William James's conceptualization of short-term memory expressed in terms of subjective experience. Primary memory was said to hold information to which the individual was recently exposed. The information was experienced as part of the psychological present and could be retrieved with little effort. (cf. **secondary memory**)

Primary reinforcer A stimulus whose power to reinforce behavior is innate. In practice, this means that one need not perform a training procedure to make the stimulus reinforcing.

Primary stimulus generalization Generalization from one stimulus to another on the basis of physical similarity. (cf. **secondary stimulus generalization**)

Proactive facilitation (PF) A phenomenon in which information acquired at one point in time enhances retention of information acquired at a later time.

Proactive inhibition (PI) A phenomenon in which information acquired at one point in time decreases retention of information acquired at a later time.

Pseudoconditioning In classical conditioning, a phenomenon in which a stimulus not previously paired with the unconditioned stimulus elicits the unconditioned response due to a heightened sensitivity to stimuli in general.

Punishment A procedure in which presentation or termination of a stimulus after a response occurs results in a decrease in the future probability of the response. (See also, **time-out**)

Recall test A test of memory in which a subject must partially or totally reproduce an item of information rather than identify it among a group of alternatives. (cf. **recognition test**)

Recency effect The tendency to recall more words from the end of a list than from the middle when the order of recall is unconstrained.

Recency principle In behavior theory, a principle stating that the response last evoked by a stimulus is the one most likely to be evoked by the stimulus on its next presentation, other factors being equal.

Reception procedure In studies of concept formation, a procedure in which the researcher rather than the subject arranges the sequence of stimuli from which the subject is to deduce a concept. (cf. **selection procedure**)

Recognition test A test of memory in which a subject must identify an item of information to which he or she has been exposed when presented with that item and a set of alternatives. (cf. **recall test**)

Reflex A relatively simple, involuntary response to a stimulus. Operationally, "involuntary" means that the stimulus evokes the response with an extremely high probability. This effect of the stimulus may either be innate ("unconditioned reflex") or learned ("conditioned reflex").

Reinforcement In classical conditioning, the procedure of establishing or maintaining a conditioned response by presenting an unconditioned stimulus at a specified interval before or after the conditioned stimulus. In operant conditioning, the procedure of increasing the probability of a response by presenting a reinforcer at a specified interval after the response occurs.

Reinforcer In classical conditioning, the unconditioned stimulus used to establish or maintain the response to the conditioned stimulus. In operant conditioning, a stimulus which, when presented or removed after a response occurs, increases the future probability of the response.

Releaser The stimulus that elicits a fixed action pattern.

Remote association In serial verbal learning, a type of association thought by Ebbinghaus and subsequent investigators to develop between nonadjacent items in the list during practice.

Repression In Freudian theory, a process said to block recall of painful or anxiety-provoking experiences.

Respondent Skinner's term for a reflexive response, one controlled by an antecedent stimulus rather than by its consequences.

Retroactive facilitation (RF) A phenomenon in which information acquired at one point enhances retention of information acquired at an earlier time.

Retroactive hypermnesia Unusually vivid recall of events preceding a traumatic experience, the period of heightened recall extending backward from the trauma by as much as 24 hours.

Retroactive inhibition (RI) A phenomenon in which information acquired at one point in time decreases retention of information acquired at an earlier time.

Retrograde amnesia Inability to recall a traumatic experience, with recall of prior events increasing as a function of their temporal distance from the trauma.

Reversal shift A type of discrimination learning task widely used to study concept formation in lower animals, children, and adults. It consists of two phases and is designed to be used jointly with another type of discrimination task, a "nonreversal shift." In the first phase of the procedure, subjects receive reinforcement for selecting that stimulus of a pair which exhibits a particular value on a dimension (e.g., the smaller of two stimuli). The stimuli also differ on a second dimension that is not correlated with reinforcement (e.g., the dimension of brightness). In the second phase of the reversal shift, the dimension originally correlated with reinforcement remains so, but subjects receive reinforcement for selecting the stimulus with the opposite value on that dimension (e.g., the taller of the two stimuli). In the second phase of the nonreversal shift, the dimension originally correlated with reinforcement becomes uncorrelated and subjects receive reinforcement for selecting the stimulus with a particular value on the other dimension (e.g., the darker of the two stimuli). Of primary interest are the rates of learning in the second phases of the reversal and nonreversal shifts. A comparison of these rates is said to reveal the extent to which subjects formed a true concept of the solution to the discrimination problems.

Reversibility The capacity of operant behavior to change as a function of the conditions of reinforcement; in particular, its capacity to return to a particular state after the conditions associated with a different state have been removed and the original conditions have been reinstituted.

Savings score A measure of retention that compares the amount of practice required to learn a task with the amount of practice required to relearn the task after a delay. Greater reductions in practice reflect higher degrees of retention. The savings score, expressed as a percentage of original learning, is calculated as follows:

$$\frac{(\text{Number of trials to learn}) - (\text{number of trials to relearn})}{(\text{Number of trials to learn})} \times 100$$

Scanning In certain formation problems, a type of strategy in which the subject formulates an hypothesis about which attributes of a stimulus are relevant to the definition of a concept. Information is sought that is consistent with the hypothesis until contrary evidence is discovered, at which point the hypothesis is changed. In "successive scanning," the subject entertains one hypothesis at a time. In "simultaneous scanning," the subject considers two or more hypotheses at the same time.

Schedule of reinforcement In research on operant conditioning, a rule stating the conditions under which a response will be reinforced.

Secondary memory William James's conceptualization of long-term memory in terms of subjective experience. Recalling an event was said to entail an active search process, and the event, once retrieved, created the impression of having occurred in the past rather than in the present moment. (cf. **primary memory**)

Secondary stimulus generalization Generalization from one stimulus to another on the basis of learned rather than physical similarity. (cf. **primary stimulus generalization**)

Selection procedure In research on concept formation, a type of procedure in which the subject rather than the researcher arranges the sequence of stimuli from which the concept is to be inferred. (cf. **reception procedure**)

Selective attention Responsiveness to a particular subset of the stimuli impinging on the sense receptors at a given time.

Semantic conditioning A form of classical conditioning in which the conditioned stimulus and/or the unconditioned stimulus is a word, phrase, or sentence.

Semantic memory Memory for words and verbal information. (cf. **episodic memory**)

Sensorimotor phase In Piaget's theory, a phase of intellectual development, starting at birth and continuing until the child is approximately two years of age, that is characterized by increasing coordination of sensory and motor capacities with relatively little mental activity.

Serial anticipation procedure A procedure for studying the acquisition of verbal or pictorial items in a fixed sequence. Each item appears for a specified period during which the subject attempts to state the next item in the sequence. Presentation of that item serves as feedback on the subject's response and as a signal to state the next item in the list.

Serial position curve In the analysis of serial anticipation learning, a function that depicts the number of errors a subject has made during practice at each serial position in the list. Typically, the number of errors increases to a maximum at or just past the middle of the list and then decreases.

Set One's orientation or approach to a learning task.

Shaping In operant conditioning, a procedure for establishing new forms of behavior by reinforcing successive approximations to the behavior.

Sight-word method A method for teaching word recognition in which one learns to identify words by their visual patterns. (cf. **phonics**)

Simultaneous conditioning A type of classical conditioning in which the conditioned stimulus begins at precisely the same time as the unconditioned stimulus.

Simultaneous scanning See **scanning**.

Solution shift See **reversal shift**.

Sound spectrograph The laboratory instrument used to make spectrograms of speech sounds.

Span of immediate memory The maximum number of items of information to which one can attend at any given moment. The memory span is often measured by determining how many letters or digits a person can repeat in the original order immediately after the items have been presented. The limit of the memory span is generally seven items, plus or minus two.

Spectrogram A type of graph that depicts the frequency and intensity characteristics of speech sounds. The vertical axis of the graph represents the range of possible frequencies and the horizontal axis represents time. Those frequencies that have contributed to a sound over a period of time are indicated by horizontal lines running across the graph at heights corresponding to the positions of the frequencies on the vertical axis. The darkness of the lines reflects the intensities with which the frequencies were emitted.

Spontaneous recovery In classical and operant conditioning, the tendency of a response that has undergone extinction to reappear at a fraction of its original strength after a period in which there has been no opportunity to make the response.

Stop A speech sound produced by blocking and then releasing the flow of air through the vocal tract (e.g., the sounds of p, t, and d).

Substitution A technique for constructing mental images to assist memory for pairs of words. A mental picture is invented in which one of the words is represented as performing a function normally associated with the other word. For example, with the words "tree-table," the tree could be represented as a long banquet table with diners seated on either side of it.

Successive scanning See **scanning**.

Superstition Behavior maintained by adventitious reinforcement, i.e., reinforcement that occurs by coincidence rather than as a consequence of the response.

Surface structure The grammatical relationships prevailing among the words in a sentence. (cf. **deep structure**)

Symbolic modeling Acquisition of a new form of behavior through observation of a model on film or tape. (cf. **live modeling**)

Temporal conditioning A type of classical conditioning in which the uncon-

406

ditioned stimulus is presented at prearranged intervals without a conditioned stimulus.

Temporal contiguity principle In behavior theory, the principle that two events that occur at approximately the same time will tend to become associated.

Theorem In some psychological theories, a formal statement about behavior that has been deduced from a broader principle and is expressed in sufficiently precise terms to be tested empirically. (cf. **postulate**)

Theory of identical elements A theory developed by Thorndike to explain transfer of learning from one task to another. The theory states that the degree of transfer depends on the number of "elements" that the original task has in common with the transfer task, i.e., on the similarity between the tasks. (cf. **doctrine of formal discipline**)

Time-out A form of punishment in which stimuli associated with reinforcement are removed after an undesired response occurs.

Trace conditioning A type of classical conditioning in which the conditioned stimulus is presented and terminated before onset of the unconditioned stimulus.

Transfer A phenomenon in which the information or skill acquired in one task increases or decreases the rate of learning in another task.

Transposition Generalization of a relationship from one pair of stimuli to another pair.

Tropism An innate tendency to orient toward or away from a stimulus.

Unconditioned response (UCR) An inborn, reflexive response to a stimulus.

Unconditioned stimulus (UCS) A stimulus that elicits a reflexive response innately. (See also, **reinforcer**)

Unvoiced sound A speech sound produced without vocal cord vibration (e.g., the sounds of sh and ch).

Variable interval schedule (VI) A plan for reinforcing operant behavior under which reinforcement is administered for the first response that occurs after a prearranged interval has elapsed since the last reinforcement, the duration of the interval varying randomly from one reinforcement to the next. Responses that occur before expiration of an interval do not produce reinforcement.

Variable ratio schedule (VR) A plan for reinforcing operant behavior under which reinforcement is administered after the organism makes a prearranged number of responses, the number varying randomly from one reinforcement to the next.

Verbal mediation Use of a word, phrase, or sentence to facilitate associative learning. Verbal mediation takes two forms: (1) The mediator states a relationship between the two items to be remembered; (2) The mediator occurs as a response to one item and tends to elicit the other item due to preexisting associations. In this role, the mediator does not express a relationship between the items, but rather functions as a link in a chain of stimuli and responses.

Vicarious experience An experience initiated by and resembling an experience displayed by another person.

Vocal tract A region encompassing the throat, mouth, and nasal passages that is responsible for the production of speech sounds.

Voiced sound A speech sound produced with vocal cord vibration (e.g., the sounds of *i* and *n*).

Von Restorff effect In serial anticipation learning, the tendency of a subject to acquire an item in the middle of a list faster if the item has a distinctive appearance than if it closely resembles the other items.

X-class In the pivot grammar of young children, the larger of two hypothetical classes of words from which the child was said to select one of the words in a two-word utterance. Typically, the X-word was uttered second in the sequence. (See also, **pivot grammar, pivot word**)

Bibliography

Ainslie, G. W. Specious reward: A behavioral theory of impulse and control. *Psychological Bulletin*, 1975, **82,** 463-496.

Allport, G. W. *Personality: A psychological interpretation*. New York: Holt, 1937.

Amsel, A. The role of frustrative nonreward in continuous reward situations. *Psychological Bulletin*, 1958, **55,** 102-119.

Amsel, A. Partial reinforcement effects on vigor and persistence. In K. W. Spence and J. T. Spence (Eds.) *The psychology of learning and motivation*. (Vol. 1) New York: Academic Press, 1967.

Archer, E. J. Re-evaluation of the meaningfulness of all possible CVC trigrams. *Psychological Monographs*, 1960, **74,** Whole No. 497.

Asch, S. Reformulation of the problem of associations. *American Psychologist*, 1969, **24,** 92-102.

Atkinson, R. C., and Raugh, M. R. An application of the mnemonic keyword method to the acquisition of a Russian vocabulary. *Journal of Experimental Psychology: Human Learning and Memory*, 1975, **104,** 126-133.

Atkinson, R. C., and Shiffrin, R. M. Human memory: A proposed system and its control processes. In K. W. Spence and J. T. Spence (Eds.) *The psychology of learning and motivation*. (Vol. 2) New York: Academic Press, 1968.

Ausubel, D. P., Stager, M., and Gaite, A. J. H. Retroactive facilitation in meaningful verbal learning. *Journal of Educational Psychology*, 1968, **59,** 250-255.

Ausubel, D. P., Stager, M., and Gaite, A. J. H. Proactive effects in meaningful verbal learning. *Journal of Educational Psychology*, 1969, **60,** 59-64.

Averbach, E., and Corriell, A. S. Short-term memory in vision. *Bell System Technical Journal*, 1961, **40,** 309-328.

Ayllon, T., and Azrin, N. *The token economy: A motivational system for therapy and rehabilitation*. New York: Appleton-Century-Crofts, 1966.

Azrin, N. H., and Holz, W. C. Punishment. In W. K. Honio (Ed.) *Operant behavior: Areas of research and application*. New York: Appleton-Century-Crofts, 1966.

Azrin, N. H., Rubin, H., O'Brien, F., Ayllon, T., and Roll, D. Behavioral engineering: Postural control by a portable operant apparatus. *Journal of Applied Behavior Analysis*, 1968, **1,** 99-108.

Babkin, B. P. *Pavlov*. Chicago: University of Chicago Press, 1949.

Baddeley, A. D. The influence of acoustic and semantic similarity on long-term memory for word sequences. *Quarterly Journal of Experimental Psychology*, 1966, **18**, 302-309.

Baddeley, A. D., and Warrington, E. K. Amnesia and the distinction between long- and short-term memory. *Journal of Verbal Learning and Verbal Behavior*, 1970, **9**, 176-189.

Baer, D. M. A technique of social reinforcement for the study of child behavior: Behavior avoiding reinforcement withdrawal. *Child Development*, 1962, **33**, 847-858.

Baer, D. M., and Sherman, J. A. Reinforcement control of generalized imitation in young children. *Journal of Experimental Child Psychology*, 1964, **1**, 37-49.

Bandura, A. Influence of model's reinforcement contingencies on the acquisition of imitative responses. *Journal of Personality and Social Psychology*, 1965, **1**, 589-595.

Bandura, A. *Principles of behavior modification*. New York: Holt, Rinehart, Winston, 1969.

Bandura, A., Blanchard, E. B., and Ritter, B. Relative efficacy of desensitization and modeling approaches for inducing behavioral, affective, and attitudinal changes. *Journal of Personality and Social Psychology*, 1969, **13**, 173-199.

Bandura, A., and Huston, A. C. Identification as a process of incidental learning. *Journal of Abnormal and Social Psychology*, 1961, **63**, 311-318.

Bandura, A., Ross, D., and Ross, S. A. A comparative test of the status envy, social power, and the secondary-reinforcement theories of identification. *Journal of Abnormal and Social Psychology*, 1963, **67**, 527-534.

Bandura, A., and Walters, R. H. *Social learning and personality development*. New York: Holt, Rinehart, Winston, 1963.

Barnes, J. B., and Underwood, B. J. "Fate" of first-list associations in transfer theory. *Journal of Experimental Psychology*, 1959, **58**, 97-105.

Bartlett, F. C. *Remembering: A study in experimental and social psychology*. Cambridge: Cambridge University Press, 1932.

Bass, M. J., and Hull, C. L. The irradiation of a tactile conditioned reflex in man. *Journal of Comparative Psychology*, 1934, **17**, 47-65.

Baumeister, A. A. Serial memory span thresholds of normal and mentally retarded children. *Journal of Educational Psychology*, 1974, **66**, 889-894.

Black, A. H., Osborne, B., and Ristow, W. C. A note on the operant conditioning of autonomic responses. In H. Davis and H. M. B. Hurwitz (Eds.) *Operant-Pavlovian Interactions*. Hillsdale, N.J.: Erlbaum, 1977.

Bloom, L. *Language development: Form and function in emerging grammar*. Cambridge, Mass.: M.I.T. Press, 1970.

Bousefield, W. A. The occurrence of clustering in the recall of randomly arranged associates. *Journal of General Psychology*, 1953, **49**, 229-240.

Braine, M.D.S. The ontogeny of English phrase structure: The first phase. *Language*, 1963, **39**, 1-13.

Brainerd, C., and Allen, T. Experimental inductions of the conservation of "first-order" quantitative invariants. *Psychological Bulletin*, 1971, **75**, 128-144.

Breland, K., and Breland, M. The misbehavior of organisms. *American Psychologist*, 1961, **16**, 681-684.

Broadhurst, P. L. Emotionality and the Yerkes-Dodson Law. *Journal of Experimental Psychology*, 1957, **54,** 345-352.

Brown, J. Some tests of the decay theory of immediate memory. *Quarterly Journal of Experimental Psychology*, 1958, **10,** 12-21.

Brown, J. S. *The motivation of behavior.* New York: McGraw-Hill, 1961.

Brown, R. W. Development of the first language in the human species. *American Psychologist*, 1973, **28,** 97-106.

Brown, R. W., and Bellugi, V. Three processes in the child's acquisition of syntax. *Harvard Educational Review*, 1964, **34,** 133-151.

Brown, R. W., and McNeill, D. The "tip-of-the-tongue" phenomenon. *Journal of Verbal Learning and Verbal Behavior*, 1966, **5,** 325-337.

Bruner, J. S., Goodnow, J., and Austin, G. *A study of thinking.* New York: Wiley, 1956.

Campbell, B. A., and Sheffield, F. O. Relation of random activity to food deprivation. *Journal of Comparative and Physiological Psychology*, 1953, **46,** 320-322.

Catania, A. C., and Reynolds, G. S. A quantitative analysis of the responding maintained by interval schedules of reinforcement. *Journal of the Experimental Analysis of Behavior*, 1968, **11,** 327-383.

Cermak, L. S. *Improving your memory.* New York: Norton, 1975.

Champion, R. A., and Jones, J. E. Forward, backward and pseudoconditioning of the GSR. *Journal of Experimental Psychology*, 1961, **62,** 58-61.

Cherry, E. C. Some experiments on the recognition of speech, with one and with two ears. *Journal of the Acoustical Society of America*, 1953, **25,** 975-979.

Chomsky, N. *Syntactic structures.* The Hague: Mouton, 1957.

Chomsky, N. *Aspects of the theory of syntax.* Cambridge, Mass.: M.I.T. Press, 1965.

Chomsky, N. *Language and mind.* New York: Harcourt, Brace, World, 1968.

Chung, S., and Herrnstein, R. J. Choice and delay of reinforcement. *Journal of the Experimental Analysis of Behavior*, 1967, **10,** 67-74.

Collins, A. M., and Quillian, M. R. Retrieval time from semantic memory. *Journal of Verbal Learning and Verbal Behavior*, 1969,**8,** 240-247.

Conrad, R. Acoustic confusions in immediate memory. *British Journal of Psychology*, 1964, **55,** 75-84.

Craik, F. I. M., and Lockhart, R. S. Levels of processing: A framework for memory research. *Journal of Verbal Learning and Verbal Behavior*, 1972, **11,** 671-684.

Crespi, L. P. Quantitative variation of incentive and performance in the white rat. *American Journal of Psychology*, 1942, **55,** 467-517.

Davidson, W. S. Studies of aversive conditioning for alcoholics: A critical review of theory and research methodology. *Psychological Bulletin*, 1974, **81,** 571-581.

Denes, P. B., and Pinson, E. N. *The speech chain: The physics and biology of spoken language.* Garden City, N.Y.: Anchor-Doubleday, 1973.

DiCara, L. V. Learning in the autonomic nervous system. *Scientific American*, 1970, **222,** 30-39.

Dilley, M. G., and Paivio, A. Pictures and words as stimulus and response items in paired-associate learning. *Journal of Experimental Child Psychology*, 1968, **6**, 231-240.

Dore, J., Franklin, M. B., Miller, R. T., and Ramer, A. L. H. Transitional phenomena in early language acquisition. *Journal of Child Language*, 1976, **3**, 13-28.

Ebbinghaus, H. *Memory*. Originally published, 1885. Republished (Translation by H. A. Ruger and C. E. Bussenius), New York: Dover, 1964.

Eimas, P., Siqueland, E., Jusczyk, P., and Vigorito, J. Speech perception in early infancy. *Science*, 1971, **171**, 303-306.

Eriksen, S. C. Learning theory and the teacher, II: Transfer of learning. *Memo to the Faculty*, Ann Arbor Center for Research on Learning and Teaching, 1969, No. 34. Reprinted in W. C. Morse and G. M. Wingo (Eds.) *Classroom Psychology*. Glenview, Ill.: Scott, Foresman, 1971.

Ervin-Tripp, S. M. Imitation and structural change in children's language. In E. H. Lenneberg (Ed.) *New directions in the study of language*. Cambridge, Mass.: M.I.T. Press, 1964.

Estes, W. K. The statistical approach to learning theory. In S. Koch (Ed.) *Psychology: A study of a science*. (Vol. 2) New York: McGraw-Hill, 1959.

Fantino, E., and Cole, M. Sand-digging in mice: Functional autonomy? *Psychonomic Science*, 1968, **10**, 29-30.

Fantino, E., Kasdon, D., and Stringer, N. The Yerkes-Dodson Law and alimentary motivation. *Canadian Journal of Psychology*, 1970, **24**, 77-84.

Ferguson, E. S. The mind's eye: Nonverbal thought in technology. *Science*, 1977, **197**, 827-836.

Fleck, S. Family dynamics and origin of schizophrenia. *Psychosomatic Medicine*, 1960, **22**, 333-344.

Fodor, J. A., and Bever, T. G. The psychological reality of linguistic segments. *Journal of Verbal Learning and Verbal Behavior*, 1965, **4**, 414-420.

Fraser, C., Bellugi, V., and Brown, R. Control of grammar in imitation, comprehension and production. *Journal of Verbal Learning and Verbal Behavior*, 1963, **2**, 121-135.

Freibergs, V., and Tulving, E. The effect of practice on utilization of information from positive and negative instances. *Canadian Journal of Psychology*, 1961, **15**, 101-106.

Fuller, G. D. Current status of biofeedback in clinical practice. *American Psychologist*, 1978, **33**, 39-48.

Garcia, J., and Koelling, R. A. Relation of cue to consequence in avoidance learning. *Psychonomic Science*, 1966, **4**, 123-124.

Gardner, B. T., and Gardner, R. A. Comparing the early utterance of child and chimpanzee. In A. Pick (Ed.) *Minnesota Symposium in Child Psychology*. (Vol. 8) Minneapolis: University of Minnesota Press, 1974.

Gardner, R. A., and Gardner, B. T. Teaching sign language to a chimpanzee. *Science*, 1969, **165**, 664-672.

Gibson, E. J. *Principles of perceptual learning and development*. New York: Appleton-Century-Crofts, 1969.

Gibson, J. J., and Gibson, E. J. Perceptual learning: Differentiation or enrichment? *Psychological Review,* 1955, **62,** 32-41.

Glanzer, M., and Cunitz, A. R. Two storage mechanisms in free recall. *Journal of Verbal Learning and Verbal Behavior,* 1966, **5,** 351-360.

Goldin-Meadow, S., and Feldman, H. The development of language-like communication without a language model. *Science,* 1977, **197,** 401-403.

Gruen, G. E. Experiences affecting the development of number conservation in children. *Child Development,* 1965, **36,** 963-979.

Guthrie, E. R. *The psychology of learning* (Revised Edition). Magnolia, Mass.: Peter Smith, 1952.

Guthrie, E. R. Association by contiguity. In S. Koch (Ed.) *Psychology: A study of a science.* (Vol. 2) New York: McGraw-Hill, 1959.

Guthrie, E. R., and Horton, G. P. *Cats in a puzzle box.* New York: Rinehart Press, 1946.

Guttman, N. Equal reinforcement values for sucrose and glucose solutions as compared with equal sweetness values. *Journal of Experimental Psychology,* 1954, **47,** 358-361.

Guttman, N., and Kalish, H. I. Discriminability and stimulus generalization. *Journal of Experimental Psychology,* 1956, **51,** 79-88.

Hailman, J. P. How an instinct is learned. *Scientific American,* 1969 (December), **221,** 98-106.

Hall, R. V., Lund, D., and Jackson, D. Effects of teacher attention on study behavior. *Journal of Applied Behavior Analysis,* 1969, **2,** 143-157.

Harlow, H. F. The formation of learning sets. *Psychological Review,* 1949, **56,** 51-65.

Hartman, T. F. Dynamic transmission, elective generalization, and semantic conditioning. In W. F. Prokasy (Ed.) *Classical Conditioning.* New York: Appleton-Century-Crofts, 1965.

Heidbreder, E. The attainment of concepts: II. The problem. *Journal of General Psychology,* 1956, **51,** 229-238.

Hellyer, S. Supplementary report: Frequency of stimulus presentation and short-term decrement in recall. *Journal of Experimental Psychology,* 1962, **64,** 650.

Herrnstein, R. J. Method and theory in the study of avoidance. *Psychological Review,* 1969, **76,** 49-69.

Herrnstein, R. J. The evolution of behaviorism. *American Psychologist,* 1977, **32,** 593-603.

Hilgard, E. R. A perspective on the relationship between learning theory and educational practices. In E. R. Hilgard (Ed.) *Theories of Learning and Instruction.* Chicago: National Society for the Study of Education, 1964, pp. 402-415.

Hingten, J. N., and Trost, F. C., Jr. Shaping cooperative responses in early childhood schizophrenics. Paper read at American Psychological Convention, Los Angeles, 1964. Reprinted in R. Ulrich, T. Strachnik, and J. Mabry (Eds.) *Control of human behavior.* Glenview, Ill.: Scott, Foresman, 1966.

Holen, M. C., and Oaster, T. R. Serial position and isolation effects in a classroom lecture simulation. *Journal of Educational Psychology,* 1976, **68,** 293-296.

Holland, J. G. Human vigilance. *Science,* 1958, **128,** 61-67.

Holland, J. G. Teaching machines: An application of principles from the laboratory. *Journal of the Experimental Analysis of Behavior,* 1960, **3,** 275-287.

Holt, E. B. *Animal drive.* London: Williams and Norgate, 1931.

Holz, W. C., Azrin, N. H., and Ayllon, T. Elimination of behavior of mental patients by response-produced extinction. *Journal of the Experimental Analysis of Behavior,* 1963, **6,** 407-412.

Horton, D. L., and Kjeldergaard, P. M. An experimental analysis of associative factors in mediated generalization. *Psychological Monographs,* 1961, **75** (No. 11).

Hovland, C. I., and Weiss, W. Transmission of information concerning concepts through positive and negative instances. *Journal of Experimental Psychology,* 1953, **45,** 175-182.

Hull, C. L. Knowledge and purpose as habit mechanisms. *Psychological Review,* 1930, **37,** 511-525.

Hull, C. L. Goal attraction and directing ideas conceived as habit phenomena. *Psychological Review,* 1931, **38,** 487-506.

Hull, C. L. *Principles of behavior.* New York: Appleton-Century-Crofts, 1943.

Hull, C. L. *Essentials of behavior.* New Haven, Conn.: Yale University Press, 1951.

Hull, C. L. *A behavior system: An introduction to behavior theory concerning the individual organism.* New Haven, Conn.: Yale University Press, 1952.

Ince, L. P. Modification of verbal behavior through variable interval reinforcement in a quasi-therapy situation. *Behavior Research and Therapy,* 1968, **6,** 439-445.

Jaffee, P. G., and Carlson, P. M. Modeling therapy for test anxiety: The rule of model affect and consequences. *Behavior Research and Therapy,* 1972, **10,** 329-339.

James, W. *Principles of psychology.* Originally published, 1890. Republished, New York: Dover, 1950.

Jenkins, J. G., and Dallenbach, K. M. Oblivescence during sleep and waking. *American Journal of Psychology,* 1924, **35,** 605-612.

Jensen, A. R. Spelling errors and the serial position effect. *Journal of Educational Psychology,* 1962, **53,** 105-109.

Jensen, A. R., and Rohwer, W. D. What is learned in serial learning? *Journal of Verbal Learning and Verbal Behavior,* 1965, **4,** 62-75.

Jones, M. C. The elimination of children's fears. *Journal of Experimental Psychology,* 1924, **7,** 382-390.

Kamin, L. J. The effects of termination of the CS and avoidance of the US on avoidance learning. *Journal of Comparative and Physiological Psychology,* 1956, **49,** 420-424.

Kelleher, R. I. Discrimination learning as a function of reversal and non-reversal shifts. *Journal of Experimental Psychology,* 1956, **51,** 379-384.

Keller, H. *The story of my life.* Garden City, N.Y.: Doubleday, 1954.

Kellogg, W. N. Communication and language in a home raised chimpanzee. *Science,* 1968, **162,** 423-427.

Kendler, H. H., and D'Amato, M. R. A comparison of reversal shifts and non-reversal shifts in human concept formation behavior. *Journal of Experimental Psychology,* 1955, **49,** 165-174.

Kendler, H. H., and Kendler, T. S. Vertical and horizontal processes in problem solving. *Psychological Review,* 1962, **69,** 1-16.

Kendler, T. S., and Kendler, H. H. Reversal and nonreversal shifts in kindergarten children. *Journal of Experimental Psychology,* 1959, **58,** 56-60.

Kendler, T. S., Kendler, H. H., and Wells, D. Reversal and nonreversal shifts in nursery school children. *Journal of Comparative and Physiological Psychology,* 1960, **53,** 83-88.

Keppel, G., and Underwood, B. J. Proactive inhibition in short-term retention of single items. *Journal of Verbal Learning and Verbal Behavior,* 1962, **1,** 153-161.

Kohler, W. Nachweis einfacher strukturfunktionen beim schimpanses und beim hauschuhn. (Originally published, 1918). Translated and republished in W. D. Ellis (Ed.) *A source book of gestalt psychology.* London: Kegan, Paul, Trench, Trubner, 1938.

Kohler, W. *The mentality of apes.* Originally published, 1925. Republished, New York: Liveright, 1973.

Koppenaal, R. J. Time changes in the strengths of A-B, A-C lists: Spontaneous recovery? *Journal of Verbal Learning and Verbal Behavior,* 1963, **2,** 310-319.

Kopstein, F., and Roshall, S. Learning foreign vocabulary from pictures vs. words. *American Psychologist,* 1954, **9,** 407-408.

Krechevsky, I. "Hypothesis" versus "chance" in the pre-solution period in sensory discrimination-learning. *University of California Publications in Psychology,* 1932, **6** (No. 3), 27-44 (a).

Krechevsky, I. The genesis of "hypotheses" in rats. *University of California Publications in Psychology,* 1932, **6** (No. 4), 45-64 (b).

Kuhn, D. Inducing development experimentally: Comments on a research paradigm. *Developmental Psychology,* 1974, **10,** 590-600.

Lenneberg, E. H. Understanding language without ability to speak: A case report. *Journal of Abnormal and Social Psychology,* 1962, **65,** 419-425.

Lenneberg, E. H. *Biological foundations of language.* New York: Wiley, 1967.

Lewis, D. J. Partial reinforcement: A selective review of the literature since 1950. *Psychological Bulletin,* 1960, **57,** 1-28.

Lewis, D. J., and Maher, B. A. Neural consolidation and electroconvulsive schock. *Psychological Review,* 1965, **72,** 225-239.

Liberman, A. M., Harris, K. S., Hoffman, H. S., and Griffith, B. C. The discrimination of speech sounds within and across phoneme boundaries. *Journal of Experimental Psychology,* 1957, **54,** 358-368.

Lillard, P. P. *Montessori—A modern approach.* New York: Schocken Books, 1972.

Limber, J. Language in child and chimp? *American Psychologist,* 1977, **32,** 280-295.

Lippman, M. Z., and Shanahan, M. W. Pictorial facilitation of paired-associate learning: Implications for vocabulary training. *Journal of Educational Psychology,* 1973, **64,** 216-222.

BIBLIOGRAPHY

Lobb, H., and Childs, R. Verbal control and intradimensional transfer of discrimination learning in mentally retarded vs. intellectually average subjects. *American Journal of Mental Deficiency*, 1973, **78**, 182-192.

Loftus, E. F., and Loftus, G. R. Changes in memory structure and retrieval order over the course of instruction. *Journal of Educational Psychology*, 1974, **66**, 315-318.

Lorayne, H. *Remembering people*. New York: Stein & Day, 1975.

Lorayne, H., and Lucas, J. *The memory book*. New York: Stein & Day, 1974.

Lovaas, O. I., Berberich, J. P., Perloff, B. F., and Schaeffer, B. Acquisition of imitative speech by schizophrenic children. *Science*, 1966, **151**, 705-707.

Lovaas, O. I., and Simmons, J. Q. Manipulation of self-destruction in three retarded children. *Journal of Applied Behavior Analysis*, 1968, **1**, 1-12.

Luria, A. R. *The role of speech in the regulation of normal and abnormal behavior*. New York: Liveright, 1961.

Mackintosh, N. J. Selective attention in animal discrimination learning. *Psychological Bulletin*, 1965, **64**, 124-150.

Mandler, G., and Sarason, S. B. A study of anxiety and learning. *Journal of Abnormal and Social Psychology*, 1952, **47**, 166-173.

Manning, A. A., Schneiderman, N., and Lordahl, D. S. Delay vs. trace heart rate classical discrimination conditioning in rabbits as a function of ISI. *Journal of Experimental Psychology*, 1969, **80**, 225-230.

Matazarro, J. D., Ulett, G. A., and Saslow, G. Human maze performance as a function of increasing levels of anxiety. *Journal of General Psychology*, 1955, **53**, 79-95.

Mawhinney, V. T., Bostow, D. E., Laws, D. R., Blumenfeld, G. J., and Hopkins, B. L. A comparison of students studying—behavior produced by daily, weekly, and three-week schedules. *Journal of Applied Behavior Analysis*, 1971, **4**, 257-264.

McGaugh, J. L. Time-dependent processes in memory storage. *Science*, 1966, **153**, 1351-1358.

McGeogh, J. A. Forgetting and the law of disuse. *Psychological Review*, 1932, **39**, 352-370.

McNeill, D. Developmental psycholinguistics. In F. Smith and G. A. Miller (Eds.) *The genesis of language: A psycholinguistic approach*. Cambridge, Mass.: M.I.T. Press, 1966.

McNeill, D. *The acquisition of language: The study of developmental psycholinguistics*. New York: Harper and Row, 1970.

Melton, A. W. Implication of short-term memory for a general theory of memory. *Journal of Verbal Learning and Verbal Behavior*, 1963, **2**, 1-21.

Melton, Q. E., and Irwin, J. M. The influence of degree of interpolated learning on retroactive inhibition and the overt transfer of specific responses. *American Journal of Psychology*, 1940, **53**, 173-203.

Miller, G. A. The magical number seven, plus-or-minus two: Some limits on our capacity for processing information. *Psychological Review*, 1956, **63**, 81-97.

Miller, N. E. Studies of fear as an acquirable drive: I. Fear as motivation and fear reduction as reinforcement in the learning of new responses. *Journal of Experimental Psychology*, 1948, **38**, 89-101.

416

Miller, N. E. Learning of visceral and glandular responses. *Science*, 1969, **163**, 434-445.

Miller, N. E. Biofeedback and visceral learning. In *Annual Review of Psychology*. Palo Alto, Calif.: Annual Reviews, Inc., 1978.

Miller, N. E., and Dollard, J. *Social learning and imitation*. New Haven, Conn.: Yale University Press, 1941.

Milner, B. Visually-guided maze learning in man: Effects of bilateral hippocampal, bilateral frontal, and unilateral cerebral lesions. *Neuropsychologia*, 1965, **3**, 317-338.

Milner, B. Amnesia following operation on the temporal lobes. In C. W. M. Whitty and O. L. Zangwill (Eds.) *Amnesia*. London: Butterworks, 1966.

Milner, B. Disorders of memory after brain lesions in man—Preface: Material-specific and generalized memory loss. *Neuropsychologia*, 1968, **6**, 175-179.

Milner, B., Corkin, S., and Teuber, H. L. Further analysis of the hippocampal amnesic syndrome: 14-year follow-up study of H.M. *Neuropsychologia*, 1968, **6**, 215-234.

Mischel, W. Theory and research on the antecedents of self-imposed delay of gratification. In B. Maher (Ed.) *Progress in experimental personality research*. (Vol. 3) New York: Academic Press, 1966.

Mischel, W. Processes in delay of gratification. In L. Berkowitz (Ed.) *Advances in experimental social psychology* (Vol. 7). New York: Academic Press, 1974.

Montessori, M. *The Montessori method*. New York: Frederick A. Stokes Co., 1912.

Montessori, M. *Dr. Montessori's own handbook*. Originally published, 1914. Republished, Cambridge, Mass.: Robert A. Bentley, Inc., 1964.

Mowrer, O. H. The autism theory of speech development and some clinical applications. *Journal of Speech and Hearing Disorders*, 1952, **17**, 263-268.

Mowrer, O. H. *Learning theory and behavior*. New York: Wiley, 1960 (a).

Mowrer, O. H. *Learning theory and the symbolic process*. New York: Wiley, 1960 (b).

Mowrer, O. H. The psychologist looks at language. *American Psychologist*, 1954, **9**, 660-694.

Mowrer, O. H., and Lamoreaux, R. R. Avoidance conditioning and signal duration—A study of secondary motivation and reward. *Psychological Monographs*, 1942, **54** (No. 5), Whole No. 247.

Mussen, P. Early socialization: Learning and identification. In *New directions in psychology*. New York: Holt, Rinehart, Winston, 1967.

Myrow, D. L., and Anderson, R. C. Retroactive inhibition of prose as a function of the type of test. *Journal of Educational Psychology*, 1972, **63**, 303-308.

Navarick, D. J., and Fantino, E. Self-control and general models of choice. *Journal of Experimental Psychology: Animal Behavior Processes*, 1976, **2**, 75-87.

Neisser, U., and Weene, P. Hierarchies in concept attainment. *Journal of Experimental Psychology*, 1962, **64**, 640-645.

Nelson, K. E., Carskaddon, G., and Bonvillan, J. D. Syntax acquisition: Impact of experimental variation in adult verbal interaction with the young child. *Child Development*, 1973, **44**, 497-504.

Newman, S. E., and Saltz, E. Isolation effects: Stimulus and response generalization as explanatory concepts. *Journal of Experimental Psychology*, 1958, **55**, 467-472.

Nisan, M., and Koriat, A. Children's actual choices and their conception of the wise choice in a delay-of-gratification situation. *Child Development*, 1977, **48**, 488-494.

Noble, C. E. An analysis of meaning. *Psychological Review*, 1952, **59**, 421-430.

Oller, D. K., Wieman, L. A., Doyle, W. S., and Ross, C. Infant babbling and speech. *Journal of Child Language*, 1976, **3**, 1-12.

Osgood, C. E. The similarity paradox in human learning. *Psychological Review*, 1949, **56**, 132-143.

Paivio, A., and Yarmey, A. D. Pictures versus words as stimuli and responses in paired-associate learning. *Psychonomic Science*, 1966, **5**, 235-236.

Paivio, A., and Yuille, J. C. Mediation instructions and word attributes in paired-associate learning. *Psychonomic Science*, 1967, **8**, 65-66.

Pavlov, I. P. *Conditioned reflexes* (Translated by G. V. Anrep). London: Oxford University Press, 1927.

Pavlov, I. P. The reply of a physiologist to psychologists. *Psychological Review*, 1932, **39**, 91-127.

Perin, C. T. Behavior potentiality as a joint function of the amount of training and the degree of hunger at the time of extinction. *Journal of Experimental Psychology*, 1942, **30**, 93-113.

Peterson, L. R., and Peterson, M. J. Short-term retention of individual verbal items. *Journal of Experimental Psychology*, 1959, **58**, 193-198.

Peterson, R. A., Wright, R. L. D., and Hanlan, C. The effects of extending the CS-UCS interval on the effectiveness of the conditioning treatment for nocturnal enuresis. *Behavior Research and Therapy*, 1969, **7**, 351-357.

Piaget, J. *Psychology of intelligence*. London: Routledge and Kegan Paul, 1950.

Piaget, J. *The origins of intelligence in children*. New York: Norton, 1952.

Premack, A. J., and Premack, D. Teaching sign language to a chimpanzee. *Scientific American*, 1972, **227** (October), 92-99.

Premack, D. Toward empirical behavior laws: I. Positive reinforcement. *Psychological Review*, 1959, **66**, 219-233.

Pressley, M. Imagery and children's learning: Putting the picture in developmental perspective. *Review of Educational Research*, 1977, **57**, 585-622.

Rachlin, H. *Introduction to modern behaviorism*. San Francisco: Freeman, 1970.

Rachlin, H. C., and Green, L. Commitment, choice, and self-control. *Journal of The Experimental Analysis of Behavior*, 1972, **17**, 15-22.

Raymond, M. J. The treatment of addiction by aversion conditioning with apomorphine. *Behavioral Research and Therapy*, 1964, **1**, 287-291.

Razran, G. Sentential and propositional generalization of salivary conditioning to verbal stimuli. *Science*, 1949, **109**, 447-448.

418

Rescorla, R. A. Pavlovian conditioning and its proper control procedures. *Psychological Review,* 1967, **74,** 71-80.

Rescorla, R. A., and Solomon, R. L. Two-process learning theory: Relationships between Pavlovian conditioning and instrumental learning. *Psychological Review,* 1967, **55,** 151-182.

Revusky, S. and Garcia, J. Learned associations over long delays. In G. H. Bower (Ed.) *The psychology of learning and motivation* (Vol 4). New York: Academic Press, 1970.

Revusky, S., and Taukulis, H. Effects of alcohol and lithium habituation on the development of alcohol aversions through contingent lithium injection. *Behavioral Research and Therapy,* 1975, **13,** 163-166.

Reynolds, G. S. Behavioral contrast. *Journal of the Experimental Analysis of Behavior,* 1961, **4,** 57-71. (b)

Reynolds, G. S. Attention in the pigeon. *Journal of the Experimental Analysis of Behavior,* 1961, **4,** 203-208. (a)

Rheingold, H. L., Gewitz, J. C., and Ross, H. W. Social conditioning of vocalizations in the infant. *Journal of Comparative and Physiological Psychology,* 1959, **52,** 68-73.

Riess, B. F. Genetic changes in semantic conditioning. *Journal of Experimental Psychology,* 1946, **36,** 143-152.

Riess, B. F. Semantic conditioning involving the galvanic skin reflex. *Journal of Experimental Psychology,* 1940, **26,** 238-240.

Rips, L. J., Shoben, E. J., and Smith, E. E. Semantic distance and the verification of semantic relations. *Journal of Verbal Learning and Verbal Behavior,* 1973, **12,** 1-20.

Ross, S. M. Frequency and duration of hierarchy item exposure in a systematic desensitization analogue. *Behavior Research and Therapy,* 1973, **11,** 303-312.

Ross, J., and Lawrence, K. A. Some observations on memory artifice. *Psychonomic Science,* 1968, **13,** 107-108.

Rotter, J. B. *Social learning and clinical psychology.* Englewood Cliffs, N.J.: Prentice-Hall, 1954.

Rowher, W. D., Jr., Lynch, S., Suzuki, N., and Levin, S. R. Verbal and pictorial facilitation of paired-associate learning. *Journal of Experimental Child Psychology,* 1967, **5,** 294-302.

Ruebush, B. K. Interfering and facilitating effects of test anxiety. *Journal of Abnormal and Social Psychology,* 1960, **60,** 205-212.

Rumelhart, D. E., Lindsay, P. H., and Norman, D. A. A process model for long term memory. In E. Tulving and W. Donaldson (Eds.) *Organization and memory.* New York: Academic Press, 1972.

Rundus, D. Analysis of rehearsal processes in free recall. *Journal of Experimental Psychology,* 1971, **89,** 63-77.

Russell, M. A. H., Armstrong, E., and Patel, U. A. Temporal contiguity in electric aversion therapy for cigarette smoking. *Behavior Research and Therapy,* 1976, **14,** 103-123.

Sailor, W. Reinforcement and generalization of productive plural allomorphs in two retarded children. *Journal of Applied Behavior Analysis,* 1971, **4,** 305-310.

Samuels, S. J. Attentional processes in reading: The effect of pictures on the acquisition of reading responses. *Journal of Educational Psychology,* 1967, **58,** 337-347.

BIBLIOGRAPHY

Schaar, K. "You are too fast afoot, Senator." *APA Monitor,* 1977 (April), p. 14.

Scoville, W. B., and Milner, B. Loss of recent memory after bilateral hippocampal lesions. *Journal of Neurological and Neurosurgical Psychiatry,* 1957, **20,** 11-21.

Sechenov, I. M. *Reflexes of the brain.* Originally published, 1863. Republished, Cambridge, Mass.: M.I.T., 1965.

Seligman, M. E. P. On the generality of the laws of learning. *Psychological Review,* 1970, **77,** 406-418.

Seward, J. P. An experimental study of Guthrie's theory of reinforcement. *Journal of Experimental Psychology,* 1942, **30,** 247-256.

Schaffer, L. S. The Golden Fleece: Anti-intellectualism and social science. *American Psychologist,* 1977, **32,** 814-823.

Sheffield, F. D., and Roby, T. B. Reward value of a non-nutritive sweet taste. *Journal of Comparative and Physiological Psychology,* 1950, **43,** 471-481.

Shuell, T. J., and Kepper, G. Learning ability and retention. *Journal of Educational Psychology,* 1970, **61,** 59-65.

Sidman, M. Two temporal parameters of the maintenance of avoidance behavior by the white rat. *Journal of Comparative and Physiological Psychology,* 1953, **46,** 253-261.

Sigel, I. E., Saltz, E., and Roskind, W. Variables determining concept conservation in children. *Journal of Experimental Psychology,* 1967, **74,** 471-475.

Skinner, B. F. *The behavior of organisms: An experimental analysis.* New York: Appleton-Century-Crofts, 1938.

Skinner, B. F. "Superstition" in the pigeon. *Journal of Experimental Psychology,* 1948, **38,** 168-172.

Skinner, B. F. Are theories of learning necessary? *Psychological Review,* 1950, **57,** 193-216.

Skinner, B. F. *Science and human behavior.* New York: MacMillan, 1953.

Skinner, B. F. *Verbal behavior.* New York: Appleton-Century-Crofts, 1957.

Skinner, B. F. Teaching machines. *Science,* 1958, **128,** 969-977.

Skinner, B. F. *About behaviorism.* New York: Alfred A. Knopf, 1974.

Skinner, B. F. Herrnstein and the evolution of behaviorism. *American Psychologist,* 1977, **32,** 1006-1012.

Slamecka, N. J. An inquiry into the doctrine of remote associations. *Psychological Review,* 1964, **71,** 61-76.

Slamecka, N. J. Differentiation versus unlearning of verbal associations. *Journal of Experimental Psychology,* 1966, **71,** 822-828.

Spence, K. W. The nature of discrimination learning in animals. *Psychological Review,* 1936, **43,** 427-449.

Spence, K. W. The differential response in animals to stimuli varying within a single dimension. *Psychological Review,* 1937, **44,** 430-444.

Sperling, G. The information available in brief visual presentations. *Psychological Monographs,* 1960, **74,** Whole No. 498.

Spooner, A., and Kellogg, W. N. The backward conditioning curve. *American Journal of Psychology,* 1947, **60,** 321-334.

Spring, C., and Capps, C. Encoding speed, rehearsal, and probed recall of dyslexic boys. *Journal of Educational Psychology*, 1974, **66**, 780-786.

Staats, A. W., Staats, C. K., and Heard, W. G. Language conditioning of meaning to meaning using a semantic generalization paradigm. *Journal of Experimental Psychology*, 1959, **57**, 187-191.

Stratton, G. M. Retroactive hypermnesia and other emotional effects of memory. *Psychological Review*, 1919, **26**, 474-486.

Suppes, P. C., and Morningstar, M. Computer-assisted instruction. *Science*, 1969, **166**, 343-350.

Talkington, L., Hall, S., and Altman, R. Communication deficits and aggression in the mentally retarded. *American Journal of Mental Deficiency*, 1971, **76**, 235-237.

Talkington, L. W., and Altman, R. Effects of film-mediated aggressive and affectual models on behavior. *American Journal of Mental Deficiency*, 1973, **77**, 420-425.

Taylor, J. A. The relationship of anxiety to the conditioned eyelid response. *Journal of Experimental Psychology*, 1951, **41**, 81-92.

Thorndike, E. L. Animal intelligence: An experimental study of the associative processes in animals. *Psychological Review Monographs*, Supplement #2, Whole No. 8, 1898.

Thorndike, E. L. *The psychology of learning*. New York: Teachers College, 1913.

Thorndike, E. L. *Educational Psychology: Briefer Course*. New York: Teachers College, 1914.

Tighe, L. S. Effect of perceptual pretraining on reversal and non-reversal shifts. *Journal of Experimental Psychology*, 1965, **70**, 379-385.

Tighe, L. S., and Tighe, T. S. Discrimination learning: Two views in historical perspective. *Psychological Bulletin*, 1966, **66**, 353-370.

Tolman, E. C. *Purposive behavior in animals and men*. New York: Appleton-Century-Crofts, 1932.

Tolman, E. C. Cognitive maps in rats and men. *Psychological Review*, 1948, **55**, 189-208.

Tolman, E. C. Principles of purposive behavior. In S. Koch (Ed.) *Psychology: A Study of a Science* (Vol. 2). New York: McGraw-Hill, 1959.

Tolman, E. C., and Honzik, C. H. Introduction and removal of reward and maze performance in rats. *Univ. of Calif. Publications in Psychology*, 1930, **4**, 257-275.

Tolman, E. C., Ritchie, B. F., and Kalish, D. Studies in spatial learning: II. Place learning versus response learning. *Journal of Experimental Psychology*, 1946, **36**, 221-229.

Tulving, E. Episodic and semantic memory. In E. Tulving and W. Donaldson (Eds.) *Organization and Memory*. New York: Academic Press, 1972.

Tulving, E., and Pearlstone, Z. Availability versus accessibility of information in memory for words. *Journal of Verbal Learning and Verbal Behavior*, 1966, **5**, 181-191.

Tulving, E., and Psotka, J. Retroactive inhibition in free recall: Inaccessibility of information available in the memory store. *Journal of Experimental Psychology*, 1971, **87**, 1-8.

Underwood, B. J. Retroactive and proactive inhibition after five and forty-eight hours. *Journal of Experimental Psychology*, 1948, **38**, 29-38.

Underwood, B. J. Interference and forgetting. *Psychological Review*, 1957, **64**, 49-60.

Underwood, B. J. Degree of learning and the measurement of forgetting. *Journal of Verbal Learning and Verbal Behavior*, 1964, **3,** 112-129.

Underwood, B. J., and Postman, L. Extraexperimental sources of interference in forgetting. *Psychological Review*, 1960, **67,** 73-95.

Underwood, B. J., and Richardson, J. Verbal concept learning as a function of instructions and dominance level. *Journal of Experimental Psychology*, 1956, **51,** 229-238.

Underwood, B. J., and Schulz, R. W. *Meaningfulness and verbal learning.* Philadelphia: Lippincott, 1960.

Wallace, P. Animal behavior: The puzzle of flavor aversion. *Science*, 1976, **193,** 989-991.

Wambold, C. L., Jedlinski, K., and Brown, L. Improving the sequential memory performance of trainable mentally retarded youngsters: A learning strategies approach. *Journal Special Education*, 1976, **10,** 41-46.

Warrington, E. K., and Weiskrantz, L. An analysis of short-term and long-term memory defects in man. In J. A. Deutsch (Ed.) *The physiological basis of memory*. New York: Academic Press, 1972.

Watkins, M. J. When is recall spectacularly higher than recognition? *Journal of Experimental Psychology*, 1974, **102,** 161-163.

Watson, J. B. *Behaviorism.* Originally published, 1924. Republished, New York: Norton, 1970.

Waugh, N. C., and Norman, D. A. Primary memory. *Psychological Review*, 1965, **72,** 89-104.

Weiss, R. F., Buchanan, W., Alstatt, L., and Lombardo, S. P. Altruism is rewarding. *Science*, 1971, **171,** 1262-1263.

Wiggins, J. S., Renner, K. E., Clore, G. L., and Rose, R. J. *Principles of personality.* Reading, Mass.: Addison-Wesley, 1976.

Williams, S. B. Resistance to extinction as a function of the number of reinforcements. *Journal of Experimental Psychology*, 1938, **23,** 506-521.

Winschel, J. F., and Lawrence, E. A. Short-term memory: Curricular implications for the mentally retarded. *Journal of Special Education*, 1975, **9,** 395-408.

Winters, J. J., Jr., Attlee, L. C., and Harvey, F. Paired-associate learning of EMR adolescents and nonretarded children as a function of methods of presentation of training. *American Journal of Mental Deficiency*, 1974, **79,** 70-76.

Wittrock, M. C. Effect of certain sets upon complex verbal learning. *Journal of Educational Psychology*, 1963, **54,** 85-88.

Wolfe, J. B. Effectiveness of token rewards for chimpanzees. *Comparative Psychology Monographs*, 1936, **12,** No. 60.

Wolpe, J. *Psychotherapy by reciprocal inhibition.* Stanford: Stanford University Press, 1958.

Wolpe, J., and Lazarus, A. A. *Behavior therapy techniques.* Oxford: Pergamon Press, 1966.

Woodring, G. P. Reform movements from the point of view of psychological research. In E. R. Hilgard (Ed.) *Theories of learning and instruction.* Chicago: National Society for the Study of Education, 1964. Pp. 286-305.

Yates, F. A. *The art of memory.* Chicago: University of Chicago Press, 1966.

Yerkes, R. M., and Dodson, J. D. The relation of strength of stimulus to rapidity of habit-formation. *Journal of Comparative Neurology,* 1908, **18,** 459-482.

Yukl, G., Wexley, K. N., and Seymour, J. D. Effectiveness of pay incentives under variable ratio and continuous reinforcement schedules. *Journal of Applied Psychology,* 1972, **56,** 19-23.

Zeaman, D., and House, B. J. The role of attention in retardate discrimination learning. In N. R. Ellis (Ed.) *Handbook of mental deficiency.* New York: McGraw-Hill, 1963.

Zeiler, M. D. The ratio theory of intermediate size discrimination. *Psychological Review,* 1963, **70,** 516-533.

Zimmerman, B. J., and Dialessi, F. Modeling influences on children's creative behavior. *Journal of Educational Psychology,* 1973, **65,** 127-134.

(Acknowledgments continued)

Fig. 3.8 After G. Yukl, K. N. Wexley, and J. D. Seymour, Effectiveness of pay incentives under variable and continuous reinforcement schedules. *Journal of Applied Psychology*, **56,** 1972, 21–22. Copyright 1972 by the American Psychological Association. Reprinted by permission.

Figs. 3.9 and 3.10 From J. G. Holland, Human vigilance, *Science*, **128,** 1958, 63, 64. Reprinted by permission.

Fig. 4.1 From P. L. Broadhurst, Emotionality and the Yerkes-Dodson Law, *Journal of Experimental Psychology*, **54,** 1957, 346, 348. Copyright 1957 by the American Psychological Association. Reprinted by permission.

Figs. 4.2 and 4.3 From E. Fantino, D. Kasdon, and N. Stringer, The Yerkes-Dodson Law and alimentary motivation, *Canadian Journal of Psychology*, **24,** 1970, 79, 81. Reprinted by permission.

Fig. 4.4 From J. A. Taylor, The relationship of anxiety to the conditioned eyelid response, *Journal of Experimental Psychology*, **41,** 1951, 88. Copyright 1951 by the American Psychological Association. Reprinted by permission.

Fig. 4.6 Graph from L. J. Kamin, The effects of termination of the CS and avoidance of the US on avoidance learning, *Journal of Comparative and Physiological Psychology*, **49,** 1956, 422. Copyright 1956 by the American Psychological Association. Reprinted by permission.

Fig. 4.7 From D. J. Navarick and E. Fantino, Self-control and general models of choice, *Journal of Experimental Psychology: Animal Behavior Processes*, **2,** 1976, 83. Copyright 1976 by the American Psychological Association. Reprinted by permission.

Fig. 4.8 From H. Rachlin and L. Green, Commitment, choice, and self-control, *Journal of the Experimental Analysis of Behavior*, **17,** 1972, 16. Copyright 1972 by the Society for the Experimental Analysis of Behavior, Inc. Reprinted by permission.

Fig. 5.1 From N. E. Miller and J. Dollard, *Social Learning and Imitation*. New Haven: Yale University Press, 1941. Reprinted by permission.

Fig. 5.2 From D. M. Baer, A technique of social reinforcement for the study of child behavior: Behavior avoiding reinforcement withdrawal, *Child Development*, **33,** 1962, facing p. 848. © The Society for Research in Child Development, Inc. Reprinted by permission.

Fig. 5.3 From D. M. Baer and J. A. Sherman, Reinforcement control of generalized imitation in young children, *Journal of Experimental Child Psychology*, **1,** 1964, 44. Reprinted by permission.

Fig. 5.4 From A. Bandura, Influence of model's reinforcement contingencies on the acquisition of imitative responses, *Journal of Personality and Social Psychology*, **1,** 1965, 592. Copyright 1965 by the American Psychological Association. Reprinted by permission.

Figs. 5.5, 5.6, and 5.7 From A. Bandura, E. B. Blanchard, and B. Ritter, Relative efficacy of desensitization and modeling approaches for inducing behavioral, affective, and attitudinal changes, *Journal of Personality and Social Psychology*, **13,** 1969, 183 and 185, 186, 188. Copyright 1969 by the American Psychological Association. Reprinted by permission.

Fig. 6.2 From I. Krechevsky, The genesis of "hypotheses" in rats, *University of California Publications in Psychology*, **6,** 1932, 46. Reprinted by permission of the University of California Press.

Fig. 6.5 From L. V. DiCara, Learning in the autonomic nervous system, *Scientific American,* January 1970, 33. Copyright © 1970 by Scientific American, Inc. All rights reserved.

Page 170 From W. Kohler, *The Mentality of Apes.* New York: Liveright, 1973, pp. 39-40. Reprinted by permission.

Fig. 7.1 From S. Asch, Reformulation of the problem of associations, *American Psychologist,* **24,** 1969, 95. Copyright 1969 by the American Psychological Association. Reprinted by permission.

Fig. 7.2 From M. Z. Lippman and M. W. Shanahan, Pictorial facilitation of paired-associate learning: Implications for vocabulary training, *Journal of Educational Psychology,* **64,** 1973, 217. Copyright 1973 by the American Psychological Association. Reprinted by permission.

Fig. 7.4 From A. R. Jensen, Spelling errors and the serial position effect, *Journal of Educational Psychology,* **53,** 1962, 107. Copyright 1962 by the American Psychological Association. Reprinted by permission.

Fig. 7.5 From S. E. Newman and E. Saltz, Isolation effects: Stimulus and response generalization as explanatory concepts, *Journal of Experimental Psychology;* **55,** 1958, 469. Copyright 1958 by the American Psychological Association. Reprinted by permission.

Fig. 7.7 From M. G. Dilley, and A. Paivio, Pictures and words as stimulus and response items in paired-associate learning, *Journal of Experimental Child Psychology,* **6,** 1968, 236. Reprinted by permission.

Fig. 7.12 From D. L. Horton and P. M. Kjeldergaard, An experimental analysis of associative factors in mediated generalization, *Psychological Monographs,* **75,** 1961, 3. Copyright 1961 by the American Psychological Association. Reprinted by permission.

Fig. 8.1 From M. Montessori, *Dr. Montessori's own Handbook,* published by Robert Bentley, Inc., Cambridge, Mass., 1964. Reprinted by permission.

Figs. 8.2 and 8.4 From H. H. Kendler and T. S. Kendler, Vertical and horizontal processes in problem solving, *Psychological Review,* **69,** 1962, 5, 10. Copyright 1962 by the American Psychological Association. Reprinted by permission.

Figs. 8.5 and 8.6, pages 232-233 From M. Montessori, *Dr. Montessori's own Handbook,* published by Robert Bentley, Inc., Cambridge, Mass., 1964. Reprinted by permission.

Table 8.1 From U. Neisser and U. Weene, Hierarchies in concept attainment, *Journal of Experimental Psychology,* **64,** 1962, 641. Copyright 1962 by the American Psychological Association. Reprinted by permission.

Fig. 8.7 From B. J. Underwood and J. Richardson, Verbal concept learning as a function of instructions and dominance level, *Journal of Experimental Psychology,* **51,** 1956, 236. Copyright 1956 by the American Psychological Association. Reprinted by permission.

Figs. 9.1 and 9.2 From P. B. Denes and E. N. Pinson, *The Speech Chain,* pp. 359, 361. Copyright © 1963 by Bell Laboratories, Inc. Reprinted by permission of Doubleday & Company, Inc.

Fig. 9.3 From A. M. Liberman, K. S. Harris, H. S. Hoffman, and B. C. Griffith, The discrimination of speech sounds within and across phoneme boundaries. *Journal of Experimental Psychology,* **54,** 1957, 359, 361. Copyright 1957 by the American Psychological Association. Reprinted by permission.

ACKNOWLEDGMENTS

Fig. 9.4 From P. Eimas, E. Siqueland, P. Jusczyk, and J. Vigorito, Speech perception in early infancy, *Science*, **171**, 1971, 304. Copyright 1971 by the American Association for the Advancement of Science. Reprinted by permission.

Fig. 9.5 From Noam Chomsky, *Language and Mind*, pp. 25, 26. © 1968 by Harcourt Brace Jovanovich, Inc. Reprinted by permission.

Fig. 9.6 From O. H. Mowrer, The psychologist looks at language, *American Psychologist*, **9**, 1954, 666-668. Copyright 1954 by the American Psychological Association. Reprinted by permission.

Fig. 9.7 From D. Premack and A. J. Premack, Teaching language to an ape, *Scientific American*, October 1972, 92. Copyright © 1972 by Scientific American, Inc. All rights reserved.

Fig. 9.8 From S. Goldin-Meadow and H. Feldman, The development of language-like communication without a language model, *Science*, **197**, 1977, 402. Copyright 1977 by the American Association for the Advancement of Science. Reprinted by permission.

Figs. 10.1 and 10.2 From B. Milner, S. Corkin, and H. L. Teuber, Further analysis of the hippocampal amnesic syndrome: 14-year follow-up study of H. M., Neuropsychologia, **6**, 1968, 224, 226. Copyright 1968 by Pergamon Press, Ltd. Reprinted by permission.

Fig. 10.3 After R. C. Atkinson and R. M. Shiffrin, Human memory: A proposed system and its control processes. In K. W. Spence and J. T. Spence (eds.) *The Psychology of Learning and Motivation*, Vol. 2. New York: Academic Press, 1968. Reprinted by permission.

Fig. 10.4 From D. Rundus, Analysis of rehearsal process in free recall, *Journal of Experimental Psychology*, **89**, 1971, 66. Copyright 1971 by the American Psychological Association. Reprinted by permission.

Fig. 10.5 From M. Glanzer and A. R. Cunitz, Two storage mechanisms in free recall, *Journal of Verbal Learning and Verbal Behavior*, **5**, 1966, 358. Reprinted by permission of Academic Press.

Fig. 10.6 From A. D. Baddeley and E. K. Warrington, Amnesia and the distinction between long- and short-term memory, *Journal of Verbal Learning and Verbal Behavior*, **9**, 1970, 179. Reprinted by permission of Academic Press.

Fig. 10.7 After A. A. Baumeister, Serial memory span thresholds of normal and mentally retarded children, *Journal of Educational Psychology*, **66**, 1974, 891. Copyright 1974 by the American Psychological Association. Reprinted by permission.

Fig. 10.8 From C. L. Wambold, K. Jelinski, and L. Brown, Improving the sequential memory performance of trainable mentally retarded youngsters: A learning strategies approach, *Journal of Special Education*, **10**, 1976, 45. Reprinted by permission of Grune & Stratton, Inc.

Fig. 11.1 After H. Ebbinghaus, *Memory* (originally published 1885). Republished (translation by H. A. Ruger and C. E. Bussenius) in 1964 by Dover Publications, Inc., New York. Used by permission.

Fig. 11.2 After F. C. Bartlett, *Remembering: A Study in Experimental and Social Psychology*. New York: Cambridge University Press, 1932. Reprinted and reissued 1977. Used by permission.

426

Fig. 11.3 After J. G. Jenkins and K. M. Dallenbach, Oblivescence during sleep and waking, *American Journal of Psychology*, **35**, 1924, 609. Used by permission of the University of Illinois Press.

Figs. 11.5 and 11.6 After D. L. Myrow and R. C. Anderson, Retroactive inhibition of prose as a function of the type of test, *Journal of Educational Psychology*, **63**, 1972, 306. Copyright 1972 by the American Psychological Association. Reprinted by permission.

Fig. 11.8 From E. Tulving and J. Psotka, Inaccessibility of information available in the memory store, *Journal of Experimental Psychology*, **87**, 1971, 4. Copyright 1971 by the American Psychological Association. Reprinted by permission.

Fig. 11.9 From R. W. Brown and D. McNeill, The "tip-of-the-tongue" phenomenon, *Journal of Verbal Learning and Verbal Behavior*, **5**, 1966. Reprinted by permission of Academic Press.

Figs. 11.10 and 11.11 From A. M. Collins and M. R. Quillian, Retrieval time from semantic memory, *Journal of Verbal Learning and Verbal Behavior*, **8**, 1969, 241, 244. Reprinted by permission of Academic Press.

Fig. 11.12 From E. F. Loftus and G. R. Loftus, Changes in memory structure and retrieval order over the course of instruction, *Journal of Educational Psychology*, **66**, 1974, 317. Copyright 1974 by the American Psychological Association. Reprinted by permission.

Figs. 12.1 and 12.2 From H. Lorayne, *Remembering People*. Copyright © 1975 by Harry Lorayne. Reprinted by permission of Stein and Day Publishers.

Pages 381-383 From J. S. Wiggins, K. E. Renner, G. L. Clore, and R. J. Rose, *Principles of Personality*. Reading, Mass.: Addison-Wesley, 1976, pp. 408-410. Reprinted by permission.

Author Index

Kety, S. S., 9
Kjeldegaard, P. M., 207
Koelling, R. A., 30, 31, 38
Kohler, W., 170, 171, 172, 174, 237, 326
Koppenaal, R. J., 337
Kopstein, F., 195, 196
Koriat, M., 104, 105
Krechevsky, L., 174
Kuhn, D., 235

Lamoreaux, R. R., 101
Lawrence, E. A., 314
Lawrence, K. A., 339, 340, 343
Laws, D. R., 72
Lazarus, A. A., 44, 46
Lenneberg, E. H., 271, 276, 279, 280
Levin, S. R., 199
Lewis, D. J., 76, 345
Liberman, A. M., 262
Lillard, P. P., 217
Limber, J., 286
Lindsay, P. H., 351
Lippman, M. Z., 187, 188, 201
Lobb, H., 231
Locke, J., 26, 204, 209, 210
Lockhart, R. S., 312, 313, 315
Loftus, E. F., 353, 354
Loftus, G. R., 353, 354
Lombardo, S. P., 73
Lorayne, H., 363, 364, 365, 369, 371, 375
Lordahl, D. S., 34
Lovaas, O. I., 64, 130, 131
Lucas, J., 363, 364, 371
Lund, D., 61, 63
Luria, A. R., 49, 50, 225
Lynch, S., 199

Mabry, J., 65
Mackintosh, N. J., 230
Maher, B. A., 345
Mandler, G., 100
Manning, A. A., 33
Maslow, A., 342
Matazarro, J. D., 99
Mawhinney, V. T., 72
McGaugh, J. L., 345
McGeoch, J. A., 327, 329, 330, 337
McNeill, D., 282, 346, 347, 349
Melton, A. W., 311, 312
Melton, Q. E., 335, 336

Miller, G. A., 296, 307, 308
Miller, N. E., 85, 116, 117, 118, 119, 120, 121, 122, 126, 166, 167, 168, 384
Miller, R. T., 276
Milner, B., 293, 294, 295, 299
Mischel, W., 104
Montessori, M., 8, 216, 217, 219, 223, 224, 231, 232, 314
Morningstar, M., 68
Mowrer, O. H., 29, 101, 125, 126, 145, 165, 227, 271, 273, 275, 280, 285
Mussen, P., 124, 125
Myrow, D. L., 330, 331, 332, 333, 335

Navarick, D. L., 108
Neisser, U., 241, 242, 248
Nelson, K. E., 281
Newman, S. E., 192
Newton, I., 157
Nissan, M., 104, 105
Noble, C. E., 202
Norman, D. A., 312, 351

Oaster, T. R., 192
O'Brien, F., 86
Ockham, W., 149, 163, 300
Oller, D. K., 272
Osborne, B., 167
Osgood, C., 207

Paivio, A., 196, 203
Patel, U. A., 36, 38
Pavlov, I. P., 21, 24, 26, 27, 28, 29, 31, 34, 35, 36, 41, 42, 44, 48, 56, 58, 59, 80, 102, 117, 146, 148, 149, 164, 273
Pearlstone, Z., 340, 341
Perin, C. T., 159
Perloff, B. F., 130
Peterson, L. R., 300, 311, 312
Peterson, M. J., 300, 311, 312
Peterson, R. A., 29
Piaget, J., 219, 234, 235, 236, 237, 239, 245, 382, 383
Postman, L., 338
Premack, D., 82, 83, 284
Pressley, M., 200
Proxmire, W., 1, 2, 10
Psotka, J., 343

Quillian, M. R., 309, 349, 350, 351, 352

Subject Index

Applied research
in education, nature of, 6-7
general definition, 2-3
and technological development, 7,
12-13
Association
cognitive vs. behavioristic views,
185-186
concept of, in philosophical thought,
25-26
remote and direct, in serial learning,
194-195
Attention, 230-231
Avoidance behavior, 86-87, 101-104,
165
Aversion therapy
for alcoholism, 35-36
for cigarette addiction, 37-38

Basic research
on animal behavior, relevance of, 11
general definition, 2-3
on learning, nature of, 4-6
and technological innovation, 7-10,
11-12, 219
Behavioral contrast, 171-172
Behaviorism
Guthrie's approach, 149-153
Hull's approach, 156-159, 160-163
and "hypothesis-testing" in animals,
144-145, 174-175
nature of, 168-169, 250, 325-326
Pavlov's contribution to development of,
28, 102-103
and response- vs. place-learning issue,
143-144, 173-174
Skinner's radical approach, 163
Thorndike's approach, 154-155, 174
and transposition issue, 171
Watson's approach, 142, 145-149,
175-176

Biofeedback, 168

Classical conditioning
and anxiety, 98-99
basic procedure, 29
biological constraints on, 30-31
and discrimination, 41-42
and extinction, 34-35
and generalization, 41-44, 49
and language, 48-49, 273-276
vs. operant conditioning, 59, 147-148,
164-167
Pavlov's work, 21-22, 26-27, 102-103
and personality, 98-99
and reinforcement, 34-35
Rescorla's contingency concept, 39-40
and temporal contiguity principle,
29-33, 36-44
types of, 31-34
Cognitivism
and gestalt psychology, 169-170
and "hypothesis-testing" in animals,
144-145, 174-175
information processing approach, 175,
296
nature of, 142-143, 168-169, 250,
325-326
and response- vs. place-learning issue,
143-144, 173-174
Tolman's approach, 173-175
and transposition issue, 171
Concept learning
and concrete vs. abstract concepts,
245-248
and "conservation," 235-237, 237-239
and language, 224-229, 261-264
and logical complexity, 217, 239-243
and mental retardation, 229-233
and perception, 223-224, 231-233
and positive vs. negative instances,
243-245

436